American Foreign Policy & Process

American Foreign Policy & Process

Sixth Edition

James M. McCormick

Iowa State University

 CENGAGE

Australia • Brazil • Mexico • Singapore • United Kingdom • United States

American Foreign Policy & Process,
Sixth Edition
James M. McCormick

Publisher: Suzanne Jeans

Executive Editor: Carolyn Merrill

Development Editor: Michael B. Kopf,
S4Carlisle Publishing Services

Assistant Editor: Scott Greenan

Editorial Assistant: Eireann Aspell

Media Editor: Laura Hildebrand

Brand Manager: Lydia LeStar

Senior Rights Acquisition Specialist:
Jennifer Meyer Dare

Manufacturing Planner: Fola Orekoya

Art and Design Direction, Production
Management, and Composition:
PreMediaGlobal

Cover Image: © Rob Marmion/Shutterstock

For product information and technology assistance, contact us at
**Cengage Customer & Sales Support, 1-800-354-9706
or support.cengage.com.**

For permission to use material from this text or product, submit
all requests online at **www.cengage.com/permissions.**

Library of Congress Control Number: 2012955710

ISBN-13: 978-1-4354-6272-4
ISBN-10: 1-4354-6272-6

Cengage
20 Channel Street
Boston, MA 02210
USA

Cengage is a leading provider of customized learning solutions
with employees residing in nearly 40 different countries and sales
in more than 125 countries around the world. Find your local
representative at: **www.cengage.com.**

Cengage products are represented in Canada by Nelson Education, Ltd.

To learn more about Cengage platforms and services, register or access
your online learning solution, or purchase materials for your course,
visit **www.cengage.com.**

Printed in the United States of America
3 4 5 6 7   23 22 21 20 19

To the students in my U.S. Foreign Policy classes over the past four decades

Brief Contents

Contents

Documents
and Document
Summaries, Figures,
Maps, and Tables

DOCUMENTS AND DOCUMENT SUMMARIES

FIGURES

MAPS

TABLES

INSTRUCTOR SUPPLEMENTS:

Companion Web Site for McCormick's American Foreign Policy and Process, 6e

ISBN-13: 9781133950288

This password-protected website for instructors features all of the
free student assets such as interactive web-quizzing, plus a new
instructor's manual, book-specific PowerPoint® presentations,
and an updated test bank. Access your resources by logging into
your account at www.cengage.com/login.

Preface

The sixth edition of *American Foreign Policy and Process* has been revised and updated and now covers policy and process developments through the Obama administration. The book is intended to serve as a comprehensive text for the first course in U.S. foreign policy and as a supplemental text in a global politics or comparative foreign policy course where American actions are analyzed. It also remains appropriate as a ready reference for the first graduate course in the study of American foreign policy or the foreign policy process.

Values and beliefs remain as the basic organizing theme for the text because policy actions are always taken within a value context. Yet, this emphasis on values and beliefs is not necessarily presented in a way to promote a particular point of view. Instead, the intent is to portray how values and beliefs toward foreign affairs have changed over the course of the history of the republic and how U.S. foreign policy has thus changed from its earliest years and through the Obama administration.

The text is again divided into three parts to accomplish this goal. In Part I, the first six chapters of the volume, I provide an overview of the beliefs that have shaped American foreign policy throughout its history (Chapter 1), the Cold War years (Chapter 2), the post-Vietnam era and the end of the Cold War (Chapters 3 and 4), the post–Cold War and post–9/11 years (Chapter 5), and the current era (Chapter 6). In each of the chapters, I utilize a wide variety of foreign policy actions to illustrate the values and beliefs of the particular period and administration. In Part II, which consists of Chapters 7–12, I examine in some detail the policy-making process by identifying the role of various institutions and groups—the executive (Chapter 7), Congress (Chapter 8), several bureaucracies (Chapters 9 and 10), political parties and interest groups (Chapter 11), and the media and the public at large (Chapter 12) in that process and assess how each competes to promote its own values in American foreign policy. In each chapter, too, I evaluate the relative importance of these institutions and groups in the foreign policy process. In Part III, which consists of a single concluding chapter (Chapter 13), I discuss several foreign policy divisions today—among America's political elites or leaders, between the American public and their leaders, and the increasing polarization between the political parties—and the implications of such divisions for shaping American foreign policy in the future.

Those familiar with the earlier editions will immediately recognize both continuity and change with the sixth edition. Although Chapter 1 has largely remained intact from the previous edition (albeit with a brief new section outlining an alternative view of America's past), Chapters 2–5 reflect a reorganizing from the previous edition to provide students with greater coherence in understanding the changes in American foreign policy—during the Cold War, after the Vietnam War, and since the end of the Cold War and the events of 9/11. Chapter 6 is entirely new and focuses on the foreign policy actions of the Obama administration. Chapters 7–12 reflect continuity in structure with the past editions, but each one has been carefully updated to reflect changes in actions of these important foreign policy institutions at home. At the same time, I should note that each chapter has been trimmed in length to reflect only the most important information and most appropriate illustrations from current policy actions. Chapter 13 represents a substantial revision with the addition of a section on current political party differences at home and a more focused discussion of major policy alternatives for the future at the end.

The sixth edition has retained some of the instructional features to the text, but some changes have been made to reflect a sharper focus on only the essentials. Maps continue to be used frequently in Part I to assist students in locating various countries and regions as they are being discussed. The use of tables and figures throughout the chapters has been retained. However, I have reduced the number and now focus only on the most important ones. Document and document summaries have been pared, and they are now used only for the most crucial pieces of historical items. The ones that have been retained ought to allow students to use these first-hand sources for more fully understanding American policy. I have continued to highlight in bold the key names and arguments in each chapter in order to make the discussion more accessible and more "reader friendly," but the number of highlights has been sharply reduced.

In the course of completing the sixth edition, I have incurred a number of debts to individuals and institutions, and I want to take the opportunity to acknowledge my thanks to them publicly. First of all, colleagues at other institutions offered their comments and suggestions for improving the book by carefully reviewing the fifth edition: John W. Dietrich, Bryant University; Jungkun Seo, University of North Carolina, Wilmington; James Seroka, Auburn University; and Jeannie Grussendorf, Georgia State University. For their extensive reviews and very helpful suggestions, I am most grateful. Also, a substantial portion of Chapter 6 was previously published as a chapter in Steven E. Schier's *Transforming America*; hence, I am grateful to Rowman & Littlefield Publishers, Inc., for allowing me to use that material here.

Second, colleagues in the Department of Political Science at Iowa State University provided moral support, especially as I sought to balance my administrative, teaching, and research responsibilities in completing this revision. For their friendship and encouragement, I will be forever grateful. Several of my graduate and undergraduate assistants—Nicholas Lauen, Kirk Galster, Aaron Calhoun, and Bob Beyer—were very helpful in collecting some specific pieces of data, tracking down information to update various chapters, and assisting with the bibliography, and I am in their debt for such timely assistance. I also want to thank Shirley Barnes for her help, on very short notice, with the creation or updating of some new tables and figures for this edition.

Third, I am grateful to Cengage Learning for its support and encouragement as I was completing the sixth edition. I particularly want to thank Carolyn Merrill, Executive Editor, Political Science, at Cengage/Wadsworth for keeping me on a tight schedule and my development editor, Michael Kopf, for his assistance in getting the chapters ready for publication. Thanks, too, to my copyeditor, Margaret Sears, and the production editor, Preetha Sreekanth, for making that part of the process operate smoothly and efficiently.

Fourth, I thank the thousands of students in my U.S. Foreign Policy courses over the past four decades for their interest and patience in enduring many of the arguments presented here. Their questions and comments have been a source of both satisfaction and inspiration for me in my teaching these courses. As such, I would like to dedicate this edition to them for their contribution in helping me write this text.

Finally, I am indebted to Carol as always for listening so patiently—and continuously—as I sought to complete this edition. Unwittingly, her patience, her encouragement, and her suggestions enabled me to complete this edition more quickly than I thought possible.

All of these individuals and institutions (and others whom I may have inadvertently omitted) deserve my sincere thanks. As always, though, final responsibility for the book rests with me, and any errors of fact and interpretation are mine alone.

PART I

Values and Policies in American Foreign Affairs

In Part I of *American Foreign Policy and Process*, we survey the beliefs and values that have been the basis of America's foreign policy actions. Although we provide an overview of the beliefs that have shaped American foreign policy throughout its history, we place special emphasis on the period from the end of World War II to the present—the era of America's greatest global involvement. Values and beliefs have been chosen as the basic organizing scheme because policy actions are always taken within such a context. The beginning analyst who can appreciate how belief systems influence policy choices will be in a good position to understand the foreign policy actions of a nation.

Values and beliefs cannot be understood in isolation, however; their importance is useful only within the context of actual foreign policy behavior. Thus, as an aid in appreciating how beliefs and attitudes have shaped this behavior, we provide a narrative of foreign policy actions that reflect the underlying belief systems during various periods of U.S. diplomatic history. It is our hope that by understanding both beliefs and actions, the reader will come away better able to interpret the foreign policy of the United States.

To accomplish these ends, Part I is divided into six chapters and analyzes the foreign policy approaches during differing periods of the American Republic and for several administrations, particularly those over the past four decades.

CHAPTER 1 America's Traditions in Foreign Policy 3

- Chapter 1 analyzes the effects of two important traditions in the history of American foreign policy, a commitment to isolationism and a reliance on moral principle as foreign policy guides, and how those values and beliefs continue to influence American policy today.

CHAPTER 2   America's Global Involvement and the Emergence of the Cold War   33

• Chapter 2 discusses the emergence of the Cold War and the components of the containment policy that was developed against the expansion of international communism. This chapter also outlines the values and beliefs that shaped American policy during these years (the Cold War consensus) and the international events that challenged this Consensus.

CHAPTER 3   After the Missile Crisis and the Vietnam War: Realism and Idealism in Foreign Policy   75

• Chapter 3 analyzes the effects of the Cuban Missile Crisis and the Vietnam War in stimulating new foreign policy perspectives to replace the Cold War consensus. The chapter also compares the values and beliefs of the realist approach during the Nixon administration with the idealist approach during the Carter administration.

CHAPTER 4   The Return and End of the Cold War: The Reagan and Bush Administrations   115

• Chapter 4 analyzes the Reagan administration's bipolar approach to the world, one closely reminiscent of the Cold War policies, and the George H. W. Bush administration's approach, a combination of realism and idealism as the Cold War was ending and a new era beginning.

CHAPTER 5   Foreign Policy after the Cold War and 9/11: The Clinton and Bush Administrations   159

• Chapter 5 continues this assessment of the values and beliefs of recent administrations by comparing the foreign policy approach of the Clinton administration after the end of the Cold War and the foreign policy approach of the George W. Bush administration after the events of September 11, 2001.

CHAPTER 6   Change and Continuity in Foreign Policy: The Barack Obama Administration   211

• Chapter 6 outlines the foreign policy approach of the Obama administration and the degree of change and continuity that he has brought to American foreign policy during his tenure in office.

CHAPTER **1**

America's Traditions in Foreign Policy

Wherever the standard of freedom and Independence has
been or shall be unfurled, there will her heart, her benedictions
and her prayers be. But she goes not abroad, in search of monsters
to destroy. She is the well-wisher to the freedom and independence
of all. She is the champion and vindicator only of her own.

SECRETARY OF STATE JOHN QUINCY ADAMS
JULY 4, 1821

Do not think . . . that the questions of the day are mere questions
of policy and diplomacy. They are shot through with the principles of life.
We dare not turn from the principle that morality and not expediency
is the thing that must guide us and that we will never condone
iniquity because it is most convenient to do so.

PRESIDENT WOODROW WILSON
OCTOBER 1913

Politics, at its roots, deals with values and value differences among individuals, groups, and nations. Various definitions of *politics* attest to the central place that values play in political life. For example, political scientist Harold Lasswell has written that politics "is the study of influence and the influential. . . . The influentials are those who get the most of what there is to get."[1] What there is to get, he continues, is values, such as "*deference, income, and safety.*"[2] Robert Dahl, drawing on Aristotle and Max Weber, notes that what seems to be common across these definitions is that they deal with values such as power, rule, and authority.[3] David Easton's famous definition of politics is even more explicit in its assessment of the relationship between politics and values as "the authoritative allocation of *values.*"[4] According to this definition, authority structures (for example, governments) distribute something, and that something is values.

Values refer to "modes of conduct and end-states of existence" that guide people's lives. They are "abstract ideals" that serve as an "imperative" for action.[5] Further, they are viewed as "goods" (in an ethical, not a material, sense) that ought to be obtained or maintained by a person or a society. In the Declaration of Independence, for instance, the values of life, liberty, and the pursuit of happiness were explicitly stated as reasons for founding the United States, and they came to serve as guides to political action in the earliest days of the nation. Indeed, these values remain important to this day. Liberty, or freedom, is emphasized again and again by American political leaders as one value that differentiates this nation from so many others.

VALUES, BELIEFS, AND FOREIGN POLICY

Because the essence of politics is so closely related to achieving and maintaining particular values, the analysis of **values and beliefs** is a deliberate choice as the organizing theme for our study of U.S. foreign policy.[6] Further, because values and beliefs are the motivation for individual action—and because we make the assumption that foreign policy is ultimately the result of individual decisions—their importance for our analysis becomes readily apparent. By identifying the values and beliefs that American society fosters, we ought to be in a good position to understand how they have shaped our actions toward the rest of the world.

Social psychologists have analyzed the relationships among values, beliefs, and the behavior of individuals. Milton Rokeach, for example, defines beliefs as propositions "inferred from what a person says or does" whose content "may *describe* an object or situation as true or false; *evaluate* it as good or bad; or *advocate* a certain course of action as desirable or undesirable." Individuals thus may have numerous beliefs, but some are more central than others in accounting for their behavior. These core beliefs are values. As Rokeach notes, "A value is a type of belief, centrally located within one's total belief system, about how one ought, or ought not, to behave, or about some end state of existence worth, or not worth, attaining." Although these values are likely to be few in number, they are crucial to an understanding of the attitudes and behaviors that an individual expresses.[7] By extension, nation-states operate as individuals do because they ultimately comprise individuals.

The use of values and beliefs (or "ideas," as Judith Goldstein and Robert Keohane call them[8]) as our organizing scheme fits broadly within the constructivist tradition in the study of foreign policy and international relations. This focus contrasts with that of other principal models of analysis offered in recent years: the rational actor model, the organizational process model, and the governmental or bureaucratic politics model.[9] However, although each of these has something to offer in helping us analyze foreign policy, none emphasizes the role of values and beliefs in the behavior of nations.

- The **rational actor model**, for example, begins with the assumption that nations (like individuals) are self-interested and seek to maximize their payoffs (or outcomes) when making foreign policy decisions. The key to understanding foreign policy is to identify a state's policy preferences and their rank orderings. The source of these state preferences and their relative ordering, however, has not been well explored.

- The **organizational process model** focuses more on identifying the decision-making routines of policy makers. Thus it sees foreign policy behavior less as the result of clear choices and more as a function of organizations following standing operating procedures. In large measure, the values and beliefs of the policy makers are assumed and not fully analyzed.

- The **bureaucratic politics model** pays some attention to values and beliefs (because each bureaucracy has institutional beliefs that it seeks to maximize). Still, the primary explanatory focus here is on the competition among bureaucracies, based on their relative power and influence.

The foreign policy models just described have much to offer (and careful readers will note that we use them in various ways throughout the book). However, an initial focus on values and beliefs will enable a fuller understanding of America's foreign policy decisions.

Some Cautions

There are potential difficulties in focusing on values and beliefs and in assuming a direct analogy between individuals and nation-state behavior:

- Factors such as the idiosyncratic personality traits of some leaders, the dynamics of the bureaucratic environment, and the restraints of the governmental process will intrude on a complete identification of a nation's values and beliefs.[10]

- The very definition of national values is likely to be problematic. Whose values are we to identify? Should they be those of leaders or the public? With both the public and the elite, the array of values—religious and secular—in a pluralist society is considerable. Our analysis focuses primarily on the values held by political elites, but the values and beliefs of the public, by necessity, will be considered from time to time.

- By focusing on values and beliefs, and using them as an explanation for U.S. foreign policy, we are close to relying on the national character (or, more generally, the political culture) explanation of behavior.[11] As A. F. K. Organski has written, the national character approach makes several key assumptions:

  (1) that the individual citizens of a nation share a common psychological make-up or personality or value system that distinguishes them from citizens of other nations, (2) that this national character persists without major changes over a relatively long period of time, and (3) that there is a traceable relationship between individual character and national goals.[12]

Such assumptions are difficult to maintain, and thus there are limits to the national character approach as a meaningful explanation of foreign policy, and it cannot be relied on completely. However, in a more limited sense, to identify the "basic attitudes, beliefs, values, and value orientations" of a society as a beginning point for analysis, its use is appropriate because individuals (and hence, nations) make decisions within the context of a particular set of values and beliefs.[13]

Rationales for the Values Approach

Although we acknowledge and recognize the difficulties just described, we believe that the values approach is a sufficiently useful first step in policy analysis that it warrants more coverage than it has received. Moreover, our analysis does not contend that certain values and beliefs are unchangeable, although surely some are less changeable than others. Rather, we will assess the changes in value emphasis and consistency, especially in the past several decades, during which the United States has been an active and continuing participant in the global arena.

Beyond its utility, the values approach is especially germane to the study of American foreign policy for at least three additional reasons. First, the nation was explicitly founded on particular sets of values, and these values made it view itself as "different" (or "exceptional") from the nations of the Old World.[14] In this view, politics was to be conducted not on the principles of power politics but on the basis of democratic principles. In the view of many, then, America should act in the world only according to its moral principles or in defense of them, and at all times domestic values were to be the guide to political behavior.

Second, because some American values toward international affairs have changed in recent years, understanding these changes is especially important for U.S. foreign policy analysis. America, for example, moved from its isolationist past to an active globalism in the post–World War II years. Indeed, a particular set of values often labeled the Cold War consensus came to dominate American policy actions during this period. In the post–Vietnam period (roughly 1973–1990), for example, the value orientation of the various American administrations toward the world changed a number of times—from the realism of Richard Nixon to the idealism of Jimmy Carter and back to the Cold War realism of Ronald Reagan and George H. W. Bush. In the post–Cold War era, Bill Clinton initially emphasized greater global and economic engagement and the promotion of democracy and then reverted to a focus on political–military concerns. In the post–9/11 period, George W. Bush made similar shifts in his foreign policy values and emphases, propelled most dramatically by the terrorist attacks on the United States in the fall of 2001. His administration started with a unilateralist emphasis, moved toward multilateralism (at least for a time) in its war on terrorism, and largely reverted to a unilateralist approach (although it was able to forge a "coalition of the willing") in initiating the Iraq War in March 2003. Largely as a response to the Bush years, Barack Obama called for a return to greater multilateralism and the creation of a "multi-partner world" to address pressing global issues. With such discernible shifts throughout the recent history of U.S. foreign policy and the current search for a definitive set of foreign policy values, a familiarity with both past value approaches and their policy implications is important as the United States looks toward the twenty-first century.

Third, the lack of consensus on foreign policy at either the elite or the mass level in American society today invites the use of a values approach. According to several national surveys, no foreign policy of the post–Vietnam, post–Cold War, and post–9/11 eras has been fully embraced by the American public or its leaders. Indeed, both are divided as to the set of values that should guide American policy in the future.[15] The domestic divisions between elites and the public and within the public over the Iraq War convey this continuing gulf, as does the continuing partisan divisions over the direction of foreign policy currently.

Finally, and on a normative level, there have lately been efforts by prominent political scientists to revitalize the role of values in foreign policy and international politics and in the study of foreign policy decision making.[16] The constructivist tradition in the study of international politics, as well, invites an emphasis on ideas, values, and culture as core concepts in an understanding of the behavior of states.[17]

In this first chapter, then, we begin our analysis by sketching the historical values and beliefs of American society; we then suggest how those beliefs and values have influenced foreign policy, especially in the first century and a half of the nation.

THE UNITED STATES: A NEW DEMOCRATIC STATE

Numerous scholars have noted that the United States was founded on values different from those of the rest of the world.[18] It was to be a **democratic nation** in a world governed primarily by monarchies and autocracies. Indeed, according to one historian, America's founders "didn't just want to believe that they were involved in a sordid little revolt on the fringes of the British Empire or of European civilization. They wanted to believe they were coming up with a better model . . . a better way for human beings to form a government that would be responsive to them."[19] In the words of Thomas Jefferson, the new American state was to be "the solitary republic of the world, the only monument of human rights . . . the sole depository of the sacred fire of freedom and self-government, from hence it is to be lighted up in other regions of the earth, if other regions shall ever become susceptible to its benign influence."[20] Because of its democratic emphasis at the outset of the nation, America developed with the belief that it was unique and possessed a set of values worthy of emulation by others. In this sense, the country emerged as deeply ideological (although Americans do not readily admit this) and not always tolerant of contrary views.[21] In short, **American "exceptionalism"** came to be a key tradition in guiding American actions abroad.

A Free Society

In 1776, the United States was explicitly conceived in **liberty and equality**, in contrast to other nations where ascription and privilege were so important.[22] It emerged as an essentially free society in a world that stressed authority and order. In large measure, this new American state was dynamic, classless, and free, unlike Europe, which was largely classbound and restrictive.[23] (Revolutionary France does not fit this description, but "classbound and restrictive" certainly describes politics under the Concert of Europe, the power arrangement dominated by the conservative regimes of Prussia, Russia, and Austria after the defeat of Napoleon Bonaparte.[24]) Thus, the American Revolution had been fought in defiance of the very principles by which Europe was governed. In this sense, there developed a natural aversion to European values—and foreign policies—which further reinforced America's beliefs in its uniqueness.

The fundamental American beliefs that were perceived to be so different from those of Europe can be summarized as classical liberalism, especially as espoused by seventeenth-century thinker John Locke.[25] In the liberal tradition, the individual is paramount and the role of government is limited. Government's task is to do only what is necessary to protect the life and liberty of its citizens. Citizens are generally left alone, free to pursue their own goals and to seek rewards based solely on their abilities.

Equality before the Law

From such a concern for the individual, personal freedom and personal achievement naturally emerged as cherished American values. Yet equality before the law was also necessary to ensure that all individuals could maximize their potential on the sole basis of their talents. In a society that placed so much emphasis on the freedom of the individual, this equality for all was viewed not as equality of outcomes (substantive equality) but as equality of opportunity (procedural equality).[26] Although all citizens were not guaranteed the same ultimate station in life, all should (theoretically) be able to advance as far as their individual capabilities would take them.

Thus, although equality of opportunity was important, the freedom to determine one's own level of achievement remained the dominant characteristic of this new society. In his January 2005 inaugural address, President George W. Bush reiterated this core American principle: "From the day of our Founding, we have proclaimed that every man and woman on this earth has rights, and dignity, and matchless value, because they bear the image of the Maker of Heaven and earth."[27] In his 2009 inaugural address, President Barack Obama also repeated this theme: "The time has come to reaffirm our enduring spirit . . . to carry forward that precious gift, that noble idea passed on from generation to generation: the God-given promise that all are equal, all are free, and all deserve a chance to pursue their full measure of happiness."[28]

One prominent visitor to the United States in 1831 and 1832 recognized these distinctive American values. In *Democracy in America*, in which he catalogued his travels, **Alexis de Tocqueville** expressed amazement at the country's social democracy ("The social condition of the Americans is eminently democratic; this was its character at the foundation of the colonies, and it is still more strongly marked at the present day"); its equality ("Men are there seen on a greater equality in point of fortune and intellect, or, in other words, more equal in their strength, than in any other country of the world, or in any age of which history has preserved the remembrance"); and its popular sovereignty ("If there is a country in the world where the doctrine of the sovereignty of the people can be fairly appreciated, where it can be studied in its application to the affairs of society, and where its dangers and its advantages may be judged, that country is assuredly America").[29] To be sure, Tocqueville raised concerns about this equality and its implication for governance in domestic and foreign policy matters; nevertheless, his admiration for America as a different kind of nation was indeed profound.[30]

The Importance of Domestic Values

America's early leaders differed from their European counterparts in a third important way: their views on the relationship between domestic values and foreign policy. Unlike European rulers of the time, most American leaders did not view foreign policy as having primacy over domestic policy, or as a philosophy whereby the power and standing of the state must be preserved and enhanced at the expense of domestic well-being. Nor did they view foreign policy values and domestic policy values as distinct from one another, with one moral value system guiding domestic action and another, by necessity, guiding international action. Instead, most saw foreign policy as subordinate to domestic interests and values. According to a recent analysis of Thomas Jefferson's beliefs on the relationship between the domestic and foreign policy arenas, "The objectives of foreign policy were but a means to the ends of protecting and promoting the goals of domestic society, that is, the individual's freedom and society's well-being."[31]

The Dual Emphasis on Isolationism and Moral Principle

America's values and beliefs came to have important consequences for its foreign policy. Because the United States adopted a democratic political system, developed strong libertarian and egalitarian values, and believed in the primacy of domestic over foreign policy, two important traditions quickly emerged: an emphasis on isolationism in decisions regarding involvement abroad and an emphasis on moral principle in shaping that involvement.[32] Both traditions were surely viewed as complementary and perpetuated unique American values: the former by reducing U.S. involvement in world affairs, and particularly those of Europe; the latter by justifying U.S. involvement abroad only for sufficient ethical reasons.

At times, these two traditions pulled policy makers in different directions (one based on the impulse to stay out of world affairs, the other on the impulse to reform world affairs through unilateral action), but both came to dominate American foreign policy actions.

THE ROLE OF ISOLATIONISM IN AMERICAN FOREIGN POLICY

Philosophical and practical reasons led the United States in an isolationist direction. Philosophically, because democratic values were so much at variance with those of the rest of the world, many early Americans came to view foreign, and especially European, nations with suspicion.[33] They feared that their values would be compromised by those of other states and that international ties would only entangle them in alien conflicts. From the beginning, therefore, there was a natural inclination to move away from global involvement and toward **isolationism**. Throughout the greatest part of its history, in fact, isolationism best describes America's foreign policy approach.[34]

Although philosophical concepts were influential, this isolationist orientation was also guided by important practical considerations. First, the United States was separated geographically from Europe—the main arena of international politics in the eighteenth and nineteenth centuries—and from the rest of the world. Thus, staying out of the affairs of other nations seemed a practical course. Second, because the United States was young and weak, with a small army and a relatively large land mass, seeking out adversaries and potential conflicts abroad would hardly be prudent. Third, domestic unity—a sense of nationalism—was as yet limited and merited more attention than foreign policy. And fourth, the overriding task of settling and modernizing the American continent provided reason enough to adopt an isolationist posture.[35]

Two Statements on Isolationism

Early in the history of the country, two statements—**Washington's Farewell Address** and the **Monroe Doctrine**—effectively described America's policy of isolationism and set limits on its application. Washington's Farewell Address of September 1796 was originally meant to thank the American people for their confidence in his leadership, but it also warned of threats to the continuance of the republic. George Washington admonished American citizens not to become involved in factional groups (political parties), sectional divisions (such as East versus West, North versus South), or international entanglements. His comments on the dangers of international involvements explain much of what isolationism was to mean for American foreign policy for the next century and a half.

America's attitude toward the world, Washington said, should be a simple one:

> Observe good faith and justice toward all nations. Cultivate peace and harmony with all. In the execution of such a plan nothing is more essential than that permanent, inveterate antipathies against particular nations and passionate attachments for others should be excluded, and that in place of them just and amicable feeling toward all should be cultivated.[36]

Moreover, he warned against the danger of forming close ties with other states:

> a passionate attachment of one nation for another produces a variety of evils. Sympathy for the favorite nations, facilitating the illusion of an imaginary interest in cases where no real common interest exists, and infusing into one the enmities of the other, betrays the former into a participation in the quarrels and wars of the latter without adequate inducement or justifications.[37]

Finally, Washington provided a "rule of conduct" for the United States, warning that any involvement in the Byzantine politics of Europe would not be in America's best interest:

> The great rule of conduct for us in regard to foreign nations is, in extending our commercial relations to have with them as little political connection as possible. So far as we have already formed engagements let them be fulfilled with perfect good faith. Here let us stop. Europe has a set of primary interests which to us have none or a very remote relation. Hence she must be engaged in frequent controversies, the causes of which are essentially foreign to our concerns. Hence, therefore, it must be unwise in us to implicate ourselves by artificial ties in the ordinary vicissitudes of her politics or the ordinary combinations and collisions of her friendship or enmities.[38]

In sum, Washington's strong belief was that although the foreign policy of the United States should not be one of total noninvolvement (because economic ties with some states were good and useful, and amicable diplomatic ties with others were commendable), he strongly opposed the establishment of permanent political bonds to other countries. More important, he directly warned against any involvement in the affairs of Europe.

Whereas Washington's Farewell Address outlined a general isolationism, the Monroe Doctrine set forth specific guidelines for U.S. involvement in international affairs. Named after President James Monroe's seventh annual message to Congress, delivered on December 2, 1823, this doctrine was promulgated in part as a response to the possibility of interference by the European powers in the affairs of the American continents, especially at a time when certain South American states were moving toward independence or had just achieved it.[39] Monroe's message contained several distinct and identifiable themes: an end to European colonization of Latin America and for "maintenance of the *status quo*" there; the differences in the political systems of Europe and America; and U.S. intentions not to interfere in European affairs.[40]

Monroe stated the first of these themes by declaring that the American continents were "henceforth not to be considered as subjects for future colonization by any European power" because such involvement would affect the "rights and interests" of the United States. Near the end of the message, he highlighted the differences in policies between the United States and Europe toward each other and toward Latin America:

> Of events in that quarter of the globe [Europe] with which we have so much intercourse and from which we derive our origin, we have always been anxious and interested *spectators*. . . . In the wars of the European powers in matters relating to themselves we have never taken any part, nor does it comport with our policy so to do. . . . With the movements in this hemisphere we are of necessity more immediately connected and by causes which must be obvious to all enlightened and impartial observers. The political system of the allied powers is essentially different in this respect from that of America. These differences proceed from that which exists in their respective Governments. . . . We owe it, therefore, to candor and to the amicable relations existing between the United States and those powers to declare that we should consider any attempt on their part to extend their system to any portion of this hemisphere as dangerous to our peace and safety. With the existing colonies or dependencies of any European power we have not interfered and shall not interfere. But with the Governments who have declared their independence and maintained it, and whose independence we have, on great consideration and on just principles, acknowledged, we could not view any interposition . . . by any European powers in any other light than as the manifestation of an unfriendly disposition toward the United States.[41]

With these words, the Monroe Doctrine gave rise to the "two spheres" concept in American foreign policy by emphasizing the differences between the Western and Eastern Hemispheres—that is, the New World versus the Old.[42] As Washington had earlier, Monroe spoke out against political involvement in the affairs of Europe, but he went further in declaring that the U.S. policy of political noninvolvement did not apply to Latin America. By asserting that the "rights and interests" of the United States would be affected by European involvement in the Western Hemisphere, his doctrine made clear that the United States did, indeed, have political interests beyond its borders.

Together, Washington's Farewell Address and the Monroe Doctrine are a valuable guide to understanding early America's isolationism in global affairs. The principles they enunciate were generally reflected in U.S. diplomacy throughout much of the nineteenth century and into the twentieth, and their words became the basis of the nation's continuing foreign policy.

The Isolationist Tradition in the Nineteenth Century

As a result of America's isolationism in foreign policy during the nineteenth century, there emerged a severe restriction on treaty commitments that would bind it politically to other nations. In fact, one prominent historian has pointed out that

Table 1.1 Content of International Agreements by the United States

Content	1778–1899	1947–1960
Alliance	1	1,024
Amity and Commerce	272	3,088
Boundary	32	4
Claims	167	105
Consular Activities	47	212
Extradition	47	12
Multilateral	37	469
Territorial Concessions	18	4
Total	621	4,918

Sources: Calculated from Igor I. Kavass and Mark A. Michael, *United States Treaties and Other International Agreements, Cumulative Index 1776–1949, Volume 2* (Buffalo, NY: Wm. S. Hein & Co., 1975); and from Igor I. Kavass and Adolf Sprudzs, *United States Treaties Cumulative Index 1950–1970, Volume 2* (Buffalo, NY: Wm. S. Hein & Co., 1973). For a discussion of how the table was constructed, see the text and note 45.

the United States made no alliances between the treaty with France in 1778 and the Declaration of the United Nations in 1942.[43] A survey of American treaties, however, shows that it did in fact enter into a number of "political" agreements—for example, extradition, navigation of the seas, treatment of nationals, and amity and friendship—but none of these could be construed as "entangling."[44] Instead, they served primarily to facilitate amicable trade relations.

Table 1.1 is a summary of the agreements the United States made from its founding to the twentieth century and, for comparison, from 1947 to 1960.[45] The first column of data, for 1778–1899, confirms the emphasis on economic and limited political ties in the early history of the nation, with agreements on amity and commerce and claims (largely economic) constituting about 70 percent of the total. Even agreements with more direct political elements, such as those dealing with consular activities and extradition, were largely routine, involving good relations with other states rather than controversial political issues. Only pacts that dealt with boundary issues and territorial concessions (the Louisiana Purchase, the purchase of Alaska, the Oregon Treaty, the Gadsden Treaty) might be considered controversial, and even those make up less than 10 percent of all commitments. The single true alliance between 1778 and 1899 was the treaty with France, which was ultimately allowed to lapse in 1800.[46]

Table 1.1's data for 1947–1960—the initial period of America's active engagement in global affairs—show a strikingly different pattern of commitments. First, their number is markedly higher—rising from just over 600 in a 120-year period to over 4,900 in a 14-year period. Second, although economic agreements (amity and commerce) still constituted the largest single type (about 63 percent), alliances and multilateral commitments now made up over 30 percent of the total. To be sure, these ties were broadly defined—dealing with military bases, defense pacts and mutual security agreements, and military missions—but they nevertheless demonstrated a level and scope of involvement much different from those in the early years. Similarly, the number and kind of multilateral pacts are distinctive in the two periods. In 1947–1960, the number of such pacts was over 10 times greater than in 1778–1899, and their content reflected a new dimension. At least 15 percent of the multilateral pacts in the immediate postwar years were defense commitments. There were no such pacts registered in the earlier period.

In short, then, the comparative data bring into sharp relief the differences between America's global involvement in the late eighteenth century and the entire nineteenth century and its global involvement since 1947. A brief survey of its diplomatic history during the nineteenth century will further demonstrate America's commitment to the principles of Washington and Monroe. For example, President James K. Polk, in his first address to Congress on December 2, 1845, reaffirmed the tenets that Monroe had set down twenty-two years earlier: "It should be distinctly announced to the world as our settled policy, that no future European colony or dominion shall, with our consent, be planted or established on any part of the North American continent."[47] Polk was not explicitly referring to the ongoing dispute with the British over the Oregon Territory, but the implication (in the view of at least one noted diplomatic historian) was clear.[48] Similarly, Polk expressed concern over rumors that the British were about to acquire territory in the Yucatán and in another message to Congress (on April 29, 1848) declared, "[the] United States would not permit such a deal, even with the consent of the inhabitants."[49]

During this same period, the United States concluded the **Clayton-Bulwer Treaty**, which stipulated that neither Britain nor the United States would "obtain or maintain for itself any exclusive control" over a canal across the Isthmus at Panama and that neither would "exert or maintain fortification commanding the same, or in the vicinity thereof, or fortify, or colonize, or assume, or exercise any dominion over Nicaragua, Costa Rica, the Mosquito Coast, or any part of Central America."[50] Although some later viewed this pact as a mistake because it gave standing to the British in the Western Hemisphere, it did allow U.S. involvement in the political affairs of Latin America to continue. Consistent with the prescriptions of the Monroe Doctrine, it also was an attempt to regulate Europe's involvement there.[51]

Late in the nineteenth century, during the presidency of Grover Cleveland, American policy makers again invoked the principles of the Monroe Doctrine to support Venezuela's claim against the British over a boundary dispute between Venezuela and British Guiana. On July 29, 1895, Secretary of State Richard Olney sent a note to Great Britain stating that it was violating the Monroe Doctrine with its involvement and that the United States could not permit any weakening of this policy. The British, with good reason, rejected the American complaint. President Cleveland responded angrily by asking Congress for funds to establish a commission to investigate the boundary dispute; he got them quickly, thus fueling war fever over what was a relatively minor issue.[52] This incident illustrates the continuing influence of the Monroe Doctrine on American foreign policy throughout much of the nineteenth century.[53]

If we couple these episodes with efforts to expand control over the American continent through the policy of "manifest destiny" in the 1800s, we can once again specify the degree and extent of isolationism. Moreover, many of these actions had a unilateral bent to them, further specifying the nature of American actions abroad.

An Alternate Interpretation of American Foreign Policy from Its Beginning

As these examples illustrate, the United States was not wholly isolationist, especially with regard to the Western Hemisphere in the nineteenth century, and thus some scholars challenge the degree of isolationism by the United States from its beginning and have advanced compelling alternate interpretations of America's past. Foreign policy analyst Walter Russell Mead particularly disputes "the tendency to reduce the American foreign policy tradition to a legacy of moralism and isolationism." Instead, he argues that "after a rocky start the young American republic quickly established itself as a force to be reckoned with."[54] That is, the founders created a successful alliance to defeat the British, secured the Louisiana Purchase from the French at the time of the Napoleonic Wars, annexed Florida, incorporated Texas, and used "deft American diplomacy" to thwart the Confederacy from gaining assistance from Britain and France during the Civil War. And, within a generation, Mead contends, "the United States became a recognized world power while establishing an unchallenged hegemony in the Western Hemisphere."[55] Furthermore, the individuals chosen as the early presidents (from the founding of the Republic through the Civil War period) had extensive experience in foreign policy, either as secretaries of state, cabinet or diplomat representatives, or generals in the military before taking office. As a result, these early presidents were interested in, and understood, foreign policy, unlike later presidents. In this sense, foreign policy was crucial to America's evolution, and the United States was hardly divorced from world politics at its beginning.

In his sweeping study *Union, Nation, or Empire*, diplomatic historian David Hendrickson also contends that foreign policy was an abiding interest for the early American presidencies.[56] Indeed, Hendrickson argues that the early leaders utilized foreign policy actions as ways to foster national unity. One of Hendrickson's principal themes was that foreign policy discussions were exploited to prevent these seemingly uniformed states from becoming a set of competing entities as had happened in Europe. That is, foreign policy discourse and actions fostered unity within the new Republic.[57]

Perhaps one of the most forthright statements on this alternate view of America's past has been offered by international relations scholar Hans Morgenthau. He explicitly rejected the notion that the new Republic was divorced or isolated from foreign policy from its beginning. Instead, he argues that the United States acted in the national interest from the outset of the Republic and up to the beginning of the twentieth century, even though many of its leaders did not acknowledge that fact. From the beginning of the country, and perhaps up to William McKinley's presidency, national interest politics (or realism) shaped U.S. actions abroad, although moral principles may have been utilized from time to time. Yet Morgenthau does contend "the full flowering of its [America's] political wisdom was coeval with its birth as an independent nation."[58] That is, the founders and the early national leaders recognized the American national interest of the United States and acted based upon it. They recognized that the American interests were served in the Western Hemisphere by preventing any European power to intervene there. As a result, the young Republic always "pursued policy aiming at the maintenance of the balance of power in Europe"[59] because it prevented any European power the ability to interfere or intervene in the Western Hemisphere.

During the first decade or two of the country (the Federalist period), Morgenthau contends that American foreign policy was "realistic" because its leaders thought and acted "in terms of power."[60] Washington's neutrality proclamation war against France by other European powers, including his decision not to honor America's commitment to France, was less a reflection of a commitment to isolationism by the young Republic and instead a recognition of the country's national interests. Further, other early presidents, Thomas Jefferson and John Quincy Adams, may be described as "ideological" in their appeal to moral principles to defend their foreign policy, but they, too, acted "in terms of power."[61] Jefferson's actions in dealing with England and France during the Napoleonic Wars reflected his concern for "the ever changing distribution of power."[62] John Quincy Adams and the Monroe Doctrine (which Adams actually wrote) were the essence of combining moral principle and power politics. That is, the Monroe Doctrine seemingly safeguarded America's isolationism (by its refusal to be involved in European affairs), but it also assured that the Western Hemisphere would stay under American dominance. This political realism in American foreign policy lasted only for a few more decades. By the end of the 1800s, Morgenthau argues, the "utopian period" began, and American foreign policy was steered by moral principles both in concept and in behavior. Such a change in direction was detrimental for the United States, in Morgethau's realpolitik view.[63]

Although Morgenthau viewed McKinley's presidency as the start of this "utopianism" in American foreign policy, diplomatic historian Robert Ferrell identified a somewhat earlier beginning, and he labeled it "the new manifest destiny" pursued by the United States.[64] More precisely, if one labels the first half of the 1800s as completing "manifest destiny" across the North American continent, this "new manifest destiny" involved the spreading of U.S. interest overseas "to noncontinental possessions in the Caribbean, Pacific, and Far East."[65] In this connection, Ferrell argues that the American "mission" in the world was transformed in the latter half of the 1800s: "before the Civil War the usual statement of the doctrine of mission had been that the United States should be a witness, in confident but quiet modesty, for democratic principles; after the war the doctrine of mission changed from witnessing to proselytizing."[66] The United States wanted to enhance its involvement beyond its traditional dominance in the Western Hemisphere, and it now sought an active role in world affairs. Ferrell summarizes this expansion by contending it "was virtually a carbon copy of the contemporary imperialism of European powers in Africa and Asia." In all, then, "there was, undeniably an American imperialism at the end of the nineteenth century."[67]

The Spanish-American War of 1898 is usually identified as a prime example of this new manifest destiny, although Ferrell points to American actions over Samoa, Chile, and the Hawaiian Islands decades earlier. Several factors motivated American involvement in this war: the U.S. desire to come to the defense of Cubans who were believed to be ill-treated by the Spanish; Spanish reform efforts that Americans viewed as unsatisfactory; the sinking of the USS *Maine*; and perhaps a personal attack on President McKinley, too.[68] In this sense, moral indignation and American mission seemed to come together to produce this war. The war, however, had important territorial consequence for the United States. It gained control of several territories from Spain: the Philippine Islands (after Admiral Dewey had destroyed the Spanish fleet in Manila Bay); Puerto Rico in the Caribbean; and Guam in the western Pacific. During the same time period, the United States annexed the Hawaiian Islands and announced the Open Door Policy toward China. Included in that statement was a seeming commitment to prevent "foreign encroachment" on Chinese territory.[69] By these actions, and in this interpretation, American global involvement and American imperialism were proceeding apace.

A Renewed Isolationist Tradition in the Early Twentieth Century

Despite the appeal of imperial expansion for some American leaders, global isolationism and noninvolvement still had an unmistakable appeal as the guiding principle, particularly in dealing with Europe in the early twentieth century. Only when moral principle justified intervention in European affairs could isolationism be abandoned temporarily, as World War I illustrates (and as we discuss shortly). Even then, intervention was largely a last resort, justified in strong moral tones by President Woodrow Wilson. Several social, economic, and political actions, largely directed toward Europe, also illustrate that isolationist sentiment continued to dominate American thinking and policy at this time.

In social policy, perhaps the most notable development in the early twentieth century was the passage of the **National Origins Act of 1924**, which restricted further immigration from southern and eastern Europe and prohibited all immigration from Asia. This was largely a reaction to the American fear of communism at the time (the so-called red scare) and the fear of aliens that had also shaken the country. Importantly, it also represented an attempt to control foreign influences.

In economic policy, the **Smoot-Hawley tariff of 1930** was passed, imposing high tariffs on foreign products to be sold in the United States. Such protectionist legislation was yet a further attempt to isolate the nation from global economic influences. Further, in the words of one analyst, "the belief . . . that the Depression stemmed from forces abroad against which the United States had to insulate itself . . . also gave a 'protective' tariff an irresistible symbolic appeal."[70]

In the political arena, the isolationist impulse was equally pronounced. After World War I, a "return to normalcy" was the dominant theme, implying a more isolationist and pacifist approach toward world affairs. This return to normalcy was manifested in America's refusal to join the **League of Nations** established after the war; its refusal to recognize the Soviet Union (until 1933) and other regimes of which it disapproved; its attempt to outlaw international war with the signing of the Kellogg-Briand Pact in 1928; and its effort to limit global armament through a series of conferences in the 1920s and again in the early 1930s. The 1920s also saw the emergence of a strong pacifist movement, which brought the founding of more than fifty peace societies across the country. Efforts such as these to eliminate international conflicts were viewed as moral reparation for involvement in World War I and as a way to prevent such involvement in the future. They show that international reform was wholly consistent with domestic reform in the minds of many Americans at this time.[71]

Involvement in Latin America in the Twentieth Century

America's isolationism and noninvolvement were not the guiding principles of its policies toward Latin America, as they were of its policies toward the rest of the world in the new century. Instead, in the 1904 **Roosevelt Corollary to the Monroe Doctrine**, President Theodore Roosevelt refined the meaning of Monroe's message and in so doing expanded U.S. involvement in the Western Hemisphere. Now American intervention would be undertaken, if deemed necessary, as a means of blunting European interference in the affairs of some Western Hemisphere states that had not paid their debts.

In a letter to Congress on December 6, 1904, Roosevelt stated the rationale for his corollary:

> Chronic wrongdoing, or an impotence which results in a general loosening of the ties of civilized society, may in America, as elsewhere, ultimately require intervention by some civilized nation, and in the Western Hemisphere the adherence of the United States to the Monroe Doctrine may force the United States, however reluctantly, in flagrant cases of such wrongdoing or impotence, to the exercise of an

international police power. Our interests and those of our southern neighbors are in reality identical. They have great natural riches, and if within their borders the reign of law and justice obtains, prosperity is sure to come to them. While they thus obey the primary laws of civilized society they may rest assured that they will be treated by us in a spirit of cordial and helpful sympathy. We would interfere with them only in the last resort and then only if it became evident that their inability or unwillingness to do justice at home and abroad had violated the rights of the United States or had invited foreign aggression to the detriment of the entire body of American nations.[72]

Ironically, the Monroe Doctrine had been initiated to prevent intervention from abroad, but it was now used to justify American intervention closer to home.

The Roosevelt Corollary was quickly implemented in 1905 by American intervention in the Dominican Republic to manage its economic affairs and to prevent any other outside interference. Similar financial and military interventions followed, with American forces occupying the Dominican Republic from 1916 to 1924, Haiti from 1915 to 1934, Nicaragua from 1912 to 1925 and 1926 to 1933, and Mexico for a time in 1914. In addition, the United States established a protectorate over Panama from 1903 to 1939 and over Cuba from 1898 to 1934 (see Map 1.1).[73]

The Monroe Doctrine in the Present Era

Since World War II, moreover, the Monroe Doctrine has hardly lost its relevance for American policy. In 1954, the United States supported a coup to overthrow Jacobo Árbenz Guzmán's government in Guatemala after Árbenz initiated domestic reforms and obtained arms from the Soviet bloc. Both the fear of communism in the Western Hemisphere and the Monroe Doctrine figured prominently in this support of the coup.[74] Three years after Fidel Castro seized power in Cuba in 1959, a U.S.-backed force of Cuban exiles attempted to topple his regime in April 1961. Known as the Bay of Pigs, this invasion ended in disaster but it was defended as an effort to stop the spread of communism in the Western Hemisphere. In 1962, the Monroe Doctrine again justified the American blockade against Cuba after the discovery of Soviet missiles there. In his address to the nation during the **Cuban Missile Crisis**, President John F. Kennedy declared that these missiles violated "the traditions of this nation and the Hemisphere."[75] In April 1965, when Communists were allegedly seizing power in the Dominican Republic, President Lyndon Johnson sent in some 23,000 U.S. and Organization of American States (OAS) forces to protect American citizens and to restore a government more to America's liking.

Over the past four decades, the tenets of the Monroe Doctrine have continued to shape American foreign policy in the Western Hemisphere. In September 1979, when the presence of up to 3,000 Soviet combat troops in Cuba was revealed, Senator Richard Stone of Florida cited this as one reason those troops had to be removed. When successful political revolutions occurred in El Salvador and Nicaragua in 1979, the United States immediately became concerned that they would produce "Soviet beachheads" at America's back door. Moreover, the Reagan administration challenged the new Marxist-led Sandinista government in Nicaragua and, by late 1981, had initiated a covert operation to support the Contras, a counterrevolutionary force committed to its overthrow. When Congress stopped funding for the Contras from late 1984 to late 1986, administration officials devised a scheme to continue its support by secretly selling arms to Iran and transferring part of the profits from those sales to the Nicaraguan rebels. This operation became known as the **Iran–Contra affair**.

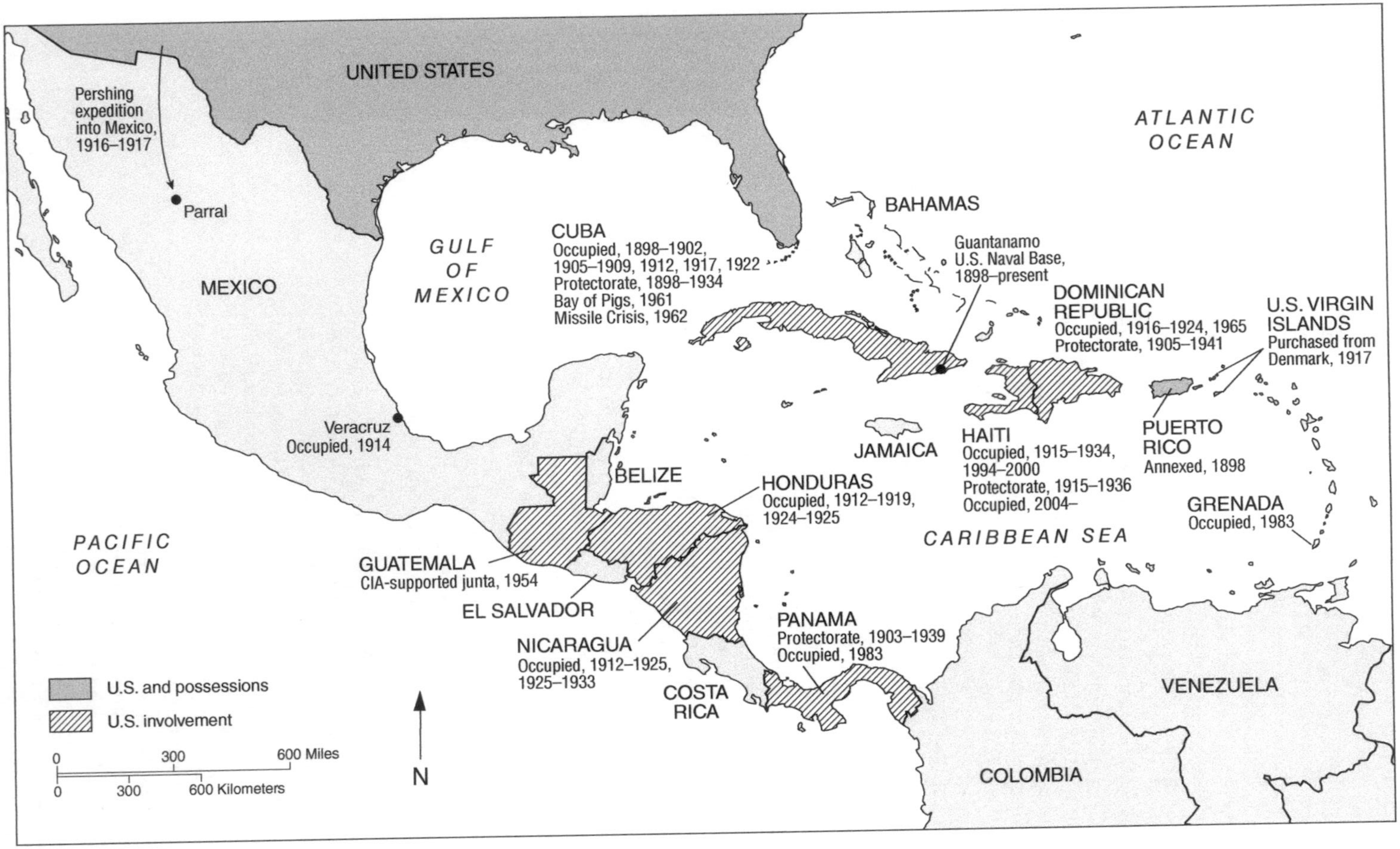
UNITED STATES
Pershing expedition into Mexico, 1916–1917
Parral
MEXICO
GULF OF MEXICO
Veracruz
Occupied, 1914
CUBA
Occupied, 1898–1902, 1905–1909, 1912, 1917, 1922
Protectorate, 1898–1934
Bay of Pigs, 1961
Missile Crisis, 1962
BAHAMAS
Guantanamo U.S. Naval Base, 1898–present
ATLANTIC OCEAN
DOMINICAN REPUBLIC
Occupied, 1916–1924, 1965
Protectorate, 1905–1941
U.S. VIRGIN ISLANDS
Purchased from Denmark, 1917
PUERTO RICO
Annexed, 1898
HAITI
Occupied, 1915–1934, 1994–2000
Protectorate, 1915–1936
Occupied, 2004–
JAMAICA
GRENADA
Occupied, 1983
BELIZE
HONDURAS
Occupied, 1912–1919, 1924–1925
CARIBBEAN SEA
PACIFIC OCEAN
GUATEMALA
CIA-supported junta, 1954
EL SALVADOR
NICARAGUA
Occupied, 1912–1925, 1925–1933
PANAMA
Protectorate, 1903–1939
Occupied, 1983
COSTA RICA
VENEZUELA
COLOMBIA
U.S. and possessions
U.S. involvement
0 300 600 Miles
0 300 600 Kilometers
N

MAP 1.1 U.S. Involvements in Central America and the Caribbean, 1898–2004

Source: The involvement data for 1898–1939 are taken from the map in Walter LeFeber's *The American Age* (New York: W. W. Norton and Company, 1989), p. 233. The subsequent American involvements have been added.

During the 1980s, both the Reagan and Bush administrations were heavily in-volved in Panama. The United States worried about the corrupt regime of Manuel Antonio Noriega and its implication for American influence in that country. General Noriega, who had been in power since the violent death of General Omar Torrijos in 1981, reportedly had made huge profits from the drug trade that traversed Panama, and in turn his regime had become increasingly repressive. The Reagan administra-tion sought and obtained his indictment in absentia on drug smuggling in Miami and undertook various efforts to oust him from power through American economic and diplomatic actions.

After a military coup covertly supported and encouraged by the Bush admin-istration failed in October 1989, the United States employed a military force totaling about 25,000 to overthrow the Noriega regime two months later. Noriega was captured, brought to the United States, and convicted and imprisoned for drug trafficking.

When in 1994 the Clinton administration attempted to remove General Raoul Cédras and restore democratically elected President Jean-Bertrand Aristide to power in Haiti, the Monroe Doctrine hovered in the background as an important policy justification. The administration had been reluctant to intervene or remain in other trouble spots around the world (such as Bosnia, Somalia, or Rwanda), but the prox-imity of Haiti and its location in the Western Hemisphere (as well as the promotion of democracy) became part of the rationale for its occupation by American troops in September 1994.

The George W. Bush administration took an equally keen interest in the Western Hemisphere with its support for legislation to aid Colombia in its fight against drug trafficking, including the continuing use of American military advisors, and in its ef-fort to promote a free trade zone among the states in the region. In late February 2004, the pattern continued. President Bush directed U.S. Marines into Haiti to re-store and maintain order after President Aristide fled the country, apparently with American encouragement.

In Venezuela, the actions of the government of Hugo Chávez—its nationalizing of various sectors of the economy, its increasingly close ties with Cuba, and its continu-ing anti-American rhetoric—have drawn the attention and concern of the United States. Likewise, the Bush and Obama administrations' interest in Cuba remains in-tense as Fidel Castro's health deteriorates, as Fidel's brother Raul has assumed the presidency, and as the future of leadership in that country remains in doubt.

In short, the imperative to keep the Western Hemisphere free of outsiders and to keep the Monroe Doctrine alive continues. The American view, since at least Theodore Roosevelt, is largely that it should use its power to establish and maintain order in this region of the world.

THE ROLE OF MORAL PRINCIPLE IN AMERICAN FOREIGN POLICY

The founding of the United States with a unique set of values, as well as the nation's development in the context of political isolationism, yielded another important di-mension of American foreign policy: **a reliance on moral principle** as a guide to world affairs.[76] Americans did not feel comfortable with international politics (espe-cially power politics as practiced in the Old World), and largely honored the impera-tive of both Washington and Monroe to stay out of foreign entanglements. This policy generated a distinct approach to the world when the country did become involved in international issues. Political scientist John Spanier and others have argued that discernible American attitudes developed toward such important political concepts as the balance of power, war and peace, and force and diplomacy as a result of these global experiences.[77]

More generally, moral values (as opposed to political interests) became an important feature of American policy making. On occasion, moral fervor led to policies that seemed more like crusades seeking to right a perceived wrong. At times, too, as some have contended, this rhetoric of morality could be cynically used to mask the use of power politics.

Before we proceed, we should note that our discussions are not intended to convey that moral principles are absent in the actions of other nations or that they underlie only the actions of the United States. To be sure, all nations are governed by particular value codes, although they clearly differ (at least in emphasis) from one state to another. What we do mean to convey, however, is that the United States as a nation has been particularly sensitive to reconciling its actions with moral principle, perhaps more so than many others. Indeed, the religious underpinnings of America's founding—and their continued impact to this day—account perhaps a large part for a reliance on moral principle in foreign affairs.[78] As we will subsequently discuss, fidelity to those principles has not always been sustained in action; yet the very concern for moral principle is nonetheless an important characteristic of U.S. foreign policy, especially when compared to other national traditions at the beginning of the American Republic.

Moral Principle and the Balance of Power

The **balance-of-power** concept, which has dominated policy making in Europe since the inception of the nation-states, is predicated on several key assumptions:

- That all states want to prevent large-scale war and preserve the existence of at least the major states in the international system
- That all states are fundamentally motivated in their foreign policy by power considerations and national interests
- That states are willing and able to join alliances (and to change them) to prevent the dominance of any one state
- That there are few domestic political constraints preventing states from acting in the political arena[79]

The essence of the balance of power concept is thus the adroit use of diplomacy and bargaining, but it holds that force and violence can—and should—be used to perpetuate the system.

Until several decades ago, the United States rejected philosophically virtually all of the key assumptions of balance-of-power politics.[80] American society has maintained that foreign policy should be motivated not by interests and power considerations but by moral principles, and that domestic values should be the sole basis for foreign policy behavior. As Henry Kissinger, a critic of American antipathy toward power politics, has observed: "It is part of American folklore that, while other nations have interests, we have responsibilities; while other nations are concerned with equilibrium, we are concerned with the legal requirements of peace."[81]

These **views on war and peace** and **force and diplomacy** follow from Americans' views on power politics. Because they have rejected the balance-of-power concept, most would find little comfort in Carl von Clausewitz's dictum that war is "the continuation of political activity by other means."[82] Instead, they have generally perceived war and peace as dichotomous: either one or the other exists. Intermediate conditions in which limited force is used (such as to settle border disputes or achieve some limited objectives, such as in Bosnia in 1995 or Kosovo in 1999, the lingering peacekeeping and peace-building operations in Iraq after 2003, and the counterinsurgency effort in Afghanistan, especially since 2009) are not always understandable or tolerable to many Americans. When war does break out, and the country must become involved, an all-out effort should be made to win. If the cause is sufficiently important in the first place, should not the effort be complete and total? Alternatively, if the cause is not important, why should U.S. forces be committed at all?

The continued impact of this view of war and peace to the present is illustrated by public reaction to the "limited wars" the United States has engaged in over the past five decades. For many Americans, the Korean and Vietnam wars were extraordinarily frustrating because an all-out military effort was not undertaken. Instead, a mixture of military might and diplomacy was employed. As a result, the outcomes—prolonged stalemate in the first, defeat in the second—were unsatisfactory. Even the highly successful U.S. effort in the Persian Gulf War of 1991 did not end satisfactorily for some because, once again, political restraints entered the process. In particular, segments of the public (including the American general in charge of the coalition forces against Iraq) were unhappy that the United States did not "finish the job."

More generally, American peace building, peacemaking, and humanitarian interventions (for example, Somalia in 1992–1993, Bosnia in 1995 and after, and Kosovo in 1999) have received decidedly mixed support from the American public and explain in part the initial impulse of the George W. Bush administration in 2001 to reduce American actions abroad. The reactions to the Iraq and Afghanistan wars exhibit many of these same sentiments. As the reconstruction efforts dragged on and as American casualties mounted in Iraq, nearly three quarters of the public viewed the war as a mistake by 2007. That year also saw presidential approval plummet, with President Bush's approval rating reaching the low 30 and high 20 percent range. The same "war fatigue" exists for the Afghanistan War, which has been going on for more than ten years.

In contrast to this attitude on limited war is the American public's response to the "**war on terrorism**" immediately after 9/11. When President Bush issued his clarion call for an all-out effort against terrorism that included all actions necessary, the public responded with the highest levels of support ever received by an American president.[83] With initial success in the attack on the Taliban in Afghanistan in 2001 and the quick toppling of Saddam Hussein in Iraq in 2003, support remained high. However, as these wars dragged on into the latter part of the decade and beyond and quick success was not in sight, support fell. In all, then, Americans support all-out efforts on war and peace, but they become more skeptical of in-between measures and expect quick and decisive results.

The public's view of force and diplomacy parallels its attitudes toward peace and war. Americans generally believe that when a nation resorts to force, that force should be sufficient to meet the task at hand. There should be no constraints of "politics" once the decision to use force has been made. As a consequence, combining force and diplomacy (as in the balance-of-power approach) is not understandable to large segments of the American people because it appears to compromise the country's moral position. Again, the Korean and Vietnam wars illustrate this point. In both instances, Americans did not understand or accept "talking and fighting." Thus, Nixon's and Kissinger's efforts to combine force and diplomacy ("coercive diplomacy") were criticized by both the political right and the political left because they suggested a certain amoralism in American foreign policy.

American diplomacy itself has historically been heavily infused with this moral tradition. Historian Dexter Perkins notes that the reliance on moral principle has produced a certain "rigidity" in U.S. dealings with other nations. By its very nature diplomacy requires compromise on competing points, he argues, but when "every question is to be invested with the aura of principle, how is adjustment to take place?"[84] John Spanier similarly notes that, given that moral principle is so prevalent in American policy making, it has traditionally been difficult for Americans to understand how compromise is possible or necessary on some questions in global politics.[85] When to compromise, and on what principles, thus remains a source of debate.

Moral Principle and International Involvement

Before 1947, when the United States finally committed itself to global involvement, American engagement in international affairs was generally tied to explicit violations of international ethical standards by other states. Four prominent instances—the **War of 1812**, the **Spanish-American War**, **World War I**, and **World War II**—can be used to illustrate the importance of moral principle as a justification for U.S. involvement and foreign policy actions.[86]

The War of 1812   The first instance in which isolationism was abandoned in favor of moral principle occurred when Congress voted a declaration of war against Great Britain in June 1812. It did so only after various efforts to avoid involvements with France and England—the dominant European powers of the time—and only after what it perceived as continuous violations of an important principle of international law: freedom of the seas for neutral states.[87]

Under a series of policy directives to limit Napoleon's power and enhance its own, the British government barred American commerce from France and from any continental ports that barred the British. Further, it barred from conducting commerce any neutral American vessel that had not passed through a British port or paid British customs duties. U.S. ships violating such standards were subject to seizure. (France, under Napoleon, imposed similar restrictions on American shipping, but for a variety of reasons the United States responded to the British with greater hostility.[88]) These actions infuriated the United States and were characterized by American leaders as blatant violations of freedom of the seas. In addition to the seizure of American vessels, the British, in their effort to control the seas, began the impressment of American sailors from American vessels, forcing them into the British navy (from which the British alleged they were deserters). Impressment was yet another challenge to America's freedom of commerce and the seas and was seen as besmirching U.S. honor. America's involvement in this war proved costly and ultimately unpopular and the final results largely confirmed the status quo. However, it does suggest the potency of moral principle in guiding early American action.[89]

The Spanish-American War   As noted earlier, several arguments were advanced to justify the Spanish-American War of 1898, largely based on moral principle: the harsh Spanish treatment of the Cubans, the sinking of the American battleship *Maine*, and the personal affront to President McKinley by the Spanish ambassador in a private letter (in which McKinley was portrayed as a "bidder for the admiration of the crowd" and as a "common politician"[90]). Fewer arguments for American participation were made on the basis of how it might affect the national interest; instead, in one view, moral arguments provided the dominant rationale.[91] As we noted earlier, too, this war encouraged the United States to pursue territorial expansion abroad with its seizure of the Philippines, the Hawaiian Islands, and Wake Island in the Pacific, albeit without the same moral umbrage as taking over Cuba.

World War I American participation in the First World War in 1917 and 1918 was also justified in terms of a moral imperative rather than as a response to the demands of the European balance of power. Only for sufficient ethical reasons did the United States feel compelled to enter this European conflict. In this case, the ethical justification was provided by Germany's violation of the principle of freedom of the seas and the rights of neutrals through its unrestricted warfare in the Atlantic.[92]

The outrage that occurred in 1915, the sinking of the British passenger ship RMS *Lusitania* (and later the ship *Sussex*) and the accompanying loss of American lives provided sufficient reason to temporarily abandon isolationism. The proximate events that precipitated the U.S. entry into the war, however, were the German announcement of its unrestricted submarine warfare in February 1917 and Germany's **Zimmermann Telegram to Mexico** that sought to prod that country into war with the United States.[93] Additional moral justification was reflected in the slogans devised to boost American participation: World War I was to be a "war to end all wars" and a campaign to "make the world safe for democracy."

World War II Although the United States had been assisting the allies prior to its formal involvement in the Second World War (1941–1945), its reentry into the world conflict could be justified only as a response to a moral violation. The Neutrality Act of 1939, for example, had reduced restrictions on arms sales and allowed the United States to supply its allies, France and Britain. The Destroyers for Bases deal with Great Britain—in which the United States gained naval and air bases in Newfoundland and certain Caribbean islands in exchange for fifty destroyers—was completed in September 1940.[94] In March 1941, moreover, Congress passed the Lend-Lease Act, which provided additional aid.[95]

Nevertheless, it was not until the Japanese bombing of Pearl Harbor, Hawaii, on December 7, 1941, which President Franklin Delano Roosevelt called "a date which will live in infamy," that the United States finally had a wholly satisfactory reason for plunging into the conflict.[96] Consistent with its attitude, it felt compelled to seek "absolute victory," as Roosevelt said. Hence, a total war effort was mounted that ultimately led to the unconditional surrender of the Japanese in September 1945, only a few months after victory in Europe.

Implications for U.S. Involvement

In general, the examples just described demonstrate that the United States has been reluctant to give up its isolationism and has done so only for identifiable moral reasons. Unlike other states, it has traditionally agreed to international involvement only in response to perceived violations of clearly established principles of international law and not to the requirements of power politics. As a consequence, sustained American engagements in the world of power politics have been decidedly few and have been entered into only in special circumstances.

After the first three global engagements discussed here, the United States moved back to its favored position of isolationism; none brought about a basic change in American foreign policy orientation. (The significance of World War II is considerably different; Chapter 2 discusses its impact on U.S. foreign policy.) After the War of 1812, for example, America immediately reaffirmed its policy of noninvolvement in European affairs and warned against European interference in the Western Hemisphere via the Monroe Doctrine of 1823.

The strong American affinity for isolationism was vividly demonstrated at the end of World War I with the rejection of the idealistic foreign policy proposed by President Wilson. "**Wilsonian idealism**," as it came to be called, attempted to shake the United States from its isolationist moorings and encourage it to become a continuing participant in global affairs. This idealism, largely borne out of President Wilson's personal beliefs, consisted of several key tenets.

- Moral principle should be the guide to U.S. actions abroad.
- The Anglo-American values of liberty and liberal democratic institutions are worthy of emulation and promotion worldwide. Indeed, they are necessary if world peace is to be realized.
- The old order, based on balance-of-power and interest politics, must be replaced by an order based on moral principles and cooperation by all states against international aggression.
- The United States must continue to take an active role in bringing about these global reforms.[97]

For Wilson, then, moral principle would serve as a continuing guide to global involvement, but the interests of humankind and global reform would take precedence over any narrowly defined national or state interest.

The most complete description of the new world that Wilson envisioned can probably be found in his **Fourteen Points**, which he delivered to a joint session of Congress in January 1918 and which became the basis for the Paris Peace Conference held at the end of World War I.[98] This new order, he declared, would ban secret diplomacy and foster international trade among nations and would emphasize self-determination and democracy for nations. In his speech, Wilson set forth several specific requirements resolving nationality and territorial issues in Central Europe at the time (see Document 1.1.)

Point 14 of Wilson's plan is particularly notable—and was ultimately troubling to many Americans—because of its explicit rejection of isolationism. It called for the establishment of a collective security organization—a **League of Nations**—that would rid the world of balance-of-power politics and create a new order based on universal principles. The League would exploit the cooperative potential among states and emphasize the role of collective (that is, universal) action to stop warfare and regulate conflict. Thus, it would require its members to be involved in the affairs of the international system. If the United States were to join, it would be permanently involved in international politics and would be an active participant in global reform efforts. In essence, Wilson's collective security proposal would have moved the United States away from isolationism and would have produced a strong moral cast to American involvement and to global politics generally.

Document 1.1   Wilson's Fourteen Points

I. Open covenants of peace, openly arrived at. . . .

II. Absolute freedom of navigation upon the seas. . . .

III. The removal, so far as possible, of all economic barriers and the establishment of equality of trade conditions among all the nations. . . .

IV. Adequate guarantees given and taken that national armaments will be reduced to the lowest point consistent with domestic safety.

V. A free, open-minded, and absolutely impartial adjustment of all colonial claims. . . .

VI. The evacuation of all Russian territory and . . . a settlement of all questions affecting Russia . . . [and] an unhampered and unembarrassed opportunity for the independent determination of her own political development and national policy. . . .

VII. Belgium . . . must be evacuated and restored without any attempt to limit the sovereignty which she enjoys in common with all other free nations.

VIII. All French territory should be freed and the invaded portions restored, and the wrong done to France by Prussia in 1871 in the matter of Alsace-Lorraine, which has unsettled the peace of the world for nearly fifty years, should be righted. . . .

IX. A readjustment of the frontiers of Italy should be effected along clearly recognizable lines of nationality.

X. The peoples of Austria-Hungary . . . should be accorded the freest opportunity of autonomous development.

XI. Rumania, Serbia, and Montenegro should be evacuated; occupied territories restored; Serbia accorded free and secure access to the sea; and the relations of the several Balkan states to one another determined by friendly counsel along historically established lines of allegiance and nationality. . . .

XII. The Turkish portions of the present Ottoman Empire should be assured a secure sovereignty, but the other nationalities . . . under Turkish rule should be assured . . . [an] opportunity of autonomous development, and the Dardanelles should be permanently opened as a free passage to the ships and commerce of all nations. . . .

XIII. An independent Polish state should be erected . . . [with] political and economic independence and territorial integrity . . . guaranteed by international covenant.

XIV. A general association of nations must be formed under specific covenants for the purpose of affording mutual guarantees of political independence and territorial integrity to great and small states alike.

Source: Taken from a speech by President Woodrow Wilson to a joint session of the U.S. Congress as reported in *Congressional Record* (January 8, 1918), 691.

Wilson's dream of a League of Nations became a reality for a time, but without the participation of the United States—the U.S. Senate failed to approve the Versailles peace treaty by the necessary two thirds vote. Indeed, on two of three roll calls, the treaty even failed to obtain majority support.[99] Clearly, despite America's long-standing rejection of balance-of-power politics, it remained unwilling to increase its global involvement in order to destroy it. Instead, it reaffirmed its isolationist beliefs and in the 1920s reverted to "normalcy," remaining in that posture throughout the 1930s.

The return to isolationism was manifested in another way in the interwar years. As the situation in Europe began to polarize and conflict seemed once again imminent, the United States passed a series of neutrality acts, in 1935, 1936, and 1937, that sought to prevent the export of arms and ammunition to belligerent countries and to restrict travel by American citizens on the vessels of nations at war.[100] The ultimate aim, of course, was to reaffirm U.S. noninvolvement and to reduce the prospects of the country being drawn into war through these means. Although President Roosevelt had, by 1939, asked for and received certain alterations in these neutrality acts,[101] it was not until the Japanese attack on Pearl Harbor that the United States was fully shaken from its isolationist stance.

CONCLUDING COMMENTS

A reliance on isolationism and moral principle largely forms the essence of America's past foreign policy,[102] and the values and beliefs that underlie this reliance continue to influence its international orientation. Although this interpretation represents the dominant view of the early history of the Republic, other analyses challenge this view. Opposing interpretations point to the realist or national interest underpinnings of American foreign policy; they also point to its expansionist tendency across the American continent and in global politics during the first century of the United States. In this sense, the careful reader needs to weigh these differing interpretations.

Nonetheless, the American approach to the world surely took a decided and recognizable turn in response to the shock of World War II; the substantial destruction of the major European powers of France, Britain, and Germany; the emergence of the Soviet challenge; and the onset of the Cold War. These events and phenomena would lead to the rejection of global noninvolvement, even as a commitment to moral principles as a guide to policy was retained.

With the collapse of the Soviet Union, the end of the Cold War, and the emergence of terrorism on American soil by the early twenty-first century, the appeal of some traditional foreign policy values resurfaced. This can be seen in the Bush administration's initial adoption of a more unilateralist (and isolationist) approach to the world, and then after the attacks of September 11, 2001, a commitment to a new globalism against terrorism. The Obama administration moved toward a greater multilateralism on a variety of issues, even as it continued to pursue a foreign policy driven by American domestic values.

In the next five chapters, we will highlight the changes in America's foreign policy values and beliefs from post–World War II to post–9/11. We will not only demonstrate how these historical traditions have changed during this period but also illustrate how they have continued to influence successive administrations and their policies. In Chapter 2, we will examine the global political and economic factors that shook the United States from its isolationist moorings and propelled it into global politics. At the same time, we will see how moral principle as a guide to policy remained largely intact.

Notes

1. Harold D. Lasswell, *Politics: Who Gets What, When, How* (New York: Whittlesey House, 1936), p. 3.

2. Ibid. Emphasis in original.

3. Robert A. Dahl, *Modern Political Analysis,* 2nd ed. (Englewood Cliffs, NJ: Prentice-Hall, 1970), pp. 4–6. Also see Christian Bay, *The Structure of Freedom* (New York: Atheneum Publishers, 1965), pp. 20–21, for another discussion of the definition of politics.

4. David Easton, *The Political System* (New York: Alfred A. Knopf, 1953), p. 90. Emphasis added.

5. Milton Rokeach, *Beliefs, Attitudes and Values* (San Francisco: Jossey-Bass, 1968), pp. 124, 159–160.

6. We will use the terms *values* and *beliefs* interchangeably throughout this book. These concepts (along with attitudes), although distinct, are very closely related, as discussed in Rokeach, *Beliefs,* pp. 113 and 159–160.

7. See Milton Rokeach's discussion under "Attitudes" in the *International Encyclopedia of the Social Sciences* (New York: The Macmillan Company and The Free Press, 1968), pp. 449–457. The quotations are at pp. 450 and 454, respectively. Emphasis in original.

8. Judith Goldstein and Robert O. Keohane, "Ideas and Foreign Policy: An Analytic Framework," in Judith Goldstein and Robert O. Keohane, eds., *Ideas and Foreign Policy: Beliefs, Institutions, and Political Change* (Ithaca, NY, and London: Cornell University Press, 1993), pp. 3–30. Some of the discussion of the models in the next paragraphs draws on Goldstein and Keohane. For good introductions to constructivism and its role in foreign policy analysis, see Stephen M. Walt, "International Relations: One World, Many Theories," *Foreign Policy* 110 (Spring 1998): 29–46, and Jack Snyder, "One World, Rival Theories," *Foreign Policy* 145 (November/December 2004): 53–62.

9. For an argument for the rational actor model as a way to explain foreign policy, see Stephen Krasner, *Defending the National Interest: Raw Materials Investment and U.S. Foreign Policy* (Princeton: Princeton University Press, 1978), and for all three models, see the seminal discussions in Graham Allison, *Essence of Decision* (Boston: Little, Brown and Co., 1971).

10. Lloyd Jensen, in *Explaining Foreign Policy* (Englewood Cliffs, NJ: Prentice Hall, 1982), surveys the research done within the context of these various factors to explain foreign policy.

11. For a discussion of how the political culture concept can be used to explain a nation's behavior, see Gabriel Almond and Sidney Verba, *The Civic Culture* (Boston: Little, Brown and Co., 1963).

12. A. F. K. Organski, *World Politics* (New York: Alfred A. Knopf, 1968), p. 87.

13. Kenneth W. Terhune, "From National Character to National Behavior: A Reformulation," *Journal of Conflict Resolution* 14 (June 1970): 259. For more discussion by Terhune and others on national character, see Howard Bliss and M. Glen Johnson, *Beyond the Water's Edge: America's Foreign Policies* (Philadelphia: J. B. Lippincott Co., 1975), pp. 93–98.

14. For two recent discussions of American "exceptionalism" and its effect on foreign policy, see Francis Fukuyama, *America at the Crossroads: Democracy, Power and the Neoconservative Legacy* (New Haven and London: Yale University Press, 2006), and Stephen Halper and Jonathan Clarke, *The Silence of the Rational Center* (New York: Basic Books, 2007).

15. See, for example, Benjamin I. Page with Marshall M. Bouton, *The Foreign Policy Disconnect* (Chicago and London: The University of Chicago Press, 2006).

16. See Joseph S. Nye, *Nuclear Ethics* (New York: The Free Press, 1986); Stanley Hoffmann, *Duties beyond Borders: On the Limits and Possibilities of Ethical International Politics* (Syracuse: Syracuse University Press, 1981); and Robert W. McElroy, *Morality and American Foreign Policy: The Role of Ethics in International Affairs* (Princeton, NJ: Princeton University Press, 1992). The McElroy volume brought the Nye and Hoffmann books to my attention at p. 3, for which I am grateful.

17. Walt, "International Relations," pp. 40–41.

18. See, for example, Seymour Martin Lipset, *The First New Nation* (Garden City, NY: Anchor Books, 1967); Russel B. Nye, *This Almost Chosen People* (East Lansing: Michigan State University Press, 1966); John G. Stoessinger, *Crusaders and Pragmatists* (New York: W.W. Norton and Company, 1979), pp. 3–7; Edmund Stillman and William Pfaff, *Power and Impotence: The Failure of America's Foreign Policy* (New York: Vintage Books, 1966), pp. 15–59; Paul A. Varg, *Foreign Policies of the Founding Fathers* (East Lansing: Michigan State University Press, 1963), pp. 1–10; and John Spanier, *American Foreign Policy Since World War II*, 9th ed. (New York: Holt, Rinehart and Winston, 1982), pp. 1–14. Spanier's essay is perhaps the best brief treatment of this and related topics discussed here. Its utility will be readily apparent.

19. Professor Frank A. Cassell (chairman, Department of History, University of Wisconsin–Milwaukee) made this characterization in a 1989 Independence Day interview. See Jerry Resler, "Living On: U.S. as Model Would Please Founder," *Milwaukee Sentinel*, July 4, 1989, part 4, p. 1.

20. Quoted in Robert W. Tucker and David C. Hendrickson, "Thomas Jefferson and Foreign Policy," *Foreign Affairs* 69 (Spring 1990): 136.

21. George F. Kennan made this point about the ideological roots of American society by noting the isolated development of the United States and the Soviet Union. This development in relative isolation from the rest of the world produced a strong sense of righteousness. See his "Is Detente Worth Saving?" *Saturday Review*, March 6, 1976, 12–17.

22. Lipset, in *The First New Nation*, uses the values of equality and achievement as the basis of his analysis.

23. This description, as noted in Spanier, *American Foreign Policy*, at p. 7, was true for most Americans, but not all. Some were clearly excluded from the political process—notably blacks, women, Native Americans, and many who held no property.

24. Gordon A. Craig and Alexander L. George, *Force and Statecraft*, 3rd ed. (New York and Oxford: Oxford University Press, 1995), pp. 27–31.

25. On his view of the goals and limits of government, see John Locke, *Two Treatises of Government*, portions of which are reprinted in William Ebenstein, *Great Political Thinkers: Plato to the Present*, 3rd ed. (New York: Holt, Rinehart and Winston, 1965), pp. 404–408, in

particular. Also see the discussion of classical liberalism in Everett C. Ladd, Jr., "Traditional Values Regnant," *Public Opinion* 1 (March/April 1978): 45–49; and Charles W. Kegley and Eugene R. Wittkopf, *American Foreign Policy: Pattern and Process*, 4th ed. (New York: St. Martin's Press, 1991), pp. 249–250.

26. These values are discussed in Ladd, "Traditional Values and Regnant," and some evidence is presented on the American commitment to these values and beliefs at the time.

27. "President Sworn-In to Second Term," January 20, 2005, at http://www.whitehouse.gov/news/releases/2005/01/print/20050120-1.html, June 7, 2007.

28. "President Barack Obama's Inaugural Address," January 21, 2009, at http://www.whitehouse.gov/blog/inaugural-address, January 26, 2012.

29. Alexis de Tocqueville, *Democracy in America*, edited and abridged by Richard D. Heffner (New York: New American Library, 1956), pp. 49, 54, and 56 for the quoted passages.

30. See ibid. and David Clinton, "Tocqueville's Challenge," *The Washington Quarterly* 11 (Winter 1988): 173–189.

31. Tucker and Hendrickson, "Thomas Jefferson and Foreign Policy," p. 139. For a discussion of how Jefferson's views were shared by other early leaders, see pp. 143–146. On the difficulty of Jefferson actually making this distinction work, see pp. 146–156.

32. See Spanier, *American Foreign Policy*, pp. 6 and 12. Previously, *isolationism* and *moralism* were used as summary terms. The use of *moralism*, however, may have a pejorative connotation for some (and it has surely been used that way). That is not the intent here. Rather, it is to convey the important role that values have played in the way America has thought about its involvement in the global arena. Hence, moral principle as a guiding tradition will be used here.

33. Dexter Perkins, *Hands Off: A History of the Monroe Doctrine* (Boston: Little, Brown and Co., 1941), pp. 3–26.

34. See Cecil V. Crabb, Jr., *Policy-Makers and Critics: Conflicting Theories of American Foreign Policy* (New York: Frederick A. Praeger, 1976), pp. 1–33, for an extended discussion of this isolationist tradition.

35. Ibid., pp. 7–15, which discusses several different dimensions of isolationism in America's past.

36. "Washington's Farewell Address," *Annals of the Congress of the United States*, 4th Cong., 2nd sess., 1786–1797, 2877.

37. Ibid.

38. Ibid., p. 2878.

39. Albert Bushnell Hart, *The Monroe Doctrine: An Interpretation* (Boston: Little, Brown & Co., 1916), pp. 20–68.

40. These themes are succinctly discussed in Evarts Seelye Scudder, *The Monroe Doctrine and World Peace* (Port Washington, NY: Kennikat Press, 1972), pp. 15–20. The quote is at p. 19. Emphasis in original.

41. "President's Message," *Annual of the Congress of the United States*, 18th Cong., 1st sess., 1823–1824, 22–23. Emphasis added.

42. Several scholars have emphasized how the Monroe Doctrine, more than any other policy statement, formalized and solidified the U.S. isolationist tradition in world affairs—at least toward Europe. See, for instance, Perkins, *The Evolution of American Foreign Policy* 2nd ed. (New York: Oxford University Press, 1966), pp. 33–38; Nye, *This Almost Chosen People*, p. 184; and Spanier, *American Foreign Policy*, p. 6.

43. Thomas A. Bailey, *The Man on the Street: The Impact of American Public Opinion on Foreign Policy* (New York: MacMillan, 1948), p. 251.

44. A survey of all international agreements during the early history was undertaken using the listing compiled by Igor I. Kavass and Mark A. Michael, *United States Treaties and Other International Agreements Cumulative Index 1776–1949, Volume 2* (Buffalo, NY: William S. Hein and Company, 1975), pp. 3–130. For the latter period, the data source was Igor I. Kavass and Adolf Sprudzs, *United States Treaties Cumulative Index 1950–1970, Volume 2* (Buffalo, NY: William S. Hein and Company, 1973), pp. 11–444, and some additional agreements from the first source for the years 1947–1949 at pp. 526–615.

45. The table was constructed using the sources listed in note 44. The category labels were derived largely from the descriptions of the agreements given in the first source. For manageability and convenience, agreements in different years in the 1778–1899 period were segmentally categorized (such as 1778–1799, 1800–1850, and so on), and the overall results were collapsed and categorized. For the second part of the table (1947–1960), the same categories were used. Although the content of the categories is relatively self-evident, the alliance, amity and commerce, and multilateral categories deserve some comment. The alliance category consisted primarily of formal military commitments, but it also included establishing military bases, signing mutual security agreements, and sending military missions to other countries. The amity and commerce category included a wide array of commercial, health and sanitation, technical cooperation, educational, aviation, and postal agreements, among others, and commitments for friendly relations with other states. The multilateral category included all agreements that were designated as such by the source. The actual content of those pacts covered a wide array of issues, but the multilateral designation was retained to show the degree to which the United States committed itself to groups of other states during this period.

   Finally, some agreements overlapped the categories, and some judgments were made to place them in one category rather than another. Others categorizing the pacts might come up with a different classification and slightly different results. It is unlikely, however, that the general pattern of the results would be changed.

46. Perkins, *The Evolution of American Foreign Policy*, p. 30, reports that the French alliance was not renewed in that year.

47. Thomas A. Bailey, *A Diplomatic History of the American People* (New York: F. S. Crofts and Co., 1942), p. 238.

48. Ibid.

49. Hart, *The Monroe Doctrine*, p. 115.

50. Robert H. Ferrell, *American Diplomacy: A History*, 3rd ed. (New York: W.W. Norton and Company, 1975), p. 231.

51. Ibid., pp. 231–232.

52. For a discussion of the various challenges to the Monroe Doctrine in the latter half of the nineteenth century, see Scudder, *The Monroe Doctrine*; and Hart, *The Monroe Doctrine*.

53. See Perkins, *The Evolution of American Foreign Policy*, pp. 35–36, on this point and on the general applicability of the Monroe Doctrine and its declining influence (pp. 32–36).

54. Walter Russell Mead, *Special Providence* (New York: Alfred A. Knopf, 2001), p. 7. This section draws from, and uses the information from, my "Diplomatic History" in Steven W. Hook and Christopher M. Jones, *Routledge Handbook of American Foreign Policy* (New York and London: Routledge, 2012), especially pp. 23–24.

55. Mead, *Special Providence*, p. 8.

56. David C. Hendrickson, *Union, Nation, or Empire: The American Debate over International Relations, 1789–1941* (Lawrence: University Press of Kansas, 2009).

57. Robert J. McMahon, "Book Review of *Union, Nation, or Empire: The American Debate over International Relations, 1789–1941*," *Political Science Quarterly* 125 (Spring): 168–169.

58. Hans Morgenthau, "The Mainsprings of American Foreign Policy," in James M. McCormick (ed.), *A Reader in American Foreign Policy* (Itasca, IL: F.E. Peacock, 1986), p. 33.

59. Ibid., p. 34.

60. Ibid., p. 38.

61. Ibid.

62. Ibid., p. 41.

63. Ibid, pp. 42–43.

64. Robert H. Ferrell, *American Diplomacy: A History* (New York: W.W. Norton, 1959), p. 169.

65. Ibid.

66. Ibid., p. 173.

67. Ibid., p. 170.

68. Ibid., pp. 182–187 and 192–200, and George F. Kennan, *American Diplomacy, 1900–1950* (New York: Mentor Books, 1951), pp. 12–17.

69. Ferrell, *American Diplomacy: A History,* pp. 185 and 211, and Kennan, *American Diplomacy, 1900–1950,* p. 34.

70. Robert Dallek, *The American Style of Foreign Policy* (New York: Alfred A. Knopf, 1983), p. 110. The discussion here is based on pp. 92–122.

71. Ibid., p. 96–97, in which Dallek discusses the various implications of the pacifist movements during this period.

72. *Congressional Record*, December 6, 1904, 19.

73. Ferrell, *American Diplomacy,* pp. 395–415. The American occupations and protectorates in the Caribbean are outlined by Walter LaFeber, *The American Age: United States Foreign Policy at Home and Abroad Since 1750* (New York: W.W. Norton and Company, 1989), p. 233.

74. Walter Lefeber, *Inevitable Revolutions: The United States in Central America* (New York: W.W. Norton and Company, 1984), pp. 111–126, especially pp. 118–123.

75. President Kennedy's address to the nation can be found in Robert F. Kennedy, *Thirteen Days* (New York: Signet, 1969), pp. 131–139. The quoted passage is at p. 132.

76. See Dexter Perkins, *The American Approach to Foreign Policy* (Cambridge, MA: Harvard University Press, 1962), pp. 72–97, for a cogent discussion of moral principles as a guide in American foreign policy.

77. See Spanier, *American Foreign Policy,* pp. 9–11; and Stoessinger, *Crusaders and Pragmatists,* pp. 5–7.

78. For a recent assessment of the important role of religion in America's founding and beyond, see Jon Meacham, *American Gospel* (New York: Random House, 2006), especially pp. 3–113.

79. A discussion of the assumptions, aims, and means of the balance of power can be found in Edward V. Gulick, *Europe's Classical Balance of Power* (Ithaca, NY: Cornell University Press, 1955), pp. 3–91.

80. Changes in American policy makers' attitudes and beliefs toward a balance-of-power system occurred dramatically during the years in which Henry Kissinger was responsible for formulating American policy. This will be discussed in Chapter 3.

81. Henry A. Kissinger, *American Foreign Policy,* exp. ed. (New York: W.W. Norton and Company, 1974), pp. 91–92.

82. Carl von Clausewitz, *On War,* edited and translated by Michael Howard and Peter Paret (Princeton: Princeton University Press, 1976), p. 87. Spanier, *American Foreign Policy,* p. 10, also raises this point and discusses the dichotomous view of war and peace upon which we draw.

83. See the job approval chart in David W. Moore, "Bush Approval at 50%, Tied for Lowest of Presidency," The Gallup Organization, http://www.gallup.com/content/default .asp?ci=9742, March 11, 2004.

84. Perkins, *The American Approach*, p. 77.

85. Spanier, *American Foreign Policy*, p. 11.

86. These instances are discussed in George F. Kennan, *American Diplomacy 1900–1950* (New York: Mentor Books, 1951); Robert Endicott Osgood, *Ideals and Self-Interest in America's Foreign Relations* (Chicago: The University of Chicago Press, 1953); and Ferrell, *American Diplomacy*, pp. 123–153.

87. Harry L. Coles, *The War of 1812* (Chicago: The University of Chicago Press, 1965), pp. 1–37; and Ferrell, *American Diplomacy*, pp. 136–141.

88. Coles, *The War of 1812*, pp. 1–37; and Ferrell, *American Diplomacy*, pp. 136–141.

89. Ibid., p. 142.

90. Kennan, *American Diplomacy 1900–1950*, p. 14; and Ferrell, *American Diplomacy*, p. 353.

91. For a critical assessment of the impact of popular sentiment on this conflict, see Kennan, *American Diplomacy 1900–1950*, pp. 15–16.

92. Ferrell, *American Diplomacy*, pp. 456–462; and Kennan, *American Diplomacy 1900–1950*, pp. 50–65.

93. Ferrell, *American Diplomacy*, pp. 468–469.

94. Ibid., pp. 556–558.

95. P.L. 77–11, March 11, 1941. 55 Stat 31.

96. Speech by President Franklin D. Roosevelt to a joint session of Congress. The quotation can be found in the *Congressional Record*, 77th Cong., 1st sess., Vol. 87, December 8, 1941, 9519.

97. On Wilson's beliefs, see John G. Stoessinger, *Crusaders and Pragmatists: Movers of Modern American Foreign Policy*, 2nd ed. (New York: W.W. Norton and Company, 1985), pp. 8–27; and Michael H. Hunt, *Ideology and U.S. Foreign Policy* (New Haven, CT: Yale University Press, 1987), pp. 125–136, especially pp. 129–135.

98. For a listing of the Fourteen Points and a discussion of the Paris Conference, see Ferrell, *American Diplomacy*, pp. 482–492. The depiction of the new order draws on Hunt, *Ideology and U.S. Foreign Policy*, p. 134.

99. Robert Ferrell, *American Diplomacy: The Twentieth Century* (New York: W.W. Norton and Company, 1988), p. 153.

100. See the text of the Neutrality Act of 1935 (August 31, 1935) or the Neutrality Act of 1936 (February 29, 1936) for a full treatment of the restrictions on arms exports and travel by Americans. Both are reprinted in Nicholas O. Berry, ed., *U.S. Foreign Policy Documents, 1933–1945: From Withdrawal to World Leadership* (Brunswick, OH: King's Court Communications, 1978), pp. 25–27 and 32.

101. See the Neutrality Act of 1939 (November 4, 1939), reprinted in ibid., pp. 58–60.

102. See Howard Bliss and M. Glen Johnson, *Beyond the Water's Edge: America's Foreign Policies*, chap. 4, for a discussion of other values that have shaped the American style. Also see Hoffmann, *Gulliver's Troubles, or the Setting of American Foreign Policy* (New York: McGraw-Hill, 1968), chaps. 5 and 6.

CHAPTER **2**

America's Global Involvement and the Emergence of the Cold War

It is logical that the United States should do whatever it is able to do to assist in the return of normal economic health in the world. . . . Our policy is directed not against any country or doctrine but against hunger, poverty, desperation and chaos. Its purpose should be the revival of a working economy in the world so as to permit the emergence of political and social conditions in which free institutions can exist.

SECRETARY OF STATE GEORGE C. MARSHALL

JUNE 5, 1947

It is clear that the main element of any United States policy toward the Soviet Union must be that of a long-term, patient but firm and vigilant containment of Russian expansive tendencies.

MR. X [GEORGE F. KENNAN]

JULY 1947

Wor) orld War II plunged the United States into global affairs. By the end of 1941, the country had committed itself to total victory, and its involvement was to prove crucial to the war effort. However, because of its central importance to allied success, and its substantive involvement in international affairs, the United States found it difficult to change course in 1945 and revert to the isolationism of the past. To be sure, the first impulse was in this direction. Calls were heard for massive demobilization of the armed forces, cutbacks in the New Deal legislation of President Franklin Roosevelt, and other political and economic isolationism efforts.[1] Even so, at least three sets of factors militated against such a course and propelled the United States in the direction of global power:

- The global political and economic conditions of 1945 to 1947
- The decision of leading political figures within the United States to abandon isolationism after World War II
- Most important, the rise of an ideological challenge from the Soviet Union

In this chapter, we first examine these factors and how they led to the end of isolationism, the adoption of globalism, and the embrace of the Cold War consensus at home. In turn, we set out the military, economic, and political dimensions of this new globalist involvement—falling under the rubric of the containment doctrine—and we discuss how it both became universal in scope and remained moral in content. The containment doctrine produced a distinct set of American foreign policy values, beliefs, and actions, summarized under the heading of the Cold War consensus that held sway for a number of years.

THE POSTWAR WORLD AND AMERICAN INVOLVEMENT

The international system that the United States faced after the defeat of Germany and Japan was considerably different from any that it had in its history: the traditional powers of Europe were defeated or had been ruined by the ravages of war; the global economy had been significantly weakened; and the Soviet Union, a relatively new power equipped with a threatening ideology, had survived—arguably in better shape than any other European nation. Yet the United States was in a relatively strong political, economic, and military position, which seemed to imply the need for sustained U.S. involvement despite the nation's isolationist past.

Such a decision for involvement was made neither quickly nor automatically; rather, it seemed to come about over the course of several years and largely through the confluence of several complementary factors. We begin our discussion with a brief description of three of these factors and suggest how they interacted to move the United States toward sustained global involvement.

The Global Vacuum: A Challenge to American Isolationism

The first important factor that contributed to America's decision to move away from isolationism was the **global political and economic conditions** of the international system immediately after World War II. The land, the cities, and the homes, along with the economies, of most European nations had been devastated.

Sizeable portions of the land had been flooded, scorched, or confiscated. What land remained for cultivation was in poor condition, leading to widespread hunger and a flourishing black market in food. The industrial sectors of these nations, along with the major cities, were badly damaged or in total ruins. London, Vienna, Trieste, Warsaw, Berlin, Rotterdam, and Cologne, among others, bore the scars of war, and millions of people were homeless—by one estimate, 5 million homes had been destroyed, with many more millions badly damaged. In a word, Europe was a "wasteland."[2]

European economies were weak, in debt, and driven by inflation. Britain, for example, had had to use up much of its wealth to win the war and, with a debt of about $6 billion at war's end, was forced to rely on American assistance to remain solvent.[3] France, the Netherlands, Belgium, and other European states were in no better shape, having to rely, in varying degrees, on American assistance to meet their financial needs. Foreign and domestic political problems also faced these states. Several British and French colonies were demanding freedom and independence, Britain faced domestic austerity, and the French struggled at home with governmental instability and worker discontent. With such problems at home and abroad, neither country was in a position to assert a prominent role in postwar international politics.

The conditions in Germany and Italy further contributed to the political and economic vacuum in Europe. Both had been defeated, and Germany was divided and occupied. Italy was left with a huge budget deficit in 1945–1946 (300 billion lire by one estimate) as well as an extraordinarily high rate of inflation. Germany also was in debt, owing nearly nine times what it had at the beginning of the war.[4] Overall, Europe, which for so long had been at the center of international politics and for so long had shaped global order, was ominously weak, both politically and economically.

In contrast to postwar Europe, the United States was healthy and prosperous. Its industrial capacity was intact, and its economy was booming. In the mid-1940s, the United States had growing balance-of-trade surpluses and huge economic reserves. For example, whereas Europe had trade deficits of $5.8 billion and $7.6 billion in 1946 and 1947, America in those years had trade surpluses of $6.7 billion and $10.1 billion. Furthermore, American reserve assets—about $26 billion—were substantial and growing.[5]

The military might of the United States, too, seemed preeminent. American troops occupied Europe and Japan. The nation had the world's largest navy ("The Pacific and the Mediterranean had become American lakes," in the words of one historian[6]). And, of course, it alone had the atomic bomb. In this sense, then, the country possessed the capacity to assume a global role. Moreover, the international environment seemed highly conducive to both the possibility and the necessity of America taking on a dominant role in global affairs.

American Leadership and Global Involvement

A second factor that encouraged the United States to abandon its isolationist strategy was the **change in worldview** among American leaders during and immediately after World War II. Most important was President Franklin Roosevelt's long-held conclusion that America's response to global affairs after World War I had been ill-advised and that such a response should not guide post–World War II foreign policy.[7] Instead, Roosevelt had decided that continued American involvement in global affairs was necessary and, early on in the war, had revealed his vision of a future world order.

Roosevelt's Plan The first necessity in Roosevelt's plan was the total defeat and disarming of the adversaries, with no leniency shown toward aggressor states. Second was a renewed commitment by the United States and other countries to prevent future global economic depressions and to foster self-determination for all states. Third was the establishment of a global collective security organization with active American involvement. Finally, above and beyond these efforts, was Roosevelt's belief that the allies in war must remain allies in peace in order to maintain global order.[8]

This last element was the core of Roosevelt's global blueprint.[9] American involvement in world affairs and its cooperation with the other great powers were essential. Indeed, Roosevelt's design envisaged a world in which postwar cooperation among the principal powers (the United States, Great Britain, the USSR, and China) would yield a system in which they acted as the "**Four Policemen**" to enforce global order. In other words, whereas in Wilson's League of Nations all states were to work together to stop warfare and mediate conflict, only the great powers would now have this responsibility. Such a vision bore a striking and unmistakable resemblance to traditional balance-of-power politics, although Roosevelt was unwilling to describe it in such terms.

Strategy: Building Wartime Cooperation To make this global design a reality, two major tasks confronted Roosevelt's wartime diplomatic efforts. One was directed toward building wartime cooperation that would continue after the war. The other was directed toward jarring the United States from its isolationist moorings and positioning the country in such a way that it would retain a role in postwar international politics. To realize the first goal, cooperation with the Soviet Union was deemed essential. Unlike some of his advisors and some State Department officials, Roosevelt believed that such cooperation was possible after the end of World War II. He believed that the Soviet Union was motivated, in the shorthand of Daniel Yergin, more by the "**Yalta Axioms**" (the name is taken from the 1945 wartime conference in which political bargains were struck between East and West) than by the "**Riga Axioms**" (the name is taken from the Latvian capital city where a U.S. mission was located that "issued constant warning against the [Soviet] international menace" in the 1920s and 1930s).[10]

In the Yalta view, the Soviet Union was much like other nations in terms of defining its interests and fostering its goals on the basis of power realities (the Yalta Axioms) rather than being driven primarily by ideological considerations (the Riga Axioms). As Yergin contends, "Roosevelt thought of the Soviet Union less as a revolutionary vanguard than as a conventional imperialist power, with ambitions rather like those of the Czarist regime."[11] Because of this perceived source of Soviet policy, Roosevelt judged that the Grand Alliance among the United States, Great Britain, and the Soviet Union would be able to continue on a "businesslike" level as long as each recognized the interests of the other. Further, according to one well-known political analyst, there was another reason for Roosevelt to think that this cooperation could continue: the power of personal diplomacy.[12] Because he had steered American policy toward the recognition of the Soviet Union, shared Joseph Stalin's anxiety over British imperialism, and seemed to acknowledge Soviet interests in the Baltics and Poland, working together would be possible.

To facilitate postwar cooperation with the Soviets, Roosevelt made a concerted effort throughout the war to foster good relations. The United States extended **Lend-Lease assistance** to the Soviet Union (albeit not as rapidly as the Soviet Union wished) and agreed to open up a second front against the Germans to relieve the battlefield pressure the Soviets faced (albeit not as soon as they wanted). Through the several wartime conferences—Tehran, Cairo, Moscow, and Yalta—Roosevelt gained an understanding of the Soviets' insecurity regarding their exposed western borders, and he recognized the need to consider this factor when dealing with them. At the same time, he became increasingly convinced that he could work with "Uncle Joe" Stalin and that political bargains and accommodations were possible.

Strategy: A Role in Postwar International Politics   Among the wartime conferences, the one that bears most directly on postwar arrangements was Yalta, held in that Crimean resort during February 1945. Not only did this conference reach agreement on a strategy for victory but it also appeared to achieve commitments on the division and operation of postwar Europe. Such understandings were important because they signaled continued American interest and involvement in global affairs—specifically Europe. They also signaled that the competing interests of states were subject to negotiation and accommodation. Spheres of influence and balance-of-power politics were expressly incorporated in these agreements, and the major powers were to be primarily responsible for carrying them out.[13]

Specifically, Roosevelt, Stalin, and British Prime Minister Winston Churchill agreed to zones of German occupation to be held by the Americans, British, French, and Soviets. Second, they conceded some territory to the Soviets at the expense of Poland. (In turn, Poland was to receive some territory from Germany.) Third, they allowed an expansion of the Lublin Committee, which was governing Poland, to include Polish government officials who were in exile in London as a way of dealing with the postwar government in Poland. Fourth, they proclaimed the **Declaration of Liberated Europe**, which specified free elections and constitutional safeguards of individual freedom in the liberated nations. Finally, the conferees produced an agreement on the Soviet Union's entry into the war against Japan and on the veto mechanism within the Security Council of the United Nations.[14]

In light of subsequent events, Roosevelt has been highly criticized for the bargains that were struck at Yalta. The Soviets obtained several territorial concessions and, in the space of a few short years, were able to gain control of the Polish government as well as the governments of other Eastern European nations. Roosevelt's rationale was that only by taking into account the interests of the various parties (including the Soviets) was a stable postwar world possible. Moreover, he also appeared to consider Soviet insecurity about its western border when making some of these arrangements. Finally, and perhaps most important, Soviet troops already occupied the Eastern European states in question.[15] Any prospects of a more favorable outcome for the Western states appeared to be more hopeful than possible.

Despite these criticisms, the Yalta agreements do mark the beginning of an American commitment to global involvement beyond the war. This commitment is further reflected in the agreement regarding the operation of the UN Security Council and in the subsequent conference on the UN charter held in San Francisco during April 1945.[16]

The Rise of the Soviet Challenge

The third factor that propelled America's international involvement was the rise of the **Soviet ideological challenge** by late 1946 and early 1947. Although the commitment to a global role for the United States was no less true of President Roosevelt's successor, Harry S. Truman, and his principal foreign policy advisors, the emergence of the Soviet challenge steeled and solidified American resolve during this period. Truman's foreign policy approach was not nearly as well developed as that outlined by Roosevelt's postwar plan, but there was no inclination on his part to reject continued American involvement in the world.

Wilsonian Idealism   Prior to assuming the presidency, Truman had displayed a commitment to an international role for the United States. In particular, he agreed with Woodrow Wilson that America should participate in world affairs through a global organization. As a consequence, Truman worked in the Senate to gain support for the emergent United Nations. At the same time, like Wilson, he saw the United States as a moral force in the world and was somewhat suspicious of the postwar design epitomized by the Four Policemen plan.[17] Nonetheless, he supported Roosevelt's plan and worked to put it into practice.

The Wartime Situation   Truman's commitment to global involvement was aided by the circumstances at the time he became president. Roosevelt had died just after the conclusion of the Yalta Conference, just prior to the United Nations Conference in San Francisco, and just before the Allied victory. As a result, he felt the Yalta agreements had to be implemented, the United Nations needed to become a reality, and the war had to be won. In all of these areas, President Truman followed his predecessor.

The Views of Truman's Advisors   Truman's closest advisors were influential in reinforcing his commitment to a leading global role for the United States. These included key advisors such as Admiral William D. Leahy, Ambassador Averell Harriman, Secretary of State Edward R. Stettinius, and Secretary of War Henry Stimson.[18] Later, Secretary of State James Byrnes, Undersecretary of State (and later Secretary of State) Dean Acheson, and Navy Secretary James V. Forrestal became Truman's key policy advisors. They, too, promoted an active global involvement, especially with their less favorable view of the Soviet Union, although, according to historian Ernest May, "their prejudices and predispositions can serve as only one small element" in the change of American policy toward the Soviet Union.[19]

Nevertheless, the issue soon became less one of whether there should be American global involvement and more one of its extent. Fueled by negative assessments of the Soviet Union by seasoned diplomatic observers, Truman's advisors increasingly focused on the threat posed by international communism generally and by the Soviets specifically.[20] In time, the shape and scope of America's role became largely a consequence of the perceived intentions of Soviet ideology.

Truman's Early Position   In the first months after assuming office, Truman followed Roosevelt's strategy for peace and American involvement by trying to maintain great-power unity. As he said, "I want peace and I am willing to work hard for it: . . . to have a reasonably lasting peace, the three great powers must be able to trust each other." Likewise, he remained faithful to the requirements of the Yalta agreements and tried to cajole Stalin into doing the same by demanding of Soviet Foreign Minister Molotov: "carry out your agreements."[21]

A Changing Environment   By the time of the **Potsdam Conference** (July 1945), President Truman was increasingly being urged to get tough with the Soviets

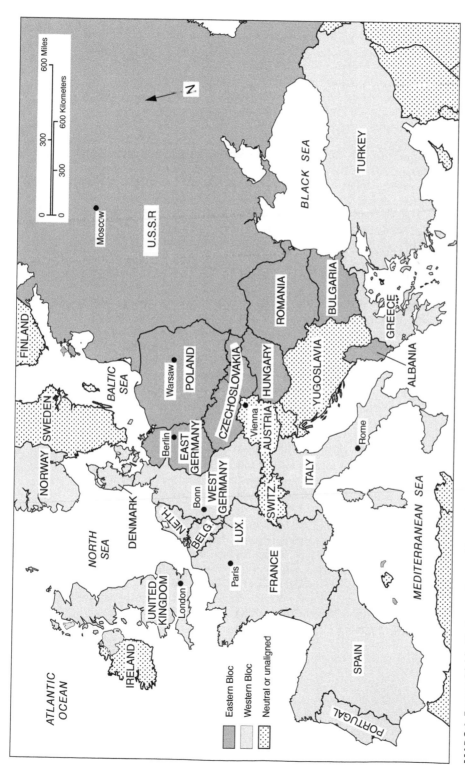

MAP 2.1 Europe Divided between East and West after World War II

while still seeking postwar cooperation. Although the accommodation that came out of Potsdam over German reparations and German boundaries, as well as other agreements, was deemed tolerable, American officials ultimately came away uneasy over the future prospects of Soviet–American relations.[22] Subsequent meetings in London (September 1945), on peace treaties for Finland, Hungary, Romania, and Bulgaria, and in Moscow (December 1945), on adherence to the Yalta agreements, reinforced this uneasiness and highlighted the growing suspicion between the United States and the Soviet Union.[23]

The end of 1945 and the early months of 1946 seemed to mark a watershed in Soviet–American relations.[24] By this time, the American public, Congress, and the president's chief advisors were lobbying for tougher action against Soviet noncompliance with the Yalta agreements and with Soviet efforts to undermine the governments in Eastern Europe. Coupled with these domestic pressures were ominous statements by Stalin, Churchill, an American diplomat, George Kennan, and a Soviet ambassador, Nikolai Novikov, about American and Soviet intentions toward the world.

Stalin Attacks Capitalism   In a speech on February 9, 1946, Soviet leader Joseph Stalin alarmed American policy makers by attacking capitalism, suggesting the inevitability of war among capitalist states, and calling for significant economic strides to meet the capitalist challenge. About the dangers from capitalist states he stated: "Marxists have repeatedly declared that the capitalist world economic system conceals in itself the elements of general crisis and military clashes." He further asserted that "the party intends to organize a new powerful advance in the national economy. . . . Only under these circumstances is it possible to consider that our country will be guaranteed against any eventuality."[25]

Although the meaning and intent of Stalin's remarks inevitably fostered some debate (one analysis suggests that Stalin did not want a "new war" and said so through 1947), and that his comments "constituted about one-tenth of the address,"[26] their ultimate effect on American policy makers was profound. Indeed, in the assessment of two prominent diplomatic historians of this period, Stalin's meaning was clear: "war was inevitable as long as capitalism existed," and "future wars were inevitable until the world economic system was reformed, that is, until communism supplanted capitalism. . . ."[27]

Churchill's Response   On March 5, 1946, Winston Churchill reciprocated by articulating the West's fear of the East in his famous "**Iron Curtain speech**" at Westminster College in Fulton, Missouri. He called for "a fraternal association of the English-speaking peoples . . . a special relationship between the British Commonwealth and Empire and the United States" to provide global order because "from Stettin in the Baltic to Trieste in the Adriatic, an iron curtain has descended across the Continent. Behind that line lie all the capitals of the ancient states of Central and Eastern Europe." Moreover, these states and many ancient cities "lie in what I must call the Soviet sphere," Churchill continued, "and all are subject in one form or another, not only to Soviet influence but to a very high and, in many cases, increasing measure of control from Moscow."[28]

This speech was a frontal attack on the Soviet Union, and, like Stalin's, it suggested the impossibility of continued Soviet–American cooperation in the postwar world because of differing worldviews. Importantly, President Truman seemed to be giving some legitimacy to such a view by accompanying Churchill to Missouri.[29]

Kennan's Perception from Moscow At about the same time that these two speeches were delivered, **George Kennan**, an American diplomat serving in Moscow, sent his famous "**long telegram**" to Washington. (The actual date of the message is February 22, 1946.) In it, he outlined his view of the basic premises of the Soviet world outlook, the "Kremlin's neurotic view of world affairs," the "instinctive Russian sense of insecurity," and the "official" and "subterranean" actions against free societies. Soviet policies, Kennan argued, would work vigorously to advance Soviet interests worldwide and to undermine Western powers. "In general," Kennan noted near the end of his message, "all Soviet efforts on [an] unofficial international plane will be negative and destructive in character, designed to tear down sources of strength beyond reach of Soviet control."

Kennan was equally pointed in the concluding section of his message:

[W]e have here a political force committed fanatically to the belief that with US there can be no permanent modus vivendi, that it is desirable and necessary that the internal harmony of our society be disrupted, our traditional way of life be destroyed, the international authority of our state be broken, if Soviet power is to be secure. Finally, it is seemingly inaccessible to considerations of reality in its basic reactions. For it, the vast fund of objective facts about human society is not, as with us, the measure against which outlook is constantly tested and reformed, but a grab bag from which individual items are selected arbitrarily and tendentiously to bolster an outlook already preconceived.[30]

Kennan's view of the Soviet Union has come to be known as the **Riga Axioms** (in contrast to the Yalta Axioms, which President Roosevelt had adopted), which held that ideology, not the realities of power politics, was the important determinant of Soviet conduct. These statements by Stalin and Churchill and the circulation of Kennan's "long telegram" within the Washington bureaucracy increased the clamor for a changed perception toward the Soviet Union, leading to a "get tough" policy on the part of the United States. They also permanently changed the U.S. role in global affairs.

Another telegram in September 1946, sent by the Soviet ambassador to the United States, **Nikolai Novikov**, to the Kremlin, completed this circle of mutual suspicion. In that telegram, Novikov asserted that "the foreign policy of the United States, which reflects the imperialist tendencies of American monopolistic capital, is characterized by a striving for world supremacy. . . . All the forces of American diplomacy—the army, the air force, the navy, industry, and science—are enlisted in the service of this foreign policy." Furthermore, he outlined the various actions carried out by the United States to comport with this perceived policy, including its efforts "directed at limiting or dislodging the influence of the Soviet Union from neighboring countries" and its efforts at preparing "for a future war" against the Soviets.[31] As diplomatic historian John Lewis Gaddis has noted, the telegram "reflected Stalin's thinking" and was "ghost-authored" by Soviet Foreign Minister V. M. Molotov.[32] In this sense, it reflected the official view of the Kremlin at the time.

In essence, then, Kennan's and Novikov's telegrams solidified "a particular worldview and analytical framework that had been established" in both countries with the result that "confrontation escalated as each side pursued a diplomacy that aimed to counter the perceived expansionism of the other."[33]

AMERICA'S GLOBALISM: THE TRUMAN DOCTRINE AND BEYOND

The immediate American response to calls to "get tough" was reflected in its policy over Soviet troops remaining in Iran in March 1946. Under the **Tripartite Treaty of Alliance** signed by Iran, the Soviet Union, and Great Britain in January 1942, Allied forces were to be withdrawn from Iranian territory within six months after hostilities ended. By March 2, 1946—six months after the surrender of Japan—all British and American forces had indeed withdrawn, but Soviet forces remained. The Soviets were sending in additional troops, were continuing to meddle in Iranian politics, and apparently had designs on Turkey and Iraq from their Iranian base.[34]

The American leadership decided to stand firm on the withdrawal of Soviet forces. Secretary of State James Byrnes and British Foreign Minister Ernest Bevin delivered speeches that made the West's position clear. In late February 1946, Secretary Byrnes claimed:

> We have joined our allies in the United Nations to put an end to war. We have covenanted not to use force except in the defense of law as embodied in the purposes and principles of the [UN] Charter. We intend to live up to that covenant. . . .
>
> But as a great power and as a permanent member of the Security Council *we have a responsibility to use our influence to see that other powers live up to their covenant.* . . .
>
> We will not and we cannot stand aloof if force or threat of force is used contrary to the purposes and principles of the Charter. We have no right to hold our troops in the territories of other sovereign states without their approval and consent freely given.[35]

Later, on March 16, Byrnes reiterated American resolve, repeating some of his earlier themes. Faced with British and American resolve as expressed in such speeches and with an imminent UN Security Council session on the Iranian issue, the Soviet Union sought a negotiated solution. In early April 1946, an agreement was reached that called for the withdrawal of all Soviet forces from Iran by the middle of May 1946.[36] The Soviets' actions demonstrate that when America adopted a tougher policy line toward the Soviet Union, it was able to achieve results.

Despite the initial success of this firmer course in early 1946, the real change in America's Soviet policy (and ultimately its policy toward the rest of the world) was not fully manifested until a year later. The occasion was the question of aid to two strategically important countries, **Greece and Turkey**.

The Greek government was under pressure from a Communist-supported national liberation movement; Turkey was under political pressure from the Soviet Union and its allies over control of the Dardanelles (the straits that provide access to the Mediterranean from the Soviets' Black Sea ports) and over territorial concessions to the Soviets in Turkish–Soviet border areas.[37] Because the British had indicated to the Americans in February 1947 that they could no longer aid these countries, the burden apparently now fell to the United States to see that these states remained stable. Accordingly, President Truman decided to seek $400 million in aid for them.

The granting of aid in itself was not a sharp break from the past, as the United States had provided assistance to Greece previously in 1946.[38] What was dramatic was the aid request's *form*, *rationale*, and *purpose*. The form was a formal speech delivered by Truman to a joint session of Congress on March 12, 1947. The rationale was even more dramatic: the need to stop the expansion of global communism. Most startling was the purpose: to commit the United States to a global strategy against this communist threat.

In his speech, in which he announced what has come to be known as the **Truman Doctrine**, the president first set out the conditions in Greece and Turkey that necessitated this assistance. Then he more fully outlined the justification for his policy and identified the global struggle that the United States faced. America must *"help free peoples to maintain their free institutions and their national identity against aggressive movements that seek to impose on them totalitarian regimes."* Moreover, such threats to freedom affected U.S. security: *"totalitarian regimes imposed on free peoples, by direct or indirect aggression, undermine the foundations of international peace and hence the security of the United States."* At this juncture in history, he continued, the nations of the world faced a decision between two ways of life: one free, the other unfree; one based *"on the will of the majority,"* the other on *"the will of a minority"*; one based on *"free institutions,"* the other on *"terror and oppression."* The task for the United States, therefore, was a clear one: *"we must assist free peoples to work out their own destinies in their own way."* Truman had clearly drawn the challenge to the Soviet Union. The Cold War had begun.[39]

The specific policy that the United States was to adopt in this struggle with the Soviet Union was one of **containment**. This term was first used in an anonymously authored article in *Foreign Affairs* magazine in July 1947. (Its author was quickly identified as George Kennan, by then the head of the policy planning staff at the Department of State, who based it on his original "long telegram" sent to the State Department a year earlier.) According to "Mr. X," the appropriate policy to adopt against the Soviet challenge was "a long-term patient but firm and vigilant containment of Russian expansive tendencies." Specifically, he called for the application of "counter-force at a series of constantly shifting geographical and political points" against Soviet actions. By following such a policy, the United States might, over time, force "a far greater degree of moderation and circumspection . . . and in this way . . . promote . . . tendencies which must eventually find their outlet in either the breakup or the gradual mellowing of Soviet power."[40]

Kennan identified a number of conditions within the Soviet system that would aid containment in achieving its goal. The population "in Russia today," he noted, "is physically and spiritually tired," the impact of the Soviet system on the young remained unclear, and the performance of the Soviet economy "has been precariously spotty and uneven."[41] Finally, the issue of succession was decidedly incomplete:

> The future of Soviet power may not be by any means as secure as Russian capacity for self-delusion would make it appear to the men in the Kremlin. That they can keep power themselves, they have demonstrated. That they can quietly and easily turn it over to others remains to be proved.[42]

Although Kennan was confident that a steady course would be successful, he was imprecise regarding what the counterforce or containment toward the Soviet Union should entail. As a result, the response by American policy makers, which Kennan later criticized,[43] was to embark on a series of sweeping military, economic, and political initiatives from 1947 through the mid-1950s to control international communism.

ELEMENTS OF CONTAINMENT: REGIONAL SECURITY PACTS

The first, and probably principal, containment initiative was the establishment of several regional political-military alliances. In September 1947, the **Rio Pact** (formally known as the Inter-American Treaty of Reciprocal Assistance) was signed by the United States and twenty-one Latin American republics. In April 1949, the **North Atlantic Treaty Organization (NATO)** was set up by the United States, Canada, and ten Western European nations (rising to thirteen in the 1950s and fourteen by 1982). Two other important pacts were established: the **ANZUS Treaty** in September 1951,[44] and the Southeast Asia Collective Defense Treaty in September 1954. The former involved the United States, Australia, and New Zealand. The latter included the United States, Great Britain, France, Australia, New Zealand, Pakistan, the Philippines, and Thailand, forming what became known as the **Southeast Asia Treaty Organization (SEATO)**. (A protocol was added to provide security protection for South Vietnam, Cambodia, and Laos. This would become most important in light of America's subsequent involvement in the Vietnam War.[45]) Map 2.2 shows these organizations and the areas they covered.

One other collective security pact was created during this period, the **Central Treaty Organization (CENTO)**, although the United States was not a direct member. CENTO evolved from a bilateral agreement of mutual cooperation between Iraq and Turkey (the so-called Baghdad Pact of February 1955) and was formally constituted in 1959 with the inclusion of the United Kingdom, Pakistan, and Iran. Through an executive agreement with Turkey, the United States pledged to support the security of its members and to provide various kinds of assistance. In addition, the United States actively participated in CENTO meetings and assisted with its joint undertakings. Because of U.S. involvement and indirect support, CENTO was actually another link in U.S. global security arrangements initiated in the immediate postwar years.

All of these defense agreements provided for assistance when organization members were confronted by armed attacks, threats of aggression, or even internal subversion (in the case of SEATO). For the ANZUS, SEATO, Rio, and CENTO pacts, however, response was not automatic. Instead, each of the signatories agreed, in the main, "to meet the common danger in accordance with its constitutional processes."[46] NATO is usually identified as an exception for at least two reasons: (1) The commitment by the parties to respond to an attack appears to be more automatic than in other pacts. (2) Its organizational structure developed much more fully than did that of the others.

First, Article 5 of the NATO agreement seemed to call for an automatic armed response to an attack by the signatories:

> The Parties agree that an armed attack against one or more of them in Europe or North America shall be considered an attack against them all, and consequently they agree that, if such an armed attack occurs, each of them . . . will assist the Party or Parties so attacked by taking forthwith, individually and in concert with the other

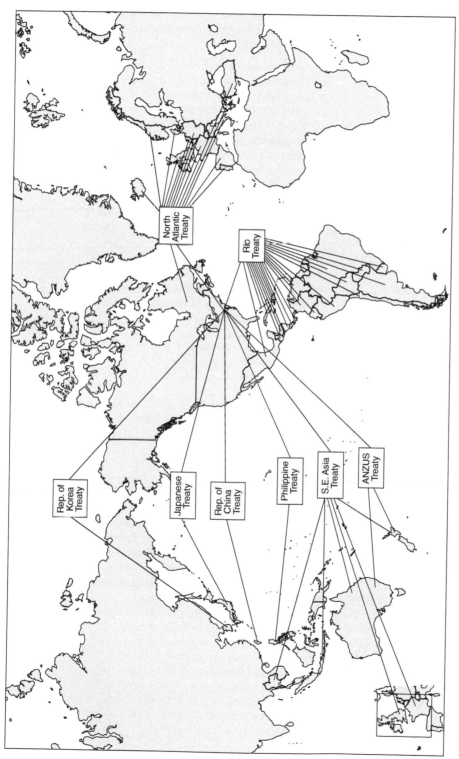

MAP 2.2 U.S. Collective Defense Arrangements

Parties, such action as it deems necessary, including the use of armed force, to restore and maintain the security of the North Atlantic area.[47]

However, constitutional scholar Michael Glennon has cautioned against too facile an interpretation of this article. As he notes, a party to the pact could take actions it "deems necessary," but troops were not necessarily required automatically. Indeed, at the time, Secretary of State Dean Acheson, in commenting on this treaty provision, downplayed the automaticity of troop commitments, acknowledging that only Congress had that authority. Still, both Acheson and Truman's congressional allies vigorously opposed a reservation that would have fully spelled out the limits of the NATO commitment. The Truman administration apparently wanted to maintain some ambiguity, both to accommodate critics at home and to reassure allies abroad.[48] Thus, the NATO commitment appears a bit different from that of other pacts during this time.

Second, the members of NATO established an integrated military command structure and called for the commitment of forces (although they would remain under ultimate national command) by members.

In both of these ways, NATO proved the most important of the regional security pacts because it involved the area of greatest concern for American interests and because Europe was regarded as the primary area of potential Soviet aggression.

In addition to the regional military organizations, a series of bilateral defense pacts were established in Asia to combat Soviet and Chinese aggression. Completed with the Philippines (1951), Japan (1951), the Republic of Korea (1953), and the Republic of China, or Taiwan (1954), they resulted from two major political events in Asia in the late 1940s and early 1950s: the Communist triumph in China under Mao Tse-tung in 1949 and the outbreak of war in Korea in 1950.[49] (This latter event will be discussed shortly.)

With these bilateral treaties in the early 1950s, the mosaic of global security was largely completed. Moreover, Map 2.2 indicates that the United States was quite successful in forming alliances in most areas that were not directly under Soviet control.

Two prominent regions, Africa and the Middle East, were still not directly covered by any security arrangements. Here too, however, some elements of containment were evident. In Africa, for instance, the colonial powers still held sway, and thus the continent was largely under the Western European containment shield.[50] Security efforts in the Middle East were more complex. Although the regimes were mainly traditional monarchies, stirrings of nationalism and pan-Arabism within Egypt under Gamal Abdel Nasser and their spread throughout the Arab world made treaty commitments difficult. Added to these factors were America's close ties to Israel over the festering Arab–Israeli conflict. Still, the United States did initiate one important security proposal in this volatile area: the so-called **Eisenhower Doctrine**.

The Eisenhower Doctrine arose from a speech given by President Dwight D. Eisenhower to a joint session of Congress on perceived trouble in the Middle East and the need to combat it. "If power-hungry Communists should either falsely or correctly estimate that the Middle East is inadequately defended, they might be tempted to use open measures of armed attack," Eisenhower declared. He asked Congress for authority to extend economic and military assistance as needed and to use armed force "to assist any such nation or group of such nations requesting assistance against armed aggression from any country controlled by international communism,"[51] and Congress complied. U.S. security commitments were now truly global in scope.

ELEMENTS OF CONTAINMENT: ECONOMIC AND MILITARY ASSISTANCE

The second set of initiatives to implement the containment strategy focused on economic and military assistance to friendly nations. From the late 1940s through the mid- and late 1950s, aid reaching over $10 billion in 1953 was provided to an ever-expanding number of nations throughout the world. Although the initial goal of this assistance was to foster the economic well-being of the recipients, the ultimate rationale, especially after 1950, was *strategic* and *political*: to ensure the stability of countries threatened by international communism and to build support for anticommunism on a global scale. Three important programs reflect the kinds of U.S. assistance during this period as well as its change in orientation over time:

- The Marshall Plan
- The Point Four program
- The mutual security concept[52]

The Marshall Plan

Proposed in a speech by **Secretary of State George Marshall** at Harvard University's June 1947 commencement exercises, the Marshall Plan remains the United States' best-known assistance effort. In his address, Marshall called for Europeans to draw up a plan for economic recovery and pledged American economic support for it. As a consequence of this speech and subsequent European–American consultations, President Truman asked Congress for $17 billion over a four-year period, from 1948 to 1952, to revitalize Western Europe.

The enormity of this aid commitment becomes apparent when compared to the approximately $1 billion in assistance offered to Eastern Europe after the collapse of the Iron Curtain in 1989 and 1990. Its size is also reflected in the fact that the Marshall Plan constituted about 1.2 percent of the GNP of the United States at the time. In contrast, the amount of U.S. development assistance in recent years has constituted well under 0.5 percent of U.S. GNP; in 2010, it constituted only 0.21 percent of the Gross National Income (a measure closely equivalent to GNP).[53]

The rationale for the Marshall Plan was the rebuilding of the economic system of Western Europe. As a key U.S. trading partner, a healthy Europe was important to America's economic health. Beyond economic concerns, though, were political concerns. If Europe did not recover, the region might well be subject to political instability and perhaps Communist penetration and subversion. According to one analysis of Marshall Plan decision making, this "threat" dimension became particularly important in the late stages of deliberations (February through April 1948, just prior to the plan's enactment).[54] In this sense, then, by the time of its formal passage by Congress, the **European Recovery Program**, as the Marshall Plan was formally known, had clear elements of the containment strategy.

Point Four

The Marshall Plan proved remarkably successful in fostering European recovery, but President Truman envisioned a broader plan of assistance for the rest of the world. He announced his Point Four program, the fourth point in his inaugural address, on January 20, 1949. The aim of this program was to develop the essentials of the Marshall Plan, which was then under way in Western Europe, on a global scale. Unlike the Marshall Plan, though, Point Four was less a cooperative venture and more a unilateral effort on the part of the United States, although America's allies might also become involved. In essence, it would provide industrial, technological, and economic assistance to underdeveloped nations,[55] and in this sense it represented an imaginative and substantial commitment to global economic development.

The Mutual Security Concept

Although Point Four had some of the ambitious economic—and undoubtedly political—motivations that the Marshall Plan had, it did not receive sufficient funding authorization from Congress[56] and instead was quickly replaced by a new, more explicitly political approach known as mutual security. The **mutual security approach** emphasized aid to nations combating communism and strengthening U.S. security and the security of the "Free World." In addition to the change in rationale was a change in the kind of assistance: from primarily economic and humanitarian to military by the early and mid-1950s. Although economic aid was not halted during this period, now it was more likely given to bolster the overall security capability of friendly countries.

These changes in aid policy can be explained by the deepening global crisis that the United States perceived in the world. Tensions between the Soviet Union and the United States were rising over Soviet actions in Eastern Europe and its potential actions toward Western Europe. The Korean War had broken out, apparently with Soviet compliance, and the Chinese Communists later entered the conflict, again evoking concern over Communist intentions. Domestically, too, there was an increased sense of Communist threat led by the verbal assaults of Senator Joseph McCarthy of Wisconsin against various individuals and groups for being "soft on communism." All in all, America's national security was perceived to be under attack, and this required some response.

The first manifestation of the new aid strategy was the **Mutual Defense Assistance Act of 1949**[57]—signed after the completion of the NATO pact and after the Soviets had tested an atomic bomb—which provided for military aid to Western Europe, Greece, Turkey, Iran, South Korea, the Philippines, and the "China area." The strategic locations of these countries are obvious: most bordered the Soviet Union or mainland China. Although the amount of aid called for was relatively small, its significance lay in the fact that it was the initial effort in U.S. military aid.

The **Mutual Security Act of 1951** marked the real beginning of growth in military assistance funding. Equally important, its language dramatically illustrated the linkage between the new aid policy and American security. The goals of the act were

> to maintain the security and to promote the foreign policy of the United States by authorizing military, economic, and technical assistance to friendly countries to strengthen the mutual security and individual and collective defenses of the free world, [and] to develop their resources in the interest of their security and independence and the national interest of the United States.[58]

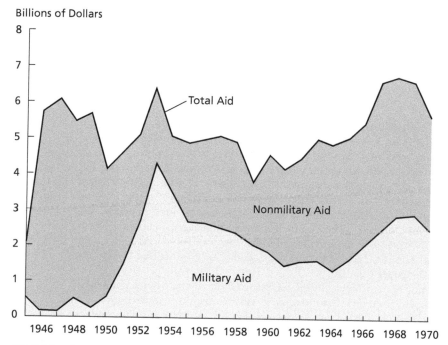

FIGURE 2.1 Patterns in Foreign Aid, 1945–1970 (Net Grants and Credits)

Source: *The Statistical History of the United States from Colonial Times to the Present* (New York: Basic Books, Inc., 1976), pp. 274, 872.

With successive mutual security acts like this one, American global assistance, and particularly military assistance, increased, as did the number of recipient countries. As Figure 2.1 shows, military aid came to dominate the U.S. assistance effort. Even with the addition of food aid under Public Law 480 in 1954 and some technical and developmental assistance to particular countries (such as Yugoslavia and Poland),[59] military assistance was often greater than nonmilitary assistance until about 1960. By that time, a new approach, one motivated more explicitly by development considerations, was being contemplated and was finally implemented by the Kennedy administration in 1961 with the establishment of the Agency for International Development (AID). Still, the political rationale for economic aid—as a way to save America's friends from Soviet (and Chinese) communism—continued.

ELEMENTS OF CONTAINMENT: THE DOMESTIC COLD WAR

The third element in the strategy of containment was primarily domestic, with the aim of making the American people aware of the Soviet threat and changing American domestic priorities to combat it. In essence, this aspect of containment might be labeled the *domestication* of the Cold War. One important document, drawn up by the National Security Council in April 1950 and entitled *NSC-68*, summarized the goals of this effort and provides a guide to the subsequent domestic and international changes that occurred. Along with the Korean War, discussed in the next section, *NSC-68* solidified America's commitment to the containment policy course.

NSC-68: Defense

NSC-68 was the result of a review of American foreign and domestic defense policies by State and Defense Department officials under the leadership of Paul Nitze. (Because the report remained classified until 1975, it gives us a unique picture of the thinking of American officials unrestrained by the fear of public disclosure.) The document itself is a rather lengthy statement that begins by outlining the current international crisis between the Soviet Union and the United States and goes on to contrast the foreign policy goals of Washington and Moscow in much the same vein as that of the Truman Doctrine, albeit in much harsher language. Document 2.1 excerpts portions of *NSC-68* that depict these alternate views of the world.[60] Note the way that Soviet and American goals are characterized and the conflict that the United States now faced is portrayed.

NSC-68 outlined four policy options for responding to the Soviet challenge: (1) continuing current policies; (2) returning to isolationism; (3) resorting to war against the Soviet Union; and (4) "a rapid build-up of political, economic and military strength in the Free World." After careful analysis along military, economic, political, and social lines, the study recommended a rapid buildup of American and allied strength as "the only course which is consistent with progress toward achieving our fundamental purpose. The frustration of the Kremlin design requires the free world to develop a successfully functioning political and economic system and a vigorous political offensive against the Soviet Union."[61]

What distinguishes *NSC-68* from other elements of containment is its emphasis on a domestic response to the Soviet threat. Along with calling for aid to allies and the promotion of anticommunism around the world, it offered substantial commentary on the need to build up America's military capacity and elicit greater support against the Soviet challenge at home.

The U.S. military, *NSC-68* contended, was inferior to the Soviet military in the number of "forces in being and in total manpower." The amount of defense spending was also relatively low, about 6 to 7 percent of U.S. GNP compared to more than 13 percent of Soviet GNP. In response, *NSC-68* called for a rapid buildup of the American military establishment as a countermeasure. Indeed, *NSC-68* went beyond this important general demand by proposing a new policy on military budgeting: in the future, it might be necessary to meet defense and foreign assistance needs by reducing federal expenditures in other areas—and by increasing taxes.[62] In effect, this policy was to make defense spending the number-one priority in the federal budget. Instead of a residual category of the budget, it was to become the focal point of future allocation decisions.

NSC-68 made at least one other significant statement on military planning. In the body of the report (not specifically in its conclusions), it called for the United States to "produce and stockpile thermonuclear weapons in the event they prove feasible and would add significantly to our net capability."[63] Although this reference is relatively oblique in context, it was significant in timing. During this period, the Truman administration was embroiled in a debate over the building of the H-bomb.

Document 2.1 Excerpts from NSC-68, April 14, 1950

FUNDAMENTAL DESIGN OF THE UNITED STATES

The fundamental purpose of the United States is laid down in the Preamble of the Constitution. . . . In essence, [it] is to assure the integrity and vitality of our free society, which is founded on the dignity and worth of the individual.

FUNDAMENTAL DESIGN OF THE KREMLIN

The fundamental design of those who control the Soviet Union and the international communist movement is to retain and solidify their absolute power, first in the Soviet Union and second in the areas now under their control. In the minds of the Soviet leaders, however, achievement of this design requires the dynamic extension of their authority and the ultimate elimination of any effective opposition to their authority. . . . The United States, as the principal center of power in the non-Soviet world and the bulwark of opposition to Soviet expansion, is the principal enemy whose integrity and vitality must be subverted or destroyed by one means or another if the Kremlin is to achieve its fundamental design.

NATURE OF THE CONFLICT

The Kremlin regards the United States as the only major threat to the achievement of its fundamental design. There is a basic conflict between the idea of freedom under a government of law, and the idea of slavery under the grim oligarchy of the Kremlin. . . . The idea of freedom, moreover, is peculiarly and intolerably subversive of the idea of slavery. But the converse is not true. The implacable purpose of the slave state to eliminate the challenge of freedom has placed the two great powers at opposite poles. It is this fact which gives the present polarization of power the quality of crisis.

The assault on free institutions is world-wide now, and in the context of the present polarization of power a defeat of free institutions anywhere is a defeat everywhere. . . .

In a shrinking world, which now faces the threat of atomic warfare, it is not an adequate objective merely to seek to check the Kremlin design, for the absence of order among nations is becoming less and less tolerable. This fact imposes on us, in our own interests, the responsibility of world leadership. It demands that we make the attempt, and accept the risks inherent in it, to bring about order and justice by means consistent with the principles of freedom and democracy. . . . Coupled with the probable fission bomb capability and possible thermonuclear bomb capability of the Soviet Union, the intensifying struggle requires us to face the fact that we can expect no lasting abatement of the crisis unless and until a change occurs in the nature of the Soviet system.

Source: A Report to the National Security Council, April 14, 1950, pp. 5–9. Declassified on February 27, 1975, by Henry A. Kissinger, assistant to the president for National Security Affairs.

NSC-68: Internal Security

A second important domestic issue discussed in the report concerned America's moral capabilities. These, too, were vulnerable, as the Soviets might well seek to undermine America's social and cultural institutions by infiltration and intimidation:

> Those that touch most closely our material and moral strength are obviously the prime targets, labor unions, civic enterprises, schools, churches, and all media for influencing opinion. The effort is not so much to make them serve obvious Soviet ends as to prevent them from serving our ends, and thus to make them sources of confusion in our economy, our culture and our body politic.[64]

Hence, internal security and civilian defense programs were necessary to "assure the internal security of the United States against dangers of sabotage, subversion, and espionage." And the government must "keep the U.S. public fully informed and cognizant of the threats to our national security so that it will be prepared to support the measures which we must accordingly adopt."[65] In essence, efforts must be made to protect the American people against subversion and to gain their support for Cold War policies.

To a considerable degree, the *NSC-68* recommendations became American policy in the early 1950s, sparked by American involvement in the **Korean War**. Defense expenditures escalated to more than 10 percent of the GNP and generally stayed above 8 percent throughout the 1960s. Similarly, defense spending as a percentage of the federal budget rose sharply after *NSC-68* to more than 50 percent and remained over 40 percent for all the years of the Johnson administration. A parallel growth occurred in the size of the U.S. armed forces, with the number of military personnel under arms reaching over 22 per 1,000 population in the early 1950s and remaining at about 14 per 1,000 throughout the height of the Vietnam War. (Figure 2.2 provides a summary of these trends during the 1946–1968 period.[66]) Additionally, the H-bomb program was given the go-ahead, and thus nuclear weapons became a part of America's defense strategy.

Efforts to ensure internal security were undertaken as well. As we have already noted, Senator Joseph McCarthy initiated his campaign against "communists" within the government; the public, too, raised questions about Communist subversion. Various investigations by the **House Un-American Activities Committee** of the 1950s and 1960s reflect this growing concern with Soviet penetration, as do FBI and CIA surveillance activities in this area (which the Church Committee investigations of intelligence activities were to reveal in the mid-1970s). Efforts to impose loyalty oaths, too, reflect this trend toward national security consciousness.

In short, political attacks, from the schoolroom to the boardroom, produced a widespread fear of veering too far from the mainstream on foreign policy issues. To a remarkable degree, a foreign policy consensus was the result of the political and psychological effects of the Cold War, and foreign policy debate suffered. When it did occur, it was more often on foreign policy tactics than on fundamental strategy.[67]

KOREA: THE FIRST MAJOR TEST OF CONTAINMENT

Although the events in Greece and Turkey stimulated the emergence of containment in 1947, the first major test of this policy, and the event that brought the Cold War fully into existence, occurred in Korea. On June 25, 1950, North Korea attacked South Korea, an action that quickly engaged the Soviet Union, China, and the United States in a confrontation on the Korean peninsula. For the United States in particular it provided the raison d'être for fully implementing the various elements of the containment strategy just outlined.

American Involvement in Korea

A brief description of the Korean conflict, its origins, and the extent of U.S. involvement will illustrate the significance of this war for American postwar policy.

Korea had been annexed by the Japanese in 1910 and was finally freed by American and Soviet forces at the end of World War II. By agreement between the Soviet Union

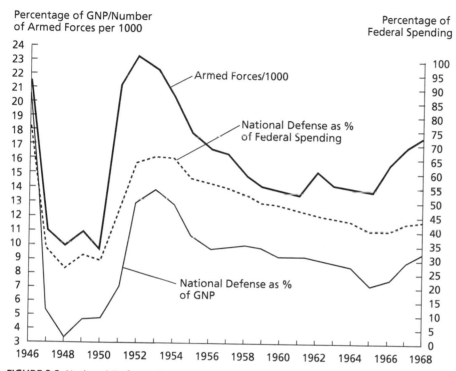

FIGURE 2.2 National Defense Expenditures and U.S. Armed Forces per 1,000 Population, 1946–1968

Sources: The data for national defense as a percentage of federal spending and GNP are taken from Alice C. Moroni, *The Fiscal Year 1984 Defense Budget Request: Data Summary* (Washington, DC: Congressional Research Service, 1983), p. 13. Total National Defense data, rather than only Department of Defense data, are used here. The two totals are usually very close (p. 14). The armed forces percentages were calculated from total population (Part 1, p. 8) and armed forces (Part 2, p. 1141) data in U.S. Bureau of the Census, *Historical Statistics of the United States, Colonial Times to 1970, Bicentennial Edition, Parts 1 and 2* (Washington, DC: U.S. Government Printing Office, 1975)

and the United States, Korea was then temporarily divided along the 38th parallel, with Soviet forces occupying the North and U.S. forces occupying the South (see Map 2.3). Despite several maneuvers by both sides, this division assumed a more permanent cast when a UN-supervised election in the South resulted in the establishment of the **Republic of Korea** on August 15, 1948, and when the adoption of a constitution in the North resulted in the creation of the **Democratic People's Republic of Korea** on September 9, 1948.[68] Both regimes claimed to be the government of Korea, and neither would recognize or accept the legitimacy of the other. Although Soviet and American occupying forces left in 1948 and 1949, respectively, the struggle between North and South (with the support of their powerful allies) was not finished.

The struggle soon erupted into sustained violence in mid-1950, when North Korea attacked South Korea and the two regimes' powerful allies were brought back into the conflict. Indeed, the United States viewed this attack on the South as Soviet-inspired and Soviet-directed,[69] and a great deal of scholarship has been directed at whether this view was accurate.[70] A former undersecretary of state at the time, U. Alexis Johnson, has made the essential point in this debate: "Whatever prompted Kim [Kim Il-Sung,

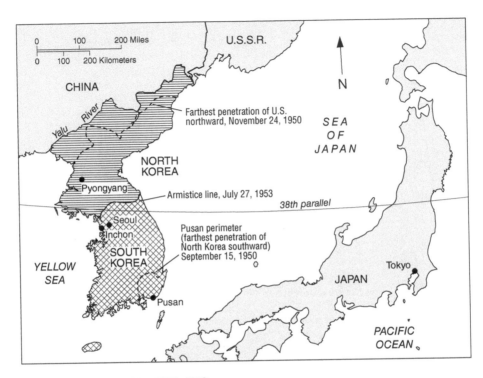

MAP 2.3 The Korean War, 1950–1953

the North Korean leader] to order the attack, this is certain: At the time no responsible official in the United States or among our allies seriously questioned that the aggression was Soviet-inspired and aimed principally at testing our resolve."[71] With this overriding perception, the United States had little recourse but to respond, thus making the containment doctrine a reality.

Within days of the North Korean attack on South Korea, President Truman ordered American air and naval support for the beleaguered South Korean troops and dispatched the Seventh Fleet to patrol the Formosa Strait to prevent Communist Chinese actions against the nationalist government on Taiwan. In addition, he sought and quickly obtained United Nations Security Council condemnation of the attack and support of a collective security force to be sent to aid the South Korean forces under U.S. direction. (The UN action was made possible by the Soviet Union's boycott of Security Council sessions because the China seat had not been given to the Communist government led by Mao Tse-tung, which meant that the Soviet Union was unable to exercise its veto.) Although some fourteen other nations ultimately sent forces to Korea, the bulk of the war effort was America's.[72] Indeed, the commander of all UN and U.S. forces was General Douglas MacArthur.

The American-led effort in Korea fared badly at first. After the allied troops were driven to a small enclave around Pusan in Southeast Korea, the North Koreans were poised to overrun the entire peninsula. In September 15, 1950, however, General MacArthur executed his Inchon landing near Seoul behind North Korean lines, and, within a matter of weeks, proceeded across the 38th parallel. Although this invasion was brilliant as a strategic move, it alarmed the Chinese when MacArthur's forces moved ever northward, coming within miles of the Chinese border.[73]

China had warned the West indirectly, through Indian channels in September 1950, that it would not "sit back with folded hands and let the Americans come to the border."[74] However, the warning was not taken seriously by U.S. policy makers. As early as mid-October 1950, **Chinese People's Volunteers** began crossing the border to aid North Korea, and by late November 1950, more than 300,000 were fighting alongside the North Koreans against UN and U.S. forces. This massive Chinese intervention drove allied forces back across the **38th parallel**, the "temporary" dividing line between North and South Korea. Stalemate ensued.

General MacArthur proposed that U.S. forces carry the war into China as a way to resolve the conflict. However, because President Truman had ordered him not to make public statements without administration approval and because administration policy was to limit the conflict, MacArthur was relieved of command for insubordination. This action caused an outpouring of support for him and vilification of President Truman.[75]

By and large, the American people continued to support the proposition that once a war was undertaken, it should be fought to victory and not be limited by political constraints. The Truman administration felt otherwise. As General Omar Bradley, chairman of the Joint Chiefs of Staff, put it, "So long as we regarded the Soviet Union as the main antagonist and Western Europe as the main prize" a massive invasion of China "would involve us in the wrong war at the wrong place at the wrong time and with the wrong enemy." In other words, involvement in a land war in Asia would lead "to a larger deadlock at greater expense" and would do little to contain Soviet designs on Western Europe.[76]

By July 1951, truce talks were arranged and fighting ceased, for the most part, by the end of the year. An armistice did not come about for another year and a half, however, because of the prolonged controversy that developed over the repatriation of prisoners of war and because the American election had made Korea an important issue. An uneasy peace eventually resulted with the establishment of a demilitarized zone between North and South.

The Korean War, as the first test of containment, however, brought numerous lessons for American policy makers for the future course of the Cold War.[77]

Korea and Implications for the Cold War

Political scientist Robert Jervis argues that American involvement in Korea "shaped the course of the Cold War by both resolving the incoherence which characterized U.S. foreign and defense efforts in the period 1946–1950 and establishing important new lines of policy."[78] American involvement resolved that incoherence by matching its perceived sense of threat from the Soviet Union and international communism with policies consistent with it. As new actions were undertaken in at least three areas, the political rhetoric of the late 1940s became the policy of the 1950s.

The first effect of the Korean War was a sharp increase in the American defense budget and the militarization of NATO. Although *NSC-68* had called for military increases, greater military expenditures did not result until U.S. involvement in Korea and were largely sustained after it. Note from Figure 2.2 how high military spending (either as a percentage of the GNP or as a percentage of the budget) remained throughout much of the 1950s. Similarly, directly on the heels of American involvement in Korea came the establishment of an integrated military structure in NATO and the eventual effort to rearm West Germany. The threat of Soviet expansionism had been made real with the actions in Asia.

A second effect of the Korean War was that it brought home to American policy makers the need to maintain large armies and to take action against aggression, wherever it appeared. Limited wars, too, might be necessary, however unpopular.[79] In this view, if the United States did not confront aggression in one dispute, its resolve in others would be questioned, and, indeed, the Korean experience had raised this doubt. After all, Secretary of State Dean Acheson had seemed to indicate, in a speech in January 1950, that the Korean peninsula was not within America's Asian "defense perimeter."[80]

A third effect of the Korean War was to solidify the American view that a Sino–Soviet bloc promoting communist expansion was a reality and that the need to combat it was real. The Chinese intervention on the side of North Korea illustrated the extent to which the Soviet Union controlled China. Indeed, the view that "China and Russia were inseparable was a product of the war."[81] Moreover, the various bilateral pacts in Asia were established after the conflict was under way.

In sum, the outbreak of the Korean War and American involvement in it brought about a dramatic correspondence between U.S. policy and actions.

Yet a fourth impact, beyond Jervis's discussion, seems reasonable, especially if we keep in mind the date on which *NSC-68* was issued (April 14, 1950) and when the Korean War began (June 25, 1950). In many ways, the actions in Korea gave further credence to the global portrait outlined in *NSC-68*, as well as to the need for rapid changes in the security arrangements of America and the free world. In relatively short order, that is exactly what happened.

A preeminent American diplomatic historian of this generation, John Lewis Gaddis, summarized **the principal importance of the Korean War** in this way: "the real commitment to contain communism everywhere originated in the events surrounding the Korean War, not the crisis in Greece and Turkey [in 1947]."[82]

THE COLD WAR CONSENSUS

The Cold War environment, and the initial encounter of the Korean War, created an identifiable foreign policy consensus among the American leadership and the public at large. This consensus was composed of a set of beliefs, values, and premises about America's role in the world and served as an important guide for U.S. behavior during the height of the Cold War (the late 1940s to the late 1960s). Lincoln P. Bloomfield has compiled an extensive list of U.S. foreign policy values in his book *In Search of American Foreign Policy*.[83] Table 2.1 reproduces a portion of that list, which will serve as a starting point for our discussion of the **Cold War consensus**.

America's Dichotomous View of the World

Bloomfield reminds us of the dichotomous view most Americans held of the world: one group of nations led by the United States and standing for democracy and capitalism, another group led by the Soviet Union and standing for totalitarianism and socialism. Even this dichotomy is not wholly accurate, however, as the United States came to define the "**Free World**" not in a positive way—by adherence to democratic principles of individual liberty and equality—but in a negative way—by adherence to the principles of anticommunism. Thus, the "Free World" could equally include the

Table 2.1 The American Postwar Consensus in Foreign Policy

- Communism is bad; capitalism is good.
- Stability is desirable; in general, instability threatens U.S. interests.
- Democracy (our kind, that is) is desirable, but if a choice has to be made, stability serves U.S. interests better than democracy.
- Any area of the world that "goes socialist" or neutralist is a net loss to us and probably a victory for the Soviets.
- Every country, and particularly the poor ones, would benefit from American "know-how."
- Nazi aggression in the 1930s and democracy's failure to respond provides the appropriate model for dealing with postwar security problems.
- Allies and clients of the United States, regardless of their political structure, are members of the Free World.
- The United States must provide leadership because it (reluctantly) has that responsibility.
- "Modernization" and "development" are good for poor, primitive, or traditional societies, and they will probably develop into democracies by these means.
- In international negotiations the United States has a virtual monopoly on "sincerity."
- Violence is an unacceptable way to secure economic, social, and political justice—except when vital U.S. interests are at stake.
- However egregious a mistake, the government must never admit having been wrong.

Source: In Search of American Foreign Policy: The Humane Use of Power by Lincoln P. Bloomfield. Copyright 1974 by Oxford University Press, Inc. Reprinted by permission of the author.

nations of Western Europe (including the dictatorships of Spain and Portugal through the mid-1970s) and the military regimes of Central and South America—because both embraced anticommunism. Such an "alliance" provided a ready bulwark against Soviet expansion.

U.S. Attitudes toward Change

A substantial part of the Free World structure was grounded in an abiding concern over Soviet expansion, but a second concern was also present: U.S. attitudes toward **stability and change**. During this period, change in the world was viewed suspiciously. It tended to be seen as Communist-inspired and therefore something to be opposed. Stability was generally the preferred global condition.

Change was feared because it might lead to enhanced influence (and control) for the Soviet Union. This gain in influence could occur directly (by a nation's formal incorporation into the Soviet bloc) or indirectly (by a state's adopting a "neutral" or "nonaligned" stance in global affairs). As a consequence, Americans tended to be skeptical of new states following the **"nonaligned" movement** initiated by Prime Minister Nehru of India and President Tito of Yugoslavia, among others. At this time, such a movement represented a loss for America's effort to rally the world against revolutionary communism.

Change was even more troublesome for the United States when it appeared in a nationalist and revolutionary environment. Even though Americans tended to sympathize philosophically with nationalist and anticolonialist movements, global realities, as viewed by American policy makers, often led them to follow a different course. J. William Fulbright, senator from Arkansas and former chairman of the Senate Foreign

Relations Committee, described this dilemma in dealing with nationalism and communism in a revolutionary setting:

> we are simultaneously hostile to communism and sympathetic to nationalism, and when the two become closely associated, we become agitated, frustrated, angry, precipitate, and inconstant. Or, to make the point by simple metaphor: loving corn and hating lima beans, we simply cannot make up our minds about succotash.[84]

The resultant American policy, as Fulbright goes on to state, was often to oppose communism rather than to support nationalism.

American Intervention to Stall Communism

The fear of change was manifested in a dramatic way: the several American military interventions (either directly or through surrogates) in the 1950s and 1960s to prevent Communist gains. A few instances will make this point. In 1950, of course, U.S. military forces were deployed to help the South Koreans in the Korean War. In 1953, the United States was involved in the toppling of Prime Minister **Mohammed Mossadegh** of Iran and the restoration of the Shah. In 1954, the CIA assisted in the overthrow of the **Jacobo Árbenz Guzmán** government in Guatemala because of the fear of growing Communist influence there. And in 1958, President Eisenhower ordered 14,000 marines to Lebanon to support a pro-Western government from possible subversion by Iraq, Syria, and Egypt.

The early 1960s saw three more interventions for a similar reason. In April 1961, the **Bay of Pigs** invasion of Cuba, planned and organized by the CIA, was attempted without success. It was launched to topple the Communist regime of Fidel Castro, who had seized power in 1959. In 1965, President Lyndon Johnson ordered the Marines to Santo Domingo, **Dominican Republic**, to protect American lives and property from a possible change in regimes; communist involvement was the rationale. Finally, of course, the Vietnam War, which began substantially in the early 1960s (although U.S. involvement went back to at least 1946), was justified by the desire to prevent the fall of **South Vietnam** and subsequently all of Southeast Asia, to the Communists.[85]

Beyond these direct interventions, the military was used in another way during the height of the Cold War. Two foreign policy analysts, Barry M. Blechman and Stephen S. Kaplan, provide some useful data on this topic in their examination of the **"armed forces as a political instrument."** Blechman and Kaplan state: "[a] political use of the armed forces occurs when physical actions are taken by one or more components of the uniformed military services as part of a deliberate attempt by the national authorities to influence, or to be prepared to influence, specific behavior of individuals in another nation without engaging in a continuing contest of violence."[86] By this definition, then, a naval task force that is moved to a particular region of the world, troops put on alert, a nonroutine military exercise begun, and the initiation of reconnaissance patrols may all be examples of the use of armed forces to further one state's political goals toward another country.

Blechman and Kaplan identify some 215 incidents from 1946 to 1975 that illustrate the use of armed forces for political goals. Of those, 181 occurred during the height of the Cold War (1946–1968). The top half of Table 2.2 shows the breakdown of these incidents from the administrations of Truman through Johnson. President Eisenhower used the military most frequently (he was in office longer than the other

Table 2.2 Use of American Military Force during Eight Administrations, 1946–1988 (Categorized by Regions)

Administration	Latin America	Europe	Middle East and North Africa	Rest of Africa	Asia	Total
Truman	5	16	7	1	6	35
Eisenhower	18	6	13	2	19	58
Kennedy	17	6	4	2	11	40
Johnson	13	11	6	5	13	48
Nixon	6	2	9	—	12	29
Ford	—	1	4	1	6	12
Carter	3	2	4	4	5	18
Reagan	25	1	35	4	9	74
Regional Totals	87	45	82	19	81	

Sources: Calculated by the author from Barry M. Blechman and Stephen S. Kaplan, *Force Without War: U.S. Armed Forces as a Political Instrument* (Washington, DC: The Brookings Institution, 1978), pp. 547–553, for the years 1946–1975; Philip D. Zelikow, "The United States and the Use of Force: A Historical Summary," in George K. Osborn, Asa A. Clark IV, Daniel J. Kaufman, and Douglas E. Lute, eds., *Democracy, Strategy, and Vietnam* (Lexington, MA: D. C. Heath and Company, 1987), pp. 34–36, for the years 1975–1984; and from data generously supplied by James Meernik of the University of North Texas for 1985–1988. See the text and these sources for a definition of an incident in which military force is used.

presidents); however, presidents Kennedy and Johnson had the highest average use. Latin America and Asia were the most frequent areas where U.S. forces were deployed for all Cold War presidents except for Truman, who, as one might suspect, was most interested in Europe.

Overall, then, even though the number of direct military interventions is relatively limited, the use of armed forces as a political instrument was frequent during the period of Cold War consensus. Blechman and Kaplan conclude that "when the United States engaged in these political-military activities, the outcomes of the situations at which the activity was directed were often favorable from the perspective of U.S. decision makers—at least in the short term."[87] About long-term outcomes, though, Blechman and Kaplan are less sanguine; nevertheless, this consequence of the Cold War consensus appeared to be popular among policy makers.

The bottom half of Table 2.2 shows the American use of force for the last two decades of the Cold War—from the Nixon through Reagan administrations.[88] During this period, the use of military force waned somewhat, with 133 incidents—down from the previous 181. This decline occurred across all areas of the world, except for the Middle East and North Africa, where the use of force rose dramatically (by 60 percent), from 30 incidents through 1968 to 52 from 1969 through 1988. With the dramatic events in this region for all American administrations—the **Yom Kippur War** of 1973 (Nixon), the **Egyptian–Israeli and Syrian–Israeli disengagement agreements** (Ford), the **Camp David Accords** in 1978 (Carter), and the **Lebanon intervention** in 1982 (Reagan)—this increase becomes more understandable, but is still quite remarkable.

When the use of force in this latter part of the Cold War years is analyzed by administration, it can be seen that all presidents—except Ronald Reagan—relied on it less than did their predecessors during the first two decades of the Cold War. Reagan, by contrast, accounted for more than 55 percent of all uses of American force. In all, his administration more often employed American forces than any other administration in the postwar period. This conclusion holds even when we take into account that Reagan served longer than any of the others except for Eisenhower. Still a comparison of the eight years of the Reagan administration with the eight years of the Eisenhower administration shows that Reagan's use of force was greater than Eisenhower's by slightly over 25 percent (74 versus 58 incidents).

Displays of force and occasional violence came to be justified to defend American interests. Challenges to national security (increasingly defined as global security) were not to go unmet, with the justification that confronting potential aggressors was essential to world peace. The so-called **Munich syndrome**, the fear of appeasing an aggressor as Neville Chamberlain had done with Adolf Hitler, became another theme of American Cold War thinking. Drawing on historical analogies such as this as a guide to present policy was an important source in shaping a response to aggression.[89]

The United States as Model

Given the nature of the perceived global struggle, a final important theme emerged from this postwar consensus. The United States came to believe that it alone could "solve" the problems of the poor and emerging nations through its technological skills,[90] and that it could offer itself as the model for achievement of development and democracy. As a result of these beliefs, large-scale development efforts were initiated, particularly in the 1960s. Such a policy came to be viewed as markedly paternalistic, however, and some states viewed it warily. It also led to frustration for Americans when development did not occur as rapidly as envisioned or when democracy did not result. Nonetheless, America's self-confidence during the 1950s and 1960s seems to summarize nicely the general value orientation that the United States employed to achieve its view of global order and to oppose the Soviet Union's strategy.

THE PUBLIC AND THE
COLD WAR CONSENSUS

Bloomfield's list (from Table 2.1) provides an excellent summary of Cold War consensus, but it does not convey how deeply held its views were among the American public during the late 1940s and 1950s. Fortunately, some public opinion survey data are available that provide additional support for Bloomfield's generalizations.[91] In particular, they depict prevailing American attitudes toward the perceived threat from international communism, the use of American troops to combat it abroad, and, more generally, public attitudes regarding how relations with the Soviet Union should be conducted.

Table 2.3 summarizes the results to a survey question asked on three occasions in 1950 and 1951: "In general, how important do you think it is for the United States to try to stop the spread of communism in the world?" On average, 80 percent of the American public answered with "very important" and another 8 percent answered with "fairly important." Only 5 percent saw stopping communism as "not important." When a similar question was asked two years earlier about the threat of communism spreading to specific regions and countries, the results were virtually the same.[92] Between 70 and 80 percent agreed with the statement that if Western Europe, South America, China, or Mexico were to become communist it would make a difference to the United States.

Table 2.3 Attitudes toward Stopping the Spread of Communism, 1950–1951

In general, how important do you think it is for the United States to try to stop the spread of communism in the world—very important, only fairly important, or not important at all?

Survey Date	Very Important	Fairly Important	Not Important	Don't Know
January 1950	77%	10%	5%	8%
April 1950	83	6	4	7
June 1951	82	7	4	7

Source: Eugene R. Wittkopf, *Faces of Internationalism: Public Opinion and American Foreign Policy,* Table 6.1 (p. 169). Copyright 1990, Duke University Press. Reprinted with permission.

The public was also quite willing to use American force to stop the spread of communism, even if it meant going to war. In two surveys, one in 1951 and another in 1952, the public was asked the following: "If you had to choose, which would you say is more important—to keep communism from spreading, or to stay out of another war?" Less than 30 percent chose to stay out of war, and about two-thirds were willing to take action. Further, about the use of American forces to stop communist attacks against particular countries or regions, the response was usually overwhelmingly favorable. Regarding the Philippines, the American-occupied zone in Germany at the time (and what eventually became West Germany), and Formosa, the public favored going to war with the Soviet Union if these attacks happened. Similarly, it favored using force if Central or South America were attacked by another country. Indeed, Americans appeared willing to sustain a worldwide effort to stop communism, even if it included the use of armed force.[93]

Short of force, the public expressed support for efforts to stop communism, and it was generally quite willing to provide economic and military assistance to countries threatened by communism. As political scientists Benjamin Page and Robert Shapiro report, "By March 1949, for example, NORC [the National Opinion Research Center] found solid support for military aid to Europe (60% approving), for continuing the Marshall Plan (79%), and for maintaining or increasing the level of [European] recovery spending (60%)."[94] Further, in surveys by NORC between January 1955 and January 1956, the average level of support for economic aid for countries opposing Communist aggression was about 81 percent. Finally, in six surveys in 1950 and 1951, support for military assistance averaged 57 percent.[95]

By the end of World War II, the public was highly suspicious of dealing with the Soviet Union. As Page and Shapiro also report, a large majority felt as early as March 1946 that the United States was "too soft" on the Soviet Union; by March 1948, that percentage had increased to 84 percent.[96] Further, they report that the percentage of the public expecting cooperation with the Soviet Union dropped precipitously from mid-1945 through mid-1949 to roughly 20 percent, across all educational levels.[97] This wariness of the Soviet Union was to continue throughout the Cold War years.

In short, after summarizing a wealth of American survey data on the early Cold War period, Page and Shapiro conclude: "The U.S. public accepted the logic of the Cold War and favored appropriate policies to carry it out."[98]

CHALLENGES TO THE COLD WAR CONSENSUS

The values and beliefs of the Cold War consensus, however, had begun to be challenged as early as the mid- to late 1960s, predominantly because of the changing world environment, which was increasingly multipolar rather than bipolar. New power centers began to appear within the Communist world, among the Western allies, and between the developed world and the Third World.[99]

The Sino–Soviet Split

The split between the People's Republic of China and the Soviet Union, the two largest Communist powers, challenged the Cold War assumption about the basic unity of international communism and the degree to which it was directed from Moscow. Throughout the height of the Cold War, the United States had treated communism as a monolithic movement that everywhere took its orders from the Soviet Union. When China and the Soviet Union became increasingly antagonistic toward one another in the late 1950s and early 1960s, the West, and the United States in particular, was forced to rethink this assumption.

In many ways, the Sino–Soviet split should not have been surprising to U.S. policy makers, as both *historical rivalries* and *social-cultural differences* had long characterized Soviet–Chinese relations. Historically, the Soviet Union had always coveted access to and control over Asia and, in turn, had always feared the growth of Chinese influence. Likewise, the Chinese had always perceived Russia as an "imperialist" power that threatened their sovereignty and territorial integrity. Territorial disputes date back at least to the signing of the Treaty of Nerchinsk in 1659 and continued into the nineteenth and twentieth centuries with the disintegration of China at the hands of outside, including Russian, powers.[100]

On a cultural level, too, deep suspicions had permeated Soviet and Chinese views of one another. The Soviets viewed a possible invasion by the "Mongols" from the East with grave concern and the Chinese regarded the Soviet commissars with similar apprehension. To the Chinese, the Russians were "foreigners" and "barbarians," intent on destroying the glories of Chinese culture and society. Although the other "imperialist" powers were driven from China with Mao's successful revolution of 1949, the Soviets remained. Their continued presence reinforced Chinese hostility.

Despite these profound suspicions, a formal alliance was forged between the Soviet Union and the People's Republic of China in 1950, raising the belief in official Washington that past differences had been resolved rather than temporarily shelved. In fact, mutual self-interest apparently dictated this formal tie. The China of **Mao Tse-tung**, although successful in its domestic revolution, was still weak and not fully an independent actor in global affairs. The Soviets, badly in need of global partners in a world of capitalist powers, had much to gain by allying with their new ideological partner.[101]

Nevertheless, new differences between the two Communist giants quickly began to grow and were superimposed on the disputes of the past. These new difficulties were mainly *economic* and *ideological*. The Soviet Union provided economic and technological assistance to China, but it was insufficient. The low aid levels frustrated the Chinese aim of self-sufficiency, a goal that the Soviet Union did not share. Most important, the Soviet Union refused to help the Chinese build an independent nuclear force, and it is this refusal that has been identified by some as the catalyst for the new Sino–Soviet split.[102]

On an ideological level, Mao's brand of communism, unlike Nikita Khrushchev's, did not call for "peaceful coexistence" with the West.[103] Nor did it call for emulating the Soviet model of heavy industrialization as the road to modernization and socialism. Further, the Soviets and the Chinese disagreed over the de-Stalinization movement, engaged in a continuous debate over the degree of diversity allowable among Communist states and parties, and adopted differing views on the nature of the worldwide revolutionary movement.[104] In short, Mao's proclamations on the "correct" interpretation of Marxism-Leninism were increasingly perceived as direct challenges to Soviet leadership of the Communist world.

By the late 1950s and into the early 1960s, the traditional Sino–Soviet split reemerged full blown. American officials slowly began to recognize this global reality and to see the need for a policy that did not homogenize the Communist powers.

Disunity in the East and West

A second readjustment in America's view of the Communist world as wholly unified occurred in Eastern Europe when differences emerged within the **Warsaw Pact**—the military alliance between the Soviet Union and its Eastern European neighbors. Although these were nowhere as severe as the Sino–Soviet split, they again suggested that some change was needed in the unidimensional way in which the United States viewed and approached the Communist world during the Cold War.

Uprisings in East Germany in 1953 and Poland in 1956, outright revolt in Hungary later in 1956, and the call for communism "with a human face" in Czechoslovakia by 1968 all signaled a changed Eastern Europe. Considering also Yugoslavia's long-standing independent Communist route, Albania's departure from the Warsaw Pact in 1968, and Romania's break with Eastern Europe over the recognition of West Germany in 1967, it became clear that Eastern Europe was hardly the model of alliance unity.

In this sense, exploiting the internal differences within the Eastern bloc was yet another way of moving these nations away from Soviet control. Furthermore, the Eastern-bloc nations themselves sought to expand economic advantage through diplomatic contact and recognition.[105] There were yet other reasons for the United States to change its strategy of strict bloc-to-bloc relations if these economic and political opportunities were not to be lost.

But readjustments in this unified East–versus–unified West definition of global politics were not confined to disharmony among the Communist states. If the Soviet Union faced challenges from the People's Republic of China and Eastern Europe, America faced them within its own NATO alliance. By the early 1960s, the United States could no longer automatically expect the Western European states to follow its foreign policy lead. More accurately, it could no longer dictate Western policy. With the economic recovery of France and West Germany and the emergence of the **European Common Market**, a number of European states wanted a more independent role in world affairs—or at least wanted to not be subservient to American policy prescriptions.

The best example of the need for a perceptual readjustment within the Western bloc was over the foreign policy pursued by France under President **Charles de Gaulle** (1958–1969), the undisputed leader of the Western European challenge to U.S. leadership. Under de Gaulle, France sought to restore some of its lost glory by relaxing its strong linkage with the United States, weakening overall American influence over Western European affairs, and improving ties with the Soviet Union and Eastern Europe. De Gaulle's ultimate goal, in fact, was to break the "hegemonic" hold on Europe of both the Soviet Union and the United States and to establish a "community of European states" from the "Atlantic to the Urals."[106] In his global design, France would once again play a central role in European politics.

To accomplish this, de Gaulle undertook a series of initiatives to reduce American influence and weaken Soviet control over the continent. First, in 1958, shortly after gaining the French presidency, he reportedly proposed a **three-power directorate** for the NATO alliance, under which policy decisions would be made only with the unanimous consent of the United States, Great Britain, and France. In effect, his proposal would give France a veto over NATO policy. Second, despite American objections, de Gaulle announced his plan to develop an independent French nuclear capability, the *force de frappe*, and refused to join in American and British (and later German) plans for an integrated nuclear force. Third, and perhaps most dramatically, he announced in 1965 that France would withdraw from the military structure of NATO in 1966. This last act was probably the single most potent challenge to Western unity. With France's military withdrawal, the appearance of political divisions within NATO became a reality.

Both the Kennedy and Johnson administrations favored a strong, unified Europe, closely allied to the United States. De Gaulle did not favor such close American involvement in European affairs. Instead, he took a series of other actions to reshape Western European politics more in accord with his views and as a further means of frustrating American dominance. To this end, he sought to reshape the European Common Market, increase French–German ties (at the expense of American–German ties), and isolate Great Britain.

De Gaulle first attempted to reduce the supranational components of the Common Market—the power of the European Commission, for example—and to increase the emphasis on intergovernmental components within it. To accomplish this, he proposed the Fouchet Plan, which was both a broadening of the Common Market arrangements to include political, cultural, and defense activities and a lessening of centralized control. Although this plan was ultimately rejected, it caused considerable controversy and division within the European Community. De Gaulle's second move was to veto British entry into the Common Market, on two different occasions (1963 and 1967), fundamentally because Britain was too close to the United States. Finally, de Gaulle sought, largely unsuccessfully, to forge a strong alliance between France and West Germany. His strategy, once again, was to break the close ties between the United States and the Federal Republic. In the main, he was rebuffed by successive German chancellors, although he did manage to put into effect the **German-French Treaty of Friendship** in January 1963.[107]

Bridges across East and West

Although de Gaulle's actions were not the only source of dissension within the Western Alliance, they did represent the most consistent pattern of movement away from the bipolar world of the Cold War. But his challenge to this bipolarity did not stop with his actions toward America and Western Europe. He also opened up contacts with Eastern Europe and took policy steps clearly at odds with the mentality of bloc-to-bloc relations of the previous decade. These actions alarmed the Americans because de Gaulle was operating unilaterally, outside the Western Alliance, but they undoubtedly pleased the Eastern Europeans because they granted these nations some legitimacy in the eyes of the West. Their effect on the Soviets was probably mixed because while granting recognition to Eastern Europe, they had the potential effect of undermining Warsaw Pact unity.

De Gaulle's Eastern Europe strategy was first to increase social, cultural, and economic ties and then to proceed toward political accommodation. For instance, educational exchanges, tourism, and trade between France and Eastern Europe increased dramatically. More important, perhaps, France initiated political contacts with the Eastern Europeans at the highest levels of government.

In the first part of his political campaign to "**build bridges**" to the East, de Gaulle sent his foreign affairs minister to several Eastern European countries. Dramatic in itself, this step was in response to numerous East European political officials' visits to France. Even more dramatic was de Gaulle's decision to visit Eastern Europe himself, making official visits to the Soviet Union in June 1966, Poland in September 1967, and Romania in May 1968. He also accepted invitations to visit Czechoslovakia, Hungary, and Bulgaria, but these trips were not made before he left office.[108] The significance of De Gaulle's contacts cannot be overstated, given that Western policy was not to offer official diplomatic recognition to the Eastern European governments because of their failure to recognize West Germany.

Throughout these visits, and despite acknowledged differences, mutual calls for reconciliation were made. De Gaulle's characterization of Europe's division into blocs as "artificial" and "sterile" epitomizes his continuing effort to break the political divisions of the Cold War,[109] and, indeed, his efforts were an impetus to greater contact between East and West. For instance, West Germany's accommodative policy toward East Germany (known as **Ostpolitik**) was slowly nurtured from 1966–1969 and came to fruition soon after.

French initiatives were also important harbingers of changes in the politics of Europe. For Americans, they once again demonstrated the difficulties of conducting **bipolar** policy in a world that was increasingly **multipolar**.

The Nonaligned Movement

In the post–World War II years, another major political force was unleashed to challenge the bipolar view of the world: the desire for independence by colonial territories, especially throughout Asia and Africa. In fact, more than ninety nations were granted or achieved political independence from their colonial overseers from 1945 through 1980. Fourteen became independent in the years from 1945 to 1949, nine from 1950 through 1959, forty-three from 1960 to 1969, twenty-six from 1970 through 1979, eight from 1980 to 1989, twenty-four from 1990 to 2000, and one after 2000.[110]

This surge of independence began in Asia and northern Africa. Pakistan, India, and the Philippines, among others, gained their independence in the late 1940s, whereas Tunisia, Cambodia (Kampuchea), Morocco, Libya, and Malaysia, among others, gained theirs by the mid-1950s. The decolonization of Africa mainly occurred in the early 1960s, although Ghana and Guinea led the way in the late 1950s. By the end of the 1960s, in fact, some sixty-six new nations were part of the international system, and this process continued into the 1970s, albeit at a slower pace.

The decolonization movement proved to be a third major challenge to the bipolar approach that underlay American foreign policy during the Cold War. The new states generally refused to tie themselves into the formal East–West bloc structure and, instead, followed an independent, nonaligned foreign policy course. To demonstrate their independence, they actually started a nonaligned movement.

The founder of the nonaligned movement was **Jawaharlal Nehru** of India, who as early as 1946 had stated that India "will follow an independent policy, keeping away from the power politics of groups aligned one against another."[111] He continued his efforts on behalf of this movement once he reached power, helping to organize the **Conference of Afro–Asian States** held at Bandung, Indonesia, in 1955. This conference is sometimes cited as the initial step in the development of a nonaligned movement because it was the first time that former colonial territories met without any European powers in attendance. However, the tone of the debate and the principles adopted later were criticized as not fully reflecting nonalignment principles.[112]

The more formal institutionalization of this movement was the **Belgrade Conference** in September 1961. Spurred on by the organizational efforts of Nehru as well as leaders such as Josip Broz Tito of Yugoslavia, Nasser of Egypt, Kwame Nkrumah of Ghana, and Sukarno of Indonesia, this conference of twenty-five nations produced a statement of principles for a "third way" in world politics.[113]

In effect, the nonaligned states wanted not only to reject bloc politics but also to expand their numbers. They saw their contribution to world peace as directly opposite to the way world politics had been conducted up to that time. That is, they would take an active part in world affairs through their own initiatives and in their own way, without going through the coordinated actions of a bloc of states. More specifically, they would reject military alliances with the superpowers (including the hosting of military bases) that, in effect, extended the politics of the Cold War through intermediaries. In this sense, nonalignment did not mean noninvolvement or rejection of global politics, but it did mean the rejection of international politics as it had been played out during the Cold War.[114]

The nonaligned movement proved highly successful, and its adherents rapidly increased. In less than a decade, the movement's membership had doubled, with fifty-three nations attending the Third Summit Meeting in Lusaka, Zambia, in September 1970.[115] The new members were primarily colonial territories that had gained their independence in the early to middle 1960s. Essentially, the new participants in world politics were joining the ranks of the nonaligned.

The United States was always a bit skeptical of the nonaligned movement and the degree of its independence in world politics. Indeed, a continuous debate existed from the movement's inception over how "nonaligned" it was, given that its pronouncements were often more critical of the West than of the East and typically more critical of capitalism than socialism. Further, several prominent nonaligned nations had close ties with the Soviet Union. Cuba, Vietnam, and Afghanistan, among others, could hardly be viewed as "nonaligned" in global politics during much of the movement's history. Despite this anomaly, the movement itself provided yet another reason for American policy makers to conclude that global politics would no longer conform to their image of East versus West.

CONCLUDING COMMENTS

In Chapter 1, we noted that isolationism and moralism were America's twin legacies from the past. The Cold War and the containment strategy appear to represent a sharp break from this heritage, at least with respect to isolationism. On one level, of course, the United States abandoned isolationism for a policy of globalism.[116] On another level, this globalism was largely a unilateralist approach, a strategy of going it alone in the world or at least of attempting to lead other nations in a particular direction. In other words, much as the original isolationism was unilateralist, so, too, was containment. It represented a U.S. strategy to reshape global order through its own design and largely through its own efforts.

The heritage of moral principle is more readily evident in the Cold War period and containment. The universal campaign that the United States initiated was highly consistent with its past: moral accommodation of Soviet communism, and all communism, was simply not acceptable. In fact, some even sought to "roll back," rather than just contain, it. Like the efforts in America's past (the War of 1812, the Spanish-American War, World War I, and World War II), then, the containment strategy represented an all-out attempt, in this case, to confront the moral challenge from the Soviet Union and all it represented. Moral values, moreover, once again served as a primary justification for American policy.

The Cold War consensus among American leaders and the public also emerged in the late 1940s and the early 1950s, which the Korean War only served to solidify. This consensus provided the rationale for the complete implementation of containment during the rest of the 1950s and 1960s and guided U.S. policy for the next several decades, although its assumptions were challenged by the emergence of the Sino–Soviet split, the fissures with the East and West, and the nonaligned movement. In addition, as we take up in the next chapter, the Cuban Missile Crisis and the Vietnam War brought into question the Cold War consensus and produced alternate foreign policy approaches by the differing administrations in the subsequent decades.

Notes

1. Joseph M. Jones, *The Fifteen Weeks* (New York: The Viking Press, 1955), pp. 89–99.

2. The term is from Richard Mayne's Chapter 2 title in *The Recovery of Europe 1945–1973* (Garden City, NY: Anchor, 1973), pp. 27–52. The discussion here draws on this chapter as well as on page 14 on the extent of decolonization.

3. Ibid., pp. 39–40.

4. Ibid.

5. Stephen E. Ambrose, *Rise to Globalism: American Foreign Policy 1938–1976* (New York: Penguin Books, 1976), p. 1. A good discussion of the economic strength of the United States in the immediate postwar period can be found in Joan Edelman Spero, *The Politics of International Economic Relations*, 2nd ed. (New York: St. Martin's Press, 1981), pp. 23–30 and 33–41. The economic data cited are at p. 36.

6. Ambrose, *Rise to Globalism*, p. 16.

7. John Lewis Gaddis, *The United States and the Origins of the Cold War 1941–1947* (New York and London: Columbia University Press, 1972), p. 1. See also Daniel Yergin, *Shattered Peace: The Origins of the Cold War and the National Security State* (Boston: Houghton Mifflin Company, 1977), pp. 42–68.

8. Gaddis, *Origins of the Cold War*, p. 2.

9. Yergin, *Shattered Peace*, pp. 43–46.

10. Ibid., pp. 17–68. The quote about Riga is at p. 19.

11. Ibid., p. 55. See the "Grand Alliance" identified at pp. 4 and 49.

12. Michael McGwire, "National Security and Soviet Foreign Policy," in Melvyn P. Leffler and David S. Painter, eds., *Origins of the Cold War: An International History* (London and New York: Routledge, 1994), p. 61.

13. See the discussion of the Yalta agreements in Robert H. Ferrell, *American Diplomacy: A History*, 3rd ed. (New York: W. W. Norton and Company, 1975), pp. 594–603.

14. Ibid.

15. James Lee Ray, *Global Politics*, 2nd ed. (Boston: Houghton Mifflin Company, 1983), p. 30.

16. For some evidence that the United States was already planning a sustained global involvement during World War II, see Melvyn P. Leffler, "National Security and U.S. Foreign Policy," in Leffler and Painter, eds., *Origins of the Cold War*, pp. 18–19.

17. Yergin, *Shattered Peace*, pp. 71–73.

18. Ibid Also see Gaddis, *Origins of the Cold War*, pp. 200–206.

19. Ernest R. May, *"Lessons" of the Past: The Use and Misuse of History in American Foreign Policy* (New York: Oxford University Press, 1973), pp. 20–22. The quotation is from p. 22.

20. Ibid., pp. 22–32, discusses these diplomatic assessments and their impact on Truman and his advisors.

21. Harry S. Truman, *Year of Decision* (New York: Doubleday and Co., 1955), p. 99. The earlier passage is quoted in Gaddis, *Origins of the Cold War*, p. 232.

22. For a recent description and assessment of the Potsdam Conference, see Charles L. Mee, Jr., *Meeting at Potsdam* (New York: M. Evans and Co., 1975).

23. Gaddis, *Origins of the Cold War*, pp. 263–281.

24. Ibid., pp. 282–312.

25. Both passages were originally from *Pravda*, the Communist Party newspaper, and were quoted in B. Thomas Trout, "Rhetoric Revisited: Political Legitimation and the Cold War," *International Studies Quarterly* 19 (September 1975): 264 and 266.

26. The "new war" remark is quoted from *Pravda* and is from Trout, "Rhetoric Revisited," p. 265, as is this assessment. The second quotation is from Trout at p. 269.

27. The first quote is from Walter Lafeber, *America, Russia, and the Cold War 1945–1975* (New York: John Wiley and Sons, 1976), p. 39; and the second is from Gaddis, *Origins of the Cold War*, p. 299.

28. The text of this speech can be found in Robert Rhodes James, ed., *Winston S. Churchill, His Complete Speeches 1897–1963, Volume VII: 1943–1949* (New York: Chelsea House Publishers, 1974), pp. 7285–7293. The quoted passages are at pp. 7289 and 7290, respectively.

29. Yergin, *Shattered Peace*, p. 176.

30. The complete text of the "long telegram" can be found in Kenneth M. Jensen, ed., *Origins of the Cold War: The Novikov, Kennan, and Roberts "Long Telegrams" of 1946* (Washington, DC: United States Institute of Peace, 1991), pp. 17–31. The quoted phrases, in order, are at pp. 20, 23, 28, and 29. The last passage can also be found in George F. Kennan, *Memoirs 1925–1950* (Boston: Little, Brown and Co., 1967), p. 557.

31. The quoted passages are from "The Novikov Telegram, Washington, September 27, 1946," reprinted in Kenneth M. Jensen, ed., *Origins of the Cold War: The Novikov, Kennan, and Roberts "Long Telegrams" of 1946*, rev. ed. (Washington, DC: United States Institute of Peace, 1993), at pp. 3, 14, and 16.

32. John Lewis Gaddis, *The Cold War: A New History* (New York: The Penguin Press, 2005), p. 30. Also see Viktor L. Mal'kov in Jensen, *Origins of the Cold War: The Novikov, Kennan, and Roberts "Long Telegrams" of 1946*, rev. ed., pp. 73–79, especially at p. 75 regarding Molotov's role.

33. Ibid., p. 74.

34. The discussion draws on Jones, *The Fifteen Weeks*, pp. 48–58, especially at pp. 48–49 here.

35. Quoted in Jones, *The Fifteen Weeks*, p. 54. Emphasis in original.

36. Ibid., p. 56. Jones does point out that the Soviets apparently got some concessions for their withdrawal.

37. Lafeber, in *America, Russia, and the Cold War*, pp. 50–59, provides a useful description of the situation in Greece at this time; Jones, in *The Fifteen Weeks*, pp. 59–77, describes the situations in Greece and Turkey during 1946 and 1947.

38. These characteristics of the Truman Doctrine are from Lafeber, *America, Russia, and the Cold War*, p. 53.

39. The "Truman Doctrine" speech can be found in *House Documents, Miscellaneous*, 80th Cong., 1st sess., Vol. 1 (Washington, DC: Government Printing Office, 1947), Document 171. Emphasis added here. John Lewis Gaddis, in *Strategies of Containment* (New York: Oxford University Press, 1982), pp. 65–66, asserts that the Truman Doctrine was not so much meant as a call to attack "communism" as it was to attack "totalitarianism" in general. Truman's reference to two ways of life referred to totalitarianism versus democracy. Only later did the commitment to contain communism really develop. See his "Was the Truman Doctrine a Real Turning Point?" *Foreign Affairs* 52 (January 1974): 386–402.

40. George Kennan reprinted his July 1947 article from *Foreign Affairs* entitled "The Sources of Soviet Conduct" in *American Diplomacy 1900–1950* (New York: Mentor Books, 1951). The quoted passages are at pp. 99 and 105.

41. Mr. X [George Kennan], "The Sources of Soviet Conduct," in James M. McCormick, ed., *A Reader in American Foreign Policy* (Itasca, IL: F. E. Peacock Publishers, 1986), pp. 68–69.

42. Ibid., pp. 70–71.

43. Kennan, in his *Memoirs 1925–1950*, pp. 354–367, contends that the implementation of containment by such sweeping actions was not what he had intended. He envisioned a more limited, more measured response than what resulted. Also see his views on the Truman Doctrine at pp. 313–324. A more recent summary of Kennan's views on containment are available in "Containment Then and Now," *Foreign Affairs* 65 (Spring 1987): 885–890.

44. ANZUS was seen as protection against Japanese expansion into the South Pacific in light of the experience of World War II, as well as against an anticommunist alliance in the face of the Korean War. For an extended discussion of ANZUS from the perspective of one of the partners, see Malcolm McKinnon, *Independence and Foreign Policy: New Zealand in the World Since 1935* (Auckland: Auckland University Press, 1993).

45. A brief description of the development of these organizations, and the charter of each one, can be found in Ruth C. Lawson, *International Regional Organizations: Constitutional Foundations* (New York: Praeger, 1962). The subsequent discussion of CENTO is also based on this source.

46. The Rio Pact did not have this language, but it did state that the "Contracting Parties may determine the immediate measures which it may individually take in fulfillment of the obligation." Quoted in Michael Glennon, *Constitutional Diplomacy* (Princeton, NJ: Princeton University Press, 1990), p. 207.

47. *NATO Handbook* (Brussels: NATO Office of Information and Press, 1992), p. 144.

48. This discussion draws on the analysis and documentation by Glennon, *Constitutional Diplomacy*, pp. 209–214. The statements from Acheson are at pp. 210–211.

49. On the evolution of American policy toward China and Asia in the late 1940s and early 1950s, see Thomas H. Etzold, "The Far East in American Strategy, 1948–1951," in Thomas H. Etzold, ed., *Aspects of Sino-American Relations Since 1784* (New York: New Viewpoints, 1978), pp. 102–126. On the Korean War, see Allen S. Whiting, *China Crosses the Yalu* (Stanford, CA: Stanford University Press, 1960); and John W. Spanier, *The Truman-MacArthur Controversy and the Korean War* (New York: W. W. Norton and Company, 1965). On the importance of the Korean War in instigating the containment policy and producing the Cold War, see Gaddis, "Was the Truman Doctrine a Real Turning Point?" and Robert Jervis, "The Impact of the Korean War on the Cold War," *The Journal of Conflict Resolution* 24 (December 1980): 563–592.

50. In fact, the original NATO pact (subsequently altered in January 1963) covered "the Algerian Departments of France" in its security network. In this limited sense, a small part of Africa was originally included in NATO. See Article 6 of the NATO charter in *NATO Handbook*, p. 144, on this point.

51. The speech by President Eisenhower can be found in *House Documents, Miscellaneous,* 85th Cong. 1st sess., Vol. 1 (Washington, DC: Government Printing Office, 1957–1958), Document 46. The first quote is from this document. The latter quote is from Public Law 85–7, which was passed on March 9, 1957, to put the Eisenhower Doctrine into effect.

52. This section draws largely on the fine summary of American foreign aid policy between 1945 and 1964 presented in *Congress and the Nation 1945–1964* (Washington, DC: Congressional Quarterly Service, 1965), pp. 160–186.

53. The text of Secretary of State Marshall's address can be found in *New York Times,* June 6, 1947, 2. The Soviet Union and the Eastern European states were invited to participate in the Marshall Plan under the original formulation. Although Poland and Czechoslovakia showed some initial interest, the Soviets quickly vetoed their efforts. See Ferrell, *American Diplomacy*, pp. 634–635. The percentage of GNP for the Marshall Plan was calculated from data presented in U.S. Bureau of Census, *Historical Statistics of the United States, Colonial Times to 1970, Parts 1 and 2*, Bicentennial ed. (Washington, DC: Government Printing Office, 1970). U.S. aid efforts over time can be found in the yearly reports by Development Co-Operation (Paris: Organization for Economic Cooperation and Development). The datum for 2010 is from the OECD, http://www.oecd.org/dataoecd/54/41/47515917 .pdf, accessed February 5, 2012.

54. Gilbert Winham, "Developing Theories of Foreign Policy Making: A Case Study of Foreign Aid," *The Journal of Politics* 32 (February 1970): 41–70.

55. President Truman's 1949 inaugural address with the Point Four provision can be found in *Senate Documents, Miscellaneous*, 81st Cong., 1st sess., Vol. 1 (Washington, DC: Government Printing Office, 1949), Document 5.

56. See Robert A. Pastor, *Congress and the Politics of U.S. Foreign Economic Policy 1929–1976* (Berkeley: University of California Press, 1980), p. 269.

57. *Congress and the Nation 1945–1964,* p. 166.

58. The Mutual Security Act of 1951 can be found as Public Law 82–165, passed on October 10, 1951.

59. Aid was given to some countries in order to bolster their economies and their political will to retain some independence from Moscow. See *Congress and the Nation 1945–1964*, pp. 161–162.

60. "A Report to the National Security Council, *NSC-68*," Washington, DC, April 14, 1950, p. 13.

61. Ibid., p. 54.

62. Ibid., p. 57. The quoted phrase on military strength is from *NSC-68* at p. 31; the information on spending is at p. 25. On these points and others on *NSC-68*, see John C. Donovan, *The Cold Warriors: A Policy-Making Elite* (Lexington, MA: D. C. Heath and Company, 1974), pp. 81–96.

63. *NSC-68*, p. 39.

64. Ibid., p. 34.

65. Ibid., p. 63.

66. Similar data are reported in James L. Payne, *The American Threat* (College Station, TX: Lytton Publishing Company, 1981), p. 291.

67. See Howard Bliss and M. Glen Johnson, *Beyond the Water's Edge: America's Foreign Policies* (Philadelphia: J. B. Lippincott Co., 1975), pp. 3–10, for a discussion of the "costs of consensus" and for another set of assumptions that make up the postwar consensus.

68. For various accounts of the Korean War, on which we relied for this summary, see John G. Stoessinger, *Why Nations Go To War*, 5th ed. (New York: St. Martin's Press, 1990), pp. 55–83, especially p. 61; Spanier, *The Truman-MacArthur Controversy and the Korean War*, especially pp. 23–26; Young W. Kihl, *Politics and Policies in Divided Korea: Regimes in Contest* (Boulder, CO: Westview Press, 1984), pp. 27–42; and Whiting, *China Crosses the Yalu*.

69. See, for example, Stoessinger, *Why Nations Go to War*, p. 61; and Spanier, *The Truman-MacArthur Controversy*, pp. 23–26.

70. John Merrill in *Korea: The Peninsular Origins of the War* (Newark: University of Delaware Press, 1989), has catalogued five explanations for the outbreak of the war: (1) Moscow ordered the North Koreans to invade the South; (2) the South Koreans provoked the North into an attack; (3) the South Koreans, in conjunction with the United States, initiated the war; (4) the deeply divided North Koreans "sprang the war on their unsuspecting Soviet allies"; and (5) the war was the result of regional politics initiated by the Soviet Union "to bring the independently minded Chinese leadership back into line and to frustrate American plans to establish a permanent military presence in Japan." The quoted passages are at pp. 19 and 48, respectively.

    Another recent study, quoting a North Korean official, argues that Stalin "reluctantly consented" to the surprise attack on the South: "Stalin was giving a nod to the general idea of an invasion but had made consultations with Mao a condition for his unequivocal assent to any future detailed plan of action." See Sergei N. Goncharov, John W. Lewis, and Xue Litai, *Uncertain Partners: Stalin, Mao, and the Korean War* (Stanford, CA: Stanford University Press, 1993), p. 144. The first quotation, from Goncharov et al., is that of the North Korean official, although the second is the judgment of these authors. In July 1994, South Korean officials announced that Soviet documents provided to them by Russian President Boris Yeltsin a month earlier "showed that Soviet dictator Josef Stalin and Chinese leader Mao Tse-tung approved Kim Il-Sung's attack on South Korea in June 1950." See Sam Jameson, "Kim Plotted Korean War, South Claims," *Des Moines Register*, July 21, 1994, 10A.

71. Quoted in Frederick H. Hartmann and Robert L. Wendzel, *America's Foreign Policy in a Changing World* (New York: Harper-Collins College Publishers, 1994), p. 222. The original source is U. Alexis Johnson, *The Right Hand of Power* (Englewood Cliffs, NJ: Prentice-Hall, 1984), p. 99.

72. Stoessinger, *Why Nations Go to War*, p. 67.

73. See the chronology of events in Whiting, *China Crosses the Yalu*, and in John E. Mueller, *War, Presidents, and Public Opinion* (New York: John Wiley and Sons, 1973), among others, on whom we rely.

74. As quoted in Whiting, *China Crosses the Yalu*, p. 93.

75. On the firing and its implications for American foreign policy, see Spanier, *The Truman-MacArthur Controversy and the Korean War*.

76. Bradley is quoted in Robert H. Ferrell, *American Diplomacy: The Twentieth Century* (New York: W. W. Norton and Company, 1988), pp. 284–285.

77. Mueller, *War, Presidents, and Public Opinion*, pp. 25–27.

78. Jervis, "The Impact of the Korean War on the Cold War," p. 563.

79. These effects are derived from Jervis, "The Impact of the Korean War on the Cold War."

80. In a speech to the Press Club on January 12, 1950, Secretary of State Dean Acheson indicated that the U.S. "defensive perimeter runs along the Aleutians to Japan and then goes to the Ryukyus. We hold important defense positions in the Ryukyu Islands, and these we will continue to hold. . . . The defensive perimeter runs from the Ryukyu to the Philippine Islands." Korea was thus outside this defense line. See Dean Acheson, *Present at the Creation* (New York: W. W. Norton and Company, 1969), p. 357.

81. Jervis, "The Impact of the Korean War on the Cold War," p. 584.

82. Gaddis, "Was the Truman Doctrine a Real Turning Point?" p. 386.

83. Lincoln P. Bloomfield, *In Search of American Foreign Policy: The Humane Use of Power* (New York: Oxford University Press, 1974).

84. J. William Fulbright, *The Arrogance of Power* (New York: Vintage Books, 1966), p. 77. His conclusion on American policy choice in this dilemma is at p. 78.

85. See the Rusk-McNamara Report to President Kennedy in Neil Sheehan, Hedrick Smith, E. W. Kenworthy, and Fox Butterfield, *The Pentagon Papers as Published by the New York Times* (New York: Bantam Books, 1971), p. 150, for a statement of American objectives in Southeast Asia.

86. Barry M. Blechman and Stephen S. Kaplan, *Force Without War* (Washington, DC: The Brookings Institution, 1978), p. 12. The examples are at p. 13. Emphasis in original.

87. Ibid., p 517. Their skepticism over the long term is at p. 532.

88. The use-of-force data for mid-1975 through late 1984 were taken from Philip D. Zelkow, "The United States and the Use of Force: A Historical Summary," in George K. Osborn, Asa A. Clark IV, Daniel J. Kaufman, and Douglas E. Lute, eds., *Democracy, Strategy, and Vietnam* (Lexington, MA: D. C. Heath and Company, 1987), pp. 34–36; the data for 1985–1988 were generously supplied by James Meernik of the University of North Texas from his research on this topic.

89. As Ernest May points out, however, American policy makers have often used historical analogies inappropriately by preparing for the last war. See *"Lessons" of the Past*, especially the discussion of the Korean War and Truman's use of the 1930s as the analogue for U.S. policy, pp. 81–86.

90. On this "skills thinking" in the American approach to foreign policy, see Stanley Hoffmann, *Gulliver's Troubles, or the Setting of American Foreign Policy* (New York: McGraw-Hill, 1968), pp. 148–161.

91. See, for example, the discussion of polling results from the early Cold War period in Benjamin I. Page and Robert Y. Shapiro, *The Rational Public: Fifty Years of Trends in Americans' Policy Preferences* (Chicago: University of Chicago Press, 1992). I am also indebted to Eugene Wittkopf for sharing some public opinion poll results with me and allowing their inclusion here. A more complete analysis of some of the public opinion data from the Cold War years discussed here is presented in Eugene R. Wittkopf and James M. McCormick, "The Cold War Consensus: Did It Exist?" *Polity* 22 (Summer 1990): 627–653.

92. Ibid., p. 633.

93. Ibid.; and Eugene R. Wittkopf, *Faces of Internationalism: Public Opinion and American Foreign Policy* (Durham: Duke University Press, 1990), p. 178.

94. Page and Shapiro, *The Rational Public*, p. 201.

95. Wittkopf and McCormick, "The Cold War Consensus: Did It Exist?" p. 635.

96. Page and Shapiro, *The Rational Public*, p. 200.

97. Ibid., pp. 203–204.

98. Ibid., p. 202.

99. In his review and critique of Henry Kissinger's approach to international politics, Richard Falk identifies some of these characteristics as the basis for the growth of multipolarity and shows how they fit into Kissinger's foreign policy design. See Richard Falk, "What's Wrong with Henry Kissinger's Foreign Policy," *Alternatives* 1 (March 1975): 86. An earlier analysis of the "challenge to consensus" can be found in Howard Bliss and M. Glen Johnson, *Beyond the Water's Edge: America's Foreign Policies* (Philadelphia: J. B. Lippincott, 1975), pp. 1–26. Their analysis focuses primarily on the impact of Vietnam.

100. For an informative discussion of these historical antipathies, see Harrison E. Salisbury, *War between China and Russia* (New York: W.W. Norton and Company, 1969), pp. 13–52. For two other lucid discussions of this dispute, see John G. Stoessinger, *Nations in Darkness:, Russia, and America*, 3rd ed. (New York: Random House, 1978), pp. 212–218; and Robert C. North, *The Foreign Relations of China*, 2nd ed. (Encino and Belmont, CA: Dickenson Publishing Company, 1974), pp. 112–122.

101. Stoessinger, *Nations in Darkness*, pp. 214–215.

102. For an examination of the centrality of military issues in the Sino–Soviet split, see North, *The Foreign Relations of China*, pp. 41–46, 121.

103. Ibid., pp. 116–120.

104. These issues and others are discussed in Donald S. Zagoria, *The Sino-Soviet Conflict 1956–1961* (Princeton, NJ: Princeton University Press, 1962).

105. The extent of these East–West contacts is analyzed in Josef Korbel, *Détente in Europe: Real or Imaginary?* (Princeton, NJ: Princeton University Press, 1972).

106. For a summary of de Gaulle's vision of European and global politics, on which we rely, see Korbel, *Détente in Europe*, pp. 40–60; Alfred Grosser, *French Foreign Policy under de Gaulle* (Boston: Little, Brown, 1965), especially pp. 13–28; Edward A. Kolodziej, *French International Policy under de Gaulle and Pompidou* (Ithaca, NY: Cornell University Press, 1974), especially pp. 19–390; Edward A. Kolodziej, "Revolt and Revisionism in the Gaullist Global Vision: An Analysis of French Strategic Policy," *The Journal of Politics* 33 (May 1971): 448–477; Roy C. Macridis, "The French Force de Frappe," and William G. Andrews, "de Gaulle and NATO," in Roy C. Macridis, ed., *Modern European Governments: Cases in Comparative Policy Making* (Englewood Cliffs, NJ: Prentice Hall, 1976), pp. 75–116.

107. On this point, see Josef Joffe, "The Foreign Policy of the German Federal Republic," in Roy C. Macridis, ed., *Foreign Policy in World Politics*, 5th ed. (Englewood Cliffs, NJ: Prentice Hall, Inc., 1976), p. 141.

108. This discussion draws on Korbel, *Détente in Europe*, pp. 40–60.

109. Ibid., p. 58.

110. The dates of independence for the new nations from 1945 to 2006 were taken from Bruce Russett, Harvey Starr, and David Kinsella, *World Politics: The Menu for Choice*, 6th ed. (Boston: Bedford/St. Martin's Press, 2000), pp. 492–498 and their 8th ed. (Belmont, CA: Thomson/Wadsworth, 2006), pp. 535–541.

111. Richard L. Park, "India's Foreign Policy," in Roy C. Macridis, ed., *Foreign Policy in World Politics*, 5th ed. (Englewood Cliffs, NJ: Prentice Hall, Inc., 1976), p. 326.

112. On this point, see the discussion in Peter Willetts, *The Non-Aligned Movement: The Origins of a Third World Alliance* (London: Frances Pinter Ltd., 1978), p. 3.

113. See Roderick Ogley, ed., *The Theory and Practice of Neutrality in the Twentieth Century* (New York: Barnes and Noble, 1970), pp. 189–194.

114. For two important discussions of nonalignment, see Cecil V. Crabb, Jr., *The Elephants and the Grass: A Study of Nonalignment* (New York: Frederick A. Praeger, 1965); and Willets, *The Non-Aligned Movement*, especially pp. 17–31.

115. See Table 1.1 in Willets, *The Non-Aligned Movement*, for a summary of the various nonaligned conferences and their membership.

116. For an extended discussion of the following argument in a similar vein, and one from which we draw, see Edmund Stillman and William Pfaff, *Power and Impotence* (New York: Vintage Books, 1966), especially at pp. 15 and 58–59.

CHAPTER 3

After the Missile Crisis and the Vietnam War: Realism and Idealism in Foreign Policy

Let every nation know, whether it wishes us well or ill, that we shall pay any price, bear any burden, meet any hardship, support any friend, oppose any foe to assure the survival and the success of liberty.

PRESIDENT JOHN F. KENNEDY
JANUARY 1961

In honor of the men and women of the armed forces of the United States who served in the Vietnam War. The names of those who gave their lives and of those who remain missing are inscribed in the order they were taken from us.

INSCRIPTION ON THE VIETNAM VETERANS MEMORIAL
WASHINGTON, D.C.
DEDICATED APRIL 27, 1979

In this chapter, we first examine two other serious challenges to the postwar consensus: the impact of the Cuban Missile Crisis in October 1962 and America's Vietnam policy, particularly from 1965 to the early 1970s, on American domestic environment, and then we turn to assess two alternative approaches to the direction of foreign policy over the following decade. The approach of the Nixon administration pursued one foreign policy, whereas the Carter administration pursued another. Neither succeeded in replacing the shattered Cold War consensus, but each emphasized alternate ways of shaping America's role in the world.

CHALLENGES TO THE COLD WAR CONSENSUS AT HOME

Although the Cuban Missile Crisis of 1962 and the Vietnam War were foreign policy events, their impact was as much domestic as foreign, and they profoundly affected America's thinking about its role in the world. They brought home to American leaders and to the American people—in a most dramatic fashion—the limits of the United States in influencing the Soviet Union and the Third World, and they illustrated the limited extent to which American beliefs and values were able to create the global design the Cold War consensus envisioned. In particular, Vietnam produced a full-blown domestic debate over the conduct of American foreign policy, and it is often cited as having signaled the death knell of the Cold War consensus.

The Missiles of October: The First Crisis of Confidence

The **Cuban Missile Crisis** of October 16–28, 1962, was the closest that the United States and the Soviet Union had come to nuclear confrontation since the advent of atomic power. It began when Cuba, under the leadership of **Fidel Castro** since 1959, and having by this time declared itself a "Marxist-Leninist" state, turned to the Soviet Union for assistance against alleged American intrigues. The crisis centered on the introduction of Soviet "offensive" intermediate-range ballistic missiles into Cuba during the fall of 1962. Such Soviet actions were in violation of its stated commitment to introduce only "defensive" weapons.

On the discovery of the missiles on October 16, 1962, President John Kennedy set out to devise an appropriate strategy to remove them from territory only ninety miles from American shores. After a week of highly secret deliberations through his Executive Committee of the National Security Council, he finally announced on October 22, 1962, that a naval quarantine would be set up in an 800-mile ring around Cuba to interdict further missile shipments (see Map 3.1). Furthermore, he threatened the Soviet Union with a nuclear response if the Cuban missiles were used against the United States. A series of other measures, through the Organization of American States, the United Nations, and bilateral contacts with the Soviet Union, were undertaken to remove the missiles already in place.

After another week of tense confrontation and exchanges of diplomatic notes, the Soviets agreed to remove the missiles under United Nations supervision. The United States, in exchange, pledged not to attempt to overthrow the Castro regime. Subsequent information about the crises, uncovered through a series of conferences in the late 1980s and early 1990s among American, Soviet, and Cuban participants, revealed that the United States and the Soviet Union struck another, informal, exchange: the Soviet Union would remove its threatening missiles from Cuba; the United States would remove its threatening missiles from Turkey.[1]

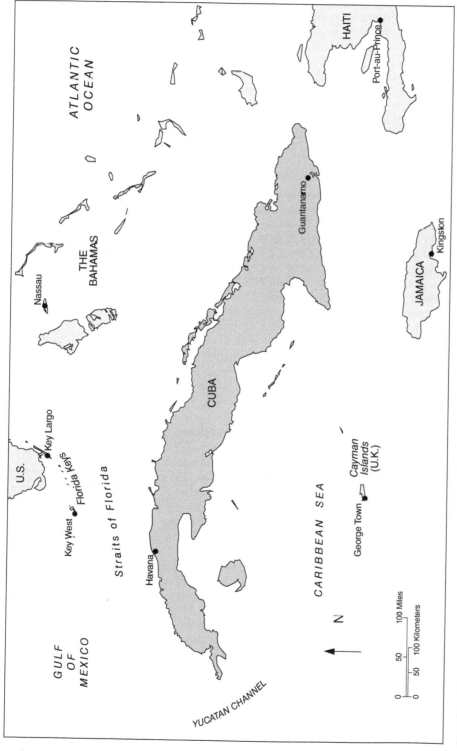

MAP 3.1 Cuba

The Missile Crisis has long been the subject of analysis and reanalysis, and it has yielded various lessons for Soviet–American relations during the Cold War and for nuclear relations generally.[2]

Lesson 1: The Risk of Nuclear Annihilation First, the crisis fully brought home to both Soviet and American leaders (and their populaces) that nuclear annihilation was a real possibility—mutual assured destruction, or MAD, was no longer an abstract theory. Although the United States may have been relatively safe from Soviet nuclear attacks in the 1950s, the development of intercontinental missiles—and even intermediate-range missiles such as those that had been placed in Cuba—demonstrated that this safety no longer existed. Americans were now vulnerable to Soviet nuclear weapons, just as the Soviets were to the U.S. nuclear arsenal.

Political analysts Len Scott and Steve Smith conclude that, with the new data available on the crisis, this lesson is even clearer today. "Recent sources," they report, "seem to show absolutely clearly that U.S. decision-makers were extremely worried about the prospect of any Soviet nuclear response, so much so that the result was to nullify the enormous nuclear superiority that the United States enjoyed at the time."[3] Two other analysts, James Blight and David Welch, writing from new material and from the review conference discussions, identify the "**perceptions of risks**" as the primary "meta-lesson" to be drawn from the crisis.[4]

Put differently, mutual survival proved more important than the unilateral interests of either country. Despite their avowed antipathy toward one another, then, neither the Soviet Union nor the United States wanted to back the other into a corner where all-out war (and nuclear holocaust) or surrender was the only option. This caution is reflected in the various personal accounts of the decision making at the time and in the importance that was attached to "placing ourselves in the other country's shoes" during the crisis.[5]

Lesson 2: The Possibility of Rational Policy Making Both the United States and the Soviet Union proved capable of rationally evaluating their national interests and global consequences during the crisis. This was especially important for American policy makers. Because of the Cold War consensus, Americans had tended to view skeptically Soviet decision making. Being so consumed with Marxist-Leninist ideology, could the Soviets assess the costs and the consequences of their actions and respond prudently? The answer was clearly yes, as reflected in the outcome of the crisis and in the subsequent scholarly research on it.[6] Rational policy making with the Soviet Union might just be possible.

Yet some recent assessments also make clear the need to go beyond the rational policy-making assumption in drawing any lessons from this dramatic episode. First, **reliance on the "rational actor"** alone fails to account "for the values and priorities of the president. For that, cognitive models are required."[7] That is, an understanding of the values, beliefs, and perceptions of the leaders in the crisis and the roles they played is important for understanding the successful resolution of the crisis and represents a useful lesson to take away from it. Second, **organizational and bureaucratic factors in policy making** during the crisis (see Chapters 9 and 10) actually produced more nuclear risks than previously thought. Policy managers were, in fact, less successful in controlling the actions of their subordinates in the field than many might want to believe.[8] One recent analysis that focuses on the crisis, for example, makes this point dramatically by noting that, during this period, "the U.S. nuclear command system clearly did not provide the certainty in safety that senior American leaders wanted and believed existed at the time."[9]

Lesson 3: The Likelihood of Mutual Accommodation   Finally, and perhaps most important, the crisis brought home the reality that the Soviet Union and the United States were going to be major participants in international relations for a long time and that each might just as well devise policies that would acknowledge the interests and rights of the other. In other words, neither superpower was capable of dislodging the other from its place in world politics quickly or easily. For the Americans, any vision of "**rolling back communism**" was illusory at best; for the Soviets, any vision of capitalist collapse was myopic. In this way, the Americans and the Soviets learned that accommodation with their major adversary was possible—and necessary—for mutual survival. Somewhat ironically, the nuclear showdown over the missiles in Cuba has been cited as the beginning of détente between the Soviet Union and the United States.

In sum, the Cuban Missile Crisis—even with the Soviets' humiliation over the removal of its missiles from Cuba—challenged the Cold War view that the Soviet Union or communism could be quickly and easily dislodged from global politics. A foreign policy based solely on this assumption was therefore likely to be frustrating and self-defeating. (Although this point is difficult to demonstrate, the Soviet Union probably learned similar lessons about the United States.) At the same time, and equally important, the crisis illustrated the possibility of negotiating with an implacable foe—even over the most fundamental questions—and of accommodating a world of different political and social systems.

VIETNAM

American involvement in Vietnam began at the end of World War II and lasted for almost thirty years, until the evacuation of American embassy personnel from Saigon at the end of April 1975 (see Map 3.2). It spanned six administrations, from Harry S. Truman's to Gerald Ford's. Guided largely by the values and beliefs of the Cold War consensus, Vietnam nevertheless produced the most divisive foreign policy debate in the history of the republic and ultimately produced a major foreign policy defeat for the United States. At home, its most important outcome was that it signaled a change in Cold War foreign policy—at least until the Reagan administration in the 1980s.

Before we assess the overall impact of Vietnam, we will present a brief sketch of American involvement there.

The Origins of Involvement, 1945–1963

President Franklin Roosevelt gave the first hint of American interest in Indochina with his preference for an international trusteeship arrangement over the countries that today are Cambodia, Laos, and Vietnam near the end of World War II. However, the events of the immediate postwar years and the rise of the Cold War propelled the United States in a different direction. The Truman administration had serious reservations about identifying itself with colonialism, but Soviet actions toward Eastern Europe, Communist success in China, and uncertainty about the political leanings of **Ho Chi Minh**—the leader of the Vietnamese independence movement—ultimately

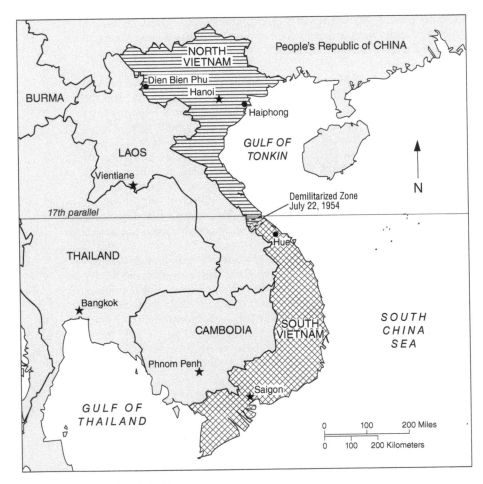

MAP 3.2 Vietnam, 1954–1975

led the United States to assume "a distinctly pro-French 'neutrality.'" As a result, Truman began providing clandestine economic and military assistance to France in the late 1940s in its war against the Vietminh (the followers of Ho Chi Minh).[10]

After the outbreak of the Korean War, which seemed to confirm Washington's suspicions about Soviet global intentions, American involvement in the war in Indochina deepened. More than $133 million of military hardware was committed to the French for Indochina, and another $50 million was sent in economic and technical assistance to the governments that they had established. Throughout the rest of the Truman administration, the United States provided more and more military and economic assistance, until American aid constituted 40 percent of the war's total cost.[11]

The Eisenhower administration took the rationale for American involvement in Vietnam one step further by invoking much of the language of the Cold War and by continuing to increase assistance to the noncommunist, French-backed Vietnamese government. In a 1954 news conference, President Dwight D. Eisenhower referred to the "**falling dominoes**" in Southeast Asia, and Secretary of State John Foster Dulles hinted at the role of the Chinese Communists in causing the unrest there.[12] Yet the administration did not go much beyond providing economic and military assistance and, in fact, explicitly ruled out the use of American forces to rescue the French from defeat at the decisive battle of **Dien Bien Phu** with the Vietminh in 1954. Instead, it sought a negotiated outcome at a **1954 Geneva conference on Indochina**.[13] That conference called for an armistice between the parties, a temporary division of the country at the 17th parallel, and elections in 1956 to decide on reunification. The United States did not actively participate in this conference nor did it sign the accords or endorse them. The proposed all-Vietnam election scheduled for 1956 was never held.

The United States quickly became the principal supporter of the noncommunist South Vietnamese government of Premier (later President) **Ngo Dinh Diem**, who came to be identified as "America's Mandarin," as he sought to replace French influence with close American ties.[14] Moreover, Eisenhower and Dulles believed that Ngo Dinh Diem represented the best prospect for developing a noncommunist Vietnam. Between 1955 and 1961, the United States provided $1 billion in aid to Diem, and by 1961, South Vietnam was the fifth largest recipient of U.S. foreign assistance.[15] Even so, the stability of the Diem government remained precarious throughout the late 1950s.

On taking office in 1961, President John F. Kennedy expanded this military and economic assistance and contemplated sending in American military forces to prevent the fall of South Vietnam. He did not quite take that step, but instead incrementally enlarged the number of American military "advisors" from 685 when he took office to about 16,000 by the time of his assassination.[16] By one account, Kennedy did not give an "unqualified commitment to the goal of saving South Vietnam from Communism."[17] Nonetheless, his actions took the United States further down the path to military involvement, and Kennedy may well have continued in that direction had he lived to remain in office.[18]

American Military Involvement, 1964–1975

It was President Lyndon Johnson who fully transformed U.S. involvement in South Vietnam from a political to a military one. He both broadened and deepened America's commitment to preserve a noncommunist South Vietnam, and it was ultimately he who decided to send in American combat forces.

As the stability of the South Vietnamese government worsened (some nine changes of government occurred from the time of the coup against President Ngo Dinh Diem in November 1963 until February 1965) and as North Vietnamese and Vietcong successes increased, the Johnson administration sought a new strategy.[19] At least as early as February 1964, American clandestine operations were under way against North Vietnam; these operations ultimately led to attacks by the North Vietnamese on two American destroyers, the *Maddox* and the *C. Turner Joy* in the Gulf of Tonkin in North Vietnam in August 1964. The Johnson administration quickly used these attacks to seek congressional approval of an American military presence in Southeast Asia.[20] In a matter of hours, Congress approved the **Gulf of Tonkin resolution**, which authorized the president to take "all necessary measures" in Southeast Asia (see Chapter 7).

For the Johnson administration, this resolution became the equivalent of a dec-laration of war, and U.S. retaliatory air strikes were quickly ordered. By December 1964, air attacks against North Vietnamese infiltration routes through Laos had be-gun, and by February 1965, "**Operation Rolling Thunder**," a bombing strategy to weaken North Vietnam's resistance and bring it to the negotiating table, was initiated. By March 1965, the first American ground troops had landed, and a rapid buildup in these forces was ordered in July.[21] Indeed, the number of forces continued to escalate until they ultimately reached over a half million American soldiers by late 1968.

Despite this vast commitment of personnel and matériel, the war went badly for the South Vietnamese and the United States. The **Tet offensive** (named for the lu-nar New Year) perhaps more than any other event brought this home to Americans. Tet consisted of widespread attacks by the North Vietnamese and the Vietcong (or the National Liberation Front of South Vietnam) over a six-month period beginning at the end of January 1968. It was ultimately a military failure for the North, cost-ing it tens of thousands of lives, but it was a political success in that it demonstrated the continuing vulnerability of South Vietnam through many years of war. More-over, Tet's impact within the United States was immediate, causing a sharp drop in American optimism.[22] Indeed, the political pressure on President Johnson became so severe that in March 1968 he voluntarily withdrew from consideration as a candidate for reelection.

President Richard Nixon, elected as Johnson's successor in part on a commitment to change Vietnam policy, adopted a different strategy. He began to decrease American military involvement through a policy of "**Vietnamization**"—whereby the South Vietnamese military would replace American soldiers—and he pursued peace negoti-ations (begun originally in mid-1968 in Paris) through both open and secret channels.

With Vietnamization, American forces in Vietnam were reduced from about 543,000 shortly after Nixon took office to about 25,000 by the end of his first term.[23] As part of this strategy, the United States invaded Cambodia in April 1970 with the expressed purpose of wiping out its North Vietnamese sanctuaries and safe havens. To many Americans, this action appeared to be a widening of the war. Protests erupted across the country, and tragedy struck Kent State University in Ohio and Jackson State University in Mississippi when students were killed during campus protests. Further opposition to the war resulted.

After a North Vietnamese offensive in the spring of 1972 had been repulsed and after further American bombing of the North near the end of the negotiations, a cease-fire agreement, formally called "**The Agreement on Ending the War and Restoring the Peace**," was signed on January 27, 1973. The agreement followed continuous U.S. involvement since 1965 and the loss of more than 58,000 American and countless Vietnamese lives.[24]

The cease-fire called for the withdrawal of all American troops and the return of prisoners of war. In addition, it allowed the North Vietnamese to keep their military forces in South Vietnam, and it left open the question of South Vietnam's future. On balance, it was less a "peace with honor," as it was portrayed at the time, and more a mechanism for enabling the United States to extricate itself from Vietnam.[25]

Although the cease-fire reduced the level of fighting and provided a way for the United States to bring its troops home, it did not totally end the war or America's involvement. The end actually came two years later, during the Ford administration, with the fall of Saigon and the final evacuation of all American personnel on **April 30, 1975**. The fall of Saigon was a humiliating defeat for a policy based on preventing communist success in South Vietnam. This defeat produced searching policy reflection at that point, but not before the basic premises of Vietnam had come under scrutiny and become the subject of intense debate.

Lessons from Vietnam

Several political and military explanations have been offered for America's defeat. Some have focused on U.S. military tactics and the very nature of "limited war."[26] They believe that the **policy of "graduated response"** did not allow the United States to take maximum advantage of its military capabilities. Others point to the failure to adjust military strategy to the unconventional nature of the war and to the futility of "search-and-destroy" against the adversary.[27] Still others point to the political problems associated with the war. The "legitimacy" of the South Vietnamese government remained a problem, and its shaky domestic support weakened the war effort.[28] By contrast, the determination and will of the North Vietnamese were much greater than many policy makers had thought. Even under the pressure of intensive bombing and high causalities, they continued to fight. Other explanations fault the loss of support for the war back home and the nature of American leadership.[29] Neither the American public nor Congress was willing to sustain its support for the war—some because they believed that it was not being prosecuted fully; others because they no longer believed that the conflict was either moral or ethical.

For all of these reasons, the Vietnam foreign policy defeat, and various explanations for it, produced a significant reexamination of the Cold War consensus and contributed substantially to its undermining (or at least its revision). Indeed, there were several domestic consequences for foreign policy from the Vietnam War that had a profound effect on the direction of future American actions abroad.

Consequence One: The U.S. Role The Vietnam War led to the **questioning of the U.S. role** in the world. Should it be responsible for political activity everywhere—especially in a country half a world away with only the most tangential relationship to American national security? Was the American public willing to support and legitimize such responsibility? Was the public willing to support a policy that had only the loftiest goals in international affairs?

Americans' response to these questions, by the early 1970s, was generally a resounding no. There were limits to American power, there were limits to America's responsibility, and there were limits to how much globalism the American public would tolerate. The future scope of the U.S. role in global affairs would have to be much more limited.

Consequence Two: Questions of Strategy Vietnam created a greater hesitancy in fighting limited war and a belief that a different strategy would be needed if such a war were to be pursued. By the late 1970s and early 1980s, the U.S. military leadership became increasingly uneasy about quickly deploying American forces abroad and came to demand from their political leaders clearer missions, adequate resources, and reasonable "exit" strategies. This **"Vietnam Syndrome"** was most dramatically played out during the Persian Gulf War of 1991, when General Colin Powell, chairman of the Joint Chiefs of Staff, and General Norman Schwarzkopf, commander of American forces in the Middle East, sought and obtained an overwhelming force level to drive the Iraqis from Kuwait. More recently, this syndrome was in the minds of policy makers as they contemplated actions in the Balkans in the mid-1990s, in Afghanistan after September 11, 2001, and in Iraq in 2003.

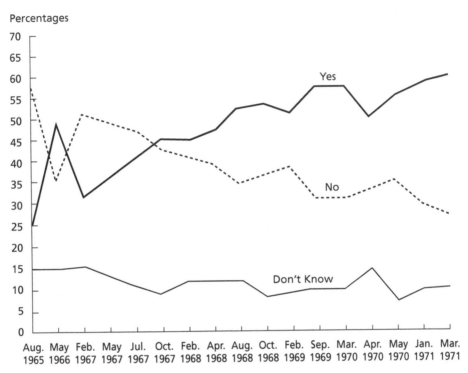

Percentage of responses to the question: "In view of the developments since we entered the fighting in Vietnam, do you think the U.S. made a mistake sending troops to fight in Vietnam?" (Gallup Organization data)

FIGURE 3.1 The "Mistake" Question on Vietnam

Source: Adapted from a portion of Table 3.3 in John E. Mueller, War, *Presidents and Public Opinion* (New York: John Wiley and Sons, 1973), pp. 54–55.

Consequence Three: Open Public Debate   Because of Vietnam, **foreign policy goals now became a ready source of public debate**. Public opinion challenged its leadership's policies on the war, and by 1968 and early 1969 a majority of Americans viewed it as a "mistake."[30] (See the public opinion data in Figure 3.1.) Moreover, after the Tet offensive of 1968, the number of "hawks" declined, although the public still did not favor immediate withdrawal. That would come by late 1969, however, when support for withdrawal rose to almost 70 percent.[31] In Congress, too, divisions were apparent between "liberals" and "conservatives" and between "hawks" and "doves" on foreign policy.[32] Such divisions are in sharp contrast to the philosophies of just a few years earlier, when liberals and conservatives, despite their domestic differences, often stood together on foreign policy. After the Vietnam experience, no such harmony was evident.

Consequence Four: The Collapse of the Cold War Consensus   Following from the first three consequences is the shattering of the values and beliefs consensus that had guided the conduct of foreign policy since the end of World War II. No longer could the American foreign policy elite depend on general public support for their foreign policy goals and actions. They were equally divided among themselves about the role of the United States in world affairs.

More than any other event, the Vietnam War appears responsible for the ultimate destruction of the Cold War consensus and for the reassessment of America's approach to international affairs. Moreover, the public, not just policy makers, had seemingly changed its views from what it had embraced in the 1950s. In the post-Vietnam era, the threat of communism remained real to most Americans, but they were no longer as enthusiastic about using economic and military aid or American soldiers to combat it. The public was much more favorable to greater accommodation with the Soviet Union and less inclined to confront it.[33]

Thus, Vietnam, coupled with the other Cold War challenges that we discussed earlier, produced a foreign policy vacuum. However, the nation's readiness to accept new ideas in dealing with the rest of the world offered a unique opportunity for succeeding presidents to develop new foreign policy approaches. Consequently, each new administration for the next two decades attempted to initiate a change of direction. We will now survey the realist and idealist approaches of the Nixon and Carter administrations as two initial responses to this foreign policy vacuum. The Nixon administration employed a "power politics" or "realist" approach, whereas the Carter administration employed a "global politics" or "idealist" approach.[34] Although neither administration succeeded in creating a new foreign policy consensus (indeed, each met with substantial criticism and resistance), each brought with it a distinct and identifiable worldview to fill the vacuum created after the height of the Cold War had passed.

REALISM AND IDEALISM AS FOREIGN POLICY CONCEPTS

The concepts of *realism* and *idealism*, both of which have been widely used to describe the behavior of individuals and states in the study of foreign policy, require some discussion before we proceed.[35] Each is an *ideal type*, which means that individuals and states are closer to one than the other but do not match either perfectly. Early postwar presidents (e.g., Truman and Eisenhower) may have combined elements of realism and idealism, but they did not match these types as well as Nixon, Jimmy Carter, and Ronald Reagan did in their foreign policy making. Realism and idealism, then, serve as important ways to think about the foreign policy of these presidents even if neither concept fully describes them.

The realist approach is based on several key assumptions: (1) the nation-state is the primary actor in world politics; (2) interest, defined as power, is the primary motivating force for the actions of states; (3) the distribution or balance of power (predominantly military power) at any given time is the key concern of states; and (4) state-to-state relations (not domestic politics) shape how one nation responds to another. For the realist, because human nature is ultimately flawed, efforts at universal perfection in global politics are shortsighted and ultimately dangerous. Instead, morality in foreign policy is largely defined by what is good for the state and for its place in international politics.

In this view, foreign policy is fraught with conflict, with each state seeking to further its interests and warily monitoring the activities of others. Balance-of-power politics predominates because all states are concerned with the relative distribution of power at any one time, and all are trying to maximize their own power and standing.

The idealist approach starts with a different set of assumptions: (1) the nation–state is only one among many participants in foreign policy; (2) values, rather than interests, are predominant in shaping foreign policy; (3) the distribution of power is only one of many important values, with social, economic, and military issues equally important; and (4) overall global conditions, not relationships between states, should dominate foreign policy thinking. For the idealist, human nature can be changed, improving humankind is a laudable goal, and universal values should be the basis of action.

In the idealist view, foreign policy should be a cooperative process between states and groups, with joint efforts undertaken to address the problems facing humankind, whether political, military, economic, or social. International institutions (such as international and regional organizations) and rule-based international law are crucial to shaping global politics, and politics based on balance of power are largely to be eschewed.

REALISM AND THE NIXON ADMINISTRATION

The Nixon administration's foreign policy was closer to the realist tradition than that of earlier postwar presidents. It was based on the principles of the balance of power and was anchored in a global equilibrium among the United States, the Soviet Union, and the People's Republic of China (and later Japan and Europe). The realist perspective would enable the United States to play a more limited global role and exploit substantial amounts of regional power (and power centers) to foster American interests. At the same time, it would allow the United States to remain an important, even dominant, participant in global affairs. It should be kept in mind that this new realism in foreign policy was precipitated by the events surrounding the Vietnam War. Indeed, the Nixon administration was as much consumed by Vietnam as it was by the reordering of superpower relations. Both factors pointed the United States toward a different foreign policy emphasis for the Nixon administration.

The Nixon Approach to Foreign Policy

Several dimensions of Nixon's policy design were foreshadowed in a *Foreign Affairs* article he wrote almost two years before he took office.[36] Nixon emphasized two points: (1) the importance of bringing the People's Republic of China back into the world community and (2) a more limited future role for the United States in regional disputes. The United States, Nixon wrote, "cannot afford to leave China forever outside the family of nations. There is no place on this small planet for a billion of its potentially most able people to live in angry isolation." At the same time, he argued for a "policy of firm restraint" to persuade Beijing to accept the "basic rules of international civility."

Nixon also foreshadowed a change in American policy toward regional conflict: "Other nations must recognize that the role of the United States as world policeman is likely to be limited in the future." If U.S. assistance is requested, it must come only after a regional collective effort has failed and only when a collective request for help is made. Unlike the Vietnam experience, direct U.S. intervention must be reduced or limited.

Other essential elements of Nixon's approach to the world were described more fully in his **State of the World Report to the Congress** in early 1970,[37] in which he outlined his plan for a new world "structure of peace." Three principles defined the "Nixon Doctrine" and were driven in no small measure by his desire to shape a post-Vietnam role for the United States:

- Peace would require a partnership with the rest of the world
- Peace would require strength to protect U.S. national interests
- Peace would require a willingness to negotiate with all states to resolve differences

These principles meant that America's role was to be diminished and its power was to be shared with others in the preservation of world order. Such a design also meant that the United States would act to protect its interests and would do so primarily through its military might. Furthermore, it would welcome the opportunity to negotiate with other states to resolve outstanding differences. This design was some distance away from the postwar consensus that had put so much stock in the ability of the United States to carry the burden of responsibility for the "Free World."

President Nixon made two other important observations in this speech. First, he recognized that the world was multipolar: ". . . the nature of that world has changed—the power of individual Communist nations has grown, but international Communist unity has been shattered." Second, he acknowledged the power of nationalism in the developing world, and he implied that this nationalism should not be equated with Communist penetration: "Once, many feared that they [the new nations] would become simply a battleground of cold-war rivalry and fertile ground for Communist penetration. But this fear misjudged their pride in their national identities and their determination to preserve their newly won sovereignty." In all, then, Nixon's foreign policy design pointed to a new foreign policy approach for the United States and represented a sharp break with the postwar consensus.[38]

Henry Kissinger and World Order

Whereas President Nixon's statements outlined the key components of a new policy approach, his national security advisor, and later secretary of state, Henry Kissinger, provided a more complete exposition of what that approach would look like in practice. To appreciate Kissinger's policy making, we must begin with his basic philosophy of international politics, which grew out of years of academic writing and his practical foreign policy experience in previous administrations.

For Henry Kissinger, the essential problem in the postwar world was structural: the lack of a *legitimate international order*.[39] Both the United States and the Soviet Union had seen the world in terms of absolutes and had tried to impose their own views of world order. Neither had succeeded. As a result, there was now a "revolutionary" and multipolar international system characterized by (1) the emergence of many states and new centers of power, (2) the growth of vast new technologies that created great disparities in power, and (3) the appearance of a diversity of political purposes by the new states and power centers.

These factors made it difficult to establish or maintain any legitimate order. Thus, according to Kissinger, the most important challenge confronting the United States was "to develop some concept of order in a world which is bipolar militarily but multipolar politically." To create such order, he argued, the United States must think more along the lines of **balance-of-power politics**. Although America's idealism of the past should not be abandoned, the requirements of global equilibrium should give

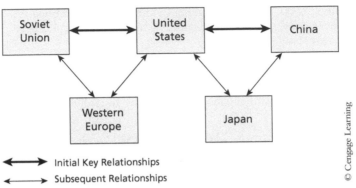

© Cengage Learning

FIGURE 3.2 Principal Participants in the Balance-of-Power System Conceptualized by Nixon and Kissinger

such idealism some "perspective." The United States should not be afraid to pursue its interests, it should not be afraid to pursue equilibrium, and it should not be afraid to think in terms of power.[40]

What Kissinger proposed was an international order in which *stability* was a fundamental goal rather than absolute peace, a goal so essential in America's past. Only by achieving a stable international system would international peace become possible because competing powers would recognize each other's rights.[41] This situation would hold the best prospect for achieving international peace because no state would attempt to impose its views on the international system.

To achieve stability and equilibrium, the legitimacy of both states and the international system had to be recognized. A prerequisite for such legitimacy was for states to accept each other's rights and interests and to contain their revolutionary fervor. Kissinger (and President Nixon) therefore proposed a "structure of peace" based on a **"pentagonal" balance of power** among the United States, the Soviet Union, The People's Republic of China, Western Europe, and Japan (see Figure 3.2).[42] The emphasis would be on gaining some accommodation among the first three, later adding Western Europe and Japan.

An important requirement of Kissinger's design was that those states that failed to respect the rights and interests of others would not go unpunished. That is, if a state took action outside its "traditional area of interest," other states should take action to demonstrate that this violation of the required "norms of international conduct" would not be tolerated. For instance, if the Soviet Union provided economic or military support to revolutionary forces in Angola—an area where it had no historical tie—as it did in 1975, a response must be made. That response might be a change in the bilateral relationship between the United States and the Soviet Union (such as reducing trade or the prospects of future arms negotiations) or in the multilateral relationship in the disputed area itself (such as direct assistance to the factions opposing the Soviet-backed group in Angola). Whichever the action, its intent would be to remind the offending state of the limits of acceptable international behavior and to demonstrate that attempts at expansion (which would upset international stability) would not be overlooked. In this way, conflict itself would contribute to stabilizing international order.

This method of dealing with violations came to be known as *linkage* in the Nixon–Kissinger system. Put differently, behavior in one foreign policy arena (for example, bilateral trade agreements) was inevitably linked to behavior in another (for example, aid to insurgents in a Third World nation).

It is significant that Nixon and Kissinger did not link foreign and domestic arenas. For them, linkage did not mean, for example, predicating arms agreements on changes in domestic conditions within the Soviet Union. Regardless, the importance of linkage to Nixon and Kissinger should not be minimized; it was indeed at the heart of their foreign policy strategy.

By having all states accept the legitimacy of the rights and interests of all other states, and by employing linkage, Kissinger believed that the United States could achieve global stability. In the short run, the success of this strategy meant the United States, the Soviet Union, and the People's Republic of China would abandon their universal goals of shaping international politics to their own ends. Furthermore, it meant that a policy of cooperation would be mixed with a policy of competition among these states. This approach, which came to be labeled *détente*, or relaxation of tensions between the superpowers, was an attempt to build some predictability into international politics. In the long run, if this approach could be institutionalized, a global order based on balance-of-power principles would become a reality.

Domestic Values and Foreign Policies

Along with bringing a policy of accommodation with adversaries to American foreign policy, Kissinger challenged four precepts of past American approaches to the world. First, he believed that diplomacy (or the "**statesman**" as he labeled it in his essay on the subject[43]) was the key to the resolution of disputes and to the conduct of international politics. As he said, "negotiation is the mechanism of stability because it presupposes that maintenance of the existing order is more important than any dispute within it." Moreover, he was willing to negotiate outstanding differences between states as the principal means of achieving stability.

Second, Kissinger adopted a different attitude toward the use of force and the combining of force with diplomacy, perhaps best summarized as "**Negotiate when possible, use force when necessary**." Furthermore, he believed in the use of relative levels of force in efforts to achieve foreign policy goals. Such an attitude toward force, and the degree of force to be used, was wholly at odds with America's past.

Third, Kissinger's view was that domestic values should not dominate American foreign policy and that policy should not be excessively moralistic; otherwise, he argued, it becomes dangerous, especially in a pluralistic world.[44] The United States should be guided by its historical values, but it should evoke them in the world rather than impose them on it. Finally, Kissinger wanted a clear demarcation between domestic politics and foreign policy. In particular, he did not want Congress to impose conditions on the "statesman's" operations in the international system. Thus, he vigorously opposed restraints on trade with the Soviet Union because of its treatment of Jews who sought to emigrate. Human rights standards were perfectly acceptable in domestic politics, but he believed they were unacceptable in foreign policy. Put differently, a state's domestic policies mattered less to Kissinger than the way that state treated the United States. The principal guide to American foreign policy should be the **relations *between* nations, not the domestic conditions *within* them**.[45]

THE NIXON–KISSINGER WORLDVIEW IN OPERATION

Many of Nixon and Kissinger's views on world order, the use of force and diplomacy, and the role of domestic values were manifest in American foreign policy actions from 1969 through 1976.[46] As such, they stimulated some important criticisms.

Developing Sino–Soviet–American Détente

Almost immediately after assuming office, Nixon and Kissinger set out to establish their model of world order. By November 1969, the first discussions with the Soviet Union over nuclear accommodation were under way—the **Strategic Arms Limitation Talks (SALT)** held in Geneva, which proceeded through several sessions before agreement was reached in 1972. At the **Moscow Summit** in May 1972, President Nixon and Soviet President Leonid Brezhnev signed the **SALT I accords**, which consisted of two agreements. One, the **Interim Agreement on Offensive Strategic Arms**, limited Soviet and U.S. offensive nuclear weapons; the other, the **Anti-Ballistic Missile Treaty**, limited the development of defensive nuclear weapons. These pacts were the first to stabilize a structure of world order between the two superpowers and institute a "balance of terror" between them. They became synonymous with the notion of détente.

The Moscow Summit meetings produced more than military accommodation between the United States and the USSR; they also produced a series of political, economic, and social/cultural arrangements. In one political agreement ("**Basic Principles of Relations Between the United States and the Union of Soviet Socialist Republics**"), the principle of linkage was presumably institutionalized, with each country pledging not to take advantage of the other, either "directly" or "indirectly." An economic commitment was made to improve trade relations, and a joint commission was established for that purpose. Four social/cultural agreements were also signed in Moscow calling for U.S.–Soviet cooperation in protecting the environment, enhancing medical science and public health, joint space exploration (including the 1975 Apollo–Soyuz flight), and furthering science and technology.[47]

The essence of détente with the Soviet Union was in place with these 1972 agreements because broad avenues of cooperation had been opened in a relationship that was still competitive. An important part of the three-pronged global order seemed to be operating.

Similar efforts at achieving global stability were initiated with the other major player in the Nixon–Kissinger design: the People's Republic of China. In late 1970, Premier Zhou Enlai gave the first hints of an interest in establishing contact with the United States.[48] The United States responded quickly and positively. By mid-1971, Kissinger made a secret trip to China in order to pave the way for a Nixon visit to that long-isolated country. On July 15, 1971, Nixon appeared on American radio and television with the shock announcement that he had been invited to China, had accepted the invitation, and would go there as soon as arrangements could be worked out. Nixon's visit took place in February 1972 and, by any analysis, was a huge success.

The **Shanghai Communiqué** resulted from this meeting. Issued from that Chinese city on February 28, 1972,[49] it reflected the differing worldviews of the two nations but also provided areas of global and bilateral commonalties. For instance, the communiqué reflected some movement on the question of Taiwan through confirmation by both sides that there was only "one China"; it opposed "hegemony" in the world (a not-so-subtle strategy by the United States to use the "China card" to influence Soviet behavior); and it called for efforts at normalization of relations (although full diplomatic relations would not be achieved until the Carter administration). It also opened up trade and other contacts between the American and Chinese peoples. Overall, the communiqué did not produce the cooperation that the Moscow Summit did, but it did sow the seeds. Indeed, it was remarkable in a more profound sense: After more than thirty years, formal contact between harsh adversaries was begun. The Asian component of the Kissinger–Nixon global design seemed to be falling into place.

The last component of this détente strategy was the **Final Act of the Conference on Security and Cooperation in Europe** signed in Helsinki, Finland, on August 1, 1975.[50] The signing came after President Nixon had left office but while Henry Kissinger still dominated policy. It signaled efforts to expand détente to all European states.

The conference itself was composed of thirty-five countries from Eastern and Western Europe and the United States and Canada. The Final Act (or the **Helsinki Accords** as it is sometimes called) was a political statement rather than a legally binding treaty of international law. It was composed of three "baskets" of issues, with each containing provisions for enhancing cooperation among the signatories. The first basket dealt with principles of conduct and ways to reduce military tension; the second dealt with efforts to enlarge economic, technological, and environmental cooperation; and the third dealt with ways to foster closer social/cultural interactions.

The Final Act was not viewed as an end in itself; instead, it was seen as the beginning point of an evolving cooperative process in Central Europe, much like the Moscow and Shanghai agreements of 1972. In this sense, with the Helsinki Accords, the "relaxation of tensions" and the stability of the international order that Nixon and Kissinger had envisioned expanded to all of central Europe.

Indeed, the policy of détente had a particular appeal for the European states. It conveyed an easing of political tensions in a region that had been the focal point of the Cold War. It had the potential of enhancing economic cooperation across the "Iron Curtain." And it looked forward to uniting cultures and families divided by the Cold War. West Germany, with its policy of *Ostpolitik* (Eastern policy) toward East Germany, would seemingly benefit immediately, but other countries of central Europe would as well.

Force and Diplomacy in the Third World

Two events illustrate the importance of the combination of force and diplomacy in Nixon and Kissinger's policy making. The first involved negotiations over ending the war in Vietnam; the second was the use of "**shuttle diplomacy**" in the Middle East. From the outset of his tenure as national security advisor, Kissinger saw negotiations as the key to ending the Vietnam War.[51] To this end, a two-track system of secret and open negotiations was put into effect immediately after Nixon's election. This did not produce quick results, however. In an attempt to get the peace talks moving, force—in this case the escalation of force—was added. For Nixon and Kissinger, force could be used to demonstrate U.S. resolve in holding to its bargaining position and to prod an adversary into serious negotiations.

In April 1970, Kissinger and Nixon agreed to an American "incursion" into Cambodia—a neutral country—essentially escalating the war (although secret bombing attacks had previously occurred). In May 1972, when negotiations were again stalled, the United States began the bombing and blockading of Hanoi and Haiphong.[52]

Yet again, after Kissinger had so solemnly announced that "peace is at hand" in late October 1972 and stated that only a few details were left to iron out, the final negotiations abruptly hit another snag. President Nixon responded by intensifying the bombing of North Vietnam in December.[53] By late January 1973, a Vietnam disengagement was signed in Paris.

The other major illustration of combining force and diplomacy occurred in the Middle East in response to Arab initiation of force in the **Yom Kippur War** of October 1973 and to the oil embargo by the Arab oil states. At first, the United States used military assistance to reinforce Israel, but then Kissinger used his considerable diplomatic skills to negotiate a series of disengagement pacts among Israel, Egypt, and Syria. These agreements began to untangle the Middle East conflict, but they had, perhaps, more importance in turning the oil spigot back on for the United States. Intermittently, over a period of months from 1973 through 1975, Kissinger shuttled between Cairo, Tel Aviv, and Damascus to hammer out two disengagement agreements over the Sinai Peninsula, between Egypt and Israel, and one over the Golan Heights, between Israel and Syria. Such diplomatic actions brought into sharp relief the central role of the "statesman" in negotiations. Although Kissinger's further efforts were ultimately stalled by intransigence on both sides, his results to that point illustrated how powerful diplomacy could be in moving toward international order.

Human Rights and Foreign Policy

As the final part of their policy making, Kissinger and Nixon separated American domestic values and American foreign policy actions. This separation was perhaps best illustrated in their policy toward **authoritarian and totalitarian regimes**. For instance, Nixon and Kissinger were reluctant to publicly confront the Chilean and Greek juntas about violations of human rights because of their overriding importance to global order. Similarly, they maintained their tacit support of South Africa despite its apartheid policy of legally separating races in social and political life. Once again, strategic considerations became an important motivating force for the Nixon administration.

Toward totalitarian regimes, Nixon and Kissinger seemed to operate on a similar dichotomy. For instance, Kissinger opposed official Washington recognition for Aleksandr Solzhenitsyn when he was expelled from the Soviet Union. He also opposed the Jackson–Vanik Amendment to the Trade Act of 1974, which essentially made free emigration a requirement for any U.S. trading partner seeking mostfavored-nation status. (Because of its restrictions on emigration, most-favored-nation trading status had been denied the Soviet Union.) For Kissinger, domestic politics in any state were to be subordinated to international politics. To the extent that domestic situations were to be addressed, "quiet diplomacy"—secret representations to the offending regime—was the correct approach.

Criticisms of the Nixon–Kissinger Foreign Policy Approach

Despite their foreign policy successes in the 1970s, Nixon and Kissinger's approach was subject to criticism both for its content and for its style. These criticisms came from analysts across the political spectrum.

From the Left, political scientist Richard Falk offered the most telling critique in an essay aptly entitled "What's Wrong with Henry Kissinger's Foreign Policy?"[54] Falk focused on the **lack of moral content** and the irrelevance of Kissinger's global design to the last quarter of the twentieth century. Kissinger's concern with order and stability ignored the more important questions of peace and justice in global affairs. In Falk's view, the most pressing issues of international politics were not power and domination, as Kissinger emphasized, but hunger, poverty, and global inequity, which Kissinger's approach had no direct way of dealing with; rather, it was predicated upon preserving the nation-state system and attempting to manage it by moderating conflict among a few strong Northern Hemisphere states. Such a view represented its "underlying conceptual flaw."[55] Kissinger's "**cooperative directorate among great powers**," according to Falk, was shortsighted in more fundamental ways as well: it accepted as inevitable the persistence of large-scale misery and repression, and it enabled the disfavored many to be kept under control by the favored few.[56]

From the Right, the Kissinger approach was criticized in terms of **moral relativity**. In particular, political conservatives viewed détente as morally bankrupt because it gave international status and recognition to regimes that the United States had largely rejected previously as totalitarian and illegitimate. The opening to the People's Republic of China was particularly troubling because the United States had never recognized or interacted much with the regime of Mao Tse-tung. Suddenly, this situation changed. Although the change was not as abrupt with the Soviet Union, the effect was largely the same.

William F. Buckley, a leading conservative spokesperson, put this criticism in a slightly different way, arguing that détente was based on an "**ideological egalitarianism**" in which there were no fundamental differences between American, Soviet, and Chinese societies. As he noted in a televised interview with Henry Kissinger, the Chinese had been most often described as "warlike," "ignorant," "sly," and "treacherous" in a 1966 American poll in the United States. One month after President Nixon's return from China in 1972, however, the description had changed dramatically. Now, the Chinese were most often described as "progressive," "hard-working," "intelligent," "artistic," and "practical."[57] The regime in Beijing (at that time) had hardly changed its policy at all; only American policy had changed. Thus, according to Buckley's critique, détente had the effect of reducing the ideological distinction between the United States and the Communist states almost overnight.

Yet a third criticism from the Right, and hardly divorced from the other two, was that détente connoted **a "no win" strategy** against communism. By accepting the legitimacy of the key Communist states and by working with them, the United States was perpetuating, not undermining, them, which presumably had been the U.S. aim for three decades.

Détente was criticized from yet another quarter. A former Kennedy and Johnson administration official did not see the policy as particularly new or as necessarily advantageous to the United States in terms of policy abroad or decision making at home.[58] On a policy level, détente did not represent a new attitude toward the Soviet Union, nor had it produced many benefits for the West. Neither had Soviet political cooperation significantly improved. On a decision-making level, the Nixon–Kissinger style was inappropriate for a great power and a democratic society. Kissinger's "lonely cowboy" policy making limited the foreign policy agenda, with the result of "a policy that ignore[d] relations with nations that happen . . . to be outside the spotlight, and . . . encourage[d] a practice of haphazard improvisation."[59] Further, this "policy of maneuver," by the "Master Player," was built on secrecy and personalism, which were hardly consistent with a democratic society. By tradition, policies must be fully explained to the American public, which Nixon and Kissinger did not want to do.

A Break with Tradition

In short, opponents (and even admirers) appeared on both the political Right and the political Left to charge that Nixon–Kissinger "power politics" was fundamentally amoral and inconsistent with America's past, and that its decision-making style challenged democratic traditions. America's approach to the world had come a considerable distance from its traditional past. It had moved away from an emphasis on both moral principle and isolationism; instead, it moved toward embracing the basic elements of realism. No longer a postwar moral crusade driven largely by fervent anticommunism, policy making was now driven by the principles of pragmatism and "power politics." Support for this approach was to wane rather quickly, and the 1976 presidential election, fought at least in part over the question of the morality of American foreign policy, produced a new president—one committed to a foreign policy based on moral standards.

IDEALISM AND THE CARTER ADMINISTRATION

Jimmy Carter's run for the presidency in 1976 was based on making American foreign policy compatible with the basic goodness of the American people. He came to office pledged to restore integrity and morality to American diplomacy. In keeping with his fundamental beliefs and values, his policy making had more **idealist** elements than could be seen in the approaches of earlier postwar presidents. Carter sought to reorient America's foreign policy away from a singular emphasis on adversaries, especially the Soviet Union (as had characterized the policies of Nixon–Ford–Kissinger) and toward a truly global emphasis. Four major policy areas would be highlighted:

- An emphasis on domestic values in foreign policy
- The improvement of relations with allies and resolution of regional conflicts
- A de-emphasis on the Soviet Union as the focus of U.S. policy
- The promotion of global human rights[60]

By the last year of his term, despite his initial idealism, Carter had reverted to a policy much more consistent with the realist policies of his predecessors.

The Carter Approach to Foreign Policy

From the outset, President Carter highlighted the **importance of domestic values** as a guide to American foreign policy. In this sense, his approach was consistent with the reliance on moral principle so evident in America's historical past, and in sharp contrast with that of the previous two administrations. For Carter, domestic values were to be preeminent in the shaping of policy; the United States must "stand for something." Even more, it should serve as a model for other nations.

In his inaugural address, President Carter stated these beliefs forcefully: "Our Nation can be strong abroad only if it is strong at home. And we know that the best way to enhance freedom in other lands is to demonstrate here that our democratic system is worthy of emulation."[61] He went on to say that the United States would not act abroad in ways that would violate domestic standards. In a similar vein, in a 1977 commencement address at Notre Dame, Carter emphasized the moral basis of American policy: "I believe we can have a foreign policy that is democratic, that is based on fundamental values, and that uses [the] power and influence which we have for humane purposes."[62] In addition to a moral basis of policy, President Carter called for a different style of policy making—one that would be "open and candid" and not one that would operate "by manipulation" or through "secret deals." Such references apparently were to what he saw as the style Kissinger adopted.

Finally, although he recognized that moral principle must be the guide, he acknowledged that foreign policy cannot be "by moral maxims." The United States would try to produce change rather than impose it. In this sense, Carter believed that there were limits to what the United States could do in the world. These limits would need to be recognized, but America could not stand idly by. Rather, it should play a constructive and positive role in shaping a new world order, "based on constant decency in its values and on optimism in our historical vision."[63]

Carter and Global Order: New States and Old Friends

The focus of the Carter administration also reflected its view of the world. Policy would not focus simply on the anticommunism inherited from the past. (Carter said, "We are now free of that inordinate fear of communism which once led us to embrace any dictator who joined us in that fear.") Instead, his administration would carry out **a policy of global cooperation**, especially with the newly influential countries in Latin America, Africa, and Asia but also with the industrial democracies of the world. The aim of such an effort would be "to create a wider framework of international cooperation suited to the new and rapidly changing historical circumstances."[64] Moreover, it would move beyond seeking global stability among the strong to recognizing the reality of the new states and their place in the world order.

Within this global context, **crucial regional trouble spots of the world** were to be important areas of concentration. Efforts at resolving the seemingly **intractable problems of the Middle East** were to have a high priority in the Carter administration. Moreover, the **festering problems of southern Africa**—Rhodesia, Namibia, and South Africa, for example—would need solutions if a more just and peaceful global order were to evolve. Similarly, the **problems with Panama and the Canal**, and their potential for generating hostility toward the United States in the Western Hemisphere, were part of the Carter strategy of addressing regional conflicts as a stepping-stone to a more stable international order.

A second major point in Carter's global approach was the **improvement of relations with Western Europe and Japan**. This emphasis on better trilateral relations was in part another response to the previous administration's emphasis on improving relations with adversaries. For instance, Kissinger's much heralded "Year of Europe" for 1973 was essentially stillborn as pressing Middle East problems arose. The result was the appearance of fissures in America's ties with its traditional friends.

Carter and the Soviet Union

With such a global emphasis, the **centrality of the Soviet–American relationship was downgraded**. Détente with the Soviet Union was not abandoned, but it was placed in a larger context of global issues. In particular, President Carter was committed to joint efforts at strategic arms control and made them the continuing and central aspect of U.S.–Soviet relations. The broad comprehensive détente of previous administrations was not the aim of the Carter administration. Economic, sociocultural, and political cooperation could continue, but only on the basis of mutual advantage. Crucial here was that such cooperation would not be linked to the overall quality of the relationship between the United States and the Soviet Union. In this sense, the "linkage" notion of the past was jettisoned.[65]

In essence, Carter's approach assumed that the world order of the late 1970s and early 1980s would not be achieved merely by harnessing the Soviet–American relationship. Détente had neither produced stability nor addressed critical global and regional issues. Instead, it had encouraged a variety of critics at home and abroad and had diverted attention from important global concerns. In short, the heart of international politics in this period had moved beyond this bilateral relationship, and any vision of an improved world along the Kissinger design was now politically infeasible.

Carter's initial approach toward the Soviets deeply offended and confused them. It was offensive because the Soviet Union had commanded the bulk of America's attention since 1945 and because it had gained superpower status only five years before via the Moscow agreements of May 1972. Now this status was apparently being denied. Carter's approach also confused the Soviets because they saw themselves as critical in dealing with conflict in the world, especially in the nuclear age. Despite their centrality to questions of war and peace, however, the Carter administration seemed to be shoving the Soviets aside. They did not know how to react to America's emphasis on moral principle and globalism as espoused by Carter or to the emphasis on human rights.

Carter and Human Rights

Indeed, the pivotal new focus of the Carter administration was its **emphasis on human rights**,[66] which can be gleaned from his inaugural address:

> Our commitment to human rights must be absolute. . . . Because we are free, we can never be indifferent to the fate of freedom everywhere. Our moral sense dictates a clear-cut preference for those societies that share with us an abiding respect for individual human rights. We do not seek to intimidate, but it is clear that a world which others can dominate with impunity would be inhospitable to decency and a threat to the well-being of all people.[67]

This philosophy was to be the guiding moral principle for American foreign policy. The United States would not conduct "business as usual" with nations that grossly and consistently violated the basic rights of their citizens. Instead, it would require that states change their domestic human rights behavior if they wished amicable relations with the United States. Although President Carter made it clear that the human rights criterion would not be the only consideration, he maintained "that a significant element in our relationships with other governments would be their performance in providing basic freedoms to their people."[68]

The human rights issue appealed to Carter because of his strong personal and religious beliefs about individual dignity and because of its strong domestic appeal, especially after Vietnam, Watergate, and revelations of CIA abuses. The "something" that the United States would stand for in the world would now be what it had historically embraced: the freedom of the individual. At the same time, the issue of human rights appealed across the political spectrum and thus would be domestically attractive.

Conservatives would approve because it would presumably condemn Communist nations for their totalitarian practices; liberals, because the United States would now reexamine its policy toward authoritarian states.

THE CARTER WORLDVIEW IN OPERATION

In the main, Carter's initial foreign policy strategy was well received by the American public because it represented a reemergence of American idealism with a clear emphasis on traditional American values and beliefs. Coupled with the idealism of the Carter approach, however, was the realization of the limits of American power. Although the United States could assist in the shaping of global order, it did not have the power to direct the international system of the 1970s—a system so diverse and complex that no nation or group of nations could impose its views of international order. In this sense, the Carter strategy was partly compatible with Kissinger's: the United States must evoke a global order through its actions. However, the focal point of this new order was considerably different from that of the past.

In spite of initial support for his policies, Carter met with criticism and challenge in two areas (improving human rights and dealing with the Soviet Union) but with some success in a third (resolving Third World conflicts).

Improving Human Rights

Definition and Policy Almost immediately, the Carter administration faced **the problem of clearly defining human rights** and establishing a consistent application of its policy on a global basis. Although President Carter had originally sought to focus his policy on the humane treatment of all individuals—and their freedom from torture and arbitrary punishment for expressing political beliefs—his administration initially defined it to include the promotion of political, economic, and social rights of all individuals.[69] Such a broad definition left the United States open to criticism in this area, especially in its promotion of economic rights for all. As a result, the United States was seen as espousing a policy that it did not adhere to itself.

Furthermore, the administration was not always clear as to how human rights were to fit into policy regarding other states. That is, should the human rights condition be the defining criterion for dealing with another nation, or should it be only one of several? After some review and discussion, the administration seemed to settle on the latter. For example, Secretary of State Cyrus Vance cautioned against a "mechanistic formula" for the human rights campaign in his speech to the University of Georgia Law School, and President Carter recognized the limitation of "rigid moral maxims" in his Notre Dame speech.[70] As a result, though, the administration seemed to lose some of its enthusiasm for human rights, and a detectable pullback in this policy occurred over its first year in office.

Implementation A second problem also arose. **How was the human rights campaign going to be put into effect?** How far was the United States willing to go to bring about change? Was it willing to stop all contact with nations alleged to be violating human rights? Was it going to cut all diplomatic, economic, and military ties to offending states? Or was the United States going to continue these ties or modify them in line with more responsive behavior? After all, was this not a better way to exercise influence over another nation than stopping all contact and thus all means of influence? In short, what were the best tactics for encouraging human rights improvements in target nations?

In fact, aid—particularly military aid—was cut off to principal offender nations such as Chile, Argentina, Uruguay, Guatemala, Nicaragua, Vietnam, Cambodia, Uganda, and Mozambique,[71] and economic aid was used to encourage human rights improvements in other states. The primary instrument used with states with poor human rights records was diplomatic "jawboning"—publicly and privately conveying to offending foreign governments American dissatisfaction. Clearly, there were limits to how far the United States could or wanted to go in the human rights area.

Applicability   A third major problem was this: **to whom should the human rights policy apply?** The paradox of the Carter approach was evident when nations saw the United States calling for the free exercise of human rights, particularly in the Soviet Union and Latin America, but providing economic and military assistance to nations often cited as having serious human rights violations, such as South Korea, the Philippines, and Iran. Juxtaposing human rights policy against the demands of realpolitik became a central dilemma for the Carter administration and a constant target of attack by its critics.

The apparent problem of selective application received criticism from two directions. Neoconservatives argued that human rights standards as practiced by the United States vis-à-vis "moderately repressive" but friendly regimes was, in effect, undermining these states and American global influence. The unintended result of this action might well be the overthrow of these imperfect regimes by ones opposed to U.S. interests—as happened, for example, in Iran and Nicaragua. Whatever the merits of human rights, these critics said, the requirements of global balance-of-power politics could not be wholly ignored.[72] In this sense, quiet, as well as intergovernmental, semigovernmental, and nongovernmental, efforts were necessary to pursue human rights in the international system.[73]

From an international perspective, critics argued that the administration's policy was yet another way to impose American values on the other nations. Moreover, they claimed, because it reflected both the lack of political realism and the importance of American moral principle in shaping foreign policy, it was another American attempt to shape global politics. As well-intentioned as the human rights goal was, it would prove inappropriate for the diverse international system and would ultimately be dysfunctional for global order. Such a refrain was heard from Third World leaders and even from some American allies, notably France and Germany.

Positive Effects   Carter's human rights campaign did have some positive effects. The number of countries that could show an **improved human rights record** increased slightly, although much greater gains would be necessary if global conditions were to be substantially changed. Still, the Carter administration registered tangible instances of improvement. The Dominican Republic made a turn toward democracy; elections were announced in Peru, Ecuador, and Bolivia for 1978; Colombia, Malaysia, Honduras, Morocco, and Portugal, among others improved conditions; Sudan, Nepal, Indonesia, Haiti, and Paraguay released political prisoners in the first year of the policy; and torture apparently declined.[74]

More significant, perhaps, American prestige was enhanced in various areas of the world. The United States began to stand for particular political values, which resulted in a more receptive attitude toward its initiatives, especially within the developing world. Perhaps the greatest demonstration of this impact was in Africa, where the black nations of southern Africa, in particular, began to have confidence in the Carter administration and American policy. Through the vigorous efforts of Andrew Young, President Carter's ambassador to the United Nations, the frontline states around white-ruled Rhodesia (Angola, Botswana, Mozambique, Tanzania, Zambia) began to believe that the Carter administration was willing to seek a just solution to Rhodesia's problems (Rhodesia is now Zimbabwe), as well as those of Namibia and South Africa. Moreover, the pivotal African state of Nigeria expressed its confidence by receiving President Carter for an official visit.[75]

Finally, President Carter seemed to see the greatest benefit of his human rights policy as **the intangible change in atmosphere and in attitude toward individual liberties** on a worldwide scale during his years in office. As he notes, "The lifting of the human spirit, the revival of hope, the absence of fear, the release from prison, the end of torture, the reunion of a family, the newfound sense of dignity" were the ultimate measure of the worth of the human rights policy."[76]

Negative Effects On the negative side, the human rights campaign caused friction with friendly but human rights–deficient nations. This strained relations with Nicaragua, Argentina, Brazil, Iran, and South Korea among others, and contributed to problems with the Soviet Union. It was particularly challenging to détente because it implied an "intervention" in the internal affairs of other states. Nonintervention in internal affairs, by contrast, had been the benchmark of détente that evolved under the Nixon–Ford–Kissinger administrations.[77]

Beyond its apparent violation of national sovereignty, the campaign for human rights threatened the Soviet Union in a more fundamental way: By fostering individual freedom of expression and tolerating diversity, it directly affronted totalitarian control at home and foreshadowed a weakening of Soviet control over Eastern Europe. As a result, the Soviet Union attacked Carter's policy, contending that the United States itself was guilty of human rights violations because of its failure to ensure economic rights for its citizens given insufficient employment, inadequate health care, and unsatisfactory social welfare benefits. Furthermore, the atmosphere surrounding relations between the United States and the Soviet Union was affected, as Foreign Minister Andrei Gromyko implied, after initial arms control discussions had broken down in April 1977.[78]

Dealing with the Soviet Union

The essential aim of the Carter administration was to downgrade the dominance of Soviet–American relations in foreign policy and to concentrate efforts primarily in other areas of the world. As one analyst has aptly put it, the goal was to contain the Soviet Union not by directly confronting it as in the past, but "by drying out the pond of possible Soviet mischief" through resolving global issues.[79] If global problems were addressed, intrusions by the Soviets would be much less likely and thus they would be contained.

Despite his initial intention, it never became possible to downgrade America's relationship with the Soviets. **Carter's failure to establish a clear and consistent policy toward the Soviet Union** was probably the greatest shortcoming of his initial foreign policy plan. At least three different reasons may be cited for this.

Soviet Centrality First, the Soviets would not allow the United States to downgrade their centrality to global politics. Their prestige was damaged by the Carter policy because they had put great effort into achieving superpower military and political parity. After finally achieving it with the 1972 agreements, they were unwilling to play "second fiddle" on global issues. Thus, the Soviets challenged Carter on human rights, but they also attacked him on arms control, despite their desire for it. More important, they challenged Carter's attempt to focus on issues in the Third World. The Soviets sought inroads to the Western Hemisphere, especially in Central America through Cuba (or so the United States believed). They also did not restrain the Vietnamese in Asia and continued their military deployments there. Finally, they continued to pressure Western Europe through an increase in their military capabilities.[80]

Competing Perspectives in the Administration Second, officials within the Carter administration were divided over how best to deal with the Soviet Union. Carter's two top advisors, **Secretary of State Cyrus Vance** and **National Security Advisor Zbigniew Brzezinski**, took differing views on this issue. Vance appeared to be committed to Carter's globalist perspective and wanted to deal with the Soviets on a piecemeal basis without linkage. Brzezinski appeared to be of two minds,[81] formally rejecting the notion of linkage as the guide to American policy in dealing with the Soviets yet adopting a policy stance that seemed markedly close to it. In fact, the first time that the Soviets took significant actions in a "third area"—they supported sending Cuban troops to Ethiopia—he resurrected aspects of the original Kissinger formula for dealing with Soviet–American relations. He wanted to confront the Soviets directly and to downgrade any remaining elements of détente. To Brzezinski, Soviet activities in the Horn of Africa should affect the SALT negotiations, and he said so directly.[82]

Others within the Carter administration—Vance, Secretary of Defense Harold Brown, and the president himself—were not willing to go as far as Brzezinski on this issue, and he eventually lost out in this debate. It was disputes like this—over how to deal with the Soviets, and especially how multilateral events were to affect bilateral relations between the two superpowers—that dominated the Carter administration's agenda during its first three years.

American Domestic Attitudes A third factor that made it difficult for the United States to move away from a perception of the Soviets as dominant in foreign policy matters was American domestic beliefs. **A true dualism existed in the minds of Americans.** Most supported détente by a wide margin, but they were also increasingly wary of growing Soviet power vis-à-vis the United States. Additionally, they continued to see the Soviet Union as central to U.S. foreign policy.[83]

Accompanying this dual attitude was a shift away from support for cuts in defense spending, which had been so strong in the immediate post-Vietnam years. By 1977, and especially by 1978, support for more defense spending was increasing and public willingness to use military force against Soviet incursions was becoming more evident.[84] Thus, from the viewpoint of domestic politics, the Soviet–American relationship still seemed crucial, and the Carter administration was no doubt aware of these changing beliefs and the need to accommodate them in its foreign policy.

For various reasons, then, the relationship between the Soviet Union and the United States could not be downgraded in American foreign policy despite the Carter administration's initial hopes. Moreover, the inability to fully integrate the primacy of this relationship into its foreign policy design and its "strategic incoherence" plagued the administration throughout its four years.[85]

Resolving Third World Conflicts

The greatest success for the Carter administration in implementing its global design was its treatment of Third World conflicts. During his administration, President Carter was able to alleviate, if not resolve, conflict in Central America over the Panama Canal, in the Middle East between Egypt and Israel, and in southern Africa over Rhodesia and Namibia. Finally, although his establishment of formal diplomatic relations between the People's Republic of China and the United States can hardly be characterized as a Third World event, it was important for lessening regional conflict in Asia.

The Panama Canal Perhaps Carter's greatest success was the resolution of the Panama Canal dispute. For more than two decades, the United States had been negotiating the transfer of the Canal and the Canal Zone to Panamanian sovereignty. The failure to resolve this dispute had undermined American influence in Central and South America and thus was one of the issues that President Carter was determined to address.

Indicative of the importance of Panama was the fact that the first **Presidential Review Memorandum** of the Carter administration dealt with the Panama Canal.[86] With such a central priority, American and Panamanian negotiators set out to reach an agreement, and in a few short months, they succeeded. By September 1977, moreover, the two treaties that constituted the agreement were ready for an elaborate signing ceremony in Washington. All Latin American countries were invited to witness the signing, which was a triumphant occasion for the Carter administration.

One of the pacts, the **Panama Canal Treaty**, called for the total transfer of Canal control to Panama by the year 2000, with intermediate stages of transfer during the twenty-two years of the pact. The second agreement, the **Neutrality Treaty**, to become effective in the year 2000 and to be of unlimited duration, stated that the Canal would be permanently neutral, secure, and open to the vessels of all nations in time of peace and war; the United States and Panama would agree to maintain and defend this neutrality. President Carter viewed these pacts as clearly compatible with his goals of reducing regional conflict and fostering global justice. Both would minimize anti-American feelings and enhance American prestige and influence abroad.[87]

The Middle East In the Middle East, a constant regional trouble spot, the initial strategy of the Carter administration was to seek a comprehensive settlement through a Geneva conference cosponsored with the Soviet Union. However, the Israelis were reluctant to participate, and the Arabs demanded maximum Palestinian participation.[88] Israel's fear was that it would be outvoted in such a conference by the larger number of Arab states and the Soviet Union, leading to an outcome that would be far from their liking.

In November 1977, however, **President Anwar Sadat of Egypt** took a dramatic step to move the process along, announcing that he was willing to go to Jerusalem to seek peace. **Prime Minister Menachem Begin of Israel** quickly issued an invitation for Sadat to speak to the Israeli Parliament, and on November 19, 1977, Sadat landed in Jerusalem for three days of discussions.[89]

The importance of this visit cannot be overstated. It broke the impasse that had blocked the Middle East peace process since the shuttle diplomacy of Kissinger, it established the precedent of face-to-face negotiations between Arabs and Israelis, and it raised hopes for real progress.

Such hopes were soon dashed. Both sides still held strong positions on the fundamental questions of Arab lands and Israeli security. (See Map 3.3 for the territories in dispute between Israel and its neighbors at that time.) By the summer of 1978, another impasse had set in despite President Carter's mediation efforts. At this juncture, Carter took a bold gamble by inviting President Sadat and Prime Minister Begin to Camp David, the presidential retreat, for in-depth discussions. After thirteen days of intense negotiations, "**A Framework for Peace in the Middle East**" was agreed to by the parties and witnessed by Carter.[90]

The signing of the **Camp David Accords** on September 17, 1978, was another highlight of the Carter foreign policy (see Document Summary 3.1). Real progress had been made in addressing the Middle East conflict. Furthermore, in March 1979, Egypt and Israel signed a peace treaty based on the Camp David framework. A comprehensive peace settlement ultimately eluded the Carter administration, however, as all the Arab states except Egypt refused to accept and participate in the Camp David framework.

Rhodesia, Namibia, and South Africa The Carter administration achieved some success in southern Africa (see Map 3.4) over the question of Rhodesia and Namibia. America's role was not as direct as in the Panama Canal and the Middle East, but it was nonetheless important. Specifically, the administration adopted a strong stand for black majority rule in these areas and assisted the British in achieving a successful

---

Document Summary 3.1   The Camp David Accords between Egypt and Israel, September 1978

THE FRAMEWORK FOR PEACE IN THE MIDDLE EAST

The Framework for Peace in the Middle East called for a "just, comprehensive, and durable settlement of the Middle East conflict through the conclusion of peace treaties based on **Security Council Resolutions 242 and 338.**" (Those resolutions called for an exchange of land by Israel—the territories seized in the June 1967 war—for peace with its Arab neighbors and an end to the state of war.) It consisted of two parts.

The first part dealt with resolving the conflict over the West Bank of the Jordan and the Gaza Strip, which Israel had seized, calling for the establishment of a self-governing authority within these territories "for a period not exceeding five years." By at least the third year of that self-governing authority, "negotiations will take place to determine the final status of the West Bank and Gaza and its

relationship to its neighbors and to conclude a peace treaty between Israel and Jordan. . . ." These negotiations will involve representatives from Egypt, Israel, Jordan, and "representatives of the inhabitants of the West Bank and Gaza. . . ."

The second part called for Egypt and Israel "to negotiate in good faith with a goal of concluding within three months from the signing of this Framework a peace treaty between them." Under this treaty, ultimately signed in March 1979 in Washington, D.C., Israel returned the Sinai Peninsula to Egypt, and Israel and Egypt ended their state of war, recognized one another, and established diplomatic relations.

Source: This description is drawn from the framework, which was printed in *The Camp David Summit*, Department of State Publication 8954 (Washington, DC: Office of Public Communications, Bureau of Public Affairs, September 1978).

MAP 3.3 Israel and its neighbors, 1977

Source: Boundaries taken from http://www.dartmouth.edu/~gov46/israeli-egypt-1975.gif

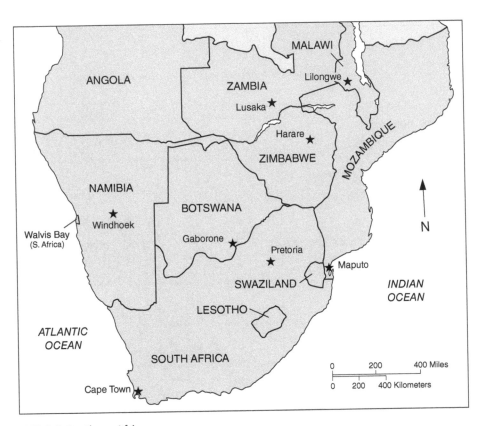

MAP 3.4 Southern Africa

outcome for Rhodesia. The United States, with the assistance of other Western states, maneuvered the South African government to accept a UN resolution on the transfer of power in Namibia.[91] Map 3.4 shows these territories in southern Africa.

In the case of Rhodesia, the Carter administration ceased trade with the white-dominated government and imposed economic sanctions in the first year of its term, bringing U.S. policy in line with long-standing UN actions. Even when the white-minority government and black leaders reached an **"internal settlement"** in 1978, the administration refused to lift these sanctions because dissident factions in exile had not participated in the settlement talks. By adopting such a stance despite considerable opposition within Congress, the United States gave impetus to British efforts to achieve a comprehensive settlement involving all parties. This settlement was ultimately worked out in the Lancaster House negotiations in London during the fall of 1979, and the agreement was put into effect in 1980.[92] Majority rule was obtained in the former Rhodesia, and the Carter administration rightly claimed credit for its role.

The same posture that was successful in Rhodesia was adopted toward South Africa: a firm stance against apartheid and a call for the transfer of control of Namibia to majority rule. Under U.S. and international policy pressure, South Africa agreed to **UN Resolution 435** on this issue. The transfer met numerous snags, however, and was not implemented during the Carter years. (In fact, it was not fully implemented until 1990.) Nonetheless, the promotion of American domestic values of respecting human rights and fostering majority rule won praise for the United States throughout Africa.

People's Republic of China   Carter's final major foreign policy success was his decision to establish **formal diplomatic relations** with the People's Republic of China on January 1, 1979. Although this caused initial difficulties with Taiwan (because formal diplomatic relations and a security treaty had been broken with the Taiwanese government), it was generally hailed as a milestone in American foreign policy. Opening relations with Beijing reduced hostilities between the United States and China and had the potential of easing conflicts in East Asia. At the same time, though, it created another uncertainty in America's approach to its traditional adversary, the Soviet Union, and reinforced the Soviets' view that the Carter administration was more interested in dealing with other states than with them.

REALISM IN THE LAST YEAR:
A RESPONSE TO CRITICS

By 1979, Carter's foreign policy had become the subject of considerable criticism on the grounds that it was inconsistent, incoherent, a failure, and, according to one critic, responsible for a decline in America's standing abroad.[93] In fact, although some successes in Carter's global approach might be identified, too many problems were evident, without a clear strategy for dealing with them.

- A revolution in Iran that replaced the Shah (whom the Carter administration had supported) with a markedly anti-American regime
- A revolution in Nicaragua, with the United States adopting a policy that pleased neither the Somozistas nor the Sandinistas
- The stalled Middle East peace effort, with Arab rejection of the Camp David framework
- The continuing growth of Soviet power without an American response

On all of these fronts, a certain malaise seemed to have set into Carter's foreign policy, marked by indecision and the inability to act. For this reason, a change in policy direction might well have been anticipated. In fact, two international events ultimately proved the catalyst to Carter's change of direction. The **seizure of American hostages in Iran** in November 1979 and the **Soviet invasion of Afghanistan** a month later were watershed events in the global approach of the Carter administration.[94] Despite the effort to move its focus away from the Soviet Union, they brought that nation back into focus for America—the former indirectly, because it raised the prospect of Soviet inroads into the Middle East and Southwest Asia; the latter directly, because it projected the Soviet Union once again into the center of global affairs.

American Hostages in Iran

The November 1979 seizure and holding of sixty-three Americans in the U.S. Embassy in Tehran, Iran, produced what was perhaps the Carter administration's greatest foreign policy challenge. It raised real concerns among the American public over the U.S. role and its effectiveness in global politics. Fanning this concern was an

ABC nightly news program called *America Held Hostage: Day*—(the day was changed nightly to emphasize how long the Americans were held) that catalogued the daily events surrounding the hostage taking. Significantly, this crisis generally and the program particularly soon conveyed how seemingly powerless the United States was and how much its global image had been damaged. Yellow ribbons (after a popular song of the time) appeared throughout the country signaling Americans' wait to welcome back the hostages. The longer the crisis continued, the greater the administration's policy dilemma became.

The hostage crisis produced a clear change in policy orientation and direction by the Carter administration, with national self-interest now dominant. Rather than trying to accommodate Third World demands, as it had been attempting in previous years, it now took a variety of steps—breaking diplomatic relations, seizing Iranian assets, imposing sanctions, and ultimately attempting a military rescue of the hostages—as a means of demonstrating resolve. Such actions also connoted a return to a realist perspective in foreign policy and away from Carter's initial idealism. Unfortunately, this strategy failed to yield quick results, and the American hostages were held for **444 days**. They were freed immediately after Carter left office on January 20, 1981.

The Soviet Invasion of Afghanistan

The Soviet invasion of Afghanistan also had a pronounced effect both on President Carter's view of the Soviet Union and on his foreign policy toward it. Carter himself poignantly summarized this in an ABC television interview at the time: "My opinion of the Russians has changed most drastically in the last week [more] than even in the previous 2½ years before that."[95] The invasion also had the immediate impact of moving him away from his global approach, with the Soviet Union only one among many countries, toward **the bilateral approach of the past**, with the Soviet–American relationship at the center of policy making. New policy actions quickly followed from this orientation. Not all of the earlier initiatives were jettisoned, but the issue areas that he had earlier emphasized were deemphasized.

The Carter administration adopted a series of responses to the Soviet Union over the invasion of Afghanistan:

- The ratification of the **SALT II treaty was shelved** in the U.S. Senate
- High-technology sales to the Soviet Union were halted
- Soviet fishing privileges in American waters were restricted
- A **grain embargo** was imposed on the Soviet Union[96]
- An **American boycott of the 1980 Summer Olympics in Moscow** was announced

Global Events and Soviet–American Relations

Global events were now increasingly interpreted through lenses that focused on their effect on Soviet–American relations, with the principal U.S. efforts during 1980 centered on rallying friends to contain the Soviet Union. Moreover, it was during this time that such global goals as arms transfer control were downplayed as a signal to the Soviets of American determination. For instance, discussions were held with Beijing about arms sales to China. Furthermore, the United States began an effort to shore up its ties in the Persian Gulf and in Southwest Asia. Military aid was quickly offered to

Pakistan, and National Security Chief Zbigniew Brzezinski made a highly publicized trip to the Khyber Pass as a show of determination regarding Afghanistan. Contacts were also made with friendly regimes in the Middle East to gain base and access rights for the United States in case of an emergency. Finally, the development of the **U.S. Rapid Deployment Force**—elite troops that could respond quickly to an emergency anywhere in the world—was given top priority.

As a further signal to the Soviet Union, Carter in his 1980 State of the Union Address warned that "an attempt by any outside force to gain control of the Persian Gulf region will be regarded as an assault on the vital interests of the United States. It will be repelled by use of any means necessary, including military force."[97] Quickly labeled the **Carter Doctrine**, this statement was highly reminiscent of an earlier era with its Cold War rhetoric and its reliance on the essential elements of containment. Nonetheless, it accurately set the tone for the final year of the Carter administration and the policy shift that had occurred.

Foreign Policy and the 1980 Campaign

Despite President Carter's attempt to change his foreign policy direction, the perception of ineffectiveness continued to haunt him. As a consequence, foreign policy, with particular emphasis on the Iranian and Afghan experiences, became an important campaign issue in the 1980 presidential election.[98] Now, however, instead of focusing on what was "good and decent," as in 1976, the Republican challenger to President Carter, Ronald Reagan, called for a policy to "make America great again." This was surely a call to move away from the idealism of the early Carter years. Yet it was also a call to pursue the kind of foreign policy that President Carter himself had tried to initiate in his last year in office.

CONCLUDING COMMENTS

After the traumatic episode of the Cuban Missile Crisis, the agonizing and humiliating experience of the Vietnam War, and the shattering of the Cold War consensus, American foreign policy immediately went through two pendulum swings in its approach to foreign policy over the succeeding decade. The Nixon administration pursued political realism, as a guide to its foreign policy actions, whereas the Carter administration, through the bulk of its tenure, pursued political idealism. Neither was able to put into place a new consensus that was embraced by the American public, and each was subject to stinging criticisms by adversaries. Moreover, candidate Reagan sought the presidency on just such a critique of the Carter administration and offered yet another approach to American foreign policy. In Chapter 4, we examine the Reagan approach and that of his successor, George H. W. Bush.

Notes

1. Theodore Sorensen, one of President Kennedy's advisors and editor of Robert Kennedy's book on the missile crisis, now acknowledges "that the missile trade had been portrayed as an explicit deal in the diaries on which the book was based, and that he [Kennedy] had seen fit to revise that account in view of the fact that the trade was still a secret at the time, known to only six members of the ExComm." This quote is from James G. Blight and David A. Welch, *On the Brink: Americans and Soviets Reexamine the Cuban Missile Crisis*, 2nd ed. (New York: The Noonday Press, 1990), p. 341. Sorensen made this admission at the 1989 Moscow Conference on the Cuban Missile Crisis.

2. See Blight and Welch, *On the Brink*, but also see Len Scott and Steve Smith, "Political Scientists, Policy-makers, and the Cuban Missile Crisis," *International Affairs* 70 (October 1994): 659–684, which summarizes and analyzes various old and new interpretations of events and lessons from the crisis by incorporating the findings from the various academic analyses and the review conferences held on this topic.

3. Scott and Smith, "Political Scientists, Policy-makers, and the Cuban Missile Crisis," p. 681.

4. Blight and Welch, *On the Brink*, p. 347.

5. Robert F. Kennedy, *Thirteen Days* (New York: Signet Books, 1969), p. 124.

6. See, for example, the study of Ole R. Holsti, Richard A. Brody, and Robert C. North, "The Management of International Crisis: Affect and Action in American-Soviet Relations," in Dean G. Pruitt and Richard C. Snyder, eds., *Theory and Research on the Causes of War* (Englewood Cliffs, NJ: Prentice Hall, 1969), pp. 62–79.

7. Scott and Smith, "Political Scientists, Policy-makers, and the Cuban Missile Crisis," p. 680.

8. See ibid., especially pp. 682–683.

9. Scott Sagan, *The Limits of Safety: Organizations, Accidents, and Nuclear Weapons* (Princeton, NJ: Princeton University Press, 1993), p. 151, as quoted in Scott and Smith, "Political Scientists, Policy-makers, and the Cuban Missile Crisis," p. 682.

10. George C. Herring, *America's Longest War: The United States and Vietnam, 1950–1975* (Philadelphia: Temple University Press, 1986), pp. 7–10. The quote is at p. 10.

11. These data are primarily from Leslie H. Gelb with Richard K. Betts, *The Irony of Vietnam: The System Worked* (Washington, DC: The Brookings Institution, 1979), p. 46. But also see Herring, *America's Longest War*, pp. 18 and 19, for the first two pieces of data.

12. Gelb with Betts, *The Irony of Vietnam*, pp. 50, 51.

13. See the chapter "The Decision Not to Intervene in Indochina 1954," in Morton Berkowitz, P. G. Bock, and Vincent J. Fuccillo, *The Politics of American Foreign Policy* (Englewood Cliffs, NJ: Prentice Hall, 1977), pp. 54–74. Also see Sheehan et al., *The Pentagon Papers, New York Times* ed., pp. 13–22; Herring, *America's Longest War*, pp. 41–42; and Timothy J. Lomperis, *The War Everyone Lost—and Won* (Washington, DC: CQ Press, 1984), p. 48, on the Geneva Accords.

14. On the role of the United States in backing Diem and the "America's Mandarin" label, see Stanley Karnow, *Vietnam: A History* (New York: Viking Press, 1983), pp. 206–239.

15. On the level of support, see Herring, *America's Longest War*, p. 57.

16. The information in this paragraph and earlier is from Sheehan et al., *The Pentagon Papers*, pp. 76, 78, and 83.

17. Ibid., p. 107.

18. See Richard K. Betts, "Misadventure Revisited," in James M. McCormick, ed., *A Reader in American Foreign Policy* (Itasca, IL: F. E. Peacock Publishers, Inc., 1986), p. 100, for this assessment.

19. On the changes in Vietnamese governments, see Lomperis, *The War Everyone Lost—and Won*, p. 62.

20. See Sheehan et al., *The Pentagon Papers*, pp. 236–237, for the chronology of events in 1964. For the controversy regarding what really happened in the Gulf of Tonkin, see Herring, *America's Longest War*, pp. 119–123.

21. Sheehan et al., *The Pentagon Papers*, pp. 308–309, 459–461.

22. Lomperis, *The War Everyone Lost—and Won*, pp. 76–79. On the Tet offensive, also see Karnow, *Vietnam: A History*, pp. 515–566.

23. Lomperis, *The War Everyone Lost—and Won*, p. 82. On the Cambodian invasion, see pp. 83–85.

24. According to the fact sheet issued by the Vietnam Veterans Leadership Program of Houston, Inc., 57,704 deaths occurred in the Vietnam War. The number of names inscribed on the Vietnam Veterans War Memorial in Washington, D.C., however, is 58,132. On the last "Easter Invasion," see Lomperis, *The War Everyone Lost—and Won*, pp. 87–90.

25. See Lomperis, *The War Everyone Lost—and Won*, p. 94, for terms of the negotiated settlement and Herring, *America's Longest War*, pp. 255–256, for this assessment of it.

26. One recent assessment of this view is George C. Herring, *LBJ and Vietnam: A Different Kind of War* (Austin: University of Texas Press, 1994) at pp. 178–186, although he also focuses significantly on the role of President Johnson and his leadership style.

27. On these explanations, see Herring, *LBJ and Vietnam*, pp. 276–278.

28. See Lomperis, *The War Everyone Lost—and Won*, for a thorough examination of the national legitimacy question. For the many lessons of Vietnam, see Gelb with Betts, *The Irony of Vietnam*, pp. 347–369.

29. Ibid.; and Herring, *LBJ and Vietnam*.

30. See Table 3.3, on public opinion survey results regarding support and opposition to the Vietnam War, in John E. Mueller, *War, Presidents and Public Opinion* (New York: John Wiley and Sons, 1973), pp. 54–55.

31. Page and Shapiro, *The Rational Public*, pp. 232–235.

32. For one summary of the literature on domestic policy/foreign policy divisions among liberals and conservatives, see Bruce Russett, "The Americans' Retreat from World Power," *Political Science Quarterly* 90 (Spring 1975): 1–21, especially pp. 14 and 15.

33. Eugene R. Wittkopf and James M. McCormick, "The Cold War Consensus: Did It Exist?" *Polity* 22 (Summer 1990): 627–653 discusses the public's view in the post-Vietnam period.

34. The approach of the Ford administration (1974–1976) is not treated separately here because Henry Kissinger continued to serve as national security advisor (through 1975) and as secretary of state (through 1976).

35. For a detailed listing of the assumptions of realism and idealism, see Charles W. Kegley, Jr., "The Neoliberal Challenge to Realist Theories of World Politics: An Introduction," in Charles W. Kegley, Jr., *Controversies in International Relations Theory* (New York: St. Martin's Press, 1995), pp. 4–5. For another statement of the idealism/liberalism tradition in international politics, see Robert O. Keohane and Joseph S. Nye, Jr., *Power and Interdependence*, 2nd ed. (Glenview, IL: Scott, Foresman/Little Brown, 1989).

36. Richard M. Nixon, "Asia after Viet Nam," *Foreign Affairs* 46 (October 1967): 111–125. The quoted passages are at pp. 121, 123, and 114.

37. Richard M. Nixon, *U.S. Policy for the 1970s, A New Strategy for Peace. A Report to the Congress* (Washington, DC: Government Printing Office, February 18, 1970). The quoted passages are at pp. 2 and 3. For the earlier statements on some of these principles, see Richard M. Nixon, "Informal Remarks in Guam with Newsmen, July 25, 1969," and "Address to the Nation on the War in Vietnam, November 3, 1969," in *Public Papers of the Presidents of the United States, Richard Nixon 1969* (Washington, DC: U.S. Government Printing Office, 1971), pp. 544–556 and pp. 901–909, respectively. Indeed, the "Nixon Doctrine" is sometimes referred to as the "Guam Doctrine."

38. For a more detailed and recent treatment of Nixon's approach to foreign policy, including additional comparisons with earlier post–World War II presidents and America's historical traditions, see Henry Kissinger, *Diplomacy* (New York: Simon & Schuster, 1994), pp. 703–718.

39. This section draws on Kissinger's important essay "Contemporary Issues of American Foreign Policy," appearing as chap. 2 in Henry A. Kissinger, *American Foreign Policy*, 3rd ed. (New York: W. W. Norton and Company, 1977), pp. 51–97. The quoted passage is at p. 79.

40. Ibid., pp. 91–97.

41. See Henry A. Kissinger, *A World Restored: Metternich, Castlereagh and the Problems of Peace 1812–1822* (Boston: Houghton Mifflin Company, 1957) on the importance of stability, especially p. 1.

42. President Nixon's commitment to the balance of power and to this pentagonal world is discussed in "An Interview with the President: 'The Jury Is Out,'" *Time*, January 3, 1972, p. 15, and quoted in Kissinger, *Diplomacy*, p. 705: "I think it will be a safer world and a better world if we have a strong, healthy United States, Europe, Soviet Union, China, Japan, each balancing the other, not playing one against the other, an even balance."

43. For a description of the "statesman," see Kissinger's essay "Domestic Structure and Foreign Policy," in James N. Rosenau, ed., *International Politics and Foreign Policy*, rev. ed. (New York: Free Press, 1969), pp. 261–275. The quoted passage on the importance of negotiations to stability is at p. 274.

44. Kissinger, *American Foreign Policy*, pp. 120–121.

45. For a further analysis of the dimensions of Kissinger's approach, and a strong critique of it, see Richard A. Falk, "What's Wrong with Henry Kissinger's Foreign Policy?" *Alternatives* 1 (1975): 79–100.

46. Once again, the analysis includes the years extending through 1976 (although President Ford came to office in August 1974) because Henry Kissinger continued to direct foreign policy.

47. "U.S.-U.S.S.R. Exchange Programs," *GIST* (Washington, DC: Department of State, April 1976).

48. See the excerpts from Henry Kissinger's *White House Years* (Boston: Little, Brown, 1979) on China in *Time*, October 1, 1979, 53–58.

49. The Shanghai Communiqué is reprinted in Gene T. Hsiao, ed., *Sino-American Detente and Its Policy Implications* (New York: Praeger Publishers, 1974), pp. 298–301.

50. This discussion draws on "Conference on Security and Cooperation in Europe," *Department of State Bulletin* 77 (September 26, 1977): 404–410. The notion of "baskets" to summarize their work came from the conference itself (p. 405).

51. See his essay in *American Foreign Policy*, exp. ed. (New York: W.W. Norton and Company, 1974), pp. 99–135.

52. See John G. Stoessinger, *Henry Kissinger: The Anguish of Power* (New York: W.W. Norton and Company, 1976), pp. 62–63.

53. Ibid., p. 73.

54. Falk, "What's Wrong with Henry Kissinger's Foreign Policy?" pp. 79–100.

55. Ibid., p. 98.

56. Ibid., p. 99.

57. William F. Buckley, Jr., "Politics of Henry Kissinger," transcript of *Firing Line*, originally broadcast on the Public Broadcasting System, September 13, 1975, p. 5. Mr. Buckley was quoting from Gallup polls.

58. George W. Ball, *Diplomacy for a Crowded World* (Boston: Atlantic Monthly/Little Brown, 1976), pp. 108–129.

59. Ibid., p. 15. The other quotes are at pp. 13 and 14.

60. This global perspective (and changes in it) is discussed in part in Leonard Silk's brief analysis of an address by Zbigniew Brzezinski, "Economic Scene: New U.S. View of the World," *New York Times*, May 1, 1979, D2; and in an address by Cyrus Vance, "Meeting the Challenges of a Changing World," Address before the American Association of Community and Junior Colleges in Chicago, reprinted in *Department of State Bulletin* 79 (June 1979): 16-19.

61. Jimmy Carter, "Inaugural Address: The Ever-Expanding American Dream," *Vital Speeches* 43 (February 15, 1977): 258.

62. Jimmy Carter, "Humane Purposes in Foreign Policy," Department of State News Release, May 22, 1977, 1 (from his commencement address at the University of Notre Dame).

63. Ibid., p. 2.

64. Ibid., pp. 1, 5.

65. See the discussion in Elizabeth Drew, "A Reporter at Large: Brzezinski," *The New Yorker*, May 1, 1978, 90–130 (especially pp. 117-121), on the extent to which linkage was applied.

66. Although the Carter administration is usually identified with human rights, congressional action on this issue began at least in 1973 with hearings by the International Organizations and Movements Subcommittee, headed by Donald Fraser. On this point, see the discussion in Harold Molineu, "Human Rights: Administrative Impact of a Symbolic Policy," in John C. Grumm and Stephen L. Wasby, eds., *The Analysis of Policy Impact* (Lexington, MA: Lexington Books, D. C. Heath and Company, 1981), pp. 24–25.

67. Carter, "Inaugural Address of President Jimmy Carter: The Ever-Expanding American Dream," p. 259.

68. Jimmy Carter, *Keeping Faith* (New York: Bantam Books, 1982), p. 145.

69. See the Carter administration's comprehensive description of human rights categories in *Human Rights and U.S. Foreign Policy* (Department of State Publication 8959, Washington, DC: Bureau of Public Affairs, Department of State, 1978), pp. 7–8. Secretary of State Cyrus Vance had outlined these same categories in a speech at the University of Georgia School of Law on April 30, 1977 (*Department of State Bulletin* 76 [May 23, 1977]: 505–508).

70. See Lincoln P. Bloomfield, "From Ideology to Program to Policy," *Journal of Policy Analysis and Management* 2 (Fall 1982): 7, for the Notre Dame speech reference and a reference to Secretary Vance's April comments. The specific reference to a "mechanistic formula" is in Secretary Cyrus Vance, "Human Rights and Foreign Policy," *Department of State Bulletin*, 76 (May 23, 1977), p. 506, which reprinted Vance's University of Georgia Law School speech.

71. In reality, some nations (Argentina, Brazil, and Guatemala, for example) simply rejected American military assistance after attacks on their human rights records by the United States. See Charles W. Kegley, Jr., and Eugene R. Wittkopf, *American Foreign Policy: Pattern and Process*, 2nd ed. (New York: St. Martin's Press, 1982), p. 595.

72. These arguments are developed by Jeane J. Kirkpatrick in "Dictatorships and Double Standards," *Commentary* 68 (November 1979): 34–45; and "Human Rights and American Foreign Policy: A Symposium," *Commentary* 79 (November 1981): 42–45.

73. See, for example, the proposal by William F. Buckley, Jr., in "Human Rights and Foreign Policy," *Foreign Affairs* 58 (Spring 1980): 775–796. Also see Arthur Schlesinger, Jr., "Human Rights and the American Tradition," *Foreign Affairs* 57 (Winter 1978/1979): 503–526, for his view on intergovernmental and nongovernmental organizations.

74. See Department of State, *Report on Human Rights Practices in Countries Receiving U.S. Aid. Submitted to the Committee on Foreign Relations*, U.S. Senate and Committee on Foreign Affairs, U.S. House of Representatives (Washington, DC: Government Printing Office, 1979), pp. 4–5; Bloomfield, "From Ideology to Program to Policy," p. 9; and Warren Christopher, "The Diplomacy of Human Rights: The First Year," speech to the American Bar Association, February 13, 1978 (Washington, DC: Department of State, 1978).

75. See Colin Legum, "The African Crisis," in William P. Bundy, ed., *America and the World 1978* (New York: Pergamon Press, 1979), pp. 633–651.

76. Carter, *Keeping Faith*, p. 150.

77. See, for example, the Helsinki Accords discussed earlier.

78. Christopher S. Wren, "After a Rebuff in Moscow, Detente Is Put to the Test," *New York Times*, April 1, 1977, IA and 8A.

79. Stanley Hoffmann, "Carter's Soviet Problem," *The New Republic* 79 (July 29, 1978): 21. On this point and for a discussion of other Carter difficulties discussed here, see Stanley Hoffmann, "A View from at Home: The Perils of Incoherence," in Bundy, ed., *America and the World 1978*, pp. 463–491.

80. Most significant, perhaps, the Soviet Union began the deployment of the SS-20s, its intermediate-range ballistic missiles, in the late 1970s.

81. Such a dualism in Brzezinski's thinking about the Soviets probably should not have been unexpected. His academic career had been largely made on the basis of a strong anti-Soviet view. Thus, his concern with global issues was a more recent phenomenon.

82. Drew, "A Reporter at Large: Brzezinski," p. 117.

83. John E. Rielly, ed., *American Public Opinion and U.S. Foreign Policy 1979* (Chicago: The Chicago Council on Foreign Relations, 1979), pp. 5 and 15.

84. Bruce Russett and Donald R. Deluca, "'Don't Tread on Me': Public Opinion and Foreign Policy in the Eighties," *Political Science Quarterly* 96 (Fall 1981): 381–399.

85. Stanley Hoffmann, "Requiem," *Foreign Policy* 42 (Spring 1981): 11.

86. Carter, *Keeping Faith*, p. 157.

87. Ibid., p. 184.

88. Ibid., p. 292.

89. Ibid., pp. 296–297.

90. Department of State, *The Camp David Summit*, Publication 8954 (Washington, DC: Bureau of Public Affairs, Office of Public Communications, Department of State, September 1978).

91. See UN Security Council Resolution 435 in *Resolutions and Decisions of the Security Council, Security Council Official Records: Thirty-Third Year* (New York: United Nations, 1979), p. 13, for the resolution that South Africa eventually said that it would work to put into effect.

92. See Henry Wiseman and Alastair M. Taylor, *From Rhodesia to Zimbabwe: The Politics of Transition* (New York: Pergamon Press, 1981).

93. For an analysis of Carter's foreign policy from this perspective, see Robert W. Tucker, "America in Decline: The Foreign Policy of 'Maturity,'" in William P. Bundy, ed., *America and the World 1979* (New York: Pergamon Press, 1980), pp. 449–488.

94. The impact of these events on Carter's foreign policy is discussed in Richard Burt, "Carter, Under Pressure of Crises, Tests New Foreign Policy Goals," *New York Times*, January 9, 1980, A1 and A8, on which we rely.

95. "My Opinion of the Russians Has Changed Most Drastically," *Time*, January 14, 1980, 10.

96. These actions are outlined in a speech that Carter gave to the nation on January 4, 1980. The speech can be found in *Vital Speeches of the Day* 46 (January 15, 1980): 194–195.

97. Jimmy Carter, "State of the Union 1980," *Vital Speeches of the Day* 46 (February 1, 1980): 227.

98. Poll results suggested that the failure to secure the quick release of the American hostages contributed significantly to the electoral defeat of Jimmy Carter in 1980.

CHAPTER 4

The Return and End of the Cold War: The Reagan and Bush Administrations

General Secretary Gorbachev, if you seek peace, if you seek
prosperity for the Soviet Union and Eastern Europe, if you seek
liberalization: Come here to this gate! Mr. Gorbachev, open this gate!
Mr. Gorbachev, tear down this wall!

PRESIDENT RONALD REAGAN

JUNE 12, 1987

The world leaves one epoch of cold war and enters another epoch. . . .
The characteristics of the cold war should be abandoned.

FORMER SOVIET PRESIDENT MIKHAIL GORBACHEV

DECEMBER 1989

In this chapter, we analyze the foreign policy values, beliefs, and approaches of the Ronald Reagan and George H. W. Bush administrations as the Cold War was ending and as a new era was emerging. The Reagan administration largely brought a realist approach back to American foreign policy after the idealism of the Carter years, but it also brought a particular idealism by resurrecting the values of the Cold War. The Bush administration largely followed the realism of the Reagan years, although more the accommodative approach to major power relations of the second Reagan term. At the same time, the Bush administration sought to build a "new world order" after the dramatic demise of the Cold War, beginning with the collapse of the Berlin Wall in 1989, the reunification of Germany a year later, and the implosion of the Soviet Union in 1991. These events, too, precipitated yet another direction in American foreign policy.

REALISM AND THE REAGAN ADMINISTRATION

Just as Jimmy Carter shifted away from the foreign policies of the Nixon–Ford–Kissinger years, Ronald Reagan sought to chart a different course from the one Carter had pursued. Reagan campaigned for the presidency on the principle of **restoring American power** at home and abroad, and his foreign policy was aimed at reflecting such power. Whereas Carter had attempted to move away from the power politics of the Kissinger era and away from a foreign policy that focused directly on adversaries—particularly the Soviet Union—Reagan embraced the need for power—especially military power—and the need to focus on the Soviet Union and its expansionism. During its second term, however, the Reagan administration sought and successfully obtained some accommodation with the Soviet Union, although without altering its anti-Soviet approach in the Third World.

The Values and Beliefs of the Reagan Administration

President Reagan did not bring with him a fully developed foreign policy design, but he did bring a strongly held worldview. For him, the prime obstacle to peace and stability in the world was the Soviet Union and particularly Soviet expansionism. The principal foreign policy goal of the United States, therefore, was to be the **revival of the national will** to contain the Soviet Union and the restoration of confidence among friends that America was determined to stop communism. Furthermore, the United States had to make other nations aware of the danger that Soviet expansionism represented.

The ideological suspicion with which President Reagan viewed the Soviet Union was highlighted dramatically at his first news conference in January 1981, in which he stated that the Soviet leadership was committed to "world revolution" and that "they reserved unto themselves the right to commit any crime; to lie; to cheat," as a means of obtaining what they wanted.[1] In 1983, echoing that first news conference, he assailed the morality of the Soviet Union once again and denounced it as an "evil empire" with which the United States, in his judgment, remained in a moral struggle.[2]

Such a consistently hostile view brought to mind comparisons with the U.S. foreign policy orientation of the 1950s, when the Cold War consensus was dominant. It surely stood in contrast to Carter's view only four years earlier that "we are now free of that inordinate fear of communism."[3] On the contrary, Reagan's view implied the centrality of the Soviet Union and its foreign policy objectives to American actions abroad. Indeed, to many observers, such a posture suggested the emergence of a new Cold War.[4]

The Reagan Administration's Policy Approach

Despite the ideological cohesion that seemed to permeate the Reagan administration, its translation into a working foreign policy was not readily apparent to observers. In fact, charges were immediately made by policy analysts that the Reagan administration had no foreign policy because it appeared to have no coherent strategy for reaching its goals. Critics complained that rhetoric served as policy—a failing that was particularly accented by the Reagan administration's having come into office determined to bring coherence and consistency to foreign affairs, which they charged the Carter administration had been unable to do.[5]

This criticism is a bit overstated. In 1981, Secretary of State Alexander Haig provided a statement of principles and the underlying rationale for dealing with the world early in his tenure. Describing his approach as a "strategic one," Haig said that American foreign policy behavior was based on four important pillars:

- The restoration of economic and military strength
- The reinvigoration of alliances and friendships
- The promotion of progress in the developing countries through peaceable changes
- A relationship with the Soviet Union characterized by restraint and reciprocity[6]

He pointed out that none of these pillars would be pursued independently and that policy initiatives based on any one must support the others. The glue that would hold the pillars together was the Soviet–American relationship because, as Haig indicated, it "must be at the center of our efforts to promote a more peaceful world."[7]

Rebuilding American Strength

The Reagan administration quickly called for an increase in military spending, proposing a $1.6 trillion defense buildup over a six-year period (1981–1986). Although the buildup was across the entire military—from a larger navy to a modernized army and air force and from the development of a new rapid deployment force to better pay for military personnel—it was the **strategic modernization plan** that attracted much of the attention in the early part of the Reagan presidency.[8]

Under this plan, each component of America's nuclear triad—land-based missiles, sea-based nuclear missiles, and intercontinental nuclear-armed bombers—would be modernized, and the strategic command and control structures—the technical communication facilities that provide direction for U.S. nuclear forces[9]—would be upgraded to guard against any possible Soviet first strike. The Reagan administration also pursued two actions to improve America's nuclear capability—one regional, the other global. On a regional level, it proposed to carry out the NATO alliance's **Dual-Track decision of 1979**. In accord with that decision, new intermediate-range or theater nuclear weapons would be deployed in Western Europe if negotiations on theater nuclear arms control failed. On a global level, President Reagan called for the United States to "embark on a program to counter the awesome Soviet missile threat with measures that are defensive." Such a defensive system "could pave the way for arms control measures to eliminate . . . [nuclear] weapons themselves."[10] Formally called the **Strategic Defense Initiative**

(SDI) but more commonly known as "Star Wars" after the popular motion picture, critics viewed this proposal as a further escalation of the arms race.

Reinvigorating America's Allies

The reinvigoration of the allies basically meant upgrading the military strength of the West and allied support of the political leadership of the United States globally. In the military area, as noted, the United States succeeded in persuading Western Europeans to go forward with the rearmament component of the Dual Track decision: Deployment of the 572 Pershing II and cruise missiles began by late 1983, after arms negotiations stalled.[11]

The administration also hoped to persuade the Europeans to accept a greater defense burden as a means of counteracting growing Soviet power in their region, and the Japanese to assume greater military responsibility in East Asia. Appeals were made to the Europeans to follow America's lead in enacting sanctions against the Soviet Union and Poland after the imposition of martial law in Poland in late 1981, although their success was limited. The United States also tried to stop the Europeans from completing their natural gas pipeline arrangement with the Soviets at about the same time. Later, the Reagan administration sought (unsuccessfully) to impose sanctions on the Europeans themselves over their failure to follow American wishes.[12]

Bolstering Friends in the Developing World

The meaning of the third pillar—a commitment to progress in the Third World—reflected a sharp shift in U.S. strategy toward friendly developing countries. As compared to the Carter administration, the Reagan administration changed policy in three distinct ways. First, unlike President Carter, who sympathized with Third World aspirations, Reagan challenged those nations to pull themselves up by their bootstraps and seek improvement through private enterprise. The administration soon developed the **Caribbean Basin Initiative** as a model for utilizing the private sector to stimulate development. This plan provided for an increase in economic assistance to the Caribbean region by $350 million, but it was preferential trade access to the American market for the Caribbean states and increased American investments in the region that were its key development components.[13]

Second, the administration increased U.S. reliance on military assistance as an "essential" element of American policy. Thus, it scrapped the arms transfer policy of the Carter administration and, following a plan more attuned to its philosophical orientation, announced that it would provide military assistance to "its major alliance partners and to those nations with whom it has friendly and cooperative security relationships."[14]

Third, American policy would now focus on how regional conflicts would be analyzed and acted upon by the United States. No longer would they be assessed on the basis of regional concerns alone. Conflicts in the developing world would now be recast as part of the underlying conflict that the Reagan administration saw in the world. In turn, U.S. actions in regional disputes would have to recognize that global reality. Therefore, the emphasis was on how these conflicts affected U.S.–Soviet relations. The aim was to build a "**strategic consensus**" against the Soviet Union and its proxies.[15] Only after the Soviet danger in these conflicts was addressed could regional concerns be brought into their resolution.

Restraint and Reciprocity with the Soviet Union

The fourth pillar of the Reagan administration's approach to foreign policy focused directly on the Soviet Union. Only if the Soviets demonstrated restraint in their global actions would the United States carry on normal and reciprocal relations with them. In this sense, the familiar linkage notion of the Kissinger years was to be at the heart of any relationship with the Soviet Union. Specifically, Secretary Haig stated that the United States would "want greater Soviet restraint on the use of force. We want greater Soviet respect for the independence of others. And we want the Soviets to abide by their reciprocal obligations, such as those undertaken in the Helsinki Accords." Moreover, no area of international relations could be left out of this restraint requirement. "We have learned that Soviet–American agreements, even in strategic arms control, will not survive Soviet threats to the overall military balance or Soviet encroachments . . . in critical regions of the world. *Linkage is not a theory; it is a fact of life that we overlook at our peril.*"[16]

THE REAGAN WORLDVIEW IN OPERATION

With the four pillars as a primary guide, the Reagan administration's actions toward the Soviet Union, Central America, southern Africa, and the Middle East reshaped the direction of American foreign policy.

Policy Actions toward the Soviet Union

Because the Soviet Union had exercised neither policy restraint nor reciprocity in the past, the Reagan administration did not seek to improve relations immediately. Instead, it sought to rally other states against the Soviets and adopted several initial measures to prod the Soviets into exercising international restraint.

First, administration officials publicly criticized the Soviet Union. President Reagan and Secretary Haig attacked the Soviet system as bankrupt and on the verge of collapse, charging the Soviets with fomenting international disorder.[17]

Second, the administration took direct steps to demonstrate American resolve. In addition to its strategic modernization plan, the administration called for producing and stockpiling the neutron bomb, a new kind of weapon (originally proposed during the Carter years) that killed humans but did not destroy property. Most significant, perhaps, the United States promptly imposed sanctions on both the Soviet Union and Poland in 1981 to show its dissatisfaction with the imposition of martial law by Poland's Communist government and Soviet support for it.[18]

Third, some actions were *not* taken to demonstrate that normal relations could not be reinstated until the Soviet Union showed that it could restrain itself. In this connection, the two most important omissions were the administration's refusal to move rapidly on arms control and its refusal to engage in summit meetings. In fact, arms control discussions were initially put on the back burner until the United States completed its arms buildup. Additionally, a summit meeting between the Soviet and American presidents was put off with the comment that conditions were not appropriate and that little valuable discussion would result.

Despite a relationship marked primarily by harsh rhetoric and strong action, some initial cooperation was evident. In the economic area, the Reagan administration in April 1981 lifted the grain embargo—which President Carter had put into effect after the Afghanistan invasion—despite its commitment to isolating and punishing the Soviet Union. Within a year, the administration sought to expand grain sales to the Soviets and eventually agreed to a new five-year grain deal.[19] In the military area, the administration stated that it would continue to adhere to the SALT I and SALT II limitations if the Soviets would.[20]

In the diplomatic area, Secretary of State Haig met with the Soviet foreign minister, Andrei Gromyko, during Gromyko's visit to the UN General Assembly in the fall of 1981, despite the political chill. Finally, the **Intermediate Nuclear Force (INF) talks**—on nuclear missiles with ranges only within Europe—were reluctantly begun during November 1981, much earlier than expected given the overall political climate. Seven months later, President Reagan also initiated the **Strategic Arms Reduction Talks (START)** on intercontinental nuclear weapons.[21] By November 1983, however, neither of these talks had reached any agreement, and the United States went ahead with its deployment of intermediate missiles in Europe.[22] The Soviet Union walked out of the INF negotiations and, within one month, declared that it would not proceed with the Strategic Arms Reduction Talks, either. Further, the Soviets resumed and expanded the deployment of their intermediate-range nuclear missiles in central Europe, announced the deployment of more nuclear submarines off the American coasts in retaliation for the new American weapons in Western Europe, and withdrew from the 1984 Olympic Games in Los Angeles, claiming that Soviet athletes would not be safe there.[23]

The consequence of this barrage of charges and actions by the superpowers was that by mid-1984 relations between them were "at the lowest level for the entire postwar period."[24] The "restraint and reciprocity" that the Reagan administration had initially set out to achieve had not been accomplished, but the plan of restoring the Soviet Union to the center of American foreign policy and building up U.S. defenses was well under way.

Policy Actions toward the Third World

Central America In Central America, the Reagan administration's response to the unrest in El Salvador reflected its basic foreign policy approach (see Map 4.1). It quickly moved to interpret the ongoing civil war as Soviet and Cuban directed. Calling **El Salvador** a "textbook case" of Communist aggression, the administration issued a white paper outlining the danger it posed.[25] Furthermore, testifying at a House Foreign Affairs Committee hearing in March 1981, Secretary of State Haig charged that the Communist attack on El Salvador was part of a "four-phased operation" aimed at ultimate Communist control of Central America.[26]

Military assistance and the threat of military action were the principal instruments the Reagan administration used to respond to the situation. Military aid totaling $25 million was immediately proposed for the Salvadoran government in its struggle with rebel forces, with more to come, and the number of military advisors was increased from 20 to 55 by the spring of 1981.[27] Over the next several years, El Salvador and its neighbor, Honduras, became leading recipients of U.S. foreign assistance.

A similar policy approach, and some of the administration's harshest rhetoric, was directed toward El Salvador's neighbor, Nicaragua. President Reagan described the **Sandinista-led government of Nicaragua** as "a Communist reign of terror" and the Nicaraguans themselves as "Cuba's Cubans" for their assumed aid of the Salvadoran guerrillas.[28] He also quoted directly from the Truman Doctrine of four decades earlier to justify the need for American action in the region ("I believe that it must be the policy of the United States to support free peoples . . .").[29] Charging that the

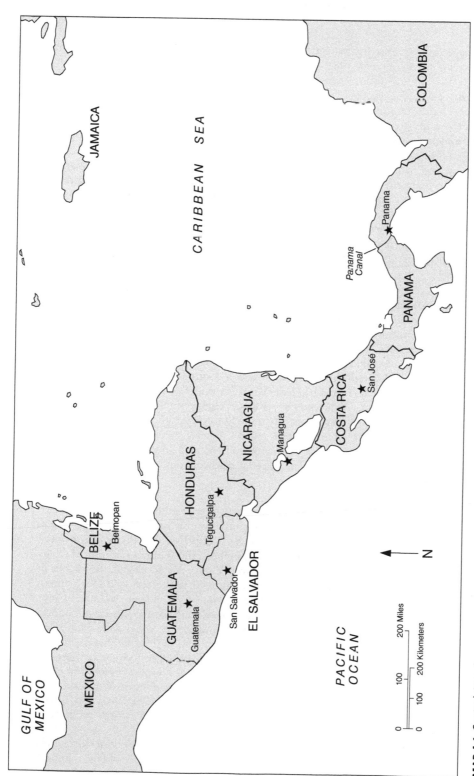

MAP 4.1 Central America

Nicaraguan government was arming the Salvadoran guerrillas, the Reagan administration, on taking office in 1981, cut off $15 million of economic aid.[30] By early 1982, in fact, the administration was conducting a clandestine operation in Honduras in support of Nicaraguan rebels, or Contras, against the Sandinista government.[31]

The hardline policy of communist containment in Latin America was perhaps manifested most dramatically with the American invasion of the Caribbean island of **Grenada** in October 1983. After Marxist Prime Minister Maurice Bishop was killed on October 19, 1983, and after a more radical group seized control, the United States agreed to join forces with the five members of the Organization of Eastern Caribbean States in an operation "to restore order and democracy." This action was officially taken to ensure the safety of between 800 and 1,000 Americans—mostly medical students—and to "forestall further chaos."[32] Within a few days, American control of the island was achieved, the Marxist regime had been replaced, and the return to a Western-style democracy was under way. This intervention demonstrated that the Reagan administration would confront Marxist regimes, with military force if necessary.

Southern Africa   The Reagan administration's actions followed a similar pattern against potential Communist gains in southern Africa. It adopted a policy of "**constructive engagement**" toward South Africa and linked any settlement in Namibia (or Southwest Africa) to the removal of Soviet-backed Cuban forces from Angola. These policies were predicated upon several key beliefs. First, South Africa was staunchly anticommunist, and, as a result, the United States should not seek a confrontational approach toward it. Second, the conflict in the region had East–West overtones that could not be overlooked. After all, South Africa was confronted by a Marxist regime in Angola backed by Cuban soldiers and Soviet arms.[33] Third, only when the South Africans felt more confident of American support could the United States try to influence them to change their apartheid policy and to seek a solution to the question of Namibia. In this region, the strategic concern of controlling communism produced a markedly different approach from the one the Carter administration had adopted.

The Middle East   The administration's primary strategy in the Middle East was also aimed at stopping any potential Communist gains. No new initiatives were proposed, nor was there much effort to proceed with the Camp David framework inherited from the previous administration. Instead, as elsewhere, the Reagan administration attempted to rally the Arab states against the Soviet Union and to engage the Israelis in a strategic understanding. A new Persian Gulf command, with the Rapid Deployment Force as part of that structure, was announced. Negotiations were held with several Middle East states regarding American base and access rights, with Egypt, Sudan, Somalia, and Oman, for example, agreeing to joint military exercises with the United States[34] and the United States obtaining military cooperation from the Israelis.[35]

The most dramatic examples of military assistance employed to bolster American influence against the Soviet Union also occurred when the United States agreed to sell technologically advanced aircraft equipment and the **Airborne Warning and Control System (AWACS)** aircraft to Saudi Arabia in October 1981, and agreed to supply forty F-16 fighter aircraft to Pakistan (an arms deal worth more than $3 billion) as part of its southwest Asia strategy.[36]

The Reagan administration's emphasis on global over local concerns ultimately proved short-lived in the Middle East. By the summer of 1982—and wholly as a result of Israel's invasion of Lebanon and its advance to Beirut—it had become fully immersed in local issues in the region. The administration sought a cease-fire between the Israelis and the surrounded Palestinian forces in West Beirut and a withdrawal of Syrian and Israeli forces from Lebanon itself. Moreover, even President Reagan played the role of mediator with a new policy initiative (labeled the **Reagan Initiative**) to serve as a follow-up to Camp David. The initiative called for a Palestinian homeland federated with Jordan, an end to Israeli settlements in the West Bank, and security for Israel.[37]

The depth of American involvement in the area reached the point of deploying American military personnel on two occasions. The administration sent a contingent of U.S. Marines into Lebanon in August 1982 as part of an effort to evacuate Palestine Liberation Organization (PLO) members from Beirut, where the Israelis had surrounded them. This mission was successfully completed without major incident. In September 1982, however, the Marines were again dispatched to Lebanon as part of a Multinational Force (MNF) composed of military personnel from several Western nations. Although the MNF was to serve as "peacekeepers" between the various Lebanese factions and as facilitators of a negotiated settlement among them, the task proved elusive and ultimately disastrous.[38] As factional feuding continued, the role of the MNF became increasingly unclear. In time, the Marines, encamped at the Beirut airport, became identified with the central government and became the target of Lebanese snipers. On October 23, 1983, a terrorist bomb attack on the barracks killed some 241 Americans.

Once again, although the Reagan administration originally intended to deal with regional issues in a global context, it became deeply involved in "local issues" in the Middle East without a well-conceived policy.

CHALLENGES TO THE REAGAN FOREIGN POLICY APPROACH

Despite the efforts of the Reagan administration to refocus American policy on the Soviet danger, the rest of the world would not easily follow its lead. Concern over—and at times rejection of—that policy's ideological tone and substance came from both international and domestic sources. These challenges made it difficult for the administration to maintain the ideological consistency that it originally intended, and they contributed to its modification over time.

International Differences

The Western European states, for example, were reluctant to follow the Reagan administration in dealing with the Soviet Union. Whether it was over martial law in Poland or the building of a natural gas pipeline from the Soviet Union to Western Europe, they were concerned with preserving contacts with Eastern Europe, not disrupting them.[39] Similarly, even though the Europeans were committed to the Dual-Track decision of 1979, they were unsure (and uneasy) about President Reagan's commitment to pursuing negotiations. With his harsh rhetoric, his strategic modernization plan, and his reluctance to proceed quickly with arms control talks, he did not seem to be following a policy of restraint. Further, the hundreds of thousands of demonstrators in London, Rome, Berlin, and Bonn protesting the Reagan arms policy created more political difficulties for European leaders.[40] Finally, some European and Latin American states refused to support either the American approach to the situation in El Salvador or its policy toward Nicaragua.[41]

Domestic Differences

The American public was increasingly skeptical of continued defense spending and expressed support for the **nuclear freeze movement**. Although Americans had been willing to go along with some increase in defense spending when the Reagan administration took office, that willingness had decreased considerably by 1983. By then, 45 percent of the American public believed that the United States was spending too much on the military, and only 14 percent believed that the United States was spending too little.[42] Similarly, public opinion polls consistently showed that more than 60 percent of Americans supported a "mutual and verifiable freeze" of nuclear weapons between the Soviet Union and the United States.[43] This nuclear freeze movement was able to turn out more than 700,000 people in New York City in June 1982 for one of the largest demonstrations in American political history. The demonstrators—individuals from a wide variety of political and social backgrounds— reflected the diversity of support for this movement.[44]

Other domestic challenges arose over Central American policy. In particular, the public expressed concern with potential American involvement in the region, especially as more American advisors were being sent there. Would American combat forces be sent? Was this involvement the beginning of another Vietnam-like quagmire in which American involvement would slowly escalate? These fears caused Secretary of State Haig to rule out the use of American troops in Central America.[45] Another argument against involvement was that local conditions in Central America, such as poverty and inequality, ought to be given greater credibility as causes of the political unrest than the Reagan administration had allowed.

POLICY CHANGE: ACCOMMODATION WITH THE SOVIET UNION

After President Reagan's resounding election to a second term in November 1984, he immediately announced that his administration would continue to do "what we've been doing."[46] In reality, however, the administration made some significant changes in its foreign policy. Reagan did not abandon his hardline position on Soviet expansionism in Third World areas, but he did make a significant change in the bilateral relationship with the Soviet Union by adopting a much more accommodationist approach and setting the stage for ending the Cold War.

Sources of Change

At least three factors contributed to the movement away from the hardline approach of the Reagan administration toward the Soviet Union:

- A change in the policy stance of the American leadership
- The emergence of new leadership and "new thinking" in the Soviet Union
- The domestic realities of the arms race between the superpowers

It is difficult to specify which of these (and presumably others as well) weighed most heavily in this policy change—or to show fully how they interacted. Nevertheless, a brief discussion of each is in order.

Policy Shifts Secretary of State George Shultz initially signaled a change in emphasis as early as October 1984, at that time declaring that linkage between Soviet behavior around the world and the quality of relations between the two superpowers was

> ... not merely a "fact of life" but a complex question of policy. There will be times when we must make progress in one dimension of the relationship contingent on progress in others. ... At the same time, linkage as an instrument of policy has limitations; if applied rigidly, it could yield the initiative to the Soviets, letting them set the pace and the character of the relationship. ... In the final analysis, linkage is a tactical question; the strategic reality of leverage comes from creating facts in support of our overall design.[47]

In other words, policy must be more flexible than it had been.

In his second inaugural address, President Reagan, too, suggested a new flexibility by committing his administration to better relations with the Soviet Union, especially in nuclear arms control. Specifically, the United States would seek to reduce the cost of national security "in negotiations with the Soviet Union." Such negotiations, however, would not only focus on limiting an increase in nuclear weapons but also they would attempt to "reduce their numbers."[48] To appreciate how significant a change this was, recall the Reagan administration's initial rejection of arms control negotiations.

"New" Thinking The second factor that contributed to the possibility of accommodation between the two superpowers was the 1985 selection of Mikhail Gorbachev as general secretary of the Communist Party in the Soviet Union and eventually as Soviet president. Gorbachev's rise to power was critical, as he brought several important conceptual changes to Soviet foreign policy thinking and a commitment to improving relations with the United States. In fact, he added two major concepts to the political lexicon of the 1980s and 1990s, *perestroika* and *glasnost*. Perestroika referred to the "restructuring" of Soviet society in an effort to improve the economy; glasnost referred to a new "openness" and a movement toward greater democratization of the Soviet system.

Such "new thinking" by the Soviet leadership, as Gorbachev himself called it, came to have important implications for Soviet–American relations. In contrast to earlier desires for "nuclear superiority," Soviet leaders began to embrace the concepts of "reasonable sufficiency" as a strategy for dealing with the West and to recognize the need for greater "strategic stability" in the nuclear balance. In such an environment, nuclear arms accommodation between the two superpowers became a viable option. Furthermore, the Soviet leadership indicated that the struggle between capitalism and socialism had changed, and so political, rather than military, solutions ought to be pursued.[49]

The Sustained Arms Race Yet a third factor may well have been the most pivotal: the increasing domestic burden of sustained military spending. The economies of both nations were being undermined and distorted by continuing confrontation. Indeed, in the Soviet Union, people's basic needs could not be met as more and more resources were diverted to the military. Gorbachev's hope of restructuring the Soviet system could not be realistically undertaken as long as military spending consumed so much of the nation's wealth. In the United States, with military budgets approaching $300 billion per year and federal budget deficits increasing, the country's economic health remained in question. Consequently, the Reagan administration could no longer count on public support for increasing military expenditures.[50]

The Return of Soviet–American Summitry

The first significant manifestation of a changed policy was the reemergence of summitry between American and Soviet leaders. Surprisingly, considering his initial reluctance, President Reagan ultimately held more summits with Soviet leaders than any other American president. In the space of about three and a half years, he held five summits with President Gorbachev,[51] each of which proved to be an important building block in improved Soviet–American ties.

The first summit between Reagan and Gorbachev, held in Geneva, Switzerland, on November 19–21, 1985, was called the "**Fireside Summit**" for the backdrop against which it took place. No important agreements emerged; rather, it was an opportunity for the leaders to get to know each other better and to exchange views on numerous issues, including arms control, human rights, and regional conflicts. In effect, this summit was a prelude to the next one.[52]

The second and third summits were arguably the most important ones of the Reagan presidency. The **October 1986 summit**, held in Reykjavik, Iceland, focused largely on seeking progress in the ongoing nuclear arms talks between the Soviet Union and the United States. Its most significant products were agreements in principle to reduce all strategic nuclear weapons 50 percent over a five-year period and to limit intermediate-range nuclear forces to one hundred warheads for each side.[53] These commitments were significant for advancing work on strategic arms reduction (START) and intermediate nuclear forces (INF) agreements. Discord remained, however, in negotiations on space-based missiles (the "Star Wars" defense systems), which threatened to undermine progress in START and INF. The INF discussions were eventually separated from the other talks, which quickly led to the completion of the **Intermediate Nuclear Forces (INF) Treaty** (discussed in the next subsection), signed at the third summit in Washington in December 1987.

The fourth summit, held in Moscow in late May and early June 1988, was primarily to exchange the instrument of ratification of the new INF Treaty, seek further progress in strategic arms negotiations, and discuss other key global issues.[54] The fifth and final Soviet–American summit of the Reagan administration was a brief one-day meeting in New York City in December 1988 during Gorbachev's visit to speak before the United Nations.[55] This was an opportunity for a final exchange of views before Reagan left office and for President-Elect George H. W. Bush to meet the Soviet leader.

The INF Treaty

The completion of the Intermediate Nuclear Forces (INF) Treaty was the most important manifestation of progress in Soviet–American relations in Reagan's second term. It was the culmination of a long series of negotiations begun in November 1981, broken off in November 1983, and resumed after a joint Soviet–American agreement to link all nuclear arms negotiations—one track on intermediate nuclear forces, a second on strategic nuclear forces, and a third on defense and space arms—in a set of "**New Negotiations**" in January 1985.[56] After the 1986 Reykjavik summit, however, the INF talks were selected for acceleration and were eventually completed and signed in December 1987.

INF called for the elimination of all intermediate-range nuclear weapons within three years and all medium-range nuclear weapons within eighteen months.[57] It also prohibited the United States and the Soviet Union from ever again possessing such weapons. In addition, it provided a series of onsite inspections for each party and set out exacting procedures on how these nuclear weapons should be destroyed. Finally, it established a Special Verification Commission that would be continuously in session to deal with any issues that might arise.

The military significance of the INF Treaty has sometimes been questioned. It required relatively few nuclear missiles to be destroyed, and each superpower retained a formidable arsenal with which to destroy the other and the rest of the world. Its political significance is less debatable, however. INF represented the first nuclear arms reduction pact in history, and it gave significant momentum to arms control and arms reduction for the future. With its incorporation of onsite inspection, it represented a new direction in the verification of arms control agreements between the superpowers.

POLICY CONTINUITY: THE REAGAN DOCTRINE AND THE THIRD WORLD

If actions toward the Soviet Union represented change, policy toward the Third World—and the perceived role of the Soviet Union in causing unrest there—represented continuity for the Reagan administration during its second term. This continuity was reflected in the formal emergence of the "**Reagan Doctrine**," which supported anticommunist movements in various locations around the world. The doctrine was demonstrated most dramatically by support of the Nicaraguan Contras, even though Congress cut off military support for that operation from 1984 to 1986. This episode, known as the "**Iran–Contra affair**" (discussed in an upcoming section) reflected the administration's determination to "stand tall" against perceived Communist penetration in Central America. At the same time, it produced a major policy inconsistency: The Reagan administration secretly abandoned its official arms embargo of Iran in an attempt to free American hostages held by Iranians.

The Reagan Doctrine

By 1985, the administration's support for anti-Communist forces in the Third World had gained such prominence and permanency that it took on a name of its own: the "Reagan Doctrine." Unlike U.S. policy that focused on containing the expansion of communism, the Reagan Doctrine espoused "providing assistance to groups fighting governments that have aligned themselves with the Soviet Union."[58] Despite the thaw in Soviet–American relations during Reagan's second term, this strategy was vigorously pursued and proved to be the main thread of continuity with the hardline policy of anticommunism that was so prominent in 1981.

What the Reagan Doctrine meant in reality was that several anti-Communist movements across three continents received both covert and overt American economic and military assistance and political encouragement in their fight against the Communist governments in power. In Asia, for example, the United States continued to support the Afghan rebels in their battle with Soviet troops and the Soviet-backed Kabul government. In Kampuchea (present-day Cambodia), it clandestinely funneled aid to groups opposing the government supported by occupying Vietnamese. As for Africa, the Reagan administration persuaded Congress to repeal its prohibition on aid to forces opposing the Angolan government, and it continued to support rebel leader Jonas Savimbi and his **National Union for the Total Independence of Angola (UNITA)** in its fight against the Marxist-supported Angolan government. In Central

America, of course, the Reagan administration continued to support the Nicaraguan Contras against the Sandinistas, even as Congress diligently attempted to end such aid.

A useful indicator of how institutionalized the Reagan Doctrine had become was the 1985 foreign aid authorization bill. Although this bill included nonmilitary humanitarian aid for the Nicaraguan Contras, support for other anti-Communist rebel groups was publicly acknowledged with a $5 million allocation to the Cambodian rebels and a $15 million "humanitarian" allocation to the Afghan people.[59] As discussed earlier, the congressional prohibition of aid to rebel forces in Angola was formally rescinded in this legislation.

The Iran–Contra Affair, 1984–1986

The episode that best illustrates the extent to which the administration embraced the Reagan Doctrine, the Iran–Contra affair from 1984 through 1986, brought together two vexing foreign policy problems for the Reagan administration.[60] The first was its dealings with the Sandinista government in Nicaragua, which it viewed as avowedly Marxist, with the intent of spreading revolution throughout Central America. The second problem was its dealings with the Iranian government led by Ayatollah Khomeini, which, along with student supporters, had seized sixty-three Americans in November 1979, held most of them hostage for 444 days, and released the remaining fifty-two on the day of President Reagan's first-term inauguration.

To deal with these two linked policy questions, the Reagan administration supported the **Nicaraguan Contras** fighting against the Sandinistas in various ways, including clandestine assistance, and continued to enforce President Carter's trade sanctions against Iran, particularly the prohibition of U.S. arms sales to that country.

Beginning in 1984, however, policies toward Nicaragua and Iran were faltering and eventually unraveled by mid-1985. Iran's actions in support of terrorism caused the first challenge to the Reagan administration's policy. As a result of U.S. participation in a multinational peacekeeping force in Lebanon in 1982 and 1983, anti-American sentiment and terrorism against the United States had risen significantly. In October 1983, terrorists bombed a U.S. Marine barracks in Lebanon. In early 1984, three Americans were seized in Beirut. In 1985, four more Americans were taken. Both the American public and President Reagan became increasingly impatient over the hostage situation. Indeed, by mid-1985, Reagan decided to reverse the long-standing policy of an arms embargo against Iran in an attempt to free U.S. hostages.

The administration's policy reversal toward Iran did not occur in isolation; rather, it quickly became tied to an attempt to save its policy of aiding the Nicaraguan Contras. In October 1984, Congress had cut off all military assistance to the Contras with the passage of the most restrictive version of the **Boland Amendments** (see Chapter 8). In light of congressional action, high administration officials almost immediately undertook efforts to keep the Contras in "body and soul together," as President Reagan had instructed. What ultimately emerged was a covert operation by private operatives to raise money and provide support for them.

The administration employed two means of raising money to support the Contras: contributions by private individuals and other governments and the clandestine sale of arms to the Iranian government. The latter effort, largely directed by **Lieutenant Colonel Oliver North** of the National Security Council, provided for several shipments of arms to Iran and for profits from those sales to be transferred to the Contras in 1985 and 1986.

It is significant that throughout the entire episode and during the investigations afterward, President Reagan consistently denied both that he knew that arms sales profits were being transferred to the Contras and that the arms sales were tied solely to the freeing of American hostages held in Lebanon.

The Iran–Contra affair affected both procedural and content aspects of American foreign policy during the last years of the Reagan administration. It damaged the clarity and the credibility of the administration's policy and challenged the way the Reagan Doctrine was being carried out. It also had a profound effect on congressional–executive relations and on public support. Yet it demonstrated the extent to which the administration was willing to enforce the Reagan Doctrine.

POLICY CHANGES TOWARD THE THIRD WORLD: THE PHILIPPINES, THE PLO, AND SOUTH AFRICA

Although adherence to the Reagan Doctrine marked the administration's approach to the Third World, three important policy changes did occur: in Southeast Asia, in the Middle East, and in Africa.

The Aquino Victory

The first change involved the Philippines and the movement toward democracy under **Corazon Aquino** in 1985 and 1986. The United States had long supported the government of **Ferdinand Marcos**, principally because of his anti-Communist credentials and because of its need to maintain its strategic military bases at Subic Bay and at Clark Field. Yet Marcos's dismal human rights record and authoritarian rule had long been a source of embarrassment and concern to U.S. policy makers. With the assassination of Senator Benigno Aquino, Jr., the leading opposition politician, and the growing strength of the New People's Army—a Marxist opposition group—and other nationalist factions, the Reagan administration came under increasing pressure to reevaluate its policy. By 1984, that reevaluation had begun with a National Security Council directive that anticipated a post-Marcos period.[61]

When President Marcos suddenly announced a "snap election" to be held in early 1986 to demonstrate his popularity, Corazon Aquino, wife of the assassinated senator and a political novice, agreed to run against him. Although Marcos was declared the election winner, accusations of voter fraud were rampant, with opposition groups surrounding the presidential palace and calling for Marcos to step down. At that juncture, the Reagan administration threw its full support behind Corazon Aquino and informed Marcos that he should resign. Within a matter of days, Marcos had left the country and taken up exile in Hawaii.

The significance of this event for the Reagan administration was that it represented a clear departure from previous policy, away from stability through support for authoritarian rule and toward human rights and democracy. This departure seemed to be particularly at odds with an administration that had previously supported Third World stability as the less dangerous way to thwart Communist expansion.

The U.S.–PLO Dialogue

A second change concerned the **Palestine Liberation Organization's (PLO)** involvement in Middle East peace negotiations. In 1975, as part of commitments associated with the second disengagement agreement between Israel and Egypt, the United States had pledged to Israel that it would have no contact with the PLO until at least two conditions were met: (1) the PLO recognized the right of Israel to exist, and (2) it accepted UN resolutions 242 and 338 as the basis for negotiations.[62] Later, a third condition for any contact between the PLO and the United States was added: the PLO would have to renounce the use of terrorism.[63] In spite of a variety of efforts by Secretary of State George Shultz in the mid-1980s, no real accommodation occurred among the parties to this ongoing dispute.

In November 1988, however, the Palestine National Council, the political assembly of the PLO, took a dramatic step to change the situation. First, it declared an independent Palestinian state in the area occupied by Israel and sought recognition from abroad. Second, and most important for U.S. policy, it moved to accept the first American condition for discussion between the parties and accepted in part the second condition. Regarding the third condition, however, it "condemned" terrorism but did not renounce it. By mid-December 1988, Yasir Arafat, head of the PLO, sensing the political value of discussions with the United States, announced his full acceptance of the three explicit conditions for U.S.–PLO dialogue and his renunciation of terrorism. Within hours, President Reagan declared that Arafat's statement met American conditions and announced a shift in American policy.[64]

Opposition to Apartheid

The third arena of change was South Africa. Although all American administrations, including Reagan's, had long opposed South Africa's policy of **apartheid**— segregation of the races—the Reagan administration's policy was one of "constructive engagement" in which "quiet diplomacy" was seen as the best way to elicit change in that strategically important country. By August 1985, however, Congress had become impatient with such a strategy and was on the verge of passing a compromise bill that would have imposed economic sanctions as a more tangible way to move the South Africans along. In a clear reversal and undoubtedly as an attempt to rescue the initiative from Congress, President Reagan issued an executive order imposing virtually the same set of sanctions that Congress had proposed.[65]

In 1986, however, the administration took no further action against South Africa. At the same time, Congress pressed ahead and passed a new, tough sanctions bill, the **Anti-Apartheid Act of 1986**, over President Reagan's veto. The policy change that President Reagan had originally put into place after congressional prodding in 1985 was now made permanent. In this sense, though, that change was more Congress's and less the administration's own.

REALISM, PRAGMATISM, AND THE
GEORGE H. W. BUSH ADMINISTRATION

George H. W. Bush, Ronald Reagan's vice president, was elected president in November 1988 less on a commitment to change the course of U.S. foreign policy and more on Americans' desire for continuity. Unlike Reagan, Bush came to office not as a foreign policy ideologue but as a pragmatist without a strongly held worldview. In this sense, Bush's initial foreign policy impulse leaned toward maintaining continuity with the recent past rather than seeking change. However, this commitment was challenged by the dramatic events that began at the end of his first year in office: the demise of the Soviet empire; the emergence of new political, economic, and social openness in Eastern Europe; and the movement toward German reunification.[66]

With the end of the Cold War at hand, President Bush had begun to modify American foreign policy by 1990 away from the anticommunist principles of the past and toward a course steered by the changes in the Soviet Union and Eastern Europe. Iraq's invasion of Kuwait in that year, and the American and allied response to it, gave further impetus to seeking a new direction for American foreign policy. Indeed, shortly after the beginning of the Persian Gulf War, Bush acknowledged as much, when he announced that "we stand at a defining hour."[67] Nonetheless, the Bush administration continued to embrace the essence of political realism, even as it sought this new direction.

The Values and Belief of the Bush Administration

Pragmatic and *prudent* were favorite terms used to describe the Bush administration's basic foreign policy values.[68] President Bush did not come to office with a grand design or with a "vision thing" (as he himself might have said) for reshaping international politics. Instead, his approach reflected the values, beliefs, and temperament of Bush himself, a moderate, middle-of-the-road professional politician who was well trained in foreign affairs—as director of the CIA, American representative to the People's Republic of China, ambassador to the United Nations, and Reagan's two-term vice president. Although at various times he claimed to be from Texas, Connecticut, or Maine, Bush had spent most of the previous twenty years deep within the Washington establishment. Thus, he was prepared for the give and take of Washington and global politics.

The Commitment to Continuity:
A Problem Solver, Not a Visionary

Bush might have described himself as a policy conservative, but he was more than that. He was a problem solver who worked well with those with whom he disagreed.[69] His underlying political philosophy might best be summarized in this way: results are more important than ideological victory; results are the best way to achieve political success.

The tenets of **realism** (Chapter 3) come the closest to describing the general principles of Bush's foreign policy making. He essentially wanted to deal with the world as it existed and sought only those changes that would not be too unsettling for the international system as a whole. Further, his administration was much more interested in relations with the strong (such as the Soviet Union and China) than with the weak (such as the Third World). In this sense, his policy orientation came closer to the balance-of-power approach that Richard Nixon, Henry Kissinger, and Gerald Ford brought to U.S. policy than to the staunchly anticommunist ideological approach of the Reagan years or the idealism most of the Carter years. Although these earlier principles continued to hold sway, the rapid unraveling of the Cold War from 1989 to 1991 compelled the Bush administration to adopt broader values and beliefs—largely from America's past—to guide U.S. policy for the future.

Bush's personal style is another reason to assert that personal values influenced his foreign policy. Unlike Reagan, Bush was actively involved in policy making—usually with a relatively small group of advisors. According to observers, he continuously "worked the phone" to accomplish his foreign policy objectives. And because he had served around the world and had been vice president for eight years, he did indeed have a close working relationship with leaders from many nations. This personal dimension was most evident during the last half of 1990 and the early part of 1991 as Bush put together, and kept together, the anti-Iraq coalition prior to and during the Gulf War.

Critics of the Bush administration viewed the president's initial pragmatic and cautious approach as indecisive, tentative, and ad hoc. Most agreed that a design was nonexistent or, more charitably, still emerging. As Theodore Sorensen, a former Kennedy administration official, put it, the early part of the Bush administration was "all tactics, no strategy."[70] William Hyland, a former official in the Ford administration, was more supportive of the Bush's cautious and pragmatic foreign policy, saying at the time, "It is the nature of the problems, however, not the style, that has dictated this approach."[71] Other questions were raised about Bush's "hand-on" policy making and the dangers that might result from it. In his administration's decision to support the failed coup attempt in Panama in October 1989, for example, the president was apparently deeply involved in its tactics, perhaps much to his regret. By contrast, and perhaps indicative of his later style, he took a more detached approach in the Gulf War, leaving most of the tactical decisions to his military advisors. Even in this case, however, he did not stay too far away from the details and was given frequent briefings and updates.[72]

BUSH'S FOREIGN POLICY APPROACH

At the outset of his administration, President Bush called for a **"policy review**," which was centered in the National Security Council system but inevitably involved the entire foreign policy machinery. The review took almost four full months to complete and its results were mainly announced not through a single document but through a series of speeches that Bush gave in April and May 1989.[73] Although these speeches failed to reveal much in the way of foreign policy departures from the Reagan administration, they conveyed a positive approach toward working with the Soviet Union and Europe.

The Policy Review: Initial Ideas and Proposals

During his 1989 commencement address at Texas A&M University, President Bush spelled out his administration's plan for dealing with the Soviet Union and for ending the Cold War: "We are approaching the conclusion of an historic postwar struggle between two visions: one of tyranny and conflict, and one of democracy and freedom.... And now, it is time to move beyond containment to a new policy for the 1990s—one that recognizes the full scope of changes taking place around the world and in the Soviet Union itself." Thus, his administration would "seek the integration of the Soviet Union into the community of nations." To achieve that aim, Bush outlined a number of changes in Soviet foreign policy that the United States would seek:

- The Soviet Union must change some of its global commitments (such as its support for the Sandinista regime in Nicaragua and its ties with Libya).

- The Soviet Union must undertake several changes in Eastern Europe, including reducing Soviet troops there and tearing down the Iron Curtain.

- The Soviet Union must work closely with the West in addressing conflicts in Central America, southern Africa, and the Middle East.

- The Soviet Union must demonstrate a substantial commitment to political pluralism and human rights and must join with the United States in "addressing pressing global problems, including the international drug menace and dangers to the environment."

For its part, the United States would commit to completion of the **START** negotiations, move toward approval of verification procedures to permit the implementation of two signed—but unratified—treaties between the United States and the Soviet Union limiting the size of nuclear tests, and support a renewal of the **"open skies" policy** between the two nations. Further, as soon as the Soviet Union reformed its emigration laws, the United States would seek a waiver of the Jackson-Vanik Amendment to free up U.S.–Soviet trade.[74]

In another early address, President Bush was equally forthcoming with an expression of hope for a new era in Europe. Regarding Eastern Europe, for instance, he applauded the emergence of democracy in Poland and offered various forms of assistance from the United States and the international community. He also expressed hope for more changes in the region. As for Western Europe, he expressed American support for unification into a single market in 1992, for the development of new mechanisms of consultation and cooperation, and for the maintenance of U.S. military forces "as long as they are wanted and needed to preserve the peace . . ." Most important, on the occasion of the fortieth anniversary of the NATO alliance, President Bush summarized his view of a new Europe in this way: "Let Europe be whole and free. . . . The Cold War began with the division of Europe. It can only end when Europe is whole."

Juxtaposed against this proposed strategy of Soviet–American cooperation and European integration, President Bush reaffirmed the commitment to a strong national security for the 1990s largely consistent with the Reagan tradition. The United States would continue "to defend American interests in light of the enduring reality of Soviet military power." It would also seek to "curb the proliferation of advanced weaponry . . . check the aggressive ambitions of renegade regimes; and . . . enhance the ability of our friends to defend themselves." His attitude toward other areas, and particularly Third World trouble spots, was equally traditional, as revealed during the Gulf War:

> In cases where the U.S. confronts much weaker enemies, our challenge will be not simply to defeat them, but to defeat them decisively and rapidly. . . . For small countries hostile to us, bleeding our forces in protracted or indecisive conflict or embarrassing us by inflicting damage on some conspicuous element of our forces may be victory enough, and could undercut political support for U.S. efforts against them.[75]

Early Actions: A Mix of Moderation, Caution, and Realism

Unlike his bold speeches on the future of Eastern Europe and on ties with the Soviet Union or even his advice on Third World trouble spots, Bush's early policy actions mainly reflected the impulses of **pragmatism** and **moderation**, albeit occasionally mixed with political realism. U.S. policy in four major trouble spots reflected this mix and set the tone for the administration's handling of the major political changes that occurred in Central Europe in late 1989 and throughout 1990.

In two early instances, the Bush administration employed its stated pragmatism and moderation. The first involved accommodation with Congress over future support for the **Nicaraguan Contras**. Realizing that Congress was in no mood to provide further military support, the Bush administration quickly fashioned a bipartisan proposal that provided some support for the Contras, as the president wanted, and committed the United States to the ongoing Central American peace process, as Congress wanted.[76] This package called for $50 million in nonmilitary aid to the Contras, pledged the Bush administration to employing diplomatic and economic measures to pressure the Sandinistas to open up their political system, and allowed congressional involvement in suspending aid if deemed appropriate.[77]

The second instance occurred in the administration's approach to the ongoing civil war in **Cambodia**. During the summer of 1990, in a sharp break with previous policy, the United States withdrew its support from the three parties opposed to the Vietnam-supported Cambodian government and agreed to direct talks with Hanoi over Cambodia's future.[78] This strategy, formulated in cooperation with the Soviet Union, was intended to motivate all parties to accept a UN peace plan, first through an internationally supervised cease-fire and then through an internationally supervised election. Indeed, within two months, the competing factions had committed themselves to the UN framework for settling the Cambodian conflict.[79]

However, the Bush administration did not practice policy accommodations everywhere, as its actions toward **Panama** and the **People's Republic of China** demonstrated. The Panamanian government of General Manuel Antonio Noriega had been an ongoing source of annoyance and trouble for the Reagan administration and had become so for the Bush administration as well. In February 1988, Noriega, a longtime CIA operative, was indicted on drug-trafficking charges by a federal grand jury in Florida and was widely reported to be involved in numerous other unsavory international activities. Although the Reagan administration had imposed economic sanctions on Panama and had employed other economic measures as a way to force Noriega's resignation,[80] none of its efforts proved successful.

The Bush administration continued these efforts. First, when Noriega nullified Panama's national election results in May 1989, it asked the Organization of American States (OAS) to investigate. The OAS condemned the actions of the Noriega government and asked that he step down, but Noriega refused. Second, President Bush declared that Noriega's handpicked regime was illegitimate, called for the installation of the democratically elected government, and declared that its ambassador to Panama, who had been called to Washington for consultations, would not return. Earlier, Bush had sent more American forces into Panama, and, for political effect, had ordered military exercises to be conducted there. Still, all measures failed to loosen Noriega's grip. Next, the Bush administration threw lukewarm support behind a coup attempt in October 1989, but it, too, failed—within hours—much to Bush's embarrassment.[81] Finally, and as a last resort, an invasion force of 13,000 troops was ordered into Panama (adding to the 11,000 already stationed there) in December 1989. The invasion succeeded in a matter of days, and Noriega was captured and returned to the United States to stand trial for drug trafficking. In essence, the Bush administration opted for and sustained a realistic approach in its decision to intervene in this case.

President Bush showed the same reliance on political realism in his policy toward the People's Republic of China. During May and early June 1989, massive prodemocracy demonstrations calling for political reforms occurred in Beijing and other Chinese cities. The government tolerated them for a time, but finally decided to put them down in a violent and bloody assault on demonstrators in Beijing's Tiananmen Square. Hundreds, and perhaps thousands, of demonstrators were killed.[82]

The Bush administration initially condemned the Chinese use of such force as a violation of human rights and threw its support behind the democracy movement. It immediately imposed a series of economic sanctions through an executive order; stopped arms sales; suspended visits between U.S. and Chinese military officials; offered humanitarian and medical assistance to those injured in the military crackdown; and instructed the U.S. immigration service to be sympathetic to Chinese students in the United States wishing to extend their stay. Yet Bush wanted to maintain ties with China, even in the context of continuing repression: "I understand the importance of the relationship with the Chinese people and the Government; it is in the interest of the United States to have good relations."[83] Indeed, the administration vetoed legislation that would have allowed Chinese students to stay in the United States after their visas had expired, and it authorized high U.S. government officials to meet with Chinese officials even though a ban on such meetings was in effect.

POLITICAL CHANGE AND EASTERN EUROPE

Nicaragua, Cambodia, Panama, and China demonstrate the mixture of moderation and realism the Bush administration practiced toward regional trouble spots. However, the imminent changes in Eastern Europe and within the Soviet Union were to pose its greatest challenge. In large measure, the Bush administration pursued the same policy mix, even as the Soviet Empire and the Soviet Union itself unraveled. Moderate and pragmatic responses, occasionally infused with doses of political realism, were still the governing principles.

The events of 1989 and 1990 can only be described as monumental in the way they shook the foundations of U.S. foreign policy. In the space of less than two years, the Soviet Empire collapsed, with most of the states of Eastern Europe moving from socialism to capitalism and from communism to democracy; the future of a divided Germany was resolved through reunification at the end of 1990; and, by the end of 1991, the Soviet Union itself had dissolved. In effect, these events seemingly resolved the central issues of the Cold War—a divided Europe and Soviet–American antagonism.

The Collapse of the Soviet Empire

The initial changes within Eastern Europe began in Poland in early 1989.[84] Although *Solidarity*, the banned Polish trade union movement, had operated for many years, its success in gaining legal status by April 1989 set in rapid motion many democratic reforms. By June 1989, Solidarity or the candidates it backed had won all of the available seats in the lower house of the Polish parliament, and 99 out of 100 seats in the upper house in free elections. By August 1989, a Solidarity member had been chosen as the first noncommunist prime minister in an Eastern European state since the end of World War II. In November 1990, the founder of the Solidarity movement, **Lech Walesa**, was elected president.

Hungary and Czechoslovakia followed a similar pattern. In January 1989, the Hungarian parliament took the first steps toward guaranteeing individual liberties, and, in October 1989, it adopted a number of sweeping democratic reforms. Parliamentary elections were held in March and April of 1990, with democratic parties and their coalition partners capturing most of the seats. The switch to democracy in Czechoslovakia was even more rapid and equally nonviolent. The first popular demonstrations for democracy occurred later (November 1989) than elsewhere, but democratic change occurred quickly once started. By early December, **Vaclav Havel**, playwright and leader of the reform movement, was named president. By June 1990, free and democratic parliamentary elections were held in Czechoslovakia with democratic reform candidates faring very well.

In East Germany, pressures for democratic reform had begun in August 1989, when East Germans began fleeing to West Germany, using Hungary, Czechoslovakia, and Austria as access routes or seeking asylum in the West German embassy in Czechoslovakia. By October 1989, the number of East German refugees numbered almost 11,000. Popular demonstrations followed, and by March 1990, free and democratic elections were held in East Germany, with the conservative Alliance for Germany obtaining the greatest percentage of votes.

Nascent democratic movements occurred in other Eastern European states, but their success was slower and generally much less complete. Dissidents in Bulgaria, Romania, Yugoslavia, and Albania called for change, but democratic reform was less assured in each case. Elections in Bulgaria, Romania, and Albania produced regimes that grew out of the still remaining Communist parties or that were closely allied with them. In the former Yugoslavia, a series of successor states emerged, but the degree of democratic reform was less immediately certain. Instead, intercommunal violence developed among the religious and ethnic groups within some of these new states (such as Bosnia) and between others (such as Serbia and Croatia).

The Reunification of Germany

The reunification of Germany was the second major Eastern European event of 1989–1990 and the one most directly related to the ending of the Cold War. Having been intentionally divided by the victorious allies at the Yalta Conference in February 1945, and having existed as two separate states since 1949, Germany was formally reunited on **October 3, 1990**.[85] If the pace of events elsewhere in Eastern Europe during the previous two years was surprisingly rapid, both the ease and speed of this reunification—from mid-1989 through the end of 1990—were, by any assessment, spectacular. The pressures for reunification began with the massive East German emigration to the West in August 1989, but the opening of the **Berlin Wall**—the most tangible symbol of a divided city in a divided nation—on **November 9, 1989**, ignited even more calls for political reunification.

Despite Soviet President Gorbachev's contention on November 15, 1989, that German unification "is not a matter of topical politics,"[86] later that month, West German Chancellor Helmut Kohl proposed a "confederation" of the two Germanys. The major wartime Allies—the United States, France, Britain, and the USSR—still retained rights over the future of Germany and, in particular, Berlin. However, this obstacle was quickly overcome at a February 1990 meeting of the foreign ministers from the Allied countries and from East and West Germany, where a reunification formula was agreed on. These so-called Four Plus Two talks called for the two Germanys to discuss plans for reunification and then to meet with the four Allied powers to resolve remaining security matters.

By May 1990, East and West Germany had worked out the terms for reunification, with existing borders agreed to. An economic union was initiated on July 1,

1990; a treaty setting out the legal and social bases of the new union was signed on August 31, 1990; a formal treaty among the Allied powers renouncing their rights and powers over German affairs was completed on September 12, 1990[87]; and formal reunification as the Federal Republic of Germany took place on October 3, 1990.[88] Finally, democratic parliamentary elections across a unified Germany were held in December 1990.

The Collapse of the Soviet Union

The Soviet Union itself was not immune to the changes that were sweeping Eastern Europe. Although not as rapid in 1989 and 1990 as they were elsewhere in Eastern Europe, change quickened by 1991, eventually producing the demise of the state itself. Initial reform efforts were largely within the limits of maintaining a modified socialist system. In August 1991, however, the Soviet Union received a dramatic jolt when a coup by Soviet hardliners against the earlier reforms failed after three days. Internal change accelerated, and there were now calls for greater regional autonomy and greater democratization. The future of the Soviet Union appeared in doubt. By late 1991, moreover, the Baltic republics had achieved independence, and a looser confederation had emerged among the other Soviet republics.

In December 1991, the Soviet Union itself collapsed, and the new nations that replaced it would challenge long-held American attitudes regarding foreign policy. In order for the significance of the changes in Europe to be appreciated, the events of 1989–1991 require a more detailed explanation.

Prior to the **August 1991 coup**, changes of two kinds occurred in the Soviet Union: (1) efforts were made to institutionalize democratic political reforms and Western-style market reforms; and (2) pressure for greater autonomy and even independence was placed on Moscow by some of the constituent republics. Indeed, democratic political reforms were essential to Gorbachev's implementation of *glasnost* and *perestroika*, his mechanism for making the country more efficient and more globally competitive (see earlier in this chapter). In March 1989, for example, in the freest election since the Revolution of 1917, voting was held for seats in the new legislative body, the Congress of People's Deputies.[89] Later that year, an effort was even made to eliminate the "leading role" of the Communist party.[90]

Market reform progressed more slowly. By the second half of 1990, a plan for a 500-day transition to a market economy was developed, but it was shelved, along with less dramatic versions of it, by the end of the year. During the last months of 1990 and early 1991, moreover, Gorbachev moved toward slowing down and even halting the political and economic liberalizations that he had initiated. Many of the internal reforms within the Soviet Union appeared stalled by the middle of 1991, and economic conditions worsened.

Equally dramatic were the demands for independence by several of the Soviet Union's constituent republics. The three Baltic states of Latvia, Lithuania, and Estonia took the boldest steps in this regard by declaring their independence or eventual independence from the central government in Moscow. In addition, Georgia and Armenia, among others, and even the largest Soviet republic, Russia, sought greater independence.

One day prior to the signing of the proposed union treaty among the Soviet republics giving them greater power, a group of hardline Communist party members and government officials (the "State Committee for the State of Emergency") deposed Gorbachev and briefly seized power. This "three-day coup" (August 18–21, 1991) collapsed for three reasons: (1) massive protests in Moscow led by the popularly elected president of the Russian Republic, Boris Yeltsin; (2) the apparent failure of the KGB to attack the protestors surrounding the Russian parliament; and (3) virtually unified international condemnation. On his return to power, Gorbachev called the failure of the coup "a majority victory for perestroika" and pledged "to move ahead democratically in all areas."[91]

Ironically, though, the coup attempt had the effect of pressuring for more fundamental reform, further weakening the central government. With his power effectively curtailed in this new environment, Gorbachev felt compelled to step down as general secretary of the Communist party. Indeed, he called for a disbanding of the party itself because of its role in the coup. Furthermore, he consulted with Yeltsin over the appointment of a number of key political offices and named several key officials from the Russian republic to leadership posts in the central government.

Increased demands for independence by the constituent republics raised doubts about the future of a unified Soviet Union. Within weeks of the coup, in fact, Lithuania, Latvia, and Estonia finally obtained full independence, and a new transitional confederative arrangement was devised between the central government and most of the other republics. Eventually, a new constitution would be formulated, giving the constituent republics more policy control.[92]

As with political change in Eastern Europe, reform within the Soviet Union took on a life of its own, and it was aided, ironically, by the coup that sought to topple those reform efforts. Pressure for formal dissolution was rapidly building and, on **December 25, 1991**, the Union of Soviet Socialist Republics was officially dead, some seventy-four years after the Bolshevik Revolution had brought it to life.

AFTER THE COLD WAR: BUSH'S POLICY TOWARD CENTRAL EUROPE

Throughout this period in Central Europe and the Soviet Union, the Bush administration was largely an **interested spectator**, not an active participant. Its policy was to encourage change without trying to shape it directly. The administration was also careful to avoid any actions that would embarrass the Soviet or Eastern European governments. Similarly, the United States refrained from any actions that might appear as gloating over the extraordinary movement to democracy and capitalism in these countries. In short, Bush's pragmatism and caution remained intact, even in a context of dynamic and dramatic global change.

Perhaps indicative of the caution practiced by the United States was President Bush's restrained reaction on the day that the Berlin Wall was opened between East and West—undoubtedly one of the most dramatic moments in recent political history. Although he claimed to be "elated" by the development, he justified his reserve by saying, "I'm just not an emotional kind of guy" and "We're handling this properly with the allies. . . ." Another administration official acknowledged the largely rhetorical nature of U.S. policy and argued for the measured American reaction to changing events: "I admit that when all is said and done it is a policy largely of stated desires and rhetoric. But what would you have us do? What we are dealing with in Eastern Europe, and to a lesser extent in the Soviet Union, is a revolutionary situation."[93]

Once revolutionary change was well under way, however, the Bush administration did outline some tangible policies regarding Central Europe, the reunification of Germany, and future relations with the Soviet Union. Toward Central Europe, the principal response was to provide some economic assistance to the new democracies and to encourage other European states (particularly the European Community) to do so as well. The funds would aid efforts to stabilize their economies; foster private enterprise; provide food aid, trade credits, and environmental funds; and support agricultural programs, technical training, and scholarship and educational exchanges with the United States.[94]

Concerning the future of Germany, the Bush administration added some realist elements to its accommodative stance, especially after the collapse of the Berlin Wall in November 1989. As early as December 1989, the administration adopted the view that German reunification should proceed, that Germany's full sovereignty should be restored, and that other states (including the United States) would necessarily lose some of their rights over German territory. Later, it also made clear that the United States would accept only a reunified Germany that remained a full member of NATO.[95] This policy position proved significant in bringing about reunification. In this respect, the Bush administration was clear on its view of Germany's future and the kind of Central Europe that it wanted to see.

AFTER THE COLD WAR: BUSH'S POLICY TOWARD THE SOVIET UNION

Toward the Soviet Union prior to its implosion, administration policy had been cautiously optimistic, albeit not fully developed. Its goal was first to formally end the Cold War and then to establish the foundation for long-term cooperation In 1989 and 1990, two major summits were held at which important agreements were signed to reach the first goal and several agreements and understandings on political, military, and economic cooperation were initiated to reach the second. The **Malta Summit**, held in November 1989, proved to be a watershed in ending the Cold War between the United States and the Soviet Union. As President Gorbachev said at Malta, "The world leaves one epoch of cold war and enters another epoch" and "the characteristics of the cold war should be abandoned."[96]

It was at Malta that the Bush administration and the Soviet leadership committed themselves to rapid progress on nuclear and conventional arms control. The administration also threw its support behind Soviet internal reforms and pledged to assist the Soviets in joining the world economy.[97] In a matter of months, the Soviet Union gained observer status in the General Agreement on Tariffs and Trade (GATT).[98]

If the Malta Summit set the tone for the end of the Cold War and for future relations, the June 1990 **Washington Summit** took several concrete steps to solidify the new U.S.–Soviet relationship. Agreements were signed (1) calling for the destruction of a substantial portion of each nation's chemical arsenal by the year 2002, (2) pledging both parties to accelerate negotiations on the Strategic Arms Reduction Treaty (START) and the Conventional (that is, nonnuclear) Armed Forces in Europe (CFE) Treaty, and (3) initiating several cultural exchange pacts.[99]

Toward the end of 1990, the Bush administration made three other important commitments that served as the capstone for the end of the Cold War in Central Europe and set the stage for European politics for the 1990s and beyond.[100] First, at the **Conference on Security and Cooperation in Europe (CSCE)** in November 1990, the United States and its NATO allies and the Soviet Union and its Warsaw Pact allies signed the **Conventional Armed Forces in Europe (CFE) Treaty**, which provided for a substantial reduction in conventional forces on both sides. Second, the two sides signed a declaration of nonaggression that officially ended the Cold War. Third, the parties to the CSCE (which includes the United States, Canada, and virtually all European states) signed an agreement to give the CSCE a greater role in European affairs.

Yet another sign of the importance that the Bush administration attached to its new relationship with the Soviet Union was signaled with its attitude and policy toward the Soviet effort to dissuade the Baltic Republics (Lithuania, Latvia, and Estonia) from pursuing independence in the spring of 1990 and the winter of 1991. In two instances, the Gorbachev government used economic sanctions and Soviet troops against them. The Bush administration decried these actions, but it did little more. In effect, the administration's commitment to political realism and good relations with the Soviet Union was more important than supporting Soviet constituent republics in their fight for independence.

In July 1991, the Bush administration took two additional policy steps—one military, another economic—as part of its effort to maintain good U.S.–Soviet relations. In the military area, President Bush and President Gorbachev met after the London economic summit of leaders of the industrial democracies (the United States, France, Britain, Canada, Germany, Italy, Japan, and the European Community) to complete work in principle on START.[101] (The agreement was formally signed about two weeks later at a hastily arranged summit in Moscow.) Under this agreement, the first in which the long-range nuclear arsenals of the two superpowers would actually be reduced, each side would decrease its nuclear warheads to 6,000 and nuclear delivery vehicles (land-based and sea-based missiles and intercontinental bombers) to 1,600. This treaty would be implemented over a seven-year period and would last for fifteen years. It also called for exchange of information between the parties on all strategic offensive weapons, twelve types of on-site inspections, and several types of cooperative procedures to ensure verification of the agreement.[102] In the economic area, another agreement called for the industrial democracies to provide economic assistance for the Soviet Union. Although financial aid would not be immediate, several measures were instituted to aid Soviet economic reform already under way, including

- "Special association" status with the International Monetary Fund and the World Bank
- Cooperation with all international economic institutions
- Restoration of trade between the Soviet Union and its Central European neighbors
- Closer contacts with leaders of the industrial democracies[103]

These actions may not have gone as far as the Soviet Union had initially hoped, but they represented an extraordinary change in its economic relationships among the United States, the West, and the Soviet Union.

In the aftermath of the August coup in the Soviet Union and with the movement to a more confederate state in late 1991, the Bush administration faced calls to initiate new and wider economic and political ties with the constituent republics and the newly independent Baltic states. Diplomatic recognition for Lithuania, Latvia, and Estonia proceeded, albeit after it was granted by several European states and the European Community,[104] and the administration promised to supply humanitarian aid as needed—that is, to the constituent republics, not the central government of the Soviet Union.[105] Yet there were limits as to how far it would go in providing massive economic assistance. In general, the Bush administration did not deviate from its policy, announced after the London summit, that in effect withheld economic aid until significant and sustained policy reforms were carried out.

THE SEARCH FOR A NEW WORLD ORDER?

With the international politics of the post–World War II period forever altered by the collapse of the Soviet Empire and the Soviet Union, the Bush administration now sought to devise a new rationale and direction for U.S. foreign policy. Change was first hinted at in an address that President Bush gave to the UN General Assembly in September 1989, but it was more fully outlined in speeches to a joint session of Congress in September 1990 and in the State of the Union address in January 1991, after Iraq's invasion of Kuwait.[106] That future direction, President Bush said, was to build **"a new world order."**[107]

Bush described the new world order as "a new era—freer from the threat of terror, stronger in the pursuit of justice, and more secure in the quest for peace, an era in which the nations of the world, East and West, North and South, can prosper and live in harmony." Such a world would be different from the one that had existed over the past forty-five years. It would be "a world where the rule of law supplants the rule of the jungle, a world in which nations recognize the shared responsibility for freedom and justice, a world where the strong respect the rights of the weak."[108] In his State of the Union address, Bush summarized this new world order as one in which "diverse nations are drawn together in common cause to achieve the universal aspirations of mankind: peace and security, freedom, and the rule of law."[109]

The president was quick to add, however, that the United States had a special role to play in creating this new world:

> For two centuries, America has served the world as an inspiring example of freedom and democracy. For generations, America has led the struggle to preserve and extend the blessings of liberty.... American leadership is indispensable.... We have a unique responsibility to the hard work of freedom.[110]

Thus, Bush's new world order, in effect, represented a reaffirmation of the values that had shaped the birth of the nation and its foreign policy actions in its earliest years (see Chapter 1). Unlike the foreign policy at the beginning of the republic, however, this emphasis was coupled with a commitment to sustained American involvement. In both tone and emphasis, moreover, the new world order of the Bush administration had the ring of **Wilsonian idealism**, which emphasized the League of Nations and collective security at the end of World War I. With the demise of the old order—that of the Cold War—the new order was grounded in the cooperation of all states and based on greater UN involvement. To be sure, Bush did not convey Wilson's fervor, and he continued to embrace political realism from time to time. Nonetheless, he did see his approach as an important departure from America's Cold War behavior.

Bush's new world order faced at least three major challenges: the Iraqi invasion of Kuwait, U.S. policy toward a post-Communist Russia, and the global disorder in Bosnia, Somalia, and Haiti.

The Persian Gulf War

The event that contributed to the idea of a new world order was Iraqi president Saddam Hussein's invasion of **Kuwait** on August 2, 1990. This action raised the question of whether the initial cooperation between the United States and the (then) Soviet Union could be sustained in a different arena and whether the global community could rally around a common emergency. As events were to unfold, this first challenge succeeded: Soviet–American cooperation held up, the global community was largely supportive of the war effort, and aggression was reversed.

In some respects, the vigorous response of the Bush administration to Iraq's action may have been unexpected. On the one hand, the Reagan administration had sought better relations with Iraq during the 1980s: diplomatic relations were restored in 1984 after having being ruptured in 1967, and the United States had "tilted" toward Iraq during the **Iran–Iraq War** from 1980 to 1988. On the other hand, Reagan had had his quarrels with Iraq: he had been displeased over Iraq's apparently mistaken attack on the **USS** *Stark* in the Persian Gulf in May 1987, resulting in the death of thirty-seven American sailors, and he had protested Iraq's use of chemical weapons against its Kurdish ethnic minority in 1988.[111]

In keeping with its realist principles, however, the Bush administration decided early on to try for better relations with Saddam Hussein for both strategic and economic reasons. Iraq's location in the Persian Gulf area was important to achieving stability in the region (see Map 4.2), and its considerable oil reserves made it crucial in global energy concerns. When Congress sought in early 1990 to enact economic sanctions against the Iraqi government over its abysmal human rights policy and its apparent effort to develop weapons of mass destruction, the administration argued against such an option.[112] In the summer of 1990, when Iraq complained that Kuwait was responsible for keeping oil prices low (and hence hurting the Iraqi economy) by overproducing its oil quota, called for an OPEC meeting to raise oil prices, and threatened an invasion, the Bush administration's policy did not really change. Furthermore, in testimony on Capitol Hill only days before the U.S. intervention, the administration issued no warning when asked whether it was considering an Iraqi invasion of Kuwait.[113]

Despite the administration's equivocation in the summer of 1990, its response to the Iraqi invasion was immediate condemnation. It demanded Iraq's withdrawal, froze all Iraqi and Kuwaiti assets in the United States, and imposed a trade embargo. The European Community and the Arab League condemned the invasion as well. Most important, the Soviet Union joined the United States in signing a joint statement issued by Secretary of State James Baker and Soviet Foreign Minister Eduard Shevardnadze.[114] A few weeks later, Bush and Gorbachev met in Helsinki, Finland, to deal with this crisis, jointly stating that "Iraq's aggression must not be tolerated."[115] Within a few weeks, about one hundred nations had condemned the invasion.

On August 8, 1990, the Bush administration announced that it was sending about 150,000 American forces into Saudi Arabia and the surrounding region to help the Saudis defend themselves against possible Iraqi aggression. President Bush outlined four policy goals that the United States sought to achieve in taking this action against Iraq:

- The "immediate, unconditional, and complete withdrawal of all Iraqi forces from Kuwait"
- The "restoration of Kuwait's legitimate government"
- The protection of American citizens in Iraq and Kuwait
- The achievement of "security and stability" in the Persian Gulf[116]

Two days later, the Arab League also voted to send forces to Saudi Arabia,[117] and within a matter of weeks, at least twenty-eight nations from virtually every continent

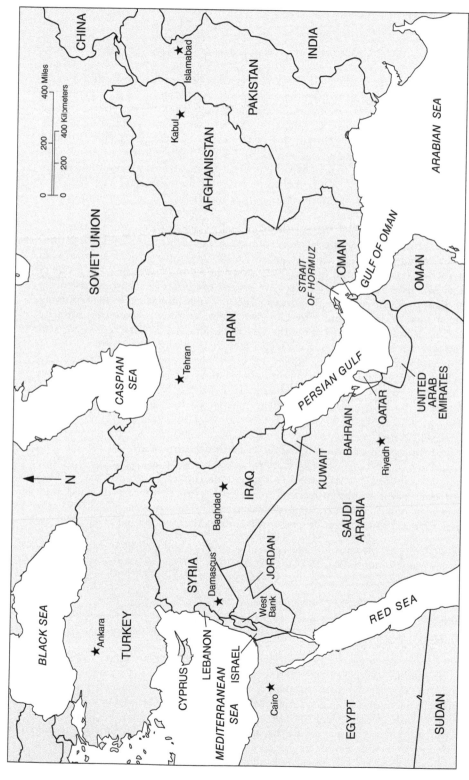

MAP 4.2 The Persian Gulf and Southwest Asia

had sent forces there. Other nations (such as Germany and Japan) pledged financial assistance.[118]

The UN Security Council also took concerted action within hours of the invasion, condemning it and demanding Iraq's immediate withdrawal. In all, it passed ten resolutions over the next several months to tighten the economic and political noose around Iraq to force it to leave Kuwait. It imposed mandatory economic sanctions, invalidated Iraq's annexation of Kuwait, and condemned its holding of foreign nationals and diplomats. The UN resolutions also expanded the trade embargo to include sea and air as well. What was remarkable about these actions was not only their rapidity but also the unanimity among the Security Council's permanent members (the United States, the Soviet Union, Britain, China, and France), a phenomenon rarely evident during the Cold War years.

On November 29, 1990, the Security Council passed its most significant resolution, authorizing member states "to use all necessary means to uphold and implement" its earlier resolutions unless Iraq left Kuwait by January 15, 1991.[119] This in effect authorized the use of force; it was only the second time the UN Security Council had authorized collective security action (the other was its response to the North Korean invasion of South Korea in 1950). When Iraq failed to leave Kuwait by the January 15 deadline and after Congress had given the president the authority to use American forces to implement the UN resolution, the anti-Iraq coalition, now totaling over a half million troops, initiated a massive bombing attack.

The attack initially failed to budge the Iraqis. However, in mid-February, Iraq agreed to withdraw, albeit with conditions. The anti-Iraq coalition rejected that plan and imposed a twenty-four-hour ultimatum on February 22, 1991, for the Iraqis to begin pulling out. When the deadline passed unanswered, the allied coalition mounted a massive ground, air, and sea assault. On February 27, 1991, President Bush declared, "Kuwait is liberated" and announced the suspension of hostilities beginning at midnight on February 28, officially ending the **Hundred Hours War**.

On March 3, 1991, the Security Council passed a resolution ending the hostilities and placing responsibility with the Iraqis for the invasion; on the same day, military commanders met in southern Iraq to formalize the terms of the cease-fire and work out arrangements for the exchange of prisoners.[120] Finally, on April 3, 1991, the Security Council passed a resolution formally ending the war and requiring Iraq

- To destroy all of its chemical and biological weapons and ballistic missile systems with a range of more than 150 kilometers
- To pay reparations to Kuwait
- To abandon its support for international terrorism
- Not to "acquire or develop nuclear weapons"
- To respect the sovereignty of Kuwait[121]

Ensuring a lasting peace ultimately proved more difficult than winning a short war. Almost immediately after the coalition victory, rebellions broke out in the north and south of Iraq.[122] In the north, the Kurds, an ethnic minority, rebelled against the Iraqi government but failed. In the south, the Shiites, a religious Muslim majority, rebelled, but failed as well. The victors, particularly the United States and NATO forces, imposed "no-fly zones" in the north and south of Iraq to ensure the safety of the Kurds and the Shiites. They also sent UN inspectors to investigate Iraq's alleged production of nuclear materials, albeit with limited success (as succeeding American administrations would discover).

Despite these problems, the Gulf War, in essence the first test of creating a new world order, produced a unified international coalition that freed Kuwait from Iraqi intervention quickly and served as an important symbol of how international disorder might be addressed in the future.

Relations with a Post-Communist Russia

A second test of the new order was the devising of appropriate **policies toward Russia** and the other successor states of the old Soviet Union. In keeping with the instincts of the Bush administration, these policies were cautionary and pragmatic economically, politically, and militarily, but significant commitments were made. By April 1992, the administration had decided on a greater commitment to economic assistance to Russia and Ukraine, prodded on by its **Group of Seven (G-7)** partners, and by the end of its term another dramatic nuclear arms reduction agreement with Russia, the **START II Treaty**, had been completed.

On the diplomatic front, the Bush administration moved quickly to establish diplomatic ties with the new republics and to foster closer ties with Russian president Boris Yeltsin. In February 1992, Bush and Yeltsin held discussions at Camp David on aid and nuclear arms, and in February 1992 Secretary of State James Baker visited Moldova, Armenia, Azerbaijan, Tajikistan, and Uzbekistan to begin normalization of relations with these new republics.[123] The highlight of these diplomatic efforts was the June 16–17, 1992, summit conference between Bush and Yeltsin in Washington, which laid the groundwork for a further reduction in nuclear weapons (what was to become the START II Treaty), enabled President Yeltsin to deliver a request to Congress for American assistance for Russia, and allowed for the development of various bilateral agreements dealing with cooperation in outer space, curbs on weapons of mass destruction, and American business activities in Russia.[124]

In the military area, two important actions were completed in 1992 and early 1993. In May 1992, a protocol to the START treaty was signed in Lisbon, Portugal, to recognize that the Soviet Union, as the original signatory of the treaty, had been dissolved and that the new republics were to be incorporated into the pact.[125] After the June summit, final negotiations on START II were also completed (although they took longer than perhaps anticipated), with the final document officially signed on January 3, 1993, about two weeks before President Bush left office. Under START II, the United States and Russia would reduce the number of their strategic nuclear warheads by at least 3,500 in two phases by 2003.[126] In addition, all multiple (or MIRVed) warheads on land-based missiles would be eliminated, warheads on either country's "heavy" (or largest) land-based missiles prohibited, and the total number of "strategic nuclear delivery vehicles" (or launchers) maintained at 1,600. In an important stipulation, START had to be fully implemented before START II could come into effect.

There was progress as well in the economic area. In 1991 and early 1992, President Bush had been criticized for his failure to be more responsive to Soviet (and then Russian) requests for assistance.[127] Undoubtedly prodded in part by that criticism, Bush announced on April 1, 1992, that the United States would participate in a $24 billion Russian aid program developed by the G-7. The plan was characterized "as a way for the United States and its allies to prevent economic collapse in Russia and thus prevent the rise of a new authoritarianism out of the rubble of the Soviet empire."[128] It was eventually written into law with the passage of the **Freedom Support Act** in October 1992, by which the United States committed itself to provide $410 million in aid, authorized a $12.3 billion increase in its support of the International Monetary Fund to aid Russia and the other former Soviet republics, supported a $3 billion multilateral effort to stabilize the Russian currency, and offered various ways of increasing American cooperation and support. A unique feature of the act authorized $800 million from the U.S. defense budget to help the former Soviet republics dismantle nuclear weapons and other weapons of mass destruction.[129] In sum, the Freedom Support Act reflected how far economic and political cooperation between the former Soviet Union and the United States had progressed in less than a year.

New Global Disorders: Bosnia, Haiti, and Somalia

The third major test for the new world order was the American policy response toward new global disorders. Three problems captured the attention of the Bush administration and epitomized the difficulty confronting American foreign policy after the Cold War: the **outbreak of ethnic fighting in Bosnia**, the **overthrow of democracy in Haiti**, and the **starvation in Somalia**. The response was different in each case, and as a result, no clear direction appeared in U.S. foreign policy. This raised questions about the role of the United States in the new world order.

Bosnia Ethnic fighting in the former Yugoslavia erupted quickly after the end of the Cold War. (See Map 4.3 for new countries created from the former Yugoslavia.) With the declaration of independence by several of its constituent populations (such as Slovenia, Croatia, and Bosnia-Herzogovina in 1991 and 1992) and the determination of Serbia to maintain control of the former Yugoslav government and much of its territory, fighting among the ethnic and religious factions within Croatia and Bosnia quickly broke out. By early 1992, an uneasy truce was in place in Croatia, but by April 1992, an ethnic war erupted in Bosnia that would become the focus of American administrations for the next several years. The fighting was among three major groups: Bosnian Serbs, Bosnian Muslims, and Bosnian Croats. There was also fighting between the Serbian government and the newly created Bosnian government, with the former seeking to extend greater Serbia and the latter seeking to maintain its independence.

The initial impulse of the Bush administration was to hold Yugoslavia together. It was reluctant to grant diplomatic recognition to the newly independent states and instead sought a negotiated outcome. As acting Secretary of State Lawrence Eagleburger said, "The [Yugoslav] republics' unilateral and uncoordinated declarations of independence, which we unsuccessfully opposed, led inexorably to civil war."[130] The preferred policy was to have the parties negotiate a settlement with help from the Europeans (through the European Union, for example) and the United Nations. Although the United States eventually supported UN sanctions on Yugoslavia and the imposition of a NATO-run "no-fly zone" over Bosnia to stop the fighting, it was unwilling to do much more. Indeed, Secretary of State Baker declared, "we don't have a dog in that fight." With that assessment, the United States would limit its help in restoring peace and stability in the new era.[131]

Haiti In Haiti, the Bush administration faced another kind of post–Cold War problem: the promotion and maintenance of democracy. Here, it adopted a somewhat different response. In September 1991, the democratically elected government of President **Jean-Bertrand Aristide** was overthrown in a military-led coup.[132] The United States was committed to Aristide's restoration, but the Bush administration

MAP 4.3 The Former Yugoslavia

primarily limited its response to diplomatic and economic measures—for example, cutting off economic assistance and freezing Haitian government assets in the United States. In turn, it joined in a trade embargo against Haiti enacted by the OAS. Despite these and other efforts, no progress was made in restoring democracy, and the Bush administration once again was disinclined to do more.

By early 1992, another and more complicating problem arose. Haitian refugees hoping to flee Haiti's failing economy and brutal regime took to a variety of boats and vessels and headed for America seeking asylum. Despite its other efforts to help the Haitians, the Bush administration ultimately ordered the U.S. Coast Guard to stop the vessels and return their passengers to Haiti. By the end of the Bush administration, democracy had not been restored and the refugees had become a presidential campaign issue. The United States and the Bush administration were clearly limiting their actions in promoting and maintaining democracy after the Cold War.

Somalia   The unrest in Somalia raised a third type of post–Cold War issue for the United States and a third type of response.[133] With the breakdown of the Somali government, starvation was running rampant by 1992, with estimates of death by starvation ranging up to 350,000. Moreover, rival "clans" were systematically hijacking relief convoys, defeating the efforts of international aid providers, so that several cities and outlying villages simply were not receiving food aid. In July 1992, the United Nations authorized the sending of UN peacekeepers to Somalia and the use of American military transport aircraft to aid the relief efforts. However, the situation continued to deteriorate.

By early December 1992, the UN Security Council passed a resolution authorizing the United States to lead a humanitarian assistance mission to Somalia. In an action dubbed "**Operation Restore Hope**," the Bush administration decided to intervene militarily, dispatching 28,000 American troops to make certain that humanitarian assistance reached the neediest people. Although this mission was carefully limited to providing food assistance and was successful initially, the Clinton administration would later expand it, and problems would develop.

CHALLENGES AND RESPONSES
TO THE NEW WORLD ORDER

Somalia evoked a markedly different reaction by the Bush administration to global disorders than had occurred in Bosnia and Haiti. Was Somalia, then, the emerging model for establishing a new global order, or was the Bush administration's basic pragmatism operating in all of these instances after the Cold War? To many critics, of course, the answer was the latter. Instead of a coherent post–Cold War foreign policy, an ad hoc foreign policy was in place. Former acting Secretary of State Eagleburger, as he was leaving office, defended the Bush administration's efforts.[134] Indeed, he argued that the administration had done much more than it was credited with in pointing the way to a future course. Moreover, he argued that the administration's alleged "ad hocism" in foreign policy was "a virtue, not a vice."

In particular, Eagleburger contended that the administration had successfully met three challenges. It had ended the Cold War peacefully by dealing successfully with several major crises—from the democratic revolution in Eastern Europe to the reunification of Germany to the collapse of the Soviet Union. It had dealt with the "instabilities generated by the Cold War's demise" (such as the Persian Gulf War and Yugoslavia), and, something critics overlooked, it had started the process of reform in global institutions, paving the way for the future. In particular, Eagleburger had in mind the development of the North American Free Trade Agreement (**NAFTA**), which created a trade organization consisting of the United States, Canada, and Mexico; the creation of the **Group of 24** (G-24) developed countries to aid Central and Eastern Europe; and the emergence of Asia-Pacific Economic Cooperation (**APEC**), an organization of eighteen nations initially stretching across the Pacific from China and Japan to Australia and New Zealand and to the United States and Canada. In the future, these largely economic organizations would be pivotal. In short, Eagleburger argued, "There was a strategy behind the President's conduct of foreign policy" and "a certain degree of 'ad hocery' is a virtue, not a vice, when you are dealing with a world in crisis and chaos. . . ."

CONCLUDING COMMENTS

The Reagan and George H. W. Bush administrations took different approaches to American foreign policy as the Cold War was changing and winding down. President Reagan sought less to impose new values to the direction of his foreign policy and more to restore earlier values, epitomized by the Cold War consensus. That is, his administration restored the moral emphasis with a focus on communism (in contrast to his predecessor) and sought to restore an American globalism reminiscent of an earlier era. Indeed, the Reagan administration largely succeeded in its effort by restoring the Soviet Union to its place at the center of American foreign policy, challenging the Soviets worldwide, and attempting to rally the nations of the noncommunist world against Soviet expansionism. During its second term, however, the administration moved from confrontation to accommodation, notably completing the first nuclear arms reduction treaty (INF) in history. Toward the rest of the world, however, it continued its staunch anti-Communist policy with a more mixed result.

George H. W. Bush continued the basic foreign policy approach of the Reagan administration's second term, albeit a policy infused with pragmatism and prudence. Nevertheless, global conditions were changing, and within a year of the end of the new administration the Cold War had begun to unravel, posing new challenges to the values and direction of American foreign policy. The Bush administration sought to deal with these changed global conditions by seeking to create a new world order based on traditional American values but also within the limits of political realism. Such an approach brought out critics who claimed the approach was ad hoc. The new administration of William Clinton, elected in November 1992, committed to change that approach.

In the next chapter, we examine that administration's new approach to foreign policy after the end of the Cold War and the changed approach yet again of the George W. Bush administration after the events of September 11.

Notes

1. "Transcript of President's First News Conference on Foreign and Domestic Topics," *New York Times*, January 30, 1981, A10.

2. "Excerpts from President's Speech to National Association of Evangelicals," *New York Times*, March 9, 1983, A18.

3. Carter, "Humane Purposes in Foreign Policy," Department of State News Release, May 22, 1977 (from Carter's commencement address at the University of Notre Dame), p. 1.

4. See, for example, Robert E. Osgood, "The Revitalization of Containment," William P. Bundy, ed., *America and the World 1981* (New York: Pergamon Press, 1982), pp. 465–502.

5. One American diplomat was quoted as saying, "Aside from opposing the Soviets, we don't really have a foreign policy." See Hedrick Smith, "Discordant Voices," *New York Times*, March 20, 1981, A2.

6. See, for example, the following statements by Alexander Haig issued by the Department of State: "A New Direction in U.S. Foreign Policy" (April 14, 1981); "Relationship of Foreign and Defense Policies" (July 30, 1981); and "A Strategic Approach to American Foreign Policy" (August 11, 1981). The four items here are quoted from "A Strategic Approach to American Foreign Policy" at p. 2, which we rely on for our subsequent analysis.

7. Ibid. Later section subtitles are from these pillars.

8. On these plans, see, for example, *Congressional Quarterly Almanac 1981* (Washington, DC: Congressional Quarterly, 1982), pp. 240–241; and Stephen Webbe, "Defense: Reagan Plans Largest U.S. Military Buildup Since Vietnam. . . ." *Christian Science Monitor*, May 1, 1981, 8–9. The latter article puts the buildup at $1.5 trillion.

9. Alexander Haig, "Arms Control and Strategic Nuclear Forces" (Washington, DC: Bureau of Public Affairs, Department of State, November 4, 1981). The elements of strategic modernization are drawn from that statement.

10. Ronald Reagan, "Peace and Security," televised address to the nation, March 23, 1983, reprinted in *Realism, Strength, Negotiation: Key Foreign Policy Statements of the Reagan Administration* (Washington, DC: Department of State, May 1984), p. 43.

11. See William P. Bundy, "A Portentous Year," in William P. Bundy, ed., *Foreign Affairs: America and the World 1983* 62 (1984): 499, on the centrality of the deployment issue in Soviet–American relations.

12. On June 18, 1982, President Reagan imposed sanctions on American subsidiaries or their licensees against supplying the Soviets over the gas pipeline. See Josef Joffe, "Europe and America: The Politics of Resentment (Cont'd)," in William P. Bundy, ed., *America and the World 1981* (New York: Pergamon Press, 1982), pp. 573–574.

13. "Caribbean Basin Initiative," *GIST* (Washington, DC: Department of State, February, 1982).

14. The White House Office of the Press Secretary, press release on arms transfer policy, July 9, 1981.

15. See the survey of Reagan's foreign policy in "A Tour of Reagan's Horizon," *Newsweek*, November 9, 1981, 34–43. The "strategic consensus" for the Middle East (p. 41) can be applied to all areas of the world during the Reagan administration.

16. Haig, "A Strategic Approach to American Foreign Policy," p. 3. Emphasis added.

17. See, for example, "Text of Haig's Speech on American Foreign Policy," *New York Times*, April 25, 1981, 4, and his characterization of the Soviet Union. Also see the chronology in Bundy, ed., *America and the World 1981*, p. 728, for President Reagan's comment at his June 16, 1981, press conference that the Soviet Union "shows signs of collapse." (The quote is from Bundy.) The text of President Reagan's remarks can be found in "The President's News Conference of June 16, 1981," *Weekly Compilation of Presidential Documents* 17 (June 22, 1981): 633.

18. On the neutron bomb, see Leslie H. Gelb, "Reagan Orders Production of 2 Types of Neutron Arms for Stockpiling in the U.S.," *New York Times*, August 9, 1981, 1. On sanctioning the Soviet Union over Poland, see the president's statement in *Weekly Compilation of Presidential Documents* 17 (January 4, 1982): 1429–1430.

19. Steven Weisman, in "Reagan Ends Curbs on Export of Grain to the Soviet Union," *New York Times*, April 25, 1981, 1 and 6, discusses the lifting of the embargo. The expansion of grain sales is reported in John F. Burns, "U.S. Will Permit Russians to Triple Imports of Grain," *New York Times*, October 2, 1981, A1 and D14. A five-year grain deal was eventually agreed to in July 1983: see Steven R. Weisman, "A New Pact Raises Soviet Purchases of American Grain," *New York Times*, July 29, 1983, A1 and D9. Also see William G. Hyland, "U.S. Relations: The Long Way Back," in Bundy, ed., *America and the World 1981*, pp. 542–543.

20. Bernard Gwertzman, "U.S. Says It Is Not Bound by 2 Arms Pacts with Soviets" *New York Times*, May 20, 1981, A11.

21. On the Haig–Gromyko meeting and for prospects on arms control talks, see Bernard Gwertzman, "U.S. and Soviet Agree to Renew Weapons Talk," *New York Times*, September 24, 1981, A1 and A10.

22. A discussion of the INF negotiations can be found in Strobe Talbott, "Buildup and Breakdown," in Bundy, ed., *America and the World 1983*, pp. 587–615. On the first deployment, see James M. Markham, "First U.S. Pershing Missiles Delivered in West Germany," *New York Times*, November 24, 1983, A14.

23. The cataloguing of these events and other Soviet actions can be found in the "Cooling Trend in Soviet Policy," *Christian Science Monitor*, May 25, 1984, 1. On the explanation for the withdrawal from the Olympics, see "U.S.–Soviet Ties Termed 'Worst Ever,'" *Des Moines Sunday Register*, May 27, 1984, 1.

24. The comment was by a Soviet official and is quoted in "U.S.–Soviet Ties Termed 'Worst Ever,'" (see note 23).

25. "Communist Interference in El Salvador," Special Report No. 80 (Washington, DC: Bureau of Public Affairs, Department of State, February 1981), p. 1.

26. See the testimony of Secretary of State Alexander Haig in *Foreign Assistance Legislation for Fiscal Year 1982*, Hearing before the Committee on Foreign Affairs, the House of Representatives, 97th Cong., 1st sess. (Washington, DC: U.S. Government Printing Office, 1981), p. 194.

27. See the chronology in Bundy, ed., *America and the World 1981*, p. 749.

28. Ibid.

29. "Reagan Says Security of U.S. Is at Stake in Central America," *Des Moines Register*, April 28, 1983, 6A.

30. "No More Aid for Nicaragua," *Today*, April 24, 1981, 13.

31. In its November 8, 1982, issue, *Newsweek* devoted its cover story to the covert war in Nicaragua. See "A Secret War for Nicaragua," pp. 42–55.

32. The justification for the Grenada invasion is taken from President Reagan's remarks on October 25, 1983. They are reprinted in "Grenada: Collective Action by the Caribbean Peace Force," *Department of State Bulletin* 83 (December 1983): 67.

33. The Reagan administration sought congressional repeal of the Clark Amendment, passed in 1976 to prohibit aid to forces in Angola. The apparent aim of such an action was to allow the United States to support Jonas Savimbi and his UNITA forces, who were still fighting the Marxist government in Angola.

34. A chronology of these various actions is presented in Bundy, ed., *America and the World 1981*, pp. 734–735. This chronology, and the subsequent chronologies in later volumes of this series, was a useful beginning for unraveling the sequence of events in the Reagan administration.

35. The United States quickly suspended this agreement after the Israelis annexed the Golan Heights in December 1981. See Raymond Aron, "Ideology in Search of a Policy," in Bundy, ed., *America and the World 1981*, p. 517.

36. Juan de Onis, "U.S. and Pakistanis Reach an Agreement on $3 Billion in Aid," *New York Times*, June 16, 1981, A1 and A15. On the importance of both the AWACS and Pakistani sales, see Carol Housa, "Arms Sale Test, U.S.-Pakistan Ties," *Christian Science Monitor*, November 12, 1981, 3.

37. On the Reagan Initiative, see "Transcript of President's Address to Nation on West Bank and Palestinians," *New York Times*, September 2, 1982, A11.

38. The explanations for sending these forces into Lebanon are contained in the reports to Congress on August 24, 1982, and September 29, 1982, and in the Multinational Force Agreement between the United States and Lebanon of September 25, 1982. All of these are reprinted in *The War Powers Resolution: Relevant Documents, Correspondence, Reports*, Subcommittee on International Security and Scientific Affairs, House Committee on Foreign Affairs (Washington, DC: Government Printing Office, December 1983), pp. 60–63 and 74–76.

39. See "Communiqué by the Common Market," *New York Times*, January 5, 1982, A7; and "Text of Declaration on Poland by the Foreign Ministers of NATO," *New York Times*, January 12, 1982, A8. Also see John Vinocur, "Bonn Says Sanctions Are Not the Solution," *New York Times*, December 30, 1981, A1 and A7.

40. In West Germany, the proposed location for most of the theater nuclear forces, the opposition to the deployment of such weapons during 1983 assisted the Greens (a new antinuclear and environmental party) in gaining some seats in the legislatures of the *Laender* (or state) governments and eventually in the *Bundestag* (the national parliament). See "Focus on the National Elections in West Germany on March 6, 1983," p. 6, and "Focus on the Results of the National Elections in the Federal Republic of Germany on March 6, 1983," p. 2. Both are published by the German Information Center.

41. Paul E. Sigmund, "Latin America: Change or Continuity?" in Bundy, ed., *America and the World 1981*, p. 636.

42. George Gallup, "Military Budget Boost Loses Support, Poll Hints," *Des Moines Sunday Register*, February 27, 1983, 5A.

43. A *Newsweek* poll as reported in the April 26, 1982, issue (p. 24), found that 68 percent of those who had heard of the nuclear freeze movement favored or strongly favored it. A *Newsweek* poll in the January 31, 1983, issue (p. 17), found that 64 percent of the public supported the nuclear freeze proposal.

44. The crowd estimates ranged from 500,000 to 700,000 or more, as reported in Paul L. Montgomery, "Throngs Fill Manhattan to Protest Nuclear Weapons," *New York Times*, June 13, 1982, 1 and 43. For a survey of how the freeze movement reflected a diverse American public, see "A Matter of Life and Death," *Newsweek*, April 26, 1982, 20–33.

45. In a March 1981 interview with Walter Cronkite, President Reagan rejected the use of U.S. armed forces. See Francis X. Cline, "President Doubtful on U.S. Intervention," *New York Times*, March 4, 1981, A1 and A22. In a December 1981 interview, Secretary Haig also ruled out American troops. On the interview, see Sigmund, "Latin America: Change or Continuity?" p. 641.

46. The quoted passage is from "Transcript of President's News Conference on Foreign and Domestic Issues," *New York Times*, November 8, 1984, 13.

47. George Shultz, "Managing the U.S.-Soviet Relationship Over the Long Term," address before the Rand/UCLA Center for the Study of Soviet International Behavior, October 18, 1984, reprinted in *Department of State Bulletin* 84 (December 1984): 2.

48. "Text of Inaugural Address," *Des Moines Register*, January 22, 1985, 4A.

49. On the changes in Soviet foreign policy, see David Holloway, "Gorbachev's New Thinking," and Robert Levgold, "The Revolution in Soviet Foreign Policy," in Bundy, ed., *Foreign Affairs: America and the World 1988/89* 68 (1989): 66–98.

50. John E. Rielly, ed., *American Public Opinion and U.S. Foreign Policy 1987* (Chicago: The Chicago Council on Foreign Relations, 1987), p. 6.

51. For summits by other presidents, see Harold W. Stanley and Richard G. Niemi, *Vital Statistics on American Politics* (Washington, DC: CQ Press, 1988), pp. 293–294.

52. See "Concluding Remarks: President Reagan, November 21, 1985," reprinted in *Department of State Bulletin* 86 (January 1986): 11.

53. "The Reykjavik Meeting," *GIST* (Washington, DC: Department of State, December 1986).

54. Steven B. Roberts, "Reagan Says He Was Moved by Contacts with Russians," *New York Times*, June 2, 1988, A16. On the third summit, see R. W. Apple, Jr., "Reagan and Gorbachev Report Progress on Long-Range Arms and Mute 'Star Wars' Quarrel," *New York Times*, December 11, 1987, 1 and 10.

55. President Reagan purposely described the occasion as not "a working summit" because there was no set agenda. See President Reagan's statement of December 3, 1988, in the *Department of State Bulletin* 89 (February 1989): 3.

56. "Joint Statement, Geneva, January 8, 1985," *Department of State Bulletin* 85 (March 1985): 30.

57. The complete text of the INF Treaty and its protocols are available in *Arms Control and Disarmament Agreements: Texts and Histories of the Negotiations* (Washington, DC: United States Arms Control and Disarmament Agency, 1990), pp. 345–444.

58. Michael Mandelbaum, "The Luck of the President," in William G. Hyland, ed., *America and the World 1985* (New York: Pergamon Press, 1986), p. 408.

59. *Congressional Quarterly Almanac 1985* (Washington, DC: Congressional Quarterly, 1986), pp. 40, 56, and 58.

60. Several sources were used for the description of events associated with the Iran–Contra affair. Among them were *Report of the Congressional Committees Investigating the Iran–Contra Affair* (Washington, DC: U.S. Government Printing Office, November 1987); *Report of the President's Special Review Board* (Washington, DC: U.S. Government Printing Office,

February 26, 1987); Peter Hayes, ed., "Chronology 1987," *Foreign Affairs: America and the World 1987/88* 66 (1988): 638–676; Peter Hayes, ed., "Chronology 1988," *Foreign Affairs: America and the World 1988/89* 68 (1989): 220–256; Clyde R. Mark, "Iran-Contra Affair: A Chronology," Report No. 86–190F (Washington, DC: The Congressional Research Service, April 2, 1987); and James M. McCormick and Steven S. Smith, "The Iran Arms Sale and the Intelligence Oversight Act of 1980," *PS* 20 (Winter 1987): 29–37. The Reagan quote on keeping the Contras "body and soul together" can be found in *Report of the Congressional Committees Investigating the Iran–Contra Affair*, p. 4. Finally, the data in this chapter on American hostages seized and released were drawn from BBC News, "Timeline: US–Iran Ties," January 16, 2009, http://news.bbc.co.uk/2/hi/middle_east/3362443.stm, July 26, 2012.

61. The change in support is from Sandra Burton, "Aquino's Philippines: The Center Holds," *Foreign Affairs: America and the World 1986* 65 (1987): 524–526.

62. Nadav Safran, *Israel: The Embattled Ally* (Cambridge, MA: The Belknap Press, 1978), p. 594.

63. Alan Cowell, "Arafat Urges U.S. to Press Israelis to Negotiate Now," *New York Times*, November 16, 1988, A1 and A10.

64. "U.S. Makes Stunning Move Toward PLO," *Des Moines Register*, December 15, 1988, 3A. On the Palestine National Council deliberations, see "The P.L.O.: Less than Meets the Eye," *New York Times*, November 16, 1988, A30; and Youssef M. Ibrahim, "Palestinian View: A Big Stride Forward," *New York Times*, November 16, 1988, A10.

65. This discussion is based on *Congressional Quarterly Almanac 1985* (Washington, DC: Congressional Quarterly, 1986), pp. 39, 40, and 85; and *Congressional Quarterly Almanac 1986* (Washington, DC: Congressional Quarterly, 1987), pp. 359–362.

66. Throughout this chapter, the term *Eastern Europe* refers to those countries that were Communist allies of the Soviet Union (East Germany, Poland, Czechoslovakia, Hungary, Romania, Bulgaria) and formed part of the "Soviet bloc" before the breakup of the Soviet Empire in 1989–1990. The term *Central Europe* refers to these countries after the breakup because it is more descriptive of their proper geographical location.

67. "Text of President Bush's State of the Union Message to Nation," *New York Times*, January 30, 1991, A8

68. These concepts are discussed in and drawn from Charles W. Kegley, Jr., "The Bush Administration and the Future of American Foreign Policy: Pragmatism, or Procrastination?" *Presidential Studies Quarterly* 19 (Fall 1989): 717–731, especially p. 717. On the Bush presidency, also see Barbara Kellerman and Ryan J. Barilleaux, *The President as World Leader* (New York: St. Martin's Press, 1991), pp. 210–216.

69. See Elaine Sciolino, "Bush Selections Signal Focus on Foreign Policy," *New York Times*, January 17, 1989, 1, for this depiction of Bush as a problem solver and not as a visionary.

70. Theodore C. Sorensen, "Bush's Timid 100 Days," *New York Times*, April 27, 1989, 27.

71. William G. Hyland, "Bush's Foreign Policy: Pragmatism or Indecision?" *New York Times*, April 26, 1989, 25.

72. Evan Thomas with Thomas M. DeFrank and Ann McDaniel, "Bush and the Generals," *Newsweek*, February 4, 1991, 27.

73. The National Security Council staff confirmed that there was not a publicly available summary of the "policy review" and that these speeches summarized the essence of the policy positions of the Bush administration at that time. The speeches, which are quoted below, were supplied by the NSC staff and consisted of the following: "Remarks by the President to the Citizens of Hamtramck," April 17, 1989; "Remarks by the President at Texas A&M University," May 12, 1989; "Remarks by the President at Boston University

Commencement Ceremony," May 21, 1989; "Remarks by the President at the Coast Guard Academy Graduation Ceremony," May 24, 1989; and "Remarks by the President at Rheingoldhalle," Mainz, Germany, May 31, 1989.

74. See Chapter 8 for a complete discussion of the Jackson-Vanik Amendment.

75. Quoted in Maureen Dowd, "Bush Moves to Control War's Endgame," *New York Times*, February 23, 1991, 5.

76. John Felton, "Bush, Hill Agree to Provide Contras with New Aid," *Congressional Quarterly Weekly Report*, March 25, 1989, 655–657.

77. See John Felton, "Hill Gives Contra Package Bipartisan Launching," *Congressional Quarterly Weekly Report*, April 15, 1989.

78. Steven Erlanger, "Hanoi's Partial Victory," *New York Times*, July 20, 1990, A1 and A2.

79. Steven Erlanger, "Ending Talks, All Cambodia Parties Commit Themselves to U.N. Peace Plan," *New York Times*, September 11, 1990, A3.

80. The following discussion draws on "U.S. Invasion Ousts Panama's Noriega," and "From U.S. Canal to Invasion . . . A Chronology of Events," *Congressional Quarterly Almanac 1989* (Washington, DC: Congressional Quarterly, 1990), pp. 595–609 and 606–607, respectively; and Stephen Engelberg, "Bush Aides Admit a U.S. Role in Coup and Bad Handling," *New York Times*, October 6, 1989, 1 and 8.

81. Engelberg, "Bush Aides Admit a U.S. Role in Coup and Bad Handling."

82. Nicholas D. Kristof, "Beijing Death Toll at Least 200; Army Tightens Control of City But Angry Resistance Goes On," *New York Times*, June 5, 1989, 1. A summary of the Bush administration's actions in this episode can be found in "Repression in China Leads to Sanctions," *Congressional Quarterly Almanac 1989* (Washington, DC: Congressional Quarterly, 1990), pp. 518–526. This summary was used here.

83. "President's News Conference on Foreign and Domestic Issues," *New York Times*, June 9, 1989, 12.

84. The chronology of events in the next three sections is based on several sources: Peter Hayes, ed., "Chronology 1989," *Foreign Affairs: America and the World 1989/90* 69 (1990); 213–257; Peter Hayes, ed., "Chronology 1990" *Foreign Affairs: America and the World 1990/91* 70 (1991): 206–248; "East Bloc Political Turmoil . . . Chronology of Big Changes" *Congressional Quarterly Weekly Report*, December 9, 1989, 3376–3377; and the chronologies in *World Book Yearbook 1990* (Chicago: World Book, 1990), and the *Britannica Book of the Year 1990* (Chicago: Encyclopaedia Britannica, 1990). For changes in Yugoslavia and Albania in 1991, see "2 Republics Split From Yugoslavia," *Des Moines Register*, June 26, 1991, 1A and 12A; and Thomas L. Friedman, "300,000 Albanians Pour into Streets to Welcome Baker," *New York Times*, June 23, 1991, 1 and 4.

85. Serge Schmemann, "Two Germanys Unite After 45 Years with Jubilation and a Vow of Peace," *New York Times*, October 3, 1990, A1 and A9.

86. Quoted in "German-NATO Drama: 9 Fateful Months," *New York Times*, July 17, 1990, A6. This article, which we used here, provides a useful chronology of the reunification process.

87. "'Two Plus Four' Treaty Signed; Germany Regains Full Sovereignty," *The Week in Germany*, September 14, 1990, 1–2. The formal name of the treaty is Treaty on the Final Provisions Regarding Germany.

88. The details of the unification treaty can be found in "Bonn, GDR Sign Unification Treaty," *The Week in Germany*, September 7, 1990, 1–2.

89. On these elections, see Bill Keller, "Soviet Savor Vote in Freest Election Since '17 Revolution," *New York Times*, March 27, 1989, A1 and A6.

90. "Reforms in the Soviet Union," *Des Moines Sunday Register*, February 11, 1990, 1C.

91. The quotations are taken, respectively, from "Gorbachev's First Remarks: 'They Failed,'" *New York Times*, August 23, 1991, A9; and his first post-coup press conference: "The Gorbachev Account: A Coup 'Against the People, Against Democracy,'" *New York Times*, August 23, 1991, A10.

92. See Serge Schmemann, "Gorbachev, Yeltsin and Republic Leaders Move to Take Power from Soviet Congress," *New York Times*, September 3, 1991, A1 and A6; "Excerpts From Soviet Congress: Time for Drastic Changes," *New York Times*, September 3, 1991, A7; and Serge Schmemann, "Soviet Congress Yields Rule to Republics to Avoid Political and Economic Collapse," *New York Times*, September 6, 1991, A1 and A6.

93. The president and the "senior Bush Administration policy maker" are quoted in Thomas L. Friedman, "U.S. Worry Rises over Europe's Stability," *New York Times*, November 10, 1989, 10.

94. "Poland, Hungary Aid Launched in 1989," *Congressional Quarterly Almanac 1989* (Washington, DC: Congressional Quarterly, 1990), pp. 503–504.

95. Karl Kaiser, "Germany's Unification," in William P. Bundy, ed., *Foreign Affairs: America and the World 1990/91* 70 (1991): 179–205.

96. The quotations are from "Transcript of the Bush-Gorbachev New Conference in Malta," *New York Times*, December 4, 1989, A12. Also see Andrew Rosenthal, "Bush and Gorbachev Proclaim a New Era for U.S.-Soviet Ties; Agree on Arms and Trade Aims," *New York Times*, December 4, 1989, A1 and A10; and Frances X. Clines, "Economic Pledges Cheer Soviet Aides," *New York Times*, December 4, 1989, A11.

97. "As Iron Curtain Falls, Superpowers Thaw," *Congressional Quarterly Almanac 1989* (Washington, DC: Congressional Quarterly, 1990), pp. 477–484.

98. Hayes, ed., "Chronology 1990," p. 208.

99. "Text of the Statement on Long-Range Arms," "Summary of U.S.–Soviet Agreement on Chemical Arms," "The Other Agreements in Brief," *New York Times*, June 2, 1990, 8.

100. James Baker, "The Gulf Crisis and CSCE Summit," *Dispatch* 1 (November 19, 1990): 273–274; Pat Towell, "Historic CFE Cuts Treaty Arms, Marks the End of Cold War," *Congressional Quarterly Weekly Report*, November 24, 1990, 3930–3932; and "CSCE Summit in Paris Shapes 'New Europe,'" *The Week in Germany*, November 23, 1990, 1. The Warsaw Pact was officially disbanded as of March 31, 1991. See Christine Bohlen, "Warsaw Pact Agrees to Dissolve Its Military Alliance by March 31," *New York Times*, February 26, 1991, A1 and A10.

101. R. W. Apple, Jr., "Superpower Weapons Treaty First to Cut Strategic Bombs," *New York Times*, July 18, 1991, A1 and A6; Thomas L. Friedman, "Bush and Gorbachev Close Era in U.S.–Soviet Relations," *New York Times*, July 18, 1991, A8; Eric Schmitt, "Senate Approval and Sharp Debate Seen," *New York Times*, July 19, 1991, A5 (including accompanying table entitled "New Limits on Strategic Weapons"); and Office of Public Affairs, U.S. Arms Control and Disarmament Agency, "Strategic Arms Reduction Talks," *Issues Brief*, April 25, 1991.

102. For further details on the treaty, see Eric Schmitt, "Senate Approval and Sharp Debate Seen," *New York Times*, July 19, 1991, A5 (including the accompanying table entitled "New Limits on Strategic Weapons"); Office of Public Affairs, U.S. Arms Control and Disarmament Agency, "Strategic Arms Reduction Talks," *Issues Brief*, April 25, 1991.

103. Steven Greenhouse, "7 Offer Moscow Technical Help," *New York Times*, July 18, 1991, A1 and A8; and "Excerpts from Talks by Gorbachev and Major: Investing and Accepting," *New York Times*, July 18, 1991, A6.

104. Andrew Rosenthal, "Baltics Recognized," *New York Times*, September 3, 1991, A1 and A8.

105. Clifford Krauss, "U.S. and Britain Will Send Some Food Aid to Republics," *New York Times*, August 30, 1991, A10.

106. See George Bush, "Outlines of a New World of Freedom," address before the 44th session of the UN General Assembly, New York City, September 25, 1989, and "Toward a New World Order," address before a joint session of Congress, September 11, 1990. Both are published by the Bureau of Public Affairs, Department of State, Washington, D.C. Also see "Text of President Bush's State of the Union Message to Nation," *New York Times*, January 30, 1991, A8.

107. President Bush's national security advisor, Brent Scowcroft, is given credit for developing this phrase and the strategy behind it. See Andrew Rosenthal, "Scowcroft and Gates: A Team Rivals Baker," *New York Times*, February 21, 1991, A6.

108. Bush, "Toward a New World Order," p. 2.

109. "Text of President Bush's State of the Union Message to Nation," *New York Times*, A8.

110. Ibid.

111. Daniel C. Diller, ed., *The Middle East*, 7th ed. (Washington, DC: Congressional Quarterly, 1990), pp. 164–165.

112. John H. Kelly, "US Relations with Iraq," statement before the Subcommittee on Europe and the Near East of the House Foreign Affairs Committee, April 26, 1990, p. 3.

113. On the evolution of the crisis, see Tom Matthews, "The Road to War," *Newsweek*, January 28, 1991, pp. 54–65. On the failure of the United States to issue a warning to Iraq, see Elaine Sciolino with Michael R. Gordon, "U.S. Gave Iraq Little Reason Not to Mount Assault," *New York Times*, September 23, 1990, 1. Matthews's article provided useful background information that we relied on for this section. On the controversy over what the American ambassador to Iraq said or did not say to Saddam Hussein prior to the crisis, see Thomas L. Friedman, "Envoy to Iraq, Faulted in Crisis, Says She Warned Hussein Sternly," *New York Times*, March 21, 1991, A1 and A7.

114. Hayes, ed., "Chronology 1990," p. 228.

115. The joint statement is reprinted in "US-USSR Statement," *Dispatch* 1 (September 17, 1990): 92.

116. George Bush, "The Arabian Peninsula: U.S. Principles," address to the nation from the Oval Office of the White House, August 8, 1990, provided by the Bureau of Public Affairs, Department of State, Washington, D.C.

117. See "How the Arab League Voted in Cairo," *New York Times*, August 11, 1990, 4.

118. The number of countries in the anti-Iraq coalition most commonly cited in public descriptions was twenty-eight, but see Steven R. Bowman, "Iraq-Kuwait Crisis: Summary of U.S. and Non-U.S. Forces" (Washington, DC: Congressional Research Service, The Library of Congress, December 27, 1990), in which slightly more nations are identified as having contributed some contingent of forces.

119. UN Security Council Resolution 678 (1990), reprinted in Marjorie Ann Browne, "Iraq-Kuwait: U.N. Security Council Resolutions—Texts and Votes" (Washington, DC: Congressional Research Service, The Library of Congress, December 4, 1990). This source provides complete texts and a summary of the previous eleven UN resolutions; "U.N. Resolutions on Iraq," *New York Times*, February 16, 1991, 6, provides a summary of these resolutions. The latter source was used for the discussion here.

120. Andrew Rosenthal, "Bush Calls Halt to Allied Offensive; Declares Kuwait Free, Iraq Beaten; Sets Stiff Terms for Full Cease-fire," *New York Times*, February 28, 1991, A1; R. W. Apple, Jr., "U.S. Says Iraqi Generals Agree to Demands 'On All Matters,' Early P.O.W. Release Expected," *New York Times*, March 4, 1991, A1, A6; and "New U.S. Hint About Hussein," *New York Times*, March 4, 1991, A6. On Iraqi and American battlefield deaths,

see Patrick E. Tyler, "Iraq's War Toll Estimated by U.S.," *New York Times*, June 5, 1991, A5; and "The Reluctant Warrior," *Newsweek*, May 13, 1991, 22.

121. Paul Lewis, "UN Votes Stern Conditions for Formally Ending War; Iraqi Response Is Uncertain," *New York Times*, April 4, 1991, A1 and A7; "UN Conditions," *Des Moines Register*, April 4, 1991, 14A; and Resolution 687 (1991) at http://www.fas.org/news/un/ iraq/sres/sres0687.htm, August 21, 2008.

122. On the outbreak of these rebellions, see, among others, "Apocalypse Near," *Newsweek*, April 1, 1991, 14–16.

123. This discussion draws on Patricia Lee Dorff, ed., "Chronology 1992," *Foreign Affairs: America and the World 1992/93* 72 (1993): 215–218, 230–233.

124. Ibid. Also see Michael Wines, "Bush and Yeltsin Agree to Cut Long-Range Atomic Warheads: Scrap Key Land-Based Missiles," *New York Times*, June 17, 1992, A1 and A6.

125. U.S. Senate, *The START Treaty*, Report of the Committee on Foreign Relations, United States Senate (Washington, DC: U.S. Government Printing Office, 1992), p. 3.

126. The treaty details are summarized more fully in "START II Treaty," *Dispatch* 4 (January 4, 1993): 5–7, from which our discussion draws.

127. See "Bush Signs Freedom Support Act," *Congressional Quarterly Almanac 1992* (Washington, DC: Congressional Quarterly, 1993), pp. 523–524.

128. Andrew Rosenthal, "Bush and Kohl Unveil Plan for 7 Nations to Contribute $24 Billion in Aid to Russia," *New York Times*, April 2, 1992, A1.

129. "Freedom Support Act Highlights," *Congressional Quarterly Almanac 1992* (Washington, DC: Congressional Quarterly, 1993), p. 526. Also see U.S. Department of Defense, "Semi-Annual Report on Program Activities to Facilitate Weapons Destruction and Nonproliferation in the Former Soviet Union," April 30, 1994.

130. Lawrence Eagleburger, "Charting the Course: U.S. Foreign Policy in a Time of Transition," Address before the Council on Foreign Relations, Washington, D.C., January 7, 1993 (Washington, DC: Bureau of Public Affairs, Department of State, 1993), p. 3. The address was later reprinted in *Dispatch* 4 (January 11, 1993): 16–19.

131. Former secretary of state James Baker is quoted in Elizabeth Drew, *On the Edge: The Clinton Presidency* (New York: Simon & Schuster, 1994), p. 139. The chronology of events here was drawn from that source and from Dorff, "Chronology 1992," pp. 221–230.

132. The sequence of events here draws on Patricia Lee Dorff, ed., "Chronology 1991," *Foreign Affairs: America and the World 1991/92* 71 (1991/92): 217–220; and Dorff, "Chronology 1992," pp. 243–245.

133. The sequence of events draws on Dorff, "Chronology 1992," pp. 248–251. Also see John R. Bolton, "Wrong Turn in Somalia," *Foreign Affairs* 73 (January/February 1994): 56–66.

134. Eagleburger, "Charting the Course: U.S. Foreign Policy in a Time of Transition" pp. 3–4.

Foreign Policy after the Cold War and 9/11: The Clinton and Bush Administrations

The successor to a doctrine of containment must be a
strategy of enlargement, the enlargement of the world's
free community of market democracies.

ANTHONY LAKE

NATIONAL SECURITY ADVISOR TO PRESIDENT CLINTON
SEPTEMBER 1993

Every nation, in every region, now has a decision to make.
Either you are with us, or you are with the terrorists. From this day
forward any nation that continues to harbor or support terrorism
will be regarded by the United States as a hostile regime.

GEORGE W. BUSH
SEPTEMBER 20, 2001

In this chapter, we analyze the foreign policy values, beliefs, and approaches of the Clinton and the George W. Bush administrations after the Cold War ended and after the attack on New York and Washington, D.C., on September 11, 2011. For the Clinton administration, we identify its initial commitment to expanding free peoples and free markets around the world and assess the extent to which it succeeded in achieving those goals during its first term. Given the altered political landscape at home, including Republican majorities in Congress, and Clinton's successful reelection to a second term, we discuss how his approach evolved from initial idealism to greater realism by the end of his time in office.

For the Bush administration, we begin by analyzing the assumptions and policy positions prior to the events of September 11, 2001, and the administration's initial commitment to classical realism. Next, we concentrate on the changes in orientation and content as a result of September 11 and the movement toward defensive realism and idealism as enunciated in the Bush Doctrine. We then discuss the seeming modification of the Bush Doctrine at the beginning of the second term with its "democracy initiative." Finally, we evaluate the key legacies that the Bush administration left to its successors.

Throughout these analyses, we survey numerous foreign policy actions to illustrate each administration's approach and we assess the values and beliefs that were now at the core of American foreign policy at the end of the twentieth century.

POST–COLD WAR FOREIGN POLICY: THE CLINTON ADMINISTRATION

Bill Clinton ran for president on the theme of change—in domestic as well as foreign policy.[1] With the end of the Cold War, candidate Clinton argued, American foreign policy must change to meet the challenges of the end of the twentieth century and to prepare for the twenty-first. Needed for this new era, he claimed, was "a new vision and the strength to meet a new set of opportunities and threats." "We face," Clinton said, "the same challenge today that we faced in 1946—to build a world of security, freedom, democracy, free markets and growth at a time of great change."[2] Indeed, he contended that the Bush administration's leadership had been "rudderless, reactive, and erratic," when the country needed leadership that was "strategic, vigorous, and grounded in America's democratic values."[3] Clinton promised to meet that need with a new direction in American policy based on its traditional domestic values.

The Values and Beliefs of the Clinton Administration

Unlike the ad hoc foreign policy the George H. W. Bush administration pursued, then, the Clinton administration's policy was determined to be rooted in a clear set of principles derived from America's past, guided by a coherent and workable strategy, and appropriate to the end of the Cold War. Domestic policy and foreign policy would be tied together because only by shoring up America's economic and social strength at home would the United States have an effective economic and security policy abroad. Indeed, candidate Clinton summarized his unified policy approach in this way: "We must tear down the wall in our thinking between domestic and foreign policy."[4]

Although American administrations often come to office with a commitment to a particular foreign policy approach, most have had to alter that approach during their years in power. This shift has occurred in some administrations from the first to the second term; for others, in response to dramatic domestic and international events;

and, for still others, in response to the electoral cycle or the rhythms of domestic politics. In this respect, the Clinton administration was no different, and the changes in emphasis over its two terms are especially important for understanding the direction of America's foreign policy after the Cold War and at the end of the twentieth century. Part of the explanation for these changes derives from Clinton's evolving interest in foreign policy and the replacement of some of his advisors, but part also comes from changes in the domestic and international environments that his administration faced. In the following sections, we discuss these factors as they relate to foreign policy during the Clinton years.

Clinton, His Foreign Policy Experience, and His Foreign Policy Advisors

Unlike President George H.W. Bush, who came to office with a broad background and interest in international affairs, President Clinton, by virtually all accounts, was largely uninterested in foreign policy making. Indeed, his background prior to assuming office was primarily confined to his two years at Oxford University, some travels in Western and Eastern Europe, and his personal anguish over American involvement in the Vietnam War. By contrast, his interest and involvement in a variety of domestic issues (educational reform and economic development, among others) as the governor of Arkansas were considerable. Thus, whereas Clinton may have justifiably been described as a **policy wonk** domestically, that label was surely less accurate globally. Indeed, his initial attitude toward foreign policy was perhaps best summarized by what the political writer Elizabeth Drew identified as the task given to Anthony Lake, Clinton's campaign foreign policy advisor and later his first national security advisor: "Keep foreign policy from becoming a problem—keep it off the screen and spare Clinton from getting embroiled as he went about his domestic business." One senior administration official acknowledged the accuracy of this assessment in 1993: **"We had hoped to keep foreign policy submerged."**[5]

Given President Clinton's limited interest and his apparent desire to keep foreign policy "submerged," the composition of his first foreign affairs team became crucial in the development and implementation of his foreign policy agenda. Although he had committed himself to appointing a cabinet that would "look like America" and did give some consideration to this idea, the top foreign policy posts of his first cabinet seemed more narrowly drawn: a very large number were filled by those who had served in the Carter administration (for example, Warren Christopher as secretary of state, Anthony Lake as national security advisor, and William Perry as his second secretary of defense), a few with Capitol Hill experience (most notably Les Aspin as his secretary of defense and Madeleine Albright as U.S. ambassador to the United Nations), and some personal and campaign friends (Mickey Kantor as trade representative, Ron Brown as secretary of commerce, Samuel [Sandy] Berger as deputy national security advisor, and Strobe Talbott, first as ambassador at large for Russia and later as deputy secretary of state).

By virtually all assessments, this team, at least through the first two years of Clinton's initial term, had considerable difficulty developing policy, explaining it to the American people, and dealing with pressing global issues. After the appointment of William Perry to replace Les Aspin, a biting commentary in the British weekly *The Economist* noted that this appointment had produced **a "stealth" foreign policy team**, comprising "the little-known Mr. Perry, the camera-shy Anthony Lake, and the low-profile Warren Christopher as secretary of state." Each one seemingly competed, the analysts claimed, "for invisibility." Yet "all too visible . . . are the global troubles they will have to cope with."[6]

Although this description is surely overdrawn, it conveys the nagging personnel problem that the Clinton administration confronted in the foreign policy arena, especially early in its first term. "The whole national security apparatus of the President was in terrible disarray," in 1993 and 1994, as one later assessment put it. "There was poor central direction from the White House and a weak N.S.C. [National Security Council] staff—the worst since the first Reagan administration. They didn't know what they didn't know."[7] A cacophony of voices without a strong leader or a strong spokesperson was developing American foreign policy, resulting in a seemingly incoherent policy for addressing the post–Cold War world. This difficulty was compounded somewhat by a president who appeared too detached to make foreign policy work effectively and by global events such as Bosnia, Haiti, Somalia, and Russia that would not let the Clinton administration isolate foreign from domestic policy.[8]

The performance of Christopher, Lake, and Perry improved from 1995 onward, and they enjoyed some foreign policy successes in Bosnia, Haiti, and the Middle East. However, the direction of American foreign policy remained unsteady and a target of criticism. One frequent critic, Senator John McCain (R-Arizona), faulted the Clinton administration for its lack of "strategic coherence," its "self-doubt," and its failure to identify key American interests.[9]

For the second term, some changes were made. First, Clinton had by then become more fully engaged in foreign policy and increasingly looked to it as a way to leave his mark. Indeed, some critics charged that his administration used foreign policy to deflect criticism from the domestic turmoil over the Lewinsky sex scandal and the impeachment that surrounded Clinton in 1997 and 1998. Second, Clinton's foreign policy team changed. Although it continued to draw on veterans of the Carter administration and close friends, it now included several individuals with experience from the first term and with broader views and backgrounds than those involved initially. To replace the relatively taciturn Warren Christopher as secretary of state, Clinton chose Madeleine Albright, who had served as American ambassador to the United Nations during his first term. His new CIA director was George J. Tenet, deputy director of the CIA at the time and a former National Security Council staffer and staff director of the Senate Intelligence Committee. Anthony Lake's deputy and Clinton's longtime personal friend, Sandy Berger, assumed the national security advisor post. To replace Secretary of Defense Perry, President Clinton chose retiring Republican senator William Cohen, a longtime student of defense and intelligence. Cohen's appointment was an attempt to shape a bipartisan foreign and defense policy with Congress, especially as he had been a frequent defender of congressional prerogatives in foreign affairs.[10]

This new team was characterized as solid (rather than distinguished) in its credentials. Yet it too had its bumps along the road in creating a consistent and coherent foreign policy, and it increasingly turned away from the idealism of the early Clinton years and toward greater reliance on political realism as a foreign policy guide. To be sure, Albright, the first woman secretary of state in American history, was more articulate and outspoken than Christopher had been. In this way, she was better able to explain the direction of foreign policy to Congress and the American public. Furthermore, she was seemingly able to rally more international support for the direction to be pursued by the United States. The new national security advisor, Berger, for the most part accommodated Albright, but, like all recent national security advisors, he came to dominate the foreign policy decision apparatus.[11]

THE CLINTON ADMINISTRATION'S EVOLVING APPROACHES TO FOREIGN POLICY

Clinton's foreign policy over two terms was marked by shifting priorities and strategies, shaped not only by his advisors but also by changes in the political and international environment. It can be seen as evolving in three phases:

- Phase one: economic engagement
- Phase two: democratic engagement (also referred to as the "strategy of enlargement," a term taken from a speech by National Security Advisor Anthony Lake)
- Phase three: selective engagement

Phase One: Economic Engagement

Initially, the Clinton administration focused on economic ties as the driving force in its dealings with the global community. At his Senate confirmation hearings as secretary of state in January 1993, Warren Christopher outlined three principles that would guide American foreign policy for the new administration: **achieving economic security, reshaping defense, and promoting democracy**. The administration's first priority was to use the international system to foster greater economic prosperity for the American people.[12] Indeed, Christopher declared that the Clinton administration would "advance America's economic security with the same energy and resourcefulness . . . devoted to waging the Cold War." This emphasis on foreign economic policy nicely wedded foreign and domestic politics—a theme that candidate Clinton had struck during this campaign when he declared that "our first foreign priority and our first domestic priority are one and the same: reviving our economy."[13]

To achieve this economic security, the Clinton administration initially committed itself to several key initiatives at home and abroad. On the domestic level, it sought to develop a program to revive the American economy and make American workers and companies more productive and competitive in the global marketplace. Included in this plan were actions to reduce budget deficits and ensure that America was a more reliable trading partner. It also sought to infuse more economic components into foreign policy making with the creation of the **National Economic Council (NEC)** as the functional economic equivalent of the National Security Council (NSC) and as a mechanism to ensure that economic matters, foreign and domestic, received a full hearing in the executive branch. Economic advisors became formal members of the national security committee structure, and several economic officials and agencies gained greater authority. The United States Trade Representative (USTR) assumed a central role in trade policy; the State Department created a new Office of the Coordinator for Business Affairs; and the Treasury and Commerce departments assumed more foreign policy responsibilities.[14]

On the international level, the Clinton administration moved quickly to complete two free trade agreements and to initiate several other multilateral and bilateral efforts to liberalize trade. The first important effort here was to complete negotiations on the North American Free Trade Agreement (NAFTA) with Canada and Mexico to move toward the elimination of tariffs on goods among these countries over a five- to fifteen-year period, grant "national treatment" for most investment among these countries, open up several service areas (such as banking, telecommunications, transportation, and government procurement) to the agreement partners, and protect intellectual property among the partners as well. Regarding this agreement, the administration began negotiations on important "side agreements" to protect worker rights and preserve environmental standards shortly after it took office. When these agreements were secured, it set up an elaborate lobbying effort to gain support in Congress for the agreement. By November 1993, the House and the Senate had passed NAFTA, although President Clinton in the end relied more on votes from Republicans than from Democrats to gain its final passage. Still, the congressional victory was hailed as an important foreign policy success of the Clinton administration—and it remains so to this day.

By November 1994, the Clinton administration had achieved a second important victory in the area of trade with the completion and approval of the Uruguay Round of the General Agreement on Tariffs and Trade (GATT) and the creation of GATT's successor, the **World Trade Organization (WTO)**. The agreement moved to cut tariffs worldwide by approximately 85 percent. Agriculture was covered under this pact for the first time, and an initial effort was made to cut agricultural subsidies as well. Furthermore, quotas on textiles from developing countries to developed countries would be eliminated over a ten-year period, and GATT would now cover international service transactions. Finally, and importantly, the WTO would become the new governing organization to regulate global trade for the future. This agreement, too, required substantial lobbying on Capitol Hill, but it was ultimately approved by about two-thirds of the House and exactly three-quarters of the Senate. Along with NAFTA, the WTO signaled the centrality of economics for Clinton's foreign policy.

With these agreements in place, President Clinton moved on to two other multilateral trading pacts. In November 1994, the administration lent its support to the Asia-Pacific Economic Cooperation (APEC) forum in its effort to establish a free trade area among its developed nation members by 2010 and to increase its total membership by 2020. A month later, Clinton proposed the establishment of a free trade area by 2005 to the thirty-four Western Hemisphere countries that were meeting at the Summit of the Americas in Miami.

Phase Two: Democratic Engagement and Enlargement

Although an economic focus dominated Clinton's foreign policy agenda during its early months (and years), changing international conditions quickly drew the administration's attention elsewhere and led to an effort to define its foreign policy more broadly. The pivotal international events were the deteriorating situation in Bosnia, the unsettled conditions in Somalia and Haiti, and the changing political landscapes in Russia and the Middle East.

In Bosnia, ethnic cleansing continued, and the administration was unable to settle on a policy that its Western European allies could support. In Somalia, the effort to transform the humanitarian mission of late 1992 into a peace- and nation-building mission in early 1993 met with strong resistance. In Haiti, the Governors Island Accord had been completed in the summer of 1993, but by fall, it had yet to be implemented. In Russia, the Yeltsin regime was meeting resistance, and the administration was forced to decide whether or not to support it. The one bright spot in foreign affairs, the

Israeli–PLO Accord of September 1993, took considerable effort to be put it into effect. In short, the international landscape called for more than economic engagement.

At home, too, discussions took another tack. One important question was whether foreign policy beyond economics was something that the United States should embrace. Although isolationism overstates the sentiments of the public and some of its leaders at the time, many Americans did support a reassessment of the breadth of U.S. commitments worldwide. Indeed, in spring 1993, the third-ranking official in the Department of State floated the idea of reducing American commitment around the world. The question of "will and wallet" now appeared in political discussions over the direction of foreign policy.

In effect, American foreign policy needed a clearer and broader road map than the Clinton administration had so far provided. By late September 1993, major foreign policy speeches by President Clinton, Secretary of State Christopher, UN Ambassador Albright, and especially National Security Advisor Lake tried to rectify this.[15] In their statements, the president and his administration officials set out the fundamental premises of Clinton's foreign policy and its basic raison d'être. Taken as a whole, these speeches indicate that the administration now embraced an even greater commitment to liberal internationalism than it did in its initial approach.

First, the administration committed the United States to global involvement and leadership in the aftermath of the Cold War. Global engagement—not isolationism or neo-isolationism—would be the administration's policy now. Christopher put it one way ("I want to assure you that the United States chooses engagement"); Albright, another ("Our nation will not retreat into a post–Cold War foxhole"). Second, the administration indicated that the United States would act in the world either unilaterally or multilaterally on a case-by-case basis. Acting only unilaterally or only multilaterally, Christopher said, was a "false polarity. It is not an 'either-or' proposition." Lake laid out the basic criterion of that choice: "[O]nly one overriding factor can determine whether the U.S. should act multilaterally or unilaterally, and this is America's interests." Third, the administration committed the United States to use force when necessary. Although "diplomacy will always be America's first choice," Albright declared, "when diplomacy fails, we have both the capacity to use force effectively and the will to do so when necessary."

It was Lake who provided the basic rationale and context for American engagement and leadership: it would be to strengthen and expand market democracies worldwide. This **"strategy of enlargement,"** as he called it, would be **the post–Cold War successor to the policy of containment**. Its primary focus, Lake stated, would be on "strengthening our democratic core in North America, Europe, and Japan; consolidating and enlarging democracy and markets in key places; and addressing backlash states such as Iran and Iraq" that challenge market democracies. In a real sense, then, the new approach was to combine the creation of liberal democracies with the development of liberal markets around the world.

Put differently, two key concepts now formed the core of the Clinton foreign policy—**free markets and free societies**—and both are essential tenets of idealism or liberal internationalism. Their foundation is the implicit assumption that cooperation, not conflict, primarily motivates the behavior of states. The former concept assumes the pacifying effects of free markets: As states cooperate in more and more so-called low-politics areas (such as trading blocs and free market agreements), they become more interested in the absolute gains that their societies can achieve and less interested in their relative gains vis-à-vis neighbors or trading partners. The latter concept assumes the pacifying effects of free societies: democracies do not fight one another; they have peaceful mechanisms for resolving their disputes, and they respect the rights of their citizens.[16] Moreover, there was to be a synergistic relationship between the two concepts: sustained economic gains by democratic states would propel continued peaceful relations, and democratic states would be equipped to peacefully pursue (and construct) more open markets.

An important implication of these two concepts was the centrality of domestic values in shaping American foreign policy. The economic emphasis of the administration's approach could, of course, have a direct effect on Americans' lives. The promotion of democracy could as well, especially because it was coupled with the promotion of human rights. In this way, the administration would seemingly appeal to the deeply held values of most Americans and would restore some idealism to America's role in the world.

Despite the intuitive appeal of the enlargement of market democracies in the world, however, this new approach gained little support at home and never provided much policy guidance abroad—except in the most abstract sense. What it did achieve, however, was to become a ready target for criticism. Unsurprisingly, Henry Kissinger declared Clinton's strategy to be lacking in "operational terms."[17] Another critic noted that it was too general and that the administration approached "foreign policy as if it were on a supermarket shopping spree, grabbing whatever it takes a fancy to. . . ."[18] Still others viewed it less as a strategy (How would the administration bring about democratic development?) and more as a set of attractive principles (Who could challenge the promotion of democracy?). Disquieting, too, was that the administration appeared to be less focused on American national interests and more on universal global values.[19]

Clinton's strategy of enlargement and his foreign policy in general also came in for criticism from within the administration itself, from Republicans on Capitol Hill, and from the American public. Secretary of State Christopher reportedly saw it as "a trade policy masquerading as a foreign policy" and refused to use the *E* (or *enlargement*) word in his policy formulations.[20] Republicans, of course, seized on its perceived failings by including several key foreign policy restrictions in their "Contract with America" during the 1994 congressional elections. Finally, in a national survey of public opinion on foreign policy conducted in late 1994, the Clinton administration's handling of foreign policy came under fire, with only 31 percent of the public judging it as "good" or "excellent."[21]

Equally important, the strategy of enlargement proved to be an incomplete guide for responding to the challenges facing the administration in 1993–1994 and beyond. Although the promotion of free markets was already a priority, it provided no instructions for how to promote democracy. It surely served as a general rationale for promoting political liberalization in Haiti or Bosnia and comported with efforts to challenge backlash states, such as Iraq or North Korea, but it did not provide much specificity about actions to be taken prior to democratic development in these states. Furthermore, it was hardly precise regarding American policy toward the Middle East, Russia, or China, or toward Rwanda and the ethnic killings there.

Phase Three: Selective Engagement

As early as January 1995, and after some stinging criticisms, the Clinton administration began to move away from the idealism that the strategy of enlargement conveyed and toward a more substantive policy rooted in realism. In a speech at

Harvard's Kennedy School of Government, Secretary of State Christopher outlined this change in direction.[22] While reaffirming a commitment to American engagement and leadership, Christopher set out a series of concrete policy priorities that, although generally compatible with the liberal internationalism set out earlier, had the ring of traditional American foreign policy goals. The United States, he declared, would seek cooperative ties with other states, build economic and security institutions, and support democracy and human rights. It would do so by liberalizing the trading order, building a new security structure in Europe, working for a comprehensive peace in the Middle East, halting the proliferation of weapons of mass destruction (WMD), and combating international crime.

A year later, in another address to the Kennedy School, Christopher outlined a similar set of foreign policy goals, but with a hierarchical ordering that seemed to signal a change in the administration's emphasis.[23] He reaffirmed the overarching principles of the previous year ("pursuing peace in regions of vital interest," "confronting the new transnational security threats," and "promoting open markets and prospects"), but the increasing emphasis on the security components of foreign policy could not be missed. The specific regional threats to peace that Christopher identified were familiar—Bosnia, Central and Eastern Europe, Russia, and such problem states as Northern Ireland, Haiti, Cyprus, Angola, Burundi, Peru, and Ecuador. The new transnational security threats ranged from the proliferation of WMD and terrorism to international criminal activities and environmental damage. Finally, and significantly, promotion of open markets was listed third and mainly reiterated the trade liberalization efforts through NAFTA and APEC, and in the Western Hemisphere. Finally, Christopher called for a continued commitment to seeking fast-track trading authority from Congress. Except in a most generous interpretation, then, the strategy of enlargement was no longer central to the administration's foreign policy actions.

The Clinton administration's altering of its foreign policy course seemed evident by the end of the first term, but change was more fully signaled at the beginning of the second. In his 1997 State of the Union address, for instance, Clinton stated that the first tasks for the United States were to "build . . . an undivided, democratic Europe" and to "shape an Asia-Pacific community of cooperation, not conflict."[24] To be sure, he mentioned the need to "expand our exports," but he also noted that the United States must "continue to be an unrelenting force for peace from the Middle East to Haiti, from Northern Ireland to Africa" and "must move strongly against new threats to our security." Further, the United States must strengthen and support its military and its diplomacy. Two months later, the new national security advisor, Samuel (Sandy) Berger, repeated these very same objectives to a Washington audience.[25]

By May 1997, the administration's **"National Security Strategy for a New Century"** report reinforced the change already under way.[26] It inverted two of the three key principles that Secretary of State Christopher had identified in 1993. (In fact, this inversion had occurred by 1994, but it can be argued that the 1997 change was much stronger in tone.) The United States' principal objectives were now, in order, "to enhance our security with effective diplomacy and with military forces that are ready to fight and win, to bolster America's economic prosperity [and] to promote democracy abroad." Traditional political-military emphases gained primacy, whereas the economic and the democracy goals lost ground. Realism, or perhaps realism "lite," now came to dominate the foreign policy agenda.

Defining Selective Engagement On a substantive level, **selective engagement implied different assumptions** from those outlined when the strategy of enlargement was announced in 1993. First, although the United States would remain engaged and lead in world affairs, it would now act (and justify its actions) on more narrowly drawn national, rather than global, interests. Its agenda, too, as the statements by Christopher, Clinton, and Berger implied, would be more specific and more narrowly chosen. Second, although the United States would not wholly eschew multilateral actions in global affairs, the administration would be more amenable to unilateral actions and would undertake them only if necessary. Third, the United States would be willing to use military force but would do so more carefully, probably more sparingly, and only after clear criteria were met. Finally, the context and goals for American engagement and leadership would focus less on remaking the international system through the expansion of market democracies and more on stabilizing relations among key states. In other words, conflict, rather than cooperation, was still a motivating force.

Thus, the United States would seek to dampen and manage conflicts rather than eliminate them quickly (that is, peacekeeping versus peace building). Put differently, and more in line with realist premises, the new emphasis would be on stabilizing the international order rather than on restructuring it. However, it was important that elements of democracy and human rights promotion continue to be commingled in the process at various points. Once again, *realism lite* is perhaps a more accurate theoretical descriptor of the administration's evolving approach.

Several types of action taken by the administration reflect this security-based attitude toward foreign policy—regarding interventions, efforts in building or rebuilding alliances, strictures on peacekeeping, the emphasis on nonproliferation, and the focus on a few key powerful states in the international system. Moreover, the actions and nonactions in Kosovo and the administration's approach to East Timor illustrate the continuance of selective engagement up to the end of Clinton's time in office. They also reveal how the administration grappled with "humanitarian interventions" in trying to devise a workable "**Clinton Doctrine**" to deal with the ethnic and communal conflict now more prevalent worldwide.

Implementing Selective Engagement Shortly after the events in Somalia, the Clinton administration made perhaps its first move in the direction of selective engagement by deciding not to take action over Rwanda but rather to step up its efforts in the Balkans. Thus, in April 1994, it refused to become deeply involved in the Rwandan genocide. Instead, it issued **Presidential Decision Directive-25 (PDD-25)** a month later, which specified several decision criteria for American involvement in UN operations under Chapter VI and VII of the UN Charter. At about the same time, it began taking more vigorous actions (including selective bombing), in an effort to stabilize the Balkan situation. Those actions reached their height in the summer and fall of 1995, both with renewed support for the Bosnian government against Serbian forces and with a strong diplomatic offensive. They eventually resulted in the Dayton Accords and the use of the NATO alliance to implement them, along with the use of American troops to stabilize the fragile peace, albeit within strict rules of engagement. In short, the Clinton administration was putting in place a more vigorous but selective effort to stabilize global politics by acting in Europe but not in Africa.

Second, the administration's actions toward its allies reflected this renewed interest in security. By late 1994, the president had endorsed the decision to go forward with

NATO expansion, despite the objection of Russian leaders and despite its possible impact on Russian domestic politics. The aim of building a **stable and secure Europe** trumped assuaging Russian fears over Western encirclement and the possibility of a divided Europe. (Anomalously of course, the decision to support NATO expansion had the side benefit of fostering European democratic development.) Similarly, the Clinton administration initiated efforts to refurbish the Japanese–American alliance and strengthen alliance ties with South Korea. It also initiated and pursued the policy of "dual containment" toward Iran and Iraq, although the administration was rather unsuccessful in obtaining the continued support of other nations in that endeavor. The Clinton administration was now willing to go it alone, however, especially with Iraq. Thus, American military forces were rapidly dispatched to Kuwait in late 1994, and the United States periodically used American air power for selective sorties against Iraq over its violations of the no-fly zones.

Third, the Clinton administration started (or enhanced) several peace initiatives to address traditional security concerns. For example, it stepped up its efforts to seek peace in the Middle East after the 1993 Israeli–PLO Accords, inaugurated a mediating role in Northern Ireland that eventually resulted in the **Good Friday Accords**, and initiated a four-power effort to obtain peace on the Korean peninsula. For a time, too, it employed a special advisor to seek movement on the Cyprus question between Greece and Turkey.

Fourth, the administration undertook at least three important actions to address the new dangers posed by the proliferation of WMD. It completed work on the **Chemical Weapons Convention** and succeeded in persuading the Senate to provide its advice and consent. Also, President Clinton signed the **Comprehensive Test Ban Treaty**, but in a stinging defeat was unable to win Senate approval for it. Furthermore, in a switch in policy for the administration, he signed the **National Missile Defense Act** in 1999. Although the decision on the extent of deployment was ultimately left to Clinton's successor, the administration, with considerable congressional prodding, was moving the nation in the direction of missile defense. In a related action in 1995, working with many other nations, the Clinton administration succeeded in making permanent the strictures in the Nuclear Nonproliferation Treaty (NPT).

Fifth, a few key states now became the focal point of policy attention—even if domestically they did not practice democracy or respect human rights. For instance, the administration supported the Yeltsin (and later Putin) regime in Russia despite human rights violations by its military in Chechnya and despite increasing concern over its growing authoritarianism. Clinton also never wavered in his policy toward China, despite its widespread human rights abuse. Fostering U.S–China trade and maintaining stability in East Asia were greater priorities.

Finally, the Clinton administration's actions over **Kosovo** and **East Timor** fully reflect the selective nature of its policy approach—both where human rights were abused and where democracy was restricted. The air campaign against Serbia over Kosovo in 1999 was strongly justified both on national interest grounds (peace in Europe, the stability of NATO) and on humanitarian values (protecting innocent lives).[27] Yet the president restricted this campaign by explicitly excluding the use of American ground forces. Administration policy toward the atrocities in East Timor also more fully reflects this selective involvement principle. Although the United States would provide logistical supplies for a multilateral operation, the Australians would largely be responsible for action on the ground.

Both President Clinton and his national security advisor, Sandy Berger, reaffirmed the administration's selective engagement approach late in the second term. In a major foreign policy address in February 1999, the president identified five major challenges confronting the United States.[28] Significantly, the list—and its structure—emphasized traditional political/military interests over economic/social concerns. The first two challenges called for renewing alliances—whether through the expansion of NATO or through refurbishing ties with Japan and Korea—and bringing Russia and China, America's principal adversaries during the Cold War, into the international system as "open, prosperous, stable nations." The third challenge also emphasized security by focusing on new international threats and dangers: drug trafficking, terrorism, proliferation, and so forth. Only the fourth and fifth challenges—creating workable trading and financial orders and promoting global freedom—had any hint of the "economic engagement" or "democratic enlargement" emphases of 1993 and 1994. Indeed, the message was clear: the United States should be engaged, it could do some good in the world, and its actions were ultimately more in the traditional political/military realm than in any other.

Berger did likewise in his summation of Clinton's foreign policy only a month or two before the administration left office.[29] In discussing the five principles that guided the administration, Berger listed four (reliance on allies in Europe and Asia, constructive relations with former adversaries, global consequences of local disputes, and new security dangers posed by technology and permeable borders) that fully fit this "selective engagement" approach and had the ring of realism. Only one (the use of economic integration to reduce economic differences) harkened back to the early Clinton years and its liberal internationalist beginnings.

THE LEGACIES OF THE CLINTON ADMINISTRATION'S FOREIGN POLICY

What were the principal legacies of the Clinton administration's foreign policy across its three phases? How did it affect the United States and the rest of the world? Although I have provided a more detailed assessment of the major policy-making and policy legacies of the Clinton administration in another analysis,[30] I draw on it here to suggest several general and specific foreign policy legacies of the Clinton years and to outline the degree of continuity and change from earlier administrations.

General Legacies

The first and most important general legacy for American foreign policy was the Clinton administration's commitment to **maintaining American involvement and leadership in global affairs after the Cold War.** As the extent of its international dealings expanded and contracted from economic to democratic engagement and from enlargement to selective engagement, the president and his administration never wavered in their basic commitment to maintaining a central role for the United States in the international system. Virtually every pronouncement spoke of this. Early on, when Peter Tarnoff, undersecretary of state for political affairs, hinted at a reduced global role, his trial balloon was promptly shot down by Secretary of State Christopher.[31] In this sense, continuity, rather than change, describes the Clinton administration's approach.

At the same time, some might well argue that the administration's interest across such a broad array of foreign policy issues—economic, political-military, sociocultural—had the effect of taking America's global role to new heights and making it difficult, if not impossible, for any subsequent administration to significantly reduce it. Consider the initial impulse of the George W. Bush administration to promote a "distinctly American internationalism." That in effect meant a lessening of U.S. involvement in some areas. Candidate Bush suggested, for example, that the presence of American forces in the Balkans and America's central role in the Middle East peace process should be reduced. Yet his administration had to alter its course on both fronts, even before the devastating events of September 11, 2001. One longtime Washington observer offered a possible explanation for why any policy change by the Bush administration might well be difficult: Clinton's had "occupied so much of the middle ground" across a broad set of foreign policy issues that it had provided little maneuvering room for its successor.[32]

A second general legacy of the Clinton years was an **expanded role for the president in foreign policy**. Despite the initial impulse of the administration to reduce the importance of foreign policy on its agenda, and despite Clinton's apparent aversion to such issues, the administration actually left office with an imperative for a greater, not lesser, executive involvement. The United States could not achieve success in foreign policy without presidential leadership, both domestically and internationally. Whether seeking to pass NAFTA or to obtain fast-track trading authority, President Clinton's participation (or nonparticipation) was crucial to the outcome. Whether negotiating NATO expansion or the refurbishment of the Japanese alliance, presidential involvement was paramount in gaining support both at home and abroad. One reason presidential leadership became necessary was the divided nature of politics in the last six years of the administration (with Republicans controlling both houses of Congress). Another was that there was less support for foreign policy without an overarching strategy such as the Cold War provided.

A third legacy of Clinton's foreign policy was the **extraordinary impact of domestic politics on foreign policy issues**. On one level, of course, it is hardly exceptional to assert that domestic politics shape foreign policy, but what is remarkable about the Clinton years is the extent to which it did so. In the first foreign policy phase, of course, the domestic effect was both by design and definition. Indeed, some of the actions in this phase were crassly calculated in terms of domestic politics. Consider this assessment of the two side agreements to the NAFTA pact negotiated in 1993: "They had to be sufficiently strong to sway domestic environmentalists and, to a lesser extent labor, in order to enable Democrats to vote for the agreement . . . while at the same time not being too strong as to alienate core Republican supporters of NAFTA and their business elites."[33] The continuance of the economic engagement phase was also driven by domestic political considerations, as the failure to gain fast-track trading authority for the president (see Chapter 8) impeded the rapid completion of further economic—particularly multilateral—pacts. Certainly the lack of movement on a trade agreement for the nations of the Western Hemisphere, the expansion of NAFTA, and more progress on an APEC accord derive in part from this failure.

In the second phase, too, the strategy of enlargement was driven by considerations of domestic politics, under the assumption that free markets and free peoples would have considerable domestic appeal. The problem was perhaps that the design was too grandiose and was viewed too skeptically by the public at large and therefore never caught on. In reality, of course, domestic politics compelled the Clinton administration to employ selective engagement after the Republicans gained control of both houses of Congress and as security questions once again (and perhaps inevitably) came to dominate the international agenda.

Finally, the limitations on American actions during the selective engagement phase flowed in large part from domestic politics. Most noteworthy, of course, was the public's aversion to the use of American ground forces abroad and the Clinton administration's policy caution as a result. Similarly, domestic politics were crucial in the NATO expansion decision, the decision to sign legislation that included the Helms-Burton amendment, the administration's changed position on missile defense, and the modification of defense policy.

Specific Legacies

Undoubtedly the Clinton administration's first and most important specific policy legacy—and an important change from earlier administrations—was **the placement of global economic policy at the center of American foreign policy**. NAFTA, WTO, about 300 other trade accords (including congressional approval of permanent normal trading relations with China in late 2000), and the initiation of several multilateral pacts in different areas of the world represent a lasting foreign policy impact. Significantly, too, Clinton's actions in the foreign economic arena made it incumbent on future American presidents to assist in managing the global economy in much the same way they have become responsible for managing the American domestic economy. To be sure, the globalization of economic policy has been a two-edged sword. Although Clinton's efforts transformed and improved the lives of citizens in many countries throughout the world, they also created innumerable dislocations for others. The prolonged and violent protests at the WTO Ministerial meetings in December 1999 (and the violent protests at the Western Hemisphere meeting in Quebec City, the European Union meeting in Göteborg, and the G-8 meeting in Genoa later) illustrate the growing concerns that these global economic transformations have produced.

A second specific policy legacy of the Clinton administration was to **stabilize the relationship between the United States and its principal alliance partners**. NATO's expansion and its prodding to undertake missions "out-of-area" are important legacies of the Clinton years. They have had the effect of moving the allies in the direction of greater security responsibilities, including the incipient development of the European Defense and Security Initiative (EDSI). The refurbishment of alliances in Asia does not appear to have progressed as far as it has in Europe. Nevertheless, the Clinton administration began that process. In this sense, alliance stability represented continuity whereas the nature of some alliance actions (for example, within NATO) represented change.

A third specific legacy was the effort to **stabilize the relationship with China and Russia** after the Cold War, which portended more continuity than change. By the end of Clinton's second term, neither nation was the strategic partner originally envisioned by the administration, but, once again, stabilization had begun. The granting of permanent normal trading relations (PNTR) to China and the expenditure of significant foreign aid to Russia were important factors in this stabilization. Moreover, they made it difficult for any future administration to turn abruptly in a different policy direction.

A fourth specific legacy was that the United States would **take the lead in conflict resolution**. Although this did not represent a significant change by the

United States or Clinton, it was an area where the administration devoted a great deal of time and energy. Its record is largely mixed, but the general conclusion is that these efforts were more positive than negative, leaving important opportunities for the administration's successors.

The Dayton Accords and the Middle East peace discussions top the list of the administration's conflict resolution efforts; the conflicts in Northern Ireland and the Korean peninsula were important as well. Yet by the end of the Clinton presidency, no significant and sustained progress had been made. None of his efforts produced the level of resolution perhaps originally hoped for. In fact, the Middle East negotiations were sharply frayed and in danger of collapse by the end of 2000 (despite the Wye Plantation Accords of 1998 and a last-ditch effort by the administration in 2000), and even with the Dayton Accords the situation in Bosnia was fragile, with the likelihood of American military presence there for some time to come. The Good Friday Accords for Northern Ireland also yielded initial promise, but, once again, they were on the verge of collapse by the end of the Clinton years. The Four-Party Talks over Korea were also stalled as a new president assumed office.

At least three other specific policy efforts had similar incomplete outcomes and represent continuity more so than change from past American actions. First, Clinton's attempts at reducing threats to global peace and stability from WMD did not progress far. To be sure, his counter-proliferation initiative, announced early in his first term, signaled the United States' intention to use both prevention and protection measures against WMD. The successful ratification of the Convention on Chemical Weapons was also an important step for creating an international organization to monitor the use of chemicals and prevent their conversion to WMD. However, the failure to gain Senate approval of the Comprehensive Test Ban Treaty, the failure to resolve the issue of missile defense (and the ABM Treaty debate), the ambiguous outcome of the 1994 agreement with North Korea over halting its nuclear weapons program, the remaining dangers from possible weapons development by Iraq, and nuclear weapons testing by India and Pakistan in 1998 all suggest that this legacy was perhaps more negative than positive and represented a real challenge for future administrations.[34]

Second, although the administration came to office with a substantial commitment to human rights and the promotion of democracy, its efforts in these areas often were overshadowed by other policy priorities. Its hesitancy to become involved in the Balkans, its reluctance to challenge China over human rights, and its decision not to become involved in Rwanda lend credence to this position. The military interdiction in Haiti, the Bosnian response under the Dayton Accords, and the actions in Kosovo suggest otherwise, but, by most measures, the promotion of democracy and human rights during the Clinton administration cannot be characterized as an unqualified success.

By its second term, the Clinton administration was actually taking a different path to the improvement of global human rights. That is, it had seemingly decided to emphasize *multilateral* and *indirect* means, although with the proviso **that unilateral and direct** means would not be wholly abandoned.[35] Increasingly, American actions would be directed at resolving conflicts and disputes and encouraging political institutions and elections as indirect ways to improve human rights, and the United States would work with other state and nonstate actors in pursuing these goals. Finally, and importantly, the negative effects of globalization would need to be incorporated into any policy addressing democracy and human rights by a new administration.

Third, the issue of when and under what conditions the United States would intervene with American force remained unresolved at the end of the Clinton years. The administration took several steps to clarify American policy, but questions continued. In May 1994, and in response to the Somalia fiasco, Clinton issued Presidential Decision Directive 25 (PDD-25), which outlined the specific conditions required for the United States to participate in multilateral peace support operations. In May 1997, the administration issued another directive, **PDD-56**, which outlined the intragovernmental procedures for preparing for, and executing, a humanitarian intervention,[36] and in June 1999, after the Kosovo bombing, President Clinton made a sweeping pledge to assist those endangered around the world: "[W]hether you live in Africa, or Central Europe, or any other place, if somebody comes after innocent civilians and tries to kill them en masse because of their race, their ethnic background or their religion, and it's within our power to stop it, we will stop it."[37]

This pledge, labeled the **Clinton Doctrine** on humanitarian intervention, seemed to represent a new departure for intervention policy.[38] However, it was controversial. Were American policy makers wholly committed to such universal action, especially in light of the limited actions over Rwanda and East Timor? Would the American people support such interventions in light of their limited support for the use of force involving internal conflicts, albeit more so for humanitarian ones?[39]

THE INTERNATIONAL SYSTEM AT THE DAWN OF A NEW CENTURY

Although the Clinton administration saw important changes in and challenges for American foreign policy after the Cold War, the shape of the international system was affected by this important global event as well. Before we turn to American foreign policy at the beginning of the new century under the George W. Bush administration, we must take stock of the global landscape at the end of the 1990s and by the year 2000. Across a wide spectrum, the international system had changed dramatically from only a few decades earlier, when the United States first committed itself to a continuous global role after World War II.

The forces of globalization—those forces that knit together peoples and societies regardless of state boundaries—had accelerated rapidly with the ending of the Cold War and affected the political, economic, and social makeup of the international community. On the political level, the number and kinds of intergovernmental and nongovernmental organizations had expanded dramatically. The magnitude of these international linkages challenged—and arguably reduced—the sovereignty of the nation-state. Among regional security organizations, for instance, NATO, the Association of Southeast Asian Nations (ASEAN) Regional Forum, and the Organization for Security and Cooperation (OSCE) were expanding their memberships, agendas, and activities in global affairs. Much the same was true for regional and global economic organizations. NAFTA had taken off and was rapidly expanding trade relations among the United States, Canada, and Mexico. The continuing efforts of the European Union to unite Europe through expanding its membership and deepening its responsibilities—including the creation of a new currency, the euro—had profound economic, political, and social implications. Likewise, APEC continued to expand and intensify its activities across Asia and the Pacific. Finally, the growth of nongovernmental organizations (NGOs)—people-to-people groups across national boundaries—had accelerated throughout the past century, especially from 1950 to the present. Some NGOs promote global human rights (Human Rights Watch, Amnesty International) or foster relief efforts (International Red Cross, Oxfam). Others advance religious beliefs and services (major religions, World Vision, Catholic Relief Services) or promote political and cultural causes across states (Socialist International, la Francophonie, al-Qaeda). Still others promote global environmental (Greenpeace) and economic goals (multinational firms such as ExxonMobil, Toyota, Mitsubishi). In all, estimates of the number of these nongovernmental organizations vary widely from a few thousand to 25,000 and even as many as 100,000 worldwide.[40] Although the exact number may be in dispute, their growth and significance across national boundaries are not.

We may blithely assume that these globalizing forces are working in a positive way to knit peoples, societies, and states together, but the reality is that each also has its dark side. In the economic realm, the freeing up of global markets has undoubtedly produced cheaper and more abundant goods in some states, but it has also harmed people and societies in states unable to compete in the global marketplace. Many workers in some countries are forced to accept low wages just to keep their jobs and to stay competitive in the global economy; some may be displaced as companies move to cheaper labor markets abroad.

The forces of globalization contribute to new security dangers. With more open and penetrable borders, trafficking in drugs and people may be less detectable. The same is true for the movement of terrorists seeking to raise havoc in the international community. The widespread use of the Internet, the ready availability of cell phones, and the increasing ease of international travel all create an international system that is more penetrable and less controllable. Finally, new environmental issues arise as global warming and global pollution recognize no national borders.

In sum, the international system at the dawn of the new century was an admixture of integrating and dividing forces that increasingly challenged nation-states and their foreign policies. New actors and issues marked the global environment. Perhaps the most significant shock to the international system in the first months of the new century was represented by the events of September 11, 2001.

BEFORE AND AFTER 9/11: THE FOREIGN POLICY OF THE GEORGE W. BUSH ADMINISTRATION

During the 2000 election campaign, George W. Bush announced that he would pursue a "distinctly American internationalism" in foreign policy,[41] largely in contrast to the liberal internationalism of the Clinton administration. He initially sought a greater emphasis on American national interests than on global interests. The events of September 11, however, quickly changed both the content of his administration's foreign policy and the process by which it was made. As a result, President Bush's foreign policy was universal in scope and viewed virtually all international actions as affecting American interests. The efforts to build a "coalition of the willing" to find and defeat "terrorists and tyrants" worldwide illustrate the universality of this approach, but the difficulties that the invasion and occupation of Iraq created also demonstrate its limitations. At the beginning of its second term, the Bush administration reiterated its commitment to democratization worldwide as yet another way to combat global terrorism, and it initiated some actions toward that goal. Yet its efforts were largely overshadowed by the continuing occupation of Iraq and the failure to end that war.

THE VALUES AND BELIEFS OF THE BUSH ADMINISTRATION: PRIOR TO SEPTEMBER 11

Because George W. Bush was philosophically inclined to follow the political realism in foreign policy of his father's administration, President Clinton's legacies were particularly unwelcome. Indeed, these legacies were a target of attack by candidate Bush and his foreign policy advisors in the 2000 election and beyond because they represented a more universal and multilateral approach than the new administration intended. Yet Bush did not come to office with much foreign policy experience or with his own vision of America's role in the world. Thus, he was highly dependent on his foreign policy advisors, and the team that he chose provides considerable insight into the direction that his foreign policy would take. For the most part, Bush selected political realists, foreign policy conservatives and neoconservatives, and veterans of recent Republican administrations.

Bush's Foreign Policy Team

Bush's **vice president, Dick Cheney**, quickly became a key advisor. Cheney, of course, had been a member of two previous administrations, as chief of staff in the Gerald R. Ford administration and as secretary of defense in the George H. W. Bush administration, and he had represented Wyoming in Congress for several terms. In this sense, he was familiar with Washington and the policy-making process. His views, too, were well established. He was generally regarded as conservative, as reflected in his voting record in Congress, but he quickly became a strong advocate of American primacy in the world. Cheney advanced his views in the Bush White House and sometimes got ahead of administration policy, especially in promoting a more vigorous approach toward Iraq in the months preceding the Iraq war.[42] Indeed, he also became identified as a leader of the "neoconservatives" in the White House. (Neoconservatives believed that "American power has been and could be used for moral purposes," that the nature of the regimes within countries affect foreign policy and require attention, and that international institutions and international law should be viewed skeptically as a guide to policy.[43] In the neoconservative view, the United States should be more assertive and robust in its foreign policy actions.)

A second crucial Bush advisor was **Condoleezza Rice**, assistant to the president for national security affairs, or national security adviser. A veteran of the George H. W. Bush administration, where she worked on the NSC staff dealing with Soviet/Russian affairs, she was now named to head the NSC and the NSC "system" (see Chapter 10). On foreign policy matters, Rice quickly became Bush's "alter ego," much as she had been during the 2000 election campaign. Although she was not viewed as a "master global strategist like Henry Kissinger" and largely saw her role as sharpening the differences among other key advisors,[44] she had ready access to the president and could surely shape the direction of policy by her (largely) private advice. Moreover, her general foreign policy orientation was more toward traditional realism than the neoconservativism that came to dominate the Bush policy-making apparatus.

In his first term, President Bush appointed **Colin Powell**, a veteran of several previous administrations and possessor of a wealth of foreign policy experience, as his secretary of state. Powell had served as national security advisor during the Reagan administration and as chairman of the Joint Chiefs of Staff during the George H. W. Bush administration and in the early days of the Clinton administration.[45] Although instinctively a political realist, Powell was probably the most moderate among Bush's key foreign policy advisors. His deputy secretary of state, Richard Armitage, who also had served in several foreign policy–making posts in the Reagan and senior Bush administrations, largely in the Department of Defense, held views compatible with Powell's, although perhaps a bit more conservative.

When Rice became secretary of state, she continued this more realist foreign policy perspective, both through her own views and through her principal aides. She appointed Robert Zoellick as deputy secretary of state.[46] He, too, had had long experience in Washington, serving as U.S. trade representative during George W. Bush's first term and in the Treasury and State departments, and as White House deputy chief of staff in the Reagan and the senior Bush administrations.

At the Department of Defense, the two top officials appointed in the first term were largely neoconservative voices on foreign policy, and both came to their positions with substantial policy-making experience. **Donald Rumsfeld** was appointed for a second time as secretary of defense, a post he had served in during the Ford administration. His Washington experience included several terms in Congress during the 1960s, a stint in the Nixon administration, and service as U.S. ambassador to NATO in the early 1970s. In 1998 and 2000, he served on commissions evaluating missile defense and national security strategy for space.[47] Rumsfeld's foreign policy views tended toward American primacy, and his policy impact became especially pronounced in the post–September 11 period. Rumsfeld's deputy secretary of defense, **Paul Wolfowitz**, shared many of Rumsfeld's views about a more vigorous and singular global role for the United States after the Cold War and after September 11. Indeed, he was also viewed as a leader of the neoconservatives in the Bush administration, who hoped to reshape American foreign policy on the Reagan model of the 1980s.[48]

When Rumsfeld resigned in November 2006, his successor was **Robert Gates**. Gates came from the presidency of Texas A&M University but had had extensive government experience in previous administrations as deputy national security adviser and CIA director during the George H. W. Bush administration and as the only CIA entry-level officer to become director of the agency in its history.[49] His global views were more those of a traditional realist and thus were highly compatible with the views of Secretary of State Rice.

George Tenet, as director of Central Intelligence, was a holdover from the Clinton administration. He, too, brought a considerable amount of Washington experience—as deputy director of the CIA before assuming the directorship, as a member of the NSC staff, and as a member of the staff of the Senate Intelligence Committee. The new administration viewed this experience as an asset. However, with the events of 9/11 and the faulty intelligence related to the initiation of the Iraq War, Tenet ultimately stepped down in 2004. He was succeeded by Porter Goss, a former CIA officer and a member of Congress for several terms. Goss had led the House Intelligence Committee prior to assuming the position as CIA director. He served for two years and was succeeded by General Michael Hayden in 2006. Hayden, a career intelligence officer in the military, a former director of the National Security Agency, and the initial deputy director of national intelligence from 2005 to 2006, thus had considerable policy-making experience in the intelligence field.[50]

In all, Bush's key advisors were Washington and foreign policy veterans. During the first term, as noted, several were more ideological and more unilateralist than their predecessors in the Clinton administration. During Bush's second term, several neoconservatives were replaced with more traditional conservatives and political realists.

CLASSICAL REALISM AND THE
BUSH APPROACH

Classical realism is based on several important assumptions about states and state behavior that had direct implications for the Bush administration's initial foreign policy approach. First, classical realists assume that states are the principal actors in foreign policy and that actions *between* states trump any efforts to change behaviors *within* them. In this sense, relations between states are the basis for evaluating a country's foreign policy, and American policy would focus principally on state-to-state relations. Second, a state's "interests are determined by its power (meaning its material resources) relative to other nations."[51] As a state's relative power increases, it seeks to expand its political influence, albeit based on a careful cost/benefit analysis. In this regard, American power could and should be used to restrain states that could clearly harm the United States and its interests, but it should be exercised carefully. Third, classical realists focus on managing relations among the major powers, as these are likely to be the major threats to the international system. A guiding principle for realists is that no great power, or coalition of great powers, should dominate or endanger a nation or a group of nations. In this sense, the United States should focus on strengthening its alliances and on challenging some states, albeit prudently and selectively.

These assumptions largely informed the policies that the Bush administration initially supported and opposed when it took office in 2001. First of all, Bush came to office seeking to develop a "**distinctly American internationalism.**"What that phrase implied was a much narrower definition of the American national interest than his immediate predecessor's and even his father's.[52] Second, candidate Bush had made clear that a top priority of his administration would be to refurbish America's alliances around the world as a tangible manifestation of managing great-power relationships. Europe and Asia would be the highest foreign policy priorities because they were home to long-time allies—and potential rivals. Third, Russia and China would be viewed more skeptically than they had been by the Clinton administration, and American military capacity would be important for exercising American influence over them. China, for example, should be viewed as an emerging power and as "a competitor, not a strategic partner."[53] Fourth, "hard power" would be preferred over "soft power" for dealing with the international system.[54] Hard power uses military capacity, sanctioning, and threats, among other coercive measures, as ways to influence the behavior of nations. Soft power relies on the appeal of American culture and American values to enable the United States to wield influence. Fifth, and in line with refurbishing alliances and with the use of hard power, the remaking and strengthening of the American military would be a top priority in terms of increased military pay and increased military spending overall.

The assumptions of classical realism also pointed to the policies that the Bush administration initially opposed. Most fundamentally, the new administration, largely in contrast to the Clinton years, sought to narrow America's foreign involvement and focus only on strategically important actions. First, the United States would not be as caught up in changing other states internally or in promoting political democracy. As Bush stated:"We value the elegant structures of our own democracy—but realize that, in other societies, the architecture will vary.We propose our principles, but we must not impose our culture."[55] Second, Bush opposed American humanitarian interventions that had no clear strategic rationale. The American military, Rice said, is neither "a civilian police force" nor "a political referee" in internecine and communal conflicts.[56] Indeed, during the 2000 election campaign, Bush demonstrated this position by indicating a willingness to pull back from American involvement in Middle East discussions, and, during his first months in office, by deciding to move away from negotiations with North Korea. Third, the Bush administration eschewed involvement with international institutions and opposed several key international agreements—rejecting the Kyoto Protocol to control global warming, opposing the Comprehensive Test Ban Treaty, and showing a willingness to withdraw from the 1972 ABM Treaty in order to deploy national missile defense. Fourth, the administration was not inclined to afford much influence to Congress or America's allies in the conduct of foreign policy. Instead, executive power in foreign affairs would be reasserted.

THE IMPACT OF SEPTEMBER 11

Much as December 7, 1941, was a "day which will live in infamy" for earlier generations of Americans, **September 11, 2001**, will be such a day for the current American generation. Indeed, Americans will always remember where they were and what they were doing when they first heard that American Airlines flight 11 crashed into the north tower of the World Trade Center, or a few minutes later when United Airlines flight 175 crashed into the south tower. Few, too, will forget where they were a little while later when American Airlines flight 77 crashed into the Pentagon and United Airlines Flight 93 crashed into a field in Pennsylvania after the passengers attempted to overpower its hijackers.

From an analytical point of view, the events of that day represent one of those **rare and spectacular political events** that can change the mindset of the public and its leaders regarding foreign policy. Such watershed events are few indeed, as one political scientist noted many years ago, but when they do occur, they can reverse or change the views of a generation or more.[57] The Vietnam War—or the "searing effects of Vietnam" to use the words of a political scientist at the time—was another of those spectacular events that had a jarring effect on attitudes toward war and peace and toward the use of American force abroad in an earlier period.[58] More recently, the collapse of the Berlin Wall and the implosion of the Soviet Union—the ending of the Cold War—might be cited as similar spectacular events. Yet September 11 appears to rank at the top because of its pervasive effect not only for the generation being socialized to politics at the time but also for the leveling effect it had on foreign policy beliefs across generations.

In a real sense, September 11 has had a more profound effect than Pearl Harbor, the Vietnam War, or the Berlin Wall for at least three reasons. First, it was the **first substantial attack on the American continent** since the burning of Washington in the War of 1812. The American public had always assumed it was secure, and 9/11 shattered that assumption. It demonstrated that no state or person was safe from those determined to do harm. Second, September 11 was fundamentally **an attack on American civilians**, not military personnel (although, to be sure, military personnel were killed at the Pentagon). Even Pearl Harbor and its devastation had fundamentally been directed at the military. Third, and important, the **terrorist attack was the deadliest in American history**—costing almost 3,000 lives and surpassing the total dead at Pearl Harbor by almost 1,000.

The effects of September 11 were profound, whether measured by the changed attitudes among the American public toward foreign policy, the changed agenda within Congress with new levels of support for the president on foreign policy issues, or the changed nature of the presidency itself.

Impact on the Public and Congress

The impact of September 11 on the American people was evident almost immediately. Hosts of Americans were suddenly flying flags from their car windows, wearing them on their lapels, and pasting them to their front windows. From people of all walks of life and from all parts of the country came a huge outpouring of support for the victims of the attacks and their families. Support, too, for President Bush and his foreign policy actions increased across party lines. His approval rating went from 51 percent just prior to September 11, 2001, to 86 percent immediately after. The "rally 'round the flag" effect (35 points) was the largest the Gallup polling organization ever recorded. Indeed, Bush's approval rating shortly reached 90 percent.[59]

After September 11, the American public's foreign policy attitudes took a sharp turn away from those it had held as recently as the 1998 Chicago Council on Foreign Relations survey.[60] Now, those attitudes supported a more robust American approach abroad. In particular, although the public continued its strong support for nonmilitary measures to address terrorism, it was now willing to endorse military measures as well, including the use of American air strikes and ground troops against terrorists and even the assassination of terrorist leaders if carried out multilaterally. The public strongly supported more spending on defense and more spending on intelligence gathering. Overall, the public was hardly a constraint on Bush's foreign policy actions after September 11; instead, it appeared to be endorsing whatever actions that the administration was already pursuing or contemplating.

September 11 had a similar effect on Congress and its role in policy making, especially when compared to its role over the previous three decades. The end of the Cold War had accelerated the pluralistic decision-making process that had emerged after the Vietnam War and had enhanced congressional influence. With the collapse of the Soviet Empire and the breakup of the Soviet Union, for instance, America's foreign policy agenda changed dramatically, and a broad array of new economic, environmental, sociocultural, and security issues now took center stage. Many of these issues allowed or required congressional action. As a result, foreign policy issues became increasingly partisan and contentious.[61]

In large measure, the events of September 11 changed all that, and, much as with the impact on public attitudes, served as a **watershed in congressional–executive relations on foreign policy**. In particular, they seem to have resurrected an aphorism popular during the height of the Cold War: "Politics stops at the water's edge." Substantively, the impact of September 11 on congressional behavior manifested itself in the high degree of bipartisan support for legislation to combat international terrorism.

Within a week of the September 11 attacks, Congress had enacted **Senate Joint Resolution 23** authorizing the president to use force "against those nations, organizations, or persons, he determines planned, authorized, committed, or aided the terrorist attacks." Just over a month later, it passed the **USA PATRIOT Act** that afforded the executive branch greater discretion in pursuing terrorist suspects and narrowed some previous civil liberty protections. Over the next several months, Congress passed several pieces of legislation waiving previous restrictions on aid to Pakistan, enhancing border security and visa entry requirements, aiding the victims of terrorism, increasing intelligence authorizations, and amending the immigration statute. Some twenty-one pieces of legislation were passed as part of the congressional response to September 11.[62]

Many of these pieces of legislations were passed with little dissent. In all, only five produced any opposition, all of it confined to the House of Representatives. And even those—the Air Transportation Safety and System Stabilization Act, the USA PATRIOT Act, the Terrorist Bombings Convention Implementation Act, the Export-Import Bank Reauthorization Act, and the National Defense Authorization Act—received only a modest number of opposing votes. In all, then, there was overwhelming congressional support for the president in the first year after September 11.

This congressional support continued in the second year as well, although not quite at the same level. In October 2002, Congress passed a joint resolution authorizing the president to use force "as he determines to be necessary and appropriate in order to defend the national security of the United States against the continuing threat posed by Iraq and enforce all relevant United Nations Security Council Resolutions regarding Iraq."[63] Passage was by a wide margin in each chamber (House, 296–133; Senate, 77–23). **The Department of Homeland Security Act of 2002** also passed by a wide margin in the House (295–133), but stalled in the Senate for a time. After the Republicans' and President Bush's success in the 2002 congressional elections, the Senate acted quickly, passing the measure by a 90–9 vote in November 2002 and establishing one of the largest governmental bureaucracies in the history of the American Republic.

Impact on the President

Finally, and importantly, the events of September 11, 2001, appeared to have had a profound impact on **George W. Bush himself**, both **personally and on his policy approach**. On the night of those tragic events, he dictated for his diary that "the Pearl Harbor of the 21st century took place today."[64] With that assessment, Bush appeared to realize that he had new responsibilities. "He was now a wartime president,"[65] as Bob Woodward noted, with all that this implied for his leadership.

Fred Greenstein, a long-time student of presidents, argues that Bush's cognitive style and his effectiveness with the public were the areas most affected by the terrorist attacks. His emotional intelligence was strengthened in that he was able to face this national tragedy, and his political skills were sharpened by his need to put together a coalition against terrorism.[66] Thomas Preston and Margaret Hermann reach a similar conclusion: "[Bush's] normal lack of interest in foreign affairs and desire to delegate the formulation and implementation of foreign policy to others . . . was forced to give way to his current, more active and involved pattern."[67] Political psychologist Stanley Renshon also argues that 9/11 was a transforming moment for the president. It helped him find "his place and his purpose." He then "turned his efforts toward transforming America's place in the world and the world in which America has its place."[68]

THE VALUES AND BELIEFS OF THE BUSH ADMINISTRATION: AFTER SEPTEMBER 11

If aspects of President Bush's leadership style were affected by the tragic events at the World Trade Center and the Pentagon, his administration's foreign policy changed as well. Although these events ironically confirmed some of the administration's assumptions about the world and its approach to it (such as the importance of hard power over soft power and the need for enhanced military preparedness), they also suggested the limits of Bush's commitment to classical realism. The administration did not do a *volte-face* in its policy, but it did change from classical realism to what we would describe as "defensive realism" that incorporated a distinct form of idealism.

Defensive Realism and "Revival Wilsonians"[69]

Defensive realism makes many of the same assumptions as classical realism, but it differs in one important aspect: the importance of "insecurity" as the motivating force for state actions. Fareed Zakaria summarizes this fundamental difference:

> While the latter implies that states expand out of confidence, or at least out of an awareness of increased resources, the former maintains that states expand out of fear and nervousness. For the classical realist, states expand because they can; for the defensive realist, states expand because they must.[70]

The new threatening environment after September 11, 2001, thus propelled the Bush administration to rethink some of its assumptions and actions—and eventually to create a new defensive security strategy.

Along with a new defensive realism, the Bush administration embraced a form of idealism in foreign affairs, especially in regard to combating international terrorism in the post-9/11 era. A nation pursuing an idealist foreign policy approach is motivated by a moral imperative and seeks to promote common values within and across states. In this sense, U.S. foreign policy became more than state-to-state relations among the strong and now sought to advance universal norms. That is, the administration would promote a worldwide imperative against terrorism even as it pursued greater global democratization. Thus, it became increasingly concerned about the actions of all states (and groups) and the internal composition of many, especially as it influenced their attitude toward terrorism. Put somewhat differently, the administration appeared to embrace the **Wilsonian tradition** in American foreign policy, albeit driven rather singularly by the imperative to combat terrorism and doing so in a particular way.[71]

This change in approach—and the Bush administration's combining of realism and idealism—might be described essentially as its adoption of what Francis Fukuyama labels "**the neoconservative legacy**." The administration came to accept that the "internal characteristics of regimes matter" in the conduct of foreign policy, that American power and capabilities can and should be used for moral purposes even within states, and that international institutions and international law should be viewed skeptically in the conduct of foreign policy. At the same time, it continued to view social engineering by governments suspiciously.[72] Walter Russell Mead labels the Bush administration adherents of the neoconservative legacy as "**Revival Wilsonians**."[73] They believed in the spread of democracy and the goodness of American intentions and actions, without Wilson's embrace of international law and institutions. This revamped Wilsonianism was driven fundamentally by domestic American values and implemented primarily by American power and American unilateralism.

Changes in Assumptions and Policy Direction

Three of Bush's initial foreign policy assumptions changed as a result of 9/11.[74] First, and perhaps most significantly, his administration moved from a narrow or particularistic foreign policy approach to a **more universal approach**. It moved from narrowing American national interests to broadening them to combat international terrorism. Second, it moved away from its rather narrowly defined unilateralism to a **greater multilateralism, albeit with a unilateralist option**. Although the United States would pursue multilateral efforts, Bush threatened to act unilaterally if multilateral support did not come—much as the war against Iraq would demonstrate. Third, the administration moved from its reliance on a stark realism in foreign policy—without much concern for the internal dynamics of states—to a version of idealism that was clearly concerned with the **internal dynamics of *some* states**. In this regard, humanitarian interventions, peacekeeping efforts, and peacemaking actions within states had now become part and parcel of Bush's foreign policy approach, much as they had for his immediate predecessor.

Several administration actions evidenced these changes in assumptions. Bush addressed a joint session of Congress shortly after September 11 to call for a new universalism. Instead of a "distinctly American internationalism," he now adopted what might be called a "**comprehensive American globalism**," defined and animated by the moral outrage against the attacks on the World Trade Center and the Pentagon. In other words, Bush committed the United States to fighting terrorism and states that support it everywhere, and with all means, asserting

> Our enemy is a radical network of terrorists, and every government that supports them. . . .
>
> Our war on terror begins with al Qaeda, but it does not end there. It will not end until every terrorist group of global reach has been found, stopped and defeated.[75]

In words reminiscent of the Truman Doctrine at the start of the Cold War, Bush outlined the **dichotomous and stark nature of the global struggle**—a struggle between the way of terror and the way of freedom, a struggle between states that support terror and those that do not, and a struggle between the uncivilized and civilized world.

> These terrorists kill not merely to end lives, but to disrupt and end a way of life. With every atrocity, they hope that America grows fearful, retreating from the world and forsaking our friends. They stand against us, because we stand in their way.
>
> [W]e will pursue nations that provide aid or safe haven to terrorism. Every nation, in every region, now has a decision to make. Either you are with us, or you are with the terrorists. . . .
>
> This is not . . . just America's fight. And what is at stake is not just America's freedom. This is the world's fight. This is civilization's fight.[76]

Bush also conveyed the multilateral nature of this new foreign policy approach in his initial speech on the war on terrorism, which was demonstrated by his administration's actions.

> Our response involves far more than instant retaliation and isolated strikes. Americans should not expect one battle, but a lengthy campaign, unlike any other we have ever seen. . . . We will starve terrorist of funding, turn them one against another, drive them from place to place, until there is no refuge or no rest. . . .
>
> We ask every nation to join us. . . .[77]

Most dramatic about Bush's new foreign policy approach were its decision to mount a coalitional effort, the speed with which it was put together, and the variety of participants that it included, especially in light of his foreign policy assumptions when he took office. On a bilateral level, for example, Russia, China, India, and Pakistan offered to provide information and support. Twenty-seven nations offered the United States overflight and landing rights in connection with its actions in Afghanistan. One hundred nations offered to provide intelligence support to the United States. On a multilateral level, the UN Security Council adopted a resolution instructing all nations to pursue terrorists and their supporters. Australia invoked Article IV of the ANZUS Treaty and declared the 9/11 attack as representing an attack on it.[78] Finally, for the first time in its history, NATO invoked Article V of the treaty, viewing the attack as an attack on all of its members.

In all, then, such a listing conveys the collective effort undertaken to address these attacks. In addition, the United States engaged cooperative efforts to freeze the financial assets of known or suspected terrorist organizations within the United States and around the world. Finally, the Office (and later Department) of Homeland Security was created, new security standards were imposed at airports, and stricter standards were initiated for immigration into the United States.

By the time that a military operation was commenced in Afghanistan on October 7, 2001, several allied countries (Britain, Canada, Australia, Germany, and France, among others) had pledged assistance. Aditionally, more than forty nations had approved American overflight and landing rights.[79] This assistance came from several continents and regions (the Middle East, Africa, Europe, and Asia). Furthermore, Operation Anaconda in Afghanistan eventually included contributions from some twenty countries from around the world.

A third dimension to this post–September 11 change was the administration's interests and actions regarding **communal and regional conflicts**. The decision to focus on the internal situation in Afghanistan is hardly surprising in light of September 11, but what is surprising is the extent to which the administration committed itself to changing or assisting in changing the domestic situations in other countries. These range from the effort to pursue the "axis of evil" countries—Iran, Iraq, and North Korea—to the commitments for military training and advisory units to the Philippines, Yemen, and Georgia, among others, for assistance with internal problems and to efforts to use American naval power around Somalia to block possibly escaping al-Qaeda fighters.

The administration's efforts to resolve conflict in the Middle East and between India and Pakistan and its reopening of discussions with North Korea also illustrate a newfound concern with the internal dynamics of various countries and regions. Almost immediately after September 11, the administration appointed a special envoy, General Anthony Zinni, to the Middle East, and Secretary of State Colin Powell traveled to India and Pakistan in an attempt to defuse the situation over Kashmir. President Bush reiterated his willingness to open discussions with the North Koreans over peace and stability on the Korean peninsula (although this was a position adopted as early as the summer of 2001). At the same time, the administration was willing to look past internal concerns with some nations (such as China, Russia, Pakistan), especially their human rights conditions, because their cooperation in the war on terrorism was more important for the United States.

In sum, the thrust of the new approach, quickly labeled the **Bush Doctrine**, was to hunt down terrorists and their supporters on a worldwide scale. In this effort the United States would seek cooperation and support from other countries but would go it alone if necessary. The globalism of this effort and the motivation for its actions represent the major transformations of the Bush administration's policy approach after September 11, 2001.

FORMALIZING THE BUSH DOCTRINE: THE *NATIONAL SECURITY STRATEGY* STATEMENT

Although its statements and actions conveyed President Bush's new foreign policy approach, the administration issued a fuller rationale for its policy direction almost exactly one year after 9/11. This was *The National Security Strategy of the United States of America*, which declared that the fundamental aim of American foreign policy was "to create a balance of power that favors freedom."[80] To create such a balance, the United States would "defend the peace by fighting terrorists and tyrants . . . will preserve peace by building good relations among the great powers . . . [and would] extend the peace by encouraging free and open societies on every continent."

This statement demonstrates how much American actions would now be motivated by the new threat environment, much as defensive realism postulated. It also conveyed the idealist and universal nature of the proposed foreign policy agenda with its concern for the internal make-up and operations of states and groups: "The United States is now threatened less by conquering states than . . . by failing ones . . . less by fleets and armies than by catastrophic technologies in the hands of the embittered few." The statement moreover recognized and accepted the fact that the United States possessed "unprecedented—and unequaled—strength and influence in the world" and acknowledged that "this position comes with unparalleled responsibilities, obligations, and opportunity."

The Bush administration outlined seven courses of action to promote its fundamental goal of promoting freedom and advancing the "nonnegotiable demands of human dignity." These included rallying nations and alliances around the world to defeat terrorism (and relying on a broad array of actions to do so); addressing (and hopefully resolving) regional conflicts to reduce their impact on global stability; and focusing on "rogue states" and terrorists who might gain access to WMD. The administration also indicated that it would seek to lead a broad coalition to promote a balance of power.

The *National Security Strategy* included commitments to ignite global economic growth, fundamentally through free trade initiatives but also through increased development assistance and the expansion of global democracies. Finally, it called for transforming national security institutions at home by improving the military and the intelligence communities and strengthening homeland security to defend peace at home and abroad.[81]

To provide a better sense of the direction of the Bush administration's foreign policy and to identify its emphases, we group these courses of actions under what appear to be the proper themes of defending, preserving, and extending the peace.

Defending the Peace

The first three courses of action explicitly focused on defending the peace against terrorists and rogue states. The administration would **rally nations and alliances** around the world to defeat terrorism. The new adversary was now "not a single political regime or person or religion or ideology" but an "elusive enemy" that would "be fought on many fronts" and "over an extended period of time. Progress would come through the persistent accumulation of successes—some seen, some unseen."[82] Moreover, a broad array of actions would be used to defeat terrorism—disrupting the funding of terrorists through various means, taking direct actions against terrorists and terrorist organizations, denying territorial sanctuaries to terrorist groups in failed countries, addressing domestic conditions that breed terrorism, and strengthening homeland security. Although the *National Security Strategy* makes clear that regional and international organizations would be used in pursuing this objective, it also states that the United States would act alone or through a "coalition of the willing" if necessary.

The second course of action to defend the peace would be to address **the regional conflicts** in the world. These conflicts could "strain our alliances, rekindle rivalries among the great powers, and create horrifying affronts to human dignity." The Bush administration committed itself to a variety of actions to reduce the impact of regional conflicts on global stability and, where possible, to aid in their resolution. However, it made clear that there were to be limits on how much the United States could and would do: "The United States should be realistic about its ability to help those who are unwilling or unready to help themselves."

A third dimension of defending the peace focused on **rogue states and terrorists** that might gain access to WMD. That is, the Bush administration would use the threat of WMD as a way to link terrorists and rogue states and to identify both as the combined enemies of American foreign policy. These rogue states, while small in number, were states "that brutalize their own people"; "display no regard for international law"; are "determined to acquire weapons of mass destruction"; "sponsor terrorism around the globe"; and "reject human values and hate the United States and everything for which it stands." In particular, the United States would have to be prepared to "deter and defend" against terrorists and rogue states, strengthen nonproliferation efforts against them, and have "effective consequence management" against the effects of WMD if deterrence failed.

Preserving the Peace

The first three courses of action would also contribute to preserving the peace, but the sixth course—**developing cooperation with other centers of power**—explicitly focused on that goal. The United States would seek to lead a broad coalition, "as broad as practicable," to promote a balance of power in favor of freedom. This coalition-building effort would involve America's traditional allies, such as NATO (and an expanded NATO), Japan, Australia, Korea, Thailand, and the Philippines, but it would also include Russia, India, and China. In this sense, the Bush administration advocated submerging differences that might exist between the United States and key countries (such as Russia, China, India, and Pakistan) in an effort to build a larger and nearly universal coalition against international terrorism. What is particularly noteworthy about this section of the document is its relative silence on the role of international organizations, save for some discussion of NATO and the European Union.

Extending the Peace

The fourth and fifth courses of action—**igniting global economic growth and expanding the number of open societies and democracies**—reflected the economic and political components of the administration's foreign policy approach (as contrasted with the security dimension so evident in the other courses of action). They also reflected its effort to bring more states into this balance of power for freedom as well as some of its idealistic underpinnings. The Bush administration's view was that economic growth "creates new jobs and higher incomes. It allows people to lift their lives out of poverty, spurs economic and legal reform, and the fight against corruption, and it reinforces the habits of liberty." Thus, the United States would be committed to "a return to economic growth in Europe and Japan" and "to policies that will help emerging markets achieve access to larger capital flows at lower costs." In particular, the Bush administration reaffirmed its commitment to global, regional, and bilateral free trade initiatives as the way to foster global economic growth and development. In the belief that protection of the environment should accompany this commitment, the administration pledged to reduce U.S. greenhouse gas intensity by 18 percent during the next ten years. (This commitment would be accomplished outside the Kyoto Protocol, however.)

For the Bush administration, development and economic growth were closely tied. The *National Security Strategy* recognized that "a world where some live in comfort and plenty, while half . . . lives on less than $2 a day, is neither just nor stable." As such, development was to be "a moral imperative" for the United States. The administration thus pledged to increase its development assistance by 50 percent, to work for reform of the World Bank and its activities to help the poor, to develop measures to document progress within countries, and to increase the amount of funding in the form of grants, as opposed to loans. At the same time, it would continue to view trade and investment as "the real engines of economic growth." Finally, the administration reiterated its emphasis on basic needs within poor countries, such as public health, education, and agricultural development.

The last course of action in the statement called for **transforming national security institutions at home**. Although such a transformation would have an impact on the defending, preserving, and expanding of peace, its priorities were improving the military and the intelligence communities and strengthening homeland security to defend the peace at home and abroad. There was a brief mention of improving diplomacy and the Department of State, but the emphasis was surely more on "hard-power" rather than on "soft-power" ways to accomplish this.

In what became the most controversial statements in the document, the Bush administration asserted that the United States must have available "**the option of preemptive actions** to counter a *sufficient* threat to our national security" (emphasis added). It concluded with the administration's commitment **to act unilaterally** if collective efforts fail: "In exercising our leadership, we will respect the values, judgment, and interests of our friends and partners. Still, we will be prepared to act apart when our interests and unique responsibilities require." These statements concerning preemption and the unilateral option would ultimately capture the most attention of critics at home and abroad and would soon undermine the administration's initial effort to produce a "grand strategy" against terrorism with broad support.

POLICY IMPLICATIONS OF THE BUSH DOCTRINE TOWARD THE WORLD

This global strategy outlined by the Bush administration had an important effect on a wide range of countries and affected the relationship with allies and adversaries. Over this next section, we provide a brief survey of this policy's impact for America's relations with several perceived rogue states (Iraq, North Korea, Iran, and Libya), with some possible adversaries (Russia and China), and with our allies, especially in Europe.

Policy toward Iraq

After Afghanistan, the first real test of the Bush Doctrine of pursuing terrorists and tyrants was, of course, the pursuit of Saddam Hussein's Iraq. Iraq became a focus of administration discussions almost immediately after September 11. In the first meetings of policy makers after the terrorist attacks, Secretary of Defense Donald Rumsfeld "raised the question of Iraq," although the Pentagon "had been working for months on developing a military option for Iraq."[83] At the time, however, because President Bush wanted more attention directed toward Afghanistan—particularly al-Qaeda and the Taliban—Iraq was placed on the back burner.

By early 2002, Iraq had once again gained the attention of President Bush and his key policy makers because Saddam Hussein's regime had used chemical and biological weapons against its own people and had started the development of a nuclear weapons program. Although its link to terrorists was still unclear to many, the possibility of the joining together of **a "rogue state"** (in the administration's definition) **with nonstate terrorist groups** was considered lethal for the United States and the international community. See Map 5.1 for the location and size of Iraq.

By summer 2002, the Iraq issue had set off a pitched debate within the administration. Some key advisors supported quick and unilateral action to remove Hussein, whereas others, most prominently Colin Powell and his deputy, Richard Armitage, argued that this had "risks and complexities" that needed more analysis.[84] In addition, the possibility of a war against Hussein had alienated Republican allies in Congress and former officials from previous administrations, notably former secretary of state Henry Kissinger and former national security advisor Brent Scowcroft. Kissinger and Scowcroft supported the need to remove Hussein, but they were concerned that the administration's plan would "alienat[e] allies, creating greater instability in the Middle East, and harming long-term American interests."

By fall 2002, the Bush administration had decided to challenge the international community and the United Nations to address the issue of WMD in Iraq by seeking a multilateral solution. In a speech to the United Nations, Bush issued just such a challenge.[85]

After five weeks of negotiation, on November 8, 2002, the UN Security Council unanimously passed **Resolution 1441**,[86] which found Iraq in "material breach" of a previous UN resolution. (This was UN Resolution 687, passed at the end of the Gulf War in 1991, which called for Iraq's disarmament of its WMD.) In addition, it required Iraq to report within thirty days on all aspects of its programs related to WMD and ordered that Iraq immediately allow UN and International Atomic Energy Agency (IAEA) inspectors back into the country. Significantly, the resolution stated, "that the Council has repeatedly warned Iraq that it will face serious consequences as a result of its continued violations of its obligations."

In accordance with Resolution 1441, Iraq provided a report to the United Nations in December 2002 on its weapons program and allowed UN and IAEA inspectors into the country. Over the next several months, the chief inspectors provided reports to the UN Security Council on the status of the inspections and the disarmament that indicated that Iraq was not fully complying with either the resolution or with the inspectors. However, the inspectors requested more time from the Security Council to complete their work.

By March 2003, the Bush administration's patience had run out on the failure of the UN Security Council to act against Iraq. At the urging of the British prime

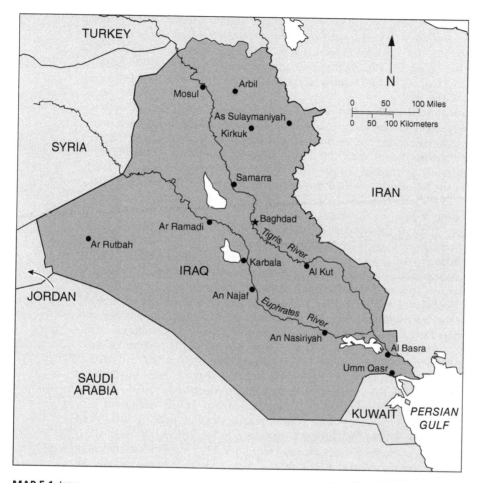

MAP 5.1 Iraq

Source: http://www.cia.gov/cia/publications/factbook/geos/iz.html.

minister, Tony Blair, the United States, Great Britain, and Spain circulated another draft UN resolution explicitly to find Iraq in "material breach" and implicitly to obtain approval for military action to enforce Resolution 1441. This new resolution never reached a vote because several nations on the council, led principally by the French and the potential use of its veto, did not support it. Indeed, France indicated that it would not support any resolution that would lead to war.

As a result, **President Bush issued an ultimatum to Iraq and its leadership on March 17, 2003**: "Saddam Hussein and his sons must leave Iraq within 48 hours. Their refusal to do so will result in military conflict, commenced at a time of our choosing."[87] When the Iraqi leadership refused to comply, the United States attacked a command bunker in Baghdad, and the war, called Operation Iraqi Freedom, began. The president took this action without another UN resolution and instead relied on the congressional resolution passed in October 2002. The administration put together a "coalition of the willing" (some forty-two nations initially), much as the *National Security Strategy* of a few months earlier had stated. Yet the United States and Great Britain carried out the principal military action, with some assistance from Australia and a few other countries. Clearly, the Bush administration was willing to act alone (or with an informal coalition) in pursuing tyrants and terrorists and in implementing its national security strategy.

The war went well and quickly for the United States and Great Britain, with the loss of relatively few lives. The United States gained **control of Baghdad by April 9**, only three weeks after the start of the war, and President Bush declared **"major combat operations" over on May 1**. Still, winning the peace and establishing a stable democratic government proved more difficult. Indeed, American deaths mounted over the following months as Iraqi resistance continued. Equally challenging was the effort to uncover clear evidence of WMD—the fundamental rationale for the war—and to capture Saddam Hussein.

By summer 2003, as the number of Americans killed in postwar Iraq increased and as WMD remained undiscovered, criticism of Bush policy by the bureaucracy and Capitol Hill began to surface. Some charged that the administration had skewed intelligence data to support its war against Iraq or had pressured intelligence analysts to provide supportive estimates.[88] The Pentagon was accused of developing its own "hardline view of intelligence related to Iraq" to justify American military actions there.[89] Even though the Bush administration denied such charges, skepticism remained and Congress initiated inquiries. In July 2003, the criticism reached a crescendo when the administration was forced to admit that American intelligence did not support a statement in the president's 2003 State of the Union Address claiming that Iraq had tried to obtain uranium from an African nation. George Tenet, director of Central Intelligence, took formal responsibility for this error,[90] but the episode reinforced the view that the administration had been determined to dig up evidence to justify military action against Iraq. The integrity of the Bush administration's policy making was called into question, and the Senate Intelligence Committee called hearings to investigate. Although Hussein was ultimately captured in December 2003, the Bush administration's foreign policy continued to face scrutiny and criticism both at home and abroad.

By this time, too, foreign policy, and the Iraq War in particular, became a central issue in the 2004 presidential election campaign. Former Vermont governor Howard Dean and Representative Dennis Kucinich, who both opposed the war in Iraq, had voiced criticism for some time, but other presidential contenders (Representative Richard Gephardt and Senator John Kerry) who had supported the war followed suit in the summer and fall of 2003. Representative Gephardt, for example, charged the president with "stunning incompetence" in foreign policy.[91] Senator Kerry accused the administration of failing to have a plan to win the peace in Iraq, pointing to the "arrogant absence of any major international effort to build what's needed."[92] Another contender for a time, Senator Bob Graham, called for further investigations into Bush's policy making. American policy toward Iraq and the Bush Doctrine more generally had become sources of domestic debate after a long post-9/11 hiatus.

Policy toward North Korea, Iran, and Libya

In his January 2002 State of the Union address, President Bush had identified North Korea and Iran, along with Iraq, as the "axis of evil." The Bush Doctrine thus had important implications for American policy toward those states as well: the administration made a sustained effort to deter their attempts to develop WMD, but its approach was markedly different from the approach toward Iraq. Deterrence and diplomatic efforts became its preferred strategy.

North Korea became a source of increased attention and international tension when, in October 2002, it informed a "visiting American delegation to Pyongyang that it had maintained a clandestine nuclear weapons program."[93] Furthermore, North Korea announced in December 2002 that it would reopen a previously closed nuclear facility at Yongbyon in violation of the 1994 Agreed Framework with the United States. A month later, North Korea renounced its adherence to the Nuclear Non-Proliferation Treaty (NPT), claiming that it needed to have a nuclear capability to deter the United States from taking action against it, especially after the perceived aggressive statements by the Bush administration.

Unlike its policy toward Iraq, however, the United States did not pursue a preemptive course; instead, the Bush administration sought to employ a multilateral diplomatic effort to deter and roll back the North Korean actions. Although North Korea called for direct, bilateral talks with the United States and initially demanded a nonaggression pact between the two countries in exchange for moving away from its nuclear program, the Bush administration held out for a joint effort made up of interested states and the international community. In August 2003, the initial **Six-Party Talks**—among the United States, North Korea, South Korea, Japan, China, and Russia—were held in Beijing.[94] Progress was slow and at best episodic and, as we will show, continued in the second term as well.

Toward Iran, the Bush policy looked more like that adopted toward North Korea than toward Iraq, even as the administration continued to insist that Iran possessed chemical, biological, and nuclear weapons. In the heady days immediately after the fall of Baghdad, the administration appeared to make a veiled threat about moving against Iran, but its comments were quickly downplayed. Instead, diplomatic and economic tracks were pursued. By December 2003, John Bolton, undersecretary of state for arms control and international security, continued to maintain that the Bush administration's basic strategy was "bilateral and multilateral pressure to end" this nuclear threat.[95] Moreover, the approach to Iran's biological and chemical weapons appeared to follow the same pattern.

The administration's strategy on Iran's nuclear policy yielded some progress by the end of 2003. In November of that year, the Board of Governors of the IAEA passed a resolution that deplored the failure of Iran to adhere to its obligations under its Safeguard Agreement pursuant to the Nuclear Non-Proliferation Treaty. Fearing that the IAEA might go to the UN Security Council, Iran agreed in mid-December to an accord that would allow UN experts "full access" to its various nuclear research facilities. The Bush administration saw the accord as "a useful step in the right direction" but remained skeptical that Iran was being fully forthcoming.[96] Like Iraq and North Korea, Iran would continue to be a challenge, but the administration's response would remain relatively the same.

Although not explicitly mentioned by President Bush in his "axis of evil" statement in 2002, Libya also became a target of administration action over its efforts to acquire WMD. The United States had imposed economic sanctions on Libya over its past involvement with terrorism, but it had also been concerned about Libya's efforts to acquire (and even use) WMD over the years. Indeed, its mercurial leader, Colonel Moammar Gadhafi had been accused of developing and using chemical weapons by Washington since the 1980s. In a key diplomatic initiative in March 2003, the Bush administration, in conjunction with Great Britain, began secret discussions with Libya at the very time that it was initiating war against Iraq. Nine months later, in late December 2003, those efforts proved successful when Prime Minister Tony Blair and President Bush announced that Gadhafi "had agreed to give up all of his nuclear, chemical, and biological weapons" and to submit to international inspections.[97] Although Libya claimed that it made this decision of its own "free will," the Bush administration cited it as bolstering its policy of confronting countries with WMD.[98] The administration's policy instruments in obtaining Libya's capitulation were largely economic and diplomatic, albeit against the backdrop of the Iraq War. In this sense, coercive diplomacy might well be a more apt description of its policy approach in the Libyan situation.

Policy with Russia and China

Although the Bush Doctrine was fundamentally directed against terrorists and states that might obtain WMD, it also had an effect on U.S. relations with other major powers, its allies, and its friends. Indeed, the events of September 11 and the application of the doctrine toward Iraq altered the approach of the Bush administration toward two key states, Russia and China. Initially, the administration sought to treat these powers more as competitors than as partners (in contrast to the Clinton administration's approach), but 9/11 changed that policy. **After September 11, both Russia and China immediately provided support for the United States, and the Bush administration reciprocated with closer ties with them.**

These closer ties began when President Vladimir Putin was the first to call the United States after September 11, declaring that "we are with you."[99] In short order, too, Putin offered his diplomatic support and Russian aid in fighting terrorism, and he expressed a willingness to work more closely with NATO. Putin also accepted the American decision to withdraw from **the Anti-Ballistic Missile (ABM) Treaty** and pledged to continue good relations despite this decision. In turn, the United States made several concessions to Russia. It agreed to a new strategic arms pact— **the Strategic Offensive Reductions Treaty (SORT)**—that further reduced the number of nuclear warheads available to the two states to a range of 1,700 to 2,200 by 2010; that designated Russia as possessing "market economy" status in the world; and that offered full membership to Russia in the Group of Eight (G-8) countries. Additionally, the United States toned down its criticism of Russian actions in Chechnya and began to encourage Russia's closer ties to NATO as well.[100] In short, a **strategic partnership** increasingly seemed to characterize the relationship.

The formal enunciation of the Bush Doctrine and the movement toward war with Iraq dampened those ties, but only modestly. Russia, as a former patron of Iraq, was not supportive of the war and announced that it would oppose such authorization by the UN Security Council. Although the war itself did not erase the progress that had been made in Russian–U.S. ties, it did cool the ties between the two states for a time. Once the major fighting was over, Russia was willing to work with the United States in the United Nations to pass resolutions calling for aid from other states and working toward democracy.

By the end of 2003, some further deterioration in relations had taken hold, especially over American concerns about Russian interference in the internal affairs of Ukraine and Georgia and about the "managed democracy" in Russia itself, where some freedoms were coming under increased pressure from the Putin government. In early 2004, the United States expressed concerns over the level of democratic participation in the Russian presidential election, which also raised Moscow's ire.

U.S.–Russian differences over Iraq remained during the balance of the Bush administration. The cooling relations between the two states appeared to be due less to Iraq than to other policy actions by Russia at home and in the "near abroad" nations. Russia's military intervention in August 2008 into the independent country (and former Soviet republic) of Georgia, now an increasingly close ally of the United States, only served to exacerbate tensions between the United States and Russia. Its delay in departing Georgia caused further tensions as well. Still, by 2008 Russia and Iraq signed agreements to write off some of Iraq's past debt, and Russia committed to an investment of up to $4 billion in the Iraqi economy.[101] In this sense, Russia, despite its policy differences with the United States, sought to stabilize Iraq even as it tried to exercise some economic and political influence there. In sum, the Iraq War had soured the close ties between Russia and the United States, but the relationship generally remained workable, despite some clear differences in interests and outlook.

The events of September 11 and then the Iraq War had a parallel effect on U.S.–Chinese relations. After September 11, China provided immediate diplomatic support in the United Nations and acquiesced in America's military action in Afghanistan. At the ensuing APEC forum in Shanghai shortly after September 11, the United States toned down its criticism of China over such vexing issues as Taiwan, its sales of missiles abroad, and its treatment of Tibetans. Additionally, a "cooperative tone continued" during President Bush's visit to Beijing in February 2002.[102]

Once again, the proclamation of the Bush Doctrine and the time immediately prior to the war with Iraq began to sour those immediate post–September 11 ties, but they did not break them. China, like Russia, was opposed to American action against Iraq, and it made its position known. It largely favored allowing more time for UN inspectors to do their work rather than using military force against Saddam Hussein's regime. China did not immediately contribute to reconstruction efforts in Iraq, but it did not veto U.S. efforts to pass resolutions to promote reconstruction.

Somewhat later, China did indeed contribute to Iraqi reconstruction. In June 2007, for example, China, like Russia, sought to exercise its influence in that country by signing four agreements with the Iraqi government.[103] These agreements focused on debt relief, but they also set up cooperation agreements between the foreign ministries of the two countries, established economic and technical cooperation, and supported human resources training. Furthermore, a short time earlier, the Chinese government had reaffirmed its commitment to maintaining the sovereignty and independence of Iraq and indicated that it would continue to work with the United States on a broad array of issues.[104] In this sense, Chinese–American relations were on an even keel, despite the effects of the war.

One Asian analyst described the relationship between the United States and China that had evolved as a **"selective partnership"** in which the two countries cooperate when they can. That is, it was neither the strategic competition that the Bush administration portended nor the strategic partnership that the Clinton administration had hoped for.[105] In this sense, the changed relationship between the two countries since the first days of the Bush administration was "one of the biggest foreign policy shifts of this administration," in the view of another Asian expert.[106]

Policy with America's Allies

If September 11 and the application of the Bush Doctrine toward Iraq had the dual effect of improving ties with Russia and China and then chilling them for a time, the same can be said of some of America's traditional allies in Europe and Canada, albeit with an important difference. That difference appears to be a more sustained chill over the implications of the Bush Doctrine. Although there were episodic changes in America's relationships with its allies from late 2003 into 2004, the general direction was a decline, despite some initial efforts by the administration at the beginning of its second term in 2005. Moreover, this chill was one of the lingering legacies of the Bush Doctrine and, more specifically, of the Iraq War.

In the immediate aftermath of September 11, U.S. ties with all European states, like other states, grew closer. As one analyst noted, "even the traditionally skeptical French press declared, 'We are all Americans.'"[107] And both allies and friends, and even adversaries, initially supported the change in Bush's foreign policy approach. The acknowledgment that America needed help from other states in fighting terrorism, its initial turn to international institutions, and its recognition of multiple actors in the international arena undoubtedly struck a responsive chord. Moreover, friends and allies accepted U.S. concern over the internal dynamics of some states and the need to address festering regional and communal conflicts. After all, Article V of the NATO pact was invoked for the first time in the fifty-nine-year history of the alliance immediately after 9/11, and virtually all European nations agreed to provide some assistance against al-Qaeda and the Taliban in Afghanistan.

This international receptivity was short-lived, however. The 2002 State of the Union Address in which President Bush identified the "axis of evil" nations and appeared to foreshadow actions against one or more of them caused immediate alarm. As the French foreign minister, Hubert Védrine, noted: "We are currently threatened by a simplified approach which reduces all problems of the world to the mere struggle against terrorism." Javier Solana Madariaga, the European Union's minister for foreign affairs, warned about "the dangers of global unilateralism," and German foreign minister Joschka Fischer called the "axis of evil" notion "not in accordance with our political ethos."[108]

Support and cooperation with allies lasted throughout the 2001–2002 campaign in Afghanistan, but relations with some European states—notably France and Germany—quickly soured as the Bush administration turned its sights on Iraq. These two states, in particular, counseled for a slower and more multilateral approach. Their opposition became particularly intense when the United States sought a second resolution in the United Nations to support the war against Iraq in early 2003. When that effort failed, the United States worked to put together a "coalition of the willing" to initiate the war. France and Germany, along with a number of other traditional allies, including Canada, refused to join. Some Western and Eastern European nations, including Spain, the Netherlands, Poland, and Italy, ultimately lent their support, but the fissure in American and Western European ties wrought by Iraq was clear.

Indeed, the divisions between France and Germany and the United States continued in the post–Iraq War period. The two European powers kept up their pressure on the United States to turn over more Iraqi reconstruction activities and political control to the United Nations. When the United States was unwilling to make these changes immediately, political differences continued. Moreover, the electoral defeat in March 2004 of the Spanish political party whose leader had supported the United States in the Iraq War, as well as the massive demonstrations in allied and friendly countries on the war's first anniversary, conveyed the opposition to the Bush Doctrine.

The administration did take some actions to improve ties with its alliance partners, and they responded in kind. In mid-2003, bilateral discussions at the G-8 summit meetings and other diplomatic initiatives (see the discussion to come) thawed the strained ties. By fall 2003, the Europeans and the Americans were cooperating on new UN resolutions on reconstruction in Iraq, which represented compromise on both sides. By the end of 2003, in a shift in policy, Germany and France indicated that they would be willing to forgive Iraq's debts and thus contribute to the reconstruction efforts.[109] In December 2003, Canada, under the leadership of a new prime minister, Paul Martin, indicated that improving the relationship with the United States was a key priority and that steps would be taken to do so.

None of the Bush's administration's actions reflected a fundamental shift from the approach adopted after September 11, 2001. Indeed, terrorist incidents in Saudi Arabia and Morocco in the spring of 2003 (attributed to al-Qaeda) and the Madrid bombing of March 11, 2004, only reinforced the administration's stance. However, mounting foreign and domestic criticism of the administration's unilateral and ideological approach appeared to introduce a cautionary note in considerations of further military responses, whether against North Korea, Iran, or elsewhere. Also, presidential popularity had declined to pre-9/11 levels, and support for the Iraq War was beginning to wane by late 2004. Still, the policy was "**stay the course**," and it applied not only to Iraq but also to the unique combination of defensive realism and limited idealism that the Bush administration had adopted in the post-9/11 period.

AFTER REELECTION: A NEW FOREIGN POLICY APPROACH?

George W. Bush won a narrow victory in the 2004 presidential election, partly on his antiterrorist foreign policy stance. However, the second-term Bush administration initially sought to alter its foreign policy approach, including the war on terrorism. The first hint of a change came in a meeting with Britain's Prime Minister Blair shortly after his reelection. At the end of that meeting, Bush declared that "[in] my second term, I will work to deepen our trans-Atlantic [sic] ties to nations of Europe." He also declared that stronger ties between Europe and America were vital to the "promotion of worldwide democracy."[110]

The Democracy Imperative

President Bush more fully signaled a modified approach in his second inaugural address and in his State of the Union Address a few weeks later. In his inaugural address, for example, he directly tied America's well-being to the expansion of freedom and liberty around the world.[111] America and the world would become secure only by promoting these principles and by using them to reconstruct the international system. "The survival of liberty in our land," he declared, "increasingly depends on the success of liberty in other lands. The best hope for peace in our world is the expansion of freedom in the world." Later in his address he added, "It is the policy of the United States to seek and support the growth of democratic movements and institutions in every nation and culture, with the ultimate goal of ending tyranny in the world."

In his State of the Union address, Bush continued to link America's well-being at home with the promotion of freedom abroad. A principal goal for his administration, he declared, would be "to pass along to our children all the freedoms we enjoy—and chief among them is freedom from fear."[112] Bush emphasized that this transformational foreign policy would not be imposed from abroad or implemented by military means. Instead, it would have to be evoked, or encouraged, by the global community.

At her Senate confirmation hearings in early 2005, Condoleezza Rice, too, was quick to outline some new central themes of the administration: to unite, strengthen, and spread democracies around the world and to do so through diplomacy. In her words, "[w]e must use American diplomacy to help create a balance of power in the world that favors freedom. And the time for diplomacy is now."[113] To be sure, such themes were not entirely new for the Bush administration. After all, the notion of creating "a balance of power favoring freedom" seemingly was straight out of the 2002 *National Security Strategy* and the discussion of promoting democracy was a theme that President Bush had enunciated in his visit to Britain in November 2003, during which he called for "the global expansion of democracy" as a key pillar of American security.[114]

What was new, however, was the initial effort that Bush and the new secretary of state undertook to assuage allies, particularly the Europeans. Rice's "peace offensive" to several European capitals was one such effort. It was generally well received, and it did not stop with that initial trip. By one analysis, Rice visited forty-nine countries in her first year and "nearly 70 percent of Rice's time abroad in 2005 was spent in Europe."[115] Bush, too, sought to send a different signal to the Europeans in 2005 by visiting NATO and the European Union headquarters and by having "long meetings" with two key European skeptics of the Bush approach, French president Jacques Chirac, and German chancellor Gerhard Schroeder.

Changes in Personnel and Policy Actions

The administration also made changes in foreign policy personnel at home as part of this seeming new direction. Early in the second term, key neoconservatives (Paul Wolfowitz and Douglas Feith at Defense and John Bolton at State) left the administration, and new pragmatists and foreign policy realists filled these important posts.[116] In particular, Robert Zoellick was appointed as deputy secretary of state, Nicholas Burns assumed the number-three position as undersecretary of state for political affairs, and Christopher Hill became assistant secretary of state for East Asian and Pacific affairs (and eventually the American lead negotiator with North Korea). Immediately after the 2006 congressional elections, Secretary of Defense Donald Rumsfeld resigned and was replaced by Robert Gates. Gates's political perspective tended more toward classical realism than the neoconservativism that had previously dominated the civilian leadership at the Pentagon.

Multilateral diplomatic initiatives began or were restarted toward two "axis of evil" countries, Iran and North Korea, and became Bush's principal foreign policy approach toward these countries. Partly as a result of Bush's trip to Europe in 2005, the "EU-3"—France, Germany, and Great Britain—agreed to work with the United States on a diplomatic initiative with Iran to forestall its potential development of nuclear weapons. This initiative ultimately led to a series of economic sanctions against Iran and to considerable unity among the United States and these key European allies over the next three years. Multilateral diplomacy remained the principal foreign policy vehicle for the Bush administration during the balance of its second term, despite some of the administration's rhetoric to the contrary.

By mid-2005, too, the Six-Party Talks over North Korea's development of nuclear weapons were resurrected, even though the North Koreans had declared several months earlier that they were "indefinitely suspending" their nuclear program. Indeed, by mid-September 2005, all parties had reaffirmed the goal of the talks as the "verifiable denuclearization of the Korean Peninsula in a peaceful manner."[117] Although the Six-Party Talks experienced ups and down over the next three years (including UN-imposed sanctions over a North Korean nuclear test), they ultimately resulted in an agreement in 2007 on the phased shutdown and eventual dismantlement of North Korea's nuclear facilities. Rapid implementation of these agreements, however, eluded the Bush administration. North Korea did submit a listing of the extent of its nuclear program in late June 2008 in accord with the Six-Party Talks, and the United States lifted trading restrictions on that country and signaled its intent to remove North Korea's designation as a "State Sponsor of Terrorism." Although the administration noted that North Korea needed to take more action to meet its obligations under the Six-Party Talks, it reaffirmed its commitment to following a multilateral diplomatic course in dealing with this "axis of evil" state.[118]

Finally, several other modest changes in the Bush administration approach near the beginning of the second term, and later, suggested a slightly different course. Some changes were made in the administration's position on foreign aid, especially more aid for Africa, and on climate change, including a statement that it was "largely a man-made problem." Halting steps, too, were evident in working with international organizations, including some favorable actions vis-à-vis the International Criminal Court and UN efforts over Darfur in the Sudan.[119] In 2007 and 2008, the Bush administration stepped up its efforts to move peace negotiations between the Palestinians and the Israelis along. It also worked collectively with its NATO allies for expansion of that organization once again, although it did not get all the new members desired. Still, by 2008, the administration had obtained unanimous support from its European NATO allies for the placement of missile shields in Poland and the Czech Republic, even in the face of repeated Russian objections.

THE IRAQ WAR AND OPPOSITION TO THE BUSH FOREIGN POLICY

Despite changes in personnel and actions, sharp doubts continued among foreign leaders and publics about the Bush administration and its foreign policy. A majority of the American public and numerous members of Congress also voiced doubts, especially about the Iraq War.

Sustained Criticism from Abroad

Skepticism about any real change in direction by the Bush administration was largely driven by the unpopularity of the Iraq War (and the unilateralist approach that it reflected), but it was also driven by Bush's rhetoric and personal unpopularity. Any goodwill created after 9/11 among Europeans, for example, quickly dissipated in the run-up to the Iraq War, and it largely did not rebound. In March 2003, at about the start of the Iraq War, only 48 percent of the public in Britain, 34 percent in Italy, 25 percent in Germany, 31 percent in France, and 14 percent in Spain expressed a favorable view of the United States.[120] Three years later, and more than a year into President Bush's second term (April 2006), the favorable percentages had improved only slightly among key European allies. Fifty-six percent of the British, 39 percent of the French, 37 percent of the Germans, and 23 percent of the Spanish expressed favorable opinions. This skepticism or downright opposition was not confined to Europe, of course. In a 2006 Pew survey of global attitudes toward the United States, only in three countries of the ten surveyed did a majority of the public view the United States favorably. These countries were Japan, India, and Nigeria. The rest (Russia, Indonesia, Egypt, Pakistan, Jordan, Turkey, and China) had favorability ratings ranging from 12 percent positive in Turkey to 47 percent positive in China.[121]

Bush's personal unpopularity undoubtedly continued to cloud any change in policy direction. In a BBC World Service poll in 2005, in only three countries (out of twenty-two surveyed) did a majority or a plurality positively view Bush's reelection. These were India and the Philippines (majorities) and Poland (a plurality). The rest, including respondents in five European countries, viewed the reelection of Bush as "negative for peace and security for the world."[122]

The skepticism of key European publics (and others) was mirrored at the governmental level. Only a few European states were willing to provide much assistance in the effort to stabilize Iraq. Even those that did withdrew or announced their withdrawal of forces, often because of opposition at home. Still, some of the states most critical of the United States over the war were willing to train Iraqi security personnel (such as Germany) and provided some resources for reconstruction (such as France). Yet there were clear limits on how far they would go to endorse the Bush administration's foreign policy approach.

With new leaders elected in Germany in November 2005 (**Chancellor Angela Merkel**) and in France in May 2007 (**President Nicolas Sarkozy**) and with the selection of **Gordon Brown** to replace Tony Blair as British prime minister in 2007, President Bush now had a new set of leaders who were generally more willing to cooperate with the United States than those (except for Blair) at the height of the Iraq War. Nonetheless, the war would hang heavy over other nations moving too close to the United States—and it would continue to impinge on any enthusiastic alliance support for the administration.

Increasing Opposition at Home

Although the Bush administration was successful in winning the White House and in keeping Republicans in control of Congress in the 2004 elections, based in part on a campaign of antiterrorism, domestic support for the president and his Iraq policy quickly began to erode by mid-2005. Indeed, public approval of the president had dropped significantly since the initiation of the war and by the beginning of 2008 hovered just slightly above 30 percent. Since March 2005, when his presidential job approval dropped to 45 percent, there had been only two instances in the weekly Gallup tracking polls (April 4–7, 2005, and May 2–5, 2005) when the president's approval rating was at 50 percent. Instead, the trend was consistently downward from March 2005, reaching its lowest level (up to that time) at 31 percent in the polling of May 5–7, 2006.[123]

With the full formation of the Iraqi government and the killing of Iraqi al-Qaeda leader, Abu al-Zarqawi, in 2006, President Bush's approval rating inched back up a bit to the high 30s and even to 42 percent, but it fell to 29 percent in July 2007, and by October 2008 it dropped to 25 percent.[124] In all, a majority of the public disapproved of his job performance for nearly all of Bush's second term—and much of that disapproval, of course, was related to foreign policy and specifically to Iraq.

The public response to the frequently asked question of whether sending troops to Iraq was a mistake also steadily eroded over the second term to where a large majority agreed with this position (see Figure 5.1.) As early as June 2004, a majority

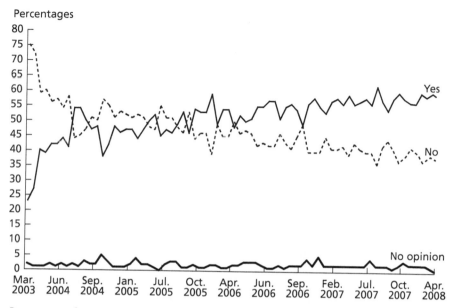

Percentage of responses to the question: "In view of the developments since we first sent our troops to Iraq, do you think the United States made a mistake in sending troops to Iraq, or not?" (Gallup Poll Organization data)

FIGURE 5.1 The "Mistake" Question on Iraq

Source: The data are from Frank Newport, "Public Situation in Iraq Getting Worse for U.S.," http://www.gallup.com and USA Today/Gallup Poll, April Wave 1, April 18–20, 2008, Final Topline.

of the public responded that the United States had "made a mistake in sending troops to Iraq" in Gallup tracking polls. Over the next year, though, a slim majority usually disagreed with this statement, but from August 2005 (with an exception of two polls) a majority of the public viewed the action as a "mistake" in the periodic polling by the Gallup organization.[125]

By April 2008, 58 percent of the public viewed the Iraq War as a mistake. In this sense, although the majority opposition to the administration's Iraq policy was probably more recent than many might believe, the general opinion that the Iraq invasion was a mistake was stable from 2005 through the end of the Bush presidency. Moreover, in his comparison of the Iraq, Vietnam, and Korean wars, political scientist John Mueller reports that what is most striking is how much more quickly domestic support eroded in the case of Iraq.[126]

The sharp drop in public support was equally matched by the rise in criticism of the Bush administration's foreign policy by analysts and members of Congress. In March 2006, the Bush administration released its second National Security Strategy statement, in which it assessed its previous four years of action in the war on terrorism and advanced its new emphasis on promoting democracy as the way that this war would be won. In a broad critique of the new strategy statement, analysts Lawrence Korb and Caroline Wadhams fault the administration for failing to learn "from the mistakes of its first term" and, more generally, for failing to advance a new and workable foreign policy approach.[127] In particular, they fault the administration for continuing to confuse preemption and preventive war, for embracing the "unachievable goal of 'ending tyranny' completely throughout the world," and failing "to make a realistic assessment of the threats to our security." Finally, and importantly, they criticize the administration's emphasis on democracy as too grandiose because it subordinated all other goals and because its vision "has been excessively focused on elections, while underemphasizing the more difficult tasks of building an overall culture of open civil society and institutions based on the rule of law." In their view, little had changed in the basic flawed policy of the Bush administration after more than five years in office (by 2006).

During this same period, congressional criticism of the Bush administration's Iraq policy began to escalate on both sides of the political aisle. Two military veterans in the Congress dramatized the changing nature of the political environment and epitomized the growing opposition in that body. In late November 2005, **Representative John Murtha** (D-Pennsylvania), the ranking Democrat on the House Subcommittee on Appropriations, a former Marine, and a supporter of the Iraq War, broke with the Bush administration and called for the withdrawal of American troops from Iraq within six months: "The military has done everything that has been asked of them. The U.S. cannot accomplish anything further in Iraq militarily. It is time to bring the troops home."[128] On the Republican side, **Senator Chuck Hagel** (R-Nebraska), a Vietnam veteran and a "media favorite" for his outspokenness on the administration's postwar Iraq policy, became an increasingly vocal critic as well.[129] One profile of Hagel characterized his determination in this way: "He did not let up, despite extreme pressure from party leaders to cool it."[130] These congressional critics were not alone, and Congress's push for greater White House accountability on the Iraq War escalated in 2005 and 2006, especially with elections on the horizon. As a result, the 2006 congressional elections became a referendum on Iraq policy specifically and on the Bush approach to foreign policy generally.

A Change in Course?

In a news conference a day after the 2006 congressional elections, President Bush characterized the results as a "thumping" for his party. Republicans lost six seats in the Senate and thirty seats in the House, and control of both chambers changed from Republican to Democratic. In short order, Secretary of Defense Rumsfeld resigned, a new commander was appointed in Iraq, and the president considered a new Iraq strategy. Within a month, the **Iraq Study Group**, an independent, bipartisan group led by former secretary of state James Baker and former congressman Lee Hamilton issued its report with seventy-nine recommendations outlining "the way forward in Iraq."

The thrust of the study group's recommendations called for the United States to launch "a new diplomatic initiative to build an international consensus for stability in Iraq and the region" and to "adjust its role in Iraq to encourage the Iraqi people to take control of their own destiny." The U.S. military "should evolve into one of supporting the Iraqi military," the report concluded, with principal responsibility left to the Iraqis themselves. Furthermore, the American government "should work closely with Iraq's leaders to support the achievement of specific objectives . . . on national reconciliation, security, and governance."[131] In short, the group called for new diplomatic initiatives toward Iraq's neighbors; reduced American military involvement, except for training and some embedded units; enhanced Iraqi progress on internal reconciliation among religious groups; and improved national governance.

President Bush indicated that he would carefully review the Iraq Study Group's recommendations, but he quickly moved in a different direction. In early 2007, he adopted a new Iraq strategy prepared by **General David Petraeus**, the coalition commander. Popularly called the "**surge strategy**," it called for an increase of American troops by about 21,000 in an effort to quell the sectarian violence and to provide the Iraqi government with time to make progress on internal political reconciliation. Congress sharply criticized this policy. Senator Hagel, for example, called the president's speech about the surge strategy "the most dangerous foreign policy blunder in this country since Vietnam."[132] The House of Representatives subsequently passed a nonbinding resolution disapproving the surge, although the Senate failed to do so.

In the ensuing months of 2007, the Democratic majority made various attempts to cut off funding for Iraq and to set a date for American withdrawal. These efforts were in response to the president's action as well as part of the Democrats' perceived election mandate. The Senate sought to invoke cloture (cutting off Senate debate) to possibly pass resolutions on troop increases, but it failed to reach the needed sixty votes. Congress passed a supplemental Iraq/Afghanistan funding measure in late April 2007 with language requiring the withdrawal of troops if certain "benchmarks" were not achieved. However, it was vetoed by President Bush on May 1, 2007, and the veto was upheld by the House a day later.[133] Other amendments (for example, the Feingold and Levin amendments) were introduced in the Senate later, but they, too, failed to pass with the required number of votes. In all, **Congress was unsuccessful with these legislative measures over the Iraq War**.

Several factors account for the president's success in staving off congressional actions. First, the veto (or even the threat of a veto) is an effective instrument for the president. Second, Bush was largely able to maintain the support of his Republican colleagues in the House and Senate, even in the face of a united Democratic opposition. Third, Senate rules requiring sixty votes to end cloture worked in Bush's favor, as did the Senate rule requiring a sixty-vote majority for a measure to pass. Finally, and importantly, Democrats (and Republicans) had to face the real difficulty of cutting off funds for the troops in the field and had to gauge the political backlash that such action might create among their constituents back home.

Although the surge strategy proved successful in dampening sectarian violence in Iraq in 2007 and into 2008, the Iraqi government's progress on national reconciliation among competing sectarian groups was markedly slow, as documented by an independent assessment by the U.S. Government Accountability Office and as confirmed by General Petraeus's testimony before Congress on two different occasions.[134] By April 2008, moreover, because of increases in Iraqi violence, Petraeus was forced to ask for a "pause" in the drawdown of surge forces started a year earlier to consolidate progress that had been achieved. Such actions, along with the continuing loss of American lives, made foreign policy, and specifically the Iraq War, a central issue in the 2008 presidential campaign. In this sense, more than five years after the start of the war, Iraq continued to cast a long shadow over the presidential candidates and over the direction of American foreign policy.

CONCLUDING COMMENTS

Much as the Clinton administration left some policies and unresolved issues for the Bush administration, the Bush administration did the same for the Obama administration. After the events of September 11, the Bush administration sought to lead a transformative foreign policy with its global war on terrorism. Although the war in Afghanistan against the Taliban and al-Qaeda met with quick success immediately after 9/11, the contested rationale for the Iraq War (that is, the existence of WMD in the hands of a rouge state), the failure of reconstruction planning and implementation after the initial invasion, and the difficulties of bringing democracy to a country fraught with sectarian divisions brought into serious question this foreign policy approach. Furthermore, the largely unilateral nature of the Iraqi invasion—despite the "coalition of the willing" veneer—the opposition of key allies, and the failure to gain UN endorsement tarnished America's image abroad and weakened its attractiveness in the international community. In short, the transformative foreign policy that the Bush administration attempted was largely left fallow by actions and events surrounding Iraq and the Iraq War.

To be sure, the administration sought to recast its foreign policy approach at the beginning of its second term into one of promoting democracy and eliminating tyranny worldwide. It tried to modify its approach—by removing or having key neoconservative advisers resign, by reaching out to the Europeans, and by initiating a number of multilateral diplomatic efforts toward Iran and North Korea and toward other international concerns, such as Darfur and the Middle East. Yet these initiatives were largely lost because of the deteriorating situation in Iraq, the stay-the-course strategy, and the administration's continued embrace of the rhetoric of the immediate post-9/11 period. Because of the dominance of the Iraq issue and the caricatured way in which the president was portrayed at home and abroad, the Bush administration, and the United States more generally, had a difficult time exercising international influence. In this sense, America's global reputation was yet another casualty of the Iraq War.

As a result, the United States faced several foreign policy challenges near the end of the first decade of the twenty-first century. Some related to specific foreign policy questions; others related to the general approach that the Bush administration adopted toward the world. Two specific foreign policy challenges were how to conclude the Iraq War and how to confront terrorism. Other concerns related to the general approach to foreign policy the Bush administration adopted. If the Clinton administration left the Bush administration a legacy of too much reliance on multilateralism, the Bush legacy is the very opposite: an inordinate reliance on unilateralism.

Two other important policy legacies of the Bush administration—preemption and preventive war—require the same kind of adjustment and clarification in dealing with the rest of the world. Once again, few states will exclude the possibility of preemptive action when survival is at stake and the threat is truly imminent, but the threat must truly be imminent or will wrongly become the rationale for a preemptive war. The reliance on unilateralism and the Bush administration's right of preemption (along with its strident rhetoric) had the effect of tarnishing America's image abroad and, more generally, of eroding its "soft power"—that is, the attractiveness of its values and culture and its ability to influence international actions.

In the next chapter, we turn to the foreign policy of the Barack Obama administration and its efforts to address these and other challenges.

Notes

1. Part of this chapter and its arguments originally appeared in James M. McCormick, "Assessing Clinton's Foreign Policy at Midterm," *Current History* 94 (November 1995): 370–374.

2. Governor Bill Clinton, "A New Covenant for American Security," address delivered at Georgetown University, December 12, 1991.

3. "Remarks of Governor Bill Clinton," Los Angeles World Affairs Council, August 13, 1992.

4. Ibid.

5. Both quotes are from Drew, *On the Edge: The Clinton Presidency* (New York: Simon & Schuster, 1994), p. 138. The first is Drew's assessment (for a similar characterization, see p. 28); the other is her quoting of a senior official.

6. "Enter Mr. Stealth," *The Economist*, January 29, 1994, A28.

7. A former National Security Council staffer during the Bush administration is quoted in Tim Weiner, "Clinton as a Military Leader: Tough On-The-Job Training," *New York Times*, October 28, 1996, A1.

8. For a discussion of these two factors, which help explain the Clinton administration's difficulty in foreign policy, see Anthony Lewis, "Foreign Policy Morass," *New York Times*, October 11, 1993, A11.

9. John McCain, "Imagery or Purpose? The Choice in November," *Foreign Policy* 103 (Summer 1996): 20–34.

10. See, for example, Gordon Silverstein, *Imbalance of Powers* (New York: Oxford University Press, 1997), pp. 5–6; and Adam Clymer, "A Career Bipartisan: William Sebastian Cohen," *New York Times*, December 6, 1996, A1 and A16.

11. Steven Erlanger, "Albright May Be Facing Unfamiliar Tests," *New York Times*, December 7, 1996, 5.

12. Warren Christopher, "Statement at Senate Confirmation Hearing before the Senate Foreign Relations Committee," January 13, 1993, reprinted in *Dispatch* 4 (January 25, 1993): 45–49.

13. "Remarks of Governor Bill Clinton."

14. See James M. McCormick, "Clinton and Foreign Policy," in Steven E. Schier, ed., *The Postmodern Presidency: Bill Clinton's Legacy in U.S. Politics* (Pittsburgh: University of Pittsburgh, 2000), pp. 78–79.

15. The four speeches were Bill Clinton, "Confronting the Challenges of a Broader World," address to the UN General Assembly, September 27, 1993; Warren Christopher, "Building Peace in the Middle East," address at Columbia University, September 20, 1993; Anthony Lake, "From Containment to Enlargement," address at John Hopkins University School of Advanced International Studies, September 21, 1993; and Madeleine K. Albright, "Use of Force in a Post–Cold War World," remarks at the National War College, September 23, 1993. All quoted passages by the various individuals in the next several paragraphs are from these addresses.

16. See McCormick, "Assessing Clinton's Foreign Policy at Midterm," pp. 370–374.

17. See Henry A. Kissinger, *Diplomacy* (New York: Simon & Schuster, 1994). A portion was excerpted in *Time*, March 14, 1994; the relevant passage is at p. 74.

18. George Szamuely, "Clinton's Clumsy Encounter with the World," *Orbis* 38 (Summer 1994): 393.

19. Michael Mandelbaum, "Foreign Policy as Social Work," *Foreign Affairs* 75 (February 1996): 16–32.

20. Douglas Brinkley, "Democratic Enlargement: The Clinton Doctrine," *Foreign Policy* 106 (Spring 1997): 121.

21. John Rielly, ed., *American Public Opinion and U.S. Foreign Policy 1995* (Chicago: The Chicago Council on Foreign Relations, 1995), p. 16.

22. Warren Christopher, "Principles and Opportunities for American Foreign Policy," *Dispatch* 6 (January 23, 1995): 41–46.

23. Warren Christopher, "Leadership for the Next American Century," *Dispatch* 7 (January 22, 1996): 9–12.

24. Bill Clinton, "Address Before a Joint Session of the Congress on the State of the Union," February 4, 1997, *Public Papers of the Presidents of the United States: William J. Clinton 1997. Book 1: January 1 to June 30, 1997* (Washington, DC: Government Printing Office, 1998).

25. Samuel R. Berger, Assistant to the President for National Security Affairs" "A Foreign Policy Agenda for the Second Term," Center for Strategic and International Studies, Washington, DC, March 27, 1997, http://astro.temple.edu/~rimmerma/Samuel_Berger.htm, July 27, 2012.

26. United States, Executive Office of the President, *A National Security Strategy for a New Century*, National Security Council, Washington, DC, May 1997, http://www.whitehouse.gov/ WH/EOP/NSC/Strategy/, August 4, 1999. In fact, in its 1994 National Security Strategy report to Congress, the Clinton administration had already placed security concerns above economic prosperity and promotion of democracy abroad, but it was not until the 1997 National Security Strategy report that "there was a new focus on enumerating priorities for America abroad." See Don M. Snider and John A. Nagl, "The National Security Strategy: Documenting Strategic Vision," in Joseph R. Cerami and James F. Holcomb, Jr., eds., *U.S. Army War College Guide to Strategy*, pp. 135–136, http://www.strategicstudiesinstitute.army. mil/pubs/display.cfm?PubID=362, August 21, 2008.

27. Bill Clinton, "Statement on Kosovo (March 24, 1999)," Miller Center, University of Virginia. http://millercenter.org/president/speeches/detail/3932, July 27, 2012.

28. Bill Clinton, "Remarks by the President on Foreign Policy," Grand Hyatt Hotel, San Francisco, California, February 26, 1999, https://www.mtholyoke.edu/acad/intrel/clintfps. htm, July 27, 2012.

29. Samuel R. Berger, "A Foreign Policy for a Global Age," *Foreign Affairs* 79 (November/ December 2000): 22–39.

30. McCormick, "Clinton and Foreign Policy," pp. 74–83.

31. J. F. O. McAllister, "Secretary of Shhhhh!" *Time International*, June 7, 1993, 26.

32. Confidential interview with a longtime Washington observer, May 2001.

33. Maxwell A. Cameron and Brian W. Tomlin, *The Making of NAFTA: How the Deal Was Done* (Ithaca, NY, and London: Cornell University Press, 2000), p. 201.

34. See Stephen M. Walt, "Two Cheers for Clinton's Foreign Policy," *Foreign Affairs* 79 (March/April 2000): 72–74, for a somewhat more positive assessment in this area.

35. James M. McCormick, "Human Rights and the Clinton Administration: American Policy at the Dawn of a New Century," in Robert G. Patman, ed., *Universal Human Rights?* (New York: St. Martin's Press, 2000), pp. 128–131.

36. Alton Frye, *Humanitarian Intervention: Crafting a Workable Doctrine* (New York: Council on Foreign Relations, 2000), pp. 77–85.

37. Ibid., p. 76.

38. Ibid., p. 74.

39. See Bruce W. Jentleson and Rebecca L. Britton, "Still Pretty Prudent," *Journal of Conflict Resolution* 42 (August 1998): 395–418, on public support for various interventions.

40. On the sources of these estimates, see James M. McCormick, "Decision-Making Processes and Actors in American Foreign Policy Formulation: Is There a Third World Lobby?" in Jurgen Ruland, Theodor Hanf, and Eva Manske, eds., *U.S. Foreign Policy Toward the Third World: A Post-Cold War Assessment* (Armonk, New York, and London: M.E. Sharpe, 2006), p. 64.

41. George W. Bush, "A Distinctly American Internationalism," speech delivered at the Ronald Reagan Presidential Library, November 19, 1999, http://www.georgewbush.com/speeches/foreignpolicy/foreignpolicy.asp.

42. See Evan Thomas, "Condoleezza Rice, Bush's Secret White House Weapon," *Newsweek*, December 16, 2002, 26, in which Rice apparently had to moderate some of Vice President Cheney's remarks on Iraq.

43. Francis Fukuyama, *America at the Crossroads: Democracy, Power, and the Neoconservative Legacy* (New Haven and London: Yale University Press, 2006), pp. 48–49.

44. Thomas, "Condoleezza Rice, Bush's Secret White House Weapon," p. 27.

45. For a biography of Colin Powell, see http://www.biography.com/people/colin-powell-9445708?page=1, July 27, 2012.

46. For a recent biography of Robert B. Zoellick, see http://web.worldbank.org/WBSITE/EXTERNAL/EXTABOUTUS/ORGANIZATION/EXTPRESIDENT/EXTPASTPRESIDENTS/EXTPRESIDENT2007/0,contentMDK:21394208~menuPK:64822289~pagePK:64821878~piPK:64821912~theSitePK:3916065,00.html, July 27, 2012.

47. The biographical information on Donald Rumsfeld and Paul Wolfowitz is from http://www.biography.com/people/donald-rumsfeld-9466907 and http://historyking.com/Biography/Biography-Of-Paul-Wolfowitz.html, July 27, 2012.

48. The commitment to this Reaganite foreign policy model is derived in part from Rumsfeld and Wolfowitz's involvement with the Project for a New American Century, in connection with which both (as well as Dick Cheney) signed a statement of principles in June 1997. The statement is available at http://www.newamericancentury.org/statementofprinciples.htm.

49. Department of Defense, "Biography: Dr. Robert M. Gates," http://www.defenselink.mil/bios/biographydetail.aspx?biographyid=115.

50. See "Bush Nominates Goss to Head CIA," August 11, 2004, http://www.cnn.com/2004/ALLPOLITICS/08/10/cia.goss/, August 23, 2008; Liza Porteus, "CIA Chief Porter Resigns," May 5, 2006, http://www.foxnews.com/story/0,2933,194419,00.html, August 23, 2008; U.S. Air Force, "General Michael V. Hayden," http://www.af.mil/information/bios/bio.asp?bioID=5746, July 27, 2012.

51. Fareed Zakaria, *From Wealth to Power: The Unusual Origins of America's World Role* (Princeton, NJ: Princeton University Press, 1998), pp. 8–9.

52. Bush, "A Distinctly American Internationalism."

53. Ibid.

54. George W. Bush, "A Period of Consequences," remarks delivered at The Citadel, September 23, 1999, http://www.georgewbush.com/speeches/defense/citadel.asp.

55. Bush, "A Distinctly American Internationalism."

56. Condoleezza Rice, "Promoting the National Interest," *Foreign Affairs* 79 (January/February 2000): 53.

57. Karl W. Deutsch, "External Influences on the Internal Behavior of States," in R. Barry Farrell, ed., *Approaches to Comparative and International Politics* (Evanston, IL: Northwestern University Press, 1966), pp. 5–26.

58. Bruce Russett, "The Americans' Retreat from World Power," *Political Science Quarterly* 90 (Spring 1975): 1–22.

59. "Rallying behind the Country's Leaders and Institutions," September 25, 2001, *Tuesday-Briefing@Gallup.com*; and Shoon Kathleen Murray and Christopher Spinosa, "The Post-9/11 Shift in Public Opinion: How Long Will It Last?" in Eugene R. Wittkopf and James M. McCormick, eds., *The Domestic Sources of American Foreign Policy: Insights and Evidence*, 4th ed. (Lanham, MD: Rowman & Littlefield, 2004), pp. 97–115.

60. For the full report of American attitudes after the events of September 11, 2001, see Marshall M. Bouton, ed., *Worldviews 2002: American Public Opinion and Foreign Policy.* Chicago: The Chicago Council on Foreign Relations, 2002, http://www.thechicagocouncil. org/UserFiles/File/POS_Topline%20Reports/POS%202002/2002_US_Report.pdf, July 27, 2012.

61. McCormick, "Clinton and Foreign Policy," pp. 60–83.

62. For the complete listing of the legislation identified by the House of Representatives as related to 9/11 as well as the accompanying votes, see my "The Foreign Policy of the George W. Bush Administration" in Steven E. Schier, ed., *High Risks and Big Ambitions* (Pittsburgh: University of Pittsburgh Press, 2004), p. 202, Table 9.1.

63. See the Iraq Resolution. Public Law 107–243 (H.J. Res. 114).

64. Bob Woodward, *Bush at War* (New York: Simon & Schuster, 2002), p. 37.

65. Ibid.

66. Fred Greenstein, "The Changing Leadership of George W. Bush: A Pre-and Post-9/11 Comparison," in Wittkopf and McCormick, eds., *The Domestic Sources of American Foreign Policy*, 4th ed., pp. 353–362.

67. Thomas Preston and Margaret G. Hermann, "Presidential Leadership Style and the Foreign Policy Advisory Process," in Wittkopf and McCormick, eds., *The Domestic Sources of American Foreign Policy*, 4th ed., p. 370.

68. Stanley Renshon, "Assessing the Personality of George W. Bush," in Eugene R. Wittkopf and James M. McCormick, eds., *The Domestic Sources of American Foreign Policy: Insights and Evidence*, 5th ed. (Lanham, MD: Rowman & Littlefield, 2008), p. 386.

69. The term is from Walter Russell Mead, *Power, Terror, Peace, and War: America's Grand Strategy in a World at Risk* (New York: Vintage Books, 2005), pp. 88–97.

70. Zakaria, *From Wealth to Power*, pp. 8–9.

71. For a critique, see Gary Dorrien, "Axis of One," *Christian Century* 120 (March 8, 2003): 30–35.

72. Fukuyama, *America at the Crossroads*, pp. 48–49.

73. Mead, *Power, Terror, Peace, and War*, at p. 94, for example.

74. Ivo Daalder and James M. Lindsay argued that the events of September 11 gave the Bush administration the opportunity to implement a foreign policy design that they had already embraced. In this sense, the administration's foreign policy was less changed than actualized by

September 11. See Daalder and Lindsay, "The Bush Revolution: The Remaking of America's Foreign Policy," a revised version of a paper presented at The George W. Bush Presidency: An Early Assessment Conference, April 25–26, 2003, originally available at http://www.brookings.edu/views/papers/daalder/20030425.pdf. Also see Daalder and Lindsay, *America Unbound: The Bush Revolution in Foreign Policy* (Washington, DC: Brookings Institution, 2003).

75. George W. Bush, "Address to a Joint Session of Congress and the American People," September 20, 2001, http://www.whitehouse.gov/news/releases/2001/09/20010920–8.html.

76. Ibid.

77. Ibid.

78. This listing is drawn from U.S. Department of State, "Operation Enduring Freedom Overview," October 1, 2001, which is discussed in greater detail in McCormick, "The Foreign Policy of the George W. Bush Administration," at pp. 207–209 and in Table 9.2 at p. 208.

79. See McCormick, "The Foreign Policy of the George W. Bush Administration," at pp. 207–209 and also see; Office of the Historian, Department of State, "The United States and the Global Coalition Against Terrorism, September–December 2001: A Chronology," December 31, 2001.

80. Interestingly, the phrase, "distinctly American internationalism" remains in this document, but it now takes on a different meaning from the meaning it had at the beginning of the administration.

81. Also see Ivo H. Daalder, James M. Lindsay, and James B. Steinberg, "The Bush National Security Strategy: An Evaluation," October, 2002, http://www.brookings.edu/research/papers/2002/10/defense-daalder, from which we draw.

82. All of the quoted materials in this section and above are taken from *The National Security Strategy of the United States* (Washington, DC: The White House, September 17, 2002), http://www.whitehouse.gov/nsc/nss/2002/index.html, August 23, 2008.

83. Woodward, *Bush at War*, p. 49.

84. Todd S. Purdom and Patrick E. Tyler, "Top Republicans Break with Bush on Iraq Strategy," *New York Times*, August 16, 2002, http://www.nytimes.com/2002/08/16/international/middleeast/16IRAQ.html?todaysheadlines, September 29, 2002.

85. See George W. Bush, "President's Remarks at the United Nations General Assembly," September 12, 2002, http://www.whitehouse.gov/news/releases/2002/09/2002/09.

86. "Text of U.N. Resolution on Iraq," Cable News Network, November 8, 2002, http://www.cnn.com/2002/US/11/08/resolution.text/.

87. George W. Bush, "President Says Saddam Hussein Must Leave Iraq Within 48 Hours," March 17, 2003, http://www.whitehouse.gov/news/releases/2003/03/20030317-7.html.

88. For an analysis of intelligence on this point, see Paul R. Pillar, "Intelligence, Policy, and the War in Iraq," Wittkopf and McCormick, eds., *The Domestic Sources of American Foreign Policy*, 5th ed., pp. 235–245.

89. Eric Schmitt, "Aide Denies Shaping Data to Justify War," *New York Times*, June 5, 2003, http://query.nytimes.com/gst/fullpage.html?res=9B01E0D91E30F936A35755C0A9659C8B63, August 23, 2008.

90. David E. Sanger and James Risen, "C.I.A. Chief Takes Blame in Assertion on Iraqi Uranium," *New York Times*, July 12, 2003, A1 and A5.

91. Thomas Beaumont, "Gephardt Takes Aim at Bush," *Des Moines Register*, July 14, 2003, 1B.

92. Dan Balz, "Kerry Raps Bush Policy on Postwar Iraq," *Washington Post*, July 11, 2003, A1 and A6.

93. Young Whan Kihl, "Nuclear Issues in U.S.-Korea Relations: An Uncertain Security Future," *International Journal of Korean Studies* 7 (Spring/Summer 2003): 79–97. The quoted passage is at p. 84.

94. Ibid., pp. 94–95.

95. See the text of remarks to be delivered by John R. Bolton, Undersecretary of State for Arms Control and International Security, to the Conference of the Institute for Foreign Policy Analysis and the Fletcher School's International Security Studies Program, December 2, 2003, http://web.lexis-nexis.com/universe/document?_m=db581af8ba8 4e819eda4030efc04a4c2&_docnum=35&wchp=dGLbVtb-zSkVb&_md5=6de8dd06a 0293b590c3fed55080cedea.

96. Vanessa Gera, "Iran to Open Nuclear Facilities to UN," *Associated Press Online*, December 18, 2003, http://web.lexis-nexis.com/universe/document?_m=221a4f9a4668a39086 1be5a6ecf8076f&_docnum=44&wchp=dGLbVlb-zSkVA&_md5=76216dc29c2cc73e8b 809758550716d7.

97. David E. Sanger and Judith Miller, "Libya to Give Up Arms Programs, Bush Announces," *New York Times*, December 20, 2003, A1 and A8.

98. Ibid., A8.

99. The items of cooperation and accommodation between Russia and the United States listed in this paragraph are drawn from Jessica T. Matthews, "September 11, One Year Later: A World of Change," *Policy Brief*, Special Edition 18 (Washington, DC: Carnegie Endowment for International Peace, 2002), p. 3.

100. Ibid., and James Steinberg, "Counterterrorism," *Brookings Review* 20 (Summer 2002): 5.

101. BBC Worldwide Monitoring, "Russia Hopes for Joint Oil, Gas and Electricity Projects with Iraq," February 11, 2008, http://www.lexisnexis.com/us/lnacademic/results/ docview/docview.do?docLinkInd=true&risb=21_T3685309766&format=GNBFI&sort =RELEVANCE&startDocNo=1&resultsUrlKey=29_T3685309770&cisb=22_T368530 9769&treeMax=true&treeWidth=0&csi=10962&docNo=4.

102. Steinberg, "Counterterrorism," p. 6.

103. BBC Worldwide Monitoring, "Chinese, Iraqi Leaders Hold Talks: Debt Relief, Cooperation Accords Signed," June 21, 2007, http://www.lexisnexis.com/us/lnacademic/results/ docview/docview.do?docLinkInd=true&risb=21_T3685378877&format=GNBFI&sort= RELEVANCE&startDocNo=1&resultsUrlKey=29_T3685378884&cisb=22_T368537888 3&treeMax=true&treeWidth=0&csi=10962&docNo=6.

104. BBC Worldwide Monitoring, "Chinese Foreign Minister Meets Iraq PM, US, Russian, EU Foreign Affairs Chiefs," May 5, 2007, http://www.lexisnexis.com/us/lnacademic/ results/docview/docview.do?docLinkInd=true&risb=21_T3685484080&format=GNBF I&sort=RELEVANCE&startDocNo=1&resultsUrlKey=29_T3685484097&cisb=22_T3 685484096&treeMax=true&treeWidth=0&csi=10962&docNo=6.

105. Peter Grier and Amelia Newcomb, "US, China Find a New Middle Way," *Christian Science Monitor*, December 11, 2003, 1, http://www.csmonitor.com/2003/1211/p01s02-woap.html. The expert quoted here is Minxin Pei from the Carnegie Endowment for International Peace.

106. Ibid. The expert quoted here is Elizabeth Economy at the Council on Foreign Relations.

107. Steinberg, "Counterterrorism," p. 6.

108. Peter Schwarz, "European Foreign Ministers Attack Bush's Policy," World Socialist Website, http://www.wsws.org/articles/2002/feb2002/euro-f15.shtml. For a discussion on this point, also see James M. McCormick, "The War on Terror and Contemporary U.S.-European Relations," *Politics and Policy* 34 (June 2006): 434, from which we draw here.

109. Dana Milbank, "The 'Bush Doctrine' Experiences Shining Moments," *Washington Post*, December 21, 2003, A26. http://web.lexis-nexis.com/universe/document?_m=5f4ea6a4 1c2db8c6aef626b89b0e4dac&_docnum=7&wchp=dGLbVlb-zSkVA&_md5=7fb3cfa95 ba18af75f73dc8c027db0d2.

110. David Stout, "Bush Vows to Improve Ties with Europeans," *International Herald Tribune*, November 13, 2004, 1 and 4. See the discussion of the following themes in McCormick, "The War on Terror and Contemporary U.S.-European Relations," pp. 436–443, from which we draw for the following discussion.

111. "President Sworn-In to Second Term," January 20, 2005, http://www.whitehouse.gov/news/releases/2005/01/print/20050120-1.html.

112. George W. Bush, "State of the Union Address," February 2, 2005, http://www.white-house.gov/news/releases/2005/01/print/20050202-11.html.

113. Hearing before the Committee on Foreign Relations, United States Senate, "The Nomination of Dr. Condoleezza Rice to be Secretary of State." 109th Cong., 1st sess., January 18–19, 2005 (Washington, DC: Government Printing Office), p 18. Also see Secretary Condoleezza Rice, "Opening Remarks by Secretary of State-Designate Dr. Condoleezza Rice," January 18, 2005 at http://merln.ndu.edu/archivepdf/nss/state/40991.pdf, July 27, 2012.

114. George W. Bush, "President Bush Discussed Iraq Policy at Whitehall Palace in London," November 19, 2003, http://georgewbush-whitehouse.archives.gov/news/releases/2003/11/20031119-1.html, July 27, 2012.

115. Philip Gordon, "The End of the Bush Revolution," *Foreign Affairs* 85 (July/August 2006): 81.

116. Ibid., pp. 81–82.

117. U.S. Department of State, "Background Notes: North Korea," February, 2008, http://www.state.gov/r/pa/ei/bgn/2792.htm, August 23, 2008.

118. See "Statement by the Press Secretary on North Korea," June 26, 2008, http://www.whitehouse.gov/news/releases/2008/06/print/20080626.html, August 19, 2008; and "President Discusses North Korea," June 26, 2008 http://www.whitehouse.gov/news/releases/2008/06/print/20080626-9.html, August 19, 2008.

119. Gordon, "The End of the Bush Revolution," p. 83.

120. Pew Global Project Attitudes, *Views of a Changing World June 2003*, p. 19.

121. Pew Global Attitudes Project, *America's Image Slips, But Allies Share U.S. Concerns Over Iran* (Washington, DC: The Pew Research Center for the People & the Press, 2006), p. 1.

122. BBC World Service Poll, "22 Nation Poll on Bush's Reelection, A BBC World Service Poll," January 19, 2005. The results are available at http://www.pipa.org/OnlineReports/Views_US/BushReelect_Jan05/BushReelect_Jan05_rpt.pdf, July 27, 2012.

123. Gallup Poll, "Presidential Approval Ratings—George W. Bush," http://www.gallup.com/poll/116500/Presidential-Approval-Ratings-George-Bush.aspx, July 27, 2012.

124. Ibid.

125. See the periodic polling results reported in Frank Newport, "Public: Situation in Iraq Getting Worse for U.S.," Gallup New Service, October 18, 2007, http://www.gallup.com/poll/102055/Public-Situation-Iraq-Getting-Worse-US.aspx, July 27, 2012.

126. John Mueller, "The Iraq Syndrome," in Wittkopf and McCormick, eds., *The Domestic Sources of American Foreign Policy*, 5th ed., p. 116.

127. Lawrence Korb and Caroline Wadhams, "A Critique of the Bush Administration's National Security Strategy," *Policy Analysis Brief* (Muscatine, IA: The Stanley Foundation, June, 2006), pp. 1 and 3 for the quoted passages.

128. David Nather, "War of Words Intensifies," *CQ Weekly Online* (November 21, 2005): 3120, http://library.cqpress.com/cqweekly/weeklyreport109-000001975373, August 23, 2008.

129. David Nather, "GOP Nominee 2008: Let the Speculation Begin," *CQ Weekly Online* (October 24, 2005): 2834, http://library.cqpress.com/cqweekly/weeklyreport109-000001925236, August 23, 2008.

130. "2008 White House Contender: Chuck Hagel," *CQ Weekly Online* (November 6, 2006): 2926, http://library.cqpress.com/cqweekly/weeklyreport109-000002398071, August 23, 2008.

131. James A. Baker III and Lee H. Hamilton, *The Iraq Study Group Report* (New York: Vintage Books, 2006).

132. David Nather, "Waging War on the Surge," *CQ Weekly Online* (January 15, 2007), 170, http://library.cqpress.com/cqweekly/weeklyreport110-000002428775, accessed October 15, 2008.

133. Liriel Higa and John Donnelly, "War Supplemental Heads to Veto," *CQ Weekly Online* (April 30, 2007): 1266–1269, http://library.cqpress.com/cqweekly/weeklyreport110-000002500138, August 23, 2008; and David Clarke, "Search for a Supplemental Compromise," *CQ Weekly Online* (May 7, 2007): 1348–1350, http://library.cqpress.com/cqweekly/weeklyreport110-000002505198, August 23, 2008.

134. See United States Government Accountability Office, "Securing, Stabilizing, and Rebuilding Iraq," GAO-07-1195 (Washington, DC: U.S. Government Accountability Office, September, 2007). General Petraeus testified before Congress in September 2007 and April 2008 on the surge strategy.

CHAPTER 6

Change and Continuity in Foreign Policy: The Barack Obama Administration*

We reject as false the choice between our safety and our ideals. . . .
Those ideals still light the world, and we will not give
them up for expedience's sake.

PRESIDENT BARACK OBAMA
JANUARY 20, 2009

[The United States] will lead by inducing greater
cooperation among a greater number of actors and reducing
competition, tilting the balance away from a multi-polar world
and toward a multi-partner world.

SECRETARY OF STATE HILLARY CLINTON
JULY 15, 2009

*This chapter is an expanded and updated version of my "The Obama Presidency: A Foreign Policy of Change?" in Steven Schier, ed. *Transforming America: Barack Obama in the White House* (Lanham, MD: Rowman & Littlefield, 2011), pp. 235–266.

Barack Obama ran for the presidency on a **policy of change**—change in domestic policy and change in foreign policy. During the 2008 nomination and election campaigns, this focus on change was the overarching theme that he struck at virtually every stop on the campaign trail. In foreign policy, Obama's emphasis on change focused on an array of issues—ending the Iraq and Afghanistan wars and bringing American troops home, "resetting" and "restarting" American relations with allies and other major powers throughout the world, engaging with adversaries to address a number of outstanding issues, and dealing with global economic and military issues, most notably nuclear proliferation. The larger aim of this "change" emphasis was to enable the United States to reengage with the world and to move away from the isolated position in which America found itself after the seeming unilateralist policies of the Bush administration. In this sense, the foreign policy approach of the Obama administration sought a distinct **change in values and beliefs** for shaping foreign policy and a marked **change in the substance** of American policy.

In this chapter, we examine the foreign policy approach and policies of the Obama administration and assess how well it has achieved this change. First, we set out the basic values and beliefs and foreign policy approach and priorities that President Obama and his team brought to American foreign policy in 2009. Next, we assess the key foreign policy actions of the Obama administration, how well they comport with its stated goals and priorities, and the degree to which they represent change from the Bush years. Finally, we identify some criticism of this new approach as well as draw some preliminary conclusions about the degree of foreign policy changes during President Obama's time in office.

VALUES AND BELIEFS OF THE OBAMA ADMINISTRATION

Although Barack Obama did not initially come to his presidential bid with a well-developed foreign policy view of the world, he quickly developed a number of important themes that he utilized during his electoral campaign. Once he entered office, those themes were refined into a series of policy priorities through several speeches and statements that he and his secretary of state, Hillary Clinton, gave to different audiences during their first year in office. By May 2010, moreover, the administration had also issued its National Security Strategy, which more fully summarized the administration's worldview.

A Liberal Internationalist Approach

The foreign policy portrait that emerged from this process was an administration with a worldview that appeared to align closely with the liberal internationalist approach to foreign policy (albeit with some realist exceptions). The liberal internationalist approach has a substantial heritage in American foreign policy, dating back at least to Woodrow Wilson and Franklin Delano Roosevelt, but it has also found more recent expression in foreign policy elements of the Carter and Clinton administrations.

A liberal internationalist approach is one that is grounded in a number of core values and beliefs about the motivations and aims of foreign policy behavior for individual states and for the United States in particular. First of all, key domestic values, such as the **promotion of democracies and individual freedoms**, are viewed as important ways to create a stable and peaceful international order. In this context, the

Obama approach would find appeal among those who see the "democratic peace" theory as the way to global order. Following this tradition, too, the basis of U.S. foreign policy would flow directly from its domestic values as a nation, even as the United States works to promote such values internationally. Second, liberal internationalism calls for promoting international cooperation and interdependence in a variety of ways as means to **knit states and peoples in a web of interdependence** to address common problems and reduce the risk of conflict. The United States would promote free trade among nations, but it also would promote cooperative actions across borders by different levels of government and among numerous civil society groups. Third, **international law** and **international institutions** are assumed to "have a modernizing and civilizing effect on states" and also fit within this liberal internationalist tradition for enhancing global cooperation and interdependence.[1] In this sense, American foreign policy would utilize regional and global organizations because they, too, are essential in linking states and the international community. Fourth, and particularly important from this perspective and its **Wilsonian roots** (see Chapter 1), the United States would not only stay involved in global affairs but also assist in bringing about a stable, liberal order through its cooperative and constructive leadership efforts. These actions would not be done in any top-down or directive way; instead, they would be evoked through cooperative actions with states and actors.

In several respects, liberal internationalism stands in considerable contrast to the foreign policy approach of the George W. Bush administration, an approach variously described as a combination of "defensive realism" and "idealism," "revival Wilsonianism," or neoconservatism (see Chapter 5). A liberal internationalist approach begins from a more **cooperative assumption** about foreign policy and global politics than the Bush administration adopted, especially after the events of September 11 that prompted Bush to announce: "either you are with us or you are with the terrorists." This approach also emphasizes the utility of multilateral means to address foreign policy, an approach that the Bush administration generally viewed skeptically from the outset of its tenure. In this sense, the Obama approach places greater reliance on diplomacy and "soft power" instruments for achieving foreign policy change, a marked contrast to the Bush administration's seeming reliance on coercive diplomacy and "hard power" instruments.

At least two important similarities in goals, however, exist between Obama's liberal internationalist and Bush's neoconservative approach: both approaches favor **fostering of democracies** and both call for **American leadership**. Yet, they differ substantially on how best to achieve these goals. The Obama approach focuses on building democracy from the bottom up, whereas the Bush approach sought, at least in practice, to impose it from the top down. Both approaches also favor American leadership, but again they differ on how to pursue that goal. The Obama approach calls for more cooperative leadership ("**partnerships**" as the Obama administration continuously describes it), whereas the Bush administration favored a more assertive American leadership to encourage followership.

Some Core Beliefs

The components of this liberal internationalist approach of President Obama and his administration evolved (as did some limitations that were ultimately placed on it). Therefore, it is worthwhile to review that evolution beginning with the presidential campaign, continuing through his initial foreign policy review, and culminating in the issuance of the national security strategy in May 2010.

Early on, Senator Obama clearly rejected the Bush administration's neoconservative approach. Writing in *Foreign Affairs* magazine in the summer of 2007, Obama explicitly called for a different kind of American leadership in the world—and one that he saw as at odds with the Bush administration: "We can neither retreat from the world nor try to bully it into submission. We must lead by deed and by example."[2] Similarly, he embraced the use of diplomacy as America's principal foreign policy option and endorsed the use of "partnerships" for dealing with a host of foreign policy issues, whether in the security or non-security areas. Furthermore, Obama called for American domestic values to serve as the guide for this new kind of engagement: "Our global engagement cannot be defined by what we are against; it must be guided by a clear sense of what we stand for."[3] Third, and importantly, he endorsed the promotion of democracy, but he explicitly rejected the imposition of democracy on other nations.[4] As he noted, "we need to invest in building capable, democratic states that can establish healthy and educated communities, develop markets, and generate wealth."[5] In other words, he sought democracy from the bottom up, not the top down or through the use of force.

Indeed, the U.S. emphasis on "partnerships" to address key foreign policy issues immediately became an important theme of Obama's approach and an important contrast from the Bush administration. On the issue of terrorism, for instance, Obama called for a movement away from such a singular focus on a military response as utilized by the Bush administration and toward a greater reliance on a collective response from the global community. He also called for new (or renewed) partnerships to address such diverse issues as strengthening the capability of NATO, building new security, economic, or social institutions in Asia (or elsewhere), and combating climate change worldwide. A similar kind of global cooperation or global partnerships would also be necessary to arrest and reverse nuclear proliferation in the world today—an issue that candidate Obama described as "the most urgent threat to the security of America and the world."[6] To accomplish this, however, Obama not only called for global cooperation to prevent Iran from obtaining nuclear weapons and to roll back the nuclear efforts of North Korea but he also called for the negotiation of "a verifiable global ban on the production of new nuclear weapons materials"[7] and for the U.S. Senate to ratify the Comprehensive Test Ban Treaty.

The Global Vision: A Multipartner World

A more precise foreign policy framework for the administration, closely aligned to the campaign themes, emerged during the first year of the administration and took even fuller shape by the middle of the second year in office. In his 2009 inaugural address, for example, President Obama once again alluded to this change in foreign policy from the Bush years with an explicit promotion of American values as the basis of policy and with an appeal for diplomacy toward adversaries: "We reject as false the choice between our safety and our ideals. . . . Those ideals still light the world, and we will not give them up for expedience's sake" and "To those who cling to power through corruption and deceit and the silencing of dissent, know that you are on the wrong side of history, but we will extend a hand if you are willing to unclench your fist." Yet, he also signaled a continuation of past foreign policy in this way: "We will not apologize for our way of life nor will we waver in its defense. And for those who seek to advance their aims by inducing terror and slaughtering innocents, we say to you now that, 'Our spirit is stronger and cannot be broken. You cannot outlast us, and we will defeat you.'"[8] As Stanley Renshon correctly noted, the former set of statements would appeal to liberals (and liberal internationalists in our parlance), whereas the latter set of statements would appeal to conservatives and political realists.[9] In all, although change was in the air, the degree of change was again mixed with a commitment to continuity in policy.

During the first several months of the administration, President Obama's foreign policy team conducted a **policy review**. The results of that review were announced through a series of presidential speeches from April to July 2009 given in several world capitals (in Europe, the Middle East, and Africa). In April 2009 in Prague, Czech Republic, he extolled the virtues of the changes that have occurred in that country in a few short years and called for cooperation and policy coordination among nations "to renew our prosperity" and "to provide for our common security." He also articulated his goal of "a world without nuclear weapons" and outlined a series of steps to move in that direction by completing a new Strategic Arms Reduction Treaty with Russia, strengthening the Nuclear Non-Proliferation Treaty, and initiating "a new international effort to secure all vulnerable nuclear material around the world within four years."[10] In June 2009 in Cairo, Egypt, Obama called for "a new beginning between the United States and the Muslims, one based on mutual interest and mutual respect" and sought to show the substantial ties between the Muslim world and the United States over the decades and centuries. Importantly, he called for "a sustained effort to listen to each other; to learn from each other; to respect one another; and to seek common ground" and he went on to state that "our problems must be dealt with through partnership; [and] our progress must be shared."[11] Even as he struck the theme of calling for more cooperation and understanding, he also outlined the key issues that challenged these two differing worlds: violent extremism; the situation among Israelis, Palestinians, and the Arab world; the dangers of nuclear weapons; and the need to promote democracy, religious freedom, women's rights, and economic development. Finally, he concluded as he had done in Prague by emphasizing that "all these things must be done in partnership."

In July 2009, Obama gave foreign policy speeches in two other capitals—Moscow, Russia, and Accra, Ghana. In both speeches, he sought to reach out to these differing audiences and to highlight the change in American policy that he wanted to initiate. In Moscow, Obama called for a "'reset' in relations between the United States and Russia." The aim, he said, would be "a sustained effort among the American and Russian people to identify mutual interests, and expand dialogue and cooperation that can pave the way to progress."[12] As he had done in the earlier addresses, he identified his **policy priorities on nuclear weapons, extremism, global prosperity, democratic promotion, and global cooperation**. In Accra, Obama once again struck this theme of international cooperation and partnership: "I see Africa as a fundamental part of our interconnected world as partners with America on behalf of the future we want for all of our children."[13] In that speech, he particularly focused on issues relating to the needs of Africa and the developing world: the need for democratic governments, development that provides opportunity, governance that strengthens public health, and the peaceful resolution of conflicts. In all these areas, the United States would stand as a partner with Africa.

At roughly the same time, Secretary of State Hillary Clinton delivered an important foreign policy address at home.[14] In that address, she committed the United States to a leadership position, albeit a particular kind; identified the basic values to inform the Obama administration's foreign policy priorities; outlined how the administration would conduct its foreign policy; and crystallized the view of the kind of international system that the administration wished to create. In particular, she stated that the United States would continue to lead in global affairs, but the nation "need[s] a new mindset about how America will use its power to safeguard our nation, expand shared prosperity, and help more people in more places live up to their God-given potential." In this "new era of engagement," Clinton contended, the United States must base its actions on "common interests, shared values, and mutual respect," and she said that the United States would advance its interests through "the power of [its] example and the empowerment of people." In addition, and importantly, she also indicated that "we will exercise American leadership to build partnerships and solve problems that no nation can solve on its own." She identified four basic values that would drive such problem-solving and policy priorities: "liberty, democracy, justice, and opportunity."

More specifically, Secretary Clinton outlined the approach that would be followed to solve important "collective action problems" in the international system. In particular, she rejected the approaches of the past and committed the administration to working toward "a different global architecture" to address the common challenges and threats in the world today. Secretary Clinton said that Americans will

> use our power to convene, our ability to connect countries around the world, and sound foreign policy strategies to create partnerships aimed at solving problems. We'll go beyond states to create opportunities for non-state actors and individuals to contribute to solutions. . . . In short, we will lead by inducing greater cooperation among a greater number of actors and reducing competition, *tilting the balance away from a multi-polar world and toward a multi-partner world.* (Emphasis added.)

Secretary Clinton also incorporated an important realist exception to her "focus on diplomacy and development" as a basic approach. When the United States is threatened, she said, "We will not hesitate to defend our friends, our interests, and above all, our people vigorously and when necessary with the world's strongest military." In other words, the unilateral option of self-reliance is still very much available.

National Security Strategy: "A Strategy of Engagement"

The national security strategy statement of May 2010 again outlined the foreign policy approach of the Obama administration.[15] Its "strategic approach," the administration declared, was grounded in three fundamental ideas: the need to rebuild the American economy as the basis for strong global leadership, a commitment to living American values at home in order to promote them credibly abroad, and a commitment to reshaping the international system in a way that it will enable the global community to address the challenges of the twenty-first century. To actualize these ideas, the overarching U.S. strategy would be a **"strategy of engagement."** This engagement, moreover, would be broad-gauged—with allies in every part of the world; with nations who are emerging as "centers of influence" (such as China, India, Russia, Brazil, South Africa, and Indonesia); and with emerging nations in the Americas, Africa, and Southeast Asia. In this sense, American engagement would involve friend and foe and would be driven by the fundamental belief that "our own interests are bound to the interests of those beyond our borders."

Such widespread engagement would be utilized to address four principal goals in order to "achieve the world we seek": (1) achieve and maintain security for the United States, allies, and partners; (2) rebuild and strengthen the American economy through an open international system "that promotes opportunity and prosperity"; (3) promote universal values abroad; and (4) work toward an international order "that can foster collective action to confront common challenges." Each of these four areas requires the United States to address specific issues to realize these principal goals, and the national security strategy discussed each in turn.

Security   The first major goal for the United States is to address multiple current security threats. These new threats range from "a loose network of violent extremists" to the dangers posed by failing states to the spread of nuclear weapons. In addition, though, these threats include "asymmetric" ones in which adversaries target space and cyberspace as ways to harm and undermine American (and, indeed, global) society.

For each of these threats, the Obama administration outlined its proposed course of actions. For terrorism, the administration called for developing a greater domestic capacity to address emergencies at home, and it remained committed "to disrupt, dismantle, and defeat al-Qaida and its affiliates" abroad in partnership with others. For the threat of nuclear and biological weapons, the administration called for strengthening the Nuclear Non-Proliferation Treaty, creating a nuclear-free Korean peninsula through the denuclearization of North Korea, and compelling Iran to move away from its pursuit of nuclear weapons. Furthermore, the administration would seek to secure all "vulnerable nuclear weapons and materials" and counter the potential of biological weapons. For the threat from failing states and unresolved conflicts, the administration called for a "responsible transition" as the United States ended the war in Iraq, endorsed a two-state solution for the Arab–Israel conflict, remained open to offering Iran "a pathway to a better future, provided Iran's leaders are prepared to take it" and offered to aid states transitioning from recent conflicts. Finally, on the threat to cyberspace, the administration vowed to work with the private sector and with other governments, "to investigate cyber intrusion and to ensure an organized and unified response to future cyber incidents."

Importantly, the administration was careful to specify its position on the use of force in addressing the terrorist threats. Although the national strategy statement indicates that the use of force "may be necessary to defend our country and allies and to preserve broader peace and security," the administration is careful to specify that it "will exhaust other options before war whenever we can, and carefully weigh the costs and risks of action against costs and risks of inaction." **In this sense, the Obama administration is more circumspect in the use of force than the strategy the Bush administration outlined its 2002 national security strategy.**

Prosperity   The second major goal of the national security strategy is to **rebuild and strengthen the U.S. economy as the basis for a continuing leadership role in the world.** The statement outlines actions that must be completed domestically and internationally to accomplish this goal. Domestically, the administration calls for improvement in the quality of American education from the elementary through the university level. The statement also commits the administration to "support programs that cultivate interest and scholarship in foreign languages and intercultural affairs," and to comprehensive immigration reform as a way to improve America's human capital. Finally, the United States must reduce the nation's deficit, reform the contracting process within the government to reduce waste and inefficiency, and increase the level of transparency so that the public can more fully follow how the taxpayers' dollars are being spent.

Internationally, the United States must expand the growth of the "integrated, global economy," even as it addresses the "economic imbalances and financial excesses."

The national security strategy statement calls on Americans to spend less and save more, double U.S. exports by 2014, and take more actions to open up markets for American products. The Obama administration will also support the **G-20 nations'** "emergence as the premier forum for international economic cooperation" in the global community, and will provide leadership to that organization, the International Monetary Fund, and the World Bank in making necessary global financial reforms. Finally, the administration called for economic changes in developing economies, although those changes should be done within the context of "long-term development" and "sustainable development."

Values   The third major goal of the national security strategy is the promotion of key fundamental values. These values are the basic fundamental individual freedoms contained in the U.S. constitution, which the Obama administration believes are universal and important to promote globally. In order to make the promotion of these values legitimate around the world, they need to be respected at home. In this sense, the United States must **prohibit the use of torture** against individuals and must adhere to the rule of law in its actions, including in dealing with terrorism. Abroad, the United States will **promote democracy and human rights** "because governments that respect these values are more just, peaceful, and legitimate." Yet, the United States "will not impose any system of government on another country." Instead, it will support and build the capacity of those states pursuing democratic development. Such assistance will be undertaken not only through working directly with other governments but also working through civil society groups to create and expand key democratic institutions. Finally, the Obama administration indicated that its emphasis on global freedom also meant "freedom from want," and that it would promote a new global health initiative, promote greater food security, and continue to respond to global humanitarian crises.

International Order   The last goal outlined in the national security statement is the establishment of **"a just and sustainable international order that can foster collective action to confront common challenges."** The Obama administration views this component of the national security strategy as crucial to the advancement of the earlier three goals.

To bring about this new order, the national security strategy statement calls a long litany of American actions and priorities. The United States will sustain its security relations with America's traditional allies in Europe, Asia, and North America; build cooperative relations with those that are the "Twenty-First-Century Centers of Influence" (such as China, India, and Russia); and expand its ties with the G-20 nations (such as Indonesia, Brazil, Saudi Arabia, Argentina, South Africa, and South Korea). In addition, the United States will work to strengthen the United Nations, devolve some responsibility for collective action to a variety of international institutions, and invest in strengthening the capacity of regional organizations across the globe as a way to enhance worldwide security.

The ultimate test of this new international order, the national security strategy points out, is the ability to obtain global cooperation to address the current system challenges. Such challenges range from climate change, ethnic, and genocidal conflict to global pandemics, transnational criminal syndicates, and issues of the "global commons"—shared seas, air, and space among nations. No one state could adequately address these issues; hence, the administration would work to achieve collective action within the international community.

THE OBAMA WORLDVIEW IN OPERATION

The foreign policy approach of the Obama administration is broad, comprehensive, and ambitious in conception—and considerably at variance with the Bush administration's approach. In this sense, the Obama approach represents a dramatic change in foreign policy orientation. The important question, however, is whether this approach has had any impact. How much of this approach has been implemented? Has the approach changed the substance of American foreign policy? Has this approach yielded greater foreign policy success than its predecessor in addressing key issues?

In an effort to reach some conclusions about these questions, we now evaluate the impact of this approach on several key foreign policy issues identified in the strategy statement. In particular, we examine the impact of the Obama approach on reengaging the United States abroad and improving America's reputation abroad; infusing American values into foreign policy (most notably over the handling and treatment of terrorist suspects and addressing the "Arab Spring"); dealing with key security relations, such as Iraq, Afghanistan, Iran, North Korea, and the Middle East conflict; restarting relations with Russia; and addressing "global commons" issues of nuclear proliferation, financial reform, and climate change.

Improving America's Global Image

In terms of reengaging the United States with the international community, the Obama approach has surely changed from the Bush administration. President Obama made important foreign policy speeches in key capitals across different continents and regions in an effort to reach out to the world and improve America's image. He has also engaged key world leaders in bilateral diplomatic summits (for instance, with Russian President Medvedev) and in a variety of multilateral forums (such as the G-8, the G-20, APEC). Furthermore, his administration appointed a large number of special envoys to address a broad range of global issues, whether over Darfur, Afghanistan, North Korea, the Middle East, or elsewhere. Finally, and importantly, the United States has increased its use of regional and international organizations in pursuit of its foreign policy goals. In all, the efforts at global engagement have been substantial and pervasive.

Indeed, this engagement, and the president's personal popularity worldwide, has had an effect on America's image abroad. In Pew Research Center polls in 2009 and 2010 across twenty-five and twenty-two countries, respectively, the "**U.S. favorability rating**" improved considerably in most countries surveyed.[16] The greatest improvement occurred in Western European countries (Britain, France, Germany, and Spain), but America's image was also more positive in particular Latin American, African, and Asian nations. The results for 2011 on this question in the Pew survey generally showed a slight downturn from 2010, although the favorability level remained strong overall.[17]

On another question in the 2009 survey, asking whether Obama "will do the right thing in world affairs," large majorities across the respondents in the surveyed countries were now more confident that President Obama would do so as compared with the results for a similar question for President Bush in 2008. The absolute levels for this "do the right thing" question in the 2010 survey continued to show considerable confidence in President Obama for most of the countries surveyed, although the percentages across all the countries were systematically lower than in 2009. Although there is not the same question in the 2011 Pew survey, there is a comparative question on the degree of "confidence in the U.S. President." These results reveal considerable confidence in Obama worldwide, but the level of confidence in 2011 declined from the 2010 level, much like the earlier comparison.[18] In this sense, some confidence worldwide in Obama's actions had begun to erode from 2009 through 2011.

Yet, the global attitudinal change witnessed in numerous countries has not occurred in most **Muslim countries**.[19] Generally the Muslim countries included in the 2009 and 2010 surveys continued to hold negative views when measured on the U.S. favorability scale or on the "do the right thing" question. In Turkey, Egypt, Jordan, Pakistan, and the Palestinian territories in the 2009 Pew survey, for example, an overwhelming number of respondents continued to have a negative view of the United States, and they expressed low levels of confidence in Obama "doing the right thing." Such patterns continued for the 2010 survey results and actually eroded for that year.

Further, the Obama administration's actions to support the pro-democracy movements in the Arab world in the spring of 2011 did not improve the U.S. favorability levels or the Muslim world's confidence level in President Obama. In Jordan, Turkey, Pakistan, Indonesia, and Lebanon, the favorability scores for the United States declined by three to eight points from 2010. Only in Egypt did the favorability rating improve from 2010 to 2011 (by three points), and in the Palestinian territories, favorability improved by three points from 2009 to 2011. Confidence inObama, too, declined or only improved marginally. From 2010 to 2011, confidence declined eleven points in Turkey and nine points in Indonesia; stayed the same in Lebanon; and improved in Egypt, Pakistan, and Jordan by two points each. For the Palestinian territories, the decline was nine points from 2009 to 2011. In all, the "views of the U.S. remain negative, as they have been for nearly a decade."[20]

Keeping these exceptions in mind about Muslim countries and some erosion of confidence in other countries as well, these results still suggest that President Obama improved the image of the United States in the global arena. This aspect of the global "soft power" quotient of the United States has improved under the Obama administration.

But has this improvement in America's soft power quotient been translated into agreement or accommodation with U.S. foreign policy, either among the global publics or policy makers? The evidence appears mixed. The 2010 Pew survey results indicate majorities in about half of the twenty-two countries now support Obama's antiterrorism policies, but majorities in many of these same countries continue to oppose the war in Afghanistan. Generally, the same conclusion on the antiterrorism policy and the war in Afghanistan remains when the 2010 data on these questions are compared with the 2011 data. Countries provide more support for the former policy than the latter.[21] On Obama's specific policy toward Iran, majorities or pluralities in about half of the surveyed countries opposed it in 2010, and most of the countries opposed Obama's policy on the Middle East conflict as well. Yet, on some important global commons issues (such as climate change, the world economic crisis, and his overall international performance), the majority or plurality of respondents in fourteen or more of the countries voiced their approval in 2010.[22] Still, the overall conclusion is that President Obama's popularity among the global publics has not fostered uniform support for his policies.

The same conclusion applies when considering the reaction of policy makers around the globe to his policy efforts. Whether seeking NATO nations to maintain or increase their troops in Afghanistan, urging the European Union (EU) nations to stimulate their economies, or prodding greater support from China over North Korean or Iranian nuclear ambitions, Obama's global popularity has not automatically produced policy support from these leaders. Instead, national interests continue to dominate policy choices by these nations and their leaders.

Perhaps the greatest series of rebuffs to Obama's policy efforts occurred during his trip to Asia in November 2010.[23] At a meeting just prior to the G-20 summit, the United States and South Korea had hoped to conclude a free trade agreement that had languished since the Bush administration. Instead, the two sides could not agree and could only insist that they would conclude the pact "in a matter of weeks." (Despite this initial setback, they did reach an accord in early December 2010 to eliminate a number of important trade barriers between the two countries.[24] Congress eventually approved this agreement at the end of 2011, and it went into effect on March 15, 2012.) Shortly afterward at the G-20 meetings, Obama also failed to get support for his proposal to stimulate global growth before working on deficit reduction from some key trading nations (such as China, Britain, Germany, and Brazil). Further, he was unsuccessful in getting any movement from the Chinese on its overvalued currency. Instead, several countries criticized the Federal Reserve's decision to weaken the U.S. dollar by pumping an additional $600 billion into circulation (and thus potentially hurting the attractiveness of their exports). Policy makers of other nations pursuing their own interests in foreign policy—and thus disagreeing with American policy at times—is hardly surprising, but their actions suggest the limitation that a change in reputation may have on support for American policy abroad. In short, **nations** (both publics and their leaders) **continue to disagree with American policy**, albeit perhaps less vocally and less disapprovingly than during the Bush years.

Incorporating Domestic Values in Foreign Policy: Guantanamo Bay and the Arab Spring

A second area where the Obama approach called for policy change was in the incorporation of domestic values in the conduct of American foreign policy. Indeed, President Obama noted that the United States did not need to compromise its values in carrying out its foreign policy. Rather, he argued, "in the long run we . . . cannot keep this country safe unless we enlist the power of our most fundamental values."[25] His implicit reference, of course, was to the Bush administration's actions toward the treatment of suspected terrorists in seeming violation of domestic and international standards. Hence, one of his first actions as president was the issuance of **three executive orders** just two days after his inauguration to reverse some of these actions. One executive order called for the CIA to close overseas prisons and to eliminate certain interrogation methods in dealing with terrorist suspects, a second directed the closing of the detention camp at Guantanamo Bay within a year's time, and the third set up a special interagency task force "to identify lawful options for the disposition of individuals captured or apprehended in connection with armed conflicts and counterterrorism operations."[26]

Despite these orders, however, the administration has been only partially successful in implementing a change in policy. The interrogation measures, based on only those outlined in the Army Field Manual, have now been adhered to; the use of water boarding, a practice that was used more than 300 times during the Bush administration, no longer occurs. The full implementation of the other directives, however, has encountered difficulty, and, indeed, not all aspects of the executive orders have been fully brought into effect. To be sure, former CIA director Leon Panetta announced in April 2009 that overseas prisons operated by the organization had been closed,[27] but the transfer of prisoners to facilities operated by other countries apparently would continue, although outside "contractors" would not be used to question the suspects.[28]

The effort to close the Guantanamo Bay prison facility and to transfer its prisoners elsewhere, in particular, met with considerable resistance. Although the administration was able to locate a domestic facility to take these prisoners (an empty maximum security prison in Illinois), Congress has blocked funding to renovate that facility, fearful of housing suspected terrorists on American soil.[29] Furthermore, public opposition to the closing of the Guantanamo facility remains significant; 60 percent of the American public in a March 2010 poll supported keeping it open.[30] The administration has also had to move back from its original position that it would transfer all detainees at Guantanamo to other prisons or put them on trial. Indeed, as early as May 2009, Obama acknowledged that his administration would continue to use military commissions to try some prisoners held at Guantanamo, despite earlier opposition to such action, and that he did not have an answer to those "detainees at Guantanamo who cannot be prosecuted yet who pose a clear danger to the American people."[31] In this sense, for these latter prisoners, they are likely to remain at Guantanamo for the foreseeable future. Furthermore, with the thwarted attacks on Christmas Day 2009 and on Times Square in May 2010, the prospects of closing Guantanamo have continued to fade, and it is now "unlikely that President Obama will fulfill his promise to close it before his term ends in 2013."[32]

The status of indefinite detention at Guantanamo and the use of indefinite detentions were confirmed by the Obama administration in March 2011 when the president issued **a new executive order confirming these policies**—an order ironically that appeared directly at variance with the ones issued after his inauguration in January 2009.[33] Yet, one official remains upbeat about the current situation and its effect on public (and global) opinion: "Closing Guantanamo is good, but fighting to close Guantanamo is O.K. Admitting you failed would be the worst."[34] As the first term of the Obama administration draws to a close, the prison at Guantanamo Bay remains open, even as the number of detainees declined, and military commissions to try some of those detainees have been scheduled.

In contrast to its seeming failed efforts to infuse American values into its policy in dealing with Guantanamo Bay, the administration acted much more consistently and decisively with its commitment to promoting American values with the emergence of the "Arab Spring" in early 2011. The **Arab Spring** referred to a groundswell of popular movements for democratic reform in several Arab countries. The movement began in Tunisia, where the long-serving leader was ultimately forced into exile after several days of popular protests in January 2011. The movement spread to Egypt with days of public protests against the thirty-year autocratic rule of President **Hosni Mubarak**, an important U.S. ally in the Middle East peace process. The administration thus faced vital crossroads with this uprising: support interests that it wanted to protect or support values that it wanted to promote. Although the administration was a bit indecisive in the opening days of the Egyptian public protests, Obama ultimately called for the departure of President Mubarak. By mid-February 2011, Mubarak resigned, and an effort at democratic transition was underway in that crucial Middle Eastern country, albeit not without difficulty.

As this Arab Spring swept other states in the Middle East, the Obama administration continued to support these democratic reform efforts—sometimes more pronounced than others. The Obama administration's most dramatic support was for Libya, where opposition forces struggled to end **Moammar Gadhafi**'s forty-year rule. As protests increased and the rebel forces in Libya began to advance, Gadhafi threatened to destroy these forces, with the potential of great loss of innocent lives. President Obama undertook a series of actions to stop these efforts by Gadhafi's forces. He evacuated the American embassy and froze Gadhafi's assets in the United States.[35] Working with allies, the administration succeeded in broadening international sanctions through **UN Security Council Resolution 1970** against the Libyan government and imposing a "no-fly zone" over Libya through **UN Security Council 1973**.[36] The latter resolution also included a provision authorizing the member states "to take all necessary measures" to protect civilians in that country. In large measure, these actions were fully consistent with the "**Responsibility to Protect**" doctrine endorsed by the global community in 2005.[37]

As a result, the administration, as part of a NATO-led coalition, moved to enforce the UN resolution, although the United States had European nations largely take the lead. Some opposition to this administration action was voiced at home by analysts who were not convinced that American interests were at stake in Libya. Indeed, in outlining his policy actions, Obama argued otherwise: "To brush aside America's responsibility as a leader and—more profoundly—our responsibilities to our fellow human beings under such circumstances would have been a betrayal of who we are."[38] In this sense, Obama's Libyan policy was carefully legitimized through its adherence to the American domestic values. By fall 2011, the policy appeared to have succeeded. Gadhafi fled the Libyan capital and was eventually captured and killed by the opposition. The Libyans then faced the daunting task of putting together a functioning democratic government.

By 2011 and into 2012, this pro-democracy movement in the Middle East had moved to other countries, and the Obama administration's policy was a bit more cautious than with Egypt and Libya. Even as the administration called for democratic reform in other Middle East nations, it was reluctant to take more action. By early 2012, **Syria** had erupted into continuing uprising between rebel forces and the government of **Bashir al-Assad**, with the death toll mounting into the thousands. The Obama administration did seek a UN Security Council resolution, similar to the one over Libya, but it was vetoed by Russia and China. As a result, the United States resorted to additional sanctions against Syria and sought similar sanctions from its European allies, but more assertive actions have not followed. In all, Syria proved more politically complicated for the Obama administration to enforce the responsibility to protect doctrine than Egypt and Libya.

Addressing Key Security Issues: Iraq, Afghanistan, Iran, and North Korea

The Obama administration inherited several security issues from the Bush administration, and it promised to change policy on them as well. In dealing with the Iraq War, the administration has surely changed courses, but, in addressing the war in Afghanistan, it has not. On the nuclear threats from North Korea and Iran, the administration has attempted an engagement approach, but with very little success so far. In all, the degree of change in either the substance or the success on the latter three issues has been limited.

Iraq Perhaps the most important policy change that candidate Obama promised during his campaign was to end American involvement in Iraq. He succeeded in that effort. Early on, he called for the **ending of all American combat operations** by August 31, 2010, with only 50,000 trainers and advisers remaining in Iraq by that date, and he promised the withdrawal of all American forces by the end of 2011. The former goal has been achieved on schedule and, in December 2011, the last truckloads of American combat soldiers crossed the border from Iraq into Kuwait.[39] At one juncture, there was some discussion of maintaining a residual American force in Iraq, but the Iraqi government and the Obama administration could not agree on whether American soldiers would get immunity from prosecution by Iraqi authorities for any criminal violations that might occur in Iraq. Moreover, American leaders refused to stay without such immunity, and Iraq's prime minister, Nouri al-Maliki, told American military officials that he did not have support for such immunity in the Iraqi Parliament.[40] Iraq represents a good example of the Obama approach in action, largely a departure from the Bush approach, although the 2011 withdrawal actually was originally negotiated by the earlier administration.[41] In all, the overall success of the U.S. policy toward Iraq remains unclear because the stability of the Iraqi government, its ability to maintain national unity, and the future of its democracy are continuing challenges for that nation.

Afghanistan If Iraq represents a movement away from the Bush approach by the Obama administration, Obama's policy toward Afghanistan resembles the Bush administration's Iraq policy beginning in 2007. To be sure, candidate Obama maintained that the **real threat from international terrorism was in Afghanistan** and that the Bush administration had "taken its eye off the ball" with the Iraq War.[42] As a result, President Obama quickly committed two additional brigades to Afghanistan upon taking office; increased the number of U.S. drone attacks against terrorist camps, both in Afghanistan and Pakistan; and appointed a new commander in Afghanistan, General Stanley McChrystal, who was ordered to conduct a review of Afghanistan policy and strategy. General McChrystal completed that review in late summer 2009, and his principal recommendation to the president was the need for a substantial increase in American military forces if there was to be a chance of success.

McChrystal's report became a source of considerable internal debate among Obama and his national security team over the next several months. At the end of this debate—one in which the president believed he had only received one real option (increasing the number of American troops)—the president largely supported the military's position.[43] That is, he ordered 30,000 more American troops—somewhat less than 40,000 requested—and opted for pursuing a counterinsurgency option (as the military preferred). In ordering the size of the troop increase and in adopting the counterinsurgency strategy, the policy choice—a "**surge strategy**"—seemed closely aligned to what President Bush had chosen in Iraq in early 2007. Indeed, the parallelism became complete a few months later when General McChrystal resigned (over some critical remarks of administration officials in *Rolling Stone* magazine) and was replaced with General David Petraeus, who had carried out the surge strategy in Iraq for the Bush administration. Still, some important differences did exist between the Obama surge strategy and Bush's. President Obama tied the strategy to a commitment to begin withdrawing American troops from Afghanistan in July 2011. Importantly, though, he conditioned the withdrawal of forces on "taking into account conditions on the grounds."[44] Furthermore, this military approach was linked to a civilian strategy to enhance the effectiveness of the Afghan government and a partnership with Pakistan building on "mutual interest, mutual respect, and mutual trust."

The new military strategy was implemented with some initial success,[45] but the civilian strategy within Afghanistan and the relationship with Pakistan did not improve appreciably over the next two years. Indeed, the stability and effectiveness of the Afghan government remained an area of concern, as have the continued ties between Pakistani military intelligence and elements supportive of the Taliban and al-Qaeda. In this sense, questions remained over how reliable a partner the Afghan government of Hamid Karzai was in seeking stability and a functioning government in that country.

American relations with Pakistan remained troubled as well—whether over the increased number of drone attacks in the tribal areas of Pakistan, the civilian casualties that occurred with such raids, or the Pakistani intelligence ties with terrorist groups attacking American forces. Furthermore, a U.S. covert operation in **May 2011** that found and killed **Osama bin Laden**, the head of al-Qaeda and the perpetrator of the 9/11 attacks, in Abbottabad, a Pakistani city with a large military installation and academy near the capital, complicated relations between the two countries. U.S. officials wondered how bin Laden could go undetected for so long in a Pakistani garrison town, and Pakistani authorities were angered by the invasion of their country's sovereignty without their knowledge.

At the NATO summit in November 2010, the alliance had outlined a plan to stay in Afghanistan through 2014, a plan the Obama administration endorsed, but these subsequent developments in 2011 and beyond began to raise questions about this timetable. The successful raid on bin Laden's compound, an action hailed as a major antiterrorism success, immediately raised doubts about the future direction of policy in Afghanistan and Pakistan. Would this action quicken the Obama administration's departure from Afghanistan because of increased domestic and international pressure? Would the Pakistani government move away from continued cooperation with the Americans because they were left out of this raid?

In the near term, the Obama administration did not seek to change the basic policy course in Afghanistan; instead, the administration's only decision was to remove the additional "surge" forces there by the end of 2012. Yet, two incidents involving the American military in the early months of 2012 in Afghanistan created another challenge to U.S. policy. One incident involved the accidental burning of the Koran on a military base, and the second involved the killing of sixteen Afghan civilians, including several children, apparently by a U.S. soldier. Both incidents produced protests against the American presence in that country. Indeed, the Afghan president, Hamid Karzai, pointedly called the American–Afghan relationship at a breaking point over the latter incident. American officials—including President Obama, Secretary of State Clinton, Secretary of Defense Panetta, and the American military commander in Afghanistan, General John Allen—continued to affirm the present policy course and to hold to the 2014 schedule. In all, then, the strategy in Afghanistan and in Iraq for the Obama and Bush administrations have proved to be similar, as one anonymous American official acknowledged in late 2010: "Iraq is a pretty decent blueprint for how to transition in Afghanistan."[46] To date, that approach in Afghanistan continues despite setbacks, a process reminiscent of the Iraq case.

North Korea In keeping with candidate Obama's commitment to engage with adversaries rather than to confront them, President Obama followed this course with North Korea and Iran during the first two years of his administration, but he achieved little tangible results with either regime with this strategy so far.

The **Six-Party Talks** (among North Korea, South Korea, China, Russia, Japan, and the United States) was the principal diplomatic vehicle used during the Bush administration to address the nuclear issue with North Korea. These talks went through seven different "rounds" with limited success, as North Korea conducted its first underground nuclear test in October 2006. By 2007, however, an apparent agreement was reached on the eventual dismantlement of the North Korean nuclear facilities in exchange for economic assistance from the United States and others, and for moving toward normalization of North Korean relations with several states, including the United States (see Chapter 5).[47] In 2008, however, the implementation of that agreement became stalled as each side accused the other of not fulfilling its commitments. By early 2009, North Korea announced that it was ending its military and political agreement with South Korea,[48] and the seeming progress on denuclearization of the Korean peninsula halted.

A new North Korean approach was dramatically evident within the first few months of the Obama administration taking office. On virtually the same day in April 2009 that President Obama was calling for a nuclear-free world in a major foreign policy address in Prague, North Korea conducted a missile test that appeared to be a violation of earlier sanctions. A little more than a month later, North Korea conducted a second nuclear test. That action precipitated the UN Security Council to enact new sanctions on North Korea. These sanctions tightened restrictions on imports and exports of military-related hardware to North Korea and called on UN members "to inspect and destroy all banned cargo to and from that country—on the high seas, at seaports and airports—if they have reasonable grounds to suspect a violation."[49] Such inspections, however, remained voluntary on the part of states (and hence weakened their overall impact), although these sanctions were described as "unprecedented" at the time.[50] Near the end of 2009, the Administration's Special Representative for North Korean Policy, Ambassador Stephen Bosworth, traveled to North Korea to try to get that country back to the Six-Party Talks, but his effort did not succeed.[51]

The administration's efforts at engaging North Korea continued to deteriorate in 2010, and as a result the administration's approach turned increasingly toward placing more sanctions on that regime. In March, a South Korean warship was sunk, killing some forty-six sailors. After an investigation, it was determined that North Korea was responsible for this action. In July 2010, the UN Security Council issued a "**Presidential Statement**" condemning this attack, although not specifically accusing North Korea of responsibility.[52] A short time after that, the Obama administration announced new unilateral economic sanctions against North Korea as yet another way to "tighten the financial vise" around the North Korean leadership, and Secretary of State Clinton announced that the United States would not engage in negotiations with North Korea until it agreed to abandon its nuclear weapons program.[53] In late November, the situation had deteriorated further with the revelation that North Korea had built a new facility for processing uranium,[54] and with the North Korean shelling of a South Korean island, which resulted in the deaths of both civilian and military personnel.[55] In all, the Obama administration's effort at engaging the North Koreans and using increased bilateral and multilateral sanctions to prod them to return to negotiations had not succeeded as measured by one important indicator: no new rounds of the Six-Party Talks were held through early 2012. Indeed, the North Koreans had indeed been seeking such a meeting, but the Obama administration, reminiscent of the Bush administration's approach, has declined until North Korea's behavior changes.[56]

With the death of the North Korean leader, **Kim Jong-il**, in late 2011, and the assumption of power by his son, **Kim Jong-un**, some movement occurred in talks between North Korea and the United States, and a **new agreement** was announced at the end of February 2012. Indeed, the United States and North Korea apparently had discussions from at least mid-July 2011 about an exchange of food assistance from the United States for a moratorium on nuclear development by North Korea. With the death of Kim Jong-il, the discussions were again stalled and the agreement was completed by the new North Korean leader. The agreement called for North Korea to suspend nuclear weapons test and the enrichment of uranium, allow international inspectors to monitor its nuclear activities at its main site, and impose a moratorium on long-range missile test in exchange for 240,000 metric tons of food in the form of nutritional supplements over a one-year period. The hope was that this agreement would lead to negotiations with North Korea over its nuclear program, although the process has been arduous with little progress. Still, the agreement was viewed at the time as a "welcome step" by a member of the policy community,[57] but the implementation of the agreement was in doubt.

Iran   A similar lack of substantial progress has occurred over efforts to engage Iran diplomatically over its nuclear ambitions as well. Over the past decade, Iran has been subject to numerous critical reports from the **International Atomic Energy Agency (IAEA)** due to its failure to adhere fully to the safeguards agreement required under the Nuclear Nonproliferation Treaty. The Bush administration was initially reluctant to engage in direct talks with Iran and instead sought to isolate and sanction the regime (including three rounds of sanctions passed by the UN Security Council). By 2006, the Bush administration did participate in the **P 5 + 1** (China, France, Germany, Russia, the United States, and the United Kingdom) talks with Iran and offered Iran a series of incentives for cooperating with the IAEA and for foregoing its enrichment and reprocessing activities.[58] No breakthrough occurred, however.

Nonetheless, the Obama administration sought to build on this diplomatic start. American officials met with Iran through the P 5 + 1 process in October 2009, albeit without notable success. Similarly, Iran did not accept an offer by the United States, France, and Russia to provide a plan for providing nuclear fuel assemblies for its research reactor with international safeguards. Instead, Iran continued its nuclear enrichment activities. As a result, the Obama administration imposed additional sanctions on Iran in an effort to isolate it internationally.

By the middle of 2010, the Obama administration succeeded in getting **several additional sanctions** placed on Iran. First, the UN Security Council passed a fourth set of sanctions against Iran in early June.[59] These sanctions largely focused on military, trade, and financial actions taken by the Islamic Revolutionary Guards in Iran, because this group plays a key role in the country's nuclear program. Second, the administration also obtained new unilateral American sanctions through congressional legislation later that month.[60] Those sanctions endeavored to restrict foreign banks that deal with Iranian banks or with the Islamic Revolutionary Guards from gaining access to the American financial system and sought to restrict gasoline suppliers from providing much-needed fuel to Iran. (Despite an abundance of oil, Iran has limited refining capacity.) Finally, the EU in late July 2010 imposed an additional series of economic sanctions on Iran.[61] Such sanctions were particularly important because the EU has such a large amount of trade with Iran.

By the end of 2011 and early in 2012, the United States and the EU imposed even more sanctions on Iran. In late December 2011, Obama signed into law a defense bill that imposed **sanctions on financial institutions** that dealt with Iran's central bank, because the bank is "the main conduit for Tehran's oil revenues." Those financial institutions that were sanctioned by this legislation "would be frozen out of U.S. financial markets."[62] Although these sanctions would be phrased in and the president could authorize waivers on national security grounds, the aim was to target Tehran's revenues from the sale of oil. In January 2012, the **EU** moved to "prohibit the import, purchase and transport of Iranian crude oil and petroleum products" and all such oil contracts would be phased out by July 1, 2012. At the present time, the EU purchases about 20 percent of Iran's exported oil. In addition, the EU will "freeze the assets of Iran's central bank" in the European community. Moreover, Catherine Ashton, the foreign policy head of the EU, indicated that the aim of these new sanctions was "to put pressure on Iran to come back to the negotiating table" over its nuclear activities.[63]

According to the administration's strategy, these kinds of sanctions were to alter Iran's "cost-benefit" calculation in pursuing nuclear weapons development. By seeking to engage Iran, promoting a norm of nuclear nonproliferation, and imposing economic sanctions, the administration sought to compel Iran to agree to negotiations over its nuclear weapons ambitions. In late summer of 2010, President Obama insisted that this approach was working,[64] although no immediate negotiations were forthcoming. Near the end of 2010, however, some movement appeared as a meeting between the P 5 + 1 and Iran was scheduled for early December. The prospects of a real breakthrough at such a meeting, though, looked dim. The more likely outcome was for continued stalemate among the two sides.[65] Moreover, the December meeting in Geneva produced exactly that result, although the two sides agreed to meet again in Istanbul, Turkey, in January of 2011.[66] The meeting, too, ended without real progress. After the late 2011 sanctions by the United States and early 2012 sanctions by the EU, Iran proposed a **renewal of talks** and Ashton, the head of foreign policy for the European Union and the diplomat representing the P 5 + 1 on issues with Iran, accepted this offer. This proposed resumption of talks comes in the context of the new sanctions, but also in the context of speculation over Israel's possible preemptive strike on Iran's nuclear installations.[67] If past is prologue, however, the prospect of these talks resolving the Iranian nuclear issue remains highly uncertain, and this issue will likely continue to vex the international community for the foreseeable future.

Confronting the Israeli-Palestinian Conflict

The administration's engagement efforts in seeking progress in resolving the Israeli-Palestinian conflict has produced a bit more movement than those with North Korea and Iran, but no significant breakthrough has occurred so far on this issue either. When the Obama administration assumed office, discussions between the two parties had broken off after an Israeli military offensive against Gaza in late 2008 in which at least 1,400 people were killed, some 5,000 injured, and numerous homes, schools, and other building were destroyed.[68] As a result, prospects for any direct talks between the two parties were slim, and the Obama administration decided to pursue a different tack in the short term.

Embracing the Bush administration's Middle East goal of creating a **two-state solution** to the conflict, the Obama administration's initial strategy was to propose the use of "**proximity talks**" with the Israelis and Palestinians as a vehicle to restart direct negotiations.[69] Under the proximity proposal, the United States, and particularly Senator George Mitchell, the U.S. Middle East Envoy, would meet with the Israelis and the Palestinians separately and seek to improve the "atmosphere for negotiations" between the parties as a way of moving back to direct negotiations between the parties.[70] Both parties eventually agreed to the American proposal, and proximity talks went on for several months, albeit not without difficulties, especially over Israel building settlements on land seized in the Six-Day War. Nonetheless, the administration's persistence paid off. On September 1, 2010, President Obama was able to announce that direct negotiations between the Israelis and Palestinians would be resumed.[71] The parties also informed the president that they thought they could complete their negotiations within one year. In these negotiations, the Israelis and Palestinians would have responsibility for them, but the Obama administration would continue to assist them in their discussions.

Even as these negotiations were being launched, skepticism remained over prospect for success. That skepticism increased as the Israeli government announced in early November 2010 that it would build 1,300 new housing units in East Jerusalem. This announcement brought condemnation from the United States, and the Palestinian negotiator charged that such action was "destroying the peace process."[72] A few days later, the Israeli government announced that it was freezing settlements for three months as part of a bargain for military aid and diplomatic support from the United States,[73] although that deal was later abandoned by the Obama administration.[74] Instead, the administration reverted to the use of "indirect talks" between the parties by Middle East Envoy Mitchell, an approach initially adopted by the administration at the beginning of its term.[75] In this sense, the Middle East peace efforts had come full circle during the Obama administration, without notable success.

In 2011 and 2012, other Middle East developments clouded the efforts to move the peace process forward by the United States and other regional participants. First, the Arab Spring, and the incipient democracy movement that it initiated, directed Arab and American attention away from the peace process. Although the expansion of democracy in the Middle East may eventually benefit the peace process, the short-term effect has been to turn attention to domestic political protests and governmental reforms in the Arab world. Second, the seeming continued effort by Iran to develop nuclear weapons created another source of tension, especially with reports that Israel viewed the time for stopping such a development as running out and that it contemplated a military strike on Iranian nuclear facilities. Indeed, at a White House meeting in March 2012, President Obama reportedly urged Israeli Prime Minister **Benjamin Netanyahu** "to give diplomacy and economic sanctions a chance to work before resorting to military action."[76] In all, the Middle East peace process is likely to remain stalled for some time.

Restarting Relations with Russia

One area where the Obama administration achieved foreign policy success was in improving relations with Russia. From the beginning of its term, the administration focused on this relationship, and it has succeeded in advancing both bilateral and multilateral cooperation with Russia. The center of this reset effort was the signing of the **New START Treaty** in April 2010, but several other cooperative efforts also marked the relationship during the first two years of the Obama administration.[77] In this sense, relations with Russia mark a significant change in policy substance and in policy success as compared to the Bush years.

By the end of the Bush administration, American relations with Russia had deteriorated in part over the American (and NATO-endorsed) decision on deploying a missile defense system in Poland and the Czech Republic and over the Russian intervention into South Ossetia region of Georgia in the summer of 2008.[78] The Russians saw the missile defense system aimed at them rather than at Iran as the Bush administration argued, and the Americans saw the Russian actions in Georgia as an effort to undermine the independence of the former Soviet republic. In this wary political environment between these two powers, the Obama administration nevertheless set out to reset relations with Russia.

The first meeting between President Obama and President **Dmitry Medvedev** occurred at the G-20 meeting in London in April 2009 and produced immediate results. Medvedev characterized Obama as "totally different" from Bush and noted the positive nature of their exchanges. Obama recognized "real differences" with Russia on some important issues, but he acknowledged that there was "a broad set of common interests that we can pursue."[79] Significantly, the leaders jointly issued a statement that they would begin negotiations on a new agreement "on reducing and limiting strategic offensive arms to replace the START Treaty,"[80] and Obama agreed to visit Moscow the following July.

At that July summit, Obama and Medvedev took further steps to improve the relationship. The two leaders announced the creation of a **Bilateral Presidential Commission between Russia and the United States**. This commission would consist of thirteen different working groups initially (although others could be created), and its goal would be to "strive to deepen our cooperation in concrete ways and to take further steps to demonstrate joint leadership in addressing new challenges ... [and] address disagreements openly and honestly in a spirit of mutual respect and acknowledgement of each other's perspective." The initial working groups ranged widely—from ones focused on nuclear energy and nuclear security, arms control and international security, foreign policy and fighting terrorism to others focused on energy and the environment, health, space cooperation, and educational and cultural exchanges. Importantly, Obama and Medvedev also announced that Russia and the United States would work on cooperative efforts to address the issue of defense against the proliferation of ballistic missiles.[81]

In mid-September 2009, the Obama administration announced an important change in the Bush administration's European **missile defense** plan. Under the revised Obama missile plan, the United States would not station radars in the Czech Republic and place ten ballistic missile interceptors in Poland. Instead the administration decided on a ten-year phased deployment of missile defense, beginning with a sea-based deployment and a transportable radar surveillance system. The target of this new missile defense plan would be short- and medium-range missiles, particularly those under development by Iran, and less on long-range missiles from that country.[82] Some say this change was a concession to Russia because such a system could be viewed as less threatening to Russia than the Bush plan, although the Russian response was somewhat mixed to this change.[83]

The cooperative relationship continued over the next year, and by June 2010, on the occasion of President Medvedev's visit to the White House, the Obama administration issued a "reset" fact sheet lauding the extent of cooperation between the two nations.[84] And, indeed, there were numerous bilateral and multilateral actions that the United States and Russia had addressed. On bilateral issues, the United States and Russia worked on moving Russia toward accession in the World Trade Organization, collaborated on addressing the global financial crisis, agreed to a new energy initiative, pursued military cooperation (including allowing ground and air transit of forces and supplies bound for Afghanistan through Russian territory), and fostered state-to-state cooperation to promote more open governance, democracy, and human rights. On multilateral issues, the United States and Russia cooperated on passing a new set of sanctions on Iran through the UN Security Council (and, in accord with that resolution, Russia agreed not to ship S-300 missiles to Iran), approving a new sanctioning resolution through the United Nations over North Korea's second nuclear test, pursuing stability and the restoration of democracy in Kyrgyzstan after the violence there in summer 2010, and developing some "confidence building" measures over dealing with Abkhazia and South Ossetia in Georgia.

All of these efforts (including numerous nongovernmental activities) reflect the change in the Russian–American relationship, but none appeared as crucial in reestablishing this relationship as the New START Treaty. This treaty (with its name a play on words to convey the changing relationship) would require Russia and the United States to reduce their deployed nuclear delivery vehicles (intercontinental ballistic missiles, submarine-launched missiles, and long-range bombers) by about 50 percent from the previous limit in the 1991 START Treaty (see Chapter 5) to 800 in total, with a maximum of 700 such vehicles deployed.[85] It would also require each side to reduce the number of nuclear warheads to 1,550. Such a total would represent a reduction of about 30 percent from the maximum level allowed under the Strategic Arms Offensive Treaty (SORT) of 2002.[86] The Obama administration viewed this treaty as important not only in improving the bilateral relationship but also in advancing its larger nuclear nonproliferation goal. By the end of 2010, the U.S. Senate had recommended ratification of this treaty, and this centerpiece of Obama's U.S–Russian and nonproliferation agenda had become a notable foreign policy success for the administration. Obama formally signed the treaty on February 2, 2011, and it went into effect a few days later.

Despite this apparent warming in relations with Russia, political differences on regional and global issues remain between the two countries. Indeed, these differences may be exacerbated in the years ahead. Although Russia, by abstaining, cooperated with the United States over the gaining passage of a 2011 UN Resolution to take actions against Libya at the beginning of the Arab Spring, it (along with China) vetoed a similar UN resolution over the uprisings in Syria in 2012. Further, Russia continued to urge a go-slow policy over Iranian and North Korean nuclear issues (although the administration did succeed in gaining new UN resolutions against both states). Further, and importantly, with the return to the Russian presidency of Vladimir Putin in the March 2012 elections, the likely prospect is that Putin will move toward a more assertive policy direction against the United States and the West in general. Although the gains of recent years will likely not be lost in the relationship, continued improvement will be more challenging.

Stabilizing Ties with China and Redirecting Attention to the Asia-Pacific

Two other issues of importance for the Obama administration were to stabilize the relationship between the United States and China and to redirect American policy toward a greater focus on Asia. Actions on the former have occupied the administration throughout its time in office; activity on the latter has been a more recent phenomenon.

The Obama administration's policy toward China was to "develop a positive, cooperative, and comprehensive relationship" with that country, in the words of Secretary of State Clinton, and support the peaceful rise of China as a major global power.[87] Since the establishment of diplomatic relations in 1979 between the United States and China, the two countries have established a number of cooperative working groups to facilitate the relationship. In this sense, the Obama administration has been no different. Much like its dialogue with Russia, the Obama administration created the **U.S.-China Strategic and Economic Dialogue** as an important mechanism to advance this cooperative relationship. Moreover, this dialogue covers a broad range of bilateral issues, such as human rights, military relations, and the issue of Taiwan; international security concerns, such as nuclear nonproliferation and UN peacekeeping issues; and global issues, such as climate change and energy concerns. In addition, the dialogue provides a venue for discussing regional security issues over the Sudan, Afghanistan, and North Korea. In addition to this ongoing dialogue, exchanges of visits between key officials of both governments (including visits between President Obama and his Chinese counterpart) have been frequent and largely productive.

Chinese-American economic relations, of course, have been especially crucial for the past three decades, and the magnitude of these ties has continued to grow during the Obama administration. China is now America's largest overseas trading partner, and the United States is China's second-largest trading partner after the EU. Moreover, the total volume of two-way trade approaches $500 billion per year, and American investment totaled some $60 billion in 2010.

Despite these efforts at a cooperative relationship, frictions have remained between the two countries in economic, social, and political areas. The Obama administration's attempts to address these issues have had only limited success. In trade relations between the two countries, the United States has had continuing concerns about the undervalued Chinese currency in the global marketplace, the restrictions placed on American access to the Chinese market, and the protection of intellectual property rights in that country. Furthermore, the ballooning trade deficit with China, reaching almost $300 billion in 2011, and the seeming dependence on China to purchase U.S. Treasury notes to fund America's budget deficit have also brought criticism of this relationship.

Human rights conditions have also been a perennial issue in China—whether it has been over the use of forced abortion for population control, the treatment of dissidents in the country (including a Nobel Prize winner), or the treatment of the Tibetan people. The Obama administration routinely raises these human rights issues and sometimes undertakes symbolic actions to demonstrate the administration's concern. For example, President Obama has twice received the Dalai Lama at the White House, much to the protest of the Chinese government, as a way to demonstrate the American position on Tibet. In general, though, except for the periodic release of some political prisoners at propitious times by the Beijing government, human rights conditions have not improved.

Finally, important strategic issues continued to trouble the relationship as well. These include the **status of Taiwan**, the territorial conflicts in the South China Sea, the modernization by the Chinese navy and its implications for American presence in Asia, and the degree of cooperation on the nuclear initiatives by North Korea and Iran. Although the United States and China agree on a one-China policy (dating back to the Shanghai Communiqué in 1972), the Obama administration, like previous administrations, has continued to supply military aid to Taiwan in accordance with the **Taiwan Relations Act of 1979**. Moreover, the Obama administration in 2010 and 2011 provided military equipment to Taiwan, much to the objection of the

Chinese government. Similarly, the United States has been concerned for some time about the Chinese territorial claims in the South China Sea, regarding the **Spratly** and **Paracel Islands**, and has routinely called for a peaceful settlement, including siding with China's opponents in these disputes. Further, the Chinese modernization of its navy, including the launch of its first aircraft carrier, has raised questions about U.S. access in the Pacific and its ability to offer protection to its key allies in the region, South Korea and Japan, as well as its commitment to Taiwan. Finally, as noted before, Chinese cooperation on halting the nuclear ambitions of North Korea and Iran has been difficult to obtain and remains a point of contention in the relationship.

Beyond China, the Obama administration has sought to make a major "**pivot**" in U.S. foreign policy toward Asia generally and away from Europe. This pivot was seemingly a goal at the outset of the administration, but the redirection was more fully actualized near the end of its third year in office through a major statement by Secretary of State Clinton. (The foreign policy issues discussed in the chapter undoubtedly limited this redirection early in the Obama tenure.) In late 2011, Secretary Clinton outlined the reasons for this refocus by noting that the Asia-Pacific region has "become a key driver of global politics," "boasts almost half the world's population," "includes many of the key engines of the global economy," and incorporates "several of our key allies and important emerging powers like China, India, and Indonesia."[88] To redirect policy toward this region, Secretary Clinton outlined an ambitious U.S. agenda—ranging from strengthening current bilateral treaty ties, developing more extensive multilateral ties in Asia, and expanding ties with India and Indonesia to promoting democracy and human rights and opening the Asian market to healthy competition that is "open, free, transparent, and fair."[89] In all, this represents a full agenda for the next decade and, if implemented, a major redirection—and change—in the focus of American foreign policy.

Initiating Global Common Issues

In addition to Chinese-American and Asia-Pacific relations, issues of the "global commons" have also been an important area where the Obama administration has moved beyond the agenda of the previous administration with its own initiatives. Nuclear nonproliferation, global financial reform, and climate change represent especially new departures by the Obama administration, but policy success with these initiatives remain elusive so far.

Nonproliferation Although the New START Treaty represents one aspect of the Obama administration's nonproliferation activities, the administration has a much broader agenda in this area. The administration is pursuing at least three other initiatives to promote nuclear nonproliferation. The first involves the Obama administration's **new directives on when nuclear weapons would be used by the United States.** Specifically, the administration committed the United States to refrain from using nuclear weapons against those nonnuclear states that are parties to the Nuclear Non-Proliferation Treaty (NPT) and those states that are fully in compliance with NPT requirements. If these nonnuclear states were to utilize biological and chemical weapons against the United States, the American response would generally be with conventional weapons (although a slight opening remains for a nuclear response in exceptional cases). Toward nuclear weapons states and those states not in compliance with the NPT, the potential use of nuclear weapons would remain, but such use would occur "only in extreme circumstances to defend the vital interests of the United States, our allies and partners."[90] In essence, then, the administration was seeking to move toward a more stable nuclear use policy and encourage other states in this direction as well.

The second initiative was President Obama's decision to convene the Washington Nuclear Security Summit in April 2010 with forty-seven countries in attendance. The goal of this summit was to address how best "to prevent terrorist, criminals, or other unauthorized actors from acquiring nuclear materials" that may be available today. The summit ended with a communiqué, a commitment to meet this goal within four years, a work plan for the future, and an agreement to meet again in 2012.[91] All of these initial commitments, however, were voluntary, and some potential or existing nuclear states (such as Iran and North Korea) and potential proliferators were not invited.[92] The second Nuclear Security Summit was held in Seoul, South Korea, in late March 2012 with a slightly larger group in attendance than in 2010; the agenda was broadened to discuss nuclear safety as well as nuclear terrorism.[93] Moreover, Obama journeyed to Seoul to participate in this summit meeting once again to show his commitment to this issue. In all, then, this initiative is an important first step on nuclear nonproliferation, but considerable work remains to be done.

The third initiative focused on a reaffirmation of the world's commitment to nonproliferation at the **2010 Nuclear Non-Proliferation Review Conference**. After some four weeks of debate and discussion among the conferees in May 2010, the review meeting did announce two important agreements: the 189 signatories to the NPT reaffirmed their commitment to it, and the parties agreed to a 2012 deadline for a Middle East conference to address unconventional weapons in that part of the world.[94] Although the Middle East conference did not take place, the reaffirmation of the NPT provides important support for the Obama administration's efforts to advance its nuclear nonproliferation agenda.

Financial Reform   Global financial reform was a second commons initiative the Obama administration advanced. The difficult economic environment that President Obama inherited as he assumed the presidency largely drove this initiative. The goal of this reform is to create a sounder financial system by standardizing banking regulations and regulating the various investment instruments used worldwide. The principal forum that the Obama administration has been using to make progress on this issue has been the G-20 summits. The U.S. effort actually began with the G-20 Washington Summit in late 2008 at the end of the Bush administration, but it has been continued at the subsequent G-20 summits in London and Pittsburgh in 2009 and in Toronto and Seoul in 2010. A global framework has now been outlined to regulate global banking capital and reserve requirements, as noted at the G-20 Summit in Seoul, but the new framework will only start to be implemented in 2013. Importantly, though, the framework will still need to be incorporated into national law by the states involved. Further, there remain other areas of work as well, such as developing a common framework on dealing with financial institutions that are "too big to fail" and protecting taxpayers from bearing these costs.[95] Finally, differences remain over the regulation of some financial instruments, such as hedge funds, with the European states seeking much greater control of such instruments than the United States.[96] With the Eurocrisis among the European Union members, there was yet another imperative for global financial reform.

Climate Change American policy on climate change under the Obama administration represents another significant change from the Bush administration. Indeed, the administration came to office with a substantial commitment to lead international environmental change and took a number of initial steps at home to promote that agenda. Early on, Secretary of State Clinton appointed a special envoy for climate change as a way to advance this agenda within the government.[97] The administration also advanced a "green jobs" agenda at home, included some $80 billion in the 2009 stimulus package to address energy issues, and announced new emission standards for new vehicles built for 2017 through 2025.[98] Further, the administration was successful in getting the House of Representatives (although not the Senate) to pass a "cap-and-trade" bill that would have imposed mandatory limits on the emission of greenhouse gases and encouraged the use of cleaner energy sources for the future.[99]

With these domestic initiatives in place, the administration seemed well positioned to argue for significant global reform at the **United Nations Conference on Climate Change in Copenhagen, Denmark**, in December 2009. Yet, this was not to be. President Obama personally attended the meeting of 192 countries, and he worked tirelessly to broker the divide between developed and developing countries on an international accord or even a commitment to a legally binding agreement. What was ultimately achieved was a three-page agreement among China, India, Brazil, and South Africa in which a commitment was made to help developing countries adapt to climate change ($30 billion a year through 2012, and a total of $100 billion by 2020). A commitment was also made to limit the increase in the global temperature below two degrees Celsius. But these commitments were political statements only, and they did not include any means of enforcement. Although Obama contended that the agreement was a "breakthrough," he also acknowledged that "this progress alone is not enough."[100]

As the Obama administration moved to the next scheduled international conference on climate change in **Cancun, Mexico**, in late November to mid-December 2010, the prospects for success seemed dim. The outcome of that meeting was described as "modest," although sufficient to continue the international effort.[101] Still, environmental legislation was highly unlikely with the new political composition of the U.S. House and Senate, and it appears unlikely that the United States can meet its financial obligations to aid the developing countries in light of the large budget deficits and economic problems at home. Nonetheless, prior to the Cancun meeting the administration's special envoy for climate change pledged to press forward with its agenda,[102] and afterward this envoy described Cancun as "a significant step forward that builds on the progress made in Copenhagen."[103]

Yet another global climate change conference took place in **Durban, South Africa**, in late 2011, and UN Secretary General Ban Ki-moon put the expectations of that conference in perspective: "The ultimate goal for a comprehensive and binding climate change agreement may be beyond our reach for now."[104] Indeed, the results of the meetings continued to be modest. An agreement was reached on a "green fund" to help poor nations deal with climate issues and to reduce deforestation. In addition, and importantly, China and India agreed "in principle" to pursue an international agreement that would apply to all parties.[105] The completion of such a climate change agreement and its implementation still remains years away. In all, the Obama administration's success with climate change remains extremely modest.

CRITICISMS OF THE OBAMA APPROACH AND ITS APPLICATION

The Obama administration's approach to changing the direction of U.S. foreign policy has not been without criticism from political opponents and political supporters. Some have argued that the administration's foreign policy reflects little change in actual behavior, even if the rhetoric is distinct from the Bush administration. Others have pointed to a series of policies that they believe are seriously flawed and ultimately dangerous for America's standing in the world. Still others view the administration's policy approach as less closely tied to a consistent liberal internationalism as initially espoused and instead one tied to political pragmatism or even political realism.

One view, for example, contends that the Obama administration's **policies do not represent a real change** from the Bush administration in a number of key areas. The adoption of the "surge strategy" in Afghanistan, for example, reflects a counterinsurgency approach similar to the one that the Bush administration adopted in Iraq. The escalation of the number of unmanned drone attacks in Afghanistan and Pakistan is another example of the continuation of the anti-terrorism policy of the past—and indeed an escalation of that policy. One analysis, for instance, notes that the Obama administration carried out a total of 239 drone attacks in its first three years, compared to only 44 such strikes during a similar time period for the Bush administration.[106] The pursuit and killing of Osama bin Laden and the drone strike on Anwar al-Awlaki also represent a continuation of this policy. Furthermore, despite candidate Obama's opposition to the USA PATRIOT Act, he renewed it during his administration. Similarly, as noted earlier, the plan to close the prison at Guantanamo Bay has largely been abandoned. In all, these actions largely represent a maintenance of the past policy rather than significant change.

Supporters of the administration, however, point to a more nuanced strategy adopted by the administration on these (mainly) antiterrorism issues. In that sense, the approach is a movement away from the Bush administration. The "**Obama doctrine**," as one analyst labeled it, involves reliance on multilateralism, drone strikes, and limited U.S. military actions best exemplified by American actions in Libya, Pakistan, and Yemen. In addition, the doctrine focuses more on the use of such force, but with greater reliance on the CIA and Special Operations Forces than previously.[107] At the same time, President Obama's deputy national security adviser has indicated that the administration would "use force unilaterally if necessary against direct threats to the United States," and "use force in a very precise way."[108] Overall, then, such an approach by the administration may be viewed as less bellicose and less focused on military actions than the Bush administration. Whether this greater reliance on covert activity will succeed is debatable, especially as the U.S. drone strikes have generated considerable backlash in several affected countries. Furthermore, these (and other actions) have seemingly expanded presidential authority in the conduct of foreign policy.[109]

Another critic is less focused on the approach. Instead, he is **more troubled by the direction of the policies** in various areas and their implications for the U.S. position in the world. Senator Lindsey Graham (R-South Carolina) views the administration's policies as alienating allies and abandoning opportunities "to guide entire regions into a closer alignment with American interests."[110] In particular, Senator Graham is critical of the administration's failure to stop the development of nuclear weapons by Iran. The administration's sanctioning regime had not been "painful and biting," to have a lasting effect. Furthermore, the administration's failure to support the "**Persian Spring**," the period of democratic protest in Iran in the summer of 2009, has also had an effect on U.S. standing in the world. The administration's decision to withdraw American forces from Iraq by the end of 2011 was also ill advised because the stability of the country and the prevention of ethnic and religious violence by the Iraqi forces remain in doubt. In addition, the administration has been insufficiently supportive of Israel "by unduly focusing on Israeli settlement policies and advocating that Israel retreat to its indefensible 1967 borders" and it has been too willing to withdraw the surge forces from Afghanistan, jeopardizing the gains that have been achieved in that country. Finally, the "leading from behind" policy in Libya, the proposal to hold trials of some "enemy combatants" from the Guantanamo Bay prison in civilian courts, and the changes in interrogation procedures for "enemy combatants" have weakened U.S. foreign policy and its global standing.

Yet another kind of criticism raises a question more generally about the overall foreign policy approach of the Obama administration and whether it represents a new approach. By this assessment, President Obama's foreign policy approach consistently conveys neither a realist nor an idealist (liberal international) approach; instead, his approach is one in which he is a **foreign policy "consequentialist."**[111] That is, the president decides "his response to every threat on its own merits." In this sense, the approach cannot be characterized as fitting into one category, and it is perhaps simply foreign policy pragmatism or even an ad hoc approach.

By this evaluation, the lack of a clear foreign policy approach has evolved for Obama from his time in public service. Although President Obama came to office with a commitment to foreign policy views of the Left as espoused by liberal internationalism, he also wanted to pursue "a strategy no longer driven by ideology and politics, but one based on a realistic assessment of the sobering facts on the ground and our interests in the region." In this sense, foreign policy realists came to dominate the Obama administration from the time of the inauguration onward as reflected in some of the antiterrorism actions and by the administration's failure to promote human rights and democracy initially.

The policy choices during the Arab Spring of 2011, however, brought the realism/idealism into sharp relief within the administration, and Obama ultimately moved to align with the idealism in the case of Egypt and Libya, especially with an embrace of the "responsibility to protect" doctrine. Nonetheless, these decisions apparently were more driven by the cases and less by a philosophical position. Hence, the foreign policy approach of the Obama administration remains unclear and remains difficult to characterize.

CONCLUDING COMMENTS

The Obama administration came to office promising foreign policy change. The degree of change so far has been limited, and the administration's policies have been subject to criticisms lately. In outlining a liberal internationalist foreign policy approach, the Obama administration has surely achieved change from the approach followed by the Bush administration. In seeking to implement that approach—whether evaluated through the changes in the substance of American policy or through the achievements that it has had—the Obama administration has had much **less success**. In this sense, continuity in several foreign policy arenas remains more prevalent than change during the Obama administration.

Indeed, several areas reflect **considerable continuity**. For instance, the Obama administration made an initial attempt to infuse domestic values into foreign policy with its three executive orders on the treatment of terrorist suspects, but the most visible symbol of the Bush policy—Guantanamo Bay—remains open and military commissions continue as well. The administration's actions during the Arab Spring, and especially with regard to Libya, reflect more fully this liberal internationalist agenda. Obama's personal popularity initially softened America's image abroad as compared to the Bush years, but that new "soft power" has not been translated very easily into support for U.S. foreign policy. Further, on major security issues, with the exception of ending the Iraq War, the Obama administration's policy reflects more continuity than change—whether addressing the Afghanistan War, the Middle East, or the nuclear threats from North Korea and Iran. Indeed, the strategy of engagement with North Korea and Iran has not yielded success; instead, relations with both countries appear to have eroded somewhat.

Still, the Obama administration has initiated **some substantive foreign policy changes**, and in at least one area it has achieved notable success. The Obama administration has begun to address a number of global commons issues with new policy approaches—whether global financial reform, climate change, or nuclear nonproliferation. The degree of success in each of these areas remains unclear, but these policies do represent new departures from the Bush years. Importantly, Obama's strategy of engagement with Russia has had a substantial effect in improving that relationship, and a New START Treaty is a crucial consequence of the "reset" in relations with that country. The administration also points to the tracking down and killing of Osama bin Laden in mid-2011.

In all, though, the administration's **foreign policy results are modest**. In this sense, the Obama administration's foreign policy is still largely a "work in progress," as one analysis described it,[112] or one with lots of "big ideas" but short on implementation, as another summarized it.[113] In this sense, foreign policy changes have been in the air since the Obama administration took office, but the requirements of global politics have seemingly moved the administration toward pragmatism and realism, much as other recent administrations have done.

Notes

1. On Wilsonianism and for this quotation, see G. John Ikenberry, "Introduction: "Woodrow Wilson, the Bush Administration, and the Future of Liberal Internationalism," in G. John Ikenberry, Thomas J. Knock, Anne-Marie Slaughter, and Tony Smith, eds., *The Crisis of American Foreign Policy: Wilsonianism in the Twenty-first Century* (Princeton: Princeton University Press, 2008), pp. 1–24

2. Barack Obama, "Renewing American Leadership," *Foreign Affairs* 86 (July/August 2007): 4.

3. Ibid., p. 14.

4. Cf. candidate George W. Bush's statement about imposing democracy during the 2000 presidential campaign in which he said the following: "We value the elegant structures of our own democracy—but realize that, in other societies, the architecture will vary. We propose our principles, but we must not impose our culture."

5. Obama, "Renewing American Leadership," p. 14.

6. Ibid., p. 8.

7. Ibid., p. 9.

8. See "Barack Obama's Inaugural Address," *New York Times*, January 20, 2009, http://www.nytimes.com/2009/01/20/us/politics/20text-obama.html, January 21, 2009.

9. Stanley A. Renshon, *National Security in the Obama Administration: Reassessing the Bush Doctrine* (New York and London: Routledge, 2010), pp. 7–8.

10. Barack Obama, "Remarks by President Barack Obama," at Hradcany Square, Prague, Czech Republic, April 5, 2009. The White House, Office of the Press Secretary.

11. Barack Obama, "Remarks by the President on a New Beginning," Cairo University, Cairo, Egypt. June 4, 2009. The White House, Office of the Press Secretary.

12. Barack Obama, "Remarks by the President at the New Economic School Graduation," Gostinny Dvor, Moscow, Russia, July 7, 2009. The White House, Office of the Press Secretary.

13. Barack Obama, "Remarks by the President to the Ghanaian Parliament," Accra International Center, Accra, Ghana, July 11, 2009. The White House, Office of the Press Secretary.

14. Hillary Clinton, "Secretary Clinton's Speech at the Council on Foreign Relations," July 15, 2009, http://www.realclearpolitics.com/articles/2009/07/15/clinton_speech_transcript_council_foreign_relations_97491.html, July 4, 2010.

15. The White House, *National Security Strategy*, May 27, 2010, http://www.whitehouse.gov/sites/default/files/rss_viewer/national_security_strategy.pdf, November 12, 2010. The following discussion is drawn from this document as well as the quoted passages.

16. The data in the following discussion are taken from Pew Global Attitudes Project, "Confidence in Obama Lifts U.S. Image around the World," July 23, 2009, http://pewglobal.org/files/pdf/264.pdf, November 12, 2010, and Pew Global Attitudes Project, "Obama More Popular Abroad than At Home, Global Image of U.S. Continues to Benefit," June 17, 2010, http://pewglobal.org/2010/06/17/obama-more-popular-abroad-than-at-home/, November 12, 2010.

17. See the comparison of Pew data for 2011 and 2010 on this favorability question with the charts at http://www.pewglobal.org/database/?indicator=1&survey=12&response=Favorable&mode=chart, March 19, 2012.

18. See the comparative charts from the Pew Global Attitudes Project at http://www.pewglobal.org/database/?indicator=6&survey=13&response=Confidence&mode=chart, access March 19, 2012.

19. Two exceptions to these results for Muslim countries are Indonesia and Lebanon (although Lebanon also has a substantial Christian population). The respondents in these two countries express favorability and confidence levels comparable to the Western European countries according to these surveys.

20. Pew Global Attitudes Project, "Arab Spring Fails to Improve U.S. Image," May 17, 2011, http://www.pewglobal.org/2011/05/17/arab-spring-fails-to-improve-us-image/, March 19, 2012.

21. Compare the results on these two questions with the data for 2010 and 2011 from the Pew Global Attitudes Project, http://www.pewglobal.org/database/?indicator=9&survey=13&response=Keep troops in Afghanistan&mode=chart and http://www.pewglobal.org/database/?indicator=8&mode=chart, March 19, 2012.

22. Pew Global Attitudes Project, "Obama More Popular Abroad than At Home, Global Image of U.S. Continues to Benefit," pp. 4–5.

23. Sewell Chan, Sheryl Gay Stolberg, and David E. Sanger, "Obama's Trade Strategy Runs into Stiff Resistance," *New York Times*, November 11, 2010, http://www.nytimes.com/2010/11/12/business/global/12group.html?src=me&pagewanted=print, November 15, 2010.

24. Sewell Chan, "South Korea and U.S. Reach Deal on Trade." *New York Times*, December 3, 2010, http://www.nytimes.com/2010/12/04/business/global/04trade.html, December 6, 2010.

25. Barack Obama, "Remarks by the President on National Security," Address at the National Archives, Washington, D.C., May 21, 2009. The White House, Office of the Press Secretary.

26. Executive Orders 13491, 13492, and 13493. January 22, 2009, Federal Register 74, no. 16 (January 27): 4893–4902, http://www.archives.gov/federal-register/executive-orders/2009-obama.html, October 29, 2010.

27. Scott Shane, "Obama Orders Secret Prisons and Detention Camps Closed," *New York Times*, January 23, 2009, http://www.nytimes.com/2009/01/23/us/politics/23GITMOCND.html, October 29, 2010.

28. "CIA Claims to Close Secret Prisons But Promises to Imprison People Somewhere Else and Oppose Prosecuting Past Crimes," April 10, 2009, http://warisacrime.org/node/41585, November 2, 2010.

29. David Welna, "Democrats Block Funding to Close Guantanamo," May 20, 2009, http://www.npr.org/templates/story/story.php?storyId=104334339, November 2, 2010.

30. Charles Savage, "Closing Guantanamo Fades as a Priority," *New York Times*, June 25, 2010, http://www.nytimes.com/2010/06/26/us/politics/26gitmo.html, November 1, 2010.

31. Obama, "Remarks by the President on National Security."

32. Savage, "Closing Guantanamo Fades as a Priority."

33. Jake Tapper and Sunlen Miller, "President Obama Orders Resumption of Military Commission Trials for Accused Detainees at Gitmo," ABC News, March 7, 2011, http://blogs.abcnews.com/politicalpunch/2011/03/president-obama-orders-resumption-of-military-commission-trials-for-accused-detainees-at-gitmo.html, May 14, 2011.

34. Ibid.

35. NPR, "Obama's Speech on Libya: 'A Responsibility to Act.'" March 28, 2011, http://www.npr.org/2011/03/28/134935452/obamas-speech-on-libya-a-responsibility-to-act, May 14, 2011.

36. See UN Security Council Resolutions 1970 and 1973 at United Nations Security Council, "Resolution 1970 (2011)," February 26, 2011, http://daccess-dds-ny.un.org/doc/UNDOC/GEN/N11/245/58/PDF/N1124558.pdf?OpenElement, July 26, 2012; and http://daccess-ddsny.un.org/doc/UNDOC/GEN/N11/245/58/PDF/N1124558.pdf?OpenElement, ; United Nations Security Council, Department of Public Information, "Security Council Approves 'No-Fly Zone' Over Libya, Authorizing 'All Necessary Measures' to Protect Civilians, by Vote of 10 in Favour with 5 Abstentions," March 17, 2011, http://www.un.org/News/Press/docs/2011/sc10200.doc.htm, July 26, 2012.

37. International Coalition for the Responsibility to Protect, http://www.responsibilityto-protect.org/index.php/about-rtop#world_summit, May 14, 2011.

38. NPR, "Obama's Speech on Libya: 'A Responsibility to Act.'"

39. Tim Arango and Michael S. Schmidt, "Last Convoy of American Troops Leaves Iraq, *New York Times*, December 18, 2011, http://www.nytimes.com/2011/12/19/world/middleeast/last-convoy-of-american-troops-leaves-iraq.html?_r=1&pagewanted=print, March 21, 2012.

40. "AP: U.S. Drops Plan to Keep Troops in Iraq," *USA Today*, October 17, 2011, http://www.usatoday.com/news/military/story/2011-10-15/Iraq-withdrawal-war-troops/50786604/1, March 21, 2012.

41. Steven Lee Meyers, Thom Shanker, and Jack Healy, "Iraqi Politics Raises Questions About U.S. Military Presence," *New York Times*, December 19, 2010, p. 1.

42. "Obama to Couric: 'We took our eye off the ball,'" *Politico,* January 14, 2009, http://www.politico.com/news/stories/0109/17460.html, November 23, 2010.

43. See Bob Woodward, *Obama's Wars* (New York: Simon & Schuster, 2010).

44. Barack Obama, "Remarks by the President in Address to the Nation on the Way Forward in Afghanistan and Pakistan," West Point, New York, December 1, 2009. The White House, Office of the Press Secretary.

45. Jim Michaels, "Obama Says Afghan Withdrawal on Track," *USA Today*, December 17, 2010, 9A.

46. Peter Baker and Rod Nordland, "U.S. Plan Envisions Path to Ending Afghan Combat," *New York Times*, November 14, 2010, http://www.nytimes.com/2010/11/15/world/asia/15prexy.html?_r=1&nl=todaysheadlines&emc=a2&pagewanted=print, November 14, 2010.

47. Wikipedia, "Six Party Talks," http://en.wikipedia.org/wiki/Six-party_talks, November 15, 2010.

48. BBC News, "North Korea Conducts Nuclear Test," May 25, 2009, http://news.bbc.co.uk/2/hi/8066615.stm, November 15, 2010.

49. United Nations Security Council, Department of Public Information, United Nations Resolution 1874, "Security Council, Acting Unanimously, Condemns in Strongest Terms Democratic People's Republic of Korea, Nuclear Test, Toughens Sanctions," June 12, 2009, http://www.un.org/News/Press/docs/2009/sc9679.doc.htm, November 16, 2010.

50. Ewen MacAskill, "UN Approves 'Unprecedented' Sanctions against North Korea over Nuclear Test," June 12, 2009, http://www.guardian.co.uk/world/2009/jun/12/un-north-korea-nuclear-sanctions, November 15, 2010.

51. United States Department of State, Bureau of East Asian and Pacific Affairs, "Background Note: North Korea," September 29, 2010, http://www.state.gov/r/pa/ei/bgn/2792.htm, November 16, 2010.

52. United Nations Security Council, Department of Public Information, "Security Council Condemns Attack on Republic of Korea Naval Ship 'Cheonan,' Stresses Need to Prevent Further Attacks, Other Hostilities in Region," July 9, 2010, http://www.un.org/News/Press/docs/2010/sc9975.doc.htm, November 16, 2010.

53. Mark Landler and Elisabeth Bumiller, "U.S. to Add to Sanctions on N. Korea," *New York Times*, July 21, 2010, http://www.nytimes.com/2010/07/22/world/asia/22military.html, November 15, 2006.

54. David E. Sanger, "North Koreans Unveil New Plant for Nuclear Use," *New York Times*, November 21, 2010, http://www.nytimes.com/2010/11/21/world/asia/21intel.html?_r=1&nl=todaysheadlines&emc=a2, November 21, 2010.

55. Mark McDonald, "'Crisis Status' in South Korea After North Shells Island," *New York Times*, November 23, 2010, http://www.nytimes.com/2010/11/24/world/asia/24korea.html, December 6, 2010.

56. Mark Landler, "Obama Urges China to Check North Koreans," *New York Times*, December 6, 2010, http://www.nytimes.com/2010/12/07/world/asia/07diplo.html?nl=todaysheadlines&emc=a2, December 7, 2010.

57. See Steven Lee Myers and Choe Sang-Hun, "North Koreans Agree to Freeze Nuclear Work: U.S. to Give Aid," *New York Times*, February 29, 2012, http://www.nytimes.com/2012/03/01/world/asia/us-says-north-korea-agrees-to-curb-nuclear-work.html?pagewanted=all, March 1, 2012, from which we draw this discussion.

58. Arms Control Association, "History of Official Proposals on the Iranian Nuclear Issue," http://www.armscontrol.org/factsheets/Iran_Nuclear_Proposals, November 24, 2010, and March 18, 2012.

59. Neil MacFarquhar, "U.N. Approves New Sanctions to Deter Iran," *New York Times*, June 9, 2010, http://www.nytimes.com/2010/06/10/world/middleeast/10sanctions.html, November 16, 2010.

60. Susan Cornwell, "Congress OKs Sanctions on Iran's Energy, Banks," *Reuters*, June 25, 2010, http://www.reuters.com/article/idUSTRE65N6RZ20100625, November 16, 2010.

61. Stephen Castle, "Europe Imposes New Sanctions on Iran," *New York Times*, July 26, 2010, http://www.nytimes.com/2010/07/27/world/middleeast/27iran.html, November 16, 2010.

62. Laura MacInnis, "U.S. Imposes Sanction on Banks Dealing with Iran, *Reuters*, December 31, 2011, http://www.reuters.com/article/2011/12/31/us-iran-usa-obama-idUSTRE7BU0GP20111231, March 21, 2009.

63. See "Iran: EU Oil Sanctions 'Unfair' and 'Doomed to Fail,'" BBC News Europe, January 23, 2012, http://www.bbc.co.uk/news/world-europe-16693484?print=true, March 19, 2012, for the quoted passages and for the quote by Catherine Ashton.

64. Marc Ambinder, "Obama Makes the Case that his Iran Policy is Working," *The Atlantic*, August 5, 2010, http://www.theatlantic.com/politics/archive/2010/08/obama-makes-the-case-that-his-iran-policy-is-working/60967/, November 16, 2010.

65. "Official: Iran, West Agree on Timing of Nuke Talks," *Washington Post*, November 16, 2010, http://www.washingtonpost.com/wp-dyn/content/article/2010/11/16/AR2010111600934.html, on November 17, 2010; and Fredrik Dahl, "Analysis: Are Iran Nuclear Talks Doomed to Fail Again?" *Reuters*, November 15, 2010, http://www.reuters.com/article/idUSTRE6AE22V20101115, November 17, 2010.

66. Steven Erlanger, "More Nuclear Talks With Iran Are Set," *New York Times*, December 7, 2010, http://www.nytimes.com/2010/12/08/world/europe/08iran.html, December 27, 2010.

67. Nicholas Kulish and James Kanter, "World Powers Agree to Resume Nuclear Talks with Iran," *New York Times*, March 6, 2012, http://www.nytimes.com/2012/03/07/world/middleeast/iran-agrees-to-inspection-of-secret-military-site-report-says.html, March 7, 2012. Also see Ronen Bergman, "Will Israel Attack Iran?" *New York Times*, January 25, 2012, http://www.nytimes.com/2012/01/29/magazine/will-israel-attack-iran.html?pagewanted=all, January 31, 2012.

68. UN News Service, "Middle East: As Proximity Talks Start, Hopes for Progress Voiced at UN," May 10, 2010, http://www.un.org /apps/new/printnewsAR.asp?nid=34643, November 17, 2010.

69. Ilene R. Prasher, "US Pushes Israelis and Palestinians to 'Proximity' Peace Talks," *Christian Science Monitor*, February 9, 2010, http://www.csmonitor.com/layout/set/print/content/view/print/279215, November 17, 2010.

70. United States Department of State, "Briefing by Special Envoy for Middle East Peace George Mitchell," November 25, 2009, http://www.state.gov/r/pa/prs/ps/2009/nov/132447.htm, November 17, 2010.

71. Barack Obama, "Remarks by the President in the Rose Garden after Bilateral Meetings," The White House, Office of the Press Secretary, September 1, 2010, http://www.whitehouse.gov/the-press-office/2010/09/01/remarks-president-rose-garden-after-bilateral-meetings, November 17, 2010.

72. Joshua Mitnick, "After GOP Victory, Emboldened Israel Seclares New Building in East Jerusalem," *Christian Science Monitor*, November 8, 2010, http://www.csmonitor.com/World/Middle-East/2010/1108/After-GOP-victory-emboldened-Israel-declares-new-building-in-East-Jerusalem, November 17, 2010.

73. Joshua Mitnick, "Netanyahu Strikes a Deal on Israeli Settlements—Could it Freeze Peace, Too? *Christian Science Monitor*, November 15, 2010, http://www.csmonitor.com/World/Middle-East/2010/1115/Netanyahu-strikes-a-deal-on-Israeli-settlements-could-it-freeze-peace-too, November 17, 2010.

74. Karen DeYoung, "U.S. Abandons Push for Renewal of Israeli Settlement Freeze," *Washington Post*, December 8, 2010, http://www.washingtonpost.com/wp-dyn/content/article/2010/12/07/AR2010120707310.html?wpisrc=nl_politics, December 8, 2010.

75. "U.S. Tries Indirect Peace Tactic," *Milwaukee Journal Sentinel*, December 14, 2010, 5A.

76. Mark Landler, "Obama Pressed Netanyahu to Resist Strikes on Iran," *New York Times*, March 5, 2012, http://www.nytimes.com/2012/03/06/world/middleeast/obama-cites-window-for-diplomacy-on-iran-bomb.html?pagewanted=all, March 6, 2012.

77. The government cables released by Wikileaks in late 2010, however, suggest a more sober and franker assessment of the Russian leaders and Russia by American diplomats than the cooperative bilateral and multilateral activities convey. See C. J. Chivers, "Below Surface, U.S. Has Dim View of Putin and Russia," *New York Times*, December 1, 2010, http://www.nytimes.com/2010/12/02/world/europe/02wikileaks-russia.html, December 2, 2010.

78. BBC News, "NATO to Back US Missile Defence," April 3, 2008, http://news.bbc.co.uk/2/hi/7328915.htm, November 19, 2010; and "Russia's Medvedev Hails 'Comrade' Obama," April 2, 2009, http://www.google.com/hostednews/afp/article/ALeqM5gEo4B1heuBvO6KK7EiBHKigO1UrA, November 19, 2010.

79. "Russia's Medvedev Hails 'Comrade' Obama."

80. The White House, Office of the Press Secretary, "Joint Statement by Dmitry A. Medvedev, President of the Russian Federation, and Barack Obama, President of the United States of America, Regarding Negotiations on Further Reductions in Strategic Offensive Arms," April 1, 2009, http://www.whitehouse.gov/the_press_office/Joint-Statement-by-Dmitriy-A-Medvedev-and-Barack-Obama/, November 19, 2010.

81. See The White House, Office of the Press Secretary, "Fact Sheet: U.S.-Russia Bilateral Presidential Commission," July 6, 2009, http://www.whitehouse.gov/thepress_office/FACT-SHEET-US-Russia-Bilateral-Presidential-Commission, November 19, 2010; The White House, Office of the Press Secretary, "Joint Statement by Dmitry A. Medvedev, President of the Russian Federation, and Barack Obama, President of the United States, on Missile Defense Issues," July 6, 2009, http://www.whitehouse.gov/the_press_office/Joint-Statement-by-Dmitry-A-Medvedev-President-of-the-Russian-Federation-and-Barack-Obama-President-of-the-United-States-of-America-on-Missile-Defense-Issues/, November 19, 2010; and United States Department of State, "Bilateral Presidential Commission Fact Sheet," October 15, 2009, http://www.state.gov/p/eur/rls/fs/130616,htm, November 20, 2010, on the commission and ballistic missile defense.

82. The White House, Office of the Press Secretary, 2009d, "Fact Sheet on U.S. Missile Defense Policy, A 'Phased, Adaptive Approach' for Missile Defense in Europe," September 17, http://www.whitehouse.gov/the_press_office/FACT-SHEET-US-Missile-Defense-Policy-A-Phased-Adaptive-Approach-for-Missile-Defense-in-Europe/, November 18, 2010.

83. Thomas Young, "Issue Brief: The Reconfiguration of European Missile Protection Russia's Response and the Likely Implications," NTI, October 9, 2009, http://www.nti.org/e_research/e3_missile_defense.html, November 18, 2010.

84. The White House, Office of the Press Secretary, "U.S.-Russia Relations: 'Reset' Fact Sheet," June 24, 2010, http://www.whitehouse.gov/the-press-office/us-russia-relations-reset-fact-sheet, November 19, 2010.

85. "The New START Treaty," Council on Foreign Relations, April 8, 2010, http://www.cfr.org/publication/21851/new_start_treaty.html, November 23, 2010.

86. Arms Control Association, Strategic Offensive Reduction Treaty (SORT), May 24, 2002, http://www.armscontrol.org/documents/sort, November 23, 2010.

87. "Background Note: China," U.S. Department of State, September 6, 2011, http://www.state.gov/r/pa/ei/bgn/18902.htm, March 25, 2012. The information in the two following paragraphs is drawn from this source.

88. Hillary Clinton, "America's Pacific Century," *Foreign Policy*, November 2011, p. 57.

89. Ibid., p. 62.

90. Nuclear Posture Review Report, U.S. Department of Defense, April, 2010, http://www
.defense.gov/npr/docs/2010%20nuclear%20posture%20review%20report.pdf, November
24, 2010; and Nuclear Posture Review Briefing, U.S. Department of Defense, April 6,
2010, http://www.defense.gov/npr/docs/10-04-06_NPR%20201%20Briefing%20-%20
1032.pdf, November 24, 2010.

91. "Communiqué of the Washington Nuclear Security Summit," Council on Foreign
Relation, April 13, 2010, http://www.cfr.org/publication/21896/communiqu_of_
the_washington_nuclear_security_summit.html, November 9, 2010.

92. "The Nuclear Security Summit," *New York Times*, Editorial, April 12, 2010, http://www
.nytimes.com/2010/04/12/opinion/12mon1.html, November 9, 2010.

93. "Nuclear Security Summit," The Dong-a Ilbo, March 18, 2012, http://english.donga.
com/srv/service.php3?biid=2012031922588, March 23, 2012.

94. Neil MacFarquhar, "189 Nations Reaffirm Goal of Ban on Nuclear Weapons," *New York
Times*, May 28, 2010, http://www.nytimes.com/2010/05/29/world/middleeast/29nuke.
html, November 24, 2010.

95. "Complete Text: G-20 Seoul Communiqué," *International Business Times*, November 12,
2010, http://www.ibtimes.com/articles/81220/20101112/communique.htm, November
22, 2010.

96. Howard Schneider and David Cho, "U.S., Europe at Odds over Global Financial
Reform," *Washington Post*, March 13, 2010, p. A01.

97. Hillary Clinton, "Appointment of Special Envoy on Climate Change Todd Stern,"
January 26, 2009, http://www.state.gov/secretary/rm/2009a/01/115409.htm,
November 23, 2010.

98. Todd Stern, "A New Paradigm: Climate Change Negotiations in the Post-Copenhagen
Era," Address to the University of Michigan Law School, October 8, 2010, http://www
.state.gov/g/oes/rls/remarks/2010/149429.htm, November 22, 2010.

99. John Carey, "House Passes Carbon Cap-and-Trade Bill," June 26, 2009, http://www
.businessweek.com/blogs/money_politics/archives/2009/06/house_passes_ca.html,
November 23, 2010.

100. John M. Broder, "Many Goals Remain Unmet in 5 Nations' Climate Deal," *New
York Times*, December 19, 2009, http://www.nytimes.com/2009/12/19/science/
earth/19climate.html, November 9, 2010.

101. John M. Broder, "Climate Talks End with Modest Deal on Emissions," *New York Times*,
December 11, 2010, http://www.nytimes.com/2010/12/12/science/earth/12climate.
html, December 27, 2010.

102. Janet Eilperin, "U.S. Plays Conflicted Role in Global Climate Debate," *Washington
Post*, November 1, 2010, http://www.washingtonpost.com/wp-dyn/content/
article/2010/10/31/AR2010103103378.html, November 1, 2010.

103. Broder, "Climate Talks End with Modest Deal on Emissions."

104. Arthur Max, "U.N. Chief: Major Climate Deal Unlikely," USATODAY.com,
December 12, 2011, http://www.usatoday.com/weather/climate/story/2011-12-06/
climate-change-conference-durban-south africa/51675778/1, March 23, 2012.

105. "Beyond Durham," *New York Times*, December 16, 2011, http://www.nytimes.
com/2011/12/17/opinion/beyond-the-durban-climate-talks.html, March 23, 2012.

106. David Rohde, "The Obama Doctrine," *Foreign Policy*, March/April 2012, http://www
.foreignpolicy.com/articles/2012/02/27/the_obama_doctrine, March 4, 2012. The next
two examples are from this source as well.

107. Ibid.

108. Ibid.

109. Ibid.

110. Senator Lindsay Graham, " Team Obama's Foreign Policy, National Review Online, November 11, 2011, http://www.foreignpolicy.com/articles/2012/02/27/the_obama_ doctrine, November 13, 2011. The quotes and the following policy positions are drawn from this essay.

111. See Ryan Lizza, "The Consequentialist," *The New Yorker* 87, no. 11 (May 2, 2011), pp. 44–55. The quoted passages in this paragraph and the subsequent ones as well as this assessment are taken from this article.

112. Ben Pershing, "Obama's Foreign Policy a Work in Progress," *Washington Post*, April 14, 2010, http://voices.washingtonpost.com/44/2010/04/rundown---041410.html, November 29, 2010.

113. David Ignatius, "Obama's Foreign Policy: Big Ideas, Little Implementation," *Washington Post*, October 17, 2010, http://www.washingtonpost.com/wp-dyn/content/ article/2010/10/14/AR2010101406505.html, November 29, 2010.

PART II

The Process of
Policy Making

Now that the reader is generally familiar with the basic values and beliefs that have shaped American policy over time, we shift our focus to policy making itself. In Part II, we examine in some detail the policy-making process and how various institutions and groups—the executive, Congress, several bureaucracies, political parties, interest groups, and the public at large—compete to promote their own values in American foreign policy. Our goals in the next six chapters are to provide essential information on the principal foreign policy makers, to assess their relative influence on the decision-making process, and to evaluate how their power has changed over time. In this way, the student may be better able to understand how and why the United States adopts particular values, beliefs, and policies in its relationships with the rest of the world.

CHAPTER 7

The President and the Making of Foreign Policy

On October 7, 2001, on my orders, U.S. armed forces began
combat actions in Afghanistan against al-Qaeda terrorists
and their Taliban supporters. . . .
I have taken these actions pursuant to my constitutional authority
to conduct U.S. foreign relations as Commander in Chief
and Chief Executive.

PRESIDENT GEORGE W. BUSH

OCTOBER 2001

I directed this action [toward Somali pirates] consistent with
my responsibility to protect U.S. citizens both at home and
abroad, and in furtherance of U.S. national security interests,
pursuant to my constitutional authority to conduct
U.S. foreign relations and as Commander in
Chief and Chief Executive.

PRESIDENT BARACK OBAMA

JANUARY 2012

In March 2011, President Barack Obama announced to the American people that he had ordered American forces to Libya to support a UN Security Council Resolution "to protect the Libyan people and to establish a no-fly zone" after Libyan leader, Moammar Gadhafi threatened to massacre his opposition. With such "brutal repression and a looming humanitarian crisis," the president said, the United States needed to act both because its national interest was at stake but also due to "our responsibilities to our fellow human beings." To justify his authority to act, Obama cited one of his constitutional powers: "As Commander-in-Chief, I have no greater responsibility than keeping this country safe. . . . I've made it clear that I will never hesitate to use our military swiftly, decisively, and unilaterally when necessary to defend our people, our homeland, our allies, and our core interests."[1]

Eight years earlier, on March 17, 2003, President George W. Bush addressed the American public, declaring that the United States would initiate military action against the government of Iraq unless Saddam Hussein left the country within forty-eight hours because the Hussein regime posed a danger with the lethal weapons that it possessed. When Hussein defied this ultimatum, Bush authorized an American attack and invasion; he, too, justified his actions by citing his constitutional power: "the United States of America has the sovereign authority to use force in assuring its own national security. That duty falls to me, as Commander-in-Chief, by the oath I have sworn, by the oath I will keep."[2] In both instances, the presidents viewed their role as preeminent in the conduct and direction of U.S. foreign policy.

Other recent presidents did the same. In October 1993, when President Bill Clinton was faced with possible congressional restrictions on his ability to use force in Haiti, he too asserted his presidential prerogative: "I think that, clearly, the Constitution leaves to the president, for good and sufficient reasons, the ultimate decision-making authority."[3] More than a decade earlier, Presidents Jimmy Carter and Gerald Ford had enunciated this long-standing view in a joint appearance. In foreign policy, there is "only one clear voice," Carter said, and that is the president's; Ford endorsed this view by adding that Congress is too large and too diverse to handle foreign policy crises.[4] Presidential dominance, in short, is the usual way to characterize U.S. foreign policy making.

Over the past several decades, however, Congress has increasingly challenged the presidency by seeking a larger role in foreign affairs. This congressional resurgence began in the early 1970s, fueled by the Vietnam War and the Watergate scandal, and resulted in several initiatives that sought to curb the executive's prerogatives. That assertiveness continued in the 1980s with major roles for Congress in shaping Central American, Middle Eastern, and Soviet–American policy. As the Cold War ended and as Republican congressional majorities were elected in the mid-1990s, Congress's initiatives did not diminish, and during this time the Clinton administration faced continuous foreign policy challenges from Capitol Hill.

At the outset of his term, President Obama issued three executive orders dealing with foreign policy, including one that called for the closing of the U.S. prison at Guantanamo Bay, Cuba, within one year. Yet, implementation of that order was quickly stymied by congressional opposition that blocked funding for a domestic facility in Illinois to house these detainees. Efforts to move the trials for these detainees from Guantanamo Bay to the mainland also prompted congressional and public opposition. Similar executive–legislative skirmishes occurred over gaining congressional approval of three free trade agreements that had languished in Congress since the Bush administration and on other foreign policy issues. In fact, the struggle between the two branches over the control of U.S. foreign policy persists to this day.

In this chapter and the following one, we examine the struggle between the president and Congress to make foreign policy. Our analysis will explore the following themes:

- Why and how the executive has dominated the foreign policy process
- Why and how Congress has tried to curb presidential power recently
- What is likely to be the relationship between the president and Congress in the twenty-first century

CONSTITUTIONAL POWERS IN FOREIGN POLICY

Under the Constitution, both the legislative and executive branches of government have been delegated specific foreign affairs powers. Both, too, are directed to share some responsibility with the other. This arrangement ensures that Congress and the president can each check the actions of the other much as they do in domestic policy. Throughout the history of the republic, however, the division of foreign policy power has often been unclear and as such has caused many political disputes. We begin our analysis by identifying the foreign policy powers of each branch and the areas of dispute between them.

Presidential Powers

Under **Article II** of the Constitution, the president is granted the plenary power to be **chief executive**, which extends to the foreign policy arena ("The Executive Power shall be vested in a President" and "he shall take Care that the Laws be faithfully executed").[5] He is also granted the power to **command the armed forces** ("The President shall be Commander in Chief of the Army and Navy of the United States") the power to be **chief negotiator** and **chief diplomat** ("He shall have power, by and with the advice and consent of the Senate, to make Treaties . . . shall appoint Ambassadors . . . and he shall receive Ambassadors and other public Ministers. . . ."). The president, in short, is to wear at least three different hats: chief executive, commander-in-chief, and chief diplomat. With such power at his disposal, he seemingly possesses the constitutional mandate to dominate foreign affairs.

This constitutional delegation of foreign policy powers to the executive branch represented a marked change from the arrangements set out by the earlier Articles of Confederation, which had no executive branch. During the period prior to 1787, Congress controlled foreign policy through its Committee on Foreign Affairs. This system did not work very well, however, and Congress's inability to manage trade, maintain and protect America's national boundaries, and deal effectively with Britain and Spain contributed to a new constitutional structure for the young republic. Indeed, according to one assessment, "*the mismanagement of foreign affairs by Congress*" contributed to the holding of the Constitutional Convention.[6]

The founders at the Constitutional Convention were in agreement on the need to strengthen national over state government, but they were divided over how strong the foreign policy powers of the executive should be. Although they were familiar with John Locke's *Second Treatise on Government*, in which various foreign policy prerogatives rested with the executive, and with Sir William Blackstone's *Commentaries on the Laws of England*, in which the king enjoyed similar prerogatives, the founders largely rejected these models. Instead, they were concerned about too much executive power and made sure that the president, in making treaties, appointments, and war and peace, shared his power with the legislative branch.[7] Even Alexander Hamilton, a strong proponent of executive power, was led to conclude that the president under the Constitution would have fewer substantive foreign affairs prerogatives than the King of England.[8]

Congressional Powers

Under **Article I** of the Constitution, Congress does in fact enjoy significant foreign policy power. It has the right to make and modify any laws and to **appropriate funds** for the implementation of any laws ("No money shall be drawn from the Treasury, but in Consequence of Appropriations made by Law"). It has the right **to provide for the national defense** and **to declare war** (Congress is authorized to "provide for the common Defence . . . ; To declare War . . . ; To raise and support Armies . . . ; To provide and maintain a Navy"). And it is delegated the responsibility to **regulate international commerce** ("To regulate commerce with foreign nations") and to use its **implied powers** (the right to "make all Laws which shall be necessary and proper" for carrying out its other responsibilities).

Constitutional scholar Louis Henkin has argued that Congress has even more of what he calls "foreign affairs powers." These are not explicitly derived from the Constitution, but derive from the fact that the United States has sovereignty and nationhood. Thus, Congress enjoys additional authority to support legislation to regulate and protect "the conduct of foreign relations and foreign diplomatic activities in the United States." These undefined powers also allow congressional legislation in such areas as immigration, the regulation of aliens, the authorization of international commitments, and the extradition of citizens to other states. Moreover, Henkin rather boldly concludes that there is no matter in foreign affairs "that is not subject to legislation by Congress."[9] In this sense, Congress has a constitutional mandate to be involved in foreign policy, just as the executive branch has.

"The Twilight Zone" and Foreign Policy

Although the nation's founders delegated separate foreign policy responsibilities to each branch, they went further by stipulating that some of those responsibilities be shared. Thus, the president is the chief executive, but Congress decides what laws are to be enforced; the president may command the armed forces, but Congress decides whether wars should be initiated; the president may negotiate treaties, but Congress (or, more accurately, the Senate) must give its advice and consent. (Table 7.1 shows three areas of shared foreign policy powers as outlined in Articles I and II of the Constitution.)

It is easier to describe the constitutional ideal of **shared foreign policy powers** than it is to put it into effective operation. Often, the actions of one branch seemingly cross over into the responsibilities of the other. The president relies on his power as commander-in-chief to initiate military actions against another nation, even though only Congress has the power to declare war. Congress can restrict the deployment of troops in a particular region, even though the president has the power to direct their deployment. What has emerged, in the words of Supreme Court Justice Robert Jackson, is "a zone of twilight in which [the president] and Congress may have concurrent authority, or in which its distribution is uncertain."[10]

The result of this shared responsibility, owing to the Constitution's ambiguity, has been an historical tension over who ultimately controls foreign policy. Perhaps one of

Table 7.1 Some Foreign Policy Powers Shared between the President and the Congress

President	Congress
War making	
"Commander in Chief of the Army and Navy of the United States"	the power "to declare war"; "to raise and support armies"; to "provide for the Common Defence"
Commitment making	
"He shall have Power . . . to make Treaties"	"provided two thirds of the Senators present concur"
Appointments	
"He shall nominate . . . and shall appoint Ambassadors"	"by and with the advice and Consent of the Senate"

© Cengage Learning

the earliest debates reflecting this tension was carried out by two founders, **Alexander Hamilton** and **James Madison**, writing under pseudonyms in the early 1790s. Hamilton (or "Pacificus," as he called himself), in defense of President George Washington's declaration of neutrality in 1793 (over France's war against Great Britain, Spain, and the Netherlands), made the classic case for a strong executive: The powers and responsibilities over foreign policy rested with the executive, except for those specifically delegated to Congress. Madison (or "Helvidius," as he called himself) viewed presidential powers in foreign affairs in a more limited way: only those powers expressly delegated to the executive were allowed under the Constitution, and there was not such an unrestrained delegation of power to that branch.[11] Moreover, other foreign policy powers were necessarily left to Congress to serve as a counterweight to the presidency. In short, no exact division of power and responsibility was spelled out.

In the modern era, several scholars attest to the difficulty of delineating the foreign policy powers of the two branches. Historian Arthur Schlesinger, in his book *The Imperial Presidency*, describes the Constitution on this issue as "cryptic, ambiguous, and incomplete," and thus as contributing to disputes between the two institutions.[12] Louis Henkin notes that "the constitutional blueprint for the governance of our foreign affairs has proved to be starkly incomplete, indeed skimpy."[13] Edward S. Corwin, the noted scholar on constitutional and presidential power, has given us probably the most often cited summary of this dilemma: the Constitution has provided "**an invitation to struggle** for the privilege of directing American foreign policy."[14]

A CYCLICAL INTERPRETATION OF FOREIGN POLICY DOMINANCE

To some analysts, a cyclical pattern of control has resulted from this "invitation to struggle": one branch dominating during a particular epoch, the other dominating during another. However, these analysts do not all see the periods of executive or legislative dominance as the same.[15] Many see the presidency as more successful than Congress over the history of the republic, especially in the post–World War II years, but others view the recent decades (that is, since the Vietnam War) as a period in which the legislative branch has attempted to wrest some foreign policy making from the executive branch. Both views merit our attention, especially as we focus on the post–World War II era of American foreign policy.

The Early Years of the Republic

According to the cyclical interpretation, during the early decades of the country, **presidential dominance in foreign policy** was on the rise and congressional involvement was often limited. When President Washington took several unilateral actions—appointing diplomats abroad, refusing to share information on the Jay Treaty, and declaring neutrality in the fighting between Britain and France—congressional involvement was minimal, thus assuring presidential ascendancy. Other early presidents—John Adams, Thomas Jefferson, and James Madison—largely followed this pattern, epitomized by the executive initiatives in securing the Louisiana Purchase and in issuing the Monroe Doctrine. Congress was not entirely kept out of the decision making in these early years, as illustrated by its role in precipitating the War of 1812. In particular, it enacted various embargo bills—especially against the British. As a result, a "congressional war" was actually initiated.[16]

Beginning with **Andrew Jackson**'s presidency and continuing until the presidency of Abraham Lincoln (with the exception of James K. Polk), **congressional involvement** in foreign policy became more assertive. Jackson, for example, deferred to Congress when action seemed called for over attacks on American ships off South America and when France was reluctant to pay claims owed to the United States. When Texas revolted against Mexico and then sought American recognition as an independent state, he turned to Congress for guidance.

During the presidency of **James K. Polk, presidential dominance** arose once again when, without asking Congress for authorization, Polk ordered the U.S. military into the territory that was disputed by Texas and Mexico. The result was an attack on American forces by Mexico and a rather quick congressional declaration of war.[17] During **Lincoln's presidency**, however, this executive dominance extended even further as Lincoln sought to hold the Union together through the Civil War. With his numerous executive actions initiated without congressional involvement, as we catalogue below, presidential power reached its height.

Congressional Dominance after the Civil War

After the Civil War, however, the "**golden age of congressional ascendancy**" emerged.[18] Congress once again asserted its role, passing a resolution to halt the acquisition of territory after Henry Seward's purchase of Alaska in 1867 and, in 1869, refusing to take action on a treaty "permitting de facto annexation of Santo Domingo." Indeed, over the next thirty years or so, congressional–executive relations were so strained that the "Senate refused to ratify any important treaty outside of the immigration context."[19]

By roughly the turn of the century, however, the pendulum began to swing back toward the executive. From Presidents William McKinley and Theodore Roosevelt to Woodrow Wilson (with Taft as the exception), **the presidency reigned** over foreign policy. Consider Roosevelt's robust action in the Western Hemisphere and McKinley's in Asia. Wilson, too, sought to enlarge the role of the presidency in foreign affairs with his proposal of a global collective security system and his endorsement of the

League of Nations. But when the Senate rejected the Versailles Treaty and membership in the nascent League of Nations, presidential dominance lost ground once again. By the time of the "**return to normalcy**" of the interwar years, Congress largely shaped foreign policy through the passage of neutrality acts to keep America out of foreign involvement and through restrictive trade and immigration laws (such as the Smoot-Hawley Tariff Act and the National Origins Act).

Despite its muscular role in the nineteenth century and into the early twentieth century, Congress's overall involvement in foreign policy was "episodic and fitful."[20] Moreover, its involvement was to change dramatically with the onset of World War II, when executive dominance emerged once again. President Roosevelt, for example, acted to aid the British in 1940 with the "destroyers for bases" deal, an arrangement in which the United States sold fifty destroyers to Britain in exchange for access rights to British bases "in the Atlantic and Caribbean,"[21] and in 1941 he obtained congressional approval for the Lend-Lease Act, an American aid effort to support the allies already fighting in Europe. With the coming of the Cold War, presidential power in foreign affairs was to increase even more dramatically. Indeed, by the late 1940s and early 1950s, executive dominance was fully in place.

EXECUTIVE DOMINANCE AFTER WORLD WAR II: THE IMPERIAL PRESIDENCY

The growth of presidential power after World War II was in part the result of long-term historical trends, but it was particularly associated with the rise of American globalism during that time. In the main, though, the president has been the dominant actor in foreign affairs owing to several key factors:

- Important historical executive precedents
- Supreme Court decisions
- Congressional deference and delegation
- The growth of executive institutions
- International situational factors

Important Historical Executive Precedents

By assuming that they controlled particular aspects of foreign policy and by taking action, the early presidents set a pattern—a **precedent**—for how future executives would act. These precedents ranged across several key foreign policy areas: negotiation with other nations, recognition of other governments, the withholding of information from Congress on certain foreign policy matters, the conduct of foreign policy, the initiation of military action and even to wage war, and the making of commitments. In this regard, Washington was particularly pivotal in establishing precedents, because he put into effect the constitutional phrase "in response to events."[22] Other early presidents followed Washington's lead and were to give the presidency preeminence in these foreign policy areas.

Negotiating with Other Nations Washington made it clear that the executive would be the representative of the United States abroad. He sent personal emissaries to represent him in negotiations and simply informed Congress of his actions.

In 1791, for instance, he informed the Senate that Gouverneur Morris, who was in Great Britain at that time, would confer with the British over their adherence to the treaty of peace. A short time later, he sent his friend Colonel David Humphreys to Spain and Portugal as his personal representative.[23]

Recognizing Other Nations When Washington received Edmond Genêt ("Citizen Genêt"), the first minister to the United States from the French Republic, he went a long way toward legitimizing that nation's revolutionary government. Similarly, when Genêt seemingly violated his power by seeking to enlist Americans against the British, it was up to Washington to demand that he be recalled.[24]

Withholding Foreign Policy Information In declining to share important diplomatic information with the House of Representatives when negotiating the Jay Treaty of 1794, Washington's rationale was that the House had no standing in the treaty process. However, the implications of his action went further. This precedent broadened executive power so that "a President feels free by the same formula to decline information even to his constitutional partner in treaty-making. . . ."[25]

Initiating Policy In unilaterally declaring neutrality between France and Britain in 1793, Washington began the tradition of presidential direction in foreign policy matters. After this declaration, Congress largely followed the president and passed a neutrality act in conformity with his wishes.[26] President Monroe followed a similar approach with his unilateral declaration of the Monroe Doctrine in 1823, although Congress still held the right to deny funding for any Western Hemisphere activity.

Other early presidents followed Washington's lead. For instance, President Adams used his executive power to extradite an individual under the Jay Treaty without congressional authorization. Likewise, he vigorously defended his right to recognize other states. President Jefferson, too, although a proponent of legislative dominance in the affairs of state, nonetheless exercised considerable individual control over the Louisiana Purchase. Still later, President Monroe refused to relinquish the president's right to recognize other governments, especially with regard to several Latin American states. The result, as Corwin concludes, was to "reaffirm the President's monopoly of international intercourse and his constitutional independence in the performance of that function."[27]

Initiating Conflicts and War Although Congress was granted the right to declare war under the Constitution, how far could the president go under the commander-in-chief clause of the Constitution before he intruded on the congressional prerogative to declare war?

Early presidents were usually careful about extending the meaning of the commander-in-chief clause. Only in the case of attacks on Americans or American forces did they occasionally provide immediate military responses, but, as Schlesinger points out, even in those instances, they were quite meticulous in involving Congress in any actions.[28] When Jefferson was faced with the question of using force against Tripoli because of its attack on American shipping, he sent U.S. frigates to the Mediterranean but supposedly limited them to defensive action. Some evidence presented by Schlesinger, however, suggests that Jefferson "sent a naval squadron to the Mediterranean under secret orders to fight the Barbary pirates, applied for congressional sanctions six months later and then misled Congress as to the nature of the orders."[29]

Moreover, at about the same time, Jefferson sent a message to Congress declaring that "his actions . . . [were] in compliance with constitutional limitations on his authority in the absence of a declaration of war."[30] In this sense, executive assertiveness in war making may have begun quite early in the republic.

By the 1840s, however, some transformation in the commander-in-chief clause was already evident. As noted earlier, Polk used his power as head of the armed forces to precipitate a declaration of war against Mexico. By moving American troops into disputed territory—resulting in a Mexican attack—he was able to obtain a war resolution from Congress.[31] **The boldest precedents** with the **commander-in-chief clause** came during Lincoln's presidency. Combining the powers granted under this clause with the executive power to see that laws were carried out, President Lincoln, according to analyst Edward Corwin, effectively made the "war power" his own. Because of the Civil War, Lincoln, without consulting Congress, "proclaimed a blockade of the Southern ports, suspended the writ of habeas corpus in various places, and ordered the arrest and military detention of persons 'who were represented to him' as being engaged or contemplating 'treasonable practices.' . . ."[32] In addition, he enlarged the army and navy, pressed into service the state militias, and called up 40,000 volunteers. Despite outcries that the president was going beyond his limits, neither Congress nor the courts challenged him. In fact, Congress approved his actions after the fact, and the Supreme Court upheld his actions in the *Prize Cases* by a narrow margin of 5 to 4.[33] Although these presidential actions were taken in the context of a civil war (and their relevance to foreign wars is debatable), this expansion of presidential power in war making was not lost on future presidents.

Congressional acquiescence to Lincoln did not produce any expansion of war making by his immediate successors, but it did establish important precedents for later commanders-in-chief.[34] The dispatch of troops to China by President McKinley in 1900, the interventions by Presidents Theodore Roosevelt and William Howard Taft in the Caribbean in the early 1900s, and even the sending of American forces to Korea (albeit with a UN resolution) were without congressional authorization. Furthermore, several interventions by the United States during the height of the Cold War (Lebanon, the Bay of Pigs, the Dominican Republic, and Vietnam) were ordered without congressional action before the fact. Indeed, Lyndon Johnson was able to boast that there was a large body of precedent for his Vietnam policy by citing the actions of previous commanders-in-chief.[35] Later, during the Vietnam War, President Richard Nixon justified the Cambodian invasion in 1970 by stating, "I shall meet my responsibility as Commander in Chief of our Armed Forces to take the action necessary to defend the security of our American men."[36]

This pattern continued throughout the 1980s, 1990s, 2000s, to the present. In 1982, President Ronald Reagan initially sent American troops into Lebanon as a "peacekeeping force" without congressional approval and justified doing so through the commander-in-chief clause. In April 1986, too, he unilaterally initiated a retaliatory attack against Libya over that country's involvement with a terrorist attack on Americans in West Berlin. In December 1989, President George H. W. Bush justified U.S. intervention in Panama on the basis of his "constitutional authority with respect to the conduct of foreign relations," his responsibility "to protect American lives in imminent danger," and "as Commander in Chief" of American military forces.[37]

President Clinton exercised the same presidential prerogative with regard to the use of force in Haiti, Bosnia, and Kosovo. When Congress raised the possibility of restricting that prerogative in Haiti in September 1993, the president, in a sharply worded letter to Senate leaders, stated that he opposed several proposed amendments at the time because they would "unduly restrict the ability of the President to make foreign policy" and because they would weaken the commander-in-chief's power.[38] In 1995, Clinton sent American peacekeeping forces to Bosnia without congressional approval as part of the NATO-led Dayton Accords. He noted that these commitments were made "in conjunction with our NATO allies" and were consistent with his constitutional authority as president.[39] In 1999, after ordering the bombing in Kosovo as retaliation against Serbian atrocities, Clinton reported to Congress but stated that he was taking such actions "pursuant to my constitutional authority to conduct U.S. foreign relations and as Commander in Chief and Chief Executive."[40]

President George W. Bush followed, and arguably expanded, these precedents, especially after the events of September 11. President Bush cited his constitutional power to initiate a military response to terrorism, dispatching American forces to Afghanistan to pursue al-Qaeda and the Taliban, as well as several countries (such as the Philippines, Yemen) to aid in combating terrorists. Although presidential authority was invoked in these cases, Congress, in an unusual move, passed a sweeping resolution granting Bush broad authority to take military actions (see the discussion of Public Law 107–40 later in this chapter) after 9/11 and later a similar resolution with regard to Iraq.[41]

President Obama has also relied on his constitutional prerogatives in sending American forces abroad. These prerogatives were most dramatically in evidence over the intervention in Libya in March 2011. Obama cited UN Resolution 1973 as well as his constitutional power as commander-in-chief as allowing him to use force there, and his attorney general provided an even fuller justification along these lines by issuing a fourteen-page report that contended that "the President had the constitutional authority to direct the use of force in Libya because he could reasonably determine that such use of force was in the national interest, [and] prior congressional approval was not constitutionally required to use military force in the limited operations under consideration."[42] According to critics, then, the commander-in-chief clause had now been expanded to include the power not only to conduct a war already begun but also to initiate one if necessary.

Making Foreign Commitments   The president has enhanced his ability to make and carry out foreign policy by executive action alone. Instead of relying on the treaty as the basic instrument of making commitments to other states, presidents have come to rely on the so-called **executive agreement**. By such precedent, the treaty power of Congress has been eroded, and its involvement in this aspect of foreign policy making has been weakened.

The **executive agreement** is made with another country by the president or the president's representative, usually without congressional involvement. Its most important difference from a treaty is that it does not require the advice and consent of the Senate, yet it has the same force of law. An executive agreement actually may take two forms. One is based solely on the constitutional power of the president ("pure"); the other is based on congressional legislation authorizing or approving the president's making of a commitment ("statutory").

The **pure executive agreement** relies on powers granted in Article II, especially the commander-in-chief clause. An example is the agreement made by the United States for use of naval facilities in Bahrain about which a State Department official testified before Congress that the "President, as Commander in Chief, has constitutional authority to make arrangements for facilities for our military personnel." The **statu-tory executive agreement** relies on some precise piece of earlier congressional authorization or a treaty. An example is the agreement with Portugal for military rights in the Azores, which was based on a 1951 defense agreement between the two countries in accordance with the 1949 NATO Treaty.[43]

Of the two, the statutory executive agreement is the more prevalent and the more controversial.[44] It allows Congress procedural involvement in the agreement process, but the extent of its substantive involvement remains an important question. It is not always clear that Congress is fully aware of the considerable discretion that it is affording the president in making commitments abroad or how far statutory authority is expanded to cover a contemplated executive agreement. In some instances, Congress may be providing legislation that might later be viewed as a "blank check" for presidential action.

Table 7.2 provides some data on the use of executive agreements (including the statutory and the pure forms in one category) versus treaties over the history of the republic. As these data show, the executive agreement was used moderately at first, but its use grew dramatically in the last century or so.[45] In the years between 1889 and 1929, the number of executive agreements was almost twice that of treaties. By comparison, in the post–World War II period, the use of executive agreements virtually exploded, dwarfing the use of treaties. Over the history of the nation, about 90 percent of all commitments have been by executive agreement. From 1950 through 1999, 94 percent of all commitments were made in this way. Our survey of international commitments executed by the United States between 2000 and 2005 provides a similar picture, with at least 90 percent taking the form of executive agreements and 10 percent or fewer take the form of treaties. In this sense, the executive

Table 7.2 Treaties and Executive Agreements, 1789–1999

Years	Treaties	Executive Agreements	Percent of Total as Executive Agreements (%)
1789–1839	60	27	31
1839–1889	215	238	53
1889–1929	382	763	67
1930–1939	132	154	54
1940–1949	116	919	89
1950–1959	138	2,229	94
1960–1969	114	2,324	95
1970–1979	173	3,039	95
1980–1989	166	3,524	95
1990–1999	249	3,524	96
Totals/Average %	1,745	16,074	90

Sources: The data for 1789–1929 are from Michael Nelson, ed., *Congressional Quarterly's Guide to the Presidency* (Washington, DC: Congressional Quarterly, 1989), p. 1104; the data for 1930–1999 are from *Treaties and Other International Agreements: The Role of the United States Senate*, a study prepared for the Committee on Foreign Relations, United States Senate (Washington, DC: Government Printing Office, 2001), p. 39. Column 3 was calculated by the author.

agreement, as an instrument for making foreign policy commitments abroad, remains predominant.[46]

Despite the limited use of the executive agreement in the first century of the republic, important commitments were made via this route. The agreement between the British and the Americans to limit naval vessels on the Great Lakes (the Rush–Bagot Agreement of 1817), for example, was made through an exchange of notes by executive representatives of the two governments, and President McKinley agreed to the terms for ending the Spanish-American War in this way as well. President Theodore Roosevelt made a secret agreement with Japan over Korea in 1905 and made a "Gentlemen's Agreement" in 1907 to restrict Japanese immigration into the United States.[47]

In the modern era, the executive agreement was used frequently and for important commitments. President Franklin Roosevelt set the pattern for recent presidents with the Destroyers for Bases deal of 1940 and the Yalta Agreement of 1945. President Harry Truman followed suit with the Potsdam Agreement and later made an oral commitment to defend the newly independent state of Israel in 1948.[48]

Following these initiatives, later postwar chief executives made numerous important political and military executive agreements on their own. As a Senate Foreign Relations subcommittee investigation reported, in the late 1960s and early 1970s, many political, military, and intelligence commitments (some verbal and some secret) were extended to Thailand, Laos, Spain, Ethiopia, and the Philippines, among others, through executive action alone, leaving Congress almost entirely in the dark.[49] Many important foreign military commitments in the postwar years were made by executive agreement.[50] These include military missions in Honduras and El Salvador in the 1950s; pledges to Turkey, Iran, and Pakistan over security in 1959; permission from the British to use the island of Diego Garcia for military purposes in the 1960s; and a military mission in Iran in 1974. The analysis further revealed that some "understandings" and arrangements with nations were handled by executive agreements—for instance, a message by President Nixon regarding aid for the reconstruction of North Vietnam as part of a peace effort and an "understanding" regarding the role of American military personnel in the Israeli–Egyptian disengagement agreement of 1975. Similarly, an executive agreement brought about the Offensive Arms Pact of the Strategic Arms Limitation Talks (SALT I) in 1972.

Recent presidents have carried out important commitments via executive agreements. In October 1994, for instance, President Clinton completed an executive agreement between the United States and North Korea over that country's future nuclear program. If this pact had been fully implemented, North Korea would forgo any nuclear weapons development program, open up its nuclear power sites to international inspection, and in return receive two light-water nuclear power reactors from an international consortium (probably Japan and South Korea).[51] The executive agreement was the Bush administration's preferred mechanism to negotiate with the Iraqi government about the future of American troops in that country during 2008. Similarly, the Obama administration used this instrument to negotiate "a strategic partnership agreement" with Afghanistan to support that country after American forces leave in 2014 and to broker an agreement with North Korea on suspending its nuclear program in exchange for some American food aid.[52]

Various pledges at summits (for instance, G-8 or G-20 meetings) or presidential meetings with foreign leaders have been via executive agreement. President George W. Bush and Russian President Vladimir Putin worked out several understandings on the war on terrorism through executive consultations. Indeed, President Bush came to several such understandings with other nations over dealing with terrorism through this mechanism. President Obama reached several agreements and understandings (on cooperation in Afghanistan, transit rights for U.S. troops through Russia going to Afghanistan, a framework on military-to-military cooperation, and the establishment of a U.S.-Russia Bilateral Presidential Commission) with Russian President Dmitry Medvedev at a Moscow Summit with this mechanism. Finally, the declarations by the Group of Eight (G-8)—the industrial democracies of the United States, Britain, France, Germany, Japan, Italy, Canada, and Russia—or the commitments by the Group of 20 (G-20)—the major developed and advanced developing countries—are made through executive agreements.

To be sure, Congress may still become involved in some of these commitments, especially if they are made to change the status of a nation under a treaty or convention (granting most favored nation trading status to China, for example) or when additional funding of some program is required (such as increasing foreign aid for Ukraine or military assistance to Afghanistan). Nevertheless, the executive agreement remains a potent foreign policy tool for the president.

Issuing Executive Orders Executive Orders are directives that the president unilaterally makes for particular areas of policy, both domestic and foreign. Some are like statutory executive agreements in that they implement a statute passed by Congress. For example, President Bush issued a directive continuing the national emergency with respect to Burma and its human rights policy under a National Emergency Act passed by Congress in May 2001.[53] Bush issued an executive order "blocking property of and prohibiting transactions with the Government of Sudan" as a way to impose sanctions on that government over its policy in Darfur and as a way to implement policy flowing from congressional passage of the Darfur Peace and Accountability Act of 2006.[54]

President Obama has also issued important executive orders on foreign policy, both to direct how policy should be implemented and to order a new direction in policy. Two days after his inauguration, the president issued three executive orders dealing with foreign policy. One called for closing all overseas prisons operated by the CIA and halting certain interrogation methods for those suspected of terrorism; a second called for the closing of the U.S. prison at Guantanamo Bay within one year; and a third set up a task force to look at lawful options for handling those apprehended for suspected terrorist activities.

Although executive orders may deal with a large array of matters, many deal with significant foreign policy issues. Indeed, political scientists Kenneth Mayer and Kevin Price's analysis of such orders over a sixty-four-year period demonstrates this point.[55] Based on stringent criteria, they found that149 of the 1,028 executive orders sampled were "significant" in their effect on policy and society. Of those 149, moreover, we estimated that 58 (or 39 percent) dealt with foreign policy. Executive orders thus afford presidents yet another avenue of influence on foreign affairs.

Issuing Presidential Signing Statements According to Philip J. Cooper, "signing statements"

> are pronouncements issued by the president at the time a congressional enactment is signed that, in addition to providing general commentary on the bills, identify provisions of the legislation with which the president has concerns and (1) provide the president's interpretation of the language of the law, (2) announce constitutional

limits on the implementation of some of its provisions, or (3) indicate directions
to executive branch officials as to how to administer the new law in an acceptable
manner.[56]

Although such statements have been used by several recent administrations as a
way to assert presidential leadership, they have gained particular prominence since the
Reagan administration, obtained renewed significance during the George W. Bush
administration, and continue to be used by the Obama administration. In part, these
statements are viewed as a mechanism for incorporating the president's interpretation
of legislation into the history of a statute that has been enacted and as a way for the
president to provide direction in the law's implementation. As one analyst put it, the
signing statement acts as "a kind of a line-item veto."[57] Presidents defend their use as
simply part of carrying out their constitutional responsibility "to take care that the
laws be faithfully executed."[58]

As Cooper has catalogued, the Bush administration issued some 108 signing statements during its first term, raising 505 constitutional objections to various parts of
congressionally passed legislation. And these statements continued to be issued in its
second term as well. Of the 505 first-term constitutional objections in the first term,
we calculated that 177 of them dealt with foreign policy or national security matters.[59] By contrast, the Obama administration issued only 21 signing statements from
2009 through February 2012, and, by our judgment, 12 of these statements dealt with
foreign policy.[60]

Illustrations from the Bush and Obama administration will convey how the administration sought to specify the interpretation of legislation to serve its ends and to
challenge legislation it thought might hamper executive direction of foreign policy. In
his signing of Congress's renewal of the USA PATRIOT Act, President Bush declared
that he would "submit to the Congress recommendations for legislative actions," as
called for in the bill, only "in a manner consistent with the President's constitutional
authority to supervise the unitary executive branch and to recommend for the consideration of Congress such measures *as he judges necessary and expedient.*"[61] Similarly, in
signing the 2009 Omnibus Appropriations Act, for instance, President Obama claimed
that the foreign affairs provisions "unduly interfere with my constitutional authority . . .
by effectively directing the Executive on how to proceed or not to proceed in negotiations or discussion with international organizations and foreign governments." He went
on to assert that he "will not treat these provisions as limiting my ability to negotiate
and enter into agreements with foreign nations." In signing several pieces of legislations
dealing with defense policy in 2011, Obama repeatedly expressed his objections to restrictions placed on the administration on the transfer of Guantanamo detainees to the
United States or to foreign countries. For these pieces of legislation, he also objected
to requirements to share sensitive information with Congress, and to requirements
that the executive branch report to Congress on foreign policy actions that it was
undertaking. In one instance (in the National Defense Authorization Act for Fiscal
Year 2012), the president declared: "My administration will . . . interpret and implement [the section of the bill] in a manner that does not interfere with the President's
constitutional authority to conduct foreign affairs and avoids the undue disclosure of
sensitive diplomatic communications."[62]

We should emphasize that signing statements and presidential assertions do not
have the force of law per se; however, the apparent aim is to place them on the record as a way to make them part of the debate if legal challenges arise. They may
thus become important, given that the division of foreign policy power between the

president and Congress continues to be murky and ill-defined. Signing statements are yet another way for the president to assert and maintain his control of the direction of American actions abroad.

In sum, executive precedents in several areas—negotiating with and recognizing other states, withholding information from Congress, taking foreign policy actions, initiating wars or interventions, making unilateral commitments, and issuing executive orders and signing statements—have given operational meaning to the delegation of executive foreign policy powers as outlined in Article II of the Constitution.

Supreme Court Decisions

The Supreme Court has also aided the president in gaining ascendancy in the foreign policy arena by issuing decisions that, with few exceptions, have supported presidential claims to dominance. It has done so in two important ways. First the Court, particularly in the twentieth century, has largely ruled on the merits in favor of the executive over Congress on foreign policy matters. Second, and increasingly in recent decades, the Supreme Court and lower courts have refused to rule on cases challenging executive authority. They have done so either because the case under consideration raised political, not legal, questions (the "**political question doctrine**") or because the case was not ready for adjudication because not all avenues had been exhausted by Congress or the plaintiff (the **"ripeness" issue**).

Some Rulings Supporting the Executive   During the past century, when the Court decided foreign policy cases, it largely ruled in favor of the executive branch. In turn, these decisions became important precedents for other cases brought before it. We highlight four important court decisions from the first half of the twentieth century that illustrate the extent to which the Supreme Court has deferred to the president in matters dealing with international politics—even prior to America's extensive global involvement after World War II. We also discuss a ruling on the "**legislative veto**" from the 1980s that had significant implications for presidential foreign policy powers. By finding in support of the president in this ruling, the Court once again provided the president considerable latitude in policy making and weakened the role of Congress.

Curtiss-Wright   The most important and most sweeping grant of presidential dominance over foreign policy was set forth in the Supreme Court's decision in *U.S. v. Curtiss-Wright Export Corporation et al.* (1936).[63] In effect, this case gave special standing to the executive in foreign policy matters.

The case dealt with a joint congressional resolution that authorized the president to prohibit "the sale of arms and munitions of war . . . to those countries engaged . . . in armed conflict" in the Chaco region of South America (Bolivia and Paraguay) if he determined that such an embargo would contribute to peace. On May 28, 1934, President Franklin Roosevelt issued such a proclamation, putting the resolution into effect. Later, in November 1935, he revoked it with a similar proclamation. As a result of the original proclamation, however, the Curtiss-Wright Corporation was indicted on the charge that it conspired to sell fifteen machine guns to Bolivia beginning in May 1934.

Several issues were raised before the Supreme Court by Curtiss-Wright to deny any wrongdoing in this matter. The corporation contended that the joint resolution was an invalid delegation of legislative power, that it never became effective because of the failure of the president to find essential jurisdictional facts, and that the second proclamation (lifting the ban) ended the liability of the company under the joint resolution.[64] The Court rejected all of these arguments, but its reasoning on the first was the most important for enlarging presidential power in foreign affairs.

The Court held that the **delegation of power** to the executive—to apply the ban or not—was not unconstitutional because the issue dealt with a question of external, not internal, affairs. In these two areas, the Court said, the powers of delegation are different. In internal affairs, the federal government can exercise only those powers specifically enumerated in the Constitution (and such implied powers as are necessary and proper), but in the external area, such limitations do not apply. Because of America's separation from Great Britain, and as a result of being a member of the family of nations, the United States possesses external sovereignty and the powers associated with it. "The powers to declare and wage war, to conclude peace, to make treaties, to maintain diplomatic relations with other sovereignties, if they had never been mentioned in the Constitution, would have vested in the federal government as necessary concomitants of nationality."[65]

Most important, the Court held that the **president** was the **representative of sovereignty** ("the President alone has the power to speak or listen as a representative of the nation"). Therefore, his authority in foreign affairs goes beyond the actual constitutional delegation of power. Furthermore, the president is to be granted considerable discretion in his exercise of these powers as compared to the domestic arena.[66] In sum, *Curtiss-Wright* made clear that the president's power in foreign policy **could not be derived only from constitutional directives**; there were "extra-constitutional" powers tied to the sovereignty of the United States and the executive's role as the representative of that sovereignty. Subsequent cases and legal analyses have challenged this interpretation, but they have not fully undermined the notion of the executive's primacy in foreign affairs.[67]

Missouri v. Holland   The case of *Missouri v. Holland* (1920) clarified, and actually enlarged, the treaty powers given to the executive. In this case, the Court held that the president's powers could not be limited by any "invisible radiation" of the Tenth Amendment to the Constitution.[68] Put differently, the power of the president in making treaties was ensured against any intrusion by states' rights advocates.

The dispute involved the constitutionality of the Migratory Bird Act, which Congress passed pursuant to a treaty between the United States and Great Britain. Missouri contended that this act was void because Article I of the Constitution did not delegate the regulation of such birds to Congress; therefore, the states were reserved this power by the Tenth Amendment. In two earlier cases, moreover—before the treaty was signed—two U.S. district courts had voided such a congressional act, but the Court now decided differently, mainly because of the intervening treaty. Justice Oliver Wendell Holmes, in his opinion for the majority, wrote that "Acts of Congress are the supreme law of the land only when made in pursuance of the Constitution, while treaties are declared to be so when made under the authority of the United States. We do not mean to imply that there are no qualifications to the treaty-making power; they must be ascertained in a different way."[69]

As a result, Holmes acknowledged that the Constitution was silent on the regulation of migratory birds, but such silence was not sufficient to support Missouri's claim. Hence, such regulation was best left to the federal government. In addition, he held that "a treaty may override" the powers of the state.[70]

Missouri v. Holland was highly significant for the **powers of the national government versus state governments**, but it also aided the president by legitimizing his use of the treaty process to add to the constitutional framework, in conjunction with the Senate. Arguably, the Court's decision reduced the implied powers of the states and Congress because those powers could be overridden through the president's treaty power.

Belmont and Pink   *U.S. v. Belmont* (1937) and *U.S. v. Pink* (1942) dealt with the legal status of executive agreements.[71] The decisions in these cases gave the president additional means of enhancing his foreign policy powers.

The *Belmont* case involved whether the federal government could recover the bank account of an American national, August Belmont, who owned obligations belonging to a Russian company before the establishment of the Soviet Union. The accounts, held in the State of New York, were being claimed by the federal government because under the **Litvinov Agreement**—which established diplomatic relations between the United States and the Soviet Union—they had been assigned to it. The state courts had held that the federal government could not claim such accounts, but the Supreme Court held otherwise. Justice George Sutherland argued that the external powers of the United States must be exercised without regard to the constraint of state law or policies.

The *Pink* case, which also dealt with the legitimacy of the Litvinov Agreement and involved some of the same issues as the *Belmont* case, was an action brought by the U.S. government against the New York State Superintendent of Insurance (Pink) to acquire the remaining assets of the First Russian Insurance Company. When the Soviet Union was established, all properties—wherever located—were nationalized. Under the Litvinov Agreement, as we noted, these assets were assigned to the government. Pink claimed, however, that the nationalization action had "no territorial effect" and that the government's action was improper.[72] The Supreme Court disagreed, with Justice Douglas stating the Court's view in this forceful passage:

> We hold that the right to the funds or property in question became vested in the Soviet Government as the successor to the First Russian Insurance Co.; that this right has passed to the United States under the Litvinov Assignment; and that the United States is entitled to the property as against the corporation and the foreign creditors.[73]

The *Belmont* and *Pink* cases are important because the Litvinov Agreement was an executive agreement. Thus, the Court's decisions have been interpreted as giving legitimacy to executive agreements as the law of the land—without any congressional action—and giving them supremacy over the rights of an individual state (the State of New York in both cases). Once again, these cases strengthened the president's hand in the conduct of foreign affairs. Moreover, Louis Henkin argues that the language and reasoning in the *Belmont* and *Pink* cases were sufficiently general to apply to any executive agreement and to ensure its supremacy over any state law.[74]

INS v. Chadha   Perhaps the most recent sweeping court decision in the foreign policy area was *Immigration and Naturalization Service v. Chadha* (1983). In this case, the Supreme Court found the "one-house legislative veto" unconstitutional. At the time of the Chadha decision, at least fifty-six statutes contained one or more legislative vetoes, including several important ones involving foreign policy.[75] The decision thus had far-ranging implications for congressional–executive relations generally and foreign policy in particular. It also illustrated the Court's continuing deference to the executive branch, often at the expense of the legislative branch.

Originally devised in the 1930s, the legislative veto was a procedural device that allowed Congress "to relegate policy making authority to the executive branch in areas constitutionally delegated to the legislature," but also "allowed Congress to retain ultimate oversight in the form of a veto power."[76] This policy mechanism grew gradually until about 1960, but its incorporation into new legislation expanded rapidly thereafter, and foreign policy and defense legislation was hardly immune to its impact. Although the legislative veto did not appear in foreign policy legislation until the 1950s and early 1960s, immigration and defense legislation had contained such vetoes since the 1940s.[77]

The legislative veto works in this way: Congress would explicitly incorporate a provision in a piece of legislation that allowed it to stop or modify the executive's subsequent implementation of the statute simply by declaring its objection. The legislative branch could register its "veto" of executive action in several ways, depending on how the statute was written: (1) passage by a single chamber by a simple majority; (2) passage by both chambers by a simple majority (a concurrent resolution in this case); or (3) in some instances, passage by a committee in Congress by a simple majority.[78] The most important point is that none of these mechanisms allowed the executive to approve or disapprove the action. When the legislative veto was incorporated within an act of Congress, Congress could pass legislation and then, unilaterally, monitor and modify its implementation by the executive branch. In this sense, congressional power was gained at the expense of executive power.

The *Chadha* case involved an East Indian student, born in Kenya and holding a British passport, who overstayed his student nonimmigrant visa and was ordered deported by the INS. He appealed the deportation, and his deportation was suspended by immigration authorities. By a provision incorporated into previous immigration legislation, however, Congress (either the House or the Senate) could pass a simple majority resolution objecting to this suspension. In this case, the House did so, in effect calling for Chadha's deportation promptly.

Once the case reached the Supreme Court, a majority of the justices held that this "legislative veto" in the earlier legislation was invalid for two important constitutional reasons. It violated the **presentment clause** of the Constitution.[79] That is, "every Bill which shall have passed the House of Representatives and the Senate, shall, before it becomes a Law, be presented to the President of the United States" for his consideration. Such a presentment did not occur in this case because the House acted unilaterally to rescind the action of the executive branch. Second, it violated the **principle of bicameralism** (that is, all legislation must be passed by majorities in both the House and the Senate).[80] As such, the legislative veto could not stand.

Although the *Chadha* decision dealt only with the "one-House" legislative veto, the Supreme Court expanded its decision about two weeks later by declaring the "two-house" veto unconstitutional as well.[81] Because the legislative veto was a prominent device used by Congress in the 1970s and early 1980s to rein in executive power in foreign affairs (as we shall discuss in Chapter 8), *Chadha* has had considerable impact on the extent of congressional resurgence against executive power.

Some Rulings Challenging the Executive Although the president has usually gotten his way with the Court on foreign policy questions, we need to highlight important instances in which he has not. One important case in the 1950s, two in the

1970s, and three in the post-9/11 era fit into this category. Still, even these successful challenges have been overshadowed by the precedents from earlier cases and the nonrulings in favor of the president in numerous others (as we discuss shortly). Furthermore, the basis for deciding against the president in some recent cases appeared less an effort to reduce his powers and more an effort to maintain some fundamental American freedoms for citizens and noncitizens.

Youngstown Sheet & Tube Co. et al. v. Sawyer Unlike the earlier cases, the Supreme Court's decision in the *Youngstown* case restricted the foreign policy powers of the president, especially as they seemed to intrude into domestic policy. In so deciding, the Court thus preserved a foreign policy role for Congress in some areas. In particular, *Youngstown*, decided in 1952, addressed the question of whether the chief executive and commander-in-chief clauses of the Constitution enabled the president to seize control of the nation's steel mills to avert a national strike and protect national security at the time of the Korean War. President Truman had made just such a claim, issuing an executive order to his secretary of commerce (Sawyer) to take over the steel mills. The Court held that such action was unconstitutional. Justice Hugo Black wrote in the majority opinion for the Court that there was **no statutory authorization** for such action:

> The President's power, if any, to issue the order must stem either from an act of Congress or from the Constitution. There is no statute that expressly authorizes the president to take possession of property as he did here. Nor is there any act of Congress to which our attention has been directed from which such a power can fairly be implied.[82]

Likewise, he contended that there was **no constitutional basis** for such an action:

> The order cannot properly be sustained as an exercise of the President's military power as Commander in Chief of the Armed Forces. . . . Even though "theater of war" be an expanding concept, we cannot with faithfulness to our constitutional system hold that the Commander in Chief of the Armed Forces has the ultimate power as such to take possession of private property in order to keep labor disputes from stopping production. . . . Nor can the seizure order be sustained because of the several constitutional provisions that grant executive power to the President.[83]

In sum, *Youngstown* made clear that there are indeed limits on the foreign policy powers of the president. This decision stands in contrast to those of earlier cases that largely deferred to the president's authority and afforded him wide discretion as well.

New York Times v. United States and U.S. v. Nixon These two presidential defeats from the 1970s are arguably less sweeping in their implications for foreign policy than *Youngstown*, but they, too, convey important limitations on executive power. In *New York Times v. United States* (1971), popularly known as the *Pentagon Papers* case, the Court held that the executive's claims of national security could not stop the publication of documents chronicling American involvement in Southeast Asia during the Vietnam War. First-amendment freedoms proved to be more persuasive than any immediate national security needs. In *U.S. v. Nixon* (1974), the Court decided that President Nixon must turn over tape recordings and records dealing with the Watergate investigation. The Supreme Court held that "neither the separation of powers nor the confidentiality of executive communications barred the federal courts from access to presidential tapes needed as evidence in a criminal case." At the same time, the Court was less than precise over whether specific claims of "national security" would have led to another result. As Chief Justice Warren Burger put it, the president did not "claim . . . [a] need to protect military, diplomatic, or sensitive national secrets," as such.[84]

Hamdi v. Rumsfeld, Hamdan v. Rumsfeld et al., and Boumediene et al. v. Bush et al.

Three recent cases, adjudicated in the context of the Bush administration's war on terrorism, also ruled that there are limitations on foreign policy actions by the executive and that individual liberties still must be protected in such circumstances.

In *Hamdi v. Rumsfeld* (2004), the Supreme Court ruled that a U.S. citizen "held in the United States as an **enemy combatant** be given a meaningful opportunity to contest the factual basis for that detention before a neutral decisionmaker." The case involved Yaser Esam Hamdi, who was born in Louisiana but had moved to Saudi Arabia at a young age. He eventually ended up in Afghanistan, where he was captured in the post–9/11 period in 2001 by a group fighting the Taliban. He was subsequently transferred to the American base at Guantanamo Bay in Cuba and held as an "enemy combatant." When the government learned that he was an American citizen, Hamdi was transferred to the United States in 2002. A habeas corpus petition was filed on his behalf, contending that he was being held in violation of the Fifth and Fourteenth amendments to the Constitution because he was not given sufficient judicial review or due process to challenge his status.

The district court essentially ruled in Hamdi's favor by noting that the government's evidence for detaining him was insufficient. The appeals court overturned that decision, but the U.S. Supreme Court reversed the appeals court, ruling that the **Authorization for Use of Military Force Resolution (AUMF)** resolution passed by Congress was sufficient authority to hold Hamdi as an "enemy combatant." At the same time, it also ruled that a U.S. citizen held as such must "be given a meaningful opportunity" to challenge his detention.[85] In other words, due process must be respected for an American citizen in the context of the war on terrorism.

In *Hamdan v. Rumsfeld* (2006), the Supreme Court ruled that Salim Ahmed Hamdan, a Yemeni national being held at Guantanamo Bay after his capture in Afghanistan in 2001, could not be put on trial before a military commission (or tribunal) for conspiracy charges brought against him. The Court ruled in Hamdan's favor because the proposed military commissions violated the **Uniform Code of Military Justice (UCMJ)** and the **Geneva Conventions**. Under the proposed military commission trial, Hamdan and his counsel would be excluded from discovery of evidence to be presented against him except for that provided at the discretion of the presiding officer. Thus, this commission would not be in compliance with the UCMJ. Furthermore, Common Article 3 of the Geneva Conventions applied to Hamdan, and the proposed military commission would not comply with the requirements of that article. Finally, the Court held that "neither the AUMF [Authorization for the Use of Military Force Resolution passed immediately after 9/11] nor the DTA [Detainee Treatment Act of 2005] could be read to provide specific, overriding authorization for the commission convened to try Hamdan."[86] In other words, the protection of individual rights— including a fair trial—trumped any foreign policy powers that the executive branch might seek to imply from these acts of Congress.

In *Boumediene et al. v. Bush et al.* (2008), the Supreme Court ruled by a 5–4 margin that detainees captured in Afghanistan and elsewhere and held as "enemy combatants" at Guantanamo Bay in Cuba were entitled to a habeas corpus hearing (challenging why they were being held) in federal court, much as any American citizen would have this privilege under the Constitution.[87] Plaintiffs in this case were challenging two previously passed legislative acts, the Detainee Treatment Act of 2005 and the Military Commissions Act of 2006, which prohibited enemy combatants from appealing their detention in federal court, permitting them only the military procedures outlined in the acts as legal recourse.

In the Court's ruling, the majority found that the detainees were "entitled to the habeas privilege" and that the alternative procedures established under the Detainee Treatment Act were "not an adequate and effective substitute for the habeas writ."[88] Moreover, the section of the Military Commission Act that followed those procedures in suspending the writ of habeas corpus was found to be unconstitutional. Thus, enemy combatants held in American custody were entitled to this same constitutional protection as citizens.

In short, these three cases reveal the limits of presidential powers—even during a period of deep concern about international terrorism—and some of the issues in them remain in contention in other cases to this day. Perhaps most significantly they reveal the ongoing tension between the pursuit of national security and the protection of individual rights.

Nonrulings Supporting the President   A second important way in which the Court has supported the executive on foreign policy has been through *nonrulings*— that is, decisions not to rule on cases brought before it. In doing so, it has allowed executive actions that have already been taken to stand.

One justification for the Court's adoption of this nondecision posture is the **"political question" doctrine**. In effect, the Court has held that the issue before it is a political, not a legal or constitutional, dispute between the branches of government—normally between Congress and the presidency—and hence is not subject to judicial remedy. Although the basis for this doctrine is not well developed or wholly understood in constitutional law, it has been invoked many times under differing circumstances:

- When the Court believed it lacked the authority to decide the case because the constitutionally prescribed activities of another branch of government were involved

- When the effective solution involved a political remedy that would favor one branch of government over another

- When the Court wanted to avoid a question brought before it[89]

Another justification for nondecisions on foreign policy cases is the **"ripeness criterion."** Here the Court has claimed that when members of Congress, for example, file suit against the president over the use of force abroad or the abrogation of a treaty, they must first use all available avenues within the political system (the legislative process and legislative routes) before pursuing a legal challenge. Only then may the issue be appropriate for judicial judgment.

In several cases, the political question and ripeness criteria have been invoked as reasons for not ruling in particular cases. A brief discussion of some of them will reveal the Court's rationale in each instance. In particular, the discussion will reveal how these nondecisions have strengthened the president's hand in the use of force as commander in chief and in the use of his treaty powers as chief diplomat.

The first prominent case deals with the breaking of the 1954 Mutual Defense Treaty with the Republic of China (Taiwan) as part of the process of establishing diplomatic relations with the People's Republic of China. In *Goldwater et al. v. Carter* (1979), several senators charged that President Carter could not terminate this treaty without either a two-thirds majority of the Senate or a majority of both houses. The Supreme Court, however, divided along several lines in rendering its judgment. Four justices held that the case was "**nonjusticiable**" because it involved a political issue; another said that is was not ripe for court action because Congress, as a body, had taken no formal action to challenge the president; and one decided the case on the merits and argued that the president acted within his constitutional power to recognize states.[90] The upshot of this ruling was to dismiss the challenge to the president and his treaty powers.

Several attempts were made to challenge the constitutionality of the Vietnam War in the 1970s, but in virtually all instances the Court refused to hear these cases because it judged them as dealing with **a political question** between the two branches.[91] Much the same reasoning, albeit with an exception or two, prevailed in the cases dealing with presidential military actions in El Salvador (*Crockett v. Reagan*, 1983), Grenada (*Conyers v. Reagan*, 1985), and the Persian Gulf (*Lowry v. Reagan*, 1987) during the 1980s and brought by members of Congress against the executive.[92] In those instances, the court held that the issue was nonjusticiable because it was a "political question" between the branches or that the court lacked jurisdiction to decide the case. In all instances, presidential action prevailed, and the congressional challenges failed.

In *Dellums v. Bush* (1990), a case involving the president's war-making powers, the decisions by the courts largely followed these precedents. In this case, fifty-four members of Congress sought a federal injunction to negate President Bush's right to go to war against Iraq without a congressional declaration of war or some congressional authorization. The federal district court in Washington, D.C., heard the case but ruled against the plaintiffs. The judge held that the issue was **not "ripe" for decision** because Congress as a body had not taken a formal stand on whether it wanted President Bush to seek a congressional authorization. Although both leaving the door open for such a decision if Congress acted and rejecting the executive's claim that the courts could not intrude into "political question" disputes, the judge's ruling still did not formally restrict executive power in this area.[93]

More recently, similar arguments were made in deciding important cases in the Clinton, Bush, and Obama administrations. In *Campbell v. Clinton* (2000), thirty-one members of Congress challenged President Clinton's decision to use American forces in the 1999 campaign against Yugoslavia in Kosovo. They claimed that the president violated the War Powers Resolution and the war powers granted to Congress by the Constitution. The district court dismissed the suit because, it argued, the plaintiffs lacked standing to sue. The appeals court concurred, ruling that the members could have sought other remedies, such as passing a law to stop the operation in Kosovo, cutting off funding, or even impeaching the president, but Congress as a body had not pursued these options.[94] In *Doe v. Bush* (2003), twelve House members, three service members, and fifteen military parents filed a lawsuit to halt the Bush administration from starting the Iraq War, arguing that the October 2002 Authorization for the Use of Military Force Against Iraq Resolution (AUFM) was an unconstitutional delegation to the executive of congressional power to declare war and that the administration's invasion of Iraq exceeded that resolution as well. In February 2003, a federal district court dismissed the case, ruling that a nonjusticiable political question was involved. Later, in March 2003, a U.S. Court of Appeals ruled that the case was not ripe for judicial review, but it did find that the 2002 congressional resolution "did not constitute an unlawful delegation of Congress's constitutional authority."[95]

In another case, *Mohamed et al. v. Jeppesen Dataplan, Inc.* (2010), a suit was filed against Jeppesen Dataplan, a subsidiary of Boeing, on behalf of individuals who were subjected to "rendition" by the American government. Rendition involved a program by the U.S. government "to gather intelligence by apprehending foreign nationals suspected of involvement in terrorist activities and transferring them in secret to foreign countries for detention and interrogation." Jeppesen Dataplan was accused of providing "flight planning and logistical support services to the aircraft and crew" for the flights involving the five plaintiffs. The original lawsuit was filed in 2007 and the Bush administration invoked the "states secrets privilege," seeking dismissal on that ground. The lawsuit went through several appeals, and the Obama administration became involved by 2009, also invoking the states secrets privilege. In September 2010, the 9th Circuit Court of Appeals decided for the government, and the Supreme Court refused to hear the case.[96] Once again, the president's position prevailed on a foreign policy issue.

Whereas the *Youngstown Steel* case seemed to argue strongly for a more balanced interpretation of constitutional powers over foreign policy, many cases over the past three decades reflect the extent to which the Supreme Court and other federal jurisdictions continue to defer to the executive, often at the expense of Congress. When "Congress is formally or clearly opposed" to the president, constitutional analyst Gordon Silverstein argues, "the Court will support Congress."[97] Increasingly, however, the Court is demanding clearer and clearer direction when Congress seeks to do so. If it does not exhaust all avenues to assert its power (satisfying the ripeness criterion) or is at all unclear in its legislative intent or ambiguous in the language that delegates authority to the president, the Court is likely to support the executive.

Congressional Deference and Delegation

A third factor that has added to presidential preeminence in foreign policy has been the degree of congressional support for presidential initiatives, particularly since World War II. Indeed, Congress has sometimes gone further than giving its support, on occasion delegating to him some of its foreign policy prerogatives. A brief survey of this phenomenon will illustrate how the president's foreign policy control has been strengthened by congressional support and how it has changed recently.

Congressional Leadership Legislative support for the president in foreign policy can be seen in the statements and policy actions of members of both houses of Congress. This support has often been couched in a commitment to bipartisanship. **"Politics stops at the water's edge"** was a frequent post–World War II refrain. This tradition of bipartisanship probably dates from the pledge of Senator Arthur Vandenberg, chairman of the Senate Foreign Relations Committee, to support President Truman in his foreign policy efforts immediately after World War II. The **Vandenberg Resolution**, for example, worked out in close consultation with the Department of State and passed in June 1948, called on the executive branch to proceed with the development of the North Atlantic Treaty and with the reforms of the United Nations. But what it also did was usher in an era of congressional–executive cooperation in the making of foreign policy. Throughout this era, and to this day, the president has generally taken the initiative, which Congress has often legitimized.[98]

Leaders of Congress, and particularly leaders of the foreign affairs committees in both House and Senate, have often—until relatively recently—viewed their role primarily as carrying out the president's wishes in foreign policy. Thomas (Doc) Morgan, chair of the House Foreign Affairs Committee from 1959 to 1976, stated this view directly: "Under the Constitution, the President is made responsible for the conduct of our foreign relations. . . ." He saw himself as "only the quarterback not the coach of the team." Moreover, congressional scholar Richard Fenno reports that Morgan saw his committee, "in *all* matters, as the subordinate partners in a permanent alliance with the executive branch. And as far as he is concerned, the group's blanket, all purpose decision rule should be: support all executive branch proposals."[99]

Senator J. William Fulbright, chair of the Senate Foreign Relations Committee from 1959 to 1974, also enunciated this commitment to bipartisanship, at least until 1965. As Morgan had done, Fulbright relied on a football analogy to express his support of, and deference to, the president: "No football team can expect to win with every man his own quarterback. . . . The Foreign Relations Committee is available to advise the President, but his is the primary responsibility."[100] Although the bipartisanship of Fulbright and the Senate Foreign Relations Committee waned with America's deepening involvement in Vietnam during the 1960s, the committee's tradition of support for the president was not entirely abandoned by subsequent leaders.

Nonetheless, by the early 1980s, Senator Charles Percy, a former chair of the Senate Foreign Relations Committee, lamented the "partisan gap" that had developed over foreign policy and renewed the call for bipartisanship "if the United States is to maintain a leadership role in the world."[101] Speakers of the House Thomas P. ("Tip") O'Neill and Jim Wright clashed bitterly with the Reagan administration over Central American policy in the 1980s. Sending American forces into Lebanon and exchanging arms for hostages with Iran and transferring profits to the Nicaraguan contras (the so-called Iran–Contra affair) further weakened congressional support for executive action. The establishment of two committees in 1987 to hold hearings on executive decision making during the Iran–Contra affair reflected the suspicion with which Congress held the president's explanation of this whole episode.

Throughout these years of confrontation, calls for bipartisanship and for greater executive prerogatives in foreign affairs were never completely silenced by congressional debate over alleged executive abuses. Indeed, President George H. W. Bush called for the "old bipartisanship" in his 1989 inaugural address. Some congressional leaders were responsive to this call, and proposals were made for increasing consultation between the White House and Congress through monthly meetings to review foreign policy issues, for congressional changes in the foreign aid bill to allow greater presidential flexibility in implementing it, and even for loosening the restrictiveness of the War Powers Resolution.[102] Although none of these could lessen the suspicions of the immediate past, they do suggest the inclination of congressional leaders to defer to the president on foreign policy.

The chair of the House Foreign Affairs Committee at the time, Dante Fascell, generally applauded this bipartisan renewal, but he also wanted the democratic process to work. In his view, "a bipartisan foreign policy does not mean a unilateral decision by the president, rubber-stamped by the Congress."[103] Fascell's successor, Lee Hamilton of Indiana, largely adopted this view on relations between Congress and the White House. He was committed to making the constitutional system work, but he conveyed traditional congressional deference to the foreign policy powers of the executive: "I do not fool myself about the role of Congress on foreign policy. It is an important actor, but presidential leadership is by far the most important ingredient in a successful foreign policy. Only the president can lead. . . . We in the Congress . . . can help and support him."[104] After the 1994 elections, however, new Republican congressional foreign affairs leadership was much less willing to defer to a Democratic president. Both Senator Jesse Helms, chair of the Senate Foreign Relations Committee, and Congressman Benjamin A. Gilman, chair of the House International Relations Committee, offered legislation to restructure the foreign affairs bureaucracy within the executive branch and proposed significant cuts in American foreign assistance. In this sense, any automatic deference toward presidential leadership seemed to be waning.

With the 2000 election of President George W. Bush, the Republican leadership in the House and the Senate was ready to defer to executive leadership on foreign policy matters. After the events of September 11, the Democratic leadership in both houses, Richard Gephardt (House minority leader), and Tom Daschle (Senate majority leader) were also quick to endorse President Bush's actions against international terrorism. The leaders of the key foreign policy committees in the House and the Senate at the time were equally supportive. By 2003, that leadership support, especially in the principal foreign policy committees, began to fray as reconstruction efforts in Iraq unraveled, human rights abuses there were revealed, and sectarian violence escalated. Moreover, with the loss of Republican control of the House and the Senate in the 2006 elections, support was further weakened, and congressional challenges became the hallmark of Democratic and even some Republican leaders. These challenges came from both the House and the Senate, and various measures were introduced and voted on to oppose the direction of American foreign policy in Iraq.

Despite Obama's substantial presidential election victory in 2008, partisan and leadership divisions on foreign policy have arguably increased, not declined, in recent years. To be sure, some congressional leaders in the foreign policy realm have expressed support for presidential actions, such as the killing of Osama bin Laden and for the post–2014 agreement reached for American assistance with Afghanistan, but partisan critiques of the administration's foreign policy have been more the norm, whether over the conditions involving the departure of American forces from Iraq at the end of 2011; the administration's policy toward Iran, Russia, and Israel; or the nuclear arms agreement with Russia. Deference to presidential leadership on foreign policy has declined sharply from the period immediately after the events of September 11.

In short, rhetorical (and actual) support for bipartisanship had waned considerably by the first decade of the twenty-first century. Yet the ability of the Congress to take legislative action to alter the direction of foreign policy has also generally proved to be elusive.

Supportive Legislative Behavior Although the bipartisanship call by congressional leaders over the years indicates deference to the president on foreign policy, a true indicator is congressional action on executive branch proposals. Aaron Wildavsky, in a classic 1966 article on the presidency, documented the level of congressional support for presidential initiatives and contended that, "In the realm of foreign policy there has not been a single major issue on which Presidents, when they were serious and determined, have failed."[105]

Wildavsky went on to demonstrate that on presidential proposals to Congress during the **1948–1964** period of his study, the president prevailed **about 70 percent** of the time **on defense and foreign policy** matters but **only 40 percent** of the time **on domestic matters**.[106] Thus, the president not only was successful on foreign policy with Congress but was also 75 percent more effective than on domestic policy. In this sense, Congress has been highly supportive of the president's wishes on issues beyond the water's edge. By Wildavsky's argument, there are "two presidencies"—one highly successful on foreign policy with Congress; another constantly in debate and conflict with Congress on domestic policy.

Other studies have shown that this extraordinary support for the president in foreign policy remained into the 1970s and beyond, a period sometimes described as producing a congressional "revolution" in foreign affairs. Lance LeLoup and Steven Shull, for instance, demonstrate that congressional approval of presidential foreign policy initiatives remained high from 1965 to 1975, although the average level of support had decreased to about 55 percent from 70 percent from 1948 to 1964.[107] They also report that a difference remained between congressional approval of foreign policy and domestic policy (55 percent compared to 46 percent on average). When LeLoup and Shull categorized the domestic policy questions into social welfare, agriculture, government management, natural resources, and civil liberties, presidential proposals in the foreign and defense area still received greater congressional support than any other individual issue.[108] In another study, Richard Fleisher and Jon Bond found that presidential foreign policy success remained substantial in both the House and the Senate through the Reagan years, although Nixon and Ford did not garner as much support as did other administrations. Similarly, Carter and Reagan did not do as well in the House as they did in the Senate compared to earlier presidents.[109]

In our calculation of the degree of presidential success from Truman to Obama on foreign policy voting in Congress, we also found that recent presidents have been enormously successful in gaining approval for issues on which they took a position. Table 7.3 shows the results of these calculations. **Overall, presidential success has been greater**, on average, **in the Senate than in the House**, but both chambers have been supportive of presidential votes. In the Senate, presidents (from Truman through Bush) averaged an 80 percent success rate, whereas in the House, they won about 69 percent of the time.[110]

Changing Legislative Behavior? Foreshadowing our discussion of congressional resurgence in the next chapter, though, increasing evidence shows congressional support for the president on foreign policy matters has waned over the years. According to political scientist Lee Sigelman, when one examines "key votes" the degree of support for the president began to decline in 1973, especially among the party in opposition to the president.[111] Moreover, he suggests that despite what Wildavsky and others contend, the difference in congressional support for presidential initiatives on foreign policy versus domestic policy, based on key votes, was small from 1957 to 1972 (74 percent versus 73 percent) and widened only slightly from 1973 to 1978 (60 percent versus 57 percent).[112] Thus, for Sigelman, the argument for greater congressional support on foreign policy matters versus domestic matters is not demonstrable when key votes are examined. Nonetheless, congressional support for the president's foreign policy agenda even on key votes was still very high, at least until 1973.

The analysis of LeLoup and Shull, along with our own analyses, provides additional evidence that executive success with Congress has weakened somewhat in recent years. LeLoup and Shull demonstrate that congressional approval of the foreign policy initiatives of Nixon and Ford was considerably lower than that of Eisenhower, Kennedy, and Johnson,[113] which shows that congressional deference began to wane in

Table 7.3 Presidential Victories on Foreign Policy Votes in the Congress: From Harry S. Truman to Barack Obama

Administration	House		Senate	
Truman	68%	(*N*=78)	77%	(*N*=110)
Eisenhower	85	(*N*=94)	88	(*N*=217)
Kennedy	89	(*N*=47)	88	(*N*=109)
Johnson	86	(*N*=111)	81	(*N*=231)
Nixon	75	(*N*=85)	80	(*N*=181)
Ford	59	(*N*=46)	76	(*N*=106)
Carter	75	(*N*=180)	85	(*N*=215)
Reagan	64	(*N*=275)	84	(*N*=325)
Bush (G. H. W.)	48	(*N*=132)	77	(*N*=127)
Clinton	47	(*N*=217)	72	(*N*=136)
Bush (G. W.)	60	(*N*=155)	77	(*N*=150)
Obama (through 2011)	79	(*N*=75)	91	(*N*=47)

Note: Entries are the percentage of presidential victories on congressional foreign policy votes on which the president took a position.

Sources: Calculated by the author and Eugene R. Wittkopf, of Louisiana State University, from congressional roll calls made available by the Inter-University Consortium for Political and Social Research and from reported votes in *Congressional Quarterly Weekly Reports* and *CQ Weekly* (various issues) through Clinton's first term. Nick Lauen, Kirk Galster, Bob Beyer, and Yong Cho assisted in collecting and coding the data for the G.W. Bush and Obama years. The president's position was based on *Congressional Quarterly Almanac* (various years), *Congressional Quarterly Weekly Reports* (various issues), and *CQ Weekly* (various issues) assessments for Eisenhower through Obama and was determined for Truman by a survey of *Congressional Quarterly Almanac* and presidential papers in collaboration with Eugene R. Wittkopf of Louisiana State University.

the 1970s. Fleisher and his colleagues have updated this analysis through Clinton's first term, and they conclude that "the level of success for minority party presidents [those whose party does not control Congress] on foreign and defense votes has declined to such low levels that it leads us to question the continued utility of trying to explain presidential-congressional relations . . . in terms of a two presidencies model."[114] (Also see Table 7.3 for a largely similar pattern for most recent administrations.)

This weakening of presidential success, however, is confined more to the House than to the Senate. Note that President Ford's success rate was only 59 percent in the House and Carter's was 75 percent; however, Reagan's reached only 64 percent, George H. W. Bush's reached 48 percent, and Clinton's reached 47 percent. In the Senate, by contrast, Carter and Reagan actually had about the same success rate as earlier presidents, although Ford's and Bush's were a bit lower. During its eight years, the Clinton administration's support was only 72 percent, the lowest of any administration since the end of World War II.

During the George W. Bush and Obama administrations, however, presidential foreign policy success bucked these recent trends, with congressional support returning to earlier higher levels. Bush received between 68 and 89 percent support in the House during the first three Congresses of his administration (with his support falling to 34 percent in the last Congress with Democratic control of that chamber) and 72 to 79 percent support in the Senate across the four Congresses of his administration. On average, though, as Table 7.3 shows, he had 60 percent support overall in the House and 77 percent support in the Senate, averages that still were somewhat higher than recent presidents. Obama's administration has done even better during the first three years of its time in office. In the 111th Congress (2009–2010), President Obama was successful on 86 percent of his foreign policy votes in the House and 94 percent of his votes in the Senate. Even with Republican control of the House in the first year of the 112th Congress (2011), his administration won on 68 percent of the foreign policy votes in that chamber and had an 85 percent success rate in the Senate. It remains to be seen, of course, whether this level of support will be sustained for future presidents, but these results do highlight the degree of deference that presidents continue to receive from Congress on foreign policy issues.

Another changing aspect of congressional behavior on foreign policy questions has been the impact of partisanship and ideology on congressional behavior. Analyses of congressional voting patterns on the antiballistic missile issue in the late 1960s and early 1970s, the Panama Canal Treaties in the late 1970s, the call for a nuclear freeze, the B-1 bomber debate, and the fight over aid to the Nicaraguan Contras in the 1980s all demonstrate that ideology in particular was a potent factor in individual members' votes, seemingly more important than presidential influence.[115] Votes on the Persian Gulf War, the North American Free Trade Agreement, and the Comprehensive Test-Ban Treaty in the 1990s also elicited partisan and ideological responses. Over the past decade, too, votes on altering the course in the Iraq War, challenging Obama over his Libyan policy, or approving free trade agreements have followed a similar course. Clearly, partisanship (and ideology) on foreign policy has begun to hold sway, much as Fleisher and his colleagues predicted and as others have reported.[116]

The originator of the **"two presidencies" thesis** recognized the substantial change in relations between Congress and the White House over the years. In a 1989 co-authored study, Aaron Wildavsky acknowledged that his earlier (1960s) argument was "time and culture bound." As the public and political parties have become more ideological, the building of bipartisan support for the president has become much more difficult in the current era. Yet Wildavsky and his co-author, Duane Oldfield, argue that the president has other means of exercising his power, much as our survey here suggests.[117] Overall, though, the foreign policy debate has become much more politicized than in it was the past.

Although we can surely conclude that there has been some change in congressional deference to the executive and in the level of conflict on foreign policy questions, **presidential success remains pronounced**. As a result, and as we will demonstrate more fully in Chapter 8, specific areas of foreign policy did elicit changes in congressional procedures in dealing with the executive, albeit with limited success.

Legislative Delegation   Not only has Congress shown its deference by its approval of presidential actions but it also has occasionally gone further, granting or delegating some of its own powers to the executive. This has most notably occurred in the president's use of armed forces as he sees fit, in the distribution of foreign aid, and in the implementation of trade policy. In effect, these delegations have transferred to the executive some congressional responsibility.

The transfer of power has been most dramatic since the end of World War II, especially in permitting the use of American armed forces at the president's discretion. In the **Formosa Resolution** in January 1955, Congress granted to President Eisenhower the power to use armed forces to defend Quemoy and Matsu from attack by Chinese Communists and to protect Formosa and the Pescadores Islands. Its language was quite sweeping in its tone: "the President of the United States is authorized to employ the Armed Forces of the United States *as he deems necessary. . . .*"[118]

Congress also granted President Eisenhower a broad mandate to deal with the threat of international communism in the Middle East. Popularly called the Eisenhower Doctrine, this congressional resolution appeared to give the president the right "to use armed forces to assist any such nation or group of nations requesting assistance against armed aggression from any country controlled by international communism."[119] Once again, what was so significant about this resolution was the apparently broad grant of power given to the executive in the making of war, although Congress slightly weakened this power by requiring the threatened country to request assistance and by declaring that the United States (not the president per se) "is prepared to use armed forces to assist" it. Furthermore, Eisenhower pledged to keep Congress informed about these activities.[120]

Another prominent grant of war making to the executive was the **Gulf of Tonkin Resolution**, approved by the House on a vote of 416–0 and by the Senate on a vote of 89–2 in August 1964 at the beginning of substantial American involvement in Vietnam. This resolution granted the president the right "to take all necessary steps, including the use of armed forces, to assist any member or protocol state of the Southeast Asia Collective Defense Treaty requesting assistance. . . ."[121] Moreover, the determination as to when to use these forces was left to the president, albeit with this expressed prior congressional approval in the resolution. The Gulf of Tonkin Resolution was eventually viewed as the "functional equivalent" of war by the Johnson administration and was used to expand American involvement in Vietnam and Southeast Asia in the 1960s.[122]

This same pattern of delegation occurred in the wake of the terrorist attacks of September 11, when both houses of Congress quickly passed a sweeping resolution granting President Bush broad military power to respond to the attacks and to pursue international terrorists. By **Public Law 107–40**,

> the president is authorized to use all necessary and appropriate force against those nations, organizations, or persons he determines planned, authorized, committed, or aided the terrorist attacks that occurred on September 11, 2001, or harbored such organizations or persons, in order to prevent any future acts of international terrorism against the United States by such nations, organizations, or persons.[123]

Much like the Gulf of Tonkin Resolution, P.L. 107–40 was overwhelmingly approved by the House (420–1) and by the Senate (98–0).

About a year later, Congress passed **Public Law 107–243** granting the president the authority to take military action against Iraq. The operative section once again afforded the president wide latitude:

> The President is authorized to use the Armed Forces of the United States *as he determines to be necessary and appropriate* [emphasis added] in order to (1) defend the national security . . . against the continuing threat posed by Iraq; and (2) enforce all relevant United Nations Security Council resolutions regarding Iraq.[124]

In both chambers, the resolution was passed by wide margins, although not as wide as with some others. In the House, the vote was 296–133; in the Senate, 77–23.

Beyond these dramatic war-making resolutions, Congress has tended to grant to the executive considerable discretion in implementing trade and foreign assistance statutes. For example, foreign assistance legislation over the years has allowed the president, "on such terms and conditions as he may determine," to provide economic support funds ". . . to promote economic or political stability," and provide military assistance that "will strengthen the security of the United States." Although this legislation imposed restrictions on the executive, considerable residual presidential authority remains.[125]

Indeed, the congressional delegation of trade responsibility to the president predates the Cold War, going back at least to the **Reciprocal Trade Agreements Act of 1934**. Under that act, the president was authorized to negotiate and implement tariff reductions of as much as 50 percent without congressional involvement. Delegation also occurred in subsequent reciprocal trade acts into the 1950s.[126] More recently, the Trade Act of 1974 and the Trade Act of 1979 authorized the president to negotiate the elimination of nontariff barriers as well. In the Omnibus Trade and Competitiveness Act of 1988, the president's prerogatives were reaffirmed in negotiating and implementing trade legislation through authorization to enter into tariff agreements, both bilaterally and multilaterally, and to change U.S. tariff schedules if he "determines such action to be in the interest of the United States." The legislation gave more power to the U.S. trade representative in implementing many of the provisions, but of course this representative is responsible to the president.[127] Congressional approval of the **North American Free Trade Agreement (NAFTA)** and American entry into the **World Trade Organizations (WTO)** yielded even more control over trade policy to the executive. The only exception in the WTO approval was a review mechanism mandating withdrawal from the organization under specified conditions.[128]

Another piece of congressional legislation, passed in the late 1970s and still in effect, had even broader implications than some of those discussed so far. Under the International Emergency Economic Powers Act, the president was authorized to declare a national emergency to deal with any "extraordinary threat, which has its source in whole or substantial part outside the United States, to the national security, foreign policy, or economy of the United States" and to "investigate, regulate, or prohibit" a wide array of largely economic actions.[129] However, this grant of authority was conditioned on several requirements dealing with consulting and reporting to Congress, and thus its seemingly broad sweep was actually to be more restrictive than what earlier legislation dating back to the Roosevelt era had allowed. Yet subsequent Supreme Court decisions in the early 1980s weakened Congress's role and, in the estimation of one analyst, "freed the president . . . to conduct widespread economic warfare merely by declaring a national emergency with respect to a particular country. . . ."[130]

Part of this authority is understandable in that individual cases could arise that Congress could not have foreseen or might not have the time or inclination to handle expeditiously. In this light, presidential discretion was reasonable because the president's responsibility was to execute the law. At the same time, it inevitably led to a greater concentration of foreign policy powers in the hands of the president—usually at the expense of the legislative branch.

The Growth of Executive Institutions

A fourth reason for presidential dominance in foreign policy has been the expansion of executive institutions. Since the end of World War II, the presidential foreign policy machinery has grown substantially, whereas the capacity of Congress has grown only modestly. As a result, presidential control of the foreign policy apparatus and information has increased sharply, leaving Congress at a distinct disadvantage in both areas.

With congressional passage of the **National Security Act of 1947**, the foreign policy machinery of the executive branch was both consolidated and enlarged.[131] This act provided for the establishment of the National Security Council, the Central

Intelligence Agency, and the organization of the separate military forces under the National Military Establishment (later the Department of Defense), with the civilian position of the secretary of defense mandated as its head. Furthermore, the Joint Chiefs of Staff was organized to advise the secretary of defense.

All of these new agencies and individuals ultimately were to assist the president in his conduct of foreign policy. The **National Security Council (NSC)**, for instance, composed of the president, vice president, secretary of state, secretary of defense, and others that the president may designate, was "to advise the president with respect to the integration of domestic, foreign, and military policies relating to the national security. . . ."[132] It has enabled him to make foreign policy with little involvement of other branches of government, and even without much involvement of the rest of the executive branch. As the NSC system has evolved—especially with the enhanced role of the national security advisor in more recent administrations—executive control of the foreign policy machinery became firmly entrenched in the office of the president. One indicator of the growth of the NSC system is the size of its staff under each succeeding president in the postwar years.

Under President Truman, for instance, NSC personnel numbered 20 in 1951. This number increased to 28 in 1955 under President Eisenhower and 50 by the time of the Kennedy administration in 1962. Under the Nixon administration, the personnel size rose to 75, dipped a bit under the Carter, Reagan, and Bush administrations, and rose to 100 by 2000 for the Clinton administration. Although the George W. Bush administration initially called for reducing the size of the staff by one-third to have a more "strategically focused operation," the number of "policy positions" was put at about 110 in 2007. Under the Obama administration, the number of NSC personnel is at "around 175 policy positions."[133] As can be seen, overall the size of the NSC staff has fluctuated over time, but it has surely grown from its initial years. More important, it has grown in power and influence in the actual formulation of foreign policy (see Chapter 9).

The **Central Intelligence Agency (CIA)** was established by the National Security Act for the purpose of developing intelligence estimates and for advising and making recommendations to the NSC. It was also to assist in coordinating the activities of other government intelligence agencies and it was assigned "to perform such other functions and duties related to intelligence affecting the national security as the National Security Council may from time to time direct."[134] This last function was used as the rationale for "covert actions" by the American government as the CIA developed.

The National Security Act also begat the **National Military Establishment** in 1947. Under this provision, the departments of the army, navy, and air force came into existence, with the secretary of defense heading this overall organizational arrangement. By 1949, as a result of amendments to the act, this had become the present **Department of Defense**. Moreover, the secretary of defense, as head of this new cabinet department, was required to be a civilian and to be "the principal assistant to the President in all matters relating to the national security."[135]

Finally, the 1947 act provided for the creation of the **Joint Chiefs of Staff**, which would consist of the army and air force chiefs of staff, the chief of naval operations, and the chairman of the Joint Chiefs. Their duties included preparing strategic plans and forces, formulating military policies, and advising the president and the secretary of defense on military matters.

By one congressional act, then, the president was provided an intelligence advisor (the director of the CIA), a military advisor (the chairman of the Joint Chiefs of Staff), and a national security advisor (the secretary of defense). In addition, he was provided with a bureaucratic mechanism for gathering intelligence (the Central Intelligence Agency), for making policy (the National Security Council), and for carrying out military operations (the National Military Establishment). All of these were in addition to the Department of State and the secretary of state—traditionally the principal foreign affairs bureaucracy and its spokesperson.

Later in the postwar period, some agencies were established to assist the president, and others assumed a larger role. Three illustrate how the executive branch continued to gain greater control over various aspects of foreign policy. In 1961, the **Agency for International Development (AID)** was established by Congress to coordinate the distribution of assistance abroad.[136] In the same year, the **Arms Control and Disarmament Agency (ACDA)** was mandated by Congress to coordinate arms control activities,[137] with its director to be the principal advisor to the president on these foreign policy questions. (In the 1990s, however, this agency was abolished and its responsibilities were folded into the Department of State.) In 1963, the Office of the Special Trade Representative was created by an executive order, and its duties have been institutionalized and expanded in subsequent trade acts passed by Congress.[138] The **U.S. Trade Representative**, for instance, is now responsible for directing all trade negotiations and for formulating trade policy. Other bureaucracies within the executive branch (such as the departments of Commerce, Treasury, Agriculture, and Justice) have also become increasingly involved in international affairs.[139]

In the post-9/11 era, Congress created the **Department of Homeland Security** in 2002 to assist the executive branch in its response to foreign (and domestic) threats. With the passage of **The Intelligence Reform and Terrorism Prevention Act of 2004**, and in response to the intelligence failures associated with the events of September 11 and the Iraq War, the position of national director of intelligence was created to coordinate and consolidate the disparate government intelligence agencies, and the National Counterterrorism Center was established to integrate intelligence on these new kinds of threats.

One important change that the Obama administration made in the national security structure was to merge the **Homeland Security Council**, a council created by President Bush after September 11 to coordinate all agencies dealing with homeland security, into the NSC. This integrated structure had been recommended by the 9/11 Commission. Although the Homeland Security Council still has the principal responsibilities on terrorism and natural disaster issues, it is now more fully coordinated into the national security system.[140] In short, with all of these agencies in place, the president and the executive branch more generally are in a better institutional position to shape foreign policy than the executive's traditional rival, Congress.

Such structural and hierarchical arrangements have markedly aided the president and his advisors in gathering information and in making rapid foreign policy decisions. Some years ago it was estimated that more than 35,000 people within the executive branch were working on matters related to foreign policy (and that number is undoubtedly higher today).[141] With so many people ultimately answerable to the president and with all of these sources of information available to him, the executive can *usually* respond quickly to an international situation, ranging from the use of military force to negotiations on arms control to the distribution of foreign assistance. By contrast, Congress *usually* does not enjoy such advantages. It is a large and often unwieldy body, with 535 members who are sometimes described as highly parochial in outlook. Congress has a cumbersome bureaucratic system, with numerous committees and subcommittees claiming foreign policy responsibilities that hinder quick decision making. It does not have many large independent information sources and so has often been highly dependent on the executive branch. Further, many complain that the size of congressional staffs has been inadequate to do the necessary background work on foreign policy questions.

Several of these criticisms of Capitol Hill are accurate, and some are being addressed by congressional reforms and changes over recent decades. Members are becoming more expert on foreign policy, and this expertise can actually work to a member's advantage within a constituency, especially as the boundaries between domestic and foreign policy erode (for example, agricultural trade policy for a Midwestern member). Information sources have expanded, too. The **Government Accountability Office** (GAO), an arm of Congress, has fourteen "teams" to address policy questions and advise members of the House and the Senate. These include four with foreign policy responsibilities—Defense Capabilities and Management, Homeland Security and Justice, International Affairs and Trade, and Acquisition and Sourcing Management.[142] The **Congressional Research Service**, a department within the Library of Congress, was expanded under the Legislative Reform Act of 1970 and now includes the Foreign Affairs, Defense and Trade Division to work on foreign policy analyses for members of Congress. The **Office of Technology Assessment**, also a creation of the 1970s, was another source of information on highly specialized topics for Congress until it was eliminated during budget-cutting efforts in 1995.[143]

Some attempts have been made over the years to streamline the congressional system and make it more effective. Because of partisan bickering, however, no proposed reforms from the discussion held by the Joint Committee on the Organization of Congress in the early 1990s were enacted into laws.[144] In 1995, when a new Republican majority took control of Congress, some changes did occur—with a reduction in the number of committees and subcommittees, new internal rules on handling and expediting legislation, and the enactment of a bill applying national workplace rules to the House and the Senate. With the Democrats gaining back control after the 2006 election, changes were made to names and structures of committees. The House and Senate Appropriations Committees now had parallel subcommittee structures; new ethics and lobbying rules were enacted; new requirements for the budget process were put in place; and new rules on the disclosure of legislative earmarked funding were added.[145] Yet these changes have seemingly not had much impact, despite the intent to increase congressional efficiency and accountability. Moreover, public perceptions of the effectiveness and the public approval of Congress remain low, with approval dropping to 10 percent in February, 2012 and remained largely in the teens for much of 2011 and 2012.[146]

International Situational Factors

Throughout the greater portion of the period since World War II, the United States made foreign policy within a Cold War environment. Such a perceived dangerous environment had the effect of muting debate over long-term goals and instead focusing on short-term tactics. Another consequence, given the dangerous global situation, was a tendency by both Congress and the American public to defer to the executive on foreign policy matters. If an emergency arose, the president, not Congress, could react immediately. If decisions had to be made about the use of force or diplomacy, the president, not Congress, was prepared to act quickly. Furthermore, with the advent of nuclear weapons and instantaneous global communication, centralized control of the foreign policy machinery seemed more necessary than ever. More generally, too, the president was often the most admired person among the American people, and this admiration created trust in his conduct of foreign affairs.[147] As a result, there was a tendency to assume that the "president knows best."[148]

In recent decades, such deference has eroded for a variety of domestic and international reasons. Although this factor cannot be wholly dismissed as a source of presidential power, now Congress and the public are more willing to question presidents on foreign policy matters. This new posture probably had its beginnings with the Watergate scandal of the early 1970s, when the credibility of President Nixon suffered greatly. President Ford's reputation, in turn, was hurt by his pardoning of the former president. Later, President Carter's foreign policy credibility was diminished by his inability to deal effectively with the Iran hostage crisis.

In the 1980s, President Reagan had a similar difficulty, at least with regard to his Central American policy. Despite his overall popularity, he was never able to obtain sustained approval for his Contra aid policy in Central America. Similarly, although President George H. W. Bush enjoyed substantial popular support, he had to fight vigorously with Congress over his policy toward China after the Tiananmen Square massacre of June 1989, he had to employ his veto power to stop restrictive trade policy toward Japan, and he had to spar with that body over his right to conduct American policy unilaterally with Iraq over its seizure of Kuwait. With the end of the Cold War, President Clinton failed to obtain the seemingly "automatic" deference that earlier presidents enjoyed on foreign policy matters. Several factors appear to account for this situation. With a direct nuclear threat to the United States having diminished as a result of the demise of the Soviet Union, the public (and Congress) seemed no longer willing to defer to the president. Americans were unsure of the future role of the United States in global affairs, and with the Clinton administration seemingly unable to define such a role satisfactorily, they were initially reluctant to embrace its policies. The events of September 11, 2001, restored support for and deference to the presidency by Congress and the public for a time. Prior to September 11, Bush's average level of support was 57 percent. Afterward, through early January 2002, it averaged 87 percent.[149] Moreover, his approval rating remained high through much of 2002 and into 2003. In this same international environment at this same time, Congress was equally supportive of presidential initiatives on terrorism, and other priorities were put aside.[150] By 2005 and beyond, though, public support for President Bush eroded with the political and social reconstruction after the Iraq War going badly. By March 2005, presidential approval dropped below 50 percent and steadily eroded. By late 2007, it was in the low to mid-30s range.[151]

Public approval for President Obama on foreign policy has fluctuated. During his first year in office, public approval on foreign policy was generally over 50 percent, but by his second year in office the public generally disapproved more than they approved of his handling of foreign affairs. During 2011, though, approval and disapproval throughout the year largely moved with events. The killing of Osama bin Laden in May of that year bolstered his approval, much as did the killing of Libyan President Moammar Gadhafi. Similarly, presidential approval increased when Obama announced the withdrawal of nearly all American forces by the end of 2011. In this sense, decisive action in the international arena appeared to bolster presidential support and deference from the public. Importantly, public approval for Obama's handling of foreign policy appeared to be consistently greater than for his handling of domestic affairs.[152]

In this sense, while most international situational factors are a source of presidential preeminence in the conduct of foreign policy for a time, they may also create problems without decisive—and successful—presidential action.

CONCLUDING COMMENTS

Historical precedents as well as Supreme Court decisions and nondecisions continue to serve as important reservoirs of presidential dominance in foreign policy making. Also important in this regard are the capacity of the executive branch to control the foreign policy bureaucracy and the demand for rapid decision making in global events (as the response to September 11 or the killing of Osama bin Laden illustrated). Legislative deference and delegation of power also aid the president, but these sources of executive strength have begun to change and are now sources of challenge to presidential power in foreign policy. Nevertheless, executive preeminence largely remains.

In Chapter 8, we focus on the major areas in which Congress has tried to reassert its foreign policy prerogatives and, by doing so, to reduce the degree of executive dominance. We then discuss how to address the inevitable policy-making conflict between the executive and legislative branches.

Notes

1. "Remarks by the President in Address to the Nation on Libya," at National Defense University, Washington, D.C., March 28, 2011, at http://www.whitehouse.gov/the-press-office/2011/03/28/remarks-president-address-nation-libya, May 8, 2012.

2. "President Says Saddam Hussein Must Leave Iraq Within 48 Hours," Remarks by the President in Address to the Nation, at http://www.whitehouse.gov/news/releases/2003/03/print/20030317-7.html, August 8, 2007.

3. Thomas L. Friedman, "Clinton Vows to Fight Congress on His Power to Use the Military," *New York Times*, October 19, 1993, A18.

4. *The McNeil-Lehrer Report*, Public Broadcasting Service, February 10, 1983.

5. Michael J. Glennon, in *Constitutional Diplomacy* (Princeton, NJ: Princeton University Press, 1990), p. 20, says that a "'plenary presidential power' is one that is not susceptible of congressional limitation." Thanks to James M. Lindsay for this point about plenary powers.

6. See Cecil V. Crabb, Jr., and Pat M. Holt, *Invitation to Struggle: Congress, the President, and Foreign Policy* (Washington, D.C.: Congressional Quarterly Press, 1980), p. 34. Emphasis in original.

7. See Louis Fisher, *Presidential War Power* (Lawrence, KS: University Press of Kansas, 1995), pp. 1–6, for this argument.

8. Federalist No. 69 can be found in Clinton Rossiter, ed., *The Federalist Papers* (New York: A Mentor Book, 1961), pp. 415–423.

9. Louis Henkin, *Foreign Affairs and the Constitution* (Mineola, NY: The Foundation Press, 1972). The quotations are at pp. 74 and 76. An early court case, *Little v. Barreme* 6 U.S. 170 (1804), reveals the degree to which Congress held sway over foreign policy and how the president yielded to its authority. See Glennon, *Constitutional Diplomacy*, pp. 3–8, for a discussion of this case.

10. Quoted in Louis Henkin, "Foreign Affairs and the Constitution," *Foreign Affairs* 66 (Winter 1987/1988): 285, from *Youngstown Sheet & Tube Co. v. Sawyer* (1952).

11. Ibid., p. 292.

12. Arthur M. Schlesinger, Jr., *The Imperial Presidency* (Boston: Houghton Mifflin Company, 1973), p. 2.

13. Henkin, "Foreign Affairs and the Constitution," p. 287.

14. Edward S. Corwin, *The President: Office and Powers 1787–1957* (New York: New York University Press, 1957), p. 171.

15. See Arthur M. Schlesinger, Jr., "Congress and the Making of American Foreign Policy," *Foreign Affairs* 51 (October 1972): 78–113; James L. Sundquist, *The Decline and Resurgence of Congress* (Washington, D.C.: The Brookings Institution, 1981), pp. 21–29; and Harold Hongju Koh, *The National Security Constitution* (New Haven, CT: Yale University Press, 1992). For a brief description of the "pendulum theory" of foreign policy powers between the president and Congress, see Thomas M. Franck and Edward Weisband, *Foreign Policy by Congress* (New York: Oxford University Press, 1979), pp. 5–6. Also, these are the sources for the discussion of the different phases in executive and legislative dominance.

16. Holbert N. Carroll, *The House of Representatives and Foreign Affairs* (Pittsburgh: University of Pittsburgh Press, 1958), p. 10. Sundquist, *The Decline and Resurgence of Congress*, pp. 22–23, views this early period slightly differently, with seemingly more power for Congress.

17. In reality, Congress passed a resolution that acknowledged that "a state of war exists." This passage is quoted in Fisher, *Presidential War Power*, p. 33.

18. The quoted phrase is from Sundquist, *The Decline and Resurgence of Congress*, p. 25.

19. The last two quoted passages are from Koh, *The National Security Constitution*, p. 86.

20. Carroll, *The House of Representatives and Foreign Affairs*, p. 14. Much of this section on the cyclical interpretation of foreign policy control also draws on James M. McCormick, "Congress and Foreign Policy," in *The Encyclopedia of U.S. Foreign Relations* (New York: Oxford University Press, 1997), pp. 312–328.

21. Fisher, *Presidential War Power*, p. 65.

22. Henkin, "Foreign Affairs and the Constitution," p. 290.

23. Corwin, *The President*, p. 206.

24. Henkin, "Foreign Affairs and the Constitution," p. 291, and Robert H. Ferrell, *American Diplomacy: A History*, 3rd ed. (New York: W.W. Norton and Company, 1975), pp. 78–79.

25. Corwin, *The President*, p. 182.

26. Schlesinger, "Congress and the Making of American Foreign Policy," p. 82. Also see Fisher, *Presidential War Power*, pp. 21–22.

27. Corwin, *The President*, p. 188.

28. Schlesinger, "Congress and the Making of American Foreign Policy," pp. 83–87. Also, however, see the 1989 edition (and its epilogue) of his *The Imperial Presidency* (Boston: Houghton Mifflin Company, 1989), p. 442 in particular.

29. Schlesinger, *The Imperial Presidency*, p. 442.

30. Johnny H. Killian, ed., *The Constitution of the United States: Analysis and Interpretation* (Washington, D.C.: Congressional Research Service, The Library of Congress, 1987), p. 338.

31. Schlesinger, "Congress and the Making of American Foreign Policy," p. 86.

32. Corwin, *The President*, p. 229.

33. For a discussion of the *Prize Cases*, see *Guide to the U.S. Supreme Court* (Washington, D.C.: Congressional Quarterly, 1979), pp. 187–189.

34. Schlesinger, "Congress and the Making of American Foreign Policy," pp. 89–91. Also see pp. 91–95 for the interventions mentioned and others by presidents without congressional authorization.

35. Francis D. Wormuth, "Presidential Wars: The Convenience of 'Precedent,'" in Martin B. Hickman, ed., *Problems of American Foreign Policy*, 2nd ed. (Beverly Hills: Glencoe Press,

1975), p. 96, for instances when President Johnson cited 125 previous cases and 137 previous cases where presidents have taken unilateral action. Also, see the discussion of the Gulf of Tonkin Resolution later in the chapter on congressional authorization for Vietnam.

36. Richard M. Nixon, "Cambodia: A Difficult Decision," *Vital Speeches of the Day* 36 (May 15, 1970): 451. This speech was originally delivered to the American public on April 30, 1970.

37. Taken from the "Letter to the Speaker of the House and the President Pro Tempore of the Senate on United States Military Action in Panama," *Weekly Compilation of Presidential Documents* 25 (December 25, 1989): 1985.

38. The quoted passages by the president are reported in Friedman, "Clinton Vows to Fight Congress on His Power to Use the Military," p. A1.

39. Ryan Hendrickson, *The Clinton Wars: The Constitution, Congress, and War Powers* (Nashville: Vanderbilt University Press, 2002), p. 87.

40. Ibid., pp. 127 and 129.

41. See P.L. 107-40 and P.L. 107-243/

42. "Authority to Use Military Force in Libya," Memorandum Opinion for the Attorney General, April 1, 2011, at http://www.justic.gov/olc/2011/authroity-military-use-in-libya.pdf.

43. These two examples are drawn from the testimony of U. Alexis Johnson, undersecretary of state for political affairs, reported in "Department Discusses Agreements on Azores and Bahrain Facilities," *Department of State Bulletin* (February 28, 1972): 279–284. The quoted passage is at p. 282. Johnson did add that Congress would have to approve the rental payment for the use of the Bahrain facilities.

44. For some evidence illustrating that the bulk of the executive agreements in the postwar period have been pursuant to statute, see Loch Johnson and James M. McCormick, "The Making of International Agreements: A Reappraisal of Congressional Involvement," *Journal of Politics* 40 (May 1978): 468–478.

45. The agreement data are in part from Michael Nelson, ed., *Congressional Quarterly's Guide to the Presidency* (Washington, D.C.: Congressional Quarterly, 1989), p. 1104. Louis Fisher in *The President and Congress: Power and Policy* (New York: Free Press, 1972), p. 45, reports similar data through 1970. See Table 7.2 for another source from the U.S. Senate.

46. The yearly treaty information for the years 2000 to 2005 is available at http://www.state.gov/s/l/treaty. The yearly listings are under the header of "Treaty Actions," but a review shows that the preponderance remains executive agreements. Along with an assistant, the author coded each entry as an executive agreement or treaty to reach the conclusion about the approximate number of each. Although the coding is not as definitive as in Table 7.2, our estimation points to the continuance of executive agreement over treaties in U.S. commitments abroad.

47. Schlesinger, *The Imperial Presidency*, pp. 86–88.

48. On this point, see "National Commitments," Senate Report 91–129, 91st Cong., 1st sess., April 16, 1969, 26.

49. The hearings on American commitments with other countries were held in 1969 and 1970 by a subcommittee of the Committee on Foreign Relations (Subcommittee on United States Security Agreements and Commitments Abroad), chaired by Senator Stuart Symington of Missouri, popularly known as the Symington Subcommittee. A summary of these hearings is reported in "Security Agreements and Commitments Abroad," *Report to the Committee on Foreign Relations of the United States Senate by the Subcommittee on Security Agreements and Commitments Abroad*, December 21, 1970.

50. Loch Johnson and James M. McCormick, "Foreign Policy by Executive Fiat," *Foreign Policy* 28 (Fall 1977): 117–138.

51. The pact was entitled "The Agreed Framework Between the United States and the Democratic People's Republic of Korea" and was signed in Geneva, Switzerland, on October 21, 1994.

52. Mark Landler, "Obama Signs Pact in Kabul, Turning Page in Afghan War," *New York Times*, May 1, 2012, at http://www.nytimes.com/2012/05/02/world/asia/obama-lands-in-kabul-on-unannounced-visit.html?_r=1&pagewanted=all&pagewanted=print, May 9, 2012; and Steven Lee Myers and Choe Sang-Hun, "North Koreans Agree to Freeze Nuclear Work; U.S. to Give Aid," *New York Times*, February 29, 2012, at http://www.nytimes.com/2012/03/01/world/asia/us-says-north-korea-agrees-to-curb-nuclear-work.html?_r=1&pagewanted=print, May 9, 2012.

53. See "Notice: Continuation of Emergency with Respect to Burma," signed by President George W. Bush on May 15, 2001, at http://www.whitehouse.gov, July 9, 2002.

54. "President Bush Signs Darfur Peace and Accountability Act," at http://usinfo.state.gov/xarchives/display.html?p=washfile-english&y=2006&m=October&x=20061014142248tn eweolc0.2076837, August 12, 2007.

55. Kenneth R. Mayer and Kevin Price, "Unilateral Presidential Powers: Significant Executive Orders, 1949–99," *Presidential Studies Quarterly* 32 (June 2002): 367–386. The author classified the significant executive order as foreign policy–related from the listing at pp. 380–384 and calculated the resulting numbers.

56. Philip J. Cooper, "George W. Bush, Edgar Allan Poe, and the Use and Abuse of Presidential Signing Statements," *Presidential Studies Quarterly* 35 (September 2005): 516–517.

57. Ibid., p. 517.

58. Ibid.

59. These totals were taken from Cooper, "George W. Bush, Edgar Allan Poe." The foreign policy objectives were derived from Table 1 at p. 522 by summing the objectives that dealt with "exclusive power over foreign policy," "authority to determine and impose national security classification and withhold information," "commander in chief powers," and "unimpeded authority to conduct negotiations for foreign affairs" in this table.

60. For a listing of all of the Obama administration's signing statement through February 2012, see John Woolley and Gerhard Peters, "The American Presidency Project," at http://www.presidency.ucsb.edu/signingstatements.php?year=2009&Submit=DISPLAY#axzz1u PfUp4Z6, May 11, 2012.

61. This signing statement and the quoted passages can be found at http://coherentbabble.com/signing statements/SSann2006.htm, p. 5, August 13, 2007. Emphasis added.

62. See Woolley and Peters, "The American Presidency Project," for these signing statements.

63. 299 U.S. 304 (1936).

64. Ibid., p. 314.

65. Ibid., p. 318.

66. Ibid., pp. 319 and 320, in which the Court more fully spells out the reasons for why the president is afforded greater discretion in foreign affairs and freedom from legislative restriction. The "extra-constitutional" description below is from Henkin, *Foreign Affairs and the Constitution*, p. 22. For another discussion (on which we draw) on the courts (and other factors) and foreign policy, see Howard Bliss and M. Glen Johnson, *Beyond the Water's Edge: America's Foreign Policies* (Philadelphia: J. P. Lippincott Company, 1975), pp. 133–137.

67. See David Gray Adler, "The Constitution and Presidential Warmaking: The Enduring Debate," *Political Science Quarterly* 103 (Spring 1988): 30–36. See especially his discussion of the *Steel Seizure Case* and *Reid v. Covert* at p. 32 as particular challenges to this broad "extra-constitutional" interpretation of presidential power. For a detailed analysis of *Curtiss-Wright*, see Glennon, *Constitutional Diplomacy*, pp. 18–34.

68. 252 U.S. 433.

69. Ibid.

70. Ibid.

71. 301 U.S. 324 (1937); 315 U.S. 203 (1942).

72. Jean Edward Smith, *The Constitution and American Foreign Policy* (St. Paul: West Publishing Company, 1989), p. 127.

73. 315 U.S. 234 (1942).

74. Henkin, *Foreign Affairs and the Constitution*, p. 185.

75. These statutes are listed in Appendix I of *INS v. Chadha* 462 U.S. 919 (1983).

76. Martha Liebler Gibson, "Managing Conflict: The Role of the Legislative Veto in American Foreign Policy," *Polity* 26 (Spring 1994): 442–443.

77. Joseph Cooper and Patricia A. Hurley, "The Legislative Veto: A Policy Analysis," *Congress & Presidency* 10 (Spring 1983): 1–24, especially at pp. 1 and 4.

78. For a fuller discussion of the origin and development of the legislative veto, see Gibson, "Managing Conflict: The Role of the Legislative Veto in American Foreign Policy," 441–472; Martha Liebler Gibson, *Weapons of Influence: The Legislative Veto, American Foreign Policy, and the Irony of Reform* (Boulder, CO: Westview Press, 1992); and Cooper and Hurley, "The Legislative Veto: A Policy Analysis," pp. 1–24.

79. These details are taken from the *Chadha* decision and from David M. O'Brien, *Constitutional Law and Politics*, vol. 1 (W.W. Norton and Company, 1991), p. 355.

80. 462 U.S. 947–959 (1983).

81. Frederick M. Kaiser, "Congressional Control of Executive Actions in the Aftermath of the *Chadha* Decision," *Administrative Law Review* 36 (Summer 1984): 242.

82. 343 U.S. 585 (1952).

83. 343 U.S. 587 (1952).

84. Quoted in Smith, *The Constitution and American Foreign Policy*, from the decision itself at p. 169. The earlier quotation is from Smith's analysis at the same page.

85. 542 U.S. 36 (2004). The description and the particulars of the case are taken from the ruling, including the syllabus of the decision. The case can be accessed at http://www.law.cornell.edu/supct/html/03-6696.ZS.html, August 22, 2008.

86. 548 U.S. 3 (2006). The other elements of the decision are also taken from the syllabus.

87. See 553 US__(2008), http://www.wilmerhale.com/boumediene, August 24, 2008; and Linda Greenhouse, "Justices Rule Terror Suspects Can Appeal in Civilian Courts," *New York Times*, June 13, 2008, http://www.nytimes.com/2008/06/13/washington/12cnd-gitmo.html?ei=5124&en=b6c3093458455a18&ex=1371009600&partner=permalink&exprod=permalink&adxnnlx=1219611903-Cx7NKJs%208cTLS/P/EEotlw&pagewanted=print, from which we draw.

88. The quoted passages are taken from the "Syllabus" of the decision in *Boumediene et al v. Bush et al.* at p. 6. See 553 U.S. ___(2008) for the full statement of the Court's decision.

89. This discussion is gleaned from Henkin, *Foreign Affairs and the Constitution*, pp. 210–215. It has been somewhat simplified. The "political doctrine" question is more complicated than this brief summary conveys and remains a complex issue of constitutional law.

90. Warren Christopher, "Ceasefire Between the Branches: A Compact in Foreign Affairs," in James M. McCormick, ed., *A Reader in American Foreign Policy* (Itasca, IL: F. E. Peacock Publishers, 1986), p. 254.

91. See, for example, *Altee v. Richardson*, 411 U.S. 911 (1973).

92. Judgments in these cases are drawn from *Crockett v. Reagan* 720 F. 2d 1355 (1983); *Conyers v. Reagan* 765 F. 2d 1124 (1985); and *Lowry v. Reagan* 676 F. Supp. 333 (D.D.C. 1987).

93. Neil A. Lewis, "Lawmakers Lose War Powers Suit," *New York Times*, December 14, 1990, A9. Also see 752 F. Supp 1141 (D.D.C. 1990).

94. The details are taken from http://www.ll.georgetown.edu/FedCt/Circuit/dc/opinions/99-5214a.html, October 31, 2000, where the opinion of the District of Columbia Circuit Court is printed for *Campbell v. Clinton*. Also see *Campbell v. Clinton*, 203 F.3d 19 (D.C. Cir. 2000).

95. See the discussion of this case in David M. Ackerman, "War Powers Litigation Initiated by Members of Congress Since the Enactment of the War Powers Resolution," CRS Report to Congress (Washington, D.C.: Congressional Research Service, The Library of Congress, March 19, 2003) at p. 12 and from where the quotation is taken.

96. For the chronology of this case, see American Civil Liberties Union, "Mohamed et al. v. Jeppesen Dataplan, Inc," November 15, 2011, at http://www.aclu.org/national-security/mohamed-et-al-v-jeppesen-dataplan-inc, October 18, 2011. The quoted passages are from the decision by the United States Court of Appeals for the Ninth Circuit, September 8, 2010, pp. 13522-13523, at http://www.ca9.uscourts.gov/datastore/opinions/2010/09/08/08-15693.pdf, October 18, 2011.

97. Gordon Silverstein, "Judicial Enhancement of Executive Power," in Paul E. Peterson, ed., *The President, the Congress, and the Making of Foreign Policy* (Norman and London: University of Oklahoma Press, 1994), pp. 23–45, especially pp. 34–45. The quoted passage is at p. 26.

98. On the Vandenberg Resolution, see James A. Robinson, *Congress and Foreign Policy-Making*, rev. ed. (Homewood, IL: The Dorsey Press, 1967), pp. 44–46. Also see Table 2-1 at p. 65, which shows the small degree of congressional initiation in foreign policy and the considerable degree of executive influence within Congress.

99. Richard F. Fenno, Jr., *Congressmen in Committees* (Boston: Little, Brown and Company, 1973), p. 71. Emphasis in original.

100. Fenno, *Congressmen in Committees*, p. 163.

101. Charles H. Percy, "The Partisan Gap," *Foreign Policy* 45 (Winter 1981/1982): 15.

102. On the "perpetual crisis in executive legislative relations" during the Reagan years and on these proposals to improve this situation in the Bush years, see John Felton, "Will Bush-Hill Honeymoon Bring Bipartisanship?" *Congressional Quarterly Weekly Report*, February 18, 1989, 332–337. The quotations are from p. 335.

103. The description of Fascell and his quotation is taken from Felton, "Foreign Affairs Committee Changes Seen Under Fascell," pp. 2622–2623.

104. Lee H. Hamilton, "American Foreign Policy: A Congressional Perspective," speech given at the Department of State, Washington, D.C., December 14, 1993.

105. Aaron Wildavsky, "Two Presidencies," *Trans-action* 3 (December 1966): 8.

106. Ibid., p. 8. For several cogent arguments questioning the utility of roll call analysis in evaluating presidential success, see James M. Lindsay and Wayne P. Steger, "The 'Two Presidencies' in Future Research: Moving Beyond Roll-Call Analysis," *Congress & The Presidency* 20 (Autumn 1993): 103–117. For some arguments supporting the use of roll call analysis, see Jon R. Bond and Richard Fleisher, *The President in the Legislative Arena* (Chicago and London: The University of Chicago Press, 1990), pp. 66–71.

107. Lance T. LeLoup and Steven A. Shull, "Congress Versus the Executive: The 'Two Presidencies' Reconsidered," *Social Science Quarterly* 59 (March 1979): 707.

108. Ibid., pp. 712–713.

109. Richard Fleisher and Jon R. Bond, "Are There Two Presidencies? Yes, But Only for Republicans," *Journal of Politics* 50 (August 1988): 747–767. Table 1 at p. 754 is the source of these conclusions. Also see, Bond and Fleisher, *The President in the Legislative Arena*, which in part addresses this issue.

110. These results were calculated from roll call data made available through the Inter-University Consortium of Political and Social Research (the Consortium bears no responsibility for the analyses and interpretations reported here) and from recorded votes reported in *Congressional Quarterly Almanac* (various years), *Congressional Quarterly Weekly Report* (various issues), and *CQ Weekly* (various issues). For the Eisenhower administration through the first two years of the George W. Bush administration, foreign policy votes on which the president took a position were identified, based on *Congressional Quarterly Almanac, Congressional Quarterly Weekly Report*, and *CQ Weekly* assessments; the president's success or failure was then calculated across each administration. The foreign policy votes for the Truman years were identified from the roll call data, and Truman's position was determined by an assessment of available *CQ Almanacs* and presidential papers. The assistance of Eugene R. Wittkopf of Louisiana State University in identifying the 1947–1996 foreign policy votes, in collecting some of the Clinton votes, and in determining Truman's position on those particular votes is appreciated. A more detailed discussion of the data collection process is reported in James M. McCormick and Eugene R. Wittkopf, "Bipartisanship, Partisanship, and Ideology in Congressional-Executive Foreign Policy Relations, 1947–1988," *Journal of Politics* 52 (November 1990): 1077–1100.

111. See Lee Sigelman, "A Reassessment of the Two Presidencies Thesis," *Journal of Politics* 41 (November 1979): 1195–1205, especially 1200–1201. Drawing on *Congressional Quarterly*, Sigelman defined a key vote as one involving "'a matter of major controversy,' 'a test of presidential or political power,' or 'a decision of potentially great impact on the nation and lives of Americans.'" The number of such votes ranged between 10 and 36 for the years of his study (p. 1199).

112. Ibid., pp. 1200–1201.

113. LeLoup and Shull, "Congress versus the Executive: The 'Two Presidencies' Reconsidered," p. 710.

114. Richard Fleisher, Jon R. Bond, Glen S. Krutz, and Stephen Hanna, "The Demise of the Two Presidencies," *American Politics Quarterly* 28 (January 2000): 21. Also see Steven A. Shull, *Presidential-Congressional Relations: Policy and Time Approaches* (Ann Arbor: The University of Michigan Press, 1997) for further evidence on the decrease of foreign policy support for presidents and the narrowing of differences between the two areas, even to showing more support for the domestic policies of some presidents. In particular, see the discussion at pp. 91–96.

115. See Robert A. Bernstein and William Anthony, "The ABM Issue in the Senate, 1968–1970: The Importance of Ideology," *American Political Science Review* 68 (September 1974): 1198–1206; James M. McCormick and Michael Black, "Ideology and Voting on the Panama Canal Treaties," *Legislative Studies Quarterly* 8 (February 1983): 45–63; James M. McCormick, "Congressional Voting on the Nuclear Freeze Resolutions," *American Politics Quarterly* 13 (January 1985): 122–136; Richard Fleisher, "Economic Benefit, Ideology, and Senate Voting on the B-1 Bomber," *American Politics Quarterly* 13 (April 1985): 200–211; James M. Lindsay, "Parochialism, Policy, and Constituency Constraints: Congressional Voting on Strategic Weapons Systems," *American Journal of Political Science* 34 (November 1990): 936–960; and Eugene R. Wittkopf and James M. McCormick, "The Domestic Politics of Contra Aid: Public Opinion, Congress, and the President," in Richard Sobel, ed., *Public Opinion in U.S. Foreign Policy: The Controversy over Contra Aid* (Lanham, MD: Rowman & Littlefield Publishers, 1993), pp. 73–103.

116. See Scot Schraufnagel and Stephen M. Shellman, "The Two Presidencies, 1984–1998: A Replication and Extension," *Presidential Studies Quarterly* 31 (December 2001): 699–707

on the waning support for the two-presidencies thesis as well as Fleisher, Bond, Krutz, and Hanna, "The Demise of the Two Presidencies," pp. 14–23.

117. Duane M. Oldfield and Aaron Wildavsky, "Reconsidering the Two Presidencies," *Society* 26 (July/August 1989): 54–59. The quotation is at p. 55. For a good summary of the some earlier debates over the "two presidencies" argument, see Steven A. Shull, ed., *The Two Presidencies: A Quarter Century Assessment* (Chicago: Nelson/Hall Publishers, 1991).

118. See P.L. 85-7, in *United States Statutes at Large*, Vol. 69 (Washington, D.C.: Government Printing Office, 1955), p. 7. Emphasis added.

119. P.L. 85-7, in *United States Statutes at Large*, Vol. 71 (Washington, D.C.: Government Printing Office, 1958), p. 5.

120. See Fisher, *Presidential War Powers*, pp. 107–110 for the controversies surrounding this resolution. Also see "'Eisenhower Doctrine' for the Middle East," *Congressional Quarterly Almanac 1957* (Washington, D.C.: Congressional Quarterly, 1957), pp. 573–579. The quote indicating that America "is prepared to use armed forces" is at p. 573. Also see Gordon Silverstein, *Imbalance of Powers* (New York: Oxford University Press, 1997), pp. 78–79.

121. P.L. 88-408. See http://www.cnn.com/SPECIALS/cold.war/episodes/11/documents/tonkin for a copy of the Resolution and Law, August 22, 2008.

122. See the testimony by Undersecretary of State Nicholas Katzenbach in "U.S. Commitments to Foreign Powers," *Hearings on S.Res. 151 Before the Senate Committee on Foreign Relations*, 90th Cong., 1st sess., August 16, 17, 21, 23, and September 19, 1967 (statement by Nicholas Katzenbach, Undersecretary of State), p. 82. Two other resolutions were passed by Congress in 1962 "expressing the determination of the United States" to use armed forces if necessary to stop Cuban aggression and to defend Berlin. Neither resolution, however, expressly granted the presidential discretion that the Formosa and Gulf of Tonkin resolutions did. See P.L. 87-733 (October 3, 1962) and H. Con. Res. 570 (October 10, 1962).

123. Public Law 107-40 can be found at the following website: http://www.gpo.gov/fdsys/pkg/PLAW-107publ40/pdf/PLAW-107publ40.pdf, August 4, 2012.

124. Public Law 107-243 can be found at the following website: http://www.gpo.gov/fdsys/pkg/PLAW-107publ243/pdf/PLAW-107publ243.pdf, August 4, 2012.

125. These passages are taken from the Foreign Assistance Act of 1961, as amended, and reported in *Legislation on Foreign Relations Through 1985* (Washington, D.C.: U.S. Government Printing Office, April 1986). The quoted passages are at pp. 32, 141, and 129, respectively.

126. See I. M. Destler, *American Trade Politics* (Washington, D.C.: Institute for International Economics and New York: The Twentieth Century Fund, June 1992), p. 12. Also see Sharyn O'Halloran, "Congress and Foreign Trade Policy," in Randall B. Ripley and James M. Lindsay, eds., *Congress Resurgent: Foreign and Defense Policy on Capitol Hill* (Ann Arbor: The University of Michigan Press, 1993), pp. 283–303.

127. The quoted passage is from P.L. 100-418 at 102 Stat. 1143. A summary of the bill is in *Congressional Quarterly Almanac 1988* (Washington, D.C.: Congressional Quarterly, Inc., 1989), pp. 209–215.

128. Stephen D. Cohen, Joel R. Paul, and Robert A. Blecker, *Fundamentals of U.S. Foreign Trade Policy* (Boulder, CO: Westview Press, 1996), p. 272.

129. 91 Stat. 1626.

130. Koh, *The National Security Constitution*, pp. 46–47. The quoted passage is at p. 47.

131. P.L. 253, in *United States Statutes At Large*, Vol. 61, part 1, 80th Cong., 1st sess., pp. 495–510.

132. Ibid., p. 496. The membership of the National Security Council has changed slightly over time. This membership represents the current required composition, although the president may invite others to participate.

133. These NSC personnel data are taken from the Budget of the United States Government for several of these years. The data for the Clinton administration in 2000 was taken from Ivo H. Daalder and I. M. Destler, "A New NSC for a New Administration," Brookings Policy Brief #68, p. 6, http://www.brook.edu.dybdocroot/comm/policybriefs/pb068/pb68.htm, July 22, 2002. The information for the George W. Bush administration is from Karen DeYoung and Steven Mufson, "A Leaner and Less Visible NSC Reorganization Will Emphasize Defense, Global Economics," *Washington Post*, February 10, 2001, pp. A1 and A6, http://washingtonpost.com/wp-dyn/world/europe/A50937-2001Feb9.html, February 12, 2001, and from Alan G. Whittaker, Frederick C. Smith, and Elizabeth McKune, *The National Security Policy Process: The National Security Council and Interagency System* (Research Report, November 2007 Annual Update) (Washington, D.C.: Industrial College of the Armed Forces, National Defense University, U.S. Department of Defense, 2007), p. 11 for "policy positions" of that administration. The data for the Obama administration is taken from the Alan G. Whittaker, Shannon A. Brown, Frederick Smith, and Ambassador Elizabeth McKune, *The National Security Policy Process: The National Security Council and Interagency System* (Research Report, August 15, 2011, Annual Update) (Washington, D.C.: Industrial College of the Armed Forces, National Defense University, U.S. Department of Defense, 2011), p. 14.

134. P.L. 253, p. 498.

135. Ibid., p. 500.

136. See P.L. 87-194.

137. See P.L. 87-297. By a reorganization plan, part of AID (effective April 1, 1999) and all of ACDA (October 1, 1999) were incorporated into the Department of State. See P.L. 105-277 at 112 Stat. 2681-797.

138. *U.S. Government Manual 1989/1990* (Washington, D.C.: Government Printing Office, July 1, 1989), p. 95.

139. For a discussion of the role of some of these bureaucracies in the foreign policy process, see Chapter 9.

140. See "National Security Council," WP Politics, at http://www.washingtonpost.com/politics/national-security-council/gIQADIUF5O_topic.html, May 10, 2012.

141. Charles W. Kegley, Jr., and Eugene R. Wittkopf, *American Foreign Policy: Pattern and Process*, 3rd ed. (New York: St. Martin's Press, 1987), p. 340.

142. For eighty-three years, the Government Accountability Office had been known as the General Accounting Office. By congressional action in 2004, its name was changed to better reflect its activities, especially the scope of its work within the federal government, and to allow it to work with private sector organizations as well. It remains an agency that works for Congress and is "independent and nonpartisan." See "What is GAO," http://www.gao.gov/about/what.html, "GAO's Name Change and Other Provisions of the GAO Human Capital Reform Act of 2004," http://www.gao.gov/about/namechange.html, and David Walker, "GAO Answers the Questions: What's in a Name?" at this website. The listing of the four teams dealing with "changing security threats and the challenges of global independences" for GAO was confirmed with a communication with an official of the agency, May 14, 2012.

143. For a discussion of these services for Congress, see *Executive Legislative Consultation on Foreign Policy: Strengthening Foreign Policy Information Sources for Congress* (Washington, D.C.: Government Printing Office, February 1982), pp. 27–37; Evelyn Howard, *The Congressional Research Service* (Washington, D.C.: Congressional Research Service, The

Library of Congress, August 14, 1989); *General Accounting Office, National Security and International Affairs Division: Organization and Responsibility* (Washington, D.C.: Government Printing Office, 1989); and http://www.gao.gov as well as note 150.

144. See "No Action Taken on Congressional Reform," *Congressional Quarterly Almanac 1993* (Washington, D.C.: Congressional Quarterly, Inc., 1994), pp. 21–29.

145. Liriel Higa, "Democrats Restore Parallel Appropriations Jurisdictions," *CQ Weekly, Online* (January 8, 2007): 126, at http://library.cqpress.com/cqweekly/weeklyreport110-000002424025, October 19, 2008; and Martin Kady II, "New Majority, New Rules," *CQ Weekly Online* (January 8, 2007): 122–124, at http://library.cqpress.com/cqweekly/weeklyreport110-000002424023, October 19, 2008.

146. Jeffrey M. Jones, "Congressional Approval Recovers Slightly, Now 17%," Gallup.Com, April 19, 2012, at http://www.gallup.com/poll/153968/congressional-approval-recovers-slightly.aspx, May 10, 2012.

147. For some evidence on how admired presidents have been in the postwar period, see John E. Mueller, *War, Presidents and Public Opinion* (New York: John Wiley and Sons, 1973), pp. 179–195.

148. The phrase is taken from Daniel Yankelovich, "Farewell to 'President Knows Best,'" in William P. Bundy, ed., *America and the World 1978* (New York: Pergamon Press, 1979), pp. 670–693, who discusses this deferential tradition in the American public and its decline in the mid-1970s.

149. The Gallup Poll, "Despite Sharp Increase in Bush Approval Since 9/11, Race Gap Persists," http://www.gallup.com/poll/5158/Despite-Sharp-Increase-Bush-Approval-Since-911-Race-Gap-Persists.aspx, January 8, 2002, August 23, 2008.

150. For an example of Congress's changed priorities after September 11, see Miles A. Pomper, "Building Anti-Terrorism Coalition Vaults Ahead of Other Priorities," *CQ Weekly Online* October 27, 2001, 2551–2558, at http://library.cqpress.com/cqweekly/weeklyreport107-000000331102, August 23, 2008. Also see Miles A. Pomper "Adversity for Ethnic Lobbies," *CQ Weekly Online* (October 27, 2001); 2558, at http://library.cqpress.com/cqweekly/weeklyreport107-000000331103, August 23, 2008.

151. The Gallup Poll, "Presidential Job Approval in Depth" at http://www.galluppoll.com/content/?ci=1723, May 24, 2007.

152. See Lydia Saad, "Obama Improves on Foreign Affairs, Struggles on Fiscal Matters," November 9, 2011, at http://www.gallup.com/poll/150650/Obama-Improves-Foreign-Affairs-Struggles-Fiscal-Matters.aspx, May 11, 2012; and Lydia Saad, "Obama's Economic Approval Rating Improves," February 9, 2012, at http://www.gallup.com/poll/152543/Obama-Economic-Approval-Rating-Improves.aspx, May 13, 2012, for data on foreign policy approval in a comparative perspective.

CHAPTER **8**

Congressional Prerogatives and the Making of Foreign Policy

Congress is not merely a "coequal" branch of government.
The framers vested the decisive and ultimate powers of war and
spending in the legislative branch. . . . American democracy places
the sovereign power in the people and entrusts to them the temporary
delegation of their power to elected Senators and Representatives.

CONSTITUTIONAL SCHOLAR LOUIS FISHER
JANUARY 2007

It's very important for the President to seek approval of the Congress [before
sending troops abroad]. The title of Commander in Chief is one thing. But the
power of the purse is the greatest power in our Constitutional system.

SENATOR ROBERT BYRD
OCTOBER 1995

The unrest at home over America's involvement in Vietnam, the perceived growth in the foreign policy powers of the president, and the weakening of executive authority as a result of the Watergate incident all contributed to efforts by the legislative branch to reassert its foreign policy prerogatives beginning in the early 1970s. Congress achieved some success in placing limits on the foreign policy powers of the president in four principal ways:

- Requiring the executive to report all commitments abroad
- Limiting the war powers of the president
- Placing restrictions on foreign policy funding
- Increasing congressional oversight of the executive branch in foreign policy making

Some of these limits have now become institutionalized practices between Congress and the president, others had been altered or largely abandoned, and, in some instances, new ones have been added. In this sense, the struggle over foreign policy continues between the two branches.

In this chapter, we review some of the foreign policy restrictions enacted by Congress over the past four decades, assess how well they have worked, and discuss how they have affected congressional–executive relations in American foreign policy making.

COMMITMENT MAKING

The first area of congressional resurgence in the 1970s involved commitment making by the executive, driven in part by the Vietnam War. This effort to rein in executive power was not particularly new, but it did prove to be more successful than an earlier attempt, in the 1950s, to control executive commitments. The two efforts differed in several ways: the earlier effort led by congressional conservatives took the form of a proposed constitutional amendment restricting the kind of treaties and executive agreements the president might initiate; the later one led by congressional liberals focused on requiring the president to report to Congress on commitments already made.

The Bricker Amendment

The 1950s effort at curbing the president was motivated by America's increasing global involvement and was led by **Senator John Bricker** of Ohio. In a series of constitutional amendments, Bricker proposed that any treaty or executive agreement that infringed on the constitutional rights of American citizens be considered unconstitutional and that Congress have the right to enact appropriate legislation to put into effect any treaty or executive agreement made by the president. Bricker was concerned that the United Nations Treaty, and human rights treaties and agreements under consideration by the UN at the time, might commit the United States to particular domestic actions and reduce congressional or state prerogatives under the Constitution.[1] He did not want these domestic actions to obtain constitutional legitimacy simply because a treaty or agreement had been made by the president.[2] In effect, his amendments were designed (1) to alter the constitutional principle established for treaties in *Missouri v. Holland* and executive agreements in *U.S. v. Belmont* and *U.S. v. Pink* (see Chapter 7); (2) to stop self-executing treaties (that is, those not requiring implementing legislation by Congress); and (3) to ensure a larger congressional role in implementing all treaties and executive agreements domestically. Several votes were taken in the Senate on these various amendment proposals. Only one ballot came close to passage, in 1954, but failed by one vote to obtain the necessary two-thirds majority needed to pass a constitutional amendment.

The Case–Zablocki Act

With escalating involvement in Vietnam, primarily through presidential initiative, and with revelations of secret commitments to a variety of nations during the 1950s and 1960s, the congressional liberals of the 1970s sought to limit executive commitments abroad.[3] In June 1969, the Senate passed a "sense of the Senate" resolution stating that the making of national commitments should involve the legislative as well as the executive branch.[4] When the executive branch went ahead with executive agreements with Portugal and Bahrain, another "sense of the Senate" resolution was passed stating that agreements with these states for military bases or foreign assistance should take the form of treaties.[5] Although these resolutions provided a way to vent congressional frustration over executive actions, they were largely symbolic because they did not legally bind the executive branch to altering its previous policies.

By the middle of 1972, however, Congress passed the first significant piece of legislation in the commitment-making area, the **Case–Zablocki Act**, named after Senator Clifford Case (R–New Jersey) and Congressman Clement Zablocki (D–Wisconsin). This law required the executive branch to report all international agreements to Congress within sixty days of their entering into force. (Classified agreements would be transmitted to the House Foreign Affairs Committee and the Senate Foreign Relations Committee under an injunction of secrecy.[6]) In 1977, this act was amended and strengthened to require that all agreements made by all agencies within the executive branch be reported to the Department of State within twenty days for ultimate transmittal to Congress under the provisions of the original act.[7]

With this reporting arrangement, Congress has enjoyed only mixed success in obtaining all agreements in a timely fashion. Although a large number of agreements (both public and classified) have been reported, the number of late transmittals remains substantial. In 1976, for example, 39 percent of all agreements were reported late; by the first half of 1978, that percentage had dropped to 32 percent.[8] By 1981, 27 percent of all agreements were still being transmitted to Congress beyond the sixty-day period; by 1988, reporting had improved, but almost one-fifth of all agreements were still reported late.[9] By 1999, the situation had changed very little, with 19 percent still being reported late.

Other agencies besides the Department of State had contributed to the tardiness of agreements in 1977, but the bulk of the late agreements in 1981 had emanated from the department itself. By 1988, the Department of State and other agencies had been about equally tardy in reporting. In the 1990s, however, State was again most frequent in late reporting. Since May 2000, however, and as part of an effort to ease the bureaucratic burden regarding reporting requirements, the executive branch has no longer had to forward reports on international commitments that were not reported in a timely manner.[10] In this sense, Congress has no guarantee of getting all agreements on time or of obtaining any explanation for late reporting.

Late reporting or nonreporting prompts congressional concern for at least two reasons: late reports are inconsistent with the procedural requirements of the legislation, and late reports can affect the substance of policy. One can readily acknowledge that the late reporting of some executive agreements dealing with administrative details (such as water and electricity agreements for American bases in a particular country) may not be problematic, but other executive agreements (such as regarding intelligence) may be. The failure of Congress to learn promptly about the latter type may well preclude it from taking any action or even staying informed on current policy.

Beyond Case–Zablocki

Although the Case–Zablocki Act required only the reporting of commitments, it did signal congressional determination to participate in the agreement-making process. In fact, some members of Congress were sufficiently dissatisfied with just the reporting requirement that they sought to go further in strengthening the legislative role in the process. Various attempts were made by members of the House and the Senate to obtain the right to reject a commitment made by the executive branch within a prescribed time period (usually sixty days). In the Senate, several measures were introduced that would have allowed both houses to veto any executive agreement within sixty days, and another measure would have allowed only the Senate the right of disapproval of executive agreements.[11] In the House, similar measures were introduced. One measure, **Executive Agreements Review Act of 1975**, proposed that both houses of Congress have the right of disapproval of executive agreements, but only for those involving "national commitments"—mainly those regarding the introduction of American military personnel or the provision of military training or equipment.[12] None of these proposals became law.

The reform initiative that went the furthest beyond simple reporting was the **Treaty Powers Resolution** first introduced in 1976. Under this resolution, the Senate could refuse to provide funding for an agreement that, in that chamber's view, should have taken the form of a treaty.[13] The emergence of this resolution (and others) set the stage for the passage of reform procedures between Congress and the executive that were incorporated into the Foreign Relations Authorization Act for Fiscal Year 1979.[14] Under the provisions of this act, the president now had to report yearly to Congress on each agreement that was late in transmittal; the Secretary of State would have to determine what arrangements constituted an international agreement; and oral agreements would now be "reduced to writing."[15] In effect, this act further strengthened the original idea behind Case–Zablocki without going much beyond it. Furthermore, the Department of State worked out an informal arrangement with the Senate Foreign Relations Committee for periodic consultation regarding which international agreements should take the form of treaties.[16]

In sum, although Congress nurtured the beginnings of a resurgence of its involvement in the commitment-making area, it was unwilling to go very far beyond the reporting mechanism as a way to control agreement making by the executive.

WAR POWERS

Frustrated over the president's use of the commander-in-chief and executive clauses of the Constitution to intervene abroad, in the 1970s Congress adopted several measures to limit his war-making ability. The first important action was the 1970 congressional repeal of the **Gulf of Tonkin Resolution**, which had allowed the president a virtual free hand in conducting the Vietnam War.[17] The repeal was more symbolic than substantive because the executive branch still claimed it had the power to continue the Vietnam War even without the resolution in place. Still, Congress was beginning to assert its role in war making.

Spurred on by the Nixon administration's indifference to the repeal of the Gulf of Tonkin Resolution, Congress began work on a proposal that would limit the president's war-making powers more generally. The resulting **War Powers Resolution (WPR)**, passed over President Richard Nixon's veto in November 1973, remains the most significant congressional attempt to reassert its control over the commitment of U.S. forces abroad.[18]

Key Provisions of the WPR

The WPR has several important provisions that require presidential consultation and reporting to Congress on the use of U.S. forces, that limit the time of deployment, and that provide Congress a mechanism for withdrawing these forces prior to any time limit. They are worth summarizing in detail.[19]

- The president could **introduce armed forces** "into hostilities or into situations where imminent involvement in hostilities is clearly indicated by the circumstances" **under only three conditions**: "(1) a declaration of war, (2) specific statutory authorization, or (3) a national emergency created by attack upon the United States, its territories, or its armed forces." For the first time, Congress specified the conditions under which the president could use the military; previously, presidential power was more discretionary and ambiguous.

- The president "in every possible instance **shall consult with Congress**" before sending American forces into hostilities or anticipated hostilities and "shall consult regularly with Congress" until those forces have been removed. Now Congress expected to be involved in the process from beginning to end.

- For those circumstances in which forces were introduced without a declaration of war, the president must submit a **written report** to the Speaker of the House and the President pro Tempore of the Senate **within forty-eight hours** of deployment, explaining the reasons for it, his relevant constitutional and legislative authority, and the "estimated scope and duration of the hostilities or involvement." The president must also "report to the Congress periodically on the status of such hostilities or situation as well as on the scope and duration of such hostilities or situation" at least every six months, if troops remained deployed.

- The resolution placed a limit on how long forces could be deployed. It specifically authorized the president to use American forces **for no longer than sixty days**, unless there had been a declaration of war or a specific congressional authorization to continue such use beyond this period. An **extension of thirty days** was possible if the president certified that military requirements precluded troop withdrawal. Unless the president reported under the appropriate section (Section 4 [a] [1]), the sixty-day time limit would not automatically begin; however, Congress might begin the sixty-day clock by invoking the resolution itself.[20]

- Finally, the resolution included a "legislative veto" provision that allowed Congress to withdraw the troops prior to the expiration of the sixty-day limit. Through a concurrent resolution (one passed by a simple majority in both houses but without presidential approval), it could specify that the troops be withdrawn immediately.

The clear intent of the war powers legislation was to stop the president from miring American troops in a conflict without a clear objective. Put more simply, it was to reduce the possibility of future Vietnams. At the same time, it was also to reassert the expressed war powers of Congress under Article I of the Constitution. Despite these combined aims, the resolution would not prevent the president from taking military action if and when necessary; instead, it would promote shared responsibility between the executive and legislative branches for dispatching American military personnel abroad.

The WPR had an important purpose in addition to its legal requirements: it served as a political and psychological restraint on presidential war making. By this legislation, the president would now have to calculate whether Congress and the American public would support the sending of American forces to foreign lands. In addition, he would need to provide formal justification for military action and might well have to submit to formal congressional scrutiny.

Presidential Compliance

The record of presidential compliance with the WPR is mixed at best. Some of the reporting requirements and the time limits on deployments, as specified, have been nominally adhered to since 1973, but controversy continues to surround the precise situations in which the resolution is applicable, the extent and manner of presidential compliance with it, and its overall effectiveness in curbing the expansion of executive power. In addition, the *Chadha* decision on the congressional veto, as noted in Chapter 7, has seemingly made the concurrent resolution provision of the law unconstitutional.

Over the past several administrations (through September 2012), 134 reports were forwarded to Congress in accordance with the provisions of the WPR.[21] (Table 8.1 lists the number of reports for each administration, and Document 8.1 illustrates them with a report sent to the Speaker of the House and the President pro Tempore of the Senate over Libya by President Barack Obama.). The Clinton administration filed the most reports, with sixty, whereas the Nixon administration did not submit any in

Table 8.1 The War Powers Resolution and Presidential Reports to Congress

Administration	Number of reports
Richard Nixon	0
Gerald Ford	4
Jimmy Carter	1
Ronald Reagan	14
George H. W. Bush	7
William Clinton	60
George W. Bush	39
Barack Obama (through September 2012)	11

Source: Richard F. Grimmett, *The War Powers Resolution: After Twenty-Eight Years*, Congressional Research Service, The Library of Congress, November 30, 2001; and Grimmett, *IB81050: War Powers Resolution: Presidential Compliance*, Congressional Research Service, Library of Congress, June 12, 2002, updated September 16, 2003, July 25, 2007, January 14, 2008, and September 25, 2012.

Document 8.1   Excerpt from a Letter from the President regarding the commencement of operations in Libya March 21, 2011

Dear Mr. Speaker: (Dear Mr. President:)

At approximately 3:00 p.m. Eastern Daylight Time, on March 19, 2011, at my direction, U.S. military forces commenced operations to assist an international effort authorized by the United Nations (U.N.) Security Council and undertaken with the support of European allies and Arab partners, to prevent a humanitarian catastrophe and address the threat posed to international peace and security by the crisis in Libya. As part of the multilateral response authorized under U.N. Security Council Resolution 1973, U.S. military forces, under the command of Commander, U.S. Africa Command, began a series of strikes against air defense systems and military airfields for the purposes of preparing a no-fly zone. These strikes will be limited in their nature, duration, and scope. Their purpose is to support an international coalition as it takes all necessary measures to enforce the terms of U.N. Security Council Resolution 1973. These limited U.S. actions will set the stage for further action by other coalition partners.

United Nations Security Council Resolution 1973 authorized Member States, under Chapter VII of the U.N. Charter, to take all necessary measures to protect civilians and civilian populated areas under threat of attack in Libya, including the establishment and enforcement of a "no-fly zone" in the airspace of Libya. United States military efforts are discrete and focused on employing unique U.S. military capabilities to set the conditions for our European allies and Arab partners to carry out the measures authorized by the U.N. Security Council Resolution.

Muammar Qadhafi was provided a very clear message that a cease-fire must be implemented immediately. The international community made clear that all attacks against civilians had to stop; Qadhafi had to stop his forces from advancing on Benghazi; pull them back from Ajdabiya, Misrata, and Zawiya; and establish water, electricity, and gas supplies to all areas. Finally, humanitarian assistance had to be allowed to reach the people of Libya. . . .

The United States has not deployed ground forces into Libya. United States forces are conducting a limited and well-defined mission in support of international efforts to protect civilians and prevent a humanitarian disaster. Accordingly, U.S. forces have targeted the Qadhafi regime's air defense systems, command and control structures, and other capabilities of Qadhafi's armed forces used to attack civilians and civilian populated areas. We will seek a rapid, but responsible, transition of operations to coalition, regional, or international organizations that are postured to continue activities as may be necessary to realize the objectives of U.N. Security Council Resolutions 1970 and 1973.

For these purposes, I have directed these actions, which are in the national security and foreign policy interests of the United States, pursuant to my constitutional authority to conduct U.S. foreign relations and as Commander in Chief and Chief Executive. I am providing this report as part of my efforts to keep the Congress fully informed, consistent with the War Powers Resolution. I appreciate the support of the Congress in this action.

BARACK OBAMA

---

the brief time it was in office after the resolution's enactment. The other administrations ranged from one by Jimmy Carter, four by Gerald Ford, seven by George H. W. Bush, eleven by Obama (through September 2012), fourteen by Ronald Reagan, to thirty-nine by George W. Bush.

The presidents' reports cover a variety of military activities under the various administrations. President Ford, for example, filed reports on the evacuations of refugees and American personnel from Vietnam and Cambodia and on the use of force to free the crew of the *Mayaguez* in May 1975. President Carter's lone report concerned the abortive 1980 attempt to rescue the American hostages in Iran. President Reagan's reports included one on the participation of military personnel in the Multinational Force and Observers (MFO) in the Sinai Peninsula in accordance with the Egyptian–Israeli Peace Treaty, and three on the deployment of forces to Lebanon in 1982 and 1983, to Grenada in 1983, and to retaliate against Libya for a Libyan-sponsored terrorist attack against Americans in 1986. President George H. W. Bush's reports focused on sending American air support to the Philippines to assist the government in restoring order and protecting American lives in 1989, dispatching 25,000 American forces to invade Panama and capture General Manuel Noriega, also in 1989, ordering forces to Saudi Arabia after the seizure of Kuwait by Iraq in August 1990, and directing actions against Iraq in the Persian Gulf War in 1991.

As noted, President Bill Clinton forwarded the most reports to Congress. Most of them covered American military deployments to Bosnia, East Timor, Haiti, Kosovo, Macedonia, and Somalia in various peacekeeping and peacemaking operations. In addition, the administration reported on the deployment of forces to evacuate Americans from such trouble spots as Cambodia, Central African Republic, Kenya, Liberia, and Rwanda. Finally, it reported on the American retaliation against Afghanistan and Sudan in 1998 after the terrorist bombing of U.S. embassies in Kenya and Tanzania and on deployment of military personnel to Yemen in 2000 after the terrorist attack on the *USS Cole*.

President George W. Bush's thirty-nine reports focused on a variety of actions, although many dealt with the war on terrorism. Roughly half involved American forces deployed in individual countries such as Afghanistan (after the events of 9/11), Bosnia (as part of the stabilization force), East Timor (in support of UN peacekeeping), Kosovo (as part of the effort to stabilize that province), Liberia (to support the evacuation of U.S. citizens), Haiti (in support of UN action), Iraq (at the start of the war in 2003), and Lebanon (to protect U.S. embassy personnel, U.S. citizens, and other international personnel). Several of them focused on antiterrorism actions in various countries and regions around the world, and many of the reports covered multiple areas. As such, they had the effect of reducing the number of individual reports as compared to previous presidents.

The eleven reports by the Obama administration (through September 2012) largely followed the Bush administration's style of filing "consolidated reports" or "supplemental consolidated reports." That is, President Obama would report to Congress on a number of military activities engaged by the United States at a particular time in one report. In December 2010, for instance, Obama reported to Congress on the American deployments in Afghanistan, Iraq, and Kosovo. In June 2011, he reported on ongoing activities in Afghanistan, a new deployment to Egypt, the transferring of military operations in Libya to NATO, and the continuing deployment to Kosovo. In at least two reports, the president informed Congress on a single deployment (on actions toward Libya in March 2011 and a hostage rescue mission in Somalia in January 2012).

Continuing Controversies

Despite these presidential reports, Congress has been dissatisfied with the level and depth of **executive notification**. Since the passage of the WPR, none of the eight presidents has fully complied with it, and each has viewed it as an unconstitutional intrusion on his commander-in-chief powers.[22] Furthermore, several controversies continue to plague its implementation.

Failure to Fully Comply Executive reservations about the resolution are evident in the fact that presidents carefully phrase their congressional reports and do not fully comply with the resolution's requirements. In virtually every report that the executive has sent forward, the same language is used. He is providing the report "in accordance with my desire that Congress be fully informed on this matter, and consistent with the War Powers Resolution."[23] **(See nearly identical language by President Obama's letter near the end of Document 8.1.)** In no report does he acknowledge compliance with the WPR. Indeed, only President Ford in his report on the *Mayaguez* incident in 1975 cites the operative section (Section 4 [a] [1]) of the resolution (and, hence, acknowledges the sixty-day deployment limitation), although he did so only after the military conflict had ceased. In a few other cases, presidents cited Section 4. Ford, for example, cited Section 4 (a) (2) on American evacuation efforts from Vietnam and Cambodia, and President Reagan cited "Section 4 (a) (2) of the War Powers Resolution," in reporting on the deployment of American military personnel in the Sinai Desert to keep the peace between Israel and Egypt. Yet that section does not set in motion the limit on deployment to sixty days.[24] Further, in a few reports, no specific reference was made to the WPR at all. Finally, and almost invariably, presidents justify their use of force on their constitutional authority as commander-in-chief and as chief executive. Consider, for example, the last paragraph in Document 8.1 in which Obama justifies the various actions taken in this way.

Failure to Report Failure to report at all has also weakened the impact of the WPR. Critics charged, for instance, that President Nixon failed to report to Congress when U.S. forces were used to evacuate Americans from Cyprus during the ethnic conflict there in 1974. President Carter raised the ire of Representative Paul Findley for his failure to report to Congress after placing some American forces on alert and for sending U.S. transport aircraft to Zaire (now Congo) during secessionist activities in that country in May 1978.[25]

President Reagan became embroiled in controversy with Congress over the applicability of the WPR to Central America and the Middle East. When the administration increased the number of American military advisors in El Salvador, it claimed that military personnel were not being introduced into hostilities, nor were they in a situation where "imminent hostilities might occur," as the resolution required.[26] Over a deployment to Lebanon, Reagan's position was that American forces, first dispatched there in 1982, were on a "peacekeeping mission" at the request of the Lebanese government and that they were neither involved in hostilities nor in any immediate danger.

Other episodes that appeared to be covered by the WPR were not reported to Congress. The Reagan administration, for instance, did not report on the navy's interception of an Egyptian airliner carrying the hijackers of the *Achille Lauro* in 1985 or on U.S. Army assistance to the Bolivian government in antidrug efforts in 1986. President George H. W. Bush failed to report to Congress on sending American military advisors to Colombia, Bolivia, and Peru as part of a new antidrug strategy and on American efforts to convey Belgian troops into Zaire during September 1991. In 1998, President Clinton did not report to Congress on American bombing of Iraq to destroy facilities capable of nuclear, biological, or chemical weapons and to attack Iraqi military targets.[27]

The Obama administration's use of American forces in Libya in 2011 also produced accusations of failure to comply with the reporting requirements of the WPR. A House resolution passed in June 2011 charged that the Obama administration had "failed to provide Congress with a compelling rationale" for its actions in Libya and failed to provide a complete statement on American "security interests and objectives in Libya."[28] Furthermore, the resolution demanded an explanation for why the administration failed to obtain congressional authorization for the use of U.S. forces in Libya. As one analyst has noted, the issue of compliance went even further. That is, even by the time of the Obama administration's submittal of this report as requested by Congress, American military action in Libya had exceeded the sixty-day limit in the WPR and was close to exceeding the ninety-day limit.[29]

In its report to the Speaker of the House, the Obama administration responded by citing the president's constitutional authority as commander-in-chief and chief executive to order such military actions and "the limited nature, scope and duration of the anticipated actions." Furthermore, the report stated, "the President is of the view that the current U.S. military operations in Libya are consistent with the War Powers Resolution and do not under the law require further congressional authorization, because U.S. military operations are distinct from the kind of 'hostilities' contemplated by the Resolution's 60 day termination provision."[30]

Failure to Consult   The "prior consultation" requirement has caused even greater difficulty between Congress and the executive branch. Members of Congress have generally held that the president has not really "consulted" with them before using American military forces, but has often merely "informed" them of his intention to do so.[31] The executive branch, however, has insisted that it has generally consulted with Congress and has kept it informed.

The evidence is mixed based on the limited instances available. President Ford, for example, "advised" the congressional leadership on his plans for the evacuation from Southeast Asia in 1975. President Reagan held a meeting with congressional leaders before the actual invasion of Grenada in 1983, after he had signed the invasion order; he also met with them after ordering the air strike against Libya in 1986, although, again, after he had directed it to be carried out. President Bush met with congressional leaders seven hours before the invasion of Panama was to begin to inform them of his decision.[32]

In other instances, when presidents have chosen not to consult with Congress, they have defended their actions by pointing to the need for secrecy in carrying out an operation, the limited time available for consultation, and the inherent presidential power to act. When President Carter, for instance, was confronted by Congress over his failure to consult prior to the Iran rescue mission in 1980, his legal counsel offered one or more of these rationales.[33] In 1989, when President Bush failed to consult Congress over his use of American aircraft to assist Corazon Aquino's government in the Philippines in avoiding an insurrection, his national security advisor, Brent Scowcroft, stated that "the nature of the rapidly evolving situation required an extremely rapid decision very late at night and consultation was simply not an option."[34]

Inadequate prior consultation also characterized the Clinton administration. His administration, for instance, did little to consult with Congress prior to its intervention in Haiti in September 1994 and subsequently acknowledged that it had adopted a strategy that was not likely to allow congressional action. Rather, according to one executive branch official, it was "to get as much positive impact as we could without opening a debate that would be harmful, not helpful."[35] One analysis, however, suggests that the Clinton administration, while acting "very much like past administrations in dealing with Congress" over war powers, did reach "out in a manner uncharacteristic of recent presidents." In particular, this analysis suggests, Clinton consulted with

Congress prior to the bombing of the headquarters of Osama bin Laden in August 1998 and prior to the bombing of Kosovo in March 1999, and used the "*rhetoric* of 'consultation'" prior to implementing the Dayton Accords over Bosnia in 1995.[36]

After the events of September 11, President George W. Bush initially indicated his willingness to consult with Congress, but his overall record was one of defending the prerogatives of the presidency with limited consultation on the use of force. In signing **Public Law 107-40** on September 18, 2001 (see Chapter 7), for example, he stated that he had enjoyed the "benefit of meaningful consultations with members of Congress" since the terrorist attack. At the same time, he reasserted the "President's constitutional authority to use force."[37]

President Obama has seemingly not moved away from this position—whether over sending more troops to Afghanistan in 2010 or committing American forces in Libya in 2011. In the latter case, in particular, it was charged that the Obama administration failed to consult before authorizing the use of American forces there. In response, the administration issued a listing of "Libya-related hearings, briefings, calls, and other communication and consultation between Congress and the Executive Branch from March 1 through June 15 [2011]."[38] In this sense, the Obama administration contended that it had consulted with Congress on this action.

The problem of eliciting regular presidential cooperation in the consultative process continues, but several questions remain about the process itself. Three, in particular, seem crucial.[39] First, **when should consultation take place**? That is, what kind of situations require discussions with Congress? Because the WPR does not spell out all such circumstances, ambiguity remains. Second, **what actions by the executive constitute consultation**? Is informing or meeting with members of Congress on a presidential decision sufficient? Or does the course of action still need to be in doubt to justify full consultation? Third, **with whom should the executive branch consult**? Is consultation (however meant) with the congressional leadership sufficient? Or should only certain foreign policy committees be involved? Congress and the executive have differing views on these items, which have yet to be resolved.

Reforming or Repealing the WPR?

Although such controversies continue to fuel the war powers debate, a larger, lingering question concerns the constitutionality of the WPR in whole or part. In his veto message back in 1973, President Nixon questioned the constitutionality of that portion of the resolution dealing with the withdrawal of troops prior to the sixty-day limit through the use of a concurrent resolution and the imposition of the sixty-day clock. In the *Chadha* decision (see Chapter 7), the Supreme Court seemingly resolved part of this question by invalidating the use of the **concurrent resolution**, or Congress's "legislative veto." Indeed, Congress acknowledged as much by passing legislation in late 1983 requiring a joint resolution for any withdrawal of troops prior to the close of the sixty-day period.[40] (A **joint resolution** requires the approval by a majority of both houses *and* the president's approval, whereas a concurrent resolution requires only congressional majorities.) The constitutionality of the time limit, identified by the executive branch as a challenge to presidential powers in foreign affairs, has yet to be resolved by the Court or even to be directly challenged there. Still, it remains a major reason that every president since Nixon has challenged the constitutionality of the WPR as a whole.[41]

Although congressional efforts have been made to change the resolution to resolve these and other concerns, none has been successful. Numerous proposals have been offered over the years. Some proposed repeal of the resolution, others suggested strengthening the consultation procedures, and still others would have dropped the sixty-day limit on the use of force and required an affirmative congressional vote on the president's use of force.[42] Indeed, in June 1995, this frustration reached a peak when the House of Representatives voted on a repeal of the WPR. By a narrow margin (217–201), the House voted not to repeal. Despite frustration over the resolution and the increasing belief of many members that the president should have a free hand in the conduct of foreign policy, a sufficient number of representatives did not want to go quite that far.

Congress's frustration over the Iraq War, and its earlier passage of the Iraq Resolution in 2002, led to another attempt to recapture the war powers in 2007. Legislation was drafted and introduced to repeal the Iraq Resolution of 2002. Although the Democratic majority acknowledged that such Senate legislation might not come up for a vote or pass if it did reach the floor, the aim was to advance the debate beyond the war itself "to a battle over directly restricting the commander in chief's war powers."[43] Despite these intentions, no such measure made it through Congress during that session, and considerable judicial and political obstacles would confront any repeal effort, as one analysis noted.[44]

In July 2008, the National War Powers Commission once again called for the repeal of the 1973 WPR. Headed by former secretaries of state James Baker and Warren Christopher, and composed of distinguished former government officials and academics, it proposed the passage of the "War Powers Consultation Act of 2009," requiring "more meaningful consultation between the president and Congress on matters of war," to replace the 1973 resolution.[45] In particular, the new measure would require (1) executive–legislative consultation before deployment of American forces, (2) definition of hostilities requiring such consultation, and (3) a congressional vote approving or disapproving American involvement within thirty days of initiation. This reform effort failed as well.

In a broader sense, and despite congressional unhappiness over presidential compliance, the WPR seems to have served at least some of its original purposes: It has generally limited the executive branch's use of military force without involving Congress in *some fashion*; it has prevented long-term military involvements (such as the Vietnam War); and, perhaps more important, it probably has made the president more circumspect and cautious in initiating foreign military actions. Indeed, political scientists David Auerswald and Peter Cowhey have demonstrated that conflicts initiated by presidents were considerably longer before the WPR than after it.[46] Although a counterfactual by definition cannot be demonstrated empirically, the WPR has probably prevented the use of U.S. ground forces in some instances (such as in Central America during the 1980s) and will likely do so in the future.

CONTROLLING THE PURSE STRINGS

A third area of congressional response to executive foreign policy power has been the use of its **funding power** (the "purse strings"). Legislative funding provisions were increasingly used in the 1970s and 1980s to achieve a variety of broad foreign policy objectives: (1) to reduce American military involvement abroad; (2) to stop covert actions in the Third World; (3) to allow congressional review of the sale of weapons and the transfer of nuclear fuels to other countries; (4) to specify trading relations with other nations; and (5) to limit the transfer of U.S. economic and military assistance to countries with gross violations of human rights, among others. In several instances, specific countries were identified by Congress and restrictions imposed on them as a means of shaping foreign policy. Specific human rights restrictions were applied to the transfer of military assistance to El Salvador, for example, and, for a time, Congress cut off all funding for the Nicaraguan Contras as a means of changing the Reagan administration's Nicaraguan policy. "Earmarking" of foreign assistance funds, too, became a particularly popular mechanism as Congress sought to influence foreign affairs.

Most of these measures are still used in the second decade of the twenty-first century, as the power of the purse remains a potent policy instrument. Longtime Democratic chairman of the Senate Appropriations Committee, Robert Byrd (D-West Virginia), bluntly reminded the Clinton administration of this power over the prospect of sending American forces into Bosnia two decades ago: "It's very important for the President to seek approval of Congress. The title of Commander in Chief is one thing. But the power of the purse is the greatest power in our Constitutional system."[47] Several differing measures used by Congress will illustrate how funding can affect the direction of American foreign policy.

Cutting Off and Conditioning Funding

First, Congress has sometimes used (or tried to use) a blunt instrument to shape foreign policy: cutting off funds for actions that it opposes. From 1966 to 1973, it cast ninety-four roll call votes on questions relating to American involvement in Southeast Asia, but only a few of them succeeded in affecting U.S. policy.[48] By 1973, however, the situation had changed, and Congress succeeded in passing a sweeping measure that stopped funding as of August 15, 1973, for military activities "in or over or from off the shores of North Vietnam, South Vietnam, Laos, or Cambodia."[49] Later, in 1975, when President Ford asked for congressional approval of new assistance to Vietnam shortly before its fall, Congress said no.[50]

Spurred by the use of funding measures to shape policy in Vietnam, Congress enacted other funding restrictions over the years. In 1975, **it cut off military and economic aid to Turkey** because of the Turkish invasion of Cyprus earlier that year.[51] (Turkey had used American-supplied weapons in violation of statutory requirements that they not be used offensively.) In 1976, it attached the **Clark Amendment**, a measure prohibiting American assistance to any group in the Angolan civil war, to the Arms Export Control Act.[52]

In the 1980s, Congress continued to use the cut-off mechanism, but now with a more nuanced approach to policy: restrictions or conditions on the use or continuance of funding. In 1981, for example, it attached a human rights reporting requirement to the International Security and Development Cooperation Act of 1981 as a condition of continued military assistance to El Salvador.[53] In 1983, it succeeded in placing a further restriction on Salvadoran military aid by specifying that 30 percent of all such aid for fiscal 1984 be withheld until those accused of murdering four U.S. churchwomen were brought to trial and a verdict rendered.[54]

In another prominent attempt to guide American foreign policy in Central America during this period, Congress relied on a combination of conditioning and cutting off aid. From 1982 to 1986, it passed a series of **Boland Amendments** to first restrict and then prevent the Reagan administration from aiding the Nicaraguan Contras in their fight against the Sandinista government.

Throughout the 1990s and to the present, Congress has continued to use the funding mechanism to shape policy and policy making. In authorization bills for foreign assistance and for the State Department, the House of Representatives sought to reshape the foreign policy bureaucracies (for example, by consolidating within the Department of State all or part of three independent agencies—the Arms Control and Disarmament Agency, the United States Information Agency, and the Agency for International Development and by making cuts in foreign assistance and eliminating some programs).[55] A long-running dispute between Congress and the executive throughout much of the 1990s was over funding for the United Nations, particularly whether American funds would be used to support abortions. This dispute was ultimately resolved near the end of the Clinton administration, but funding cutoffs do affect foreign policy making.

Over the past decade, Congress also sought to use the blunt instrument of withholding funds to convey its policy position, albeit not always successfully. In 2002, for instance, the members of the House and Senate Appropriations Committees thwarted President George W. Bush's request to transfer budget authority within the new Department of Homeland Security and even to create that department for a time.[56] In 2007, when the Democrats won control of both houses of Congress after the November 2006 elections, the new majorities sought to use the funding power to stop the Iraq War, but they were unsuccessful. In 2010, the Obama administration also experienced this legislative power when Congress blocked the president's executive order to close the prison at Guantanamo Bay, Cuba, one year after his inauguration, by refusing to provide the necessary funding to convert mainland facilities for these detainees and expressed its opposition to transferring them to U.S. soil.

Earmarking of Funds

A second way that Congress may shape foreign policy with the purse strings is through *earmarking* **funds** for particular purposes. Legislation designating funds for specific regional or functional programs (such as the African Development Foundation, refugee assistance programs) qualify as earmarks, as do prohibition on the use of funds for particular countries (such as excluding Cuba, Iran, North Korea, and Syria from assistance). Furthermore, Congress has explicitly prohibited assistance "to the government of any country whose duly elected head of government is deposed by military coup or decree."[57] The more common use of the term *earmarking*, however, refers to "specific amounts of foreign aid for individual countries."[58]

The data in Table 8.2 lists the top ten recipients of American foreign assistance for fiscal year 2012.[59] Several of these countries have these funds designated to them by the congressional legislation. For instance, Israel and Egypt have long received such "earmarked" or designated funds. Others (such as Afghanistan and Pakistan) have come to receive such designated funds in light of the efforts against international terrorism. The other top recipients on this list are important regional states, whether in the Middle East (Jordan) or throughout Africa (Kenya, Nigeria, and Ethiopia). What is important to keep in mind in reviewing this listing is how these leading recipients change, largely in response to international events, or remain the same over time, largely due to enduring American interests. Israel, Egypt, and Jordan have long been leading recipients of American assistance, but a decade earlier (in FY 2002), Colombia, Turkey, Peru, and India were among the top ten recipients of aid.[60] In large measure, these aid recipients (whether earmarked or not) reflect the priorities of American foreign policy and allow Congress to play a role in shaping them.

Although earmarks are criticized for restricting executive discretion and installing a certain rigidity into the foreign assistance program, their defenders point to them as an important and perhaps a pivotal way for Congress to shape foreign policy. At the

Table 8.2 Ten Leading Recipients of American Foreign Assistance for FY2012

	Total aid
Israel	$3.1 billion
Afghanistan	$2.3 billion
Pakistan	$2.1 billion
Iraq	$1.7 billion
Egypt	$1.6 billion
Tanzania	$752 million
Jordan	$701 million
Kenya	$652 million
Nigeria	$625 million
Ethiopia	$580 million

Source: Department of State, Foreign Operations CBJ FY2013. The data include supplementals and projected Millennium Challenge Corporation Compact disbursements in FY2012. Thanks to Jacob Parker, Office of Congressman Tom Latham, for assistance in obtaining these data.

same time, members of Congress have been reluctant to discuss such designated aid as "earmarks" because of negative political connotations associated with the term today. Instead the language utilized in the appropriations legislation is more circumspect and directs that such "funds appropriated under this heading [with a specific amount] shall be available for [a designated country]."[61] In all, the congressional intent is clear.

Specifying Trade and Aid Requirements

In the 1970s and continuing into the 1980s, Congress also sought other vehicles to ensure greater participation in foreign policy through trade and foreign aid legislation. Increasingly, it attempted to add important amendments to both kinds of legislation in order to work its will. Several of these amendments, although passed several decades ago, continue to play an important role in the policy process today.

In the early 1970s, Congress added the Jackson–Vanik Amendment to the Trade Act of 1974.[62] The **Jackson–Vanik Amendment** directed that the United States grant most-favored-nation (MFN) status only to those countries that fostered a free emigration policy and did not impose "more than a nominal tax" on citizens wishing to emigrate. Without mentioning any country by name, the amendment's clear intent was to deny MFN status to the Soviet Union. It proved successful inasmuch as the Soviets rejected this provision as an infringement on its national sovereignty. Still, the restrictions in the legislation came to affect other states and American policy toward them. Specifically, this legislation had a continuing impact on trading relations with China, especially in light of that country's dismal human rights record, and the legislation thus required a yearly exemption by the president for China to continue trading ties—until the subsequent congressional passage of legislation granting China permanent normal trading relations in 2000 (we discuss shortly).

At about the same time, Congress passed the **Nelson–Bingham Amendment** to the 1974 Foreign Assistance Act as a way for the legislative branch to have some impact on burgeoning U.S. arms sales abroad.[63] Under this legislation, Congress had the right of a twenty-day review of any intended arms sale of $25 million or more. Moreover, it reserved the right to reject such a sale by passing a concurrent resolution of disapproval. In the International Security Assistance and Arms Export Control Act of 1976, this provision was modified somewhat to allow congressional review of any offer to sell defense articles or services totaling $25 million or more or any major defense equipment totaling $7 million or more.[64] The time limit for congressional review was extended from twenty to thirty days, and the right of Congress to reject such a sale by concurrent resolution was maintained. Further, through an informal agreement with the Ford administration, Congress was afforded an additional twenty-day period of "informal notification"—a policy that has been continued by succeeding administrations.[65] This review procedure for arms sale remains in effect today, but the legislative veto provision (allow a concurrent resolution of disapproval) is no longer applicable in light of the *Chadha* decision (see Chapter 7).

In the same security assistance legislation (and in earlier economic assistance legislation), Congress added human rights considerations in U.S. dealings with other countries.[66] Under these provisions, neither security assistance nor economic assistance would be granted to any government that "engages in a consistent pattern of gross violations of internationally recognized human rights." Similar provisions were added to funding for multilateral banks, such as the World Bank, the Inter-American Development Bank, the African Development Fund, and the Asian Development Bank.[67] These provisions, too, remain in effect today and are important statements of American human rights.

In the 1990s and beyond, congressional measures specifying foreign aid and trade requirements continued. Four important measures are particularly important to note because they illustrate how Congress has come to impact policy toward differing regions of the world. In 1992, for example, Congress was instrumental in shaping the **Freedom Support Act**, the principal initial U.S. effort to provide economic assistance to the former states of the Soviet Union. Although the administration had requested broad spending discretion, Congress put limits on aid levels and subjected this aid to certain conditions. In addition, it passed legislation to assist the former Soviet republics in dismantling their nuclear weapons in accordance with the START and START II treaties.[68] The latter, popularly known as the **Nunn–Lugar amendment**, was an important initiative for dealing with the newly emerging global threat of "loose nukes." Importantly, too, these legislative instruments are still utilized to conduct relations with Russia and the former Soviet republics.

Congress also initiated and passed legislation toward a region of Africa and an important nation in Latin America during these years. The **Horn of Africa Recovery and Food Security Act of 1992**, for instance, required that the president "must certify that the [recipient] government had begun to implement peace or national reconciliation agreements, demonstrated a commitment to human rights and democracy, and held or scheduled free or fair elections" before the granting of aid.[69] Under *Plan Colombia*, a $1.3 billion foreign assistance program passed in 2000, Congress also imposed a series of conditions—aimed primarily at possible human rights violations by the military—under which the Colombian government would receive aid. In particular, Colombia was required to issue an order specifying that military personnel charged with human rights violations be tried in civilian, not military, courts and that military personnel so accused be suspended from duty. In addition, the Colombian government was required to devise a strategy to eliminate coca and poppy production by 2005 and to develop a judge advocate general corps to investigate military misconduct.[70]

In the **foreign aid** area, these specifications and conditions continue. In the FY2012 appropriations, Congress placed numerous conditions on the use of American assistance toward particular countries and groups, as it has done in the past. A few examples from the legislation will illustrate how extensively Congress seeks to specify American aid funds and, in so doing, shape foreign policy. The appropriations report, accompanying the 2012 legislation, specified that economic funds to Egypt be conditioned on the secretary of state certifying to the House and Senate Appropriations Committees "that such government is meeting its obligations under the 1979 Egypt-Israel Peace Treaty." Similarly, it directed that no funds "may be used by the Government of the United States to enter into a permanent basing rights agreement between the United States and Iraq." Further, it prohibited aid to an emergent Palestinian state (without meeting several specifications), limited the aid to the Palestinian Authority, prohibited aid to Zimbabwe "except to meet basic needs or to promote democracy," and directed aid to Uganda "for programs and activities in areas affected by the Lord's Resistance Army." At the same time, we should point out that many of these conditions (and others) in the legislation can be waived if "the Secretary of State determines and reports to the Committees on Appropriations that to do so is in the national security interest of the United States." In this sense, these conditions are not as ironclad as they might first suggest. Nonetheless, the Committee on Appropriations needs to be fully informed of these changes.[71]

In the **trade** area, Congress's record in putting its imprint on policy is perhaps uneven, but some efforts have been made to direct policy in recent years. Perhaps the most celebrated recent effort centered on denying MFN trade status to China owing to its abysmal human rights record. As noted earlier, presidents over the years had invoked an exemption clause from the Jackson–Vanik Amendment to grant the Chinese this status on a yearly basis. Resolutions objecting to the presidential exemptions were introduced and, on occasion, passed in one or both houses, only to be vetoed by the president. This pattern continued until the Clinton administration "delinked" trade policy with China and human rights. Near the end of Clinton's term, Congress actually passed new legislation granting China **permanent normal trading relations (PNTR)**.[72]

Two pieces of trade legislation passed by Congress early in the twenty-first century expanded trade with Africa and the Caribbean and restricted it with Libya and Iran. In 2000, for instance, it lowered American tariffs and removed quotas mainly on textiles from sub-Saharan Africa, the Caribbean, and Central America as a way to assist the economies in those areas. In 2001, Congress tightened sanctions on businesses that invested more than $20 million in the energy industry in either Libya or Iran and extended them for five years. This action was partly in response to Libyan involvement in the 1988 bombing of Pan Am Flight 103 and both countries' involvement with international terrorism and the development of weapons of mass destruction.[73]

Congress also put its imprint on policy toward Cuba by initiating, and passing, tougher economic sanctions against it. The **Cuban Democracy Act of 1992** directed that trade between Cuba and U.S. subsidiaries in other countries be prohibited.[74] Although the measure was opposed by the George H. W. Bush administration, and some presidential flexibility was eventually incorporated into the legislation, it did reflect a continuing congressional effort on trade policy. In 1996, after an anti-Castro plane was shot down in international waters off Cuba, Congress passed, and President Clinton agreed to sign, a measure to tighten sanctions further. Under the **Helms–Burton** legislation, foreign individuals who traded with Cuba were denied access to the United States, and foreign companies in Cuba that used property formerly belonging to Americans could be sued in American courts.[75]

Perhaps the most important congressional action in the current era has been the expansion of sanctions against Iran over its nuclear ambitions. Under the Comprehensive Iran Sanctions, Accountability, and Divestment Act of 2012, passed in the summer of 2010, the Congress importantly placed sanctions on those firms that made sales of "over $1 million (or $5 million in a one year period) of gasoline and related aviation and other fuels to Iran" and on those firms that made "sales to Iran of equipment or services . . . which would help Iran make or import gasoline." Such sanctions were viewed as crucial in trying to influence that nation's nuclear ambitions because Iran imports about 40 percent of its gasoline. Further, the Obama administration tightened sanctions on Iran's energy sector in November 2011 by issuing an executive order, utilizing the International Emergency Economic Powers Act passed by Congress in the late 1970s (see Chapter 7).[76]

Congress can place its imprint on trade policy in one more way: the refusal to vote on trade legislation. From 2007 to 2011, for instance, Congress held up passage of three free trade agreements (FTAs)—with South Korea, Colombia, and Panama—that had been negotiated by the Bush administrations over members' objections about the impact of such agreements on the American economy. The concerns in the South Korean FTA focused on that country's restrictions on the importation of American beef and automobiles, whereas the issues with the Colombia and Panama FTAs primarily focused on the lack of protections that those countries provided to their workers and money laundering, respectively. A more general concern with these pacts was their impact on American jobs and the amount of trade adjustment assistance that would be provided to displaced American workers. As a result, the Obama administration was required to negotiate a number of side agreements and to renegotiate components of these pacts to win congressional approval in late 2011.[77] In sum, then, Congress increasingly uses its funding and commerce powers to affect American foreign policy. Moreover, these vehicles will likely remain important, and their use will continue to take a variety of forms, including cutting off funds, earmarking appropriations, and imposing some form of spending restrictions on assistance or aid to particular countries.

CONGRESSIONAL OVERSIGHT

The fourth area of congressional resurgence is in the area of *oversight*, which in this case refers to Congress's reviewing and monitoring of executive branch foreign policy actions. In general, oversight has expanded because Congress has imposed more and more reporting requirements on the executive branch, and congressional committees have increased their review as well. In particular, the increase in activity by key congressional committees—Foreign Affairs (formerly International Relations) and Armed Services (briefly National Security) in the House and Foreign Relations and Armed Services in the Senate—has been much more pronounced in recent decades and has contributed to more congressional foreign policy oversight.[78] Still, the quantity and quality of congressional oversight have come in for criticism in recent years. Before we take up that critique, we first review the vehicles of congressional oversight, beginning with increased reporting requirements in recent decades.

Expansion of Reporting Requirements to Congress

The major mechanism of expanded congressional oversight of foreign policy has been the **increase in reporting requirements** imposed on the executive branch. That is, the president or the executive branch must file a written report on how a given aspect of American foreign policy was carried out. As we have noted, important pieces of foreign policy legislation already incorporate this kind of requirement (for example, the Case–Zablocki Act, the WPR, and arms sales legislation), but its extent goes beyond these specific instances. By one estimate, from the late 1980s, Congress had imposed approximately 600 foreign policy reporting requirements on the executive, a threefold increase from the early 1970s. The requirements have been described as a valuable "tool to oversee executive branch implementation of foreign policy" and as "the workhorses of congressional oversight."[79] The exact number of reporting requirements today is hard to calculate, but the totals remains substantial. Even a cursory review of the foreign aid appropriations legislation for FY2012 points to the several dozen reports required of the secretary of state to the House and Senate Appropriations Committees for various actions taken or proposed. Those instances in themselves give some sense of the magnitude of reporting currently required, despite legislation passed in the 1990s to "sunset" some of these requirements.

The three main types of reports required of the executive branch are **periodic or recurrent reports, notifications**, and **one-time reports**. The **periodic reporting requirement** directs the executive branch to submit particular information to Congress every year, every six months, or even quarterly.[80] In the mid-1970s, for example, an amendment was added to the Foreign Assistance Act that required an annual assessment of human rights conditions around the world. This report must be forwarded to Congress early in each new calendar year and becomes an important source of information on human rights globally. Another example directs the executive branch to outline the foreign policies pursued by member countries of the United Nations. The aim here is to assess how the policies of those countries comport with the policies and interests of the United States.[81] Yet another piece of legislation instructs the executive branch to prepare "a single, comprehensive and comparative analysis of the economic policies and trade practices of each country with which the United States has an economic or trade relationship."[82] Under current foreign aid legislation dealing with international security assistance, for example, the secretary of state must provide the Appropriations Committees quarterly accounting, in writing, on the use of such funding.[83]

A second kind of report, and by far the most frequent, is a **notification**, which requires the executive branch to inform Congress that a particular foreign policy action is contemplated or has been undertaken. Notifications of executive agreements or the use of military force fall into this category, but the majority involves arms sales, arms control measures, and assistance. Perhaps the most frequent notification occurs with changes in levels of funding of foreign assistance for particular countries. The executive branch must notify Congress whenever it "reprograms" economic or military assistance funds from one program or project to another in given countries and sometimes places special notification requirements for some.[84] As one illustration, consider the current foreign aid legislation where Congress requires that the secretary of state report to the Appropriations Committees, within forty-five days of the passage of the appropriations legislation and prior to the initial obligation of funding, a country-by-country listing and a proposed use of such funds "for each proposed program, project, or activity" for international narcotics control and law enforcement.[85] Similar kinds of notifications to the Appropriations Committees are required for a whole series of actions associated with foreign aid funding.

The third type of report, the **one-time report**, calls on the executive branch to examine a particular issue or question. This type is probably the most infrequent, but it can be very useful to Congress in its effort to understand an issue or to shape future policy. In the mid-1980s, with the passage of the Anti-Apartheid Act, for example, Congress called for ten one-time reports from the executive branch. They involved the degree to which the United States depended on South Africa for minerals, the kind of programs available to help black South Africans, and U.S. efforts to obtain international cooperation to end apartheid.[86] In another piece of legislation, Congress required the secretary of defense to complete "a study of the functions and organization of the Office of the Secretary of Defense" and to submit a copy to Congress within one year of enactment of the legislation.[87] Yet another recent foreign aid appropriations bill required a one-time report on the extent to which developing countries were contributing to the "greenhouse effect" and what efforts would be most beneficial in reducing harmful emissions. In the renewal of sanctions against Iran and Libya in 2001, which we discussed earlier, Congress directed the president to submit a report on the effectiveness of the sanctions during the eighteen months since their passage.[88]

In 2007, Congress directed the Bush administration to submit several one-time reports on the situation in Iraq. The U.S Troop Readiness, Veterans' Care, Katrina Recovery, and Iraq Accountability Appropriations Act of 2007 required reports to Congress on whether the Iraqi government had met some eighteen benchmarks spelled out in previous legislation. General David Petraeus, the commander of the Multi-National Force for Iraq, presented one report in rather dramatic fashion in person to Congress in September 2007, and another was prepared by the U.S. Government Accountability Office.[89] Another piece of congressional legislation commissioned an independent commission to assess the capacity and capabilities of the Iraqi Security Forces and that report was submitted in September 2007 as well.[90]

In June 2011, the House of Representatives passed a resolution directing the Obama administration to submit a report to that chamber within fourteen days on the rationale for American military activities in Libya. The House required the executive branch to explain "in detail" the American security objectives by this action and to provide an explanation for not seeking congressional authorization for this action. Indeed, the administration responded at the end of the designated period with a thirty-two-page report outlining its rationale and its defense of presidential prerogatives (as noted earlier in this chapter).[91]

These kinds of reports are, of course, informational and involve important record-keeping by the Congress, but they can be more than that. They affect policy by alerting Congress to changes or potential changes in administration aims and may well set off "fire alarms" in some quarters of the House and the Senate. For instance, reports on proposed new arms sales to Arab states or to Israel may elicit reactions from some members. Reports on new covert operations in various corners of the world may have a similar effect. As a result, some policy proposals may turn out to be stillborn or may be changed dramatically before congressional enactment. On the other hand, even a one-time or yearly report can prove to be significant. Because the Department of State must report annually on global human rights conditions, Congress may be able to use that information to monitor the changing situation within a country and use it in an attempt to impose new restrictions or lift current ones. In short, these reports are beneficial to Congress and to the policy process.

Senate Foreign Relations Committee

In the first three decades after World War II, the Senate Foreign Relations Committee was viewed as the focal point for congressional monitoring of the foreign policy actions of the president; in more recent decades, however, its influence has declined.

The committee can and does affect the foreign policy process from time to time, although perhaps not as regularly as it did in earlier decades. Several reasons account for its real and potential influence.

First, this committee has **constitutional and oversight responsibilities**. Not only is it responsible for monitoring foreign affairs but it is also required to advise on and consent to treaties and presidential nominations for various diplomatic posts.[92] The committee has been viewed as the most prestigious in the Senate (and perhaps in Congress) and provides a ready forum for members seeking to shape foreign policy and national politics. Furthermore, it provides valuable foreign policy experience for members who entertain presidential ambitions. Indeed, a number of committee members over the years have actively sought the presidential nomination of their party, including Senator John Kerry in 2004 and Senators Joseph Biden, Christopher Dodd, and Barack Obama in 2008.

Second, the quality of the **committee's leadership** in the immediate post–World War II years contributed initially to its activism and influence. Particularly prominent among recent committee chairs was Senator J. William Fulbright (D–Arkansas), who served for fifteen years. His penetrating hearings on American involvement in Vietnam contributed significantly to the national debate on this issue and to America's eventual withdrawal from Southeast Asia.[93] Further, his active involvement in the numerous reform efforts in the late 1960s and early 1970s ensured the committee's prominence in the shaping of the nation's foreign policy.

Senate Foreign Relations Committee chairs in the 1970s and 1980s did not gain the same stature as Fulbright, and the prestige and activism of the committee began to wane.[94] An exception to this generalization was Senator **Richard Lugar**, a conservative Republican from Indiana who was chair for a short time in the 1980s and again during the first decade of the twenty-first century. Although Lugar initially supported the Reagan administration,[95] he also led "by charting a course and sticking with it, working behind the scenes to build consensus through compromise and patient prodding."[96] Hence, the committee was able to exert influence on several issues during his tenure, including passage of South African sanctions and the ouster of Ferdinand Marcos in the Philippines. When Lugar served as committee chair during the George W. Bush administration, he followed a similar tack. Lugar largely supported the Bush administration's policy, but he also consistently called for greater multilateralism than the administration was pursuing. Over time, he became increasingly critical of Bush's implementation of postwar reconstruction in Iraq. In this sense, he sought to continue the more independent role of the committee and was generally admired across the partisan divide.

In the mid-1990s, Senator **Jesse Helms** (R–North Carolina) was named committee chair. His tenure illustrates how one individual can shape the direction and priorities of the committee, and he left his mark on the committee. He came to the chairmanship with a reputation for a strong ideological view in both foreign and domestic policy questions, and his views quickly came to dominate committee operations. Although Helms initially seemed to veer away from his strongly held opinions (for example, dropping his opposition to the START II treaty and his tempering of his initial hostility to the North Korean–United States nuclear agreement), he still served as a staunch watchdog over the direction of policy.[97] By mid-1995, Helms was locked in a battle with the Clinton administration over the restructuring of the foreign affairs bureaucracy and a variety of other matters. In particular, he wanted to restructure the Department of State in a way that would effectively eliminate three semiautonomous bureaucracies—the Agency for International Development (AID), the Arms Control and Disarmament Agency (ACDA), and the United States Information Agency (USIA)—and wanted to install a nongovernmental foundation to manage U.S. assistance abroad.[98]

To accomplish this reorganization, Senator Helms employed his power as chair of the Senate Foreign Relations Committee to hold up committee and Senate action on State Department promotions, some thirty ambassadorial appointments, and several important treaties, including START II and the Chemical Weapons Convention.[99] The impasse was finally broken when the Clinton administration agreed to have Senate Democrats and Republicans together come up with legislation acceptable to both sides for reshaping the foreign affairs bureaucracy.[100] Still, the episode demonstrates the ability of one committee—and, indeed, one pivotal member of it—to influence the operation of foreign policy, at least for a time.

Helms's successors were Senator **Joseph Biden** (D-Delaware) and Senator Lugar (R-Indiana). As the ranking Democrat, Biden had worked well with Helms over the years to forge some movement within the Committee. As chair, he continued to work across the aisle, though he was the principal foreign policy critic of the Bush administration, differing on such issues as the development of national missile defense, efforts to reduce American forces in Bosnia, and the level of support for Taiwan.[101] After the 2002 election, Senator Lugar returned as committee chair for his another stint in that role.

After the 2006 congressional election, Senator Biden returned once again as chair. His initial impulses were to move toward a new policy approach toward Iraq rather than dwell on past administration errors, to advance legislation on nuclear cooperation with India, and to continue his commitment to bipartisan cooperation. Importantly, though, he promised greater committee oversight of administration policy. Biden rejected the Bush attempt "to conflate every serious foreign policy and national security issue under the rubric of terrorism."[102] Biden did indeed lead more Senate Foreign Relations hearings in 2007 (although the number was limited by his run for the Democratic presidential nomination, which kept him away from Washington), but he was not able to forge the bipartisan consensus that he envisioned or to pass the Iraq legislation that he had hoped to.[103]

With the election of Obama as president and Biden as his vice president, Senator **Kerry** (D-Massachusetts) assumed the chairmanship of the Foreign Relations Committee. Kerry has long desired to serve in this role, and he quickly became a confidant of President Obama on foreign policy. He promoted several foreign policy initiatives in his new role—holding hearings with veterans of Afghanistan, seeking more aid for Pakistan, trying to persuade the Afghan president to hold a runoff election, and calling for the creation of a no-fly zone over Libya. Most significantly, perhaps, he worked with Senator Lugar, now the ranking Republican on the committee, to gain passage of the New START Treaty.[104] Despite these efforts, though, the Senate Foreign Relations Committee continues to struggle to restore its previous high profile and the substantial prestige of earlier decades.

The House Committee on Foreign Affairs

Unlike the Senate Foreign Relations Committee, the House Committee on Foreign Affairs historically was seen as less prestigious than the Senate Foreign Relations Committee and some other House committees.[105] Unlike other House committees, too, Foreign Affairs was less likely to directly assist the constituency or biennial reelection goals of House members, and it was also less useful than the Senate Foreign

Relations Committee as a springboard to national prominence on foreign policy matters. Furthermore, the House committee had a more limited agenda, confined mainly to the preparation of the foreign assistance bill, and it lacked the wide sweep of responsibilities of its Senate counterpart.[106]

In the 1970s, the House Foreign Affairs Committee underwent a series of changes that produced a considerable resurgence of activity. Its oversight function, for instance, increased sharply.[107] This newfound zeal for oversight derived from the changing composition of the committee, the structural changes in the committee system within the House of Representatives, and a resurgent interest in foreign policy matters.[108] During that time, too, the committee was increasingly composed of younger, more liberal House members, who viewed foreign policy as an important part of their legislative activities. Often elected in opposition to the Vietnam War, these members were more determined than ever to make American foreign policy accountable to Congress. Moreover, this trend of the committee being more liberal than the House as a whole continued into the 1990s and 2000s, but it has increasingly been divided ideologically, much as the House.[109]

Structural reforms within the House also assisted the invigorated oversight process. In an effort to open up the congressional process, limitations were placed on committee chairs in the appointment of subcommittee chairs (they were now elected by the committee caucus) and on the number of subcommittees that any member could chair (the new limit was one).[110] As a result, more liberal members in the 1970s and 1980s emerged as subcommittee chairs. In addition, because of some jurisdictional changes, Foreign Affairs (and consequently its subcommittees) gained more review power over international economic issues.[111] One result of this enlarged agenda was a change in subcommittee organization, from primarily regional to functional. Although the committee eventually settled on a combination of functional and regional subcommittees, the pattern of increased responsibility had been set in motion.[112]

Yet another congressional reform of the 1970s aided the House Foreign Affairs Committee. Committee and subcommittee staffs were enlarged and formally placed under the chairs. Although changes regarding the subcommittee chair's control of his or her staff were already in place, the rule changes in the House formalized them and staff grew.[113] One important consequence of these changes has been the significant increase in Foreign Affairs committee and subcommittee hearings. In the 1970s and early 1980s, these hearings numbered more than 700 in a given Congress. Since then they have fallen off a bit, but they still numbered about 500 by the end of the twentieth century.[114] In short, the Foreign Affairs Committee played a larger role in both the formulation and the review of American foreign policy from the 1970s through the early 1990s under Democratic control.

With the Republicans in control after the 1994 elections, the committee's assertiveness and legislative oversight appeared little changed. It quickly changed its name from Foreign Affairs to International Relations, reduced the number of subcommittees, and took decisive action on its principal legislative measure, the foreign aid bill. With rather remarkable speed, and under the somewhat reluctant leadership of **Benjamin Gilman** (R–New York), who had long supported foreign assistance legislation, the committee passed a pared-down foreign aid bill by mid-1995. Like the Senate measure discussed previously, this bill abolished three foreign affairs agencies—AID, ACDA, and USIA—and called for sharp cuts in total foreign assistance.[115]

When Gilman's leadership ended, **Henry Hyde** (R–Illinois) succeeded him as chair in 2001. Hyde generally adopted positions consistent with the center of

Republican thinking, but he also promoted tougher positions toward China and the Palestinian Authority. In all, though, he tended to work with the Bush administration on most issues.[116] In the aftermath of the 2006 congressional elections, Tom Lantos (D-California) first assumed the leadership of the now renamed House Foreign Affairs Committee in 2007. His tenure as chair was cut short by his death in early 2008. His successor, Howard Berman (D-California), shared many of Lantos's views on key issues, but his tenure ended with Republicans recapturing the House in the 2010 elections.[117]

In 2011, **Ileana Ros-Lehtinen** assumed the chair of the House Foreign Affairs Committee. Ros-Lehtinen, the first Hispanic woman to serve in Congress and a native of Cuba, is an outspoken advocate on a number of foreign policy issues, including her staunch opposition to Castro's Cuba and strong support for Israel, and she is a constant proponent of global human rights and a strong voice against Islamic extremism. With her background chairing several subcommittees on foreign affairs before assuming the chair of the full committee, she has a wealth of experience to draw on in leading the committee. Moreover, the ranking Democrat on the committee perhaps best summarized her capacity to lead the committee: "People greatly underestimate her skill and tenaciousness."[118]

Across party control of the committee, then, House Foreign Affairs Committee, with its subcommittees, has at times been an active participant in the oversight and legislative process over the past three decades—in some instances matching and perhaps even surpassing its Senate counterparts. In this sense, the committee exercises a somewhat more independent role in the monitoring and shaping of foreign policy than it did in the past, but it continues to labor in the shadows of the Senate Foreign Relations Committee.

Armed Services Committees in the House and Senate

The House and Senate Armed Services committees have also enjoyed a bit of a renaissance in their foreign policy oversight activities in recent years. Throughout the 1950s and 1960s, both committees were often regarded as **largely supportive of the Pentagon on key policy matters**. One study, focusing on data to 1970, found that they relied on the Department of Defense for information about military matters and "usually ratified administration proposals." Another analysis described their role up to the early 1970s both as an "advocate" and as an "overseer," with the House Armed Services Committee less of an overseer and more of an advocate than its Senate counterpart.[119] A later analysis, however, claims that the "stylized image" of the two committees as protectors of a strong national defense and of local military bases and defense contractors remains, but that two changes—a move toward yearly military authorization procedures and an innovative approach to handling military base closings—have begun to alter this image.[120]

More generally, the rule changes in Congress and in congressional procedures during the 1970s—coupled with changes in leadership—enabled the Armed Services committees to match or approach what we described as happening with the House Foreign Affairs Committee. Although the extent of legislative oversight of defense policy changed modestly at first, by the 1980s oversight activities increased with the emergence of what one political scientist has called the "outside game" in defense policy making.[121] Because Congress as a whole was increasingly more interested in scrutinizing defense policy, the committees, too, had to examine legislative policy more carefully if they were to retain any legitimacy. This did happen, but one concern has been that the committees' responsibilities will be eroded with continued Congress-wide involvement.

The congressional armed services committees have also benefited from **more assertive leadership** at various times since the 1980s. In the House, **Les Aspin** (D-Wisconsin) gained the chairmanship of the Armed Services Committee by leaping over other members with greater seniority and by being more critical of Pentagon requests than previous leaders. Aspin's successor, Ron Dellums (D-California), headed the committee for only two years, and, although traditionally an outspoken critic of the military establishment, he appeared to be a more moderate, middle-of-the-road manager than might have been initially expected.

Under Dellum's Republican successor, Floyd Spence (R-South Carolina), the committee began to revert somewhat to its advocate role for the military. With Spence as leader, the Armed Services Committee (renamed the House National Security Committee for a time) sought to implement the Republican "Contract with America" for strengthening American military capabilities through greater readiness and more defense spending. Indeed, he (and others) proposed "their own multiyear, hundred billion dollar plans to increase military spending and shift defense priorities" shortly after the beginning of the 104th Congress.[122] By the end of this session, the committee—and the House and Senate as a whole—had passed a defense spending bill surpassing what the Clinton administration had proposed.

Representative Bob Stump (R-Arizona), the chair of the House Armed Services Committee by 2001, did not match the flair and global strategy of Aspin or Sam Nunn (in the Senate), but he was a strong defender of the military. His particular area of interest was military personnel and veterans' issues.[123] Stump's successor, Representative Duncan Hunter (R-California), was equally a voice for a strong defense and a bit more assertive.

Ike Skelton (D-Missouri) succeeded Hunter as chair when the Democrats regained control of the House after the 2006 congressional elections. In some ways, Skelton was an archetypal defender of the military and its interests. He was known on Capitol Hill "as a military junkie, whose frequent lunch companions in the members' dining room are top military brass."[124] Indeed, he voted for the Iraq Resolution (among eighty Democratic members to do so), even though he raised concerns with the White House over its post-invasion planning. Skelton became disillusioned with the Iraq War, describing it as "mission impossible," and joined Representative John Murtha (D-Pennsylvania) in calling for an immediate drawdown of American forces in 2006. In 2007, he sponsored a bill that passed the House calling for redeployment of American forces from Iraq, and he continued to be an important war critic.[125] At the same time, Skelton continued to make certain that the needs of the military were met.

With Skelton's defeat and Republican control of Congress after the 2010 elections, **Howard P. "Buck" McKeon** was chosen as chair of the House Armed Services Committee. He is a strong voice for the Pentagon and has succeeded in guiding defense bills through the Congress. His aim has been not only to provide needed resources for a strong defense but also to support America's veterans. At the same time, he has worked to keep enemy combatants from being housed on American soil and continues to be strong advocate of missile defense.[126] In his strong support of the Pentagon, he thus continues a long tradition among chairs of the Armed Services Committee.

In the Senate, recent chairs have breathed new life into the Armed Services Committee. **Sam Nunn** of Georgia, chair from 1987 to 1995, did not automatically prove to be a military supporter. Instead, he, too, demonstrated a willingness to challenge the Department of Defense and the administration in office with his own defense plans.[127] At the same time, Nunn sought to improve America's armed forces by increasing efficiency within the Pentagon and enhancing conditions for military personnel. He also evidenced a streak of independence over military affairs by continuing to support economic sanctions rather than military actions prior to the Persian Gulf War and by vigorously opposing the Clinton administration's effort to overturn existing policy on homosexuals in the military. Nunn's Republican successors, Strom Thurmond (R–South Carolina) and John Warner (R–Virginia), brought altered priorities to the Senate Armed Services Committee that were more in line with its earlier tradition of receptiveness to the Pentagon's wishes. In particular, Thurmond sought to increase military spending as a means of enhancing U.S. force readiness.

Warner's successor in 2001, **Carl Levin** (D–Michigan), represented a bit more skepticism on defense policy. Although he supported the committee's tilt, he also remained a persistent critic or questioner of the administration in some cases. A student of defense issues, Levin was well versed in the intricacies of defense policy and could successfully spar with those holding opposing views. He was critical of the administration's call for national missile defense and its abandonment of the ABM Treaty, and he questioned aspects of the war on terrorism. In doing so, he continued to make the Senate Armed Services Committee an important player in responding to September 11 and in devising American defense strategy for the future.[128] After the 2002 election, Warner returned as chair, largely espousing a position fully in line with the Bush administration's wishes while still seeking to exercise some policy influence.

In 2007, with the Democrats in control of the Senate, Levin returned to head the committee. He was a vocal critic of the Bush administration's Iraq policy and was the leader of efforts to pull out American forces, including one measure in 2007 that would have required withdrawal by April 30, 2008.[129] Similarly, he has been a prominent advocate for more rights for detainees in the war on terrorism and criticized the Bush administration's military tribunals for such detainees, even as he backed military spending.[130] With his personal style and approach as committee chair, he continues to utilize the committee, more so than his predecessor did, to promote congressional oversight.

Congressional Oversight: The Recent Record

Although a good case can be made for an overall increase in congressional oversight over the past several decades, a debate has recently emerged over the degree of that oversight regarding foreign policy in recent years. In 2006, political analysts Norman Ornstein and Thomas Mann characterized the oversight activities of recent Congresses in this way: "Congressional oversight of the executive branch across a range of policies, but especially foreign and national security policy, has virtually collapsed."[131] To the extent that any oversight occurred in the first six years of the Bush administration, they argue, it has been mainly budgetary review rather than demanding and consistent review regarding policy.

Oversight of the Iraq War and its aftermath especially has been missing. Ornstein and Mann point to several reinforcing factors that might account for this: the lack of "a strong institutional identity" by members of Congress; greater loyalty to party and president than to Congress; close party divisions within Congress reducing congressional identity; and the abbreviated congressional work schedule (often three-day workweeks). The reluctance of the Bush administration to share information with Congress and the failure of administration officials to testify before relevant committees were also contributors to this decline. In a response to Ornstein and Mann,

William G. Howell and Jon C. Pevehouse remind us of another important factor that is part and parcel of congressional oversight: **partisan politics**.[132] Congressional oversight has usually been most vigorous when different parties controlled the Congress and the White House, whereas it has been most dormant when the two branches are unified.

In this sense, the recent changes in control of the White House and the Congress have undoubtedly stimulated and enhanced the oversight record. That is, after the Democrats gained control of both Houses of Congress in the congressional elections in 2006, foreign policy oversight increased of the Republican president in the White House. And after the Republicans gained control of the House in the congressional elections in 2010, similar foreign policy scrutiny occurred of the Democratic president in the White House.

MECHANISMS OF CONGRESSIONAL INFLUENCE

A useful way to summarize the congressional role in foreign policy that we have been describing so far is to use some categories of influence that prominent political scientists have developed.[133] In the broadest sense, we may categorize congressional actions on foreign policy as either **legislative or nonlegislative**. Within the legislative category, Congress can impose substantive or procedural legislation on the executive branch. Within the nonlegislative category, we can subdivide those mechanisms into institutional actions (those taken by Congress to express its view) and individual actions (those taken by members to convey their policy prescriptions).

Legislation: Substantive and Procedural

Although Congress has the ability to legislate foreign policy with a particular bill or act (for example, imposing sanctions on South Africa or Cuba, lifting the arms embargo against Bosnia, granting trade preferences to African states or Central America), such **substantive pieces of legislation are relatively rare** in terms of all congressional activities. Political scientist Barbara Hinckley reports that, on average, only about seven to eight substantive pieces of foreign policy legislation have been approved by the House of Representatives per administration from the Kennedy years to the first three years of the George H. W. Bush administration. In the Senate, that average is even lower, at five per administration. Hinckley notes that foreign policy–related resolutions, which are primarily symbolic, have increased; the amount of substantive foreign policy legislation has remained markedly stable and small over the years.[134] Moreover, given the acrimony between Congress and the Clinton administration on foreign policy matters and the now renewed partisan divisions between the Bush and Obama administrations and Congress, we would hardly expect this legislative record to improve.

Procedural legislation, however, has grown dramatically, as our earlier discussion sought to convey. In such diverse areas as war powers, commitments abroad, covert operations, foreign aid, and trade, Congress has developed a wide array of procedures for discerning executive action and, in some instances, seeking to play a more direct role in changing or altering executive policy. In addition, as political scientist James Lindsay has pointed out, these procedural measures include the reporting and monitoring of policy and the creation of new bureaucracies—and new offices within bureaucracies—to allow greater congressional insight and involvement in the process.[135] The U.S. Trade Representative (USTR), for example, was a creation of

Congress and has now been given increased powers over trade policy. Accompanying these enhanced powers, in fact, has been a requirement that five House members be designated as advisors to the USTR on trade policy issues.

Nonlegislative Actions: Institutional and Individual Actions

Nonlegislative institutional actions by Congress have also assumed an increasingly larger role in its efforts to influence foreign policy.[136] These include hearings held by standing committees, such as Senate Foreign Relations or House Foreign Affairs on American policy in Afghanistan; the use of select committees, such as those on the Iran-Contra episode in the 1980s and on intelligence failures after 9/11; and the use of a wide array of briefings by congressional caucuses to inform like-minded legislators with new information and to rally them to coordinated action, such as the Congressional Human Rights Caucus. Although such hearings (or briefings in the case of caucuses) may not, and in most instances will not, lead directly to legislation, they do serve to convey to the executive branch and to the public the congressional view on these matters.

Other nonlegislative institutional action involves formal or informal consultations with the executive branch and the passing of various kinds of nonbinding resolutions on foreign policy issues by Congress. Examples of the former would be the formal executive–congressional consultation that is called for in the WPR or the formal and informal notification procedures required for arm sales. Examples of the latter can take the form of a concurrent or two-house resolution or a single ("sense of the House" or "sense of the Senate") resolution on a current foreign policy issue. Such resolutions have been used routinely over the years.

In 1999, for instance, the Senate passed a nonbinding resolution supporting President Clinton's actions in Kosovo, while the House rejected such a resolution but passed its own directing the president to follow the WPR.[137] In 2003 and 2004, a series of nonbinding resolutions dealing with human rights conditions in various countries and regions were passed in the House and sometimes in both chambers, largely sponsored by activist members of the Congressional Human Rights Caucus.

After the 2006 congressional elections, Congress sought to pass a number of nonbinding resolutions to express its opposition to the "surge" of American forces in Iraq (an increase of about 21,000 military personnel) but also to call for the withdrawal of forces by a date certain. Indeed, the House did pass such a resolution of disapproval of the surge policy. More recently, the House and the Senate voted on several resolutions to express each chamber's views on the Obama administration's intervention in Libya. Such nonbinding actions by Congress have not always passed, or not always been followed by the administration if they are passed. Nonetheless, they do put the executive on notice about the interest and intent of Congress on particular issues.

A final nonlegislative way for Congress to express its views on foreign policy activities is through **nonlegislative individual actions**. These are myriad, but a few illustrations will demonstrate how legislators over the years have attempted to influence the foreign policy process. Some members have used newsletters and policy analyses to convey their views on foreign policy issues. Others have written individual letters directly to the president or an executive branch office or have joined with their colleagues in doing so. Still others have used the floor of the House and Senate, either during regular debate or at the beginning or end of the legislative day when time is set aside for individual members to speak. Members, too, have increasingly used television interview programs or "talk radio" to make their cases about foreign policy issues. Finally, two other intriguing nonlegislative mechanisms used by individual members of Congress are (1) dealing directly with foreign governments on foreign policy questions and (2) filing court challenges against the president to defend congressional foreign policy prerogatives. An example of the former was when House Speaker Jim Wright (D-Texas) prepared a peace plan for ending the conflict in Central America between the Contras and the Sandinista government in Nicaragua, which he circulated to regional governmental representatives and to the State Department. Examples of the latter are the several lawsuits filed by member of Congress (see Chapter 7), often over the war powers of Congress versus the powers of the commander-in-chief. In all, then, these nonlegislative individual actions or action by "policy entrepreneurs," as they have been labeled by an extensive study by political scientists Ralph Carter and James Scott, are more pronounced and influential than previously acknowledged.[138]

On balance, the various legislative mechanisms appear to have a mixed record of success, but one analyst suggests that they have an effect. As Rebecca Hersman argues, "individualized power and strong issue leaders have enhanced Congress's obstructive powers" in foreign policy. "The very strength of these obstructive powers makes them effective leverage against the executive branch."[139]

CONGRESSIONAL CHANGE AND FUTURE FOREIGN POLICY MAKING

Have all of these congressional changes over the past four decades permanently altered the foreign policy relationships between Congress and the executive that have evolved since World War II? Alternate views abound within and outside the executive and legislative branches and among political analysts as well.

The Degree of Change

Writing shortly after some of these initial reforms, congressional–executive scholars Thomas Franck, Edward Weisband, and I. M. Destler believed so.[140] They pointed to the structural and procedural arrangements that Congress put in place for dealing with foreign policy; the various pieces of legislation giving it more political clout; the larger foreign policy staffs on Capitol Hill and constituencies among the American public; and the adjustments that the president has made in his relationship with Congress (perhaps grudgingly).

Two decades later, and writing in a similar vein, analyst Jeremy Rosner pointed to "the new **tug-of-war**," between the branches, largely as a result of the ending of the Cold War. In this new environment, Rosner argues, the relationship between the two branches will vary by issue and will be dependent on the degree of presidential involvement with Congress. On issues involving security, the president will likely prevail if he takes an early and determined stance. On those not directly involving security (such as international peacekeeping or human rights), Congress will likely dominate, especially if the president does not push them. Because more issues are likely to reflect the latter than the former in the years ahead (although Rosner wrote before September 11, 2001), Congress will be "more assertive relative to the executive branch than during the late years of the Cold War."[141]

However, constitutional lawyer Harold Hongju Koh and political scientist Barbara Hinckley raised doubts about whether the changes over the years have been significant or important to the policy process. Koh argued that Congress ultimately has assented to presidential wishes because the reforms undertaken have been inadequate and the political will has been insufficient to stop the executive.[142] Hinckley was as skeptical as Koh—if not more so—about the impact of this presumed congressional activism. She argues that conflict between the two branches is "in large part an illusion." There has been "no shift from a conventional to a reform pattern of policy making, as some popular wisdom leads us to expect."[143]

Even so, considerable evidence from recent administrations seems to provide at least some support for the former view. The Reagan administration, for example, was locked in heated policy battles with Congress on several fronts. Most prominent, of course, was the six-year struggle over the funding of the Nicaraguan Contras. It also fought with Congress over, among other issues, the reflagging of Kuwaiti vessels in the Persian Gulf and congressional war powers, the imposition of economic sanctions on South Africa over its apartheid policy, and congressional initiatives on international trade policy.[144] Reagan's successor, George H. W. Bush, also sparred with Congress over both substance and procedure in foreign policy making. He used his veto power four times in his first year to alter foreign policy legislation with which he did not agree—an extraordinarily high use of the veto in such a short time.[145]

The Clinton administration experienced the same tumult with Congress over foreign policy making. The debacle in Somalia in middle to late 1993, along with the congressional response to formally end U.S. involvement there by the end of March 1994, was an early example. Later examples focused on the American military role in Bosnia and Kosovo, funding the Mexican peso bailout, and refunding the International Monetary Fund at the time of the Asian financial crisis. Perhaps the most critical debates, and the most direct losses for the president, were over Congress's failure to renew fast-track trading authority for the administration and the Senate's stinging defeat of the Comprehensive Test Ban Treaty (CTBT).

The George W. Bush administration also had its disputes with Congress. Early on, for example, members of Congress looked with skepticism on its approach toward such issues as North Korea, Russia, and missile defense. The terrorist attacks of September 11, 2001 dramatically dampened any criticism of the administration's foreign policy by members of Congress for a time, and several pieces of antiterrorism legislation sailed through the House and Senate with broad support. Yet criticism reemerged by mid-2002 and was largely in full voice after that. The conflicts between the White House and Congress escalated when the Democrats gained control of the House and the Senate in the 2006 congressional elections and as President Bush's unpopularity among the American public reached all-time lows. Iraq policy, of course, remained at the center of those criticisms, but clashes also focused on Iran, North Korea, global climate change, trade policy, and nuclear proliferation, among others.

The Obama administration has hardly been immune to these disputes with Congress over foreign policy, disputes to which we have already alluded. Almost immediately after President Obama issued an executive order about closing the prison at Guantanamo Bay, Cuba, within one year, Congress reacted to and passed legislation to stop the transferral of the enemy combatant to U.S. soil. Although the House passed a "cap and trade" energy bill to address global warming, the Senate stalled the measure and ultimately stopped it in its track. The Senate eventually gave its approval for ratification of the New START treaty with Russia, but only after obtaining several concessions on nuclear weapons policy from the administration. Both Houses of Congress delayed approval of free trade agreements, as we have noted, and gave their consent only after obtaining several changes from the Obama administration. Finally, both Houses of Congress produced a chorus of criticism of the Obama administration's actions toward Libya in 2011, and its failure to involve Congress in that initiative.[146]

Such conflicts between the branches are lamented by a number of high officials because they point to the difficulties of conducting foreign policy with a Congress constantly intruding on, or at least limiting, the president's freedom of action. A principal complaint, for instance, is that coherent foreign policy cannot be carried out with this continuous struggle between Congress and the president.[147] Moreover, virtually every president, from the time these various reforms were enacted, complained about congressional intrusions into foreign policy, and each one sought to pursue and to protect his foreign policy prerogatives. In this sense, the struggle between the two branches continues.

Congressional Reform and Policy Impact

A key question, of course, is how much effect these reforms have had on American foreign policy. For several reasons, their substantive impact has been much less widespread than might be anticipated by examining only the original legislation. This lends support to those analysts who are skeptical about the degree of congressional activism.

The first factor that supports this view is that **congressional reform measures have been invoked infrequently**. Despite the arms sales review procedures, for instance, no arms deal has actually been denied to the executive branch since 1974, although the composition and timing of some may have been altered. The human rights requirements did not markedly change the economic or security assistance policies of subsequent administrations, although they did result in the cutting off of aid to a few nations (such as Argentina, Chile) and the rejection of aid by some (such as Brazil). When necessary, legislative loopholes or exceptions were often found for strategically important states. After September 11, for instance, Congress rapidly waived sanctions against Pakistan (imposed after that country's nuclear tests in 1998) as a way to obtain its cooperation in the war on terrorism.[148]

The **apparent weak public record should not be pushed too far**, however. Some significant actions have been taken by Congress to stop executive action, and some administrations have been dissuaded from pursuing policy options because of evident congressional opposition. In the first category, the use of the Jackson–Vanik Amendment to restrict most-favored-nation status for the former Soviet Union and for China illustrates how congressional legislation can be significant. Indeed, and as noted, it took congressional action to grant China permanent normal trading relations with the United States in 2000 to resolve this issue. In the second category, the rapid completion of the Chemical Weapons Conventions by the Senate was slowed down by congressional opposition and prerogatives, and the CTBT was actually defeated in the Senate.[149] In 2008, the House of Representatives stopped a vote on a free trade agreement with Colombia when it changed the fast-track procedures by altering its rules for consideration of this measure.[150] In this sense, procedural requirements and congressional prerogatives had a tangible effect on policy.

A second factor that weakens congressional authority in foreign affairs is that much reform legislation has **"escape clauses" for the president**. If, for example, the president certifies that an arms sale must go forward for national security reasons despite a congressional rejection, he may proceed. The most-favored-nation requirement in the Trade Act of 1974 has an escape clause allowing the president to grant such status if he so wishes. The human rights requirements in the economic assistance legislation also can be waived if the executive branch certifies that aid will reach "needy people" in the recipient nation "and if either house of Congress does not disapprove the waiver within thirty days."[151]

Similarly, the Helms–Burton Amendment tightening economic sanctions against Cuba included a presidential waiver for a portion of it. Specifically, under Title III of the legislation, U.S. citizens could sue in court over properties seized by the Castro regime after the revolution, but the president was allowed to waive this stipulation if "necessary to the national interest of the United States" and if he decided the waiver would "expedite a transition to democracy in Cuba."[152] President Clinton immediately did this for six months and continued to do so throughout his second term. And this pattern of issuing waivers for this section continued for the Bush and the Obama administrations.[153]

Finally, foreign aid legislation is often filled with escape clauses that allow the president to proceed even if Congress initially prohibits some policy. In a recent foreign aid appropriations law, for example, the president could waive a provision requiring Afghanistan's cooperation over poppy eradication and interdiction and to provide additional funding to the Afghan government if he determines that such aid "is vital to the national security interests of the United States." He must so report to the Committees on Appropriations, however.[154]

A third factor that limits the effectiveness of congressional reforms is that the **legislative veto was declared unconstitutional** by the Supreme Court in *Immigration and Naturalization Service v. Chadha*.[155] Several important congressional reforms in foreign policy making (such as the WPR and the arms sales amendment) had incorporated this provision. Its removal did not wholly paralyze congressional participation in these areas, but it made it more difficult to quickly halt presidential action. For example, the president is still restricted by the sixty-day clock when sending troops abroad, but Congress cannot remove them before the clock runs out without a joint resolution (instead of the previous concurrent resolution). In effect, this kind of legislation requires a two-thirds majority to override an expected presidential veto and not just a simple majority as under the concurrent resolution procedure.

Yet a fourth factor reduces the substantive effect of the congressional reforms over the past several decades: despite the desire of Congress to assert its role in foreign affairs, **it still perceives limits as to how far it should go in restricting the executive**. Many members of Congress still rely on the president for the initiation and execution of foreign policy. In a series of lectures on congressional–executive relations near the turn of the twenty-first century, former congressman and former chair of the House Foreign Affairs Committee Lee H. Hamilton (D-Indiana) perhaps best summarized the prevailing congressional perspective: "There is simply no substitute for presidential leadership. Only the president is accountable to, and speaks for, all Americans, and possesses the authority to implement policy. On rare occasions, Congress seizes the initiative on foreign policy, but most decisions follow a proposal by the president."[156] Despite the acrimony of some members of Congress over an array of foreign policy issues with the president, there thus remains a strong residual sentiment among senators and representatives that the president should be allowed some flexibility in the conduct of foreign policy and should continue to take the lead.

In short, Congress thus seeks to be involved in the formulation of policy, in conjunction with the president, but to leave its implementation to the executive branch. Although it is unlikely to turn back to an earlier era of congressional acquiescence, Congress appears equally unlikely to pass many new restrictions on presidential power.[157] Instead, it will remain alert to its prerogatives in foreign affairs without seeking to direct policy unilaterally.

CONCLUDING COMMENTS

As Chapter 7 and this chapter have emphasized, because Congress and the president share the power to make foreign policy under the Constitution, foreign policy is likely to remain a "contest" between them for the foreseeable future. It is doubtful that either side will yield its prerogatives, or is any structural change ultimately going to alter this inherent constitutional dilemma. Instead, as Arthur Schlesinger, Jr., correctly noted at the beginning of these congressional reform efforts, the problem is "primarily political" and will undoubtedly require efforts at cooperative solutions that are procedural rather than legislative.[158] For these reasons, on both sides greater consultation and institutional respect for the other remain the best prescriptions for dealing with the continuing foreign policy debate between the president and Congress.[159]

The legislative and executive branches are the preeminent actors in foreign policy making, but they are not the only ones involved in the process. Within the executive branch in particular, diverse, and important bureaucracies—the Department of State, the Department of Defense, the National Security Council, the intelligence community, and several economic bureaucracies—can and do have a hand in policy formulation. The next two chapters analyze these key bureaucracies and begin to offer a more complete picture of the foreign policy process.

Notes

1. See Natalie Hevener Kaufman, *Human Rights Treaties and the Senate* (Chapel Hill and London: The University of North Carolina Press, 1990). For other discussions of the Bricker Amendment, see Stephen A. Garrett, "Foreign Policy and the American Constitution: The Bricker Amendment in Contemporary Perspective," *International Studies Quarterly* 16 (June 1972): 187–220; and Duane Tananbaum, *The Bricker Amendment Controversy: A Test of Eisenhower's Political Leadership* (Ithaca, NY, and London: Cornell University Press, 1988).

2. See Michael Nelson, ed., *Congressional Quarterly's Guide to the Presidency* (Washington, D.C.: Congressional Quarterly, 1989), pp. 512–513; and *Congressional Quarterly's Guide to Congress*, 3rd ed. (Washington, D.C.: Congressional Quarterly, 1982), pp. 303–304.

3. See "Security Agreements and Commitments Abroad," Report to the Committee on Foreign Relations of the United States Senate by the Subcommittee on Security Agreements and Commitments Abroad, 91st Congress, 2nd Sess., December 21, 1970, pp. 1–28. This report is available through Congressional Information Service at CIS 70 S382-17.

4. The text of the resolution can be found in the *Congressional Record*, 91st Cong., 1st sess., June 25, 1969, 17245.

5. The text of the amended resolution can be found in "Agreements with Portugal and Bahrain," Senate Report No. 92-632, 92nd Cong., 2nd sess., February 17, 1972, 1.

6. See P.L. 92-403, "United States International Agreements: Transmission to Congress," 86 Stat. 619, approved August 22, 1972.

7. See Section 5 of P.L. 95-45, "An Act to Authorize Appropriations for the Department of State for Fiscal Year 1977," for the text of the Case amendment. It is available at 91 Stat. 224, approved June 15, 1977.

8. The data are from Report of the Comptroller General of the United States, "Reporting of U.S. International Agreements by Executive Agencies Has Improved," Report ID-78-57, October 31, 1978, p. 22.

9. The late reporting by agencies in 1977 is given in ibid., p. 23; the rest of the data cited in this paragraph are from Congressional Research Service, *Treaties and Other International Agreements: The Role of the United States Senate*, A Study Prepared for the Committee on Foreign Relations, United States Senate, by the Congressional Research Service, The Library of Congress (Washington, D.C.: Government Printing Office, January 2001), pp. 226–227.

10. See the Federal Reports Elimination and Sunset Act of 1995 (P.L. 104–66), p. 38. The elimination of the reporting requirement on late transmittal was effective from May 15, 2000. Thanks to Jacob Parker in the Office of Congressman Tom Latham for assistance on this matter.

11. See Marjorie Ann Browne, Executive Agreements and the Congress, *Issue Brief Number 1B75035* (Washington, D.C.: Congressional Research Service, The Library of Congress, 1981), p. 7. Another bill by Senator John Glenn was S. 1251, 94th Cong., 1st sess., introduced on March 20, 1975.

12. See H.R. 4439, 94th Cong., 1st sess., introduced on March 6, 1975. The discussion of this measure, "Executive Agreement Review Act of 1975," can be found in the *Congressional Record,* 94th Cong., 1st sess., Vol. 121, Part 5, March 6, 1975, pp. 5557–5558.

13. For the discussion of the Treaty Powers Resolution (S. Res. 434), see the *Congressional Record,* 94th Cong., 2nd sess., April 14, 1976, 10967.

14. See Section 708 of P.L. 95-426, October 7, 1978.

15. Ibid. These reforms are also summarized in "Reporting of U.S. International Agreements by Executive Agencies Has Improved," p. 8.

16. The exchange of letters establishing this process is reproduced in "International Agreements Consultation Resolution," Senate Report 95-1171, August 25, 1978, 2–3.

17. P.L. 91-672. For the executive claim of not needing the Gulf of Tonkin Resolution to continue the war, see *Congress and the Nation, Volume III 1969–1972* (Washington, D.C.: Congressional Quarterly, 1973), p. 947.

18. The entire text of the resolution can be found in *The War Powers Resolution: Relevant Documents, Correspondence, Reports,* Subcommittee on International Security and Scientific Affairs, House Committee on Foreign Affairs, December 1983, pp. 1–6.

19. The following analysis is based on the text of the War Powers Resolution (P.L. 93-148). A section-by-section analysis is provided in Robert A. Katzmann, "War Powers: Toward a New Accommodation," in Thomas E. Mann, ed., *A Question of Balance* (Washington, D.C.: The Brookings Institution, 1990), pp. 46–49.

20. Ibid., pp. 50 and 58, on this point.

21. The cases of presidential reports to Congress discussed in this section are drawn from Richard F. Grimmett, *War Powers Resolution: After Twenty-Eight Years* (Washington, D.C.: Congressional Research Service, The Library of Congress, November 30, 2001) and Richard F. Grimmett, *IB81050: War Powers Resolution: Presidential Compliance* (Washington, D.C.: Congressional Research Service, June 12, 2002, updated September 16, 2003, July 25, 2007, January 14, 2008, and September 25, 2012).

22. Jennifer K. Elsea, Michael John Garcia, and Thomas J. Nicola, *Congressional Authority to Limit U.S. Military Operations in Iraq,* CRS Report for Congress (Washington, D.C.: Congressional Research Service, The Library of Congress, July 11, 2007), p. 15, and Grimmett, *War Powers Resolution: Presidential Compliance,* p. 2.

23. This language is taken from President Bush's report on the Panama invasion, which is printed in *Weekly Compilation of Presidential Documents* 25 (December 25, 1989): 1985.

24. Grimmett, *War Powers Resolution: After Twenty-Eight Years,* pp. 53–54.

25. Jeffrey Frank, "Vietnam, Watergate Bred War Powers Act . . . Controversy Still Surrounds Law's Effects," *Congressional Quarterly Weekly Report,* October 1, 1983, 2019.

26. See the reply to Congressman Zablocki's letter of inquiry by Richard Fairbanks, former assistant secretary of state for congressional relations, in *The War Powers Resolution: Relevant Documents, Correspondence, Reports,* pp. 52–54.

27. Grimmett, *War Powers Resolution: After Twenty-Eight Years,* p. 69.

28. The first quotation is from the resolution itself and is from Louis Fisher, "Presidents Who Initiate Wars," in James M. McCormick, ed., *The Domestic Sources of American Foreign Policy: Insights and Evidence*, 6th ed. (Lanham, MD: Rowman & Littlefield, Inc, 2012), p. 204, while the second quotation in this passage is Fisher's, also at p. 204.

29. Ibid.

30. "United States Activities in Libya," Report from the Obama Administration to Speaker John A. Boehner, June 15, 2011, at http://s3.documentcloud.org/documents/204673/united-states-activities-in-libya-6-15-11.pdf, May 16, 2012.

31. Katzmann, "War Powers: Toward A New Accommodation," p. 61.

32. Ellen C. Collier, "The War Powers Resolution: Fifteen Years of Experience," Congressional Research Service, August 3, 1988, pp. 29–31; Collier, "War Powers Resolution: Presidential Compliance," Issue Brief 81050, Congressional Research Service, The Library of Congress, February 16, 1990, p. 3.

33. See "Legal Opinion of May 9, 1980, by Lloyd Cutler, counsel to Former President Carter, on War Powers Consultation Relative to the Iran Rescue Mission," reprinted in *The War Powers Resolution: Relevant Documents, Correspondence, Reports*, p. 50.

34. Collier, "War Powers Resolution: Presidential Compliance," p. 5.

35. The official is quoted in Elaine Sciolino, "On the Brink of War, a Tense Battle of Wills," *New York Times*, September 20, 1994, A13; the White House strategy for moving toward intervention is also set forth there.

36. Ryan Hendrickson, *The Clinton Wars* (Nashville: Vanderbilt University Press, 2002), pp. 161–162. Emphasis in original.

37. Grimmett, *War Powers Resolution: After Twenty-Eight Years*, p. 46.

38. See "United States Activities in Libya," Report from the Obama Administration to Speaker John A. Boehner, pp. 26–31. The quoted passage is from p. 26.

39. Collier, "The War Powers Resolution: Fifteen Years of Experience," pp. 27–29.

40. Ibid., pp. 9–11 and Grimmett, *War Powers Resolution: After Twenty-Eight Years*, p. 9.

41. See Jennifer K. Elsea, Michael John Garcia, and Thomas J. Nicola, *Congressional Authority to Limit U.S. Military Operations in Iraq*. CRS Report to Congress, July 11, 2007, p. 15 and Grimmett, *War Powers Resolution: Presidential Compliance*, p. 2. Also see Michael J. Glennon, *Constitutional Diplomacy* (Princeton, NJ: Princeton University Press, 1990), p. 93, in which he argues that only Nixon and Reagan viewed the requirements for the withdrawal of troops in the WPR as unconstitutional.

42. Katzmann, "War Powers: Toward A New Accommodation," pp. 66–69; *Committee on Foreign Affairs, Congress and Foreign Policy 1988* (Washington, D.C.: U.S. Government Printing Office, 1989), p. 9; and Collier, "The War Powers Resolution: Fifteen Years of Experience," pp. 45–50.

43. John M. Donnelly, "Democrats Ready Next Move on the War," *CQ Weekly*, February 26, 2007, p. 609.

44. See Elsea, Garcia, and Nicola, *Congressional Authority to Limit U.S. Military Operations in Iraq*, pp. 21–26.

45. See Miller Center of Public Affairs, "The National War Powers Commission," originally issued on July 8, 2008, http://millercenter.org/policy/commissions/warpowers, July 11, 2008, for this quotation. The full report, *National War Powers Commission Report*, is also available at this site.

46. David P. Auerswald and Peter F. Cowhey, "Ballotbox Diplomacy: The War Powers Resolution and the Use of Force," *International Studies Quarterly* 41 (September 1997): 505–528. The quotation is at p. 529.

47. Quoted in Eric Schmitt, "Senators Query U.S. Role in Bosnia," *New York Times*, October 18, 1995, A12.

48. The analysis of voting during the 1966–1972 period is drawn from "Congress Took 94 Roll-Call Votes On War 1966–72," *Congress and the Nation, Volume III*, 1966–1972 (Washington, D.C.: Congressional Quarterly Service, 1973), pp. 914–945. Senator Frank Church (D-Idaho) had a defense appropriation bill amended to bar the "introduction of U.S. ground combat troops into Laos or Thailand" in 1969, and he, along with Senator John Sherman Cooper (R-Kentucky), had an amendment passed to bar "U.S. military operations in Cambodia after July 1, 1970."

49. See P.L. 93-126 of October 18, 1973.

50. *Congressional Quarterly Almanac 1975* (Washington, D.C.: Congressional Quarterly, 1976), pp. 306–315.

51. See Keith R. Legg, "Congress as Trojan Horses? The Turkish Embargo Problem, 1974–1978," in John Spanier and Joseph Nogee, eds., *Congress, The Presidency, and American Foreign Policy* (New York: Pergamon Press, 1981), pp. 107–131, especially the chronology of events at pp. 108–109 for the passage of the arms embargo.

52. See Section 404 of P.L. 94-329. 90 Stat. 757.

53. See Section 728 of P.L. 97-113.

54. See P.L. 98-151. A description of the law is provided by John Felton, "Omnibus Bill Includes Foreign Aid Programs," *Congressional Quarterly Weekly Report*, November 19, 1983, 2435–2436.

55. See Doherty, "House Approves Overhaul of Agencies, Policies," p. 1655; and Carroll J. Doherty, "Bill Slashing Overseas Aid Gets Bipartisan Support," *Congressional Quarterly Weekly Report*, June 10, 1995, 1658.

56. Curt Anderson, "Bush Seeks More Powers, Money for National Safety," *Des Moines Register*, July 17, 2002, 1A.

57. See the Conference Report on H.R. 2055, Military Construction and Veterans Affairs and Related Agencies Appropriation Act, 2012, which was the vehicle for foreign assistance legislation in the 112th Congress, 1st session. Section 7007 deals with aid prohibition to specific countries, and Section 7008 deals with aid prohibition on countries experiencing coups. Thanks to Jacob Parker at the Office of Congress Tom Latham for assistance in obtaining this report. The cited provisions here and subsequently in other notes are also in P.L. 112-74 (H.R. 2055) that was subsequently passed in Congress.

58. "Most Aid Earmarked," *Congressional Quarterly Weekly Report*, January 20, 1990, 198.

59. The data in Table 8.2 come from the Department of State, Foreign Operations CBJ, FY2013 for fiscal year 2012. The data totals include supplementals and projected Millennium Challenge Corporation Compact disbursements in FY2012. Thanks to Jacob Parker at the Office of Congress Tom Latham for assistance in obtaining this report.

60. The leading recipients for FY2002 were made available from the same source as note 60 through the good offices of Jacob Parker.

61. See the Conference report on H.R. 2055, Military Construction and Veterans Affairs and Related Agencies Appropriation Act, 2012, p. 395 regarding Economic Support Fund for Egypt and the use of this particular language.

62. See Sections 402 and 613 of the Trade Act of 1974 (P.L. 93-618).

63. See Section 36 of P.L. 93-559.

64. See Section 36h of P.L. 94-329. The dollar totals were subsequently raised to $50 million and $14 million, respectively. See John Felton, "Hill Weighs Foreign Policy Impact of Ruling," *Congressional Quarterly Weekly Report*, July 2, 1983, 1330.

65. See *Congressional Quarterly Almanac 1981* (Washington, D.C.: Congress Quarterly, 1982), p. 132.

66. The economic aid legislation was the International Development and Food Assistance Act of 1975 (P.L. 94-161). The human rights provision can be found at Section 116. In the International Security and Arms Report Control Act, the human rights provision is Section 502b.

67. See P.L. 95-118, Section 701, and P.L. 94-302, Section 28. Also see the discussion of this human rights legislation in Lars Schoultz, "Politics, Economics, and U.S. Participation in Multilateral Development Banks," *International Organization* 36 (Summer 1982): 537–574.

68. These examples are taken from Ellen C. Collier, "Congress and Foreign Policy 1992: Introduction" in Committee on Foreign Affairs, *Congress and Foreign Policy 1992* (Washington, D.C.: Government Printing Office, 1993), pp. 1–21; and U.S. Congress, Office of Technology Assessment, *Dismantling the Bomb and Managing the Nuclear Materials*. OTA-O-572 (Washington, D.C.: Government Printing Office, September 1993), p. 130.

69. Collier, "Congress and Foreign Policy 1992: Introduction," p. 6.

70. Jennifer S. Holmes, "The Colombian Drug Trade: National Security and Congressional Politics," in Ralph G. Carter, ed., *Contemporary Cases in U.S. Foreign Policy: From Terrorism to Trade* (Washington, D.C.: CQ Press, 2002), p. 103. For an update on the evolution of Plan Colombia and American aid to that country over drug trafficking, see Jennifer S. Holmes, "Colombia and U.S. Foreign Policy: Coca, Security, and Human Rights in Ralph G. Carter, ed., *Contemporary Cases in U.S. Foreign Policy: From Terrorism to Trade*, 4th ed. (Washington, D.C.: CQ Press, 2002), pp. 74–107.

71. See the Conference report on H.R. 2055, Military Construction and Veterans Affairs and Related Agencies Appropriation Act, 2012, pp. 435–439, 446 for the quotations and the specifications outlined in this paragraph. These are the same pages as in H.R. 2055 itself.

72. "Lawmakers Hand Clinton Big Victory in Granting China Permanent Trade Status," *Congressional Quarterly Almanac 2000* (Washington, D.C.: Congressional Quarterly, 2001), pp. 20–23.

73. "African-Caribbean Initiative Lowers Tariffs, Quotas on Some Foreign-Made Apparel," *Congressional Quarterly Almanac 2000* (Washington, D.C.: Congressional Quarterly, 2001), pp. 20–24; and "Iran, Libya Sanctions," *CQ Weekly*, December 22, 2001, 3039.

74. Collier, "Congress and Foreign Policy 1992: Introduction," p. 11.

75. Patrick J. Haney and Walt Vanderbush, "The Helms-Burton Act: Congress and Cuba Policy," in Ralph G. Carter, ed., *Contemporary Cases in U.S. Foreign Policy: From Terrorism to Trade*, pp. 270–290.

76. Kenneth Katzman, "Iran Sanctions," CRS Report for Congress (Washington, D.C.: Congressional Research Service, April 26, 2012, pp. 3–4, with the quoted passages from p. 4.

77. See, for example, Rosemary D'Amour, "U.S. Congress Passes Controversial Free Trade Agreements," IPS Inter Press Service, October 13, 2011, at http://ipsnews.net/news.asp?idnews=105460, May 18, 2012; and Tim Mullaney, "Auto, Ag Industries Could Gain from Trade Deals," *USA Today*, October 12, 2011, at http://www.usatoday.com/money/economy/story/2011-10-12/trade-deals-impact/50747402/1, May 23, 2012, on the pros and cons of these FTAs.

78. We do not mean to imply that other committees are not involved with foreign policy issues; rather, these are the principal foreign policy authorizing committees. Appropriations, Governmental Affairs (Senate), Government Reform and Oversight (House), Judiciary, and Select Intelligence, among others, are regularly involved as well. Further, the Foreign Operations Subcommittee of the House and Senate Appropriations committees are extraordinarily important in appropriating foreign policy funding.

79. Ellen C. Collier, "Foreign Policy by Reporting Requirement," *Washington Quarterly* 11 (Winter 1988): 81, 77. This article is the source for the subsequent discussion as well.

80. The types of report and the description of each are taken from ibid.

81. Committee on Foreign Affairs and Committee on Foreign Relations, *Legislation on Foreign Relations Through 1985* (Washington, D.C.: Government Printing Office, April 1986), p. 956.

82. *Country Reports on Economic Policy and Trade Practices*, Report to the Committee on Foreign Relations and Committee on Finance of the U.S. Senate and Committee on Foreign Affairs and Committee on Ways and Means of the U.S. House of Representatives (Washington, D.C.: Government Printing Office, February 1994).

83. See the Conference report on H.R. 2055, Military Construction and Veterans Affairs and Related Agencies Appropriation Act, 2012, pp. 413 for this reporting requirement in current legislation.

84. A more complete description of reprogramming reporting is available in James M. McCormick, "A Review of the Foreign Assistance Program," memo prepared for the Office of the Honorable Lee Hamilton, February 1987.

85. See the Conference report on H.R. 2055, Military Construction and Veterans Affairs and Related Agencies Appropriation Act, 2012, p. 399 for this requirement. It is at the same page in H.R. 2055.

86. Collier, "Foreign Policy by Reporting Requirement," p. 80.

87. See P.L. 99-433, enacted on October 1, 1986.

88. The examples of required reporting are taken from the Committee on Foreign Relations and Committee on International Relations, *Legislation on Foreign Relations Through 1994*, Volume I-A (Washington, D.C.: U.S. Government Printing Office, June, 1995), pp. 658, and "Iran, Libya Sanctions," p. 3039.

89. See United States Government Accountability Office, "Securing, Stabilizing and Rebuilding Iraq," GAO-07-1195, September 2007 and the "Benchmark Assessment Report," September 14, 2007 presented by General David Petraeus.

90. See General James L. Jones, USMC (Ret.), Chairman, *The Report of the Independent Commission on the Security Forces of Iraq*, September 6, 2007.

91. Fisher, "Presidents Who Initiate Wars," p. 204.

92. For a more complete discussion of the changing role of the Senate Foreign Relations Committee and its oversight responsibilities, see James M. McCormick, "Decision Making in the Foreign Affairs and Foreign Relations Committees," in Randall B. Ripley and James M. Lindsay, eds., *Congress Resurgent: Foreign and Defense Policy on Capitol Hill* (Ann Arbor: University of Michigan Press, 1993), pp. 115–153.

93. Congressional Quarterly, *Congressional Quarterly's Guide to Congress*, 3rd ed. p. 289.

94. Ibid.

95. Bernard Gwertzman, "Senator Planning Sweeping Hearing on Foreign Policy," *New York Times*, December 9, 1984, 20.

96. Helen Dewar, "Senate Foreign Relations Panel Founders," *Washington Post*, October 10, 1989, A12.

97. Dick Kirschten, "Where's the Bite?" *National Journal*, March 25, 1995, 739–742.

98. Ibid.

99. Elaine Sciolino, "Awaiting Call, Helms Puts Foreign Policy on Hold," *New York Times*, September 24, 1995, 1.

100. Elaine Sciolino, "Helms to Allow Action in Senate on Clinton Diplomatic Nominees," *New York Times*, September 30, 1995, 1.

101. "Foreign Relations: The Power Broker," *CQ Weekly*, May 26, 2001, 1228.

102. Elaine Monaghan, "110th Senate Committee: Foreign Relations," *CQ Weekly*, November 13, 2006, p. 3030.

103. Ibid.

104. See "John Kerry" in Michael Barone and Chuck McCutcheon, *The Almanac of American Politics, 2012* (Chicago: University of Chicago Press, 2011), pp. 774–777, especially at p. 777 at http://site.ebrary.com.proxy.lib.iastate.edu:2048/lib/iowastate/docDetail. action?docID=10502610, May 21, 2012.

105. Foreign Affairs is not ranked as the most popular committee in the House; it still ranks behind Ways and Means and Appropriations as a desirable committee assignment. See Richard F. Fenno, *Congressman in Committees* (Boston: Little, Brown and Co., 1973), pp. 16–20. For a different ranking, see Randall B. Ripley, *Congress: Process and Policy*, 2nd ed. (New York: W.W. Norton and Company, 1978), p. 166.

106. See Fenno, *Congressman in Committees*, pp. 15–151, on the importance of the Senate Foreign Relations Committee. On the limited responsibilities of the House Foreign Affairs agenda, see ibid., pp. 213–215.

107. See Fred Kaiser, "Oversight of Foreign Policy: The U.S. House Committee on International Relations," *Legislative Studies Quarterly* 2 (August 1977): 259; and Fred M. Kaiser, "The Changing Nature and Extent of Oversight: The House Committee on Foreign Affairs in the 1970s," paper presented at the 1975 Annual Meeting of the Midwest Political Science Association, Chicago, Illinois.

108. Fred M. Kaiser, "Structural Change and Policy Development: The House Committee on International Relations," paper presented at the 1976 Annual Meeting of the Midwest Political Science Association; and Fred M. Kaiser, "Structural and Policy Change: The House Committee on International Relations," *Policy Studies Journal* 5 (Summer 1977): 443–451.

109. Interviews with majority and minority staff in June 1982 reveal that they viewed the committee as more liberal than the House as a whole. Also see James M. McCormick, "The Changing Role of the House Foreign Affairs Committee in the 1970s and 1980s," *Congress & The Presidency* 12 (Spring 1985): 1–20; and McCormick "Decision Making in the Foreign Affairs and Foreign Relations Committees," pp. 132–137.

110. *Origins and Development of Congress* (Washington, D.C.: Congressional Quarterly, 1976), p. 159.

111. Kaiser, "Structural and Policy Change," p. 446.

112. For a listing of the subcommittees and for a brief history of the House Foreign Affairs Committee, see *Survey of Activities, 99th Congress* (Washington, D.C.: Government Printing Office, 1987).

113. Kaiser, "Structural Change and Policy Development," pp. 21–22.

114. See the data on committee and subcommittee hearings in Committee on International Relations, *Legislative Review Activities of the Committee on International Relations*, 104th Cong. (Washington, D.C.: Government Printing Office, 1997), p. 123.

115. Carroll J. Doherty, "Republicans Poised to Slash International Programs," *Congressional Quarterly Weekly Report*, May 13, 1995, 1334–1336; and Carroll J. Doherty, "Gilman Under Pressure," *Congressional Quarterly Weekly Report*, May 13, 1995, 1335.

116. Miles A. Pomper, "International Relations: Rep. Henry J. Hyde of Illinois," *CQ Weekly*, January 6, 2001, 17.

117. Edward Epstein, "Tom Lantos, Foreign Affairs Chairman, Dies," *CQ Weekly*, February 18, 2008, p. 448.

118. See "Biography," at http://ros-lehtinen.house.gov/aout-me/full biography, "Committees and Caucuses," at http://ros-lehtinen.house.gov/aout-me/committee-and-caucuses, May 21, 2012, and "Ileana Ros-Lehtinen" in Michael Barone and Chuck McCutcheon, *The Almanac of American Politics, 2012* (Chicago: University of Chicago Press, 2011),

pp. 408–411, at http://site.ebrary.com.proxy.lib.iastate.edu:2048/lib/iowastate/docDetail. action?docID=10502610, May 21, 2012. The quotation is from Congressman Howard Berman at p. 411.

119. The first study is by Carol Goss, cited in Edward J. Laurance, "The Congressional Role in Defense Policy: The Evolution of the Literature," *Armed Forces & Society* 6 (Spring 1980): 437, the second is "Armed Services Committees: Advocates or Overseers?" *Congressional Quarterly Weekly Report*, March 25, 1972, 673–677.

120. Christopher J. Deering, "Decision Making in the Armed Services Committees," in Randall B. Ripley and James M. Lindsay, eds., *Congress Resurgent: Foreign and Defense Policy on Capitol Hill* (Ann Arbor: University of Michigan Press, 1993), pp. 155–182.

121. See James M. Lindsay, "Congress and Defense Policy: 1961 to 1986," *Armed Forces & Society* 13 (Spring 1987): 371–401, for a discussion of these committees in the 1970s and 1980s. As he correctly notes, the Defense subcommittees on the House and Senate Appropriations committees are equally important—or even more important—players on defense policy issues.

122. Cited in Paul Stockton, "Beyond Micromanagement: Congressional Budgeting for a Post–Cold War Military," *Political Science Quarterly* 110 (Summer 1995): 239.

123. Pat Towell, "Armed Services: Rep. Bob Stump of Arizona," *CQ Weekly*, January 6, 2001, 14.

124. George Cahlink, "Hawk and Dove Allied in Wartime," *CQ Weekly Online* (November 20, 2006): 3120–3121, at http://library.cqpress.com/cqweekly/weeklyreport109-000002405288, October 20, 2008.

125. John M. Donnelly and Adam Graham-Silverman, "House Votes Again on Withdrawal," *CQ Weekly Online* (July 16, 2007): 2115–2117, at http://library.cqpress.com/cqweekly/weeklyreport110–000002550946, October 20, 2008.

126. See "Buck McKeon," in Michael Barone and Chuck McCutcheon, *The Almanac of American Politics, 2012* (Chicago: University of Chicago Press, 2011), pp. 202–204, at http://site.ebrary.com.proxy.lib.iastate.edu:2048/lib/iowastate/docDetail. action?docID=10502610, May 21, 2012; and "Biography," at http://mckeon.house.gov/aboutbuck/biography.htm, May 21, 2012.

127. See Stockton, "Beyond Micromanagement: Congressional Budgeting for a Post–Cold War Military," pp. 237–240, for mention of Nunn's and Aspin's efforts. For a fuller discussion, see Paul N. Stockton, "Congress and U.S. Military Policy Beyond the Cold War," in Ripley and Lindsay, eds., *Congress Resurgent: Foreign and Defense Policy on Capitol Hill*, pp. 235–259.

128. Pat Towell, "Armed Services: Missile Defense Skeptic," *CQ Weekly*, May 26, 2001, 1221.

129. John Donnelly, "Fall Agenda: Iraq War Policy," *CQ Weekly Online* (September 3, 2007): 2544, at http://library.cqpress.com/cqweekly/weeklyreport110-000002576963, October 20, 2008.

130. Chalink, "Hawk and Dove Allied in Wartime," p. 3120.

131. Norman J. Ornstein and Thomas E. Mann, "When Congress Checks Out," *Foreign Affairs* 85 (November/December 2006), p. 68. The complete article is from pp. 67–82.

132. William G. Howell and Jon C. Pevehouse, "When Congress Stops Wars: Partisan Politics and Presidential Power," *Foreign Affairs* 86 (September/October 2007): 95–107.

133. The subsequent discussion here draws on the insightful analyses by Eileen Burgin, "Congress and Foreign Policy: The Misperceptions," in Lawrence C. Dodd and Bruce I. Oppenheimer, eds., *Congress Reconsidered* (Washington, D.C.: CQ Press, 1993), pp. 333–363; and James M. Lindsay, "Congress and Foreign Policy: Avenues of Influence," in Eugene R. Wittkopf, *The Domestic Sources of American Foreign Policy: Insights and Evidence*, 2nd ed. (New York: St. Martin's Press, 1994), pp. 191–207.

134. See Barbara Hinckley, *Less Than Meets the Eye*, pp. 26–29, esp. Tables 2.1 and 2.2. Given Hinckley's definition of what to include and exclude as legislation (see p. 25), the congressional role might be somewhat understated. Also, it is not clear which legislation is initiated by Congress and which is initiated by the president.

135. See Lindsay, "Congress and Foreign Policy: Avenues of Influence," pp. 198–201. Also see his "Congress, Foreign Policy, and the New Institutionalism," *International Studies Quarterly* 38 (June 1994): 281–304.

136. See Burgin, "Congress and Foreign Policy: The Misperceptions," for the types of nonlegislative actions on which we draw throughout this section and for more examples of these activities.

137. Grimmett, *The War Powers Resolution: After Twenty-Eight Years*, pp. 39–40.

138. Ralph G. Carter and James M. Scott, *Choosing to Lead: Understanding Congressional Foreign Policy Entrepreneurs* (Durham & London: Duke University Press, 2009).

139. Rebecca K. C. Hersman, *Friends and Foes* (Washington, D.C.: The Brookings Institution, 2000), p. 106.

140. Thomas M. Franck and Edward Weisband, *Foreign Policy by Congress* (New York: Oxford University Press, 1979), pp. 6–9; and I. M. Destler, "Dateline Washington: Congress as Boss?" *Foreign Policy* 42 (Spring 1981): 167–180.

141. Jeremy D. Rosner, *The New Tug-of-War: Congress, the Executive Branch and National Security* (Washington, D.C.: Carnegie Endowment for International Peace, 1995).

142. Harold Hongju Koh, *The National Security Constitution* (New Haven, CT, and London: Yale University Press, 1990), p. 117.

143. Hinckley, *Less Than Meets the Eye*, pp. 5 and 47, respectively.

144. Committee on Foreign Affairs, *Congress and Foreign Policy, 1988*; and Committee on Foreign Affairs, *Congress and Foreign Policy 1987* (Washington, D.C.: Government Printing Office, 1989).

145. "Bush's Dozen Vetoes," *New York Times*, June 16, 1990, 8; and "State Department Bill Clears, But Faces Bush's Veto," *Congressional Quarterly Weekly Report*, November 18, 1989, 3189.

146. On some of these controversies between the Obama administration and the Congress, as well as the changing relationship between Congress and the executive on foreign policy over time, see James M. Lindsay, "The Shifting Pendulum of Power: Executive-Legislative Relations on American Foreign Policy," in James M. McCormick, ed., *The Domestic Sources of American Foreign Policy: Insights and Evidence* (Lanham, MD: Rowman & Littlefield, 2012), pp. 223–238.

147. John G. Tower, "Congress Versus the President: The Formulation and Implementation of American Foreign Policy," *Foreign Affairs* 60 (Winter 1981–1982): 233.

148. "Pakistan Waivers," *CQ Weekly*, December 22, 2001, 3040. Also see P.L. 107-57.

149. On the difficulties of approving the Chemical Weapons Conventions, see Hersman, *Friends and Foes*, pp. 85–104.

150. Homan, "Colombia Free-Trade Pact Held up as House Democrats Block Action," p. 949.

151. Norman J. Ornstein and David W. Rohde, "Shifting Forces, Changing Rules, and Political Outcomes: The Impact of Congressional Change on Four House Committees," in Robert L. Peabody and Nelson W. Polsby, eds., *New Perspectives on the House of Representatives*, 3rd ed. (Chicago: Rand McNally, 1977), p. 259. This description, however, was before the *Chadha* decision.

152. Haney and Vanderbush, "The Helms-Burton Act: Congress and Cuba Policy," pp. 278, 283. On the continued suspension of Title III in the Clinton and Bush administrations, see Mark P. Sullivan, "Cuba: Issues for the 108th Congress," Congressional Research

Service, The Library of Congress, January 3, 2003, RL 31740, at http://www.fpc.state. gov/21354.pdf, September 7, 2008.

153. On the suspension of Title III for the Obama administration, see Tim Bearden, "Helms-Burton Act: Resurrecting the Iron Curtain," June 13, 2011, at http://truth-out.org/ index.php?option=com_k2&view=item&id=1606.helmsburton-act-resurrecting-the-iron-curtain, May 20, 2012.

154. P.L. 110-161.

155. See Felton, "Hill Weighs Foreign Policy Impact of Ruling," pp. 1329–1330, for an assessment of the Supreme Court ruling on the legislative veto for foreign policy, and 462 U.S. 919 (1983).

156. Lee H. Hamilton, "The Role of the U.S. Congress in American Foreign Policy," Elliott School Special Lecture Series, The George Washington University, 1999–2000, p. 16.

157. These views are based on interviews with staff of the House Foreign Affairs Committee (June 1982), officials of the Department of State who deal with congressional relations (October 1981), some participant observation in the House of Representatives in 1986 and 1987, and continued observation of the political process.

158. Schlesinger, "Congress and the Making of American Foreign Policy," *Foreign Affairs* 51 (October 1972): 106.

159. For a listing of suggestions for addressing this consultation problem, see Hamilton, "The Role of the U.S. Congress in American Foreign Policy," pp. 1–10.

The Diplomatic and Economic Bureaucracies: Duplication or Specialization?

We must use what has been called "smart power": the full range or tools
at our disposal—diplomatic, economic, military, political, legal,
and cultural—picking the right tool, or combination of
tools, for each situation. With smart power, diplomacy
will be the vanguard of foreign policy.

SECRETARY OF STATE DESIGNATE HILLARY
RODHAM CLINTON
JANUARY 13, 2009

... the work we do at USTR—to open markets, level the playing field,
and keep America competitive—is enormously relevant for
hard-working families across the United States.

RON KIRK U.S. TRADE REPRESENTATIVE
MAY 15, 2012

Although the president may dominate vis-à-vis Congress in the foreign policy process, he cannot act alone. He needs information and advice from his assistants and the various foreign affairs bureaucracies within the executive branch to formulate policy; he also needs the aid of the executive branch to implement it. Thus, although it may be the president who ultimately chooses a foreign policy option—the use of force against the Taliban and al-Qaeda in Afghanistan in 2001, going to war against Iraq in 2003, or imposing sanctions against Iran or threatening North Korea over nuclear weapons development—it is the bureaucratic environment in which he operates that greatly influences his decisions and their implementation.

The variety of agencies with an interest in foreign policy may be surprising. For example, the **Department of Agriculture** may seem primarily concerned with domestic farm issues, but it also encourages the granting of foreign trade credits to countries such as Russia and Poland to promote American farm exports. Similarly, the **Department of Treasury** may monitor the money supply at home, but it also advises the president on how to respond to the global recession or to the Euro crisis. Although the **Justice Department** may be primarily interested in eradicating illegal drugs at home, it also has an interest in drug production in several South American and South Asian countries as well. One of its long-standing divisions (before it was folded into the **Department of Homeland Security**), the Immigration and Naturalization Service (INS), was responsible for monitoring America's borders, but following September 11, 2001, its successor agency **Immigration and Custom Enforcement (ICE)** became involved in developing cooperative arrangements with other countries to control international terrorism. Finally, more than any other bureaucracy, the Department of Homeland Security illustrates how domestic and foreign concerns are intermingled within an agency. This department is Janus-faced, concerned with threats to security at home and from abroad.

In short, the principal foreign policy bureaucracies that we often think of (and even those we may not immediately think of) continuously compete to get the "president's ear" on international issues and to shape an outcome favorable to them on to what they perceive as good foreign policy. With the globalization of so many issues and the growth and expansion of bureaucratic agendas, understanding domestic bureaucratic politics has become critically important to understanding American foreign policy.

BUREAUCRATIC POLITICS AND FOREIGN POLICY MAKING

The "bureaucratic politics" approach to foreign policy making stands in contrast to earlier discussions in which we emphasized the values and beliefs of American society as a whole, the values of particular presidents and administrations, or even the influence of institutions like Congress and the presidency. This approach views the emergence of policy from the interactions among the various bureaucracies as they compete to shape the nation's actions abroad. Policy thus becomes less the result of the values and beliefs of individual political actors (although they can surely have an effect) and more the result of interaction between and among several bureaucracies. Put differently, policy making is the result of the "pulling" and "hauling" among these competing institutions.[1] Compromise within and coalition building across bureaucracies become important to the way in which policy ultimately emerges. In this sense, the *process* of policy making becomes an important means of arriving at the substance of policy.

Although the bureaucratic politics model has long been used to study domestic policy, its sustained application in foreign policy dates from the early 1970s with the imaginative work by political scientist Graham Allison on the Cuban Missile Crisis and more general research by political analyst Morton Halperin.[2] These two pioneers sparked a broader interest in this approach, and it has now become a standard mode of foreign policy analysis.

This approach has had considerable applicability to foreign policy decision making over the past several decades, but examples from the George W. Bush and Barack Obama administrations will illustrate its utility for the present era as well. The Bush administration's decision making over Iraq and the Obama administration's decision making over Afghanistan will illustrate how the pulling and hauling among the bureaucracies affected the direction of policy in both instances.

During the middle of 2002, a bureaucratic policy debate arose over appropriate policy actions toward **Iraq** and the nature of the threat that it posed to the United States and the global community. Although some officials in the Bush administration favored immediate military action to remove Saddam Hussein because of his development of weapons of mass destruction, others in the Department of State, including Secretary of State Colin Powell and Deputy Secretary of State Richard Armitage, raised concerns about the "risks and complexities" of such an approach.[3] Members of Congress, too, counseled against quick military action, as did foreign policy officials from the senior Bush administration. Further, a Senate Foreign Relations Committee hearing in July 2002 illustrated the array of views on this issue. Finally, there were reportedly divided opinions even within the Department of Defense itself: civilian officials favored immediate military actions; military officials, in the Pentagon, were more cautious. Hence, a number of competing positions could potentially affect the direction of policy.

During the Obama administration, bureaucratic debates also confronted its policy actions in Afghanistan. During the spring of 2009, President Obama ordered the American commander in Afghanistan, General Stanley McChrystal, to conduct a review of the situation in that country and to make a recommendation on the way forward. McChrystal's recommendations largely called for sending more U.S. troops to Afghanistan and to pursue a counterinsurgency strategy in that country. These recommendations produced an extended debate among the president's foreign policy advisors. Vice President Joseph Biden and Richard Holbrooke (the president's special representative to Afghanistan and Pakistan) opposed sending more troops; Biden called for a counterterrorism, not a counterinsurgency, strategy. On the other side of the debate were General David Petraeus, then in charge of Central Command and the former commander in Iraq; Secretary of Defense Robert Gates; and—eventually—Secretary of State Hillary Clinton; each supported the principal recommendations of the McChrystal report. The internal policy among these various bureaucracies continued for several months and was only settled when the president announced his decision to pursue a counterinsurgency "surge strategy" in Afghanistan.[4]

The bureaucratic politics model thus allows us to apply another perspective in interpreting and understanding U.S. foreign policy. To do this, we examine each of the key foreign policy bureaucracies within the executive branch, describe its role and assess its relative influence. In this way, we can begin to evaluate how some bureaucracies succeed in the shaping of foreign policy and identify the policy areas where some bureaucracies are influential.

We analyze four central foreign policy bureaucracies in detail in this and the following chapter: the **Department of State**, the **National Security Council**, the **Department of Defense**, and **the intelligence community**. We also survey the increasingly important economic bureaucracies and their role in shaping foreign economic policy—in particular, the **Office of the U.S. Trade Representative**, the **Department of Treasury**, the **Department of Commerce**, and the **Department of Agriculture**. In the final section of Chapter 10, we bring the discussion of the various bureaucracies together by showing how they coordinate with one another through interagency groups (IGs) as part of the National Security Council system. Throughout both chapters, we discuss a crucial question of the bureaucratic politics approach: how are foreign policy choices the result of both interdepartmental coordination and interdepartmental rivalries?

THE DEPARTMENT OF STATE

The oldest cabinet post and the original foreign policy bureaucracy is the Department of State, established in 1781 under the Articles of Confederation as the Department of Foreign Affairs and becoming the Department of State in 1789 with the election of George Washington.[5] Over its 220-year history, State has evolved into a large and complex organization with a variety of functions. Its principal job, however, remains assisting the president in policy formulation on all international issues and implementing policy in America's foreign relations. In this way, the Department of State coordinates U.S. overseas programs that emanate from Washington.[6] At the same time, it has seen its influence weakened by internal and external problems over the years.

The Structure of State at Home

The **Department of State** has always been organized in a complex and hierarchical fashion, but **changes have been made to rationalize its organizational structure and gain greater operational efficiency**.[7] In particular, these changes included streamlining its internal structure through reorganization and restructuring its decision-making responsibilities. In the 1990s, the department downsized its foreign operations (about forty embassies and consulates were closed during that time). Indeed, for almost six years during the 1990s, the department did not hire or add a new Foreign Service officer; more recently, however, it has been adding new positions and requesting more. In 2010, for example, Secretary of State Hillary Clinton reported that Congress had provided funding for 1,108 new Foreign Service and Civil Service officers and that the Agency for International Development (USAID) was in the process of hiring 1,200 new Foreign Service officers. Furthermore, and in accord with the Quadrennial Diplomacy and Development Review (QDDR) in 2010, the emphasis is now on greater cooperation between these two as well as a commitment to creating a "global civilian service," including the private sector, to advance American national interests.[8]

The Secretary of State and Principal Advisors Figure 9.1 displays the internal organizational structure of the Department of State. At the top is the **secretary of state**, who is the principal foreign policy advisor to the president and who is responsible for carrying out "the President's foreign policies through the State Department and the Foreign Service of the United States."[9] The secretary now has two deputy

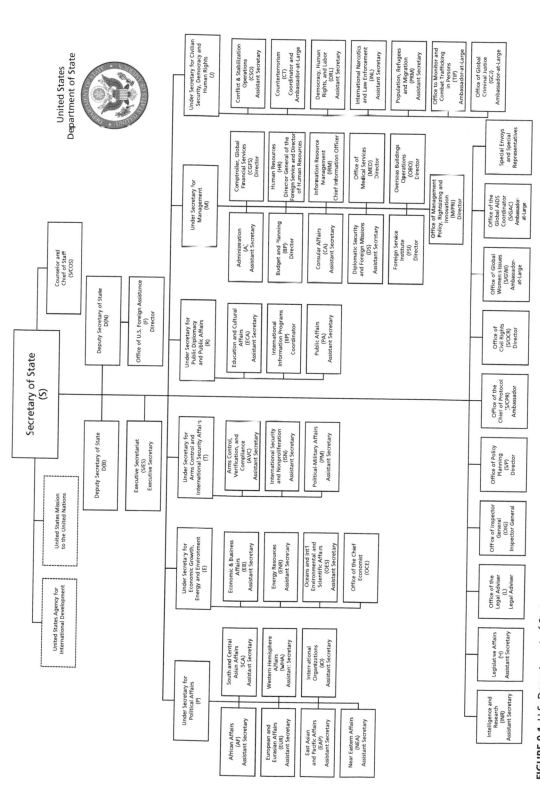

FIGURE 9.1 U.S. Department of State

Source: From the Department of State website, at http://www.state.gov/r/pa/ei/rls/dos/99494.htm.

secretaries of state. One is the deputy secretary of state for policy. That individual serves as the secretary's "principal deputy, adviser, and alter ego;" assumes the role "as Acting Secretary of State in the Secretary's absence; and assists the Secretary in the formulation and conduct of U.S. foreign policy."[10] The second deputy secretary of state is for management, serving as the "Chief Operating Officer of the Department" and "as principal adviser to the Secretary on over-all supervision and direction of resource allocation and management activities of the Department."[11] Also included at the top of the organizational structure of the department are a counselor and chief of staff and the Executive Secretariat, composed of an executive secretary and four deputies. The function of the Executive Secretariat is to coordinate activities among the secretary, deputy secretary, undersecretaries, and various bureaus. It also works with "the White House, the National Security Council, and other Cabinet agencies."[12] The Operations Center reports to the Executive Secretariat and monitors, on a twenty-four-hour basis, events and activities across the globe, serving as the "communications and crisis management center" for the department. Finally, several departmental individuals, bureaus, and activities report directly to the secretary. These include the Policy Planning Staff, the Bureau of Legislative Affairs, the Bureau of Intelligence and Research, the Office of the Chief of Protocol, the Office of the Inspector General, the Office of Legal Advisor, and the Special Envoys and Special Representatives.

The Role of Undersecretaries   An important second level of authority is the six undersecretaries, who have varying responsibilities and who report directly to the secretary. The move to a larger number of undersecretaries was completed during the Clinton administration to strengthen their role in the policy process and to have them serve as "the principal foreign policy advisors to the Secretary."[13] These officials (and their divisions) are now responsible for managing and coordinating the principal activities under their aegis and for serving as a "corporate board" to the secretary of state.

- The **undersecretary for political affairs** now oversees six regional bureaus (African Affairs, East Asian and Pacific Affairs, European and Eurasian Affairs, Western Hemisphere Affairs, Near Eastern Affairs, and South and Central Asian Affairs) and one functional bureau (International Organization Affairs).

- The **undersecretary for economic growth, energy and environment**, is responsible for four bureaus (Economic & Business Affairs, Energy Resources, Oceans and International Environmental and Scientific Affairs, and the Office of the Chief Economist).

- The **undersecretary for arms control and international security affairs** oversees a wide range of security and defense activities through the Bureau of Political-Military Affairs and two related bureaus. This undersecretary serves "as Senior Adviser to the President and the Secretary of State" for issues of arms control, nonproliferation, and disarmament and may participate in the meeting of the National Security Council on such issues as well.[14]

- The **undersecretary for public diplomacy and public affairs** is responsible for educational and cultural affairs, international information programs, public affairs, and public diplomacy. In effect, this division assumed the responsibilities of the semiautonomous U.S. Information Agency, which was folded into the Department of State in 1999.

- The **undersecretary for civilian security, democracy, and human rights** manages a number of functional bureaus dealing with democracy promotion; human rights; worker rights; environmental and scientific affairs; population, refugee, and migration issues; international narcotics and law enforcement; monitoring and combating trafficking in persons; and global criminal justice.

- The **undersecretary for management** oversees many of the common internal administrative activities of the department: the Foreign Service Institute, which provides language, political, cultural, and now business promotion training for American personnel assigned abroad, and the Human Resources Office. This secretariat also manages the bureaus of Administration, Consular Affairs, Diplomatic Security, and a variety of information resources.

An assistant secretary of state (usually there are about twenty at any given time) heads each of the departmental bureaus and answers to either the secretary's office or the appropriate undersecretary.[15] Because the reorganizations over the past two decades have emphasized the need for the undersecretaries to concentrate on broad overviews of policy, the assistant secretaries have come to possess considerably greater latitude in policy formulation and decision making. As a result, they are likely to represent their bureaus in foreign affairs interagency groups, in testimony before congressional committees or subcommittees, and perhaps with the secretary of state directly (although the chain of command goes through the appropriate undersecretary). In addition, the assistant secretaries may become important negotiators or representatives of the department with foreign governments.

Semiautonomous Agencies   Until the congressionally mandated changes in 1999, there were four semiautonomous agencies associated with the Department of State. Two of them, the United States Information Agency (USIA) and the United States Arms Control and Disarmament Agency (ACDA), were fully incorporated into the department. USIA, created in 1953, had the tasks of explaining American policy abroad, building good relations, and advising the government on foreign attitudes about the United States. ACDA, created in 1961, had responsibility for fostering global arms restraint, seeking arms control agreements, and monitoring compliance with agreements already in effect. The reasons for incorporating these agencies into State were to streamline and improve efficiency but also to provide the department with greater control over these two aspects of American foreign policy. The two remaining semiautonomous agencies connected with the Department of State complete the government's diplomatic apparatus: the **United States Mission to the United Nations** and the **United States Agency for International Development**. They are also shown at the top of Figure 9.1.

The establishment of the position of U.S. Permanent Representative to the United Nations, originally undertaken by the Clinton administration, was to allow America's UN ambassador to coordinate activities more directly with the Bureau of International Organization Affairs within the department. This representative served on the Principals Committee of the National Security Council during the Clinton administration and that practice now continues with the Obama administration.

USAID, created by Congress in 1961, is the principal foreign aid bureaucracy of the U.S. government. Its aims are twofold: to further "America's interests" abroad and to improve "lives in the developing world."[16] Organizationally, USAID works toward its goals through its regional and functional bureaus and through its various missions or posts located in countries throughout the developing world. At less than 0.50 percent of the U.S. federal budget, its budget is quite small. The president's FY2013 budget request for all State Department and USAID operations was $51.6 billion,[17] although most of those funds go for international activities managed by State and USAID and not administration per se. By combining its efforts with and working through private and voluntary organizations (PVOs) and nongovernmental organizations (NGOs) around the world, USAID points to numerous successes, such as saving more than three million lives yearly through its immunization program, raising literacy rates by 33 percent in the past twenty-five years, reducing the number of undernourished people, eradicating smallpox, and providing assistance to governments transitioning to democracy.[18]

The Structure of State Abroad

The State Department represents America through U.S. missions, usually located in a capital city and consulates in other major cities of host countries. As of March 31, 2012, there were 275 embassies, missions, consular agencies, consulates general, and other offices abroad and 10 missions at the headquarters of various intergovernmental organizations (such as United Nations, European Union, Organization of American States, and International Civil Aviation Organization).[19] In all, the United States currently has diplomatic relations with 190 nations, and there are only a few with which it presently has none: Bhutan, Cuba, Iran, and North Korea. Nevertheless, it may conduct business with some of these states through the "good offices" of other states that do have diplomatic relations with them.

The U.S. embassy is headed by a **chief of mission**, usually an **ambassador**, who is the personal representative of the president and is authorized to handle U.S. foreign relations with that country.[20] The ambassador is assisted by the deputy chief of mission (DCM), who is largely responsible for the day-to-day operation of the embassy staff. Although political, economic, consular, and administrative Foreign Service officers from State serve the embassy, representatives from several other executive departments are housed within it. The composition of the "**country team**" of a U.S. mission might consist of an agricultural counselor from the Department of Agriculture, a commercial counselor from the Department of Commerce, a labor official from the Department of Labor, an environmental officer from the Environmental Protection Agency, and both a defense attaché and a military advisory group from the Department of Defense. Other agencies may also be represented, ranging from the Drug Enforcement Agency to the Internal Revenue Service. Officials from the Central Intelligence Agency—using a cover of other positions—are often on the country team as well.

The U.S. embassy in Islamabad, Pakistan, for example, has 800 staff members, with about 550 diplomats, civil servants, and USAID officials, but the rest are "from 11 other federal agencies." As a result, Secretary Clinton noted in 2010, "A U.S. ambassador … is … responsible not only for managing civilians from the State Department and USAID but also for operating as the CEO of a multiagency mission. And he or she must also be adept at connecting with audiences outside of government, such as the private sector and civil society."[21] The size of a mission is a function primarily of the size of the nation where it is located and its perceived political and strategic importance. American missions abroad have ranged widely, from 1,100 U.S. direct hires in Germany (and an additional 800 foreign nationals) to 1 in the Former Yugoslav Republic of Macedonia. By one analysis, the median size of a U.S. mission abroad in the 1990s was roughly 100—equally divided between Americans and foreign nationals.[22] During the Iraq War, the American embassy in that country was reportedly the largest worldwide, and the size of the embassies in Afghanistan and Pakistan swelled as American involvement in those countries expanded.

As this overview indicates, the structure of the Department of State (and its affiliated agencies) appears quite large and complex. In reality, however, the department itself is one of the smallest bureaucracies within the executive branch. Currently, it has roughly 69,000 employees, of which about 7,920 are traditional Foreign Service officers, 5,710 are Foreign Service specialists, 10,631 are civil service personnel, and 37,000 are foreign nationals. (By contrast, the Department of Defense has approximately 718,000 civilian employees.[23]) State has traditionally been smaller than all but four other cabinet departments (Energy, Labor, Housing and Urban Development, and Education), and it has fewer employees than some city governments.[24] Furthermore, its operating budget is one of the smallest within the government (see the next section), especially when compared with other foreign affairs sectors, such as the Department of Defense or the intelligence community.[25]

The Weakened Influence of State

Despite its role as the principal foreign policy bureaucracy, and as the one that usually offers a nonmilitary option in policy making, the Department of State has been **criticized for its effectiveness in policy formulation and implementation**.[26] As a consequence, it has not played the dominant role in recent administrations that its central diplomatic position might imply. A departmental report formally acknowledged that it should not be the focus for foreign policy coordination. The *State 2000* report asserted "that the National Security Council (NSC) [should] be the catalyst and the point of coordination for this new, single foreign policy process."[27] In large measure, and as we discuss later, the NSC has become the center of foreign policy making.

In this sense, the *policy influence* of the Department of State is **comparatively less** than that of other government foreign policy bureaucracies. The factors that have reduced its influence are *internal*, such as its increasing budget problems, its size, its personnel, its "subculture," and the relationship between the secretary and the department; and *external*, such as the relationship between the president and the secretary, the relationship between the president and the department, the perception of the public at large, and the growth of other foreign policy bureaucracies (such as the National Security Council and the Office of the U.S. Trade Representative). Let us examine several of these factors to give some sense of this weakened influence.

The Problem of Resources The first problem that the Department of State faces in the competition to influence foreign affairs and to carry out its responsibilities is resources. Its small operating budget has been a perennial issue over the past three decades, with Congress reluctant to fund all of its needs. By contrast, funding for the Department of Defense and the intelligence community grew in the 1980s, suffered from budgetary pressures after the end of the Cold War, and expanded at the beginning of the new century as part of America's effort to combat global terrorism. State has not enjoyed such substantial budget increases.

State's administrative budget, however, has increased from about $700 million in 1979 to about $13 billion in FY2012, but the effects of inflation, congressional mandates for new departmental bureaus, and the expansion of foreign affairs responsibilities worldwide have become real problems.[28] Moreover, apart from Congress's lack of budgetary responsiveness to State's needs, Congress also has sought to block some activities with which it strongly disagrees (for example, several controversial foreign assistance programs). In February 1987, Secretary of State George Shultz became so frustrated that he commented that State's budget problems were "a tragedy." As a result, "America is hauling down the flag. . . . We're withdrawing from the world." In November 1987, the department began hinting that 1,200 jobs would have to be eliminated and several embassies and consulates around the world would have to be closed because of these mounting budget problems.[29]

During the Clinton administration, the closing of numerous foreign posts (consulates and embassies) became a reality. From 1993 to 1997, thirty-two embassies and consulates were abolished. Many were consulates in peripheral locations around the world, and their closings represented a consolidation of operations. A few, however, were embassies in places such as Equatorial Guinea, Western Samoa, and the Seychelles.[30] Nonetheless, all of these closings reduced American presence globally and increased the workload for other posts.

Reductions in State Department staff occurred as well. In May 1995, Secretary of State Warren Christopher stated that 500 positions would be eliminated to save money, streamline the policy process, and forestall even greater reductions by a Republican-controlled Congress. Six months later, the department reported that more than 1,100 jobs had been trimmed.[31] By late 2001, however, this trend had started to reverse itself with the hiring of "about 475 foreign service generalists (officers) and about 350 foreign service specialists each year. These numbers declined marginally in FY05 but should remain at similar levels."[32] By 2010, as Secretary of State Hillary Clinton pointed out, State was increasing its staff with funding for 1,108 new Foreign Service and Civil Service officers approved by Congress and USAID was in the process of adding 1,200 new Foreign Service officers.[33]

Still, each of the last three secretaries of state has appealed to Congress for increased funding for the department. One of Colin Powell's first stops after being named secretary of state in 2001 was Congress, to implore it to provide more funding. He promised reform as part of his request but was met with skepticism. As one member put it: "The most relevant question . . . is not have we provided enough money, but rather . . . is the State Department up to the task of responsibly managing the money it's been given and the mission given to it by the Congress?"[34] Bush's secretary of state, Condoleezza Rice, invoked some of the same themes as Secretary Powell at her confirmation hearings in 2005, calling for more funding and more recruitment of top personnel: "I will personally work to ensure that America's diplomats have all the tools they need to do their jobs—from training to budgets to mentoring to embassy security. I also intend to strengthen the recruitment of new personnel, because American diplomacy needs to constantly hire and develop top talent."[35] In 2009, Hillary Clinton made much the same kind of statement at her confirmation hearing: "One of my first priorities is to make sure that the State Department and USAID have the resources they need, and I will be back to make the case to Congress for full funding of the President's budget request. At the same time, I will work just as hard to make sure that we manage those resources prudently so that we fulfill our mission efficiently and effectively."[36] In short, both careful use of funding and continued evidence of reform are still necessary for the Department of State to gain additional congressional support.

In the view of those at the department, though, serious policy implications accompany these continuing funding problems. First, personnel are not adequately

CHAPTER 9   THE DIPLOMATIC AND ECONOMIC BUREAUCRACIES: DUPLICATION OR SPECIALIZATION?

349

compensated or supported. Starting salaries are relatively low (compared to similar positions in the private sector), ranging "from the mid-thirty to the mid-sixty thousand dollar range, depending on education level and prior work experience." (Another source noted that the starting salary is about $44,000 depending on initial classification, but increases are often small.)[37] As a result, top-quality staff become less easy to recruit and more difficult to keep. Concerns have been expressed that new recruits do not match the quality of those of earlier years and regular recruiting was forestalled, at least until recently. The Foreign Service exam, the principal mechanism for screening new Foreign Service officers, was not even offered for two years in the 1990s, and, as noted earlier, for a time in the 1990s no new officers were hired. Second, budget restraints mean that individuals are asked to carry greater and greater workloads, and, inevitably, the quality of their work suffers. Third, morale suffers as officials are asked to do more with less and, sometimes, even to work without pay. Both the collection of information and the implementation of policy are unlikely to be as thorough under such circumstances. From the Department of State's point of view, the continuing budget problems reduce both its incentive and its capacity for competing with other bureaucracies in shaping U.S. foreign policy.

The Problem of Size   A second problem for the Department of State, as it attempts to compete with other bureaucracies, is its size. It is at once **too large and too small**. It is too large in the sense that there are layers and layers of bureaucracy through which policy reviews and recommendations must progress. At the present time, for example, there are six geographical and more than twenty functional bureaus involved in policy making. In most instances, recommendations must go through the appropriate regional and functional bureaus before they can reach the "seventh floor," where the department's executive offices are located.

As one former secretary of state reported in his memoirs, getting things done at State can be a challenge: "Different floors of 'the building' had their own unique views on events: 'The seventh floor [where the secretary and undersecretaries are located] won't want it that way.' 'The sixth floor [where the assistant secretaries are] wants to reclama on that.' . . . 'EUR [the Bureau of European and Canadian Affairs] is out of control.'"[38] In this sense, the structure of the department hinders its overall effectiveness and reduces its efficiency in developing policy.

At the same time, the department has been criticized as **too small** because it is dwarfed by the other bureaucracies in terms of political representation in the National Security Council interagency process. Furthermore, its staff does not often carry the same political clout that staffs in other large bureaucracies do. Consider the lobbying power of Defense, Commerce, Treasury, or even Agriculture; all have large and vocal constituencies to argue their policy position with the American people, Congress, and, ultimately, the president. By contrast, the State lacks a ready constituency within the American public to offer support and to lobby for it.[39] The State Department must therefore lobby by itself—through the testimony of its officials during congressional hearings, through its informal contacts with congressional staff, through the implementation of legislative action programs (LAPs), and through the interagency process. Suffice it to say, these avenues do not always yield political success.

The Personnel and the Environment in which State Operates   Foreign Service officers, foreign policy specialists, and civil service personnel from the U.S. Foreign Service are the department's principal officials. Primary policy responsibility, however, rests with the approximately 7,920 Foreign Service officers (FSOs) who have sometimes been depicted as an "eastern elite" out of touch with the country and determined to shape foreign policy in line with their own views.[40] According to this criticism, many share the same educational background (Princeton, Harvard, Yale, Johns Hopkins, Fletcher School of Law and Diplomacy), over-represent the eastern establishment, and exhibit an inflexible attitude toward global politics. However, several careful analyses of the Foreign Service officer corps some decades ago challenged these stereotypes. Moreover, midcareer ("lateral entry") and minority recruitment efforts have been used for some years to address this issue.[41] Nonetheless, the elitist image persists, as some scholarly and popular assessments confirm, and it reduces the department's effectiveness.[42]

At least two additional personnel problems are perceived among members of Congress, the foreign affairs bureaucracy, and the public at large. One is the charge of "**clientelism**," or "clientitis."[43] That is, in an FSO's zeal to foster good relations with the country in which he or she is serving, the officer becomes too closely identified with that country's interests, sometimes at the expense of American interests and the requirements of American domestic politics. Although this criticism is largely over-drawn, it has become an important excuse for members of Congress and the executive branch who want to avoid relying too closely on State's recommendations.

Another is the **level of expertise** that State Department personnel and FSOs possess on increasingly specialized issues. Although these individuals are undoubtedly capable generalists, the level of specific knowledge on technical subjects—and some reluctance to recruit outside experts—fosters the charge that the quality of their work is inadequate:

> Critics complain the State Department studies are too long and too descriptive and often unsatisfactory. Based heavily on intuition, and almost never conceptual, many of the analyses are unaccompanied by reliable sources and information, or reflect the FSO's lack of adequate training and expertise; papers are so cautious and vague as to be of little use to policymakers who long ago concluded that such "waffling" constitutes the quintessential character of the "Fudge Factory at Foggy Bottom."[44]

Today, this criticism, too, may be overdrawn. The Department of State has increasingly developed and hired specialists and has continued to rely on consultants for particular issues. Still, Foreign Service generalists still outnumber specialists. Hence, this critique continues.

The other part of this personnel complaint is exactly the reverse: "The tendency to assume that others do not understand foreign affairs as well as the Foreign Service."[45] With the emergence of sound academic programs, research institutes, and Washington think tanks focusing on many specialized issues, and with political appointees in and out of government on a regular basis, State Department FSOs should be more willing to look to these individuals for policy advice. In part, the Obama administration has recognized this problem and Secretary of State Clinton commissioned the QDDR that called for more cooperation across agencies within the government but also for more public–private effort to promote U.S. foreign policy interests.[46]

The Subculture Problem A bureaucratic "subculture" has developed in the State Department that emphasizes the importance of "trying to be something rather than . . . trying to do something."[47] Also, "Don't rock the boat" is the dominant bureaucratic refrain. Obtaining regular promotions and ensuring career advancements become more important than creating sound, innovative policy. According to one analyst, "Subcultural norms discourage vigorous policy debate within the Department. . . . The Department is not inclined toward vigorous exploration of policy options and it is not inclined to let anyone else do the job for it."[48] Another analyst describes the subculture in this way: "The prudent course is the cautious course. 'Fitting in' has a higher value than 'standing out.'"[49]

A recent secretary of state confirms the persistence of this State Department subculture. In his experience, he says, "the State Department has the most unique bureaucratic culture I've ever encountered."[50] He acknowledges the skills of most Foreign Service officers but finds that "some of them tend to avoid risk-taking or creative thinking" because of the bureaucratic environment.[51] As a result, he believes that sole reliance on State Department officials in policy making is not possible.

The President and the Secretary of State A fifth problem for the Department of State is its relationship with the president and the secretary of state.[52] Postwar presidents and secretaries of state have often not made extensive use of the department for policy formulation. Instead, presidents have tried to be their own "secretary of state" or have relied on key advisors instead of the appointed secretary of state for advice. For these reasons, the power of the secretary in policy making may be more apparent than real. Even when the president has confidence in his appointee, the secretary sometimes chooses not to involve the department, instead relying on a few key aides. Because of these patterns, the State Department's role has once again been diminished.

The relationship between recent presidents and their secretaries of state illustrates the problem. President Richard Nixon did not view Secretary of State William Rogers as his key foreign policy advisor; instead, National Security Advisor Henry Kissinger was the primary architect of foreign policy during those years. President Jimmy Carter initially tried to create a balance in policy making between Secretary of State Cyrus Vance and National Security Advisor Zbigniew Brzezinski, but he depended more on Brzezinski for shaping his response to global politics. President Ronald Reagan came to office committed to granting more control of foreign policy to the secretary of state, but his national security advisors over the years proved to be the most influential.[53]

Even the two early post–World War II presidents who relied on the secretary of state for policy formulation did not often go beyond him to enlist the full involvement of the department. Dean Acheson and George Marshall, secretaries under President Harry Truman, were primarily responsible for making their own foreign policy without much input by State.[54] Similarly, John Foster Dulles, secretary under President Dwight Eisenhower, was given wide latitude in policy formulation.

The administrations of George H. W. Bush and William Clinton tried to combine these various policy patterns. President Bush viewed foreign policy as an area of expertise because he had served as U.S. ambassador to the United Nations, director of the CIA, and representative to the People's Republic of China. As such, he assumed a large role in policy formulation but relied on his close friend and secretary of state, James Baker, and his national security advisor, Brent Scowcroft. By contrast, during his first term, President Clinton eschewed the importance of foreign policy and largely left it to Anthony Lake, his national security advisor, and Warren Christopher, his secretary of state. In his second term, he was more directly involved, but his national security advisor, Samuel Berger, and his secretary of state, Madeleine Albright, remained key policy formulators. Still, both Bush and Clinton placed the national security advisor and his staff at the center of foreign policy making, with ultimately a lesser role for the secretary of state.[55]

President George W. Bush's first secretary of state, Colin Powell, was initially thought to have a central role in the shaping of American foreign policy. In the first several months of the administration, though, his views appeared not to dominate administration policy discussions, as the new president veered from the secretary's opinions on dealing with North Korea and Iraq.[56] Instead, Bush relied on the advice of his national security advisor, Condoleezza Rice, much as recent presidents had on theirs. Complicating the situation was the fact that the president also sought foreign policy advice from his vice president, Dick Cheney, and from his secretary of defense, Donald Rumsfeld.[57] When Rice became secretary of state in Bush's second term, this situation reversed once again. Because the president trusted Rice on key foreign policy questions, she assumed a larger role, aided by the facts that her former deputy at the NSC, Stephen Hadley, moved up to her old post and that some of the staunchest neoconservatives left the government at the beginning or into the second term.

President Obama's secretary of state, Hillary Rodham Clinton, assumed a larger role than some of her predecessors, largely because the president relied on her knowledge and experience when Obama's first national security advisor, General James Jones, proved ineffective. Jones's successor was more closely tied to the president, but Secretary Clinton continued to have some impact in the policy process, especially due to her close ties with Robert Gates, who was secretary of defense during the first three years of the Obama administration.[58]

In sum, under many of the arrangements for the past six decades—where the secretary of state was primarily responsible for foreign policy, where the president relied on other advisors for policy making, or where the president tried to be his own secretary of state—the Department of State's role in the formulation of foreign affairs has been reduced in comparison with other executive institutions and individuals.

The President and the Department According to a former Foreign Service officer, Jack Perry, **"the Foreign Service does not enjoy the confidence of our presidents."** Too often, it is perceived as potentially "disloyal" to the president and instead loyal "either to the opposition party or else to the diplomat's own view of what foreign policy should be."[59]

The percentage of **ambassadorships** that go to **political friends**—mainly large campaign contributors with limited foreign policy experience—reflects this suspicion. These appointments reduce the opportunities available for career foreign service officers, whose aspirations may be to gain ambassadorships to cap their long careers.

Although some analyses focusing on only the first year or so of an administration found a somewhat higher percentage of ambassadorial appointments going to political friends as opposed to career diplomats,[60] in fact the entire record of ambassadorial appointments from the Kennedy administration through the first three plus years (May 25, 2012) of the Barack Obama administration revealed that roughly one-third or fewer were political friends and campaign contributors. The numbers ranged from 24 percent for Carter to 32 percent for Kennedy and Reagan, to 34 percent for Obama, at present.[61]

Overall, then, these percentages have remained relatively stable over the past ten administrations, but what they fail to reveal is that some key and prestigious ambassadorships in several administrations have gone not to skilled foreign policy officials but to large campaign contributors and political allies. President Clinton, for example, appointed Pamela Harriman, who had contributed $132,000 to Democratic candidates, as ambassador to France; he also appointed a successful hotel operator in California, M. Larry Lawrence, who had donated $196,000 to the Democratic Party, as ambassador to Switzerland. Other large contributors received ambassadorial appointments to the Netherlands, Austria, and Barbados.

For the George W. Bush administration, this trend continued. By one assessment, Bush's patronage appointments exceeded those of President Clinton and President George H. W. Bush, with 36 percent being "noncareer" or "political."[62] By the end of his term, , the administration's political appointments totaled less, at 30 percent.[63] Still, ambassadorships to such prominent posts as Britain, Ireland, Canada, France, Denmark, the Vatican, and Switzerland went to prominent political donors and key political friends.[64]

Obama has not altered this pattern in making his ambassadorial appointments. Numerous "bundlers" for candidate Obama—those individuals who raised and collected large sums of campaign contributions—received government jobs, including some key ambassador position. By one assessment, President Obama nominated twenty-four bundlers to ambassadorships by mid-2011. Fourteen of these individuals had raised at least $500,000 for the campaign, and six others, $200,000 or more. Moreover, two prominent contributors received plum ambassadorial appointments. Donald H. Gips, an executive for Level 3 Communications, a telecom company, was appointed ambassador to South Africa, and David Jacobson, a Chicago lawyer, was named ambassador to Canada.[65]

Aside from the influence of money in politics, critics see **serious problems** with such appointments **from a policy point of view**. They reduce the role of the Department of State in the foreign policy process, and the appointees' inexperience may be damaging to its conduct. Furthermore, these ambassadors may feel much freer to circumvent the State Department in shaping policy and use "back channels" to the White House. In doing so, they alienate the career personnel within an embassy and further weaken an orderly foreign policy process. One senator described such appointments starkly: they are "ticking time bombs moving all over the world."[66]

A former U.S. ambassador to a small Asia-Pacific nation, and a political appointee of the Clinton administration, however, defends such political appointments. He argues that they have better access to the president than nonpolitical appointees, and the president may be more willing to listen to a personal appointee than to a career diplomat. The Australian ambassador to the United States, commenting on the American political appointments sent to his country as ambassador, made the same point in a different way: "What you want is a quality person who is taken seriously in his own capital."[67] In this view, these kinds of appointments may actually enhance American diplomacy by better serving both the United States and the host country.

The use of political appointees within the Department of State and the weighing of political loyalties in appointing Foreign Service officers as ambassadors exemplify the suspicion between State and the president. One tactic, for instance, has been to engage in a "purge" of bureaus and personnel perceived as not fully committed to the administration. The Bureau of Inter-American Affairs suffered this fate early in the Reagan administration because it was not fully in tune with White House priorities. The assistant secretary of state in charge was replaced with a career diplomat perceived as more loyal to the administration's goal, albeit lacking in Latin American experience. When the diplomat began to waver on policy, he was ultimately replaced by a political appointee who was a staunch conservative and wholly committed to aid for the Nicaraguan Contras.[68]

The George H. W. Bush administration employed a number of political appointees, particularly at the top of the State Department. Four key political operatives came from outside the department, and one of them was responsible for screening all papers that reached Secretary of State Baker. By one account, the department's attitude "evolved from deep hostility to ambivalence" toward Baker and these appointees. The career foreign service personnel "felt altogether shut out for a time. . . ."[69]

Sometimes, the policy direction of an administration can cause grumbling within State Department ranks, and some political appointments can cause problems elsewhere, notably in Congress. In early 1994, five State Department officials resigned from the Clinton administration and others protested to the secretary over Bosnia.[70] Some were surely unhappy with the administration's failure to heed the views of foreign policy analysts within the department over its policy changes, but morale in this instance still remained "level," according to one close observer.[71] For the George W. Bush administration, the appointment of staunch conservatives to two important State Department posts—John Bolton as undersecretary for arms control and international security and Otto Reich as assistant secretary for Inter-American affairs—caused delays and drew criticism from the Senate. Recently, the Obama administration's appointment of Harold Koh as State Department legal adviser created some opposition outside the department. One critic complained, for instance, that "he cares as much about—if not more about—international law and integrating that into the American judicial system than he does about protecting American prerogatives and American sovereignty."[72]

Overall, then, the role of career officials at the Department of State continues to erode as the number of political appointees, both as ambassadors and as key departmental leaders, continues. In a slightly different context, one former Foreign Service officer perhaps said it best almost two decades ago: "Creeping politicization has corrupted foreign service professionalism." In turn, he added, politicization "**has hindered American diplomacy**."[73]

The Public's View   The Department of State has never really enjoyed a sound reputation among the American public. Beyond the view that it is out of step with the nation as a whole, members of Congress and the executive branch have called for it to become more efficient and effective. State's negative public image has perhaps waned over the decades, but, along with the other restraints evident within the department, it has produced a certain caution in the department's policy choices.

THE NATIONAL SECURITY COUNCIL

The National Security Council (NSC) has enlarged its role in the foreign policy process over the last four decades. It has grown from a relatively small agency with only a policy-coordinating function to a separate bureaucracy with major policy-making responsibilities. Its head, now designated as the **assistant to the president for national security affairs (or the national security advisor)**, is viewed as a major foreign policy formulator whose influence often surpasses that of the secretaries of state and defense.

Because of this evolution, an important distinction ought to be kept in mind as we discuss two different, but related, bureaucratic arrangements operating under the "National Security Council" label. One arrangement is the "**NSC system**," which focuses on the departmental memberships on the NSC itself and the subsequent interagency working groups established by presidents to coordinate policy making across the existing bureaucracies. That coordination process remains intact and is the focus of the last portion of Chapter 10. The other arrangement, and the one that has lately been commonly discussed, is the "**NSC staff**" (or simply "the NSC"), a separate bureaucracy that has developed over the years and has increasingly played an independent role in U.S. foreign policy making.[74] The following discussion focuses on the growth of that bureaucracy and its policy-making role and leaves the discussion of the NSC system to the next chapter.

The Development of the NSC Bureaucracy

As originally constituted under the **National Security Act of 1947**, the NSC was a mechanism for coordinating policy options among the various foreign affairs bureaucracies. By statute, members were limited to the president, the vice president, the secretary of state, and secretary of defense, with the director of central intelligence (now the director of national intelligence) and the chairman of the Joint Chiefs of Staff as advisors.[75] These members, along with others that the president might choose to invite, met to consider policy options at the president's discretion.[76] Over time, the NSC system has evolved with a set of interdepartmental committees to support the NSC itself.

Table 9.1 portrays the composition of the NSC under the Obama administration. The members include those required by statute (President, Vice President, Secretary

Table 9.1 Composition of the National Security Council

Regular Attendees (Statutory and Nonstatutory)

President, Attorney	General U.S. Ambassador to the United Nations
Vice President, U.S.	Ambassador to the United Nations
Secretary of State	Assistant to the President and Chief of Staff
Secretary of Energy	Assistant to the President for National Security Affairs
Secretary of Defense	Assistant to the President and Dep. National Security Advisor
Secretary of the Treasury	
Secretary of Homeland Security	
Director of National Intelligence (attends as advisor)	
Chairman of the Joint Chiefs of Staff (attends as advisor)	

Other Attendees

When international economic issues are on the agenda, the Secretary of Commerce, the United States Trade Representative, the Assistant to the President for Economic Policy, and the Chair of the Council of Economic Advisers will attend.

When homeland security or counterterrorism issues are on the agenda, the Assistant to the President for Homeland Security and Counterterrorism will attend.

When science and technology issues are on the agenda, the Director of the Office of Science and Technology Policy will attend.

Sources: Presidential Policy Directive 1, The White House, Washington DC, February 13, 2009, at http://www.fas.org/irp/offdocs/ppd/ppd-1.pdf; and Alan G. Whittaker, Shannon A. Brown, Frederick C. Smith, and Ambassador Elizabeth McKune, *The National Security Policy Process: The National Security Council and Interagency System*, Research Report, August 15, 2011, Annual Update (Washington, D.C.: Industrial College of the Armed Forces, National Defense University, U.S. Department of Defense, 2011), pp. 12–14.

of State, Secretary of Defense, and Secretary of Energy) as well as a relatively large number of other cabinet members or key assistants to the president, including Secretary of the Treasury, Secretary of Homeland Security, Attorney General, and various key advisors to the president. As the table shows, other officials are invited for addressing international economic issues, counterterrorism issues, and science and technology issues. What is important about this composition is its inclusion of presidential economic advisors, begun by the Clinton administration, and of other officials (such as the attorney general, the president's chief of staff) who might not normally deal with foreign policy.[77] Furthermore, the NSC's size has continued to increase, largely in connection with the impact of globalization on the political process.

Under the original legislative mandate for the NSC, the assumption was that the staff of the NSC was to be small and its responsibilities focused largely on facilitating the coordination of activities among the various foreign affairs departments. Indeed, the NSC staff originally had only three major components: "(a) the Office of the Executive Secretary; (b) a Secretariat . . . and (c) a unit simply called 'the staff.'" The executive secretary and the secretariat were the permanent employees and generally coordinated the activities of the council. The staff "initially consisted wholly of officials detailed on a full-time basis by the departments and agencies represented on the Council" and was assisted by full-time support personnel.[78] Their responsibility was to prepare studies on various regional and functional questions, but they continued to maintain and coordinate their work with the respective departments from which they were drawn. Coordination across departments appeared to be more important than any independent assessment that they might undertake.

Presidents Truman and Eisenhower used the NSC as a coordinating body. Because Truman had relatively strong secretaries of state, and because he went to them for policy advice, he used NSC meetings primarily as an arena for exchanging ideas (often not attending the meetings himself until the outbreak of the Korean War). Eisenhower, by contrast, met with the NSC on an almost weekly basis and relied on it for decision-making discussions. Actual policy decisions, however, seemed to have been made outside this forum, especially as Eisenhower's secretary of state, John Foster Dulles, gained decision-making influence.[79] For neither of these presidents, though, was the NSC staff the independent policy influencer that it was to become.

Under Eisenhower, the structure and staff of the NSC bureaucracy began to gain greater definition. For instance, Eisenhower created the post of special assistant to the president for national security affairs for Robert Cutler and named him the "principal executive officer" of the NSC.[80] He also revamped and enlarged the staff structure and expanded the council's mandate and duties. Most notably, he designated the NSC as "a corporate body composed of individuals advising the President in their own right, rather than as representatives of their respective departments and agencies." In a later revision, however, he stated that "the views of their respective departments and agencies" ought to be stated as well.[81] Although Cutler and the NSC staff continued to perform their coordinating role, President Eisenhower's statements were the first hints of a more independent policy role for the NSC, and such a view would eventually become a reality in succeeding administrations.

The Rise of the National Security Advisor

During the Kennedy administration, the role of the NSC began to change, and a more prominent role for the national security advisor ("special assistant for national security affairs") emerged. Now there was more presidential reliance on key ad hoc advisors, including the national security advisor, but not on the NSC as such. In fact, few meetings of the council were held during the Kennedy years. Instead, the national security advisor became a source of policy making and was no longer just a policy coordinator. As a result of Kennedy's reorganization, the national security advisor gained a number of previous staff responsibilities. Thus, **McGeorge Bundy** became the **first national security advisor** to serve in a **policy-formulating and policy-coordinating capacity**.[82]

The role of national security advisor was enhanced even more during the administration of President Lyndon Johnson. Walt W. Rostow, successor to Bundy during much of Johnson's term, and a small group of advisors (the "Tuesday Lunch" group) played an increasingly large role, especially in formulating Vietnam policy.[83] As during the Kennedy years, the national security advisor gained influence, but the council, as a decision or discussion forum, actually declined in importance.

The full implication of this changed decision-making style became most apparent during the Nixon administration.[84] In particular, the appointment of **Henry A. Kissinger** as national security advisor further transformed the national security advisor's policy-making role. Henry Kissinger, an academic and a consultant to previous administrations, was familiar with, and critical of, the bureaucratic machinery of government. In large measure, he saw the bureaucracy as impeding effective policy making and hindering the job of the "statesman."[85] Through his considerable personal skill, Kissinger reorganized the decision-making apparatus of the foreign policy bureaucracies so that he was able to dominate it, and the NSC and staff thus became the focal point of all policy analyses.

Kissinger accomplished this transformation by creating a series of interdepartmental committees flowing from the NSC system. These committees included representatives from the principal foreign policy bureaucracies, but excluded them from ultimate authority for making policy recommendations. In fact, Kissinger set up a senior review group, which he himself chaired, for examining all policy recommendations before they were sent to the NSC and the president.[86] Even when he became secretary of state (as well as national security advisor) in September 1973, and when Gerald Ford became president in August 1974, this dominance of NSC staff continued.

The National Security Advisor: The Carter and Reagan Administrations

President Carter's initial impulse was to reduce the role of the national security advisor and his staff (partly in reaction to Kissinger's dominance in the previous eight years) and to place more responsibility in the hands of the secretary of state. More accurately, his goal was to balance the advice coming from the secretary of state with that coming from the national security advisor. Thus, the elaborate NSC committee system developed during the Kissinger years was initially pared back to only two committees.[87] Ultimately, however, Carter's national security advisor, **Zbigniew Brzezinski**, was able to play a more dominant role in the shaping of foreign policy and to work his will in the policy process because of the force of his personality, his strong foreign policy views, and the challenge of global events (such as the seizure of American diplomats in Iran in November 1979 and the Soviet invasion of Afghanistan in December 1979).[88]

Under the Reagan administration, a return to the earlier collegiality of policy making was once again attempted. Reagan's first secretary of state, Alexander Haig, came to office determined to restore the dominance of the Department of State (and especially the office of the secretary) and to make himself the "vicar" of foreign affairs. In part to facilitate this reversion, President Reagan appointed a relatively inexperienced foreign policy analyst, Richard Allen, as national security advisor. In this environment, it seemed possible that the secretary of state could reassert his dominance.

Ultimately, though, Haig was forced to resign when frictions developed among the White House staff and the secretaries of state and defense and when a new national security advisor, William Clark, who was closer to President Reagan, was appointed. Power seemed to be shifting more perceptibly back to the White House and the national security advisor. George Shultz, Haig's successor, appeared to have been given some latitude in policy making, but National Security Advisor **William Clark** soon eclipsed him. Indeed, by one assessment, in a very short time, Clark "became the most influential foreign policy figure in Reagan's entourage."[89] The shift was so perceptible that Shultz reportedly complained directly to the president that he could not do his job effectively when foreign policy decisions were made without his participation.[90]

Only under Clark's successor as NSC advisor, Robert McFarlane, and after the disclosure of the Iran–Contra affair did Shultz gain policy dominance. Because McFarlane was not personally close to President Reagan and because he felt constrained by the president's insistence on "cabinet-style" government, the pattern began to change. Still, crucial national security decision directives were issued by McFarlane's office, often without prior departmental clearance.[91]

The Iran–Contra affair that was revealed in November 1986 in one sense demonstrated the extent to which the NSC had dominated policy making (after all, the episode seemed to be directed entirely by individuals within the NSC), but it also showed the dangers of such dominance. Both investigations of this affair—the presidential inquiry, known as the Tower Commission, and two inquiries by congressional committees—cited the dangers of allowing NSC staff to carry out covert operations without presidential accountability, faulted the poor operation of the NSC system under the Reagan administration, and recommended reforms in the decision-making system itself.[92] After the firing of John Poindexter as national security advisor, his two successors—first, Frank Carlucci and then Colin Powell—were much more inclined to serve as coordinators than as formulators. As a result, Secretary of State George Shultz increasingly dominated the policy process.

The National Security Advisor: From George H. W. Bush to George W. Bush

At least by formal design, the senior Bush administration returned to a more familiar pattern of NSC dominance. President Bush placed national security advisor **Brent Scowcroft** and his deputy at the head of the policy-making machinery by appointing them as chairs of the two key coordinating committees of the NSC system: the NSC/Principals and NSC/Deputies committees (see Chapter 10 for details on these committees).[93] In this way, the NSC and its staff were in a strong position to dominate the departments of State and Defense. Further, the national security advisor, albeit in consultation with the secretaries of state and defense, was given responsibilities for establishing appropriate interagency groups to develop policy options as the need arose.

With James Baker as secretary of state and given his close personal ties to Bush, some raised doubts about Scowcroft's ability to control the process. However, his previous experience as national security advisor under President Ford and his background in bureaucratic politics allowed him to fare quite well. He did not seek the limelight, and he put together a staff that was generally applauded. He quickly undertook a broad review of American policy and became identified as the real "mover and shaker" in the foreign policy hierarchy.[94]

Clinton's first national security advisor, **Anthony Lake**, was cut from the same cloth as Scowcroft and was less like, say, Kissinger or Brzezinski in carrying out his assignment. Lake did not seek the limelight and rarely got it. By one assessment, he was "surely the only national security advisor ever to stand beside the President in a *New York Times* photograph and be described as an 'unidentified' man."[95] Instead, Lake's influence derived from his geographical closeness to the president (the proximity between his office and the Oval Office) and Clinton's limited experience and interest in foreign policy. Despite a self-effacing personal style, Lake, after the president and vice president, was perhaps "the most powerful influence on foreign affairs."[96]

Lake's successor was his former deputy, **Samuel (Sandy) Berger**, appointed in December 1996. Like Lake, Berger appeared to enjoy considerable policy influence, based on his knowledge of foreign affairs and his close ties with the president. He had previously worked for Lake in the Department of State during the Carter administration and had worked for four years as Lake's top aide on the NSC during Clinton's first term. In addition, he had a long-standing personal relationship with President Clinton, beginning with their involvement in the McGovern campaign for president in 1972. In time, Berger came to dominate the foreign policy process, eclipsing the influence of the secretary of state, Madeleine Albright.[97]

With the election of George W. Bush came the same question of whether the national security advisor would dominate the foreign policy–making process. The foreign policy credentials of the new secretary of state, **Colin Powell**, seemed to indicate that he would eclipse the national security advisor. After all, Powell had served in several previous administrations, starting with Nixon's, had been national security advisor for a time during the Reagan administration, and had been chairman of the Joint Chiefs of Staff during parts of the George H. W. Bush and Clinton administrations. Furthermore, **Condoleezza Rice**, Bush's first national security advisor, although personally close to Bush and with experience on the NSC staff of his father, indicated that she would not be a "policy initiator or implementer."[98]

Despite this initial intention to move back to a policy-coordinating role, Rice in fact came to play a major role in policy formulation and implementation. At the outset of the Bush administration, there developed some policy differences—over North Korea, China, and the role of the United States in the Middle East. In these initial struggles, the national security advisor appeared to prevail over the secretary of state. Part of the reason for this was that President Bush's "comfort level [was] highest with her," compared to other foreign policy advisors, according to one administration source.[99] The events of September 11 brought Secretary of State Powell and Secretary of Defense Rumsfeld back to center stage, pushing the national security advisor into the background. Powell and Rumsfeld largely directed the immediate American response toward the Taliban and al-Qaeda in Afghanistan. On other major foreign policy issues, however—notably national missile defense and Iraq—National Security Advisor Rice often took the lead for the administration and because more NSC meetings and discussions were now occurring, her role and influence increased.[100] Furthermore, when postwar reconstruction efforts appeared to falter in Iraq, Bush appointed Rice to head a new NSC group to coordinate policy more directly from the

White House. In this sense, it is "'madness' to think that the genie of NSC dominance [on foreign policy making] can or should be put back in the lamp."[101]

Rice's successor as national security adviser in Bush's second term was her deputy, **Stephen Hadley**. By his own admission, Hadley planned to move to the background in shaping foreign policy. He had been characterized as a "staff man," as someone who "articulates no sweeping personal vision of the world," and as someone who "has made a point of staying in the shadows." He largely saw himself as a "facilitator for the president and 'the principals' [on the NSC]."[102] In this self-defined role, he focused on longer-range policy and institutional planning regarding Iraq and Afghanistan and on more policy implementation. At the same time, he engaged in public diplomacy, both at home and abroad, although he was not always comfortable with the latter.[103] In short, he had influence but was not the designer of foreign policy in the way that some of his predecessors had been.

The National Security Advisor: The Barack Obama Administration

General James L. Jones was chosen as President Obama's first national security advisor. Jones had been critical of the Bush administration's NSC operation because the national security advisor "had little clout and failed to think strategically" about policy. Hence, Jones proposed an alternative approach to organizing and operating the NSC for the new administration. Moreover, his appointment was attractive to the new president because Jones's military background would help Obama's credibility with the Pentagon and the secretary of defense.[104]

Yet, General Jones did not prove to be effective in this role. As one analyst noted, with his military background, he was "accustomed to the prerogatives of rank and to formal, hierarchical decision structures" and that "issues should come to him in an orderly manner." Yet, President Obama operated more informally and with trusted aides. As a result, Jones was seemingly left out of the process or surprised by the policy-making process. As a result, by late 2010, Jones was replaced by Tom Donilon, the deputy national security advisor, who had had a wealth of previous experience within the NSC system. Further, "Donilon was much more adept than Jones as a staff aide, and much more in tune with the president's style and priorities."[105] Still, despite the influence of Secretary of State Hillary Clinton and Secretary of Defense Robert Gates (and subsequently, Leon Panetta), Donilon and the White House appear to continue to be the drivers of policy.

In sum, then, the modern-day **national security advisor** has now come to play at least **three roles**.[106] The most important is **a management role**. That is, the advisor is responsible for managing the policy-making process within the NSC and the NSC system, as originally intended by the National Security Act of 1947. This is a coordinating role, but it has also become one of policy shaping, especially for some recent national security advisors. The second is **an operational role**, which may assume several dimensions—making certain that the president's policy is implemented, interacting with other officials worldwide in similar roles, and occasionally executing policy (as some recent illustrations demonstrate). Finally, there is the more recent **public role** in which the national security adviser explains and defends administration policy. This has emerged because of the enlarging U.S. foreign policy agenda and because foreign policy has been increasingly politicized at home.

BUREAUCRACIES AND FOREIGN ECONOMIC POLICY MAKING

Our discussion has so far focused on two key bureaucracies that deal primarily with the political aspects of foreign policy making. In the next chapter, we focus on those that deal with military or quasi-military (covert) aspects. Here we discuss the **foreign economic policy-making bureaucracies**. Although those bureaucracies are often avoided or given cursory treatment in books on foreign policy, they are increasingly crucial to U.S. actions abroad.[107] After all, American exports (goods and services) "supported an estimated 9.7 million jobs in 2011" and exports constituted "13.8 percent of U.S. GDP in 2011—its highest share ever."[108]

As more policy questions involve issues of international economics and finance such as trade, debt policy, and investment, American foreign policy making more than ever involves foreign economic policy. Indeed, the Clinton administration recognized the importance of economic security by making economic policy makers members of the NSC and by creating the National Economic Council. The George W. Bush and Obama administrations have continued to emphasize this importance with economic representatives on the NSC.

Several bureaucracies that were often viewed as dealing only with domestic policy have over the last four decades actually assumed important foreign economic policy responsibilities. To illustrate both their breadth and growth, we will identify several of them, describe the principal ways in which they contribute to foreign policy making, and discuss some issues with which they have been recently associated. We will first discuss the newest of them, the Office of the U.S. Trade Representative, and then turn to the role of the Departments of State and Defense in economic issues. Finally, we will describe the responsibilities of the Departments of Treasury, Commerce, and Agriculture in foreign economic policy formulation. Some of these bureaucracies are more pivotal than others, and we will try to specify their relative importance.

Before we proceed, however, we ought to note several important characteristics of the foreign economic area, especially as it relates to trade policy.[109] First, only in the twentieth century (and usually dating from the passage of the **Reciprocal Trade Agreements Act of 1934**) has the executive branch assumed a lead role in this area, even though Congress still retains the constitutional prerogative to regulate foreign commerce. Second, the executive branch has increasingly been the focus for trade policy making, especially because Congress granted recent presidents **"fast-track" trading authority** (now labeled **"trade promotion authority"**) to expedite agreements on trade with other nations by negotiating trade pacts and limiting congressional action to an up-or-down vote, without amendments, of any trade agreement. Third, the formulation of trade policy is often diffuse within the executive branch. Some decisions are made wholly by a particular bureaucracy (for example, at the deputy assistant secretary level in the relevant departments), others are made at the interagency group level (through coordination among the bureaucracies), and still others are ultimately resolved by the president. Fourth, various bureaucracies are likely to deal with different aspects of international economic policy (such as import/export, international debt financing). Such dispersion reinforces the decentralization of foreign economic policy. The principal consequence of these various characteristics is that, perhaps more than for other foreign policy-making questions, the process is highly subject to the effects of bureaucratic politics.

Office of the U.S. Trade Representative

The most important foreign economic bureaucracy is the newest and the smallest: the Office of the U.S. Trade Representative (USTR). The USTR has been described as the *"primus inter pares"* (first among equals) within the executive branch and "is the titular head of 'overall' trade policy formulation, 'chief' trade negotiator for the U.S. government, and designated 'representative' of the United States in the major international trade organizations." [110] It has cabinet-level status and acts as "the president's principal trade advisor, negotiator, and spokesperson on trade issues."[111] The USTR—both the agency and the individual heading the office—also has wide-ranging responsibilities for coordinating the interagency process within the government, leading trade delegations abroad, and preparing policy questions for presidential decision making.

As a result, the USTR has been at the center of negotiations for the North American Free Trade Agreement (NAFTA), the creation of the World Trade Organization (WTO) from the General Agreements on Tariffs and Trade (GATT), negotiations with China for establishing permanent normal trading relations (PNTR), developing and promoting a series of free trade agreements, both bilaterally (for example, with South Korea and Colombia) and multilaterally (for example, the Asia Pacific Economic Cooperation [APEC] forum, the Middle East Free Trade Initiative), and resolving trade disputes with important trading partners (for example, the longstanding softwood lumber issue with Canada).

The Office of the USTR was created relatively recently, and its role in directing trade policy is even more recent. Congressionally mandated by the **Trade Expansion Act of 1962**, the USTR was formally established by an executive order in 1963.[112] Only in the 1970s and 1980s, however, were its powers and responsibilities enhanced. In the **Trade Act of 1974**, USTR gained cabinet-level status and assumed responsibility for coordinating policy on trade matters. By an executive reorganization plan in 1980, its responsibilities expanded even further when its head was designated "chief trade negotiator" and America's official representative to the major trade organizations. In addition, the USTR staff was doubled in size to about eighty. With the passage of the **Omnibus Trade and Competitiveness Act of 1988**, the powers of the USTR were reaffirmed, and the head of the office (the USTR per se) was given primary responsibility for retaliation against unfair trading partners (Section 301 of the act). Furthermore, the USTR staff continued to grow, once again almost doubling, to about 150 by the late 1990s; it is now at about 200.[113]

As Figure 9.2 shows, the USTR's organizational structure has become increasingly complex. The office has special negotiators on textile and agricultural issues, and it has two deputy USTRs, headquartered in Washington, responsible for trade with different regions and in different functional areas. A third deputy USTR has primary responsibility for monitoring WTO activities in Geneva. Finally, the office has designated staff to deal with Congress and intergovernmental affairs and to coordinate its activities with important parts of the private sector (such as labor and industry).

In the policy-making area, the USTR has primary responsibility for coordinating and chairing two important interagency committees on trade policy.[114] The first is the **Trade Policy Staff Committee (TPSC)**, which is widely represented throughout the government and encompasses more than ninety subcommittees to deal with myriad trade questions. The second is the **Trade Policy Review Group (TPRG)**, composed of the deputy USTR and undersecretary-level appointees from other

OFFICE OF THE U.S. TRADE REPRESENTATIVE

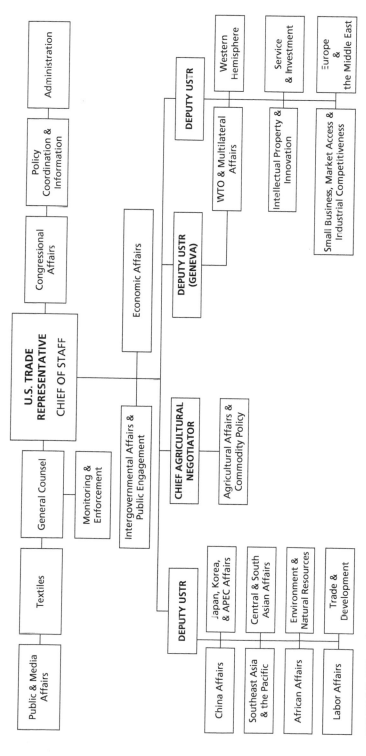

FIGURE 9.2 Office of the U.S. Trade Representative

Source: http://www.ustr.gov/sites/default/files/USTR%20rg%20org%20Chart%20Office%20only%20website%204%2013%2010%202010%20PDF.jpg, accessed June 4, 2012.

federal agencies and offices. The TPRG resolves questions that the Trade Policy Staff Committee cannot, and it addresses questions of particular policy importance. Importantly, the TPRG fits into the "NSC system" (see Chapter 10) as one of its interagency policy committees. The final component of this interagency system for trade policy making is the **National Economic Council (NEC)**,[115] established by the Clinton administration and continued by the George W. Bush and Obama administrations, to give more prominence to economic issues (both domestic and foreign) in the policy process. The NEC is headed by the president and has ultimate decision-making authority on trade policy questions theoretically beyond the USTR.

The Office of the USTR represents the convergence of trade policy making among the components just described in two important ways: it serves as a focal point for congressional involvement in policy formulation, and it serves as the formal contact point for a series of private-sector advisory groups on trade-related questions. Beginning with the Trade Act of 1974 and through expansion by subsequent legislation (for example, the Trade Acts of 1979 and 1988), five members of the House and the Senate serve as official advisors to the USTR. The private sector also has an elaborate system of USTR advisory groups to aid in shaping America's negotiating posture and general foreign trade policies. These include, among others, the Advisory Committee on Trade Policy and Negotiations, the Agricultural Policy Advisory, Industry Sector Advisory, Trade and Environment Policy Advisory, and Labor Advisory committees, all of which interact on a regular basis with the USTR. In short, the Office of the USTR, with these myriad ties and responsibilities, has become "at least nominally, the lead agency" for "U.S. trade and investment policies," and it "plays a major role in managing the interagency coordination below the cabinet level."[116]

However, political analysts Stephen Cohen, Robert Blecker, and Peter Whitney make clear that other "players" at the White House level considerably influence foreign economic policy making. Although the cabinet-level economic coordinating bodies, such as the NEC, are crucial in ultimately finalizing and ratifying policy, as noted, other White House offices, such as the economic officials on the NSC, the Council of Economic Advisors (CEA), and the Office of Management and Budget (OMB), play more secondary and advisory roles.[117]

As Cohen, Blecker, and Whitney also note, the USTR has important limits on its authority and control. Even though it may take the lead on most trade issues, it does not have the authority to handle all of them; other departments have some authority as well. It also does not have implementation authority for trade agreements: this is often the responsibility of the Departments of Commerce and Agriculture. Finally, it has to balance its mission of opening up markets worldwide with the demands of America's domestic producers. In this sense, USTR sometimes has to yield to the push and pull of other departments (like Commerce, Agriculture, or Treasury) with strong constituencies.[118]

Departments of State and Defense

Normally thought of as political-military departments, two other bureaucracies play important roles in foreign economic policy making. As our earlier discussion implied, because its goal is to coordinate security and economic policy toward the rest of the world and toward particular countries, the Department of State retains a crucial role.

Indeed, by one assessment, its influence was dominant up until World War II, but during the Cold War, as political and security concerns came to dominate its assessments, the department lost some of its clout in the economic arena. Beginning in the 1960s, State's economic role has "evolved into [that of] . . . an important participant in the making of international economic policy rather than one . . . of leadership." Although it has largely continued in that role to the present, it regained some clout with the "economics consciousness-raising" that occurred within the department in the late 1980s and 1990s. To be sure, State does watch global economic issues through its regional bureaus and its Under Secretariat for Economic Growth, Energy and Environment. It also takes the lead role in negotiating international aviation and maritime policies and participates in export control enforcement as well.[119]

Indeed, State may still be pivotal on policy if the circumstances are right. As one analyst put it, it "is sufficiently influential and ubiquitous in the decision-making process to be in a position to prevent interagency consensus on almost any international economic issue if a clear national security threat can be credibly demonstrated."[120] Immediately after September 11, for example, the circumstances may have been right for the Department of State to exercise such influence. At the same time, it must always contend with another major bureaucracy on these kinds of issues.

Although that other political-military bureaucracy, the Department of Defense, may play a less continuous and pivotal role in foreign economic policy, it can still importantly affect America's economic actions abroad, especially in advising on sensitive exports and the transfer of American technology.[121] Its role can be especially crucial when a sale of "dual-use" technology—technology with potential military and nonmilitary applications—to an unfriendly, or potentially unfriendly, country is being considered. During the Cold War years, the monitoring of such exports by Defense (and Commerce) was often pivotal. The United States developed an extensive list of restricted or prohibited trade items, and it cooperated with other Western nations through the **Coordinating Committee for Multilateral Export Controls (COCOM)** to stop the transfer of sensitive technologies to Communist states. In both arenas, Defense played a key role in assessing the impact of any transfers on national security.[122]

As the Cold War waned and finally ended in the early 1990s, both the unilateral and multilateral export control lists were sharply revised, and thus the DOD's role in the export process lessened. In the mid- to late 1980s, for example, it was unsuccessful in stopping exports to Iraq, despite objections that the dual-use technology being considered had "the high likelihood of military end use."[123] In 1992, the department was invited to assess the implications of selling new technology (for example, a new supercomputer) to China and to weigh in on whether the licensing of these sales should go forward. It opposed the sales, but because State and Commerce were on the other side for business and political reasons, its view was not persuasive.[124]

Several factors explain this lack of clout on such policy questions. First, Defense's role is more consultative than statutory. Second, unlike the Department of Commerce, Defense lacks a public constituency that might aid it in the inevitable bureaucratic clashes over technology transfers, especially in an era of trade liberalization. Third, and with particular reference to export policy, Commerce retains the final authority on issuing export licenses.[125] Finally, because the COCOM standards have been replaced by the Wassenaar Arrangement (a multilateral mechanism for monitoring the sale of dual-use goods and conventional armaments), an interagency group develops the United States' position and the Department of Defense, although it participates, does not dominate the process.[126] Much as with the Department of State, one important caveat needs to be noted about this assessment. Since the terrorist attacks of September 11, 2001, and with the increasing risk of nuclear proliferation (such as Iran), the political-security bureaucracies are more likely to be heeded than before. In this sense, Defense's assessment in interagency debate on technology and arms transfer is likely to carry more weight now than it did immediately after the end of the Cold War.

Department of the Treasury

The Department of Treasury today enjoys increased policy-making clout, especially in international financial matters. Unlike the Department of State, which has had an historical role in foreign economic matters, Treasury's rise in influence has been more recent, primarily dating from the end of World War II. Indeed, the department has been described as the "enfant terrible" in the making of international economic policy and as the bureau that now often dominates in international finance.

The growth of the Department of Treasury's policy influence has been attributed to a variety of factors:

- The relative decline of U.S. economic power globally
- The increased recognition that external economic policies affect the domestic economy
- The acknowledgment that international financial shocks need American attention
- Congressional legislation that grants the Treasury greater global economic policy responsibility
- The enhanced role of the secretary of the treasury in economic policy making

Furthermore, "the Treasury Department has undisputed jurisdiction over U.S. international monetary policy . . . and international financial policy." In addition, it is responsible for aid to former communist countries transitioning to market economies and for aid to emerging countries with currency problems. In all, only the Department of State is as interested in foreign economic policy.[127]

Although Treasury has an elaborate bureaucratic structure made up of various divisions that are potentially influential in foreign economic policy, the centers of its activity are **the Office of International Affairs and the Office of Terrorism and Financial Intelligence (TFI).** The Office of International Affairs, headed by the undersecretary for international affairs, monitors a number of foreign economic issues, including international monetary policy, coordination of policy with the G-7/8 and G-20 countries, and international financial institutions. It also addresses "transnational economic challenges, including development and climate change."[128] Deputy assistant secretaries monitor these activities, but deputy assistant secretaries also assess economic development in various regional groupings (the Middle East and Africa; Europe, Eurasia, and the Western Hemisphere; and Asia) and for the Strategic and Economic Dialogue with China.[129]

The Office of Terrorism and Financial Intelligence "develops and implements . . . strategies to combat terrorist financing domestically and internationally." It had its genesis in Executive Order 13224 issued by President George W. Bush in the aftermath of

September 11, 2001, and it has since incorporated the Office of Foreign Asset Control and the Financial Crimes Enforcement Network to carry out its objectives. Furthermore, its intelligence component (Office of Intelligence and Analysis) is part of the U.S. government's larger intelligence community (Chapter 10). The Office of Terrorism and Financial Intelligence thus plays a pivotal role not only in developing policy against terrorist financing but also in regulation and enforcement.[130] Although Treasury policy making on financial transfers by terrorist organizations has become an important focus of attention recently, the department has played a crucial role in shaping America's foreign economic policy overall, especially in responding to problems in the global economy. Several illustrations from recent decades will serve to demonstrate the department's important role in foreign economic policy.

In the 1980s, for example, Treasury was instrumental in three important initiatives to stabilize the global economy: the **Plaza Pact**, the **Baker Plan**, and the **Brady Plan**. The Plaza Pact sought to reduce the value of the dollar against other leading currencies as a means of helping the United States and world economies. It took its name from the Plaza Hotel in New York, where representatives of the United States, Japan, West Germany, France, and Great Britain met and agreed that "further orderly appreciation of the main non-dollar currencies against the dollar is desirable" and that their governments would encourage this outcome.[131]

The Baker Plan, a proposal offered by Secretary of the Treasury James Baker to the 1985 annual meeting of the World Bank and the IMF, addressed the burgeoning international debt crisis. It called for commercial banks to assist fifteen particularly indebted nations (among them Mexico, Argentina, Brazil, Nigeria, Morocco, and the Philippines) by pledging $20 billion in new loans through 1988, and for international lending institutions (such as the World Bank and the Inter-American Development Bank) to provide $9 billion more. In exchange, the debtor nations would follow "anti-inflationary fiscal and monetary policies"[132] and "strengthen their private sectors, mobilize more domestic savings, facilitate investment, liberalize trade, and pursue market-oriented approaches to currencies, interest rates, and prices."[133]

The Brady Plan, named after President George H. W. Bush's secretary of the treasury, was a debt reduction proposal,[134] under which the commercial banks in rich countries would be encouraged to write off a portion of debt owed by countries in the Third World. A variety of schemes were used. In one, international financial institutions funded poor countries' efforts to buy back a portion of their debt in exchange for some debt reduction; in another, employing "debt–equity swaps," banks received some property or asset within a country or accepted repayment of debt in local currency (probably at reduced value).

In the 1990s, Treasury was deeply involved in two major international financial crises: **the Mexican bailout of 1995 and the Asian flu, or contagion, of 1997–1998.** In December 1994, the value of the Mexican peso declined dramatically, from about 3.5 to the dollar to more than 5.5 by the end of the month. It dropped to almost 6.5 pesos to the dollar by early February 1995. The reason for this sharp drop was the weakening Mexican economy. Over the previous several years, the government, banks, and businesses had borrowed heavily to fuel Mexico's rapid economic expansion. When investor confidence eroded, the government was forced to use its revenue to protect the value of the peso in the face of increasing pressure to devalue it. By the end of 1994, that effort had largely failed, and the peso plummeted.[135]

This sharp decline in the peso's value foreshadowed a dramatic decline in Mexico's standard of living, but it also had important implications for the United States. First, a weak Mexican economy would have direct and immediate consequences for the health of the American economy.[136] Because a significant portion of Mexican debt was held by American banks, mutual funds, and insurance companies, U.S. pension plans with Mexican investments and American workers producing goods for export would both be hurt. Second, the consequences would be profound for the success of the recently implemented NAFTA. Third, reforms to make Mexico's economy more open and its political system more democratic would now be in jeopardy. Fourth, illegal immigration to the North would increase, creating social and political dislocations in the United States. Finally, the collapse of the Mexican economy would likely reverberate throughout the international economy.[137]

The Clinton administration moved quickly to devise an assistance plan for Mexico, with the Department of Treasury taking the lead in the plan's development and promotion.[138] An initial proposal called for $40 billion in new loan guarantees by the United States and about $13 billion in loans from the IMF.[139] However, this required congressional action, and opposition quickly developed in the House and Senate. As a result, President Clinton adopted an alternative strategy emanating from the Department of Treasury under which the United States provided $20 billion to forestall a default by Mexico, the IMF provided $17.5 billion in assistance, the Bank for International Settlements provided $10 billion, and Canada and Latin American countries agreed to contribute $2 billion more.[140]

In the summer of 1997, the currencies and the economies in a number of Southeast Asian countries began to collapse.[141] The collapse of the Thai baht is usually marked as the beginning point of this process, but the loss of confidence quickly spread to Indonesia, South Korea, and the Philippines, among others. With the resulting halt of large construction projects, investment faltered, banks began to fail because businesses could not pay their loans, and international investors withdrew their capital (or reduced further investment). The loss of these markets and investment opportunities had a ripple effect on the entire global economy. As a result, it was imperative for the United States to stabilize the situation.

Although the Clinton administration did not initially respond sympathetically to the Thai situation,[142] it eventually proposed a bailout plan through the IMF. After much partisan bickering and political maneuvering, Congress passed the IMF replenishment in the fall of 1998, although it required Treasury to provide various certifications to Congress over the IMF and the use of the funds.

Two more recent financial crises, the Great Recession of 2008–2009 and the Euro crisis from 2010, also demonstrate the central role of the Department of Treasury in shaping U.S. foreign economic and domestic policy. With the financial crisis that struck the United States and the world economy in September and October 2008, Henry Paulson, Bush's Treasury Secretary, was at the center of the effort to fashion a rescue or bailout package at home and cooperative efforts with the industrial democracies abroad. Indeed, Paulson proposed the Troubled Asset Recovery Program (TARP), a plan for a $700 billion bailout of failing banks as a result of collapsing mortgage-backed securities in the housing market, and Congress approved it with considerable discretion for the secretary in implementing it.[143]

President Obama's new Treasury Secretary, Timothy Geithner, continued this program, but the administration took an additional stop. The Obama administration and Treasury Secretary Geithner proposed the American Recovery and Reinvestment Act

(ARRA), a $797 billion stimulus package. This package, unlike TARP, was directed toward American consumers and not toward the banking sectors.[144] Although both of these programs were domestic economic programs, such actions impacted the global economy due to America's central role worldwide.

Similarly, as the Euro crisis—the excess debt among countries in Europe utilizing the euro as their currency, particularly in Greece, Italy, Portugal, Spain, and Ireland—emerged in 2010, the Department of the Treasury was fully engaged. The Obama administration and the Department of the Treasury encouraged European leaders to take decisive actions to address the issue. Because the European Union and the United States are closely linked economically—20 percent of U.S. exports go to Europe and more than 50 percent of American overseas assets are there—the impact of a spreading crisis would harm the already weak U.S. economy. As Treasury Secretary Geithner told a congressional committee, "We want Europe to move and we want to make sure they move more aggressively."[145] Indeed, the United States took some actions as well. Geithner consulted with European leaders on possible actions to pursue, his department worked with the IMF to support efforts by that organization to assist the European Union, and the United States, as a whole, accepted a weaker euro. In all, then, the Treasury Department and its secretary played crucial roles in formulating America's response to this continuing crisis—and continue to do so.

Department of Commerce

The fifth key department in the foreign economic policy area is the Department of Commerce. Like the Office of the USTR, Commerce benefited from the 1980 executive reorganization act by gaining a wider mandate in formulating and implementing U.S. trade policy. It now has the principal responsibility for **administering all U.S. import/export programs**.[146] Two major divisions within the department are directly involved in these tasks—**the Bureau of International Trade Administration** and the **Bureau of Industry and Security**, each headed by an undersecretary of commerce.[147]

The International Trade Administration (ITA) oversees all U.S. trade policy (except agricultural products) and assists the U.S. Trade Representative in all trade negotiations. These range from formulating and implementing foreign economic policy to shaping all import policies to promoting and developing U.S. markets. Although the USTR takes the lead role, ITA provides valuable assistance. Importantly, though, it also has the responsibility for operating the **U.S. and Foreign Commercial Service** (US & FCS), the primary agency representing American businesses seeking to export nonagricultural products. Through 109 export assistance centers within the United States and 128 commercial offices in more than 75 countries, US & FCS conducts a variety of activities to showcase American products and works with other government agencies and foreign organizations to aid American business.[148] In particular, it provides information on new markets, counsels and arranges contact between American companies and local businesses, and holds trade shows and "trade events" to demonstrate the range of American products, especially those from small and medium-sized companies.[149]

Another important function of the ITA is on the import side of the trade equation: **the enforcement of antidumping and countervailing trade statutes** to protect American businesses from unfair foreign trade practices (prior to 1980, these responsibilities rested with the Department of the Treasury). Antidumping statutues require monitoring imports from other countries to make certain that they are not being sold below "fair market value"; countervailing statutes require determining if production costs have been subsidized in a foreign country, hence making imported goods less costly on the American market.[150] In either instance, if such a determination is made, the department can recommend retaliation, and import duties may be added to the products in question.[151]

With the ever-increasing U.S. trade deficits over the past three decades and with the rising tide of protectionism in various markets, import monitoring and recommendations for appropriate responses have become crucial in U.S. foreign economic policy. Furthermore, with the completion of several multilateral and bilateral trade agreements to lower tariffs and eliminate nontariff barriers—such as NAFTA and the WTO and more recently free trade agreements with South Korea, Colombia, and Panama—these monitoring activities have taken on even more significance.

The principal foreign policy bureau in the Department of Commerce is the Bureau of Industry and Security, whose responsibilities largely focus on **the export side of foreign trade**. Industry and Security seeks to advance American national security and foreign policy "by ensuring an effective export control and treaty compliance system, and by promoting continued U.S. strategic technologies." It meets these goals through export control policies for four major multilateral agreements to which the United States is a signatory: the Australia Group agreement (chemical and biological items), the Missile Technology Control Regime (weapons technology), the Nuclear Suppliers Group (nuclear fuel transfers), and the Wassenaar Arrangement (conventional arms and dual-use goods and technologies). In addition, it monitors compliance with three nonproliferation agreements on weapons of mass destruction—the Chemical Weapons Convention, the Additional Protocol to the U.S.-International Atomic Energy Agency Safeguards Agreement, and the Biological Weapons Convention.

In all, the Bureau of Industry and Security has the responsibility to issue export licenses for some dual-use technologies, even as it monitors, controls, and prohibits others that could ultimately be used to harm the United States and its citizens. It also investigates cases of compliance and noncompliance by individuals and firms, maintains lists of individuals who were "engaging in activities contrary to U.S. national security or foreign policy interests," and enforces antiboycotting provisions of U.S. law. Finally, and importantly, the Bureau of Industry and Security engages in a variety of activities to improve America's technological base as a way to maintain its defense capacity.[152]

The Department of Commerce has gained some bureaucratic influence not only through its import and export enforcement powers but also through its efforts to open foreign markets to American products. In these areas, particularly during the Clinton administration, the department arguably had a greater impact on U.S. foreign policy than at any time since it shaped trade policy with the Soviet Union during the Nixon administration.[153] Commerce was able to obtain this influence by organizing numerous promotional trips for American corporate executives to potential U.S. markets, ranging from South Africa and Northern Ireland to China and the Middle East.[154] Furthermore, it was able to tie these efforts to domestic policy as a means of promoting greater prosperity at home, and to foreign policy as a means of promoting peace and democracy through economic development. During the Obama administration, the Commerce Department's trade promotion role continued, especially with its involvement with the National Export Initiative (an initiative to double American exports by 2015 and to support two million American jobs) and its involvement on the Export Promotion Cabinet, established by this initiative.[155]

In sum Commerce remains an important policy advocate for free trade, although sometimes selectively so, depending on the industry or service involved. For example, it might tilt a bit more in the protectionist direction with the American apparel industry because that industry is less competitive internationally. With the American information technology industry, however, it would foster freer trade because that industry is highly competitive worldwide.[156] In all, Commerce has emerged as a player in foreign economic policy, although its policy-making influence probably does not rival that of USTR or Treasury.

Department of Agriculture

The United States Department of Agriculture (USDA) enters into the foreign policy arena through its involvement with agricultural trade and aid. Under several pieces of legislation, the USDA monitors agricultural imports (and suggests quotas if necessary) and promotes U.S. agricultural exports. Under **Public Law 480 (P.L. 480)**, now called the Food for Peace Act (FPA), it has primary responsibility for providing food aid to needy countries.[157]

The **Foreign Agricultural Service (FAS)** formulates and implements agricultural trade and aid policy as part of the Farm and Foreign Agricultural Services division of the USDA. As the primary promoter of U.S. agricultural sales abroad, FAS operates in several ways. First and foremost, it relies on "agricultural counselors, attaches, trade officers, and locally employed staff" that are posted in "over 90 countries to support U.S. agricultural interests and cover 140 countries."[158] These experts have a wide array of duties, which include observing the agricultural policies of host countries, monitoring agricultural imports at home and making recommendations for quotas when necessary, analyzing worldwide agricultural trading patterns and trading prospects, and promoting American agricultural exports.

About two decades ago, the FAS opened **Agricultural Trade Offices (ATOs)** abroad as a second mechanism to promote American agricultural exports. In mid-2012, for example, there were six offices in China, three in Russia, two in Mexico, and one in Japan, as well as offices in Miami, Florida; Riyadh, Saudi Arabia; São Paulo, Brazil; Seoul, South Korea; and Taipei, Taiwan. These ATOs enable the FAS to sponsor trade exhibitions and to showcase the variety and quality of American agricultural products.[159]

FAS operates in conjunction with the **Commodity Credit Corporation (CCC)** of the USDA and export promotion programs, such as the Dairy Export Incentive Program (DEIP). These programs are additional efforts to build markets abroad. DEIP, for instance, provides exporters of American dairy products with cash supplements to make them competitive in the global marketplace when the cost of production exceeds the current price of the product. To be consistent with the requirements of the World Trade Organization, it limits its allocations, which have been used increasingly less frequently. Such subsidies sometimes lead to market clashes with other dairy exporters (such as Australia and New Zealand).[160]

On the aid side, FAS plays a central role in managing the P.L. 480 program, which provides loans and grants in the form of food assistance and offers various incentives to help developing countries expand their agricultural sectors. The U.S. food aid effort totaled $1.6 billion in FY2011, which represented a small overall percent of the total U.S. foreign assistance budget. Food aid is distributed through four measures: **P.L. 480; the Food for Progress Program; Section 416 (b); and the McGovern–Dole International Food for Education and Child Nutrition Program**. FAS is responsible for managing the food loans (Title I) of P.L. 480, whereas the Agency for International Development (AID) is responsible for food grants for emergency humanitarian and relief efforts (Title II) and for food aid that fosters food security and market reforms (Title III). Titles I and III have not been funded in recent years.[161]

The Department of Agriculture also provides food assistance through the Food for Progress (FFP) program, which aids countries that are expanding market principles in their agricultural sectors, and it operates the 416 [b] program, which donates surplus American commodities to needy countries. (This program is currently "not active.") Finally, the McGovern–Dole Program calls for the donation of American farm products and other assistance to schools and nutrition programs in "low-income, food-deficit countries that are committed to universal education."[162] Despite the mix of food aid programs, one analysis questioned both the efficiency and effectiveness of FAS aid efforts because of insufficient procurement of food, delivery issues, and inadequate oversight.[163]

The overall policy impact of the USDA (and the FAS) on international agricultural trade is mixed. On the one hand, the FAS has a "major input when agricultural trade matters are concerned" and its clout has increased "as U.S. agricultural trade has expanded."[164] When Clayton Yeutter served as secretary of agriculture during the George H. W. Bush administration, his presence boosted the USDA's clout because he had a sustained interest in trade policy (as a former U.S. Trade Representative) and was a strong believer in agricultural free trade.[165] President Clinton's appointments of Mike Espy and Dan Glickman as his secretaries of agriculture did not emphasize the international trade side of USDA as fully as Yeutter's appointment had. Yet both quickly became advocates of free trade policies as a way to strengthen American agriculture, with Espy strongly endorsing NAFTA, for example, and Glickman eventually endorsing the opening of international markets.[166]

Recent secretaries of agriculture have also taken an interest in promoting agricultural trade policy. Ann Veneman, George W. Bush's first agriculture secretary, previously served as deputy undersecretary of agriculture for international affairs and reportedly worked very well with the USTR at the time, Robert Zoellick, on matters related to developing and promoting foreign agricultural policy.[167] Veneman's successor, Mike Johanns, had an equally good working relationship with USTR Susan Schwab, was "intimately involved" in the Doha Round of world trade talks, and was very effective in developing a "rapport with developing countries."[168] Obama's secretary of agriculture, Thomas Vilsack, also had an interest in promoting agricultural trade (such as through the National Export Initiative), but he has seemingly made more of a mark in developing good rapport with domestic producers.

Yet, as most observers would note, the principal mechanism through which USDA influences overall trade policy is less the secretary and more the committee structures established by the Trade Act of 1974. Under the formula emerging from that legislation, USDA and the private sector participate in the agricultural advisory committees for trade and in the six agricultural technical advisory committees for trade, which make policy recommendations to the secretary and to the U.S. Trade

Representative. These mechanisms worked quite well in past negotiations and serve as a ready means of incorporating the public and private agricultural sectors in international trade negotiations. **The Trade Policy Staff Committee**, headed by the Office of the USTR, is an important way for USDA to contribute to the formulation of international agricultural policy. Indeed, as one official at USDA pointed out, the department (and FAS in particular) worked with the "Ag Section at USTR" to develop its overall policy.[169] In this sense, the department has an impact, but only within the usual pulling and hauling of the bureaucratic process.

CONCLUDING COMMENTS

As this chapter's review of the Department of State, the National Security Council, and several economic bureaucracies demonstrates, foreign policy making is much more complex than is often realized, and more actors are involved in it than we might immediately think. Although the Department of State is often identified as the center of U.S. foreign diplomacy, the NSC has increasingly assumed a larger role in the shaping of foreign policy. Similarly, political and military issues are often assumed to be pivotal in the foreign policy arena, but economic issues are claiming more and more attention. Hence, the role of the economic bureaucracies in foreign economic policy has been enlarged, with the Office of the U.S. Trade Representative and the Department of Treasury particularly prominent.

Although the bureaucracies discussed so far are important to policy making, others cannot be left out of this discussion. In the next chapter, therefore, we complete our survey of the foreign affairs bureaucracies by looking at the Department of Defense, several bureaucracies associated with the intelligence community, and the newly created Department of Homeland Security. We will also take a closer look at the structural and procedural arrangements of recent presidents in coordinating the policy-making process among these various bureaucracies within the executive branch.

Notes

1. Graham Allison, *Essence of Decision: Explaining the Cuban Missile Crisis* (Boston: Little, Brown and Co., 1971), p. 144. This idea is also at p. 158, where Allison quotes from Roger Hilsman's *To Move a Nation* (Garden City, NY: Doubleday Publishing, 1964), p. 6.

2. Ibid.; and Morton H. Halperin with the assistance of Priscilla Clapp and Arnold Kanter, *Bureaucratic Politics and Foreign Policy* (Washington, D.C.: The Brookings Institution, 1974).

3. Todd S. Purdom and Patrick E. Tyler, "Top Republicans Break with Bush on Iraq Strategy," *New York Times*, August 16, 2002, A1.

4. See Bob Woodward, *Obama's Wars* (New York: Simon & Schuster, 2010) for a detailed discussion of this internal debate over Afghanistan policy. On this same bureaucratic theme as here, see James M. McCormick, "Part III Introduction," in James M. McCormick, ed., *The Domestic Sources of American Foreign Policy: Insights and Evidence* 6th ed. (Lanham, MD: Rowman & Littlefield, Inc., 2012), pp. 322–323.

5. *Department of State Completes 200 Years* (Washington, D.C.: Bureau of Public Affairs, Department of State, 1982), p. 1.

6. Report of the Department of State Management Task Force, *State 2000: A New Model for Managing Foreign Affairs*, Department of State Publication 10029 (Washington, D.C.: Department of State, January 1993).

7. Much of the discussion on the organizational and structural details of the Department of State is drawn from Department of State, "Department Organization," http://www.state.gov/r/pa/ei/rls/dos/99484.htm, May 29, 2012. Earlier sources include "The United States Department of State: Structure and Organization," *Dispatch* 6 (May 1995), Supplement No. 3: 1–8; and Warren Christopher, "Department of State Reorganization," *Dispatch* 4 (February 8, 1993): 69–73.

8. Hillary Rodham Clinton, "Leading Through Civilian Power," *Foreign Affairs* 89 (November/December 2010): 13–14 for these data and the quoted passage.

9. "Secretary of State Hillary Rodham Clinton," at http://www.state.gov/secretary/, May 29, 2012.

10. "Deputy Secretary of State," at http://www.state.gov/s/d/, May 29, 2012.

11. "Deputy Secretary of State for Management and Resources," at http://www.state.gov/sdmr/index.htm, May 29, 2012.

12. "Executive Secretariat," at http://www.state.gov/s/es/index.htm, May 29, 2012.

13. Christopher, "Department of State Reorganization," p. 69. Former Secretary of State James Baker notes in his memoirs that the organization whereby the undersecretaries report to the secretary and the assistant secretaries to the undersecretaries was actually started during his time at the department during the George H.W. Bush administration. See James A. Baker III, with Thomas M. DeFrank, *The Politics of Diplomacy: Revolution, War and Peace, 1989–1992* (New York: G. P. Putnam's Sons, 1995), pp. 35–36.

14. "Under Secretary for Arms Control and International Security," at http://www.state.gov/t/, May 30, 2012.

15. "Assistant Secretaries and Those of Equivalent Rank," from the State Department Web site, http://www.state.gov/r/pa/ei/biog/c129.htm, August 16, 2002.

16. "This is USAID," at http://www.usaid.gov/about_usaid/, May 30, 2012.

17. The State Department and Budget data are from Table 1 in "Congressional Budget Justification, Foreign Assistance, Summary Tables, Fiscal Year 2013," at http://www.usaid.gov/performance/cbj/185016.pdf, May 30, 2012.

18. See a list of USAID accomplishments at "A Record of Accomplishment," http://www.usaid.gov/about/ accompli.html, May 30, 2012.

19. Bureau of Human Resources, Department of State, "HR Fact Sheet," March 31, 2012.

20. See "Organization of the Department of State Abroad," http://www.state.gov/r/pa/ei/rls/dos/436.htm, May 31, 2012. Also see "Diplomacy at Work: A U.S. Embassy," http://www.state.gov/r/pa/c61777.htm, July 21, 2002, and "A U.S. Embassy at Work," http://www.state.gov/r/pa/8710.htm, July 21, 2002.

21. Clinton, "Leading Through Civilian Power," p. 15. For a brief and interesting description of the working of an embassy and the responsibilities of political officers, see Robert Hopkins Miller, *Inside an Embassy: The Political Role of Diplomats Abroad* (Washington, D.C.: Congressional Quarterly, 1992).

22. *Overseas Presence: Staffing at U.S. Diplomatic Posts*, General Accounting Office Report (GAO/NSIAD-95-50FS, December 28, 1994): 33.

23. The data on the size and composition of the Department of State's personnel come from the Bureau of Human Resources, "HR Fact Sheet." The data on the number of civilian employees in the DOD comes from "About the Department of Defense (DOD)" at http://www.defense.gov/about/, May 31, 2012.

24. See Bureau of Public Affairs, Department of State, "The International Affairs Budget—A Sound Investment in Global Leadership: Questions and Answers," October 1, 1995, http://www.state.gov.

25. The intelligence community budget reportedly exceeds $80 billion and the defense budget currently tops $700 billion in FY2010. See Gordon Adams and Matthew Leatherman, "A Leaner and Meaner Defense" in James M. McCormick, ed., *The Domestic Sources of American Foreign Policy: Insights and Evidence* 6th ed. (Lanham, MD: Rowman & Littlefield, Inc., 2012), pp. 253–265.

26. Among some analyses that criticize the effectiveness of the Department of State are I. M. Destler, *Presidents, Bureaucrats, and Foreign Policy* (Princeton, NJ: Princeton University Press, 1974), pp. 154–190; John Franklin Campbell, "The Disorganization of State," in Martin B. Hickman, ed., *Problems of American Foreign Policy*, 2nd ed. (Beverly Hills, CA: Glencoe Press, 1975), pp. 151–170; Robert Pringle, "Creeping Irrelevance at Foggy Bottom," *Foreign Policy* 29 (Winter 1977–1978): 128–139; Andrew M. Scott, "The Department of State: Formal Organization and Informal Culture," *International Studies Quarterly* 13 (March 1969): 1–18; and Andrew M. Scott, "The Problem of the State Department," in Martin B. Hickman, ed., *Problems of American Foreign Policy*, pp. 143–151.

27. *State 2000: A New Model for Managing Foreign Affairs*, p. 4.

28. Table 1 in "Congressional Budget Justification, Foreign Assistance, Summary Tables, Fiscal Year 2013." The total reference to the "administration of foreign affairs" applies only to the Department of State. The total for the Department of State and USAID is about $51 billon for FY2012.

29. Elaine Sciolino, "Austerity at State Dept. and Fear of Diplomacy," *New York Times*, November 15, 1987, 1 and 8; and John M. Goshko, "State Dept. Budget Faces New Cuts," *Washington Post*, April 27, 1987, A6. The quoted passages are from the latter.

30. For a listing of 16 of 17 posts closed in 1993 and 1994, see *State Department: Overseas Staffing Process Not Linked to Policy Priorities*, General Accounting Office Report (GAO/NSIAD 94-228, September 20, 1994): 18–19; and for those that were scheduled for closing by the end of 1996, see U.S. State Department Daily Press Briefing, July 18, 1995. The total of 32 closures comes from Talbott, "Globalization and Diplomacy: The View from Foggy Bottom," p. 188, who was deputy secretary of state at the time.

31. See Steven Greenhouse, "Christopher to Cut Jobs at State Dept.," *New York Times*, May 7, 1995, 4; and "The International Affairs Budget—A Sound Investment in Global Leadership: Questions and Answers."

32. Personal communication with a State Department official, March 25, 2004.

33. Clinton, "Leading Through Civilian Power," p. 13.

34. Miles A. Pomper, "Powell Calls on Hill to Remedy State Department Underfunding," *CQ Weekly*, March 10, 2001, p. 548.

35. Condoleezza Rice, "Opening Remarks by Secretary of State-Designate Dr. Condoleezza Rice," Senate Foreign Relations Committee, January 18, 2005, http://www.state.gov/secretary/rm/2005/40991.htm, May 9, 2008.

36. Hillary Rodham Clinton, "Nomination Hearing to be Secretary of State," Statement before the Senate Foreign Relations Committee, Washington, D.C., January 13, 2009, at http://www.state.gov/secretary/rm/2009a/01/115196.htm.

37. Personal communication with the Bureau of Human Resources, Department of State for the latter salary estimate in May 2008. The earlier quoted passages are from "Recruiting: Frequently Asked Questions about the Foreign Service," a Department of State handout, fall 2011.

38. Baker, with DeFrank, *The Politics of Diplomacy*, p. 28.

39. On this point, see Henry T. Nash, *American Foreign Policy: Changing Perspectives on National Security* (Homewood, IL: The Dorsey Press, 1978), p. 139. Also see Nash's excellent discussion on the problems of State, from which our overall discussion draws.

40. Bureau of Human Resources, "HR Fact Sheet." This total of FSOs refers only to the "generalists." The department has another 5,710 specialist FSOs currently.

41. David Garnham, in particular, has looked at some of these Department of State stereotypes. Although he finds that the background characteristics of FSOs differ from those of the general population, he reports that they do not differ from other groups in American society on psychological flexibility. Overall, he judges that this elitism has not negatively affected the conduct of U.S. foreign policy. See his "State Department Rigidity: Testing a Psychological Hypothesis," *International Studies Quarterly* 18 (March 1974): 31–39; and "Foreign Service Elitism and U.S. Foreign Affairs," *Public Administration Review* 35 (January/February 1975): 44–51.

42. Duncan L. Clarke, "Why State Can't Lead," *Foreign Policy* 66 (Spring 1987): 135; and Baker with DeFrank, *The Politics of Diplomacy: Revolution, War, and Peace, 1989–1992*, p. 28.

43. Clarke, "Why State Can't Lead," p. 134. Also, see Baker, with DeFrank, *The Politics of Diplomacy: Revolution, War and Peace, 1989–1992*, p. 29.

44. Clarke, "Why State Can't Lead," pp. 133–134. "Foggy Bottom" refers to the area of Washington, DC, where the Department of State and several executive agencies are located. Indeed, it is so familiar to Washington residents that it has its own metro stop named "Foggy Bottom."

45. Baker with DeFrank, *The Politics of Diplomacy: Revolution, War and Peace, 1989–1992*, p. 29.

46. See Clinton, "Leading Through Civilian Power," pp. 13–24.

47. Scott, "The Problem of the State Department," p. 146. Emphasis in original.

48. Scott, "The Department of State: Formal Organization and Informal Culture," p. 6.

49. Clarke, "Why State Can't Lead," p. 136.

50. Baker, with DeFrank, *The Politics of Diplomacy*, p. 28.

51. Ibid., p. 31.

52. Nash, *American Foreign Policy: Changing Perspectives*, p. 139.

53. Hedrick Smith, *The Power Game: How Washington Works* (New York: Ballantine Books, 1988), pp. 558–562; and Theodore C. Sorensen, "The President and the Secretary of State," *Foreign Affairs* 66 (Winter 1987–1988): 231–248. But also see Leslie H. Gelb, "McFarlane Carving His Niche," *New York Times*, March 28, 1984, B10.

54. Nash, *American Foreign Policy: Changing Perspectives*, p. 100.

55. For a detailed assessment of the relationship between President Bush and Secretary of State James Baker, see Maureen Dowd and Thomas L. Friedman, "The Fabulous Bush and Baker Boys," *The New York Times Magazine*, May 6, 1990, 36. Other analyses available to assess the close ties between Bush and Baker and the enhanced role of the national security advisor during the Bush administration can be found in John Newhouse, "Profiles (James Baker)," *The New Yorker*, May 7, 1990, 50–82; and Bernard Weinraub, "Bush Backs Plan to Enhance Role of Security Staff," *New York Times*, February 2, 1989, 1 and 6. On Berger's emergence as preeminent over the secretary of state, see Jane Perlez, "With Berger in Catbird Seat, Albright's Star Dims," *New York Times*, December 14, 1999, A14.

56. Jane Perlez, "Washington Memo: Divergent Voices Heard in Bush Foreign Policy," *New York Times on the Web*, March 12, 2001, http://www.nytimes.com/201/03/12/world/12DIPL.html, March 18, 2001.

57. On the importance of Vice President Cheney in foreign policy making, see Karen DeYoung and Steven Mufson, "A Leaner and Less Visible NSC," *Washington Post*, February 10, 2001, p. A6, http://washingtonpost.com/wp-dyn/world/europe/A50937-2001Feb9.html, February 12, 2001.

58. For assessment of General Jones's role as national security adviser, see I. M. (Mac) Destler, "How National Security Advisers See Their Role," in James M. McCormick, ed., *The Domestic Sources of American Foreign Policy: Insights and Evidence* 6th ed. (Lanham, MD: Rowman & Littlefield, 2012), pp. 209–222, especially at p. 221, and Woodward, *Obama's Wars*. For an analysis that raises doubts about Clinton's impact on strategy, see Susan B. Glasser, "Head of State," 194 *Foreign Policy* (July/August 2012): 80.

59. Jack Perry, "The Foreign Service in Real Trouble, But It Can Be Saved," *Washington Post National Weekly Edition*, January 16, 1984, 21.

60. See, for example, John M. Goshko, in "Appointing Loyalists as Envoys," *Washington Post*, April 28, 1987, A16, reports that during the Reagan administration just under 40 percent of all ambassadorships went to political appointees; and Elaine Sciolino, in "Friends as Ambassadors: How Many Is Too Many?" *New York Times*, November 7, 1989, A1, A8, who reports higher figures for Kennedy through Bush when focusing only on the first few months of each administration.

61. See the American Foreign Service Association website, http://www.afsa.org/ambassadors-graph2.cfm, May 11, 2008, for career/noncareer ambassadorial appointments from the Kennedy through Clinton administrations. That site at that time showed that noncareer

ambassadorial appointments range from a low of 24 percent during the Carter administration to a high of 32 percent during the Kennedy and Reagan administrations. For the Bush and Obama administrations (through May 25, 2012, for the latter), the data are available at http://www.afsa.org/ambassadorlist.aspx, and http://www.afsa.org/ambassadorswbush.aspx, June 1, 2012. The noncareer ambassadorial appointments for Bush and Obama were 30 percent and 34 percent, respectively. This website would allow access to ambassadorial appointments for several administrations.

62. D. R. Denny, "Bush Patronage Appointments to Ambassador Exceed Father's, Clinton's," http://scholarsandrogues.wordpress.com/2007/06/25/bushs-patronage-appointments-to-ambassador-exceed-fathers-clintons/, September 7, 2008.

63. See the data for the Bush administration at American Foreign Service Association, at http://www.afsa.org/ambassadorswbush.aspx, June 1, 2012.

64. On the Clinton appointments, see Steven Greenhouse, "Clinton Is Faulted on Political Choices for Envoy Posts," New York Times, April 13, 1994, A16. On the Bush appointments, see Marc Lacey and Raymond Bonner, "A Mad Scramble by Donors for Plum Ambassadorships," New York Times, March 17, 2001, http://www.nytimes.com/2001/03/17/world/18AMBA.html, March 18, 2001, the Department of State website for chiefs of mission/country, http://www.state.gov/r/pa/ei/biog/c130.htm, July 21, 2002, and Denny, "Bush Patronage Appointments to Ambassador Exceed Father's, Clinton's," http://scholarsandrogues.wordpress.com/2007/06/25/bushs-patronage-appointments-to-ambassador-exceed-fathers-clintons/, September 7, 2008.

65. Fred Schulte, John Aloysius Farrell, and Jeremy Borden, "Obama Donors Net Government Jobs," Politico, June 15, 2011, at http://www.politico.com/news/stories/0611/56993.html, June 1, 2012.

66. Sciolino, "Friends as Ambassadors: How Many Is Too Many?" p. A8.

67. The first point is based on the author's conversation with the U.S. ambassador of a small Asia-Pacific nation, in July 1995; the Australian ambassador is quoted in Lacey and Bonner, "A Mad Scramble by Donors for Plum Ambassadorships."

68. See John M. Goshko, "Clout and Morale Decline," Washington Post, April 26, 1987, A12.

69. Newhouse, "Profiles (James Baker)," p. 76.

70. See the commentary by two former Balkan specialists in the State Department who resigned in 1993 to protest Clinton administration policy: Marshall Freeman Harris and Stephen W. Walker, "America's Sellout of the Bosnians," New York Times, August 23, 1995, A15.

71. Barry Schweid, "Warren's World," Foreign Policy 94 (Spring 1994): 143.

72. "Koh, No? Critics Decry Obama Nominee for State Department Legal Adviser," Fox News, March 31, 2009, at http://www.foxnews.com/politics/2009/03/31/koh-critics-decry-obama-nominee-state-department-legal-adviser/, May 31, 2012.

73. Perry, "The Foreign Service in Real Trouble, But It Can Be Saved," p. 21.

74. I am grateful to Smith, The Power Game, p. 589, for drawing this distinction between the two. "The NSC" is his term.

75. See Alan G. Whittaker, Shannon Brown, Frederick C. Smith, and Ambassador Elizabeth McKune, The National Security Policy Process: The National Security Council and Interagency System, Research Report, Annual Update (Washington, D.C.: Industrial College of the Armed Forces, National Defense University, Department of Defense, August 15, 2011), p. 10, on the role of the national intelligence director.

76. Membership on the NSC has varied slightly by statute over time, but these are the ones that have remained continuously.

77. See National Security Presidential Directive 1, February 13, 2001, for the list of NSC members during the George W. Bush administration, http://www.fas.org/irp/offdocs/nspd/nspd-1.htm, July 15, 2002.

78. James S. Lay, Jr., and Robert H. Johnson, "Organizational History of the National Security Council during the Truman and Eisenhower Administrations," Report prepared for the U.S. Senate, Committee on Government Operations, Subcommittee on National Policy Machinery, August 11, 1960, p. 8. It can be found at PrEx 3.2: Or 3/2 (Sudoc number).

79. I. M. Destler, "National Security Advice to U.S. Presidents: Some Lessons from Thirty Years," *World Politics* 24 (January 1977): 148–151, 153–159. Also see Nash, *American Foreign Policy: Changing Perspectives*, pp. 140, 172–174. On Truman's and Eisenhower's attendance of NSC meetings, see Lay and Johnson, "Organizational History of the National Security Council during the Truman and Eisenhower Administrations," pp. 5 and 24.

80. Lay and Johnson, "Organizational History of the National Security Council during the Truman and Eisenhower Administrations," p. 26. The characterization of Cutler as "the principal executive officer" is Lay and Johnson's.

81. Ibid., p. 30, and footnote 74.

82. For a discussion of how President Kennedy transformed the role of the national security advisor with Bundy, see I. M. Destler, "National Security Management: What Presidents Have Wrought," *Political Science Quarterly* 95 (Winter 1980–1981): 578–580; and Bromley K. Smith, "Organizational History of the National Security Council During the Kennedy and Johnson Administrations," monograph written for the National Security Council, February 1987.

83. Townsend Hoopes, *The Limits of Intervention* (New York: David McKay, 1968), for a discussion of the important influence of Rostow on LBJ, especially at pp. 20–22 and 59–62. For the identity, and critique, of the "Tuesday Lunch" group, see Irving Janis, *Victims of Groupthink* (Boston: Houghton Mifflin Company, 1972), pp. 101–135.

84. Destler, "National Security Management: What Presidents Have Wrought," p. 580.

85. Henry A. Kissinger, "Domestic Structure and Foreign Policy," in James N. Rosenau, ed., *International Politics and Foreign Policy*, rev. ed. (New York: Free Press, 1969), pp. 261–275, especially pp. 263–267.

86. See the diagram of the "Kissinger National Security Council System," in Nash, *American Foreign Policy: Changing Perspectives*, p. 197.

87. Elizabeth Drew, "A Reporter at Large: Brzezinski," *The New Yorker*, May 1, 1978, 94, reports that the initial National Security Council under Brzezinski consisted of only two committees: the Policy Review Committee and the Special Coordination Committee.

88. See the discussion of Brzezinski's role in Chapter 3. Also see Zbigniew Brzezinski, *Power and Principle: Memoirs of the National Security Advisor, 1977–1981* (New York: Farrar, Straus & Giroux, 1983).

89. Smith, *The Power Game: How Washington Works*, p. 593. The characterization of Clark's role in pushing the Strategic Defense Initiative is from pp. 594–599.

90. See "Shultz: No More Mr. Nice Guy?" *Newsweek*, August 22, 1983, 17; and "Shultz Peeved, Magazine Says," *Des Moines Register*, August 15, 1983, 8A. For Secretary of State Shultz's denial of the report, see "Aide Denies Shultz Losing His Influence," *Des Moines Register*, August 16, 1983, 1A and 2A.

91. Leslie H. Gelb, "McFarlane Carving His Niche," *New York Times*, March 28, 1984, B10.

92. *Report of the President's Special Review Board* (Tower Commission Report) (Washington, D.C.: Government Printing Office, February 26, 1987); and *Report of the Congressional Committees Investigating the Iran–Contra Affair* (Washington, D.C.: Government Printing Office, November 1987).

93. Weinraub, "Bush Backs Plan to Enhance Role of Security Staff," pp. 1, 6; and National Security Council statement, "National Security Council Organization," mimeo, April 17, 1989, 3.

94. John Barry, with Margaret Garrard Warner, "Mr. Inside, Mr. Outside," *Newsweek*, February 27, 1989, 28; and R. W. Apple, Jr., "A Mover and Shaker Behind Bush Foreign Policy," *New York Times*, February 6, 1989, 3.

95. Jason DeParle, "The Man Inside Bill Clinton's Foreign Policy," *The New York Times Magazine*, August 20, 1995, 34.

96. Ibid., p. 34.

97. "Clinton Chooses a Foreign Policy Team," *New York Times*, December 23, 1992, A13; and James Bennet, "A Trusted Adviser, and a Friend," *New York Times*, December 6, 1996, A16.

98. DeYoung and Mufson, "A Leaner and Less Visible NSC" p. A6.

99. "Condoleezza Rice; National Security Adviser," *Business Week*, February 11, 2002, p. 34, at http://proquest.umi.com/pqdweb?did=106110316&Fmt=3&clientId=60760&RQT=309&VName=PQD, September 8, 2008.

100. Ibid.

101. DeYoung and Mufson, "A Leaner and Less Visible NSC," p. A6.

102. These quotes and the assessment come from Peter Baker, "The Security Adviser Who Wants the Role, Not the Stage," *Washington Post*, January 29, 2006, p. A4.

103. Ibid.

104. Woodward, *Obama's Wars*, pp. 37–38. The quoted passage is Woodward's characterization.

105. The quoted passages are from I. M. (Mac) Destler, "How National Security Advisers See Their Role," in James M. McCormick, ed., *The Domestic Sources of American Foreign Policy: Insights and Evidence*, 6th ed. (Lanham, MD: Rowman & Littlefield, 2012), pp. 221. Also see Woodward, *Obama's Wars*, for accounts of Jones's surprise, unhappiness, and bewilderment at the policy process at, for example, pp. 124, 137–138, 196–200. For an assessment that the White House continues to dominate strategy, see Glasser, "Head of State," p. 80.

106. These roles for the national security advisor, and their brief descriptions, are drawn from Destler, "How National Security Advisers See Their Role," in James M. McCormick, ed., *The Domestic Sources of American Foreign Policy: Insights and Evidence*, pp. 209–222.

107. Two books that address these economic bureaucracies and that influenced the following discussion are Kegley and Wittkopf, *American Foreign Policy: Pattern and Process*, 5th ed. (New York: St. Martin's Press, 1996); and Howard J. Wiarda, *Foreign Policy Without Illusion* (Glenview, IL: Scott, Foresman, Little Brown Higher Education, 1990).

108. Office of the United States Trade Representative, "Benefits of Trade", at http://www.ustr.gov/about-us/benefits-trade, June 3, 2012.

109. The following principles are largely drawn from the discussion in Stephen D. Cohen, Joel R. Paul, and Robert A. Blecker, *Fundamentals of U.S. Foreign Trade Policy* (Boulder, CO: Westview Press, 1996), pp. 105–108. They are also discussed in Stephen D. Cohen, Robert A. Blecker, and Peter D. Whitney, *Fundamentals of U.S. Foreign Trade Policy*, 2nd ed. (Cambridge, MA: Westview Press, 2003), pp. 111–114.

110. Cohen, Blecker and Whitney, *Fundamentals of U.S. Foreign Trade Policy*, 2nd ed., p. 115. Emphasis added.

111. "The Office of the United States Trade Representative," at http://www.ustr.gov/about-us/mission, June 3, 2012.

112. The discussion is drawn from Cohen, *The Making of United States International Economic Policy*, 5th ed., pp. 58–60; and from Cohen, Paul, and Blecker, *Fundamentals of U.S. Foreign Trade Policy*, pp. 109, 153–154.

113. See Cohen, *The Making of United States International Economic Policy*, 5th ed., p. 60. The latest size is taken from Office of the United States Trade Representative, "About Us," at http://www.ustr.gov/about-us, June 3, 2012.

114. The Office of the United States Trade Representative, "Mission of the USTR," at http://www.ustr.gov/about-us/mission, June 3, 2012.

115. Ibid.

116. Cohen, *The Making of United States International Economic Policy*, 5th ed., p. 60, and Cohen, Blecker, and Whitney, *Fundamentals of U.S. Foreign Trade Policy*, 2nd ed., p. 115.

117. Cohen, Blecker, and Whitney, *Fundamentals of U.S. Foreign Trade Policy*, 2nd ed., pp. 116–117, and Cohen, *The Making of United States International Economic Policy*, 5th ed., pp. 61–62.

118. Cohen, Blecker, and Whitney, *Fundamentals of U.S. Foreign Trade Policy*, 2nd ed., pp. 115–116 and pp. 140–141.

119. Cohen, *The Making of United States International Economic Policy*, 5th ed., pp. 46–55. The quotes are at pp. 52 and 55, respectively.

120. Ibid., p. 53.

121. Ibid., p. 64.

122. Cohen, Paul, and Blecker, *Fundamentals of U.S. Foreign Trade Policy*, p. 47.

123. Quoted in Christopher M. Jones, "American Prewar Technology Sales to Iraq: A Bureaucratic Politics Explanation," in Eugene R. Wittkopf, ed., *The Domestic Sources of American Foreign Policy: Insights and Evidence*, 2nd ed. (New York: St. Martin's Press, 1994), p. 286.

124. Stephen D. Cohen, *The Making of United States International Economic Policy*, 4th ed. (Westport, CT: Praeger, 1994), p. 182.

125. Jones, "American Prewar Technology Sales to Iraq: A Bureaucratic Politics Explanation," p. 286.

126. Cohen, *The Making of United States International Economic Policy*, 5th ed., p. 92.

127. The quoted passages and the factors that explain Treasury's growth in influence are from ibid., pp. 47, 47–49, and 49, respectively.

128. See "About International Affairs," at http://www.treasury.gov/about/organizational-structure/offices/Pages/Office-Of-International-Affairs.aspx, June 3, 2012.

129. Ibid.

130. On the Office of Terrorism and Financial Intelligence, see http://www.treasury.gov/about/organizational-structure/offices/Pages/Office-of-Terrorism-and-Financial-Intelligence.aspx, June 3, 2012.

131. The quote is from Robert D. Hormats, "The World Economy Under Stress," in William G. Hyland, ed., *America and the World 1985* (New York: Pergamon Press, 1986), p. 469. Another source used here was Congressman Lee Hamilton, "The Decline of the Dollar," *Washington Report*, February 25, 1987.

132. S. Karene Witcher, "Baker's Plan to Relieve Debt Crisis May Spur Future Ills, Critics Say," *Wall Street Journal*, November 15, 1985, 1.

133. Hormats, "The World Economy Under Stress," p. 474.

134. The plan was devised by Undersecretary David C. Mulford. See John R. Cranford, "Members Press for Details on Brady Proposal," *Congressional Quarterly Weekly Report*, March 18, 1989, p. 572, for this point and some examples of how the plan would work; and John R. Cranford, "Brady Signals Shift in Policy Toward Debt Reduction," *Congressional Quarterly Weekly Report*, March 11, 1989, pp. 510–513, for an earlier discussion of the plan.

135. Peter Passell, "2 Views of the Peso: Wall St. vs. Main St.," *New York Times*, February 2, 1995, A6.

136. Patrick J. Lyons, "Mexico's Ripple Effects: Subtle Risks for Americans," *New York Times*, February 1, 1995, A11.

137. Bruce Stokes, "Tottering Markets," *National Journal*, February 18, 1995, 424.

138. The central role of the Department of Treasury in devising this plan can be gleaned from the active involvement of the secretary of the treasury in seeking congressional support (see, for example, David E. Sanger, "U.S. Seeks Mexican Steps in Bid to Aid Bailout Plan," *New York Times*, January 26, 1995, A14). They can also be gleaned from the importance of the undersecretary of the treasury, Lawrence Summers, in securing the agreements on the final package (see, for example Douglas Jehl, "Slow-Building Despair Led to Decision on Aid," *New York Times*, February 1, 1995, A10).

139. David E. Sanger, "Clinton Offers $20 Billion to Mexico for Peso Rescue; Action Sidesteps Congress," *New York Times*, February 1, 1995, A1.

140. Ibid.

141. For details on the Asian crisis, on which we draw here, see Ralph G. Carter and James M. Scott, "Funding the IMF: Congress versus the White House," in Ralph G. Carter, ed., *Contemporary Cases in U.S. Foreign Policy* (Washington, D.C.: CQ Press, 2002), pp. 339–363.

142. Joseph E. Stiglitz, *Globalization and Its Discontents* (New York: W.W. Norton and Company, 2002), p. 93. This book provides a stinging critique of IMF/Treasury actions during the Asian crisis, see especially pp. 89–132.

143. See "Henry M. Paulson, Jr.," *New York Times*, July 18, 2009, at http://topics.nytimes.com/top/reference/timestopics/people/p/henry_m_jr_paulson/index.html, June 4, 2012; Kimberly Amadeo, "TARP Program," About.com.US Economy, at http://useconomy.about.com/od/glossary/g/TARP.htm, June 5, 2012.

144. Kimberly Amadeo, "ARRA Details," About.com.US Economy, at http://useconomy.about.com/od/usfederalbudget/a/Economomic_Stimulus_Package_in_Detail.htm, June 5, 2012; "TARP Phase Two: Whatever Might Work," *CQ Weekly Report*, February 23, 2009, p. 404, June 4, 2012; and Robert Schmidt and Rebecca Christie, "Geithner Extends $700 Billion Bank-Bailout Program (Update3)," *Bloomberg*, December 9, 2009, http://www.bloomberg.com/apps/news?pid=newsarchive&sid=aMNX721eB9Rk, June 4, 2012.

145. For the quoted passage, see Martin Crutsinger, "Tim Geithner: Euro Crisis Could Cause Significant Damage to U.S. Economy," *Huffington Post*, October 6, 2011, at http://www.huffingtonpost.com/2011/10/06/tim-geithner-euro-crisis-_n_998112.html, June 4, 2012. For additional background, and some policy actions by the United States on this crisis, see Uri Dadush, "The Euro Crisis: A Threat to the U.S. Economy," Carnegie Endowment for International Peace, June 2, 2010, at http://www.carnegieendowment.org/2010/06/02/euro-crisis-threat-to-u.s.-economy/19w, June 6, 2012.

146. Cohen, *The Making of United States International Economic Policy*, 5th ed., p. 55.

147. See the Department of Commerce website, http://www.commerce.gov, for the list of bureaus in the department, accessed June 4, 2012. Formerly, the two bureaus were the Bureau of International Trade Administration and the Bureau of Export Administration, but the latter was changed by the Bush administration. Also see *U.S. Government Manual 2007/2008*, pp. 132–139.

148. *U.S. Government Manual 2007/2008*, pp. 137–139; Cohen, *The Making of United States International Economic Policy*, 5th ed., p. 57; and "About CS," at http://trade.gov/cs/about.asp, June 4, 2012.

149. Cohen, *The Making of United States International Economic Policy*, pp. 56–57; and Kegley and Wittkopf, *American Foreign Policy: Pattern and Process*, 5th ed., p. 414.

150. Eugene R. Wittkopf, Charles W. Kegley, Jr., and James M. Scott, *American Foreign Policy: Pattern and Process*, 6th ed. (Belmont, CA: Wadsworth/Thomson Learning, 2003), pp. 397 and 402 (note 11).

151. See Department of Commerce, "How Does the Commerce's Antidumping and Countervailing Duty Investigation Process Work?" March 20, 2012, for the procedures involves with such claims, at http://www.commerce.gov/blog/2012/03/20/how-does-commerce%E2%80%99s-antidumping-and-countervailing-duty-investigation-process-work, June 4, 2012.

152. This discussion draws on the U.S. Department of Commerce, *Bureau of Industry and Security Annual Report Fiscal Year 2010*, at http://www.bis.doc.gov/news/2011/bis_annual_report_2010.pdf, June 4, 2010. The quoted passages are at pp. 4 and 20. This report provides a complete description of the broad array of activities within this bureau at the Department of Commerce.

153. Richard W. Stevenson, "A Role as Nation's Chief Salesman Abroad," *New York Times*, April 4, 1996, A7.

154. Leslie Eaton, "A Dozen Companies Await Word," *New York Times*, April 4, 1996, A7.

155. Department of Commerce, "Commerce Secretary Gary Locke Unveils Details of the National Export Initiative," February 4, 2010, at http://www.commerce.gov/news/press-releases/2010/02/04/commerce-secretary-gary-locke-unveils-details-national-export-initiat, June 5, 2012.

156. Cohen, Blecker, and Whitney, *Fundamentals of U.S. Foreign Trade Policy*, p. 141.

157. The discussion and what follows mainly draw on *U.S. Government Manual 2001/2002*, pp. 119–122; and *U.S. Government Manual 2002/2003*, pp. 119–122; these are supplemented by Cohen, *The Making of United States International Economic Policy*, 5th ed., pp. 62–63 and Foreign Agricultural Service, "Public Law 480, Title I," at http://www.fas.usda.gov/excredits/Food Aid/pl480/pl480.asp, June 5, 2012. We also rely on several phone interviews with officials from the Department of Agriculture in Washington, DC, conducted in August 2002. I am indebted as well to my late colleague, Ross B. Talbot, for sharing his insight on agricultural policy making.

158. See "Department of Agriculture," U.S. *Government Manual 2011 Edition*, at http://www.gpo.gov/fdsys/pkg/GOVMAN-2011-10-05/xml/GOVMAN-2011-10-05-112.xml, June 5, 2012.

159. The number of ATOs was calculated from the Foreign Agricultural Service website, at http://www.fas.usda.gov/ofso/overseas_post_directory/ovs_directory_search.asp, June 5, 2012. For an earlier critical assessment of ATOs, see *International Trade: Agricultural Trade Offices' Role in Promoting U.S. Exports Is Unclear*, General Accounting Office Report (GAO/GGD-92-65, January 16, 1992).

160. See "Department of Agriculture," *U.S. Government Manual 2011 Edition*, at http://www.gpo.gov/fdsys/pkg/GOVMAN-2011-10-05/xml/GOVMAN-2011-10-05-112.xml, June 5, 2012; Farm Service Agency "About the Commodity Credit Corporation," at http://www.fsa.usda.gov/FSA/webapp?area=about&subject=landing&topic=sao-cc, June 5, 2012; and Farm Service Agency, "Program Fact Sheets," August 2011, at http://www.fsa.usda.gov/FSA/newsReleases?area=newsroom&subject=landing&topic=pfs&newstype=prfactsheet&type=detail&item=pf_20110804_dppsp_en_mpsp.html, June 5, 2012.

161. USAID, "Fact Sheet: Food for Peace—FY 2011 Programs," January 26, 2012, at http://www.usaid.gov/our_work/humanitarian_assistance/ffp/factsheets.html, June 5, 2012. This total is under Title II of P.L. 480. Food aid totals can vary depending on what is included in the calculation. On the actions on the various titles of P.L. 480, see Foreign Agricultural Service, "Public Law 480, Title I," at http://fas.usda.gov/excredits/FoodAid/pl480/pl480.asp, June 5, 2012.

162. Foreign Agricultural Service, "Food for Progress," at http://www.fas.usda.gov/excredits/Food Aid/FFP/foodforprogress.asp, June 5, 2012; Foreign Agricultural Service, "Section

416b," at http://www.fas.usda.gov/excredits/FoodAid/416b/section416b.asp, for the quote on that program; and Foreign Agricultural Service, "McGovern-Dole International Food for Education and Child Nutrition Program," February 2009, at http://www.fas. usda.gov/excredits/FoodAid/FFE/mcdfactsheet.pdf, June 5, 2012.

163. See Thomas Melito, Director of International Affairs and Trade at the Government Accountability Office, "Foreign Assistance: Multiple Challenges Hinder the Efficiency and Effectiveness of U.S. Food Aid," testimony before the Subcommittee on Agriculture, Rural Development, Food and Drug Administration, and Related Agencies, Committee on Appropriations, House of Representatives. GAO-08-83T, October 2, 2007.

164. H. Wayne Moyer and Timothy E. Josling, *Agricultural Policy Reform: Politics and Process in the EC and the USA* (New York: Harvester Wheatsheaf, 1990), pp. 120 and 124 (note 6).

165. George Athan, "Yeutter Likely to Push for Free Trade, Exports," *Des Moines Register*, December 15, 1988, 1A and 11A.

166. See Dan Looker, "The Politics of NAFTA Heat Up," *Successful Farming* 91 (September 1993): 8; and Dan Glickman, "U.S. Opportunities," Landon Lecture, Kansas State University *Vital Speeches* (October 15, 1995): 5–10.

167. The background on Secretary Veneman comes from http:www//usda.gov/agencies/ gallery/veneman.htm, August 27, 2002; and from an interview with a Department of Agriculture official on August 27, 2002. The last characterization of Veneman comes from the interview as well.

168. These assessments and quotations come from an interview with a Foreign Agricultural Service official, May 22, 2008.

169. Department of Agriculture, Foreign Agricultural Service, "Fact Sheet: Agricultural Advisory Committees for Trade," September 2011, p. 1, at http://www.fas.usda.gov/itp/ apac-atacs/FINAL%20APAC-ATACs%20Fact%20Sheet%209-15-11.pdf, June 5, 2012; phone interview with a Foreign Agricultural Service official, May 22, 2008.

The Military and Intelligence Bureaucracies: Pervasive or Accountable?

Unlike the Cold War, when we had one main adversary, we face a multitude of challenges. . . . We face insurgents and militants who cross borders to conduct attacks. We face the proliferation of dangerous weapons in the hands of terrorists, in the hands of rogue nations. We face cyber attackers. . . . We face the challenge of rising and changing powers and nations in turmoil . . .

SECRETARY OF DEFENSE-DESIGNATE LEON E. PANETTA
JUNE 2011

In my time spent in intelligence, I don't recall a more complex and interdependent array of challenges than we face today. The capabilities, technologies, know-how, communications and environmental forces aren't confined by borders, and can trigger transnational disruptions with astonishing speed.

JAMES R. CLAPPER, DIRECTOR OF NATIONAL INTELLIGENCE
FEBRUARY 2012

This chapter continues the discussion of bureaucracies and foreign policy by first examining the Department of Defense and the intelligence community. These bureaucracies increased their foreign and national security influence over the post–World War II years, but both have come under closer scrutiny lately, especially over the past decade. Our discussion assesses each bureaucracy's relative policy role and changes in each one in recent years. In addition, we discuss the creation of the Department of Homeland Security after September 11 and its implications for U.S. foreign policy. Finally, we outline the mechanisms that the executive branch uses to coordinate policy making across the different bureaucracies discussed in this and the previous chapter. Although individual bureaucracies may influence policy making directly, the combined effect of several—or the success of one bureaucracy over another—occurs most often through the interagency or interdepartmental coordination process employed by all recent presidents.

THE DEPARTMENT OF DEFENSE

The Department of Defense may well be perceived as only implementing policy, but, in fact, it contributes substantially to policy formulation. Still, although the department's overall power has grown significantly over the past seventy years, its role in foreign policy formulation remains a source of some debate. Some would contend that it is but **one bureaucracy within the foreign policy apparatus**, albeit a powerful one.[1] Others would argue that it has a pervasive effect on policy making, often surpassing the competing bureaucracies within the executive branch.[2] Still others would suggest that it is the beginning point for the "**military-industrial (and now military-political) complex**," a structure woven into American society (see Chapter 11).[3] One view especially prevalent today claims that the **military and its role ought to be substantially changed** to meet the new international threats that arose from the events of September 11, 2001, and the Iraq and Afghanistan Wars. In this connection, there is a new concern over the military–civilian gap between the department and American society at large and the implications of that gap for effective policy making. Whatever view the reader adopts about the military and its role, there can be little doubt that the Department of Defense has increased its foreign policy–making influence over the years and that such influence will likely remain for the foreseeable future, especially in the changing global environment of the early twenty-first century.

The Structure of the Pentagon

The perceived influence of the Department of Defense (DOD) begins with its considerable **size and presence**. As Figure 10.1 shows, the Pentagon (located in Arlington, Virginia, and named for its shape) is a large and complex bureaucracy organized into key divisions. These are further subdivided into a number of departments, agencies, and offices that potentially affect many areas of American life.

The DOD affects the American public through the awarding of defense contracts, through domestic and foreign jobs created for U.S. corporations, and through the men and women serving in the military. In fiscal year 2011, for example, more than $236 billion in prime defense contracts were awarded to one hundred U.S. and international corporations, individual states, and even a foreign country.[4] Virtually every state and the District of Columbia share in those awards and the thousands of jobs they create. In fact, the DOD directly and indirectly employs millions of

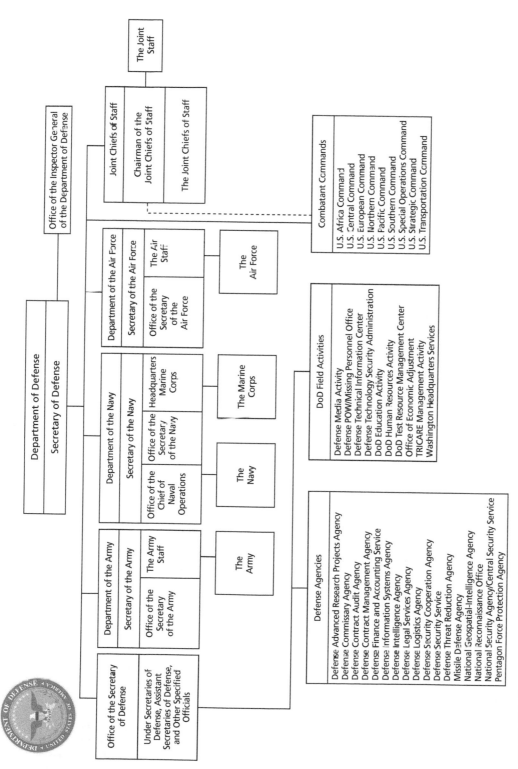

FIGURE 10.1 The Department of Defense

Source: http://odam.defense.gov/omp/Functions/Organizational_Portfolios/Organization_and_Functions_Guidebook/DoD%20Org%20chart%20December%202011.pdf, June 7, 2012.

Americans. In 2012, the department directly employed about 718,000 civilians, 1.4 million active-duty military personnel, and 1.1 million National Guard and reserve forces. In addition, "more than two million retirees and their family" were recipients of veterans' benefits. Finally, national defense outlays represent one of the largest items in the federal budget, with a fiscal year 2013 request of $614 billion.[5] In this sense, the impact of DOD expenditures on American society is pronounced and will likely remain substantial with the continuing and emergent threats in the world today.

In terms of foreign policy formulation, three sectors of the Department of Defense are pivotal: **the secretary of defense**; the **Joint Chiefs of Staff (JCS)**; and the **Office of the Secretary of Defense (OSD)**.

Office of the Secretary of Defense

The OSD is the newest, and potentially greatest, source of influence on foreign policy formulation. This office consists of the secretary of defense, the deputy secretary of defense, five undersecretaries dealing with various aspects of policy and management, and numerous assistant secretaries of defense and other staffs. As the principal staff arm of the secretary of defense, these offices deal with "policy development, planning, resource management, fiscal, and program evaluation responsibilities."[6] As the OSD has grown over the years, it has become the principal focus of policy development and administration within the DOD.

The policy division within OSD, headed by an undersecretary of defense for policy, illustrates its crucial policy-formulating function. Within this division are several important policy offices: International Security Affairs, Global Strategic Affairs, Asian and Pacific Security Affairs, Special Operations and Low-Intensity Conflict, and Homeland Defense and Americas' Security Affairs. Each is headed by an assistant secretary of defense, and each has an important stake in policy development.

Two of OSD's mid-level offices illustrate the increased policy formulation role of the DOD over the years: the **Office of International Security Affairs (ISA)** and the **Office of International Security Policy (ISP)** (now **Global Strategic Affairs**). The former, in particular, gained prominence during the Vietnam War, when it was a major source of policy advice.[7] Its responsibilities (and specifically those of the assistant secretary of defense who heads this office) include developing security policy and strategy toward nations and international organizations in Europe, the Middle East, and Africa and overseeing "security cooperation programs and foreign military sales programs in these regions." The ISA also participates in the interagency process and in international negotiations on behalf of the undersecretary of defense for policy and the secretary of defense as required.[8] Over the years, ISA had gained such prominence in policy making that it has been labeled the "little State Department" because it provides a political component to the military analysis at the Pentagon. However, as the result of structural and procedural realignments, its influence was in decline from the Richard Nixon administration through the Jimmy Carter administration.[9]

During the Ronald Reagan administration, the Office of International Security Policy (ISP) assumed a larger policy role within the DOD. Its responsibilities encompassed policy development on NATO and European affairs, including nuclear and conventional forces, strategic and theater arms negotiations, nuclear proliferation questions, and oversight of existing agreements.[10] The assistant secretary of defense for international security policy at this time, Richard Perle, was particularly prominent in speaking out on arms control. He often took the lead in shaping policy on deploying intermediate-range nuclear missiles in Europe in the early 1980s and in developing the U.S. bargaining position on both intermediate-range and long-range nuclear forces at the arms control talks in Geneva, beginning in 1981.[11]

These two offices did not receive the same recognition from the George H. W. Bush administration, but they regained their status during the Clinton years, particularly with the appointment of two assistant secretaries to head them who were prominent policy analysts on leave from Harvard University: Joseph Nye, a leading scholar of international relations and foreign policy, headed the Office of International Affairs for a time; Ashton Carter, a leading thinker and analyst in the nuclear weapons area, headed the Office of International Security Policy. Both sought an imprint on policy, and Nye, in particular, was deeply involved in shaping U.S. policy toward Asia.[12]

During the George W. Bush administration, the undersecretary of defense for policy, and the offices within his responsibility, once again gained some notoriety. After September 11, Undersecretary Douglas Feith created an intelligence team to assess whether terrorist links existed between Iraq and other countries. About a year later, in October 2002, he appointed a special planning team to prepare for a possible war with Iraq. Both teams became controversial in the aftermath of the Iraq War because of their perceived influence on the policy-making process. Indeed, the intelligence team's finding of "suspected linkages between Iraq and Al Qaeda, a conclusion doubted by the C.I.A. and D.I.A." was a particular source of interest to those assessing the quality of U.S. intelligence prior to the Iraq War.[13]

During the Barack Obama administration, a newly configured office within the OSD is the Office of the Assistant Secretary of Global Strategic Affairs. That office now has important responsibilities for policy issues currently facing the United States in the changing global environment. In particular, it has responsibility for developing "policy for the Secretary on countering weapons of mass destruction, nuclear forces and missile defense, cyber security and space issues." Moreover, this office has been involved in undertaking the Nuclear Posture, Ballistic Missile Defense, and Space Posture reviews. Furthermore, it has major responsibility for creating the policy for the Cyber Command within the Department of Defense.[14]

The Joint Chiefs of Staff

The Joint Chiefs of Staff (JCS) represents a second set of important policy advisors within the DOD. Composed of the **chief of staff of the Army**, the **chief of Naval Operations**, the **chief of staff of the Air Force**, the **commandant of the Marine Corps**, and a **vice chairman and chairman**, the JCS has been described as "the hinge between the most senior civilian leadership and the professional military."[15] Its responsibility is to provide the president and the secretary of defense with strategic planning and to coordinate the use of the armed forces if necessary. In addition, it recommends to the president and the secretary of defense the military requirements of the United States and how they are to be met. Finally, the chairman of the joint chiefs, appointed by the president with the advice and consent of the Senate, is the primary military advisor to the secretary of defense, the NSC, the Homeland Security Council (HSC), and the president.[16]

Policy-making Constraints   Despite its statutory foreign policy duties, the JCS has probably been generally less effective than the civilian side of the Pentagon in shaping American policy since World War II, for at least two reasons. First, the JCS has enjoyed only **mixed favor with presidents and with secretaries of defense** since 1947.[17] In fact, some presidents and secretaries have been at odds with the JCS and have tried to reduce its policy impact. President Dwight Eisenhower, for instance, was determined to "balance the budget and restrict military spending"—something the JCS did not favor.[18] With his own vast military experience in World War II, he did not see the need to rely on the JCS for advice and assistance, especially after it had publicly criticized his policy. Under President John Kennedy, the situation only worsened when Secretary of Defense Robert McNamara attempted to streamline and modernize the management and operation of the Pentagon. Moreover, any initial confidence that Kennedy might have had in the JCS was quickly eroded as a result of what he perceived as bad advice on the Bay of Pigs invasion in April 1961.[19]

Relations between the JCS and the president improved during the administrations of Lyndon Johnson, Nixon, and Gerald Ford. During the Johnson administration, relations warmed a bit—especially after the disaffection and ultimately the resignation of Secretary of Defense McNamara in 1967—as the president increasingly became dependent on the JCS for advice on the Vietnam War.[20] Under Nixon and Ford and when Melvin Laird was secretary of defense, the JCS was clearly in the ascendancy in terms of influence, even though it apparently did not shape critical policy positions during those years.[21]

Under the Carter and Reagan administrations, the situation changed once again, and reliance on the JCS fluctuated. Carter's major policy decisions on troop withdrawals from Korea and the scrapping of the B-1 bomber were adopted with minimal JCS involvement.[22] By contrast, the Reagan administration appeared initially to be more receptive to its views. At one point in his administration, Reagan reportedly sent written praise of the JCS's policy advice.[23] Despite such praise, however, policy making for the Reagan administration was largely located elsewhere within the executive branch and the DOD.

Second, **each joint chief's commitment to his own service has reduced the JCS's combined impact**.[24] Each member has the responsibility of managing his own military service as well as advising the president and the secretary of defense through the JCS structure. In the estimate of one defense analyst, this individual service responsibility consumes an important portion of JCS time and diminishes the JCS's foreign policy formulation role as a whole. Divided loyalties also produce policy differences, which lead to compromise recommendations that may not be vigorously supported by all.[25]

Indeed, criticisms of JCS recommendations have been particularly harsh over the years. President Carter's secretary of defense, Harold Brown, for instance, characterized JCS advice as "worse than nothing." Another former high-ranking Pentagon official labeled it "a laughing stock," and a former aide to Brown said that it was like a "bowl of oatmeal." Despite President Reagan's praise of the JCS, Secretary of Defense Caspar Weinberger rejected or ignored its advice on such major issues as the basing mode for the MX missile and the requirements of the Rapid Deployment Force.[26] Perhaps even more telling was Reagan's failure to remember the name of the chairman of the JCS during a major portion of his administration. When testifying during the Iran–Contra trial of John Poindexter, he was asked if he recognized the name of John Vessey, chairman of the JCS. He replied that the name was "very familiar," but he could not be certain as to who Vessey was.[27]

Policy-making Reforms   In the **Defense Reorganization Act of 1986** (also known as the **Goldwater-Nichols Reorganization Act** after its congressional sponsors), Congress changed the power and authority of the JCS to address its problems. These changes reduced the clout of the individual services and increased the impact of the JCS as a whole.

CHAPTER 10 THE MILITARY AND INTELLIGENCE BUREAUCRACIES: PERVASIVE OR ACCOUNTABLE?

391

One key change was to **give more power to the chairman** in policy formulation and recommendations. The chairman (and not the JCS as such) was designated as the president's primary military advisor, responsible for providing the executive with a range of military advice on any matter requested. In this way, his recommendations would not be "watered down" to accommodate his JCS colleagues. The chairman also assumed statutory responsibility for preparing strategic military plans and future military contingency plans, and for budget coordination within the military itself. Furthermore, the JCS reported directly to the chairman, as did a newly appointed vice chairman. At the same time, a member of the JCS could submit an opinion of disagreement on policy, and the chairman would be obliged to share that opinion with the president, the NSC, HSC, or the secretary of defense.[28]

A second key change was in the **command structure**. The unified Combatant Commands, or the commanders in chief (CINCs in military parlance)—those responsible for coordinating the four armed services operating in a particular region of the world—gained greater authority. Under the previous arrangement, the individual services retained substantial authority in directing forces, but under the reorganization that authority now rested with those directing multiservice operations, greatly increasing the integration of forces across the branches. As a result there are now six regional commands (Africa, European, Pacific, Northern, Central, and Southern) and three functional commands (Strategic, Special Operations, and Transportation),[29] and the CINCs have become highly influential in military operations and, as we discuss later, sometimes in policy.

In fact, the Goldwater-Nichols legislation has been characterized as "the most important piece of military legislation . . . in the last forty years . . . [and] the most dangerous."[30] In this view, the reorganization was important because it enhanced the power of the JCS chairman, but it was also dangerous because it challenged civilian control of the military. This concern was seemingly given support with the appointment of General Colin Powell as chairman of the JCS during the George H. W. Bush administration.

Described as a "military intellectual" who took a "pragmatic and collegial approach" to policy making, General Powell was well versed in all aspects of national security policy.[31] Aided by the legal basis for policy influence offered by the Goldwater-Nichols Act, he was thus poised to "become the most influential JCS chairman in U.S. history."[32] Significantly, Powell played a central role in designing the American response to Iraq's intervention into Kuwait, including the resulting American buildup in Saudi Arabia and the Persian Gulf. By one assessment, he was "responsible for shaping the U.S. military response in the gulf," and his strategy of deploying "maximum force" was fully endorsed by President Bush.[33]

When Powell continued in office during the Bill Clinton administration, policy analyst Richard Kohn argued that he was in a strong position to defy "a young, incoming president with extraordinarily weak authority in military affairs," which he initially did over Bosnia.[34] Yet as Powell pointed out after his retirement from the JCS chairmanship, the perceived crises in civil–military relations simply did not exist: "[T]hings were not out of control . . . Presidents Bush and Clinton, and Secretaries Cheney and Aspin, exercised solid, unmistakable control over the Armed Forces and especially me."[35] Nonetheless, the JCS chairman's power and influence increased with the passage of Goldwater-Nichols.

Powell's immediate successor during the Clinton years, General John Shalikashvili, also benefited from Goldwater-Nichols. He lacked Powell's significant political background in Washington (although he had served as an aide to Powell in 1991 and 1992 and represented Powell in meetings with the Department of State on occasion[36]), but he had successfully directed two politically sensitive military operations before assuming the chairmanship: aiding the Kurds in northern Iraq after the Gulf War, and, as NATO commander, planning possible air strikes in Bosnia in 1992 and 1993.[37] Thus, Shalikashvili soon proved to be an important participant in the Clinton administration's policy making over Haiti and Bosnia in 1994 and 1995 and an articulate spokesperson for the administration on Capitol Hill.

Shalikashvili's successors as chairmen of the JCS, General Henry Hugh Shelton, General Richard Myers, and General Peter Pace, did not achieve the same policy-making impact. Serving in the last years of the Clinton administration and the first year of the George W. Bush administration, General Shelton was more reserved and less assertive than his predecessors, and he was skeptical of the United States fighting small wars and engaging in peacekeeping operations.[38] Instead, he preferred to work with the troops than in the corridors of the Pentagon or the halls of Congress. Furthermore, because the attacks of September 11 occurred at the very end of his watch, Shelton was not a key player in the American response to those tragic events. As it turns out, neither were his two successors, Air Force General Richard Myers and General Peter Pace, the first Marine to be JCS chairman.[39] Both were overshadowed by Bush's secretary of defense, Donald Rumsfeld, who quickly took charge of American military policy in the post–September 11 era and was determined to assert civilian control over the military.[40]

The reduced role of recent JCS chairs produced considerable criticism of the Bush administration for undermining the military–civilian relationship within the Pentagon—and, by indirection—for weakening the reforms initiated under Goldwater–Nichols. One analyst charged in particular that the Bush administration sought to silence and overrule the military on tactics and operations and that recent JCS chairs (and the military more generally) were largely reticent on policy issues.[41] In fact, the debate was not over civilian control of the military—that was unchallenged and is constitutionally protected. Instead, the issue was whether the military, including the JCS, had been too deferential to civilian leadership over operational matters (that is, areas of military expertise) such as the number of forces required for the invasion of Iraq in 2003 and the advisability of the "surge strategy" in 2007.[42]

General Myers (and his co-author, Richard Kohn) disputed the charge that the administration overruled the military on tactics, contending that there was only the normal "pulling and hauling" between the participants on policy decisions. They deny that there had ever been a war between the civilian leadership and the military during the Rumsfeld years, but they do acknowledge that "respect, candor, collaboration, co-operation—and subordination" is necessary for effective policy making between the civilian leadership and military officials.[43]

With the appointment of Admiral Mike Mullen as Chairman of the JCS in 2007, however, the military gained a more assertive voice on policy matters. He was deeply involved in advocating for the surge strategy in Afghanistan in the first year of the Obama administration, was outspoken about the threat that the national debt posed for America's national security, and later warned that "Haqqani [terrorist] network acts as a virtual arm of Pakistan's Inter-Services Intelligence Agency" at a Senate Armed Services Committee meeting. Mullen's successor in 2011, General Martin Dempsey, is likely to be as equally outspoken, especially as he deals with the "pivot" in America's defense policy toward Asia and the budget cuts that are now facing the Pentagon.[44]

On balance, the Goldwater–Nichols Act generally benefited the JCS (albeit with exceptions), but it also significantly benefited the regional CINCs, who were given joint command over all branches of American military forces in their area. In this way, their ability to shape American policy increased. In particular, the military officials heading the regional commands around the world assumed a larger and larger role in policy formulation and implementation. In this they were aided by the decline of State Department influence through continuous budget cuts and the attrition of staff and through the diminished role of the service chiefs of the army, navy, and air force. As one analyst put it, "Washington came to rely ever more on the regional CINCs to fill a diplomatic void."[45]

Goldwater–Nichols also benefited one other component of the military structure at the Pentagon, the **Joint Staff**. Composed of officers and civilians, the Joint Staff works directly for the chairman of the JCS by advising on and formulating policy. The advice is supposed to be "politically neutral," not favoring one service over the other, but rather offered in the best interest of the nation. Analyst Stephen Saideman argues that because the Joint Staff works "on a daily basis with representatives from the State Department, the Office of the Secretary of Defense, the National Security Council, and other players in the policy-making process," it is in a good position to influence the outcome of numerous issues.[46] It may be asked to initiate a written draft policy, propose alternatives for discussion, or comment on options advanced. Although its response is not necessarily within the guidance of the chairman, the Joint Staff has an opportunity to impact the policy agenda and its direction.

In all, then, uniformed military officials—whether the chairman of the Joint Chiefs of Staff, the regional commanders in chief, or the Joint Staff—play a large role in the shaping and implementing of policy, and the Goldwater–Nichols reforms of three decades ago were important in bringing this about.

The Secretary of Defense

After the office of the secretary of defense and the JCS, the third policy advisor within the DOD is the secretary himself. Over the postwar years, the role of secretaries of defense in policy making grew considerably as their control over the department increased through the reform acts of 1953 and 1958, and as they gained greater confidence of presidents.[47] Not all analysts agree with this view. Two contend that the powers of the secretary of defense are less than the responsibilities of the office and that the secretary's relative influence can be easily overstated.[48] Nevertheless, a good case can be made that, on particular issues and in some administrations, defense secretaries often commanded as much influence as did secretaries of state. A brief survey of the most important occupants of this post supports this view, especially for recent decades.

Some Influential Secretaries: From McNamara to Rumsfeld The most influential of the twenty-three secretaries of defense since 1947 was **Robert McNamara**, who held office throughout President Kennedy's years and for most of President Johnson's term. With his close ties to both presidents, McNamara exercised more policy influence than any other cabinet officer.[49] Given a wide mandate to modernize the Pentagon, he was also allowed substantial latitude in shaping America's strategic nuclear policy. Moreover, he was the spokesperson who announced the change in strategic doctrine in two important areas: (1) the nuclear strategy toward the Soviet Union and (2) the defense strategy for NATO. In the former area, McNamara moved the United States from a position of "massive retaliation," in which it reserved the right to engage in an all-out nuclear attack for an act of aggression by the Soviet Union, to a stance of **"mutual assured destruction" (MAD)**. In this, he was instrumental in developing the **strategy of flexible response** for the United States and its European allies, which called for both conventional and nuclear forces to respond to any Soviet or Warsaw Pact aggression in central Europe.

Caspar Weinberger, secretary of defense until the last year of the Reagan administration, was an equally influential participant in the foreign policy process, particularly in bolstering defense expenditures. Aided by strong support from President Reagan, Weinberger was granted virtually all of his requests for a conventional and strategic military buildup. Only in 1983 did those requests begin to be compromised;[50] still, by fiscal year 1985, the DOD's budget authority reached the highest in real terms for any period in the 1980s—a total of $295 billion. In subsequent years, Weinberger was not as successful, with the budget declining about 3.5 percent a year from fiscal year 1986 through fiscal year 1988. Nonetheless, he had been able to move the defense budget from less than $200 billion to nearly $300 billion per year in a very brief period of time.[51] Moreover, his political influence lay in his close ties with Reagan and with the president's second national security advisor, William Clark.[52]

Friends and adversaries hailed President George H. W. Bush's secretary of defense, Richard Cheney, as "bright, articulate, fair, unflappable, and eminently likable."[53] Although his policy-making clout did not seem to match that of some of his immediate predecessors, he proved to be a competent manager of the department, where he quickly put together a plan to reduce the size of the military for the post–Cold War era, as well as an articulate spokesman for the military on Capitol Hill, where he had served as Wyoming's representative in the House for six terms. During the crisis immediately after Iraq's invasion of Kuwait in 1990 and then during the Gulf War in 1991, Cheney's stature rose appreciably.[54]

Clinton's three secretaries of defense had more mixed records in terms of policy influence. His first, Les Aspin, a congressman from Wisconsin and chairman of the House Armed Services Committee at the time of his move to the Pentagon, proved to be a better strategic thinker than a manager, and he was forced to resign by the end of the first year of the Clinton administration over Somalia and other issues.[55] Aspin's successor, William Perry, a mathematician and former undersecretary of defense for research and engineering during the Carter administration,[56] was more reserved and formal. He had earned his credentials as a Pentagon bureaucrat, enjoyed the respect of the defense brass and Congress alike, and had good managerial skills.[57] His political and policy-making skills were suspect, however, and he had little background as a public spokesperson on security issues.[58] Still, Perry proved to be more successful than initially predicted by pushing reforms within the Pentagon, emphasizing new defense technology, and promoting a new concept—preventive defense—to guide future security policy.[59] Finally, Perry's successor, former Republican senator William Cohen, brought a bipartisan cast to national security, but he did not prove to be an important shaper of foreign or defense policy. Instead, he was largely overshadowed by Secretary of State Madeleine Albright and National Security Advisor Sandy Berger.[60]

By contrast, President George W. Bush's first secretary of defense, **Donald H. Rumsfeld**, quickly returned the office to its position as an important force in the shaping of foreign and defense policy, especially in the post–September 11 period. This was Rumsfeld's second tour as secretary of defense; his first had been in the Ford administration, where he worked closely with Vice President Richard Cheney. In this sense, he was well connected to the Bush White House through Cheney and was thus perhaps poised to exercise more foreign policy influence than other secretaries of defense. He also came to office steeped in current defense issues important to candidate

Bush, and he had a mandate to undertake a "defense transformation"—an effort to change the way the United States would wage war in the twenty-first century.[61]

His initial efforts to influence policy and to effect the transformation of the military were largely undermined by his own style and by bureaucratic politics. Rumsfeld's brash and caustic approach did not win him favor with Pentagon officials or even with his policy-making counterparts in the Bush administration. His tendency to dress down senior military officials and his general brusqueness won him few friends, either in the Pentagon or on Capitol Hill.[62]

The events of September 11 had a telling effect on Rumsfeld's role within the Pentagon, and his impact on policy making changed appreciably after those events. Indeed, along with the military, he assumed a centrality in policy making that neither the military nor the secretary of defense had had in many years, and from the start he was the point person in the discussions over how to respond to al-Qaeda and the Taliban in Afghanistan. During the first set of meetings after 9/11, he immediately "raised the question of Iraq" with President Bush.[63] When the United States took action in Afghanistan in 2001 and 2002 and then later in Iraq in 2003, Rumsfeld often held press conferences to explain and defend them. Indeed, his skill in explaining policy and deflecting criticism enhanced his role in the administration.

As the reconstruction effort in Iraq stalled, as human rights abuses at Abu Ghraib were revealed, and as American deaths mounted, Rumsfeld became the target of critics over his direction of American policy; his intransigence over the course of the war only exacerbated their criticisms. Members of Congress and retired generals called for his resignation, beginning in 2003.[64]

The day after the 2006 congressional election, President Bush announced that Rumsfeld was leaving the administration, resigning just eleven days short of surpassing Robert McNamara "as the longest serving defense secretary in American history."[65] By one assessment, he had emerged "as the most powerful secretary of defense" since McNamara through his dominance of and impact on policy,[66] although his efforts to transform the military "was more promise than reality. He made a start, but these things take time, and it is clear that Iraq ha[d] denied him that time."[67]

Recent Secretaries: Gates and Panetta Rumsfeld's successor as secretary of defense in the last two years of the Bush administration was **Robert M. Gates**, a former CIA director and deputy national security adviser. His management style, his political instinct, and his goals for the DOD were considerably different from Rumsfeld's, as was his attitude toward the uniformed military. He met with the JCS in the "Tank"— the Pentagon council room—and he was described by Admiral Mike Mullen as "very open, very engaging."[68] In this sense, he represented a sharp break from Rumsfeld. Furthermore, he was more respectful of the military and more willing to take its views into account. Although his political instincts were those of a traditional political realist, he was a pragmatist who wanted to get things accomplished. He spoke favorably about expanding American diplomacy and American diplomatic presence, and as one source put it, Gates did not believe that the military could accomplish everything on its own.[69] Finally, he denied having any grand plan for the transformation of the military; rather, he had three priorities: as he put it, "Iraq, Iraq, and Iraq."[70] One analysis summarized his overall goal as "trying to salvage a war gone bad."[71]

Due to his considerable policy insights, and in a nod to bipartisanship in foreign policy, President Obama asked Gates to stay on as secretary of defense, and he remained so for the first two and half years of the administration. Indeed, he was the first secretary of defense continued by a president of a different political party. He quickly became an important ally of Secretary of State Clinton in the bureaucratic debates, especially over the direction of American policy in Afghanistan, and he became a White House favorite, with the president leaning "heavily on Mr. Gates for advice." The result was that Gates "played a central role in reshaping national security policy" during his tenure in the Obama administration.[72] Further, he gained great respect from colleagues at the Pentagon and members of Congress for his dedication to public service, his political skill, and the integrity that he brought to the position.[73] As such, Gates left public service as one of the more formidable secretaries of defense in U.S. history.

His successor was Leon Panetta, most recently the former director of the Central Intelligence Agency but also a former member of Congress and a former White House official in the Clinton administration. Although widely admired in official Washington, he faced a litany of issues—completing American withdrawal from Iraq, winding down the war in Afghanistan, dealing with significant cuts in the defense budget, and narrowing the mission of the American military[74]—and it is unclear how much decision latitude that he possesses, especially in comparison to his predecessor.

In all, although the styles and motivations of the secretaries of defense and their impact on policy varied over the past six decades, the secretary and the department remain important influences on U.S. foreign policy in the first decade of the twenty-first century, perhaps as much as at any time in the past.

THE INTELLIGENCE COMMUNITY

The growth of America's intelligence apparatus owes much to the Cold War, but its importance increased dramatically in the post–September 11 era. In a world increasingly fraught with dangers from international terrorism and political and economic instabilities, the ability of policy makers to evaluate the global political, economic, and social conditions effectively is arguably more important than ever before. With continued incidents of terrorism and civil unrest in Afghanistan, Iraq, Syria, Nigeria, and elsewhere, the possession (or the potential for possession) of nuclear weapons by a number of states (such as North Korea and Iran), and the potential for ecological calamity (such as global warming and tsunamis), sound intelligence remains as necessary now than ever before, maybe even more so.

Several congressional and independent investigations and presidential actions recognized the importance of maintaining quality intelligence. The 2003 Joint Congressional Intelligence Report into the Terrorist Attack of September 11, 2001, emphasized the continuing need for intelligence, as it outlined necessary changes in the intelligence community.[75] *The 9/11 Commission Report* likewise emphasized the need to restructure the intelligence community and to increase the degree of "jointness" among its various components.[76] President Bush issued **four executive orders** to undertake structural and institutional changes in the intelligence community, and Congress passed the **Intelligence Reform and Terrorism Prevention (IRTP) Act of 2004** later that year to reshape it through legislation. In 2009, President Obama integrated the HSC staff into the NSC staff as a means of tying together intelligence and security operations more fully.[77]

The Structure and Role of the Intelligence Community

Although the intelligence community (IC) is often associated most closely with the Central Intelligence Agency (CIA), it is much more comprehensive. There are fifteen other agencies involved in the IC, drawn from the Department of Defense, the Department of Energy, the Department of State, the Department of Treasury, the Federal Bureau of Investigation (FBI), the Coast Guard (since 2001), the Department of Homeland Security (since 2003), and the Drug Enforcement Administration (DEA, since 2006). Each of these concentrates on various aspects of information gathering and intelligence analysis (see Figure 10.2).

The IC's Traditional Components   The **CIA**, created by the National Security Act of 1947, is the oldest and the only independent agency within the IC (the others are attached to a department or other government units). The CIA has become "the primary U.S. government . . . agency for intelligence analysis, clandestine human intelligence collection, and covert action."[78] By one estimate, the CIA has more than 20,000 employees who work in one of four directorates—the Directorate of Intelligence (overseeing analysis of open and clandestine intelligence), the Directorate

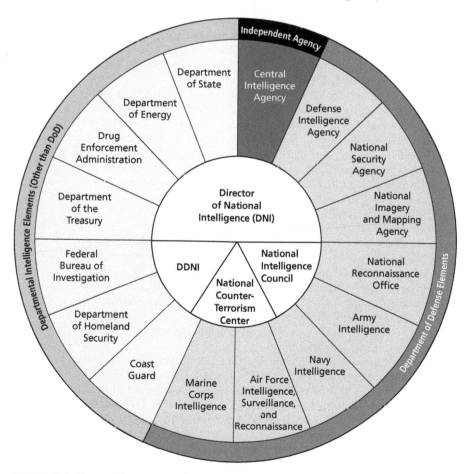

FIGURE 10.2 The Intelligence Community

Source: Information drawn from http://www.dni.gov/members_IC and "The U.S. Intelligence Community (IC), 2006" in Loch K. Johnson, ed., *Handbook of Intelligence Studies* (London and New York: Routledge, 2007), p. 363.

of Science and Technology (developing and exploiting new scientific, engineering, and technical applications for intelligence activities), the National Clandestine Service (collecting human intelligence from clandestine sources and undertaking clandestine operations), and the Directorate of Support (providing technical and human support to the other directorates).[79]

The **Department of Defense** contributes the largest number of agencies (eight) to the IC. Four of these have broad responsibilities across the military services and to other government agencies; the other four stem from the uniformed military services (army, air force, navy, and marines) and have primary responsibility (albeit shared with others) to their individual branches. Perhaps the most prominent of the four broad-gauged DOD agencies is the **Defense Intelligence Agency (DIA)**, which is "a major producer and manager of foreign military intelligence" with a large collection and analytic component for human intelligence (HUMINT), measurement and signature intelligence (MASINT), counterintelligence (CI), and Joint Staff Intelligence (J-2), among others. The DIA also directs the Defense Counterintelligence and HUMINT Center, The Central MASINT Office, the National Media Exploitation Center, and the Defense Intelligence Operations Coordination Center as well as its own Directorate for Analysis. In all, DIA has more than 16,500 military and civilians in its employ,[80] and it often rivals the CIA as the key intelligence agency within the U.S. government.

The other three agencies under DOD are the **National Security Agency (NSA)**, the **National Reconnaissance Office (NRO)**, and the **National Geospatial-Intelligence Agency (NGA)**. The NSA has responsibility for gathering signal intelligence (or SIGINT) from a variety of electronic and nonelectronic sources in foreign countries and breaking their transmission codes, and for developing secure transmission codes for several American government agencies. It is also responsible for "information assurance" for government agencies—making certain that data and transmission links are secure.[81] The NRO operates as the "nation's eyes and ears in space." Since its establishment as a classified agency in 1961 (and since its declassification in 1992), its "core responsibilities have included overseeing and funding the research and development of reconnaissance spacecraft and their sensors," "procuring the space systems and their associated ground stations, determining launch vehicle requirements . . . , and disseminating the data collected."[82] The NGA develops and analyzes global imagery intelligence. In general, it "develops imagery and map-based intelligence solutions for U.S. national defense, homeland security and safety of navigation." In this sense, NGA not only provides timely "geospatial intelligence in support of national security" but also provides intelligence on homeland security and natural disasters that may arise.[83]

The remaining components of the Intelligence Community are affiliated with other units of government that have foreign policy interests and responsibilities. The **Department of Energy's Office of Intelligence and Counterintelligence** focuses on intelligence related to nuclear issues and nuclear terrorism. The **Department of State's Bureau of Intelligence and Research** provides intelligence analysis of global political developments to the secretary of state and seeks "to provide early warning and in-depth analysis of events and trends that affect US foreign policy and national security interests." The focus of the **Department of Treasury's Office of Intelligence and Analysis**, created only in 2004, is on international financing, especially as it relates to terrorist, insurgents, and rogue state activities (also see Chapter 9). Finally, there is the **Federal Bureau of Investigation**, which has long been a member of the Intelligence Community. In 2005, President Bush created the FBI "National Security Branch (NSB)" within this agency to focus on intelligence analysis, counterterrorism, and counterintelligence, and in 2006 the Weapons of Mass Destruction Directorate was established within the NSB to focus on that issue.[84]

Other Recent Components of the IC   The U.S. Coast Guard became a member of the IC in December 2001, with its **Intelligence and Criminal Investigations Program** responsible for providing the Department of Homeland Security (where the Coast Guard is now housed) with this function. This program's mission is "to direct, coordinate, and oversee intelligence and investigative operations and activities that support all Coast Guard objectives by providing actionable . . . intelligence to strategic decision-makers, as well as operational and tactical commanders."[85] With the establishment of the Department of Homeland Security in 2003, its **Office of Intelligence and Analysis** joined the IC. The office's mission is to use "information and intelligence from multiple sources to identify and assess current and future threats to the United States" and to provide "actionable intelligence to support national and DHS decision-makers." Finally, in 2006, the Drug Enforcement Administration's **Office of National Security Intelligence** was added to the IC. This office provides intelligence gathered from DEA's worldwide drug monitoring network "to enhance U.S. efforts to protect national security, and combat global terrorism, as well as facilitate IC support to DEA's law enforcement mission."[86]

The events of September 11 motivated the addition of these new bureaucratic participants to the IC; however, the two most important structural changes were brought about by presidential executive orders and by the IRTP Act of 2004: (1) the creation of the **director of national intelligence** position and (2) the establishment of the **National Counterterrorism Center** under the director's authority. As Figure 10.2 makes clear, the director of national intelligence (DNI) is at the center of the intelligence community and is now responsible for advising the president, the NSC, other executive branches, the chairman of the JCS, military commanders, and Congress on intelligence matters. He or she is also responsible for overseeing, managing, and, importantly, integrating the entire intelligence community. These responsibilities represent a dramatic change from 1947 (the year the CIA was established under the National Security Act), when the CIA director was also the director of central intelligence (DCI), but, arguably, did not have the range of authority held by the new DNI.

The DNI oversees the IC's deputy directors, who head four directorates—one for managing the intelligence office, a second to focus on data collection, a third to ensure that the technical innovation and new development in intelligence requirements are met, and a fourth to establish high analytic standards. The Office of the DNI has ten functional units to support its intelligence activities. These range from the National Intelligence Council (NIC), which has responsibility for producing timely intelligence "estimates" on current issues and for sharing them with policy makers to the National Counterproliferation Center, which has the responsibility to obtain intelligence "to stem the proliferation of weapons of mass destruction," to the National Intelligence University, which promotes "a more effective and productive Intelligence Community through cross-disciplinary education and joint training," among seven other units.[87]

The National Counterterrorism Center, initially created by a presidential executive order (13354) and then codified into law by the Intelligence Reform and Terror Prevention Act of 2004, also is one of these key units within the DNI organization. It "serve[s] as the primary organization . . . for analyzing and integrating all intelligence" on terrorism and counterterrorism; "conduct[s] strategic operational planning for counterterrorism . . . "; "assign[s] roles and responsibilities" for counterterrorism, although it "shall not direct the execution of any resulting operations"; acts as the repository for information on suspected terrorists and international terror groups; and makes certain that all appropriate departments and agencies have access to the appropriate information for counterterrorism activities.[88]

The exact size and budget of the IC has traditionally been difficult to determine, shrouded as it is in secrecy within DOD funding. Some estimates and budget revelations became available over recent decades and show how its resources have grown. In the early 1970s, the intelligence community consisted of about 150,000 individuals, with a budget in excess of $6 billion annually, and by fiscal year 1980 it was reportedly over $10 billion.[89] In mid-1994, Congress inadvertently published the budget figure for the IC (about $28 billion) in a declassified transcript of a Senate hearing.[90] In the aftermath of the events of September 11, 2001, spending on defense, and on intelligence, increased dramatically. Indeed, in fiscal year 2007, the aggregate spending on intelligence was $43.5 billion, and the Office of the Director of National Intelligence reported that the IC had "approximately 100,000 employees.[91] By fiscal year 2010, the estimate of intelligence spending was more than $80 billion, a figure eight times greater than four decades earlier.[92]

The IC's Role in Policy Making The policy-making impact of the IC stems from its central role in gathering information about international issues and evaluating foreign policy options. Several types of intelligence developed by IC as a whole and by its components (CIA, DIA, and so on) enable it to influence the policy formulation process. These include the several daily briefs it produces for policy makers, among them the **President's Daily Brief (PDB)** and the **Worldwide Intelligence Review (WIRe)** (formerly known as the *Senior Executive Intelligence Brief* and before that as the *National Intelligence Daily*). The *PDB*—"a compilation of current intelligence items of high significance to national policy concerns prepared six days a week"—has highly restricted circulation to only the top governmental officials, whereas the *WIRe* contains a half dozen articles on a variety of subjects and is circulated more broadly within the executive branch.[93] On a regular basis, the IC develops the more familiar, and more comprehensive, intelligence reports, the **National Intelligence Estimates** (NIEs), which are in-depth analyses of a particular country, region, or issue. The number of NIEs completed each year varies by administration and by issue, and the NIEs represent "the DNI's most authoritative judgments concerning national security issues."[94] They are developed and disseminated by the National Intelligence Council (NIC), a group of senior intelligence officials and national intelligence officers (NIOs) for regional areas and functional issues.[95]

Some NIEs have been released in recent years, albeit only the unclassified portions (for example, an estimate on the threat of terrorism to the U.S homeland in July 2007 and another on Iran's nuclear program in November 2007), but most are not made available to the public. At the same time, through some leaks to the press, some information about the assessments entered the public domain. For instance, NIEs were completed on Afghanistan and Pakistan in 2010 and another on Iran in 2011, and the assessments became sources of public debate.[96]

In addition to the NIEs, the intelligence community (and the NIC specifically) produces **Special Estimates** (previously called Special National Intelligence Estimates, or SNIEs). As their name implies, these are responses to current developments around the world. Their number varies from year to year depending on changing global events.

Also distributed to policy makers is a short report on a particular topic known as a **NIC Memorandum**. In addition to these estimates and reports, each of the major intelligence agencies produces its own reports for use and reference by policy makers and analysts.[97]

Assessing the Analytic Side of the Intelligence Community

Despite its numerous reports and analyses, the IC's effectiveness in the policy process remains difficult to gauge because of the secrecy surrounding it. However, as policy makers are heavily dependent on it for information, a reasonable inference is that its influence is quite substantial. Assessments of the IC's analytic capabilities vary widely. In particular, the quality of its work, and how policy makers use it, has come under scrutiny since the events of 9/11 and the Iraq War in 2003. In order to convey a sense of the quality of intelligence and, in turn, to judge the effect of calls for its reforms, we first summarize some of the acclaims and criticisms that the IC has received in recent decades. Only then can we gauge the impact of the recent reform efforts and outline additional changes that may be needed.

Acclaim for the IC's Policy Assessments   More than three decades ago, prominent CIA critics, Victor Marchetti and John D. Marks, hinted at the quality of U.S. intelligence, especially during the Cold War. Although CIA estimates on relative U.S.–USSR strength during those years were not always successful in shaping policy and were subject to abuse on occasion, they argue that these estimates often served as a counterweight to the influence of military planners in debates between the president and Congress. They also point to the success of the agency in gathering intelligence that led to the showdown with the Soviet Union over missiles in Cuba in 1962.[98]

Others also have praised the utility of the CIA's past assessments. One points to the accuracy of its intelligence during early policy making on Southeast Asia—although its recommendations were not always followed by presidents and their advisors.[99] Reportedly, the CIA also correctly assessed the situation in the Middle East just prior to the outbreak of the Six-Day War in 1967, but policy makers were unable to take effective action to prevent this conflict.[100] The IC painted a grim picture of the Soviet economy shortly before the collapse of the Soviet Union, characterizing it as in a "near crisis," and pointed out that some modest decline in Soviet military spending had occurred.[101] Such estimates undoubtedly assisted policy makers in deciding on the degree of U.S. support for perestroika.

Other threads of evidence have emerged that point more directly to the policy influence of the CIA. Prior to the fall of Mohammad Reza Shah in 1979, for example, the agency reportedly exercised considerable influence over U.S. relations with Iran. Because the CIA assisted the Nicaraguan Contras in their opposition to the Sandinista regime, the IC enjoyed a leading role in the formulation of policy in that part of the world as well. Indeed, both the Department of State and the Department of Defense deferred to it for a time, leaving policy largely to the CIA and to key White House allies.[102] Even after Congress cut all American military assistance to the Contras in October 1984, we now know that the CIA and NSC operatives, such as Admiral John Poindexter and Lieutenant Colonel Oliver North, remained active in their support. Yet a third area of the world where the IC played a pivotal role in policy was in Afghanistan after the Soviet invasion in late 1979. The CIA ran an arms-smuggling operation there for several years until the Soviets finally withdrew by early 1989.[103] More recently, the IC in 2007 identified Osama bin Laden's courier, eventually tracked him to a residence in Abbottabod, Pakistan, and ultimately that led to the killing of Osama bin Laden in May 2011.[104]

Criticisms for the IC's Policy Assessment   Yet the IC has also been the object of severe criticism by presidents and others both for the quality of its intelligence and for its efforts to shape foreign policy. President Kennedy, in particular, lost confidence in the CIA over its recommendations, which led to the ill-fated Bay of Pigs invasion.[105] As a result, he was later reluctant to accept the agency's intelligence advice and options on Southeast Asia or the Cuban Missile Crisis and, instead, looked to other agencies and individuals. Later in the 1960s, the CIA was criticized over the loss of the intelligence ship *Liberty* during the Six-Day War in the Middle East and the capture of the Navy spy ship *Pueblo* by the North Koreans in 1968.[106]

In the 1970s, the quality of American intelligence came in for criticism yet again. The IC was criticized over the quality of its information as the Shah of Iran was losing power in 1978. In fact, President Carter was moved to send off a sharply worded memo to his key advisors: "I am not satisfied with the quality of political intelligence."[107] An "Iran Postmortem" report on intelligence lapses over the Iranian revolution of 1979 noted myriad problems in assessing the internal situation of that country and in arriving at sound intelligence estimates: lack of intelligence sources near the Shah or in any of the opposition groups; little discussion of CIA intelligence estimates within the bureaucracy or the airing of disagreements on those estimates; inadequate use of publicly available sources; and conflicting meanings drawn from the words and phrases in them.[108]

As the Cold War was ending, criticisms continued. Questionable intelligence estimates recommended the use of a grain embargo against the Soviet Union over its invasion of Afghanistan, but failed to predict the bombing of the marine barracks in Lebanon in October 1983 that killed 241 Americans. Intelligence lapses over the changing events in Eastern Europe—whether over the opening of the Berlin Wall in November 1989 or the initial reforms within the Soviet Union throughout 1989 and 1990—raised anew doubts about the CIA's analytic abilities. Even the successes during the Persian Gulf War of 1991 did not come without some intelligence failures. Estimates placed the number of Iraqi forces in the Kuwait theater at 540,000 when it was actually closer to 250,000, and the number of mobile Scud launchers at 35 when they totaled nearly 200.[109] More dramatic was the IC's failure to predict the collapse of the Soviet Union in 1991. To be sure, it did predict a Soviet economic slowdown, but it did not see the coming collapse or the political demise of the Soviet Union (although, in fairness, few others did).[110]

Criticism of the IC's analytic abilities probably reached its peak in the aftermath of the events of 9/11 and the initiation of the Iraq War. In a report issued in the summer of 2003, for example, a joint investigation by the two congressional intelligence committees investigating 9/11 noted an array of failings prior to the attacks, but two stood out: (1) available information on the terrorists and on suspicious activity by others had not been fully examined or utilized; and (2) information was inadequately shared among the CIA, FBI, NSA, and others beforehand.[111] *The 9/11 Commission Report* also pointed to these two problems: members of the intelligence community had gathered many fragmentary pieces of evidence about the 9/11 hijackers, their movements, and their intentions, but the lack of full cooperation and legal restrictions on some types of cooperation among the various components of the intelligence community made it difficult to piece the puzzle together. Yet, the report also acknowledged that some "luck" (as well as skill) would have been necessary to succeed in uncovering the hijackers with the available evidence.[112]

In the months leading up to the March 2003 war with Iraq (and even after it), controversy and criticism surrounded the IC and its assessments of that country's development of nuclear weapons. In his 2003 State of the Union Address, President Bush claimed that Iraq had sought to purchase uranium from Niger and used that claim to bolster his case that Iraq was developing nuclear weapons. Indeed, an October 2002 NIE had stated that "a foreign government service reported" on a possible arrangement between Iraq and Niger (and possibly two other countries), but it also noted that "we cannot confirm whether Iraq succeeded in acquiring uranium ore and/or yellowcake from these sources."[113] Despite this assessment (and a footnote in the NIE stating that the State Department was dubious of such a claim), Bush used the assessment. In July 2003, when the British House of Commons stated that the initial report about Niger was wrong, the administration was forced to retract the "16 words" from the State of the Union Address, and the director of central intelligence assumed responsibility for failing to delete this reference from the prepared text.[114] Overall, then, concerns have been raised over both the quality of intelligence analysis and the way in which intelligence assessments were being used by policy makers.

Some Reasons for Intelligence Problems   Several factors seem to account for the intelligence and policy failures over the years. One factor focuses on the **quality of intelligence** produced by IC analysts. As one of President George H. W. Bush's advisors put it with reference to the changes in Eastern Europe in the late 1980s and early 1990s, the CIA was "good at analyzing trends" and "poor at predicting the timing of events . . ." Testifying before Congress after the bombing of the American military complex in Saudi Arabia in the summer of 1996, Secretary of Defense William Perry pointed to another drawback of intelligence analyses: "The intelligence was not useful at a tactical level. It didn't specify the nature of the threat or the timing of the threat, and therefore it was not what we might call actionable intelligence in terms of doing our planning."[115] Another former CIA official raised questions about the adequacy of "fact-checking" by CIA analysts and possible exaggeration in the increasingly popular oral briefings of policy makers.[116] The general issue surrounding the quality of intelligence analysis was bluntly stated by a former Defense Department official: "The CIA's analysts 'collect a lot of facts and organize them very nicely. But their predictions are wrong.'"[117]

A second factor is the **excessive reliance on technology** in assessments at the expense of human intelligence and analysis. With the increasing use of satellites and electronic interception of messages, for example, there has been less reliance on agents in the field. Even those who are at work are criticized as either too timid (more interested in protecting their reputation than in taking risks) or overzealous (too often driven by ideological bias). Further, some intelligence analysts lack necessary skills. Although political analysts are plentiful, those with sociological and anthropological backgrounds, who can assess more fully the changes occurring in a foreign society, are not.[118] Evaluating the determination of Saddam Hussein and his Revolutionary Council to keep Kuwait, as well as estimating the loss of morale in the Iraqi military caused by the U.S. air war, required more than electronic intelligence in the Gulf War of 1991. Similarly, assessing al-Qaeda or similar terrorist organizations and their capabilities and intentions requires more than technical surveillance if attacks like September 11 are to be stopped or if attacks on U.S. soldiers in Afghanistan are to be prevented. To be sure, the IC recently enhanced human intelligence, but more will need to be done.

A third factor for the failure of intelligence is **competition among the various bureaucracies**. As one official noted, "In intelligence, what you foresee is often affected by where you work."[119] Indeed, the DIA's intelligence estimates are often different from the CIA's. During the Cold War, the DIA tended to be more hawkish on Soviet intentions than the CIA, and the two agencies sparred over estimates in particular regions (such as the likelihood of Soviet success in Afghanistan) or particular weapons systems (such as the capabilities of Soviet air defenses).[120] Such competing estimates occur more frequently as more diverse actors and issues complicate global politics than they did during the Cold War. In the months prior to the Iraq War, intelligence from the State Department on the danger that Iraq posed differed from that provided by the Department of Defense. Similarly, the assessments over the policies to pursue, whether over the situation in Iran or North Korea also differ by the bureaucracies and analysts involved. Under such circumstances, estimates sent to policy makers may simply become "compromises" between or among several intelligence bureaucracies, or they may allow policy makers to simply choose the one that fits most favorably with their ideology or prior beliefs.

Yet a fourth factor often identified for intelligence shortcomings is the **structure of leadership within the IC**. Until the reforms of 2004, the director of the CIA was also the head of the IC as a whole, which, as previously outlined, cuts across many foreign policy bureaucracies. Therefore, the degree to which the director could be an honest broker was called into question, whether in distilling intelligence estimates or in assigning areas of responsibility. With this kind of organizational structure, the IC's "product" was not always as useful as it might have been. Indeed, the need for separating these two roles as a necessary reform was known for some time.[121]

A final factor for intelligence shortcomings, analyst Robert Jervis argues, is the **inherent conflict between intelligence officials and policy makers**.[122] The aim of policy makers, for "both political and psychological reasons," is to obtain intelligence to reinforce their preferred policy views. The IC's aim is to produce assessments "to support better policy," not to promote a particular policy stance. Numerous factors account for this inherent conflict—(1) the "perseverance" and "confidence" that policy makers maintain in their preferred policy versus the willingness of the IC to consider alternative options, (2) differing worldviews of the two groups and their impacts on interpreting information that they receive, and (3) the timing of intelligence information provided by the IC to policy makers, either too early or too late in the process (as opposed to just right). In this sense, the IC and policy makers "are doomed to work together and to come into conflict."

Efforts at Intelligence Reform

Problems with the IC and the need for reform have long been on the agenda in Washington. Indeed, virtually all recent presidents made attempts to address them, largely without notable success. President Clinton made some structural and procedural changes, but they ultimately did not address the IC's underlying problems. Presidential Decision Directive 24, for example, abolished an existing counterintelligence facility and established a new National Counterintelligence Policy Board that would report to the president through the national security advisor and would be led by senior representatives from the NSC, the CIA, the FBI, the DOD, the Department of State, the Department of Justice, and a military service with a counterintelligence unit. The same directive created a National Counterintelligence Center, consisting of members from the FBI, the CIA, the DOD, and the military services, whose task would be to coordinate counterintelligence activities within the government. These new structures also called for closer collaboration between the FBI and the CIA in addressing counterintelligence problems.[123]

At this same time, Congress instituted changes in the intelligence community. It established a new conditional fund for covert operations, provided funds specifically for a covert operation against Iran, and pushed for the purchase of new small spy satellites to improve analytic capabilities. Yet Congress also slowed efforts to consolidate the intelligence agencies,[124] and so the structure and operation of the IC were not fundamentally altered.

After the events of September 11, however, there was a crescendo of calls to investigate what had allowed them to happen as well as to identify necessary actions to prevent such attacks in the future. Several immediate changes were made. One response was congressional passage of the **USA PATRIOT Act** in October 2001, which granted the executive branch, and particularly the IC, more investigatory tools to pursue terrorist suspects. The act narrowed some domestic civil liberties, however, and thus sparked protest. (Still, the Bush and Obama administrations have renewed the legislation, largely intact, to the present.)

A second response for intelligence reform after 9/11 came in the form of a series of recommendations by the congressional intelligence committees.[125] Their July 2003 report called for a sweeping restructuring of the IC to provide greater coordination and cooperation among its various components, and it set forth a number of specific actions for strengthening U.S. counterterrorism activities. On a structural level, the report called for Congress to make the following changes, among others:

- The creation of a statutory position of director of national intelligence that would have full authority over the entire intelligence community. The creation of a national intelligence officer for terrorism who would sit on the National Intelligence Council to make certain that terrorism received sustained attention.

- The establishment of "an effective all-source terrorism information fusion center" within the Department of Homeland Security.

- The director of national intelligence be mandated to upgrade the skill levels of intelligence personnel in counterterrorism, to promote greater information sharing among intelligence personnel and to upgrade language capabilities.

On an operational level, the report called for the following, among others:

- "[A]ction to ensure that clear, consistent, and current priorities are established and enforced throughout the intelligence community"

- The development of a comprehensive government strategy to combat terrorism

- Improvement of domestic intelligence capacities and performance of the FBI

About a year later, additional recommendations for overhauling the intelligence community came from the **National Commission on Terrorist Attacks Upon the United States** (or the **9/11 Commission**), which had been established when President Bush signed the intelligence authorization legislation for FY2003. Headed by former New Jersey governor Thomas Kean and former congressman Lee Hamilton, this commission had as its mission to prepare "a full and complete accounting of the circumstances surrounding the September 11, 2001 terrorist attacks" and to "provide recommendations to guard against future attacks."[126]

The commission's report set out forty-one recommendations for addressing terrorism worldwide, including five directed specifically at improving the structure and operation of the intelligence community:

- Unifying strategic intelligence and operational planning against Islamist terrorists across the foreign–domestic divide with a National Counterterrorism Center
- Unifying the intelligence community with a new national intelligence director
- Unifying the many participants in the counterterrorism effort and their knowledge in a network-based information-sharing system that transcends traditional governmental boundaries
- Unifying and strengthening congressional oversight to improve quality and accountability; and
- Strengthening the FBI and other homeland defenders[127]

These general recommendations led to twelve specific recommendations for improving the structure and process of the IC, many of which were consistent with the intelligence committees' recommendations (such as the creation of a national intelligence director and a national terrorism center). The commission report emphasized the need for better integration of the agencies in the IC and the need for wider sharing of intelligence information. One specific recommendation called for "rebuilding the CIA's analytic capabilities," enhancing "the human intelligence capabilities" of the clandestine service, improving the language capabilities and the diversity of officers, and "ensuring a seamless relationship between human resource collections and signal collection at the operational level."[128] It also called for a separate and open appropriations process for intelligence and the creation of either a joint committee on intelligence or two separate intelligence committees (with the power of appropriating) to enhance congressional oversight.[129] Finally, the commission recommended changes in the FBI to move it more fully into recruiting and training "a specialized and integrated national security workforce" that would complement its other components, and work on "the development of an institutional culture imbued with a deep expertise in intelligence and national security."[130]

Positive responses to these recommendations came relatively quickly, although their full implementation took longer. President Bush issued four executive orders in August 2004 that strengthened the management role of the CIA director over the community until a national intelligence director could be created, established the counterterrorism center, directed greater sharing of information among intelligence agencies, and established a presidential board to safeguard civil liberties in this new environment.[131] In December 2004, Congress passed the **Intelligence Reform and Terrorism Prevention Act (IRTP)**, which put into law the president's executive orders. For the most part, it incorporated the twelve intelligence recommendations from the *9/11 Commission Report*, although there was no mention of reforming congressional oversight arrangements.[132] In the summer of 2007, the Democratic Congress passed the September 11 Commission bill, which included many commission recommendations that had not been included in the earlier legislation. With the passage of this bill, the vice chair of the 9/11 Commission, Lee Hamilton, said that 80 percent of the commission's recommendations were now enacted.[133] Making them work and seeing that they made a difference in the IC operations remained as future tasks.

Some Recent Assessments of Intelligence Reform

To date, the record implementing these recommendations and reforms is mixed. By one analysis, the major structural changes in the IC—the creation of the director of national intelligence and the creation of the Counterterrorism Center—have not been as successful as originally envisioned when the presidential executive orders were issued and when Congress passed the IRTP Act of 2004.[134] The director of national intelligence, at a February 2008 hearing, acknowledged as much when he noted that his authority was not as substantial as the title "director" might imply. "I currently have the title of director, but the authorities created in the statute and executive order put me more in the middle of [leadership] options—coordination and integration—rather than director with directive authority."[135] Only over the CIA does the DNI have direct controlling authority; the remaining members of the IC ultimately answer to a cabinet secretary (such as the secretary of defense or the secretary of homeland security). Furthermore, there is some evidence that the DOD, the largest component of the IC, has been resistant to intelligence officers gaining experience in "joint duty status," as required by congressional legislation, and the DNI has had difficulty challenging that resistance.[136] Finally, and importantly, the DNI's budget authority is ambiguous, causing traditional turf battles and further delays in making changes.[137]

The tenth anniversary report on the 9/11 recommendations largely echoed some of these earlier concerns. Although the 2011 report acknowledges that the DNI "has increased information sharing, improved coordination among agencies, sharpened collection priorities" and made other improvement, it questioned whether the DNI is "the driving force for intelligence community integration." Indeed, it called for strengthening the DNI authority over budget and personnel, "whether through legislation or with repeated declarations from the president." Moreover, this problem of authority for the DNI has been exacerbated by having four DNIs in the first six years of the IRTP.[138]

The National Counterterrorism Center, too, was initially slow to become operative after presidential and congressional action and also came in for some criticism. At least two factors seemed to account for the slow pace of its development. First, and as noted, the DNI has limited authority to move personnel. This, of course, is a crucial lack because the purpose of the center was to integrate personnel from the larger community. Second, and equally significant, the ability of center personnel to cooperate and share information has been hampered by "rules and regulations governing who may see what intelligence data."[139] After the attempted Christmas Day bombing in 2009, for example, the National Counterterrorism Center was criticized for its inability to connect the dots over that incident and whether it had access to intercepts from the National Security Agency about this potential terrorist bomber.[140]

In this sense, then, operational success was initially viewed as modest by critics, but a more recent assessment points to substantial improvement in interagency cooperation. In 2008, an early assessment of the reforms found that "the intelligence agencies still don't work together and share their discoveries." That is, the "culture" of cooperation is still lacking across components of the intelligence community. Furthermore, the FBI has been slow to move toward the counterterrorism mission as originally intended by the reform legislation.[141] The tenth anniversary report on the 9/11 Commission recommendations, however, offers a more positive view by noting the "intelligence community transformation." That is, "progress among national agencies, and between the IC and the military in the field, has been striking . . . the level of cooperation among all levels of government is higher than ever . . . [and] the FBI has gone through dramatic change and continues to transform from an agency overwhelmingly focused on law enforcement to one that prioritizes preventing terrorism."[142]

Still, this same report noted that other areas remained to be addressed by the president, Congress, or both in terms of strengthening intelligence (and homeland security) operations in line with the original 9/11 recommendations. The report highlights three areas that seem particularly important for improving intelligence activities and oversight. Pointedly, the report notes that "congressional oversight for intelligence—and counterterrorism—is now dysfunctional." The 9/11 Commission had recommended that either a joint committee for intelligence or separate House and Senate committees that had both authorizing and appropriating powers over this jurisdiction be created. To date, Congress has done neither. Similarly, the recommendation for a board to oversee adherence to privacy and civil liberties concerns has not been fully implemented. Although the Obama administration has taken some actions, the authors of the report indicated that "the implementation of this recommendation would receive a failing mark." Finally, the report notes that the original recommendation on developing a common approach among friends and allies for dealing with "the detention and humane treatment of captured terrorists" has not been accomplished. The Obama administration made some strides in this direction, but Congress should place an agreed approach between the two branches of government "in a firm statutory basis."[143]

In sum, these reforms are a start in improving the structure and operation of the intelligence community, and they do represent more substantial changes in intelligence operations than those enacted previously. Still, as this discussion suggests, more legislation, stronger leadership (or the granting of appropriate authority to leaders), and a sustained integrative intelligence culture remain the tasks ahead. At the same time, as two former CIA officials noted, it is "unreasonable to expect 100 percent success" in the intelligence business.[144] Intelligence analyst Richard Betts delivered a similar message in discussing the "inherent enemies of intelligence," such as "a collection of mental limitations, dilemmas, contradictory imperatives, paradoxical interactions, and trade-offs among objectives" that may lead to intelligence shortcomings.[145] In this sense, future administrations will continue to grapple with improving the analytic side of intelligence, even as they will need to recognize the human limits involved in the process.

CIA "SPECIAL ACTIVITIES" AND POLICY INFLUENCE

Although analysis is a crucial IC component, it is not the only one. The other component consists of **covert operations**, and it, too, has often been criticized for its lack of accountability and control and for its considerable influence on the direction of U.S. foreign policy. Indeed, some critics have called for the elimination of these operations, on both policy and ethical grounds. They are not effective, these critics contend, and they are inconsistent with the ethical standards of the American people.[146]

Yet American covert intelligence operations, or "special activities," as they are euphemistically called, are far more numerous than we often think, and they form important aspects of foreign policy making. They have included propaganda campaigns, secret electoral campaign assistance, sabotage, assisting in the overthrow of unfriendly governments, and even, apparently, attempts at assassination of foreign officials. Covertly supplying funds to Afghan tribal groups to fight the Taliban in the fall of 2001 illustrates one type of covert action; sending covert operatives into Iraq three months prior to the 2003 war "to forge alliances with Iraqi military leaders and persuade commanders not to fight"[147] represents another; and conducting drone strikes in the tribal areas of Pakistan epitomizes yet another.

Many times, these covert activities involve counterintelligence—activities "concerned with protecting the government's secrets."[148] Part of this work involves such mundane efforts as classifying sensitive documents to keep them out of the public domain and providing adequate physical security for American secrets. Another part of counterintelligence involves infiltrating the intelligence services of foreign governments, subverting and blackmailing agents through unethical means, and using measures to thwart the techniques that are being used against the United States.

Such covert (and not so covert) operations immediately raise questions about their **compatibility with democratic values and ethical standards** as well as about how accountable agents are for their actions. The public has often been divided on the wisdom of covert operations and has expressed this uneasiness in public opinion polls. In 1995, for example, 48 percent thought covert operations were acceptable but 40 percent did not.[149] After 9/11, however, the public seemingly became more supportive of at least one type of activity. In a 2002 survey, 66 percent "favor[ed] the assassination of individual terrorist leaders" (although the question did not specify whether this should be done overtly or covertly). When the same question was asked two years later, 68 percent supported this option, and the 2010 results for this question showed 73 percent support.[150] Still, for most administrations over the years, any public ambivalence about or support for covert operations has apparently not mattered much, as such activities have been widely used. As we shall see, though, they have occasionally raised serious concerns about accountability among policy makers and the American people.

Origins and Use of Covert Operations

Under the National Security Act of 1947, the CIA was authorized not only to collect intelligence but also **"to perform such other functions and duties related to intelligence** . . . as the National Security Council may from time to time direct."[151] By successive directives from the NSC and succeeding presidents, it has continued to have that imperative. In President Reagan's 1981 executive order (still the one operating today, albeit amended during the George W. Bush administration), a covert operation is defined as

> an activity or activities of the United States Government to influence political, economic, or military conditions abroad, where it is intended that the role of the United States government will not be apparent or acknowledged publicly . . .

As this directive suggests, the mandate is broad and open-ended, but this executive order does expressly prohibit a covert action "which is intended to influence United State political processes, public opinion, policies, or media."[152]

The appeal of these measures for various presidents is unmistakable: "Clandestine operations can appear to the President as a panacea, as a way of pulling the chestnuts out of the fire without going through all the effort and aggravation of tortuous diplomatic negotiations. And if the CIA is somehow caught in the act, the deniability of these operations, in theory, saves a President from taking any responsibility—or blame."[153] In other words, they are not designed to be traceable to the White House.

The use of covert activities has indeed been substantial since World War II, even if their exact number is not readily available. According to the 1977 final report of the **Senate Select Committee on Intelligence Activities** (or **the Church Committee**, named after its chair, Senator Frank Church of Idaho), which investigated CIA covert activities over the postwar period:

> **[C]overt actions operations have not been an exceptional instrument used only in rare instances**. . . . On the contrary, presidents and administrations have made excessive, and at times self-defeating, use of covert action. In addition, covert action has become a routine program with a bureaucratic momentum of its own.[154]

The Church Committee reported that between 1949 and 1952, the director of central intelligence approved some 81 covert projects. In the Eisenhower administration, 104 were approved; in the Kennedy administration, 163; and in the Johnson administration, 142.[155]

Yet the exact totals go well beyond these numbers, as evidenced by a 1967 CIA memorandum that noted that only 16 percent of covert operations received approval from a special committee set up to monitor them. By yet another estimate, several thousand covert actions were undertaken from 1961 on, with only 14 percent reviewed by the NSC or its committees.[156] The justifications for undertaking covert operations have greatly expanded as well, "from containing International (and presumably monolithic) Communism in the early 1950s, to merely serving as an adjunct to American foreign policy in the 1970s."[157]

Covert operations were an important instrument of foreign policy for the Reagan administration and remained so for subsequent administrations. As Reagan's former national security advisor, Robert McFarlane, noted, the United States must have an option between going to war and taking no action when a friendly nation is threatened. In McFarlane's view, there must be something between "total peace" and "total war" in foreign policy.[158] Covert activity seemed to fit that middle category for a number of American administrations. Brent Scowcroft, President George H. W. Bush's national security advisor, publicly endorsed covert actions several years before serving in that role: "In many cases, covert action is the most effective, easiest way to accomplish foreign policy objectives. It is only effective if it remains covert."[159]

There is no evidence to suggest that this view has not continued during the George W. Bush and Obama administrations. One of CIA director George Tenet's first actions immediately after the 9/11 attacks, for example, was to outline for President Bush and his advisors a plan for "a full-scale covert attack on the financial underpinnings of the terrorist network, including clandestine computer surveillance and electronic eavesdropping to locate the assets of al-Qaeda and other terrorist groups." He presented a draft intelligence finding "that would give the CIA power to use the full range of covert instruments, including deadly force" against these adversaries. And he produced a document outlining "covert operations in 80 countries either underway or that he was now recommending" in the war against terrorism.[160]

The Obama administration has continued the emphasis on using covert operations, epitomized by the Navy Seals' assault on a compound in Abbottabod, Pakistan, and killing of Osama bin Laden in May 2011 at this hideout, but it is hardly confined to that example. Instead, the administration has relied routinely on covert operations to address its foreign policy objectives—whether through a substantial increase in drone strikes at terrorist camps in Pakistan and Yemen over the last several years; the development of a list of suspected terrorists to target for kill or capture, presumably by clandestine means; or through the highly secret cyber attacks on Iran's nuclear enrichment facilities that was code-named "Olympic Games."[161] More generally, the Obama administration identified an increased reliance on special operations in its 2010 Quadrennial Defense Review and implied as much in its 2012 Strategic Defense Guidance.

In sum, special (and covert) operations became an important staple of U.S. policy during the Cold War, and they remain important. **Indeed, covert operations have probably increased over the past decade.**

ACCOUNTABILITY AND COVERT ACTIONS

The Church Committee report, along with several other investigations, questioned the degree of **political accountability** for covert operations. Because the lines of accountability were not always operating, and because the CIA often carried on special activities without the full approval of the government, particularly the White House, its influence on policy was substantial, seemingly in effect to shape it.

Such discretionary powers were in operation from the agency's beginning. In the initial 1947 NSC directive on covert operations (NSC-4), no formal guidelines were established for their approval or coordination. The only requirement was that the director of central intelligence be certain, "through liaison with State and Defense, that [they] were consistent with American policy." At best, the NSC required consultation with State and Defense; it required none with the president or his representative. From 1949 to 1952, then, the director apparently granted approval for covert operations without assistance.[162]

Even when clear NSC directives were issued for committee approval of covert operations (beginning in 1955), the procedures were not without loopholes. As a CIA memorandum in 1967 reports:

> The procedures to be followed in determining which CA [covert action] operations required approval by the Special Group or by the Department of State and the other arms of the U.S. government were, during the period 1955 to March, 1963, somewhat cloudy, and thus can probably best be described as having been based on value judgments by the DCI [Director of Central Intelligence].[163]

New directives were issued in 1963 and 1970, but slippage in accountability continued. Not all covert actions were discussed and approved by the new NSC "Forty" Committee (established to review and monitor covert operations). Nor were they always coordinated with the Departments of State and Defense.[164]

Coupled with this weakness in executive branch accountability for CIA activities was the lack of any greater accountability by Congress during most of the post–World War II years. Although in principle the Armed Services and the Appropriation committees in the House and the Senate had oversight responsibility (and the CIA argued that it reported fully to the appropriate subcommittees), in practice the CIA was under only "nominal legislative surveillance" throughout much of the Cold War.[165] Committee chairs did not want to know of, or did not make concerted efforts to monitor, its activities. Congress as a whole as well seemed reluctant to make significant inquiries.

In this way, the CIA could by itself begin to shape U.S. foreign policy, although perhaps not directly. Without adequate accountability or control, it could take actions that might be outside the basic lines of American policy or, at the very least, might create difficulties for the overt foreign policy of the government, particularly once covert actions were revealed. In this sense, the influence of the covert side of the intelligence community could be quite substantial. The exact significance of this influence cannot be fully determined, owing once again to the secrecy surrounding its operation.

The Hughes–Ryan Amendment

By the early 1970s, several key events weakened congressional acquiescence to CIA covert operations and ultimately produced more congressional oversight. First was the failed Bay of Pigs invasion of Cuba in 1961, which was almost solely a CIA-designed operation and resulted in President Kennedy's increasing suspicion of reliance on the agency in policy formulation. Second was the Vietnam War, which produced a large increase in CIA covert operations and in turn more congressional interest. Third was the CIA's suspected involvement in destabilizing the Chilean government of Salvador Allende, which raised more questions about its activity. Finally, there was the "Watergate atmosphere" of 1972–1974, which emboldened Congress to challenge executive power across a wide spectrum, including intelligence activities.[166]

The first result of this new congressional interest was the Hughes–Ryan Amendment to the 1974 Foreign Assistance Act, sponsored by Senator Harold Hughes (D-Iowa) and Representative Leo Ryan (D-California). This amendment imposed some control on the initiation and use of covert activities. Its key passage is worth quoting in full:

> No funds appropriated under the authority of this or any other Act may be expended by or on behalf of the Central Intelligence Agency for operations in foreign countries, other than activities intended solely for obtaining necessary intelligence, unless and until the President finds that each such operation is important to the national security of the United States and reports, in a timely fashion, a description and scope of such operation to the appropriate committees of the Congress.[167]

Thus Hughes–Ryan required that the president be informed about covert operations (hence eliminating the "plausible denial" argument) and that he certify that each operation be "important to the national security of the United States." Further, it directed the president to report, "in a timely fashion," any operation to the "appropriate" committees of Congress. This meant the Armed Services and Appropriation committees in the House and the Senate, the Senate Foreign Relations Committee, the House Foreign Affairs Committee, and, later, the Senate and House intelligence committees, established in 1976 and 1977, respectively.

Two investigations by the executive and legislative branches recommended several other changes in intelligence operations monitoring: an executive-ordered inquiry into intelligence activities in 1975 (the Rockefeller Commission) and a legislative inquiry by the Senate in 1975 and 1976 (the Church Committee). Both called for several substantive and procedural changes in the CIA, especially regarding covert operations. New legislative acts were proposed for gaining greater oversight through joint or separate intelligence committees, through the establishment of an intelligence community charter, and through more stringent control over covert actions. The investigations also recommended consideration of a more open budgeting process, a limitation on the term of the directorship of the CIA, and consideration of appointing a director from outside the organization.[168]

Aside from the establishment of intelligence committees in each house of Congress, few of these recommendations actually became law; some, however, were incorporated in executive orders issued by Presidents Ford and Carter. In 1976, President Ford's recommendations spelled out the lines of authority over covert operations and expressly prohibited political assassination as an instrument of U.S. policy. President Carter's recommendations, in 1978, ordered the reorganization of the IC and some additional reforms.[169] Again, few reforms were translated into statutes, but the various proposals did call attention to the accountability of the IC as a whole and especially to its covert side.

The Intelligence Oversight Act of 1980

Despite efforts at greater control, the IC and its allies were successful in preventing any further legislative restrictions—most notably, proposed legislation to establish an IC charter. In fact, by 1980, the IC was able to persuade Congress to modify the Hughes–Ryan Amendment and its reporting requirements and to pass legislation that was deemed more workable.

This legislation, the Intelligence Oversight Act of 1980, retained the Hughes–Ryan provision that the president must issue a "**finding**" for each covert operation, but modified its reporting requirements. (An intelligence finding was a statement, later required to be written, in which a covert operation was defined and in which the president certified that the operation was "important to the national security of the United States.") Now, the executive branch (either the director of central intelligence or the appropriate agency head) was required to **report only to the Senate Select Committee on Intelligence and the House Permanent Select Committee on Intelligence**.[170] However, *prior notification* of all covert operations was specified in the law and not simply "in a timely fashion," as required by Hughes–Ryan. The act further required that the executive branch report to the committees any intelligence failures and any illegal intelligence activities as well as any measures undertaken to correct them.

Some reporting discretion was afforded to the president by two exemptions included in the statute. First, if the president deemed that a covert operation was vital to national security, he could limit prior notification to a smaller group (the "**Gang of Eight**," as they came to be called) listed in the statute: the chairs and the ranking minority members of the House and Senate intelligence committees, the speaker and the minority leader of the House, and the majority and minority leaders of the Senate. Even in these exceptional instances, though, the president was required ultimately to inform the entire intelligence committees "in a timely fashion."

A second more oblique, and potentially more troubling, exemption was incorporated, specifying that reporting of covert operations was to be followed "to the extent consistent with all applicable authorities and duties, including those conferred by the Constitution upon the executive and legislative branches of the Government." Although the meaning of this passage is purposefully vague, it invites the executive branch to claim constitutional prerogatives on the information it will share with the legislative branch. (And, indeed, the Reagan administration apparently invoked this exemption to defend its delay in disclosing covert operations in the Iran–Contra affair.)

With the Intelligence Oversight Act of 1980, a balance seemed to have been struck between the requirements of secrecy, as demanded by the IC and the executive branch, and those of public accountability, as sought by Congress and the American people. The IC won the repeal of the Hughes–Ryan legislative requirements, which it disliked, and Congress won the right to prior knowledge of covert actions except in rare instances.

The Iran–Contra Affair: Failed Accountability
of a Covert Operation

In late 1986, revelations surrounding the Iran–Contra affair raised questions about how accountable covert operations were to congressional directives such as the Intelligence Oversight Act. After Congress had cut off CIA funds to the Nicaraguan **Contras** through passage of the **Boland Amendment** (see Chapter 8), and after the seizure of several American hostages in Lebanon in the early 1980s, members of the Reagan administration initiated covert operations that would both assist the Contras and help free the American hostages in Lebanon through arms sales to Iran. Without President Reagan's knowledge (according to his testimony), these two operations were linked when a portion of the arms sales profits to Iran were funneled to the Contras. These actions unfolded from 1984 to 1986 with no congressional accountability or knowledge. Indeed, the House and Senate intelligence committees were kept in the dark until CIA Director William Casey testified before them on November 21, 1986.

A Failure to Comply with Existing Statutes　Critics charged that the Iran–Contra episode was an example of the executive branch's failure to comply with the requirements of the Boland Amendment and the Intelligence Oversight Act. Indeed, the joint report of the House and Senate select committees investigating this episode found several violations of legislative statutes and agreed-on congressional–executive procedures.[171] First, contrary to the prohibitions in the Boland Amendment, CIA and NSC staff in the Reagan administration established a private organization (called "the Enterprise") "to engage in covert activities on behalf of the United States." Second, the covert arms sales to Iran were carried out in a manner inconsistent with the Intelligence Oversight Act in that intelligence findings were neither properly prepared nor approved by the president in all instances; they also were not reported to Congress "in a timely fashion." Third, the transfer to the Nicaraguan Contras of a portion of the funds from the arms sales to Iran was inconsistent with government policy. Not only did it violate the Boland Amendment regarding military aid to the Contras but also it was carried out largely outside the established channels of government and represented a significant privatization of U.S. covert operations.

Recommendations of the Investigating Committees　The investigating committees further found that the episode "resulted from the failure of individuals to observe the law, not from deficiencies in existing law or in our system of governance." Therefore, their "principal recommendations . . . [were] not for new laws but for a renewal of the commitment to the constitutional government and sound processes of decision making." Nonetheless, the committees suggested that "some changes in law, particularly relating to oversight of covert operations" might be in order. First, intelligence finding should be in writing and reported in that form to Congress "prior to the commencement of a covert action except in rare instances and in no event later than 48 hours after a Finding is approved." They should include the names of all U.S. agencies involved in such operations, prohibit NSC members from participating, be limited to one-year duration, and inform all NSC members of them. Additionally, no finding should recommend illegal actions. Second, a series of executive branch changes should be made in monitoring the participation of private individuals involved in covert operations, in preserving executive documents of such operations, and in strengthening treaties regarding foreign bank records of U.S.

individuals so that the executive and congressional branches could gain access to them. Third, Congress should take steps to improve its oversight capacity by reviewing the adequacy of contempt statutes currently on the books, the effectiveness of several laws dealing with arms sales and arms transfers, and congressional procedures for safeguarding classified information.

CHANGES IN ACCOUNTABILITY FROM IRAN–CONTRA TO TODAY

Prior to the final report of the two investigating committees, President Reagan issued a **new directive** outlining several changes, all but one of which conformed with the committees' recommendations.[172] First, all executive branch agencies (and private individuals) participating in covert operations were ordered to report in the same manner as currently required of the CIA. Second, an intelligence finding was to be in writing and completed before the operation began, except when an "extreme emergency" arose. Third, oral and retroactive findings were no longer to be permitted—and all findings were to be available to members of the NSC, thus ensuring that the secretary of state and the secretary of defense would be informed of such operations. And fourth, all findings were to be limited in duration and periodically reviewed.

Concerning the notification of Congress, President Reagan's directive did not necessarily tighten reporting requirements; instead, it opened up the possibility of even more delay. That is, Reagan pledged that his administration would notify Congress within two working days after a covert operation had begun, "in all but the most exceptional circumstances," thus raising a real possibility that the reporting of more and more covert operations would be delayed until after they had begun.

In 1988 and 1989, Congress enacted several legislative remedies as a result of the Iran–Contra affair. The first dealt with "third parties" transferring American supplies to another country and specifically required that the president allow Congress thirty days to pass legislation to block such transfers. The second strengthened prohibitions on the sales of arms to countries supporting global terrorism. The third required the president to appoint an independent inspector general for the CIA as one mechanism for closer monitoring of covert actions. And the fourth, added to a foreign aid appropriations bill, prohibited the use of such aid as a lever to gain support for foreign policy actions (such as aiding the Contras).[173]

Current Covert Accountability Rules: The Intelligence Authorization Act of 1991

Through the Intelligence Authorization Act of 1991, Congress ultimately enacted new and more complete legal procedures to govern covert operations. These are the standard still in effect today.[174] In essence, these procedures finally put into statute some of the changes that were originally part of President Reagan's 1987 executive order, albeit in a more flexible way. Regarding covert operations and congressional oversight, the act[175]

- Provided the first legal definition of a covert operation
- Required that the president approve, via a written finding, all covert activity by any executive agency
- Outlawed all retroactive findings of covert actions

- Allowed the use of third parties to carry out covert operations if the intelligence committees were notified
- Generally required prior notification of the intelligence committees of all covert operations

This last requirement had two exceptions. The first was the same one outlined in the Intelligence Oversight Act of 1980: "If the President determines that it is essential to limit access to the [intelligence] finding to meet extraordinary circumstances affecting vital interests of the United States," the finding may be shared only with the so-called "Gang of Eight" leaders in the House and the Senate. The second was much broader. A finding may be withheld from the intelligence committee, without a time limit, and only require the president to inform the committee in a "timely fashion and to . . . provide a statement of the reasons for not giving prior notice." Finally, the legislation specifically required that a copy of the intelligence finding be provided to the chairs of the intelligence committees and that no fund shall be expended until the finding "has been signed or otherwise issued . . ."

Covert Actions and the War on Terrorism

Although the 1991 legislation provided a statutory basis for congressional oversight on covert operations, it did not cover or anticipate that range of issues that might arise. Two other covert intelligence issues arose in the aftermath of the events of September 11. One involved the use of **warrantless wiretapping** to obtain information and highlights the tension between individual liberties and intelligence activities. The other involved **special operations** conducted by the military, and whether they require the same accountability sought for covert operations conducted by the CIA.

The first issue involved the Bush administration's easing of the requirements in the **Foreign Intelligence Surveillance Act (FISA) of 1978** regarding the use of warrantless wiretaps against those suspected of terrorist involvement. After 9/11, President Bush ordered such wiretaps of those suspected of having ties to international terrorism, based on his constitutional powers in Article II and on Congress's passage of the Authorization for Use of Military Force (AUMF) resolution (see Chapter 7). (This action was contrary to the requirement that the government seek approval for warrantless wiretaps from the Foreign Intelligence Surveillance Court.) When this order was revealed, it encountered public opposition over its civil liberties implications and attracted attention in Congress. In 2007, Congress passed legislation altering FISA to allow the electronic surveillance of "a person reasonably believed to be located outside the United States" if the attorney general and the director of national intelligence completed a certification that met several criteria. This change was sunset to expire in early 2008 and was initially not renewed by the Democratic Congress.[176] In July 2008, however, the Bush administration succeeded in persuading Congress to pass a measure that gave "the executive branch broader latitude in eavesdropping on people abroad and at home who it believes are tied to terrorism." Furthermore, the legislation "reduce[d] the role" of the FISA court and provided legal immunity to telecommunication companies cooperating with the government wiretapping programs.[177]

Still, the controversy over electronic surveillance remained for the Obama administration. Although candidate Obama indicated that he would update FISA "to provide greater oversight accountability to the congressional intelligence committees to prevent future threats to the rule of law," President Obama nonetheless reauthorized the PATRIOT Act for four years in 2011 largely intact. This renewal included allowing roving wiretaps—("i.e., the ability of law enforcement officials to track targets if they change phones without law enforcement first consulting a judge").[178]

The second issue involved increased intelligence activities by the military in the post-9/11 period. DOD officials defend these activities as simply part of the department's "need for intelligence to support ground troops." Moreover, one senior military official testified before Congress that they are "clandestine,"[179] not covert, and thus are not subject to the same restrictions and reporting requirements as covert operations. Even if the intelligence activities of the Pentagon do not meet the legal definition of covert action, some would argue that Congress may still need to increase its oversight of these activities. Moreover, the House Intelligence Committee threatened to do just that in considering the FY2010 Intelligence Authorization Act, but so far Congress has not acted to do so.[180]

A Democratic and Ethical Challenge

Over a decade ago, Roger Hilsman, a veteran government official, called for a fundamental overhaul of the IC generally and the CIA in particular—apart from the structural or operational changes just discussed. He argued that "**the United States should get out of the business of both espionage and covert political action**"[181] because their contribution "to wise decisions in foreign policy and defense is minimal. But the cost in lives, treasure, and intangibles is high." He also contended that "covert action has been overused as an instrument of foreign policy" and has tarnished the image of the United States. Instead, the CIA's role should be only as "an independent research and analysis organization," and other intelligence operations in the rest of the government should be transferred to it.

Hilsman's argument compels us to conclude this discussion with some vexing and important questions about intelligence operations, especially covert activities, and their compatibility with democratic and ethical values. First, **how consistent are intelligence activities with American democracy**? Second, **what ethical standards do these actions portend for the United States in conducting its foreign policy**? A free and democratic society surely seems at odds with the kinds of intelligence activities that we have described. These activities stand in sharp contrast to the openness and public discussion of issues that Americans demand and promote at home. Similarly, do not some of these activities (such as entrapping and enticing foreign agents to engage in unethical conduct) affront our ethical standards? Do they not place the United States in the awkward position of endorsing the proposition that "the ends justify the means" with virtually any (unethical) behavior acceptable in the pursuit of foreign policy goals? With the antiterrorism efforts over the past decade, these questions may not be raised directly or often, as the rationale for fighting terrorism can be so easily and quickly evoked. Still, they need to be raised and addressed anew before any decisions on the structure and operation of the IC can be made.

THE DEPARTMENT OF HOMELAND SECURITY

Another result of the intelligence failures associated with September 11 was the creation of a new bureaucracy charged with ensuring homeland security. In October 2001, by executive order, the **Office of Homeland Security** was established, with its head appointed as the assistant to the president for homeland security. Its mission was "to develop and coordinate the implementation of a comprehensive national strategy to secure the United States from terrorist threats or attack."[182] Also established was the **Homeland Security Council**, consisting of the president, the vice president, the assistant to the president for homeland security, and other key cabinet secretaries, whose mission was to assist in the development of homeland security policy and to ensure its effective implementation across the government.

Within a very short time, members of Congress called for a cabinet-level department on homeland security, as a department would be answerable to both the legislative and executive branches rather than to the president alone. Although President Bush initially balked at this, he proposed just such a cabinet department in mid-2002, which the House of Representatives quickly approved by a wide margin (295–133). Senate passage was slower because of differences over work rules for department employees, but after the 2002 congressional elections, in which Republicans did better than expected, opposition disappeared. The Department of Homeland Security Act of 2002 was quickly passed by a margin of 90–9 and was signed into law at the end of November.

Like the Office of Homeland Security, the primary mission of the **Department of Homeland Security (DHS)** is to "prevent terrorist attacks within the United States; reduce the vulnerability of the United States to terrorism; and minimize the damage, and assist in the recovery, from terrorist attacks that do occur within the United States."[183] In this sense, it is the prototype "intermestic" agency within the American government—a bureaucracy with responsibilities that are both domestic and international. Although our focus here is primarily on DHS's foreign policy responsibilities, its dual role should be kept in mind throughout this discussion.

DHS formally came into existence in March 2003, when twenty-two domestic agencies from several departments were combined to create the third-largest government bureaucracy (presently more than 230,000 employees and a $59 billion budget).[184] The combination of agencies was characterized at the time as "the most significant transformation of the U.S. government since 1947, when President Truman merged the various branches of the armed forces into the Department of Defense better to coordinate the nation's defense against military threats."[185]

Even in its short time in existence, though, DHS has gone through some reorganization. Originally, it consisted of five major directorates and four divisions. At the present time, it is organized into three directorates (National Protection and Programs, Science and Technology, and Management), five offices (Policy, Health Affairs, Intelligence and Analysis, Operations Coordination and Planning, and Domestic Nuclear Detection), and several centers, agencies, and administrative units (the Federal Law Enforcement Training Center, the Transportation Security Administration [TSA], U.S. Customs and Border Protection, U.S. Citizenship and Immigration Services, U.S. Immigration and Customs Enforcement [ICE], U.S. Secret Service, Federal Emergency Management Agency [FEMA], and the U.S. Coast Guard). As shown in Figure 10.3, at the top of this organizational structure are the secretary and the Office of the Secretary. Although all of these divisions have some components that deal with foreign policy, the Directorate for National Protection and Programs, the Office of Policy, the various immigration and customs services, the TSA, and the Coast Guard are probably the most directly involved. These offices, centers, and administrative units develop policy for such areas as environmental dangers, animal diseases, and biological warfare threats, but they are also responsible for the protection of transportation, borders, and waterways.

The DHS is charged with five core missions: "preventing terrorism and managing risks to critical infrastructure; securing and managing the border; enforcing and administering immigration laws; safeguarding and securing cyberspace; and ensuring resilience

U.S. DEPARTMENT OF HOMELAND SECURITY

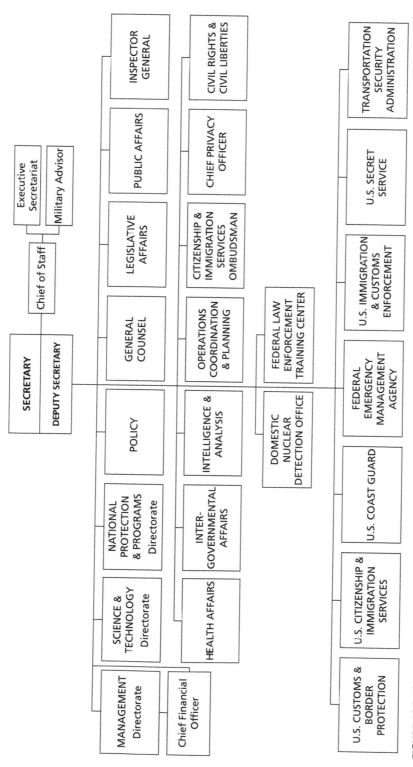

FIGURE 10.3 The Department of Homeland Security

Source: http://www.dhs.gov/xlibrary/assets/dhs-orgchart.pdf, June 20, 2012.

to disasters."[186] To carry out these missions and to give some sense of the magnitude of the responsibility of DHS, the department provides some evidence of its actions related to each of its core mission by its personnel (2011 data). For its first mission, for example, the TSA employed about 52,000 at 450 airports to screen some 603 million passengers, and the U.S. Coast Guard conducted about 37,000 patrols. To carry out its second task, DHS had several agencies involved in providing border protection, whether the 21,000 Border Patrol agents, the Coast Guard with numerous inspection of vessels, or Custom and Border Protection officers screening some 340 million travelers. For its third mission, DHS's ICE unit dealt with almost 400,000 cases of illegal aliens, and its U.S. Citizenship and Immigration Services (USCIS) held thousands of naturalization ceremonies and processed millions of verification checks across half of the states. For its fourth mission, DHS's U.S. Computer Emergency Readiness Team responded to over 100,000 incidents and released over 5,000 cyber alerts. Finally, in the area of disaster relief, FEMA dealt with "96 major disaster declarations, 29 emergency declarations, and 116 first management assistance declarations."[187]

The most widely known homeland security mechanism developed by DHS was the "Homeland Security Advisory System."[188] This was a five-level, color-coded system to warn the American public about the level of terrorist threat detected by the intelligence community, ranging from low risk of terrorist attacks (green) to severe risk of terrorist attacks (red). In 2011, however, this system was replaced by National Terrorism Advisory System (NTAS) with only two levels of alert—a simpler and more understandable system for the American public. An **Imminent Threat Alert** "warns of a credible, specific, and impending terrorist threat against the United States," and an **Elevated Threat Alert** "warns of a credible terrorist threat against the United States." Such alerts, DHS notes, "will only be issued when credible information is available."[189]

Despite all these activities, the DHS has been under attack routinely for its slow pace of organizational integration and for its failure to effectively enact homeland security measures. With its massive reorganization and its broad set of responsibilities, its growing pains have been considerable. According to one analysis early on, the department has been "hobbled by money problems, turf battles and unsteady support from the White House," all of which weakened its ability to focus on important security goals.[190]

FEMA's failures during Hurricane Katrina in 2005 and questions surrounding the security of American ports when Dubai Ports World, a company headquartered in Dubai, purchased operating control of several American seaports in 2006 raised further doubts about DHS's effectiveness in dealing with natural disasters and port security. Even though personnel changes were made at FEMA, and the Dubai Ports issue was diffused when the company transferred its port operations to its U.S. entity, the DHS remained in the spotlight.

In recent years, there is no doubt that the DHS has made considerable strides in its integration of the various units and actions to provide a homeland "that is safer, secure, and resilient against terrorism and other hazards," its stated mission. Yet, criticisms of the functioning of the homeland security remain. The tenth anniversary report on the implementation of the 9/11 Commission recommendations praised the increased cooperation within the government and DHS to deal with terrorist threats and specifically noted the creation of "72 Fusion Centers in which federal, state, local authorities investigate terrorism leads and share information" and the improvement by TSA. At the same time, however, it also pointed to several commission recommendations that have not yet been implemented. In particular, there remains a lack of sufficient integration on "unity of command and effort" in dealing with disasters,

CHAPTER 10 THE MILITARY AND INTELLIGENCE BUREAUCRACIES: PERVASIVE OR ACCOUNTABLE?

421

the need for TSA to improve its explosives screening capability to prevent another Christmas Day bomber, and the need for DHS to develop a biometric entry-exit screening system for individuals visiting the United States.[191]

In sum, the DHS has developed and implemented new policies and procedures to address possible threats, but it still has some unfinished business in addressing its broad mandate. A more general concern is whether this kind of centralized bureaucracy is the best strategy to promote homeland security. As one analysis noted when DHS was being contemplated, "Even with full Cabinet status, the secretary of a new Department of Homeland Security will not be able to coordinate the activities and actions of his many cabinet colleagues who have an interest in and share responsibility for protecting the American homeland."[192] Several years after its creation, this assessment still seems apropos.

POLICY COORDINATION AMONG COMPETING BUREAUCRACIES

For the sake of convenience and clarity, we have described the role of the various executive bureaucracies in the foreign policy process separately. Although each department, and the groups within it, may have an impact on policy, policy formulation is also coordinated across the various bureaucracies and policy makers. In the last section of this chapter, we briefly discuss how this coordination is achieved and how "bureaucratic politics" is played out among the foreign policy departments.

The National Security Coordinating System

Beginning in 1966, initially as a means of making the Department of State more fully the center of the foreign policy process, a series of **Interdepartmental Regional Groups (IRG)** were established to coordinate policy recommendations, each headed by the appropriate assistant secretary of state.[193] An IRG, for instance, might consist of representatives from Defense, USAID, the NSC, the JCS, and whatever departments were appropriate for a particular region or issue, and its principal aim would be to obtain policy advice from throughout the government. Further up in the hierarchy, a **Senior Interdepartmental Group (SIG)**, composed of higher-level representatives from the foreign policy bureaucracies and headed by the undersecretary of state, coordinated the activities of the IRGs. The SIGs were, in turn, accountable to the NSC or the various departmental secretaries.

These working groups were the principal means of stretching the policy process across departments. These groups became both a source of bureaucratic coordination and a source of competition. Still, they became the model for subsequent administrations. Succeeding presidents changed the names into **interagency groups (IGs)**, **policy coordinating committees (PCCs)**, or, currently, **interagency policy committees (IPCs)**, but their use as the principal mechanism for coordinating policy options remained. Even in the extremely hierarchical arrangements of the national security system during the Kissinger years, the use of IGs, although altered, was not wholly abandoned. Over the years, however, they have undergone an important shift, from dominance by the Department of State to greater control and direction by the National Security Council and its staff. A description of the interagency process during recent administrations (from Reagan to Obama) provides a fuller sense of how these groups facilitate both coordination and competition among the various bureaucracies and how the National Security Council increasingly directs their operation.

The NSC System from Reagan to Bush

The Reagan administration initially retained the system of SIGs and IGs of earlier administrations, but with a clear division of responsibility among the secretary of state, the secretary of defense, and the director of central intelligence for different aspects of policy.[194] Specifically, the administration established four SIGs reflecting the four major areas of national security—foreign, defense, intelligence, and international economic policy—with each headed by a representative from the Department of State, the Department of Defense, the CIA, and the Department of Treasury, respectively. Under this arrangement, each SIG created its own IGs for development and review of policy options, and each of which included representatives from other appropriate bureaus and agencies.

By the administration's second term, several changes emerged. The intelligence SIG was eventually supplanted by the National Security Planning Group (NSPG) in monitoring covert operations. The Crisis Preplanning Group and the Strategic Arms Control Group largely assumed the functions of the foreign and defense policy SIGs, and the international economic SIG was transferred to the Economic Policy Council.[195] By early 1987, the system was changed once again with the establishment of the Policy Review Group (PRG), chaired by the deputy national security advisor and composed of other subcabinet officials from various foreign policy bureaucracies. Along with the NSPG, these groups became the key forums for policy coordination in the last two years of the Reagan administration, meeting over 170 times and coordinating policy on a wide range of issues.[196] Overall, though, the Reagan system has been criticized for "an absence of orderly decision making and uncertain lines of responsibility," especially since the national security advisor did not play a central role in the process.[197]

The George H.W. Bush administration sought to streamline the coordination of the various bureaucracies and to give greater control to the national security advisor and his staff in shaping policy. As a result, a relatively simple three-tier system of committees was established leading to the NSC itself. The most important committee below the NSC for policy coordination was the NSC Principals Committee (NSC/PC).[198] This was the senior interagency group for consideration of all national security questions; it was comprised of key cabinet-level officials with foreign policy responsibilities, and it was chaired by the national security advisor. The second ranking group was the NSC Deputies Committee (NSC/DC), which reviewed the initial work of the interagency groups, or the NSC Policy Coordinating Committees (NSC/PCCs), and made recommendations to the Principals Committee. It was composed of subcabinet-level officials from the various foreign policy bureaucracies and was chaired by the deputy assistant to the president for national security affairs. The last tier in the policy coordination hierarchy, of course, was the NSC/PCCs. Comparable to the interagency groups (IGs) in earlier administrations, these developed and prepared draft policy options across departments for the administration. The NSC/PCCs were both regional, covering all areas of the world, and functional, covering particular current issues.

The Clinton administration followed the Bush model with a three-tiered coordinating system. Two of the three committees had the same names as during the Bush administration, the NSC Principals Committee (NSC/PC) and the NSC Deputies Committee (NSC/DC); a third was renamed the NSC Interagency Working Groups (NSC/IWGs) to more closely align it with the working groups employed by earlier presidents. In function, the three committees varied only slightly from those of the Bush administration.

For the Principals and the Deputies Committee, the most important difference between President Bush's and President Clinton's NSC systems was membership.[199] The Clinton administration added the U.S. ambassador to the United Nations and the assistant to the president for economic policy to the Principals Committee and invited other officials as needed. As for the NSC Deputies Committee, the Clinton administration expanded its membership and increased its workload in policy formulation and implementation. The Deputies Committee reviewed the work of all interagency working groups and apparently had special responsibilities regarding intelligence activities as well. It was designated the Deputies Committee/CM when it dealt with crisis management. Interagency working groups (NSC/IWGs) under the Clinton administration continued to be to be established by the Deputies Committee and followed the Bush model with regional and functional groupings.

Continuity with past administrations largely characterized the NSC system under George W. Bush.[200] Much as the two previous administrations did, the Bush administration adopted a three-tiered national security system. Some committee names and membership changed and a few new wrinkles were added, but there was no fundamental structural transformation.

The NSC Principals Committee (NSC/PC) during the Bush administration continued to consist of largely the same members as before, but the president also included the president's chief of staff, the vice president's national security advisor, and the deputy national security advisor. In addition, the vice president regularly attended these meetings.[201] Some members who were regular in the past (the CIA director and the chairman of the JCS) would now be only occasional attendees, and others would attend only as needed (the secretary of commerce or the USTR).

The NSC Deputies Committee (NSC/DC) continued to oversee the work of the policy coordination committees as in the previous administrations, but its membership was considerably expanded. The deputy secretary of state or the undersecretary of treasury or the undersecretary of treasury for international affairs, for instance, now participated, as did a number of other deputy secretaries or second in command from various departments or offices. In this sense, the DC had a much broader representation than it had before. Consistent with the two previous administrations, the deputy national security advisor chaired the NSC/DC, ensuring that the national security staff would largely guide these two key committees of the NSC system.

Finally, the NSC Policy Coordinating Committees (PCCs) remained "the main day-to-day [mechanisms] for interagency coordination of national security policy." PCCs were created for both regional and functional, and, by one analysis, NSC staff chaired seventeen of the twenty-six PCCs at the end of the Bush administration, reflecting the NSC's policy impact.[202]

The Barack Obama Administration and the NSC System

The Obama administration has followed the pattern of the past three administrations in relying on a three-tiered arrangement of the NSC system.[203] Like its predecessor administrations, the Obama administration has changed, and mainly expanded, the membership on the committees that comprise the system but not the fundamental structure. The Obama administration's most significant change was to integrate the Homeland Security staff into the NSC staff.

The **Principals Committee (NSC/PC)** sits at the top of the NSC system for the Obama administration. The membership of this committee, as shown in Figure 10.4, has expanded in size to incorporate more areas with national security impact, a process initiated in the Clinton administration and continued in the George W. Bush administration. The Obama administration, however, has gone further by including the secretary of energy, the secretary of homeland security, the director of the

National Security Council

NSC Principals Committee (NSC/PC)

Members:

NSA (serves as chair)
Secretary of State
Secretary of the Treasury
Secretary of Defense
Attorney General
Secretary of Energy
Director of the Office of Management and Budget
Representative of the US to the UN
Chairman of the Joint Chiefs of Staff
Chief of Staff to the President
Director of National Intelligence
Assistant to the President and
   Deputy National Security Advisor
Deputy Secretary of State
Counsel to the President
Assistant to the Vice President for National
Security Affairs

Occasional Attendees

(when international economic issues are discussed)
Secretary of Commerce
U.S. Trade Representative
Secretary of Homeland Security
Chair of the Council of Economic Advisors
Assistant to the President for Economic Policy

(when homeland security issues are discussed)
Assistant to the President for Homeland
   Security and Counter Terrorism

(when science and technology issues are discussed)
Director of the Office of Science and
   Technology Policy

NSC Deputies Committee (NSC/DC)

Members:

Assistant to the President and Deputy National
   Security Advisor (chair)
Deputy Secretary of State
Deputy Secretary of Treasury
Deputy Secretary of Defense
Deputy Attorney General
Deputy Secretary of Energy
Deputy Secretary of Homeland Security
Deputy Director of National Intelligence
Deputy Director of the Office of Management
   and Budget
Deputy to the US representative to the UN
Vice Chairman of the Joint Chiefs of Staff
Assistant to the Vice President for National
   Security Affairs

Occasional Attendees:

(when homeland security issues are discussed)
Assistant to the President for Homeland
   Security and Counter-Terrorism and Deputy
   National Security Advisor

(when international economic issues are discussed)
Deputy Assistant to the President and Deputy
   National Security Advisor

(when science and technology issues are discussed)
Associate Director of the Office of Science and
   Technology Policy

NSC Interagency Policy Committees (NSC/IPCs)

NSC/IPCs are established by the Deputies Committee and are chaired by the NSC. "The Obama administration has not released an unclassified list of IPCs. However, the IPCs of the new administration can be expected to continue to work on policy issues in most of the same areas as the PCCs that functioned during the George W Bush administration." (Alan G. Whitaker, Shannon A. Brown, Frederick C. Smith, and Ambassador Elizabeth McKune, *The National Security Policy Process: The National Security Council and Interagency System*, (Washington, D.C,: Industrial College of the Armed Forces, National Defense University, 2011), p. 17.

Examples from the Bush administration include:
Regional PCCs
Europe and Eurasia, Western Hemisphere
Functional PCCs
Democracy, Human rights, and international operations

Trade Policy Review Group

FIGURE 10.4 National Security Council System Organization in the Barack Obama Administration

Source: Presidential Policy Directive-1, February 13, 2009.

Office of Management and Budget, the attorney general, and the director of national intelligence. (The addition of the DNI is really a replacement of the director of central intelligence after the passage of the 2004 Intelligence Reform and Terrorism Prevention Act, and a process begun by the Bush administration.) In addition to the change in the regular membership on the PC, the Obama administration has also expanded the number of "occasional attendees" based on whether international economic issues, homeland security issues, or science and technology issues are on the agenda.

The Principals Committee serves "as the President's senior level policy review and coordination group," and its "mission is to ensure that, as much as possible, policy decisions brought to the President reflect a consensus within the departments and agencies."[204] International events and issues drive the frequency of the PC meetings, but they normally occur once or twice per week, except perhaps during crises. Occasionally, by one analysis, the members of the PC may meet informally to discuss key or ongoing issues. Importantly for managing the policy process, the PC is chaired by the national security advisor.

By contrast, the **Deputies Committee (DC)**, the second tier within the Obama administration's NSC system and headed by the deputy national security advisor, tends to meet daily to review policy recommendations that it receives from the third tier, **the Interagency Policy Committees (IPCs)**, and to prepare policy options and recommendations for the PC. Like the PC, the membership on the Deputies Committee has expanded in the Obama administration from previous administrations to reflect the broader national security agenda today. In large measure, the DC is the workhorse of the policy making within the NSC system because it is responsible for both shaping options for the president and the PC and for implementing policy decisions reached by the president and his advisors.[205]

The number of IPCs created and the issues that these IPCs address have in the past been the responsibility of the Deputies Committee. Although the exact number and names of the IPCs created by Obama administration have not been released, the current IPCs are assumed to be about the same as for the Bush administration.[206] That is, there were several IPCs dealing with regional issues (such as South Asia, Iran, Western Hemisphere) and even more IPCs dealing with functional issues (such as Arms Control, Biodefense, Intelligence and Counterintelligence). Membership on these IPCs involves members from various departments and agencies within the government with an interest and knowledge of the issues at hand and reflects the effort to coordinate across units in arriving at policy options. All regional IPCs are chaired by assistant secretaries of state, and most (albeit, not all) the functional IPCs are chaired by the NSC staff. In general, this arrangement ensures a dominant role for the NSC in shaping the decision-making process.

The work of these IPCs for the decision process is crucial to successful policy. That is, the IPCs "do the 'heavy lifting' in analyzing policy issues and developing policy options and recommendations that provide policy-makers with flexibility and a range of options that are policy acceptable and minimize the risk of failure."[207] These IPCs also must develop policy options that involve "coordinated actions" across departments and agencies. In a real sense, the IPCs are the starting point for foreign policy development and coordination within the U.S. government.

Finally, the Obama administration made one important change in the NSC system by its decision in May 2009 to integrate the staffs of the NSC and the HSC. This change did not affect the existence or functioning of the HSC, previously created by the Bush administration after 9/11, or the assistant to the president for homeland security and counterterrorism (who continues to report directly to the president), but the change now has the National Security staff support both the NSC and HSC.[208] In this sense, the change more fully integrated "international, transnational and homeland security matters" and placed "all policy matters under a single organizational chain of command."[209]

In all, the NSC system, especially through the coordinated work of the Deputies Committee and the Interagency Policy Committees, has effectively managed the formulation and the implementation of foreign policy for recent administrations. As such, this system has been a ready mechanism for managing conflicts between and among departments and bureaucracies.

CONCLUDING COMMENTS

The diplomatic, economic, military, and intelligence bureaucracies discussed over the last two chapters all contributed to the shaping of U.S. foreign policy in recent administrations. In the past few years, some saw their influence increase; others saw it decline. The NSC (especially the NSC staff and the national security advisor), the DOD, and key economic bureaucracies such as the Department of Treasury and the Office of the U.S. Trade Representative gained influence. By contrast, the Department of State and the intelligence community probably lost influence because of various problems over past decades. In the post–September 11 world, however, the intelligence community and the newly created Department of Homeland Security will likely regain some of that influence if they can operate efficiently and effectively. Still, the precise contribution of the bureaucracies in an administration is heavily dependent on how the president chooses to use them and on their personnel. The president is dependent on the bureaucracy for policy advice; the standing of the bureaucracy is dependent on how that advice is used.

In the next two chapters, we expand our analysis of foreign policy making by examining participants outside of the formal governmental structure. Political parties and interest groups are the focus of attention in Chapter 11, which will assess how America's two major political parties shape foreign policy and determine which interest groups, under what conditions, play a role in policy making in international affairs.

Notes

1. See Stanley Lieberson, "An Empirical Study of Military-Industrial Linkages," *American Journal of Sociology* 76 (January 1971): 562–584.

2. See, for example, Adam Yarmolinsky, *The Military Establishment: Its Impacts on American Society* (New York: Harper and Row, 1971).

3. See the chapter entitled "Is There a Military-Industrial Complex Which Prevents Peace?" in Marc Pilisuk, with the assistance of Mehrene Larudee, *International Conflict and Social Policy* (Englewood Cliffs, NJ: Prentice Hall, 1972), pp. 108–141.

4. Federal Procurement Data System– Next Generation, "Top 100 Contractors Report," at https://www.fpds.gov/fpdsng_cms/index.php/reports, June 7, 2012. The total was summed for the top 100 from this report for the DOD tab on this site.

5. The personnel data and quoted passage in this section are taken from U.S. Department of Department of Defense, "About the Department of Defense (DOD)," at http://www.defense.gov/about/, June 7, 2012. The defense expenditure data are from U.S. Department of Defense, Office of the Undersecretary of Defense (Comptroller)/Chief Financial Officer, *Overview—FY2013 Defense Budget*, February 2012, pp. 1–2, at http://comptroller.defense.gov/defbudget/fy2013/FY2013_Budget_Request.pdf, June 7, 2012.

6. Taken from United States Department of Defense, "Office of the Secretary of Defense," at http://www.defense.gov/osd, June 7, 2012.

7. See Townsend Hoopes, *The Limits of Intervention* (New York: David McKay, 1968), pp. 33–34, for a statement of the ISA's role during the Kennedy–Johnson period.

8. U.S. Department of Defense, "Assistant Secretary of Defense for International Security Affairs," at http://policy.defense.gov/isa/index.aspx, June 7, 2012.

9. See Henry T. Nash, *American Foreign Policy* (Homewood, IL: Dorsey, 1985), p. 94. By contrast, the Bureau of Politico-Military Affairs in the Department of State might be labeled the "little Defense Department" because of the military considerations in policy examined by this bureau and because of the tendency for regular personnel exchanges between this bureau and the Pentagon. On the changes in the role of ISA in the policy process, see Geoffrey Piller, "DOD's Office of International Security Affairs: The Brief Ascendancy of an Advisory System," *Political Science Quarterly* 98 (Spring 1983): 59–78.

10. *U.S. Government Manual 1989/1990* (Washington, D.C.: U.S. Government Printing Office, July 1, 1989), p. 186.

11. See Strobe Talbott, *Deadly Gambits* (New York: Vintage Books, 1985), for a discussion of the key role of Assistant Secretary of Defense Richard Perle in arms control policy.

12. See, for example, Joseph S. Nye, Jr., "The Case for Deep Engagement," *Foreign Affairs* 74 (July/August 1995): 90–102, which he published while at ISA.

13. Eric Schmitt, "Aide Denies Shaping Data to Justify War," *New York Times*, June 5, 2003, 20.

14. U.S. Department of Defense, "Assistant Secretary of Defense for Global Strategic Affairs," at http://policy.defense.gov/gsa/index.aspx, June 7, 2012.

15. Amos A. Jordan, William J. Taylor, Jr., and Lawrence J. Korb, *American National Security: Policy and Process*, 4th ed. (Baltimore and London: The Johns Hopkins University Press, 1993), p. 178. On the responsibilities of the JCS, also see Lawrence J. Korb, *The Fall and Rise of the Pentagon: American Defense Policies in the 1970s* (Westport, CT: Greenwood Press, 1979), p. 112; Korb, *The Joint Chiefs of Staff: The First Twenty-Five Years* (Bloomington: IN: University Press, 1976), p. 7; and *U.S. Government Manual 2007/2008* (Washington, D.C.: Government Printing Office, July 1, 2007), pp. 156–157.

16. *U.S. Government Manual 2012, "Joint Chiefs of Staff,"* http://www.usgovernmentmanual. gov/Agency.aspx?EntityId=tv4LVSeIL00=&ParentEId=+klubNxgV0o=&EType=jY3 M4CTKVHY=&S=7SIlhybhVKKAduGpf46/evhvfxLS8TYeEaFtP83Msuxy1RC6pzd-frQ==, August 13, 2012. On the responsibility to the Homeland Security Council, see U.S. Department of Defense, *Department of Defense Directive, Number 5100.01*, December 21, 2010, p. 14, at http://www.dtic.mil/whs/directives/corres/pdf/510001p.pdf, June 7, 2012.

17. Jordan, Taylor, and Korb, *American National Security*, pp. 178–180; and Korb, *The Fall and Rise of the Pentagon*, pp. 112–137.

18. Jordan, Taylor, and Korb, *American National Security*, p. 178.

19. Korb, *The Fall and Rise of the Pentagon*, p. 115.

20. See the discussion in Neil Sheehan, Hedrick Smith, E. W. Kenworthy, and Fox Butterfield, *The Pentagon Papers as Published by* New York Times (New York: Bantam Books, 1971), pp. 234–270, on the bombing of North Vietnam and on the acceptance of the domino theory. Although the DOD and its advisors did not get all they proposed, its influence in these decisions is still evident.

21. Jordan, Taylor, and Korb, *American National Security*, p. 179.

22. Ibid.

23. David C. Martin and Michael A. Lerner, "Why the Generals Can't Command," *Newsweek*, February 14, 1983, 22.

24. Lawrence J. Korb, "The Joint Chiefs of Staff: Access and Impact in Foreign Policy," *Policy Studies Journal* 3 (Winter 1974): 171.

25. Ibid., pp. 171–173.

26. Martin and Lerner, "Why the Generals Can't Command," p. 22.

27. "Excerpts from Reagan's Testimony on the Iran-Contra Affair," *New York Times*, February 23, 1990, A18.

28. This discussion of the Goldwater–Nichols Reorganization Act is taken from *Congressional Quarterly Almanac 1986* (Washington, D.C.: Congressional Quarterly, 1987), pp. 455–457. The last point on the sharing of opinions on policy disagreement by other JCS members is from *Department of Defense Directive, Number 5100.01*, December 21, 2010, p. 19, but this directive also outlines the considerable powers and authority of the Chairman of the JCS, pp. 14–19.

29. See the U.S. Department of Defense, "Unified Command Plan," at http://www.defense. gov/ucc/, June 8, 2012.

30. Robert Previdi, *Civilian Control versus Military Rule* (New York: Hippocrene, 1988), p. 8, as cited in Douglas Johnson and Steven Metz, "American Civil-Military Relations: A

Review of the Recent Literature," in Don M. Snider and Miranda A. Carlton-Carew, eds., *U.S. Civil-Military Relations: In Crisis or Transition?* (Washington, D.C.: The Center for Strategic and International Studies, 1995), p. 209.

31. Richard Halloran, "Bush Plans to Name Colin Powell to Head Joint Chiefs, Aides Say," *New York Times*, August 10, 1989, 1, 10.

32. Johnson and Metz, "American Civil-Military Relations," p. 210.

33. Eleanor Clift and Thomas M. DeFrank, "Bush's General: Maximum Force," *Newsweek*, September 3, 1990, 36.

34. Richard H. Kohn, "Out of Control: The Crisis in Civil-Military Relations," *National Interest* 35 (Spring 1994): 13–14, as cited in Johnson and Metz, "American Civil-Military Relations," p. 210.

35. Colin L. Powell, John Lehman, William Odom, Samuel Huntington, and Richard H. Kohn, "Exchange on Civil-Military Relations," *National Interest* 36 (Summer 1994): 23, as cited in Johnson and Metz, "American Civil-Military Relations," p. 211.

36. Pat Towell with Matthew Phillips, "Shalikashvili Wins Praise as Joint Chiefs Nominee," *Congressional Quarterly Weekly Report*, August 14, 1993, 2238.

37. Ibid.

38. Dana Priest, *The Mission* (New York: W.W. Norton and Company, 2003), pp. 21–23.

39. Stephen M. Saideman, "More Than Advice? The Role of the Joint Staff in the American Foreign Policy Process," paper presented at the annual meeting of the American Political Science Association, Chicago, Illinois, August 30, 2007, p. 3.

40. Michael C. Desch, "Bush and the Generals," *Foreign Affairs* 86 (May/June 2007): 105.

41. Desch, "Bush and the Generals," pp. 8, 97–110. In fact, there is some indirect evidence that General Pace challenged the White House over a military attack against Iran over that country's possible development of nuclear weapons. See Seymour M. Hersh, "Last Stand," in James M. McCormick, ed., *The Domestic Sources of American Foreign Policy: Insights and Evidence*, 6th ed. (Lanham, MD: Rowman & Littlefield, 2012), pp. 417–428, in which he argues that the military did "stand up" to the civilian leadership on this issue. The reference to General Pace's role is at p. 418.

42. Lawrence Korb, a former assistant secretary of defense and long-time military analyst, extended this critique to the political actions of some military officials and "the way in which President George W. Bush and his appointees have used military professionals to support their political agenda." See his "Political Generals," *Foreign Affairs* 86 (September/October 2007): 152.

43. Richard B. Myers and Richard H. Kohn, "The Military's Place," *Foreign Affairs* 86 (September/October 2007): 147 and 149.

44. On Mullen's support for General McChrystal's report on Afghanistan and the surge strategy, see Bob Woodward, *Obama's Wars* (New York: Simon & Schuster, 2010). On Mullen's statement about the Haqqani network, see Charles Hoskinson, "Mike Mullen Warns Pakistan on Terror Group," *Politico*, September 22, 2011, at http://www.politico.com/news/stories/0911/64141.html, June 8, 2012.

45. Priest, *The Mission*, p. 45.

46. Saideman, "More Than Advice?" The rest of the discussion in this paragraph draws from this analysis.

47. The reform acts strengthening the secretary's role within the DOD are "Reorganization Plan No. 6 of 1953," 67 Stat. 638–639; and the "Department of Defense Reorganization Act of 1958," P.L. 85-599, 72 Stat. 514–523.

48. See James Schlesinger, "The Role of the Secretary of Defense," in Robert J. Art, Vincent Davis, and Samuel P. Huntington, eds., *Reorganizing America's Defense: Leadership in War*

and Peace (Washington, D.C.: Pergamon-Brassey's, 1985), p. 261; and Laurence E. Lynn, Jr., and Richard I. Smith, "Can the Secretary of Defense Make a Difference?" *International Security* 7 (Summer 1982): 45–69. The former discusses the role of the secretary of defense more generally; the latter looks at it in the weapons development and acquisition process and at the impact of the bureaucracy within the Pentagon in shaping outcomes.

49. Korb, *The Fall and Rise of the Pentagon*, p. 85.

50. Theodore H. White, "Weinberger on the Ramparts," *New York Times Magazine*, February 6, 1983, 18; Alice C. Maroni, *The Fiscal Year 1984 Defense Budget Request: Data Summary* (Washington, D.C.: Congressional Research Service, The Library of Congress, February 1, 1983); and Ellen C. Collier, "Arms Control Negotiations at Home: Legislative-Executive Relations," paper presented at the Annual Meeting of the International Studies Association, March 1984, p. 8.

51. The data reported here were calculated from Table IX in Alice C. Maroni, *The Fiscal Year 1989 Defense Budget Request Data Summary*, Congressional Research Service, The Library of Congress, No. 88-182F. The data are for the National Defense function category that included the DOD and defense-related programs carried out by other agencies. If only the DOD budget is used, the average increase from 1981 to 1985 was 9.1 percent, whereas the average decline from 1986 to 1988 was 2 percent.

52. White, "Weinberger on the Ramparts," p. 18.

53. John M. Broder and Melissa Healy, "Likeable Dick Cheney Can Get Mad When He Has To," *Los Angeles Times*, March 16, 1989, 20.

54. Andrew Rosenthal, "Cheney Steps to Center of the Lineup," *New York Times*, August 24, 1990, A7.

55. See, for example, Pat Towell, "Aspin's Career a Balance of the Highs and Lows," *Congressional Quarterly Weekly Report*, May 27, 1995, 1484.

56. Charles Lane, "Perry's Parry," *The New Republic* 26 (June 27, 1994): 21–25.

57. Elizabeth Drew, *On the Edge: The Clinton Presidency* (New York: Simon & Schuster, 1994), p. 356.

58. Ibid., p. 373.

59. Lane, "Perry's Parry," p. 22.

60. See Priest, *The Mission*, p. 29, on Cohen's expertise on defense issues and some of his actions as secretary of defense.

61. James Risen, "Man in the News: A Pentagon Veteran—Donald Henry Rumsfeld," *New York Times*, December 29, 2000, at http://www.nytimes.com/2000/12/29/politics/29RUMS.html?pagewanted=all, March 18, 2001.

62. Priest, *The Mission*, pp. 23–32.

63. Bob Woodward, *Bush at War* (New York: Simon & Schuster, 2002), p. 49.

64. See Greg Newbold, "Why Iraq Was a Mistake," *Time*, April 9, 2006, at http://www.time.com/time/magazine/article/0,9171,1181629,00.html, June 2, 2008; and David S. Cloud and Eric Schmitt, "More Retired Generals Call for Rumsfeld's Resignation," *New York Times*, April 14, 2006, at http://www.nytimes.com/2006/04/14/washington/14military.html?_r=1&oref=slogin, May 29, 2008.

65. David S. Cloud, "A Still-Serving Rumsfeld Is Set for Mustering Out," *New York Times*, December 9, 2006, p. 9.

66. Michael R. Gordon, "Rumsfeld, a Force for Change, Did Not Change With the Times Amid Iraq Tumult," *New York Times*, November 9, 2006, p. 29.

67. Analyst Andrew Krepinevich is quoted in Gordon, "Rumsfeld, a Force for Change," p. 29.

68. John Barry, Richard Wolffe, and Evan Thomas (with Dan Ephron and Michael Hirsch), "Stealth Warrior," *Newsweek*, March 19, 2007, p. 28.

69. Phone interview with a former Foreign Service officer at the American Foreign Service Association, May 19, 2008. Also see Jim Hoaglund, "A Gates-Style Thaw," *Washington Post*, December 16, 2007, B07.

70. Quoted in Barry, Wolffe, and Thomas (with Ephron and Hirsch), "Stealth Warrior."

71. Ibid.

72. "Robert M. Gates," *New York Times*, Updated July 1, 2011, at http://topics.nytimes.com/top/reference/timestopics/people/g/robert_m_gates/index.html, June 10, 2012.

73. Albert R. Hunt, "U.S. Bids Farewell to Remarkable Defense Chief," *New York Times*, June 27, 2011, at http://www.nytimes.com/2011/06/27/us/27iht-letter27.html?pagewanted=all, June 10, 2012.

74. "Leon Panetta," *New York Times*, updated March 14, 2012, at http://topics.nytimes.com/top/reference/timestopics/people/p/leon_e_panetta/index.html?8qa, June 10, 2012; and Peter Baker, "Panetta's Pentagon, Without the Blank Check," *New York Times*, October 23, 2011, at http://www.nytimes.com/2011/10/24/us/at-pentagon-leon-panetta-charts-change-of-course.html?pagewanted=all, June 10, 2012.

75. *Report of the Joint Inquiry Into the Terrorist Attacks of September 11, 2001* by The House Permanent Select Committee on Intelligence and the Senate Select Committee on Intelligence, July 24, 2003 (hereafter, *Joint Inquiry Into the Terrorist Attacks*), http://new.findlaw.com/cnn/docs/911rpt/index.html, July 24, 2003.

76. See *The 9/11 Commission Report: Final Report of the National Commission on Terrorist Attacks Upon the United States* (New York: W.W. Norton and Company, 2004), chap. 13 in particular.

77. See "Presidential Study Directive-1" issued by The White House, Washington, February 23, 2009, at http://www.fas.org/irp/offdocs/psd/psd-1.pdf, June 11, 2012, on calling for a study of this possible integration. The integration of the two staffs took place a few months later. See Barack Obama, "Statement by the President on the White House Organization for Homeland Security and Counterterrorism," May 26, 2009, at http://www.whitehouse.gov/the_press_office/Statement-by-the-President-on-the-White-House-Organization-for-Homeland-Security-and-Counterterrorism/, June 17, 2012.

78. Jeffrey T. Richelson, *The U.S. Intelligence Community*, 5th ed. (Boulder, CO: Westview Press, 2008), p. 19.

79. Ibid. See p. 20 for the organizational chart of these directorates.

80. The quoted passage is from U.S. Defense Intelligence Agency, "About DIA," at http://www.dia.mil/about/, June 11, 2011; the other information is drawn from Richelson, *The U.S. Intelligence Community*, pp. 57–74.

81. Richelson, *The U.S. Intelligence Community*, pp. 30–36.

82. Ibid., p. 37. The quote about the NRO as the "nation's eyes and ears in space" is from Office of the Director of National Intelligence, "An Overview of the United States Intelligence Community for the 111th Congress," p. 14, at http://www.dni.gov/overview.pdf, June 11, 2012.

83. Ibid., p. 9. Also see Richelson, *The U.S. Intelligence Community*, pp. 42–47.

84. See Office of the Director of National Intelligence, "Members of the Intelligence Community," at http://www.dni.gov/who_what/printer_friendly/members_IC.htm, June 11, 2012.

85. "An Overview of the United States Intelligence Community," p. 24.

86. The information about these latter two intelligence units is also taken from ibid., pp. 15 and 13, respectively.

87. "An Overview of the United States Intelligence Community," pp. 1–3, for a complete description of the deputy directors and for the ten support units within the Office of the DNI.

88. Quotations are from "Primary Mission" of the National Counterterrorism Center in The Intelligence Reform and Terrorism Prevention Act of 2004 at p. 36. See http://www.nctc.gov/docs/pl108_458.pdf, October 6, 2012.

89. Victor Marchetti and John D. Marks, *The CIA and the Cult of Intelligence* (New York: Dell, 1974), p. 95, provides a breakdown of spending in the intelligence community for 1974 totaling $6.2 billion. Charles W. Kegley and Eugene R. Wittkopf report that, for fiscal 1980, the budget for the intelligence community was thought to be $10 billion, based on *Congressional Quarterly* reports. See their *American Foreign Policy: Pattern and Process* (New York: St. Martin's Press, 1982), p. 373.

90. A Senate committee first reported the aggregate budget figure. See Tim Weiner, "The Worst-Kept Secret in the Capital," *New York Times*, July 21, 1994, A11. A more detailed breakdown was reported in Tim Weiner, "$28 Billion Spying Budget Is Made Public by Mistake," *New York Times*, November 5, 1994, 54, as cited in Roger Hilsman, "Does the CIA Still Have a Role?" *Foreign Affairs* 74 (September/October 1995): 105.

91. Office of the Director of National Intelligence, "DNI Releases Budget Figure for National Intelligence Reform," October 30, 2007, at http://www.dni.gov, and "About the Intelligence Community," at http://www.dni.gov/faq_intel.htm, May 27, 2008.

92. The source for this budget figure was James Clapper, the director of national intelligence as reported in Gordon Adams and Matthew Leatherman, "A Leaner and Meaner Defense," in James M. McCormick, ed., *The Domestic Sources of American Foreign Policy: Insights and Evidence* (Lanham, MD: Rowman & Littlefield, Inc., 2012), p. 263.

93. Richelson, *The U.S. Intelligence Community*, pp. 376–381. The passage on the PDB in quoted at p. 376.

94. Office of the Director of National Intelligence, National Intelligence Council, "NIC Mission," at http://www.dni.gov/nic/NIC_about.html, June 12, 2012.

95. Ibid.

96. Richelson, *The U.S. Intelligence Community*, pp. 384.

97. Ibid., pp. 384–385.

98. Marchetti and Marks, *The CIA and the Cult of Intelligence*, pp. 291–296.

99. See Chester L. Cooper, "The CIA and Decisionmaking," *Foreign Affairs* 50 (January 1972): 221–236.

100. John H. Esterline and Robert B. Black, *Inside Foreign Policy: The Department of State Political System and Its Subsystems* (Palo Alto, CA: Mayfield Publishing Company, 1975), p. 35.

101. David E. Rosenbaum, "U.S. Sees Threats to Soviet Economy," *New York Times*, April 21, 1990, 4.

102. Philip Taubman, "CIA Taking Control of Nicaraguan Policy," *Des Moines Register*, April 20, 1984, 1A.

103. Tim Weiner, David Johnston, and Neil A. Lewis, *Betrayal: The Story of Aldrich Ames, An American Spy* (New York: Random House, 1995), p. 287.

104. The Caucus, "Timeline: The Intelligence Work Behind Bin Laden's Death," *New York Times*, May 2, 2011, at http://thecaucus.blogs.nytimes.com/2011/05/02/timeline-the-intelligence-work-behind-bin-ladens-death/, June 12, 2012.

105. See Irving Janis, *Victims of Groupthink* (Boston: Houghton Mifflin Company, 1972), pp. 14–49, for a discussion of the decision making on the Bay of Pigs invasion and the crucial involvement of the CIA. Also see Marchetti and Marks, *The CIA and the Cult of Intelligence*, p. 294, for how dissatisfied President Kennedy was over CIA action in the

Bay of Pigs and how this might have affected his view of intelligence estimates during the Cuban Missile Crisis.

106. Harry Howe Ransom, *The Intelligence Establishment* (Cambridge, MA: Harvard University Press, 1970), p. 240.

107. The portion of the note is quoted from Stansfield Turner, *Secrecy and Democracy: The CIA in Transition* (Boston: Houghton Mifflin Company, 1985), p. 113.

108. The "Iran Postmortem" report is discussed in Bob Woodward, *Veil: The Secret Wars of the CIA, 1981–1987* (New York: Pocket Books, 1987), pp. 106–108.

109. Several sources report some of these intelligence failures. See, for example, John Barry, "Failures of Intelligence?" *Newsweek*, May 14, 1990, 20–21; *NBC Nightly News*, broadcast on June 9, 1990; and Wines, "C.I.A. Faulted on Rating Soviet Economy," p. A5. On the Persian Gulf War failures, see "Intelligence Goofs," *Newsweek*, March 18, 1991, 38.

110. Joseph S. Nye, "Peering into the Future," *Foreign Policy* 73 (July/August 1994): 84–85.

111. The descriptions here are taken from "Abridged Findings and Conclusions" in *Joint Inquiry Into the Terrorist Attacks*.

112. *The 9/11 Commission Report*, pp. 254–277. The reference to "luck" (as well as skill) in finding two future hijackers is at p. 272.

113. The quoted passages are from "In Tenet's Words: 'I Am Responsible' for Review," *New York Times*, July 12, 2003, A5, but a fuller discussion of this matter can be found in David E. Sanger and James Risen, "C.I.A. Chief Takes Blame in Assertion on Iraqi Uranium," *New York Times*, July 12, 2003, A1 and A5.

114. Sanger and Risen, "C.I.A. Chief Takes Blame in Assertion on Iraqi Uranium."

115. Philip Shenon, "Saudi Bombers Got Outside Support, Perry Tells Panel," *New York Times*, July 10, 1996, A4.

116. Allan E. Goodman, "Testimony: Fact- Checking at the CIA," *Foreign Policy* 102 (Spring 1996): 180–182.

117. Quoted in Barry, "Failures of Intelligence?" p. 20. The first two quotations in this paragraph are from this article and at this page.

118. Turner, *Secrecy and Democracy: The CIA in Transition*, pp. 113–127, especially at p. 125. For another assessment of the analytic difficulties of the CIA, see Tim Weiner, "House Panel Says C.I.A. Lacks Expertise to Carry Out Its Duties," *New York Times*, June 19, 1997, A13.

119. Nye, "Peering into the Future," p. 85.

120. Barry, "Failures of Intelligence?" pp. 20–21.

121. Turner, *Secrecy and Democracy: The CIA in Transition*, pp. 273–274.

122. Robert Jervis, "Why Intelligence and Policymakers Clash," in James M. McCormick, ed., *The Domestic Sources of American Foreign Policy: Insights and Evidence* 6th ed. (Lanham, MD: Rowman & Littlefield, Inc., 2012), pp. 267–284. All quotations are taken from this chapter at pp. 268, 274, and 283, respectively.

123. "U.S. Counterintelligence Effectiveness," Statement by the Press Secretary, the White House, May 3, 1994; and "Fact Sheet: U.S. Counterintelligence Effectiveness," White House/NSC Press Office, July 19, 1994.

124. Donna Cassata, "Spy Budget Cleared for Clinton; Plan for New Agency Curbed," *Congressional Quarterly Weekly Report*, December 23, 1995, 3894–3895.

125. The following is drawn from the "Recommendations" in *Joint Inquiry Into the Terrorist Attacks* report.

126. See *Joint Inquiry Into the Terrorist Attacks* and the National Commission on Terrorist Attacks Upon the United States website, http://www.9-11Commission.gov, for its missions and initial reports. On the testimony by Clinton and Bush administration

officials before the commission, see Philip Shenon and Eric Schmitt, "Bush and Clinton Aides Grilled by Panel," *New York Times*, March 24, 2004, A1 and A16; Philip Shenon and Richard W. Stevenson, "Ex-Bush Aide Says Threat of Qaeda Was Not Heeded," *New York Times*, March 25, 2004, A1, A2; and David Johnston and Todd S. Purdum, "Missed Chances in a Long Hunt for bin Laden," *New York Times*, March 25, 2004, A1 and A20. Also, see interview with Governor Kean and Congressman Hamilton, *Fox News Sunday*, broadcast March 28, 2004.

127. *The 9/11 Commission Report*, pp. 399–400.

128. Ibid., p. 415.

129. Ibid., p. 416.

130. Ibid., pp. 425–426.

131. "Fact Sheet: President Issues New Orders to Reform Intelligence," White House/ NSC Press Office, August 27, 2004, at http://www.whitehouse.gov/news/ releases/2004/08/20040827-13.html, May 30, 2008.

132. "Recommended, and Actual, Intelligence Reorganization," *CQ Weekly Online*, December 11, 2004, 2942–2943, at http://library.cqpress.com/cqweekly/ weeklyreport108-000001453550, May 15, 2008.

133. "House Approves 9/11 Security Recommendations Bill," July 29, 2007, at http://www. foxnews.com/printer_friendly_story/0,3566,291244,00.html, June 1, 2008. Also see P.L. 110-53 or 121 STAT. 266, at http://www.ise.gov/docs/nsis/Implementing911_Act.pdf, September 11, 2008.

134. The following discussion relies on, and draws from, the excellent evaluation by Tim Sharks in "Intel: Lost in the Reshuffle," *CQ Weekly Online*, May 5, 2008, 1166–1175, at http://library.cqpress.com/cqweekly/weeklyreport110-000002716574, May 6, 2008.

135. Ibid., p. 1169.

136. Ibid.

137. Ibid.

138. National Security Preparedness Group, *Tenth Anniversary Report Card: The Status of the 9/11 Commission Recommendations*, Bipartisan Policy Center, Washington, D.C., September, 2011, p. 17, at http://bipartisanpolicy.org/sites/default/files/ CommissionRecommendations.pdf, June 13, 2012.

139. Sharks, "Intel: Lost in the Reshuffle," p. 1166.

140. Karen DeYoung, "After Attempted Airline Bombing, Effectiveness of Intelligence Reforms Questioned," *Washington Post*, January 7, 2010, A01, at http://www. washingtonpost.com/wp-dyn/content/article/2010/01/06/AR2010010605158.html, June 13, 2012.

141. Sharks, "Intel: Lost in the Reshuffle," p. 1171.

142. National Security Preparedness Group, *Tenth Anniversary Report Card: The Status of the 9/11 Commission Recommendations*, p. 11.

143. Ibid., pp. 16–17, 15–16, and 19 for these recommendations and for the quoted passages.

144. John Deutch and Jeffrey H. Smith, "Smarter Intelligence," in Eugene R. Wittkopf and James M. McCormick, eds., *The Domestic Sources of American Foreign Policy: Insights and Evidence*, 4th ed. (Lanham, MD: Rowman & Littlefield, 2004), pp. 225–226.

145. Richard Betts is quoted in Paul R. Pillar, "Intelligent Design? The Unending Saga of Intelligence Reform," *Foreign Affairs* 87 (March/April 2008): 144, as Pillar reviews Betts's book entitled *Enemies of Intelligence: Knowledge and Power in American National Security*.

146. See, for example, Hilsman, "Does the CIA Still Have a Role?"

147. Bob Woodward, *Bush at War*; and Douglas Jehl and Dexter Filkins, "U.S. Moved to Undermine Iraqi Military Before War," *New York Times*, August 10, 2003, 1.

148. Pat Holt, *Secret Intelligence and Public Policy* (Washington, D.C.: CQ Press, 1995), p. 109.

149. John E. Rielly, ed., *American Public Opinion and U.S. Foreign Policy 1995* (Chicago: The Chicago Council on Foreign Relations, 1995), p. 37.

150. See Marshall M. Bouton and Benjamin I. Page, eds., *Worldviews 2002: American Public Opinion and Foreign Policy.* (Chicago: The Chicago Council on Foreign Relations, 2002), p. 23; *Global Views 2004: American Public Opinion and Foreign Policy* (Chicago: The Chicago Council on Foreign Relations, 2004), p. 19; and Marshal M. Bouton, *Global Views 2010: Constrained Internationalism: Adapting to New Realities* (Chicago: The Chicago Council on Global Affairs, 2010), p. 43.

151. P.L. 253 in *United States Statutes at Large*, Volume 61, Part 1, 80th Cong., 1st sess., p. 498.

152. See Central Intelligence Agency, Executive Order 12333, as amended by Executive Order 13284 (2003), 13355 (2004), and 13470 (2008), at https://www.cia.gov/about-cia/eo12333.html, June 14, 2012. See Marchetti and Marks, *The CIA and the Cult of Intelligence* and the *Church Committee Report* (see note 157 below) for a discussion of the types of covert operation.

153. Marchetti and Marks, *The CIA and the Cult of Intelligence*, pp. 281–282.

154. "Foreign and Military Intelligence, Book 1," Final Report of the Select Committee to Study Governmental Operations with respect to Intelligence Activities, United States Senate (Washington, D.C.: Government Printing Office, April 26, 1976), p. 425 (hereafter, the *Church Committee Report*).

155. Ibid., p. 56.

156. Ibid., pp. 56–57.

157. Ibid., p. 57.

158. Bernard Gwertzman, "Top Reagan Aide Supports the Use of Covert Action," *New York Times*, May 14, 1984, 1, 6.

159. Scowcroft made this statement during his appearance on "President vs. Congress: War Powers and Covert Action," *The Constitution: That Delicate Balance*, Public Broadcasting Service series broadcast in 1984.

160. Woodward, *Bush at War*, at pp. 75–78, from which the information and quotations are derived.

161. See Jo Becker and Scott Shane, "Secret 'Kill List' Proves a Test of Obama's Principles and Will," *New York Times*, May 29, 2012, at http://www.nytimes.com/2012/05/29/world/obamas-leadership-in-war-on-al-qaeda.html?pagewanted=all, May 29, 2012; and David E. Sanger, "Obama Order Sped Up Wave of Cyberattacks Against Iran," *New York Times*, June 1, 2012, at http://www.nytimes.com/2012/06/01/world/middleeast/obama-ordered-wave-of-cyberattacks-against-iran.html?pagewanted=all, June 10, 2012.

162. *Church Committee Report*, pp. 49–50.

163. Ibid., pp. 51–52.

164. Ibid., p. 54.

165. Ransom, *The Intelligence Establishment*, p. 162.

166. Gregory F. Treverton, "Intelligence: Welcome to the American Government," in Thomas E. Mann, ed., *A Question of Balance* (Washington, D.C.: The Brookings Institution, 1990), pp. 72–76.

167. See P.L. 93-559, 88 Stat. 1804. The quoted passage is from section 32.

168. See *Church Committee Report*, and *Report to the President by the Commission on CIA Activities Within the United States* (Washington, D.C.: Government Printing Office,

June 1975), for a complete listing of the recommendations. The latter was named the Rockefeller Commission after its chairman, Vice President Nelson Rockefeller.

169. On this point, see Harry Howe Ransom, "Strategic Intelligence and Intermestic Politics," in Charles W. Kegley and Eugene R. Wittkopf, *Perspectives on American Foreign Policy* (New York: St. Martin's Press, 1983), p. 313. President Ford's Executive Order 11905 can be found in *Weekly Compilation of Presidential Documents* 12 (February 23, 1976): 234–243.

170. "Intelligence Authorization Act for Fiscal Year 1981," P.L. 96-450, 94 Stat. 1981–1982. This section and the following one draw on earlier work reported in James M. McCormick and Steven S. Smith in "The Iran Arms Sale and the Intelligence Oversight Act of 1980," *PS* 20 (Winter 1987): 29–37.

171. The following examples draw on the "Executive Summary" in *Report of the Congressional Committees Investigating the Iran–Contra Affair* (Washington, D.C.: Government Printing Office, 1987), pp. 3–21. The quoted phrases are from this report as well.

172. Unclassified extract from National Security Decision Directive (NSDD) 286 and "Text of Letter on Covert Operations," by President Reagan to Senator David Boren in *New York Times*, August 8, 1987, 5. See also James M. McCormick, "Prior Notification of Covert Actions," *Chicago Tribune*, September 8, 1987, 11.

173. *Congressional Quarterly Almanac 1988* (Washington, D.C.: Congressional Quarterly, 1989), pp. 498–499; and *Congressional Quarterly Almanac 1989* (Washington, D.C.: Congressional Quarterly, 1990), p. 541.

174. Alfred Cummings, "Covert Action: Legislative Background and Possible Policy Questions," CRS Report for Congress. (Washington, D.C.: Congressional Research Service, The Library of Congress, January 28, 2008), p. 6.

175. These requirements (and the quoted passages) are taken from sec. 503 of P.L. 102-88, April 14, 1991.

176. For a detailed discussion of FISA and the recent changes and issues, see Elizabeth B. Bazan and Jennifer K. Elsea, "Presidential Authority to Conduct Warrantless Electronic Surveillance to Gather Foreign Intelligence Information" Congressional Research Service Memorandum (Washington, D.C.: Congressional Research Service, The Library of Congress, January 5, 2006). Also see Elizabeth B. Bazan, "The U.S. Foreign Intelligence Surveillance Court and the U.S. Foreign Intelligence Surveillance Court of Review: An Overview," CRS Report to Congress (Washington, D.C.: Congressional Research Service, The Library of Congress, January 24, 2007); and Bazan, "P.L. 110-55, the Protect America Act of 2007: Modifications to the Foreign Intelligence Surveillance Act," CRS Report to Congress (Washington, D.C.: Congressional Research Service, The Library of Congress, February 14, 2008). The quoted passage is in the summary of the last document cited.

177. Eric Lichtblau, "Senate Approves Bill to Broaden Wiretap Powers," *New York Times*, July 10, 2008, at http://www.nytimes.com/2008/07/10/washington/10fisa.html?_r=1&oref =slogin&pagewanted=print, July 10, 2008.

178. Politifact, "The Obameter: Restrict Warrantless Wiretaps," *Tampa Bay Times*, at http:// www.politifact.com/truth-o-meter/promises/obameter/promise/180/end-warrantless-wiretaps/, June 14, 2012.

179. Cummings, "Covert Action," pp. 4–5.

180. Ibid., p. 5; and Richard A. Best, Jr., "Covert Action: Legislative Background and Possible Policy Questions," CRS Report to Congress (Washington, D.C.: Congressional Research Service, The Library of Congress, December 27, 2011), p. 9.

181. Hilsman, "Does the CIA Still Have a Role?" The quoted passages are at pp. 110, 112, and 116, respectively.

182. See "President Establishes Office of Homeland Security," Department of Homeland Security, at http://www.dhs.gov/xnews/releases/press_release_0010.shtm, June 1, 2008.

183. Taken from Section 101 of the Homeland Security Act of 2002. See P.L. 107-296 at 116 Stat .2135 or http://www.dhs.gov/xlibrary/assets/hr_5005_enr.pdf, September 11, 2008.

184. The number of personnel in DHS is taken from Janet Napolitano, "Secretary of Homeland Security Janet Napolitano's 2nd Annual Address on the State of America's Homeland Security: Homeland Security and Economic Security," January 30, 2012, at http://www.dhs.gov/ynews/speeches/napolitano-state-of-america-homeland-security. shtm, June 15, 2012. The budget figure is from Department of Homeland Security, "FY2013 Budget in Brief," p. 6, at http://www.dhs.gov/xlibrary/assets/mgmt/dhs-budget-in-brief-fy2013.pdf, June 15, 2012.

185. See "Fact Sheet: U.S. Department of Homeland Security Announces 6.8 Percent Increase in Fiscal Year 2009 Budget Request," February 4, 2008, http://www.dhs.gov/xnews/releases/pr_1202151112290.shtm, May 22, 2008.

186. Department of Homeland Security, "Executive Summary," *Quadrennial Homeland Security Review*, February 2010, p. iii, at http://www.dhs.gov/xlibrary/assets/qhsr_executive_summary.pdf, June 15, 2012.

187. For these and other data on the activities of the DHS in 2011, see Department of Homeland Security, "DHS' Progress in 2011: By the Numbers," at http://www.dhs.gov/xabout/2011-dhs-accomplishments-by-the-numbers.shtm, June 15, 2012.

188. This system is described in "Homeland Security Advisory System" and "Homeland Security Advisory System—Guidance for Federal Departments and Agencies," at http://www.dhs.gov/xinfoshare/programs/Copy_of_press_release_0046.shtm, September 11, 2008, and http://www.dhs.gov/xnews/releases/press_release_0046.shtm, March 12, 2002, September 11, 2008, and June 1, 2008, respectively.

189. Department of Homeland Security, "NTAS Public Guide," at http://www.dhs.gov/files/publications/ntas-public-guide.shtm, June 15, 2012.

190. See John Mintz, "Security Goals Compromised by Problems in Department," *Des Moines Register*, September 8, 2003, 1A and 4A, with the quote at p. 1A.

191. National Security Preparedness Group, *Tenth Anniversary Report Card: The Status of the 9/11 Commission Recommendations*. The quoted passage is at p. 11, and the discussions of the specific recommendations are at pp. 12–13, 17–18, and 18, respectively.

192. Ivo H. Daalder and I. M. Destler, "Advisors, Czars, and Councils," *The National Interest* 68 (Summer 2002): 70.

193. Esterline and Black, *Inside Foreign Policy*, p. 23. On the Kissinger reorganization, see pp. 24–26.

194. The following discussion of SIGs and IGs in the Reagan administration is based on the Statement of the President, "National Security Council Structure," January 12, 1982, reprinted in Robert E. Hunter, *Presidential Control of Foreign Policy: Management or Mishap?* The Washington Papers/91 (New York: Praeger, 1982), pp. 109–115 (also see Hunter's discussion of this system, pp. 96–102, on which we also relied); and Colin Campbell, *Managing the Presidency: Carter, Reagan, and the Search for Executive Harmony* (Pittsburgh: University of Pittsburgh Press, 1986), p. 43. In the original directive, only the first three SIGs were established. The international economic SIG was added later.

195. Campbell, *Managing the Presidency: Carter, Reagan, and the Search for Executive Harmony*, p. 43. The reference to the NSPG draws on the unclassified extract from National Security Decision Directive (NSDD) 286 at http://www.fas.org/irp/offdocs/nsdd286.htm, August 14, 2012.

196. The discussion of the changes since the Tower Commission Report of 1987 is based on Paul Schoot Stevens, "The National Security Council: Past and Prologue," *Strategic Review* 17 (Winter 1989): 61.

197. Richard A. Best, Jr., "The National Security Council: An Organizational Assessment," CRS Report to Congress (Washington, D.C.: Congressional Research Service, The Library of Congress, December 28, 2011), p. 18 for the quoted passage. The discussion of the NSC advisor during the Reagan years is at pp. 17-20.

198. The description of the George H. W. Bush administration's NSC policy coordination process is based on material provided by the Carlisle Barracks, U.S. Army War College, Pennsylvania, December 1989, and a memo from the NSC, "National Security Council Organization," April 17, 1989.

199. The descriptions of the NSC committees and the quotation about their activities during the Clinton administration are taken from *Presidential Decision Directive 2*, January 20, 1993, at http://www.fas.org/irp/offdocs/pdd/pdd-2.htm, September 12, 2008.

200. This discussion of the George W. Bush administration's NSC system is drawn from *National Security Presidential Directive 1*, February 13, 2001, at http://www.fas.org/irp/offdocs/nspd/nspd-1.htm, September 12, 2008.

201. Alan G. Whittaker, Frederick C. Smith, and Elizabeth McKune, *The National Security Policy Process: The National Security Council and Interagency System*, Research Report, November 2007 Annual Update (Washington, D.C.: Industrial College of the Armed Forces, National Defense University, U.S. Department of Defense, 2007), p. 23.

202. Ibid., p. 14, for the complete list of functional PCCs in the Bush administration and the department that is charged with chairing them.

203. See Presidential Policy Directive-1, The White House, Washington, D.C., February 13, 2009, at http://www.fas.org/irp/offdocs/ppd/ppd-1.pdf, June 17, 2012.

204. Alan G. Whittaker, Shannon A. Brown, Frederick C. Smith, and Ambassador Elizabeth McKune, *The National Security Policy Process: The National Security Council and Interagency System*, Research Report, August 15, 2011, Annual Update (Washington, D.C.: Industrial College of the Armed Forces, National Defense University, U.S. Department of Defense, 2011), pp. 31–32. The quoted passages are at p. 31.

205. Ibid., pp. 32–34.

206. Ibid., p. 17

207. Ibid., p. 34.

208. Barack Obama, "Statement by the President on the White House Organization for Homeland Security and Counterterrorism," May 26, 2009, at http://www.whitehouse.gov/the_press_office/Statement-by-the-President-on-the-White-House-Organization-for-Homeland-Security-and-Counterterrorism/, June 17, 2012.

209. Whitaker, Brown, Smith, and McKune, *The National Security Policy Process: The National Security Council and Interagency System*, p. 29.

CHAPTER 11

Political Parties, Bipartisanship, and Interest Groups

When we have been successful in national security and foreign affairs,
it has been because there has been bipartisan support.

FORMER SECRETARY OF DEFENSE ROBERT GATES

JUNE 2011

AIPAC's mission is to strengthen the ties between the United States
and its ally Israel. As America's leading pro-Israel lobby, AIPAC works
with Democrats, Republicans and Independents to enact public policy that
enhances the U.S.-Israel relationship.

MISSION STATEMENT OF THE AMERICAN ISRAEL POLITICAL
ACTION COMMITTEE (AIPAC)

AIPAC WEBSITE

JULY 2012

Beyond the president, Congress, and the bureaucracies, two other participants influence the U.S. foreign policy process: **political parties** and **interest groups**. Although these groups probably have less direct impact than the participants discussed so far, they are increasingly viewed as important to policy making. By political parties, we mean organized groups who pursue their goals by contesting elections and perhaps controlling political offices.[1] These groups can influence foreign policy decisions directly by controlling elective offices, and they can influence the decisions of those who control executive and legislative offices through criticism and debate. By *interest groups*, we mean those portions of the population who are organized and seek political goals that they are unable to achieve on their own.[2] They seek their goals through various lobbying techniques ranging from campaign contributions to a political candidate to face-to-face discussions with policy makers.

In the first half of this chapter, we examine the contribution of America's two principal political parties to the foreign policy process. We begin by focusing on the concept of bipartisanship in foreign affairs and assess its overall success since World War II. Next we examine how the Vietnam War, the end of the Cold War, and the Iraq and Afghanistan Wars weakened any bipartisanship that may have existed. Finally, we summarize evidence from the past several decades challenging the notion that bipartisanship ever existed and identify some increasingly fundamental foreign policy differences that have emerged between the parties.

In the second half of the chapter, we identify and briefly discuss several traditional foreign policy interest groups and then some newer ones that have emerged over the past three decades. We then assess the relative impact of these groups and the mechanisms that they utilize to achieve their goals within the American political system. Finally, we select two types of interest groups, economic and ethnic groups, to illustrate the importance of foreign policy interest groups generally. In this connection, we examine the relative roles of the "military-industrial complex" and the Jewish lobby on American policy making today.

POLITICAL PARTIES AND
THE BIPARTISAN TRADITION

Historically, America's two political parties did not differ in their programmatic or ideological positions on many domestic and foreign issues. Both the **Democratic and Republican parties** were more often seen **as pragmatic organizations** that adopted positions on such issues as taxation, Social Security, and health care to attract as many adherents as possible. Although this description can be overstated and tends to apply more to party followers than to party leaders, it is generally an accurate portrait of U.S. political parties, especially when compared to their European counterparts.[3]

This depiction, moreover, has been applied particularly to America's two major parties in the foreign policy arena. Despite the fact that the Republican Party more often controlled the White House, and the Democratic Party, Congress, after World War II, *bipartisanship* was frequently used to describe America's approach to foreign affairs. The origins of bipartisanship usually are attributed to the issues that the United States faced in the late 1940s and early 1950s. Because the international environment was so threatening during that period, a united approach seemed to be required for national security. In the words of one prominent politician of the time, "partisan politics . . . stopped at the water's edge."[4] By this reasoning, the national interest necessarily supplanted any partisan interest in foreign policy, and bipartisan cooperation between Congress and the president supplanted both institutional and partisan differences as well.

The exact meaning of bipartisanship, however, was not always clear, but it seemed to require at least two different, albeit complementary, kinds of cooperation between the legislative and executive branches.[5] One kind focused on achieving "unity in foreign affairs" and referred to the degree to which "policies [are] supported by majorities within each political party" in Congress. The other kind referred to a set of "practices and procedures designed to bring about the desired unity."[6] Put differently, Congress and the president would develop procedures in which each would participate and would consult with the other in the formulation of foreign policy; in turn, a majority of congressional members from both parties would support the policy developed. These two kinds of cooperation implied that **bipartisanship** would involve **collaboration in both the** *process* **of foreign policy making and its** *outcome*.

The Cold War Years and Bipartisanship

The beginning of this bipartisan effort is usually traced to the cooperation that developed between Democratic president Harry Truman and the Republican chairman of the Senate Foreign Relations Committee, **Senator Arthur Vandenberg** of Michigan, in the immediate post–World War II years. After Senator Vandenberg altered his isolationist stance and after President Truman committed himself to global involvement for the United States, the two leaders consciously sought to build a bipartisan foreign policy against Communist expansionism, and, to a large extent, they were successful. Indeed, the major foreign policy initiatives of the late 1940s were accomplished with substantial support across political parties. The passage of the Bretton Woods agreement, the UN Charter, the Greek-Turkish aid program, and the Marshall Plan, among others, garnered support from both parties and passed Congress with over 83 percent support on average.[7]

The acceptance of the Cold War consensus by the major political parties and the public at large seemingly continued this bipartisan tradition in foreign policy through the Eisenhower and Kennedy administrations and into the Johnson administration as well. Despite some party divisions over Senator Joseph McCarthy's attacks on "Communists" within the government, the "loss" of China, and the Korean War, the essential unity of the two parties remained.[8] Even with the so-called missile gap of the late 1950s that was eventually carried into the 1960 presidential campaign, the parties continued their markedly similar foreign policy orientations. In their 1956 party platforms, both expressed a desire for a bipartisan foreign policy; the Republicans expressed this sentiment again in 1960.[9]

Both **Democrats and Republicans** came to stand for a similar posture toward world affairs: **a strong national defense, active U.S. global involvement**, and **staunch anticommunism**. To be sure, some divisions existed within the two parties. The Republicans had to contend with a wing that still cherished isolationism, and the Democrats had to contend with a wing that was initially suspicious of the confrontational approach toward the Soviet Union. Further, the Democrats had to deal with popular perceptions of them as the party associated with war (but also with prosperity); in contrast, the Republicans enjoyed being perceived as the party associated with peace (but not as the party associated with recession).[10] Democratic presidents— such as Franklin Delano Roosevelt, who led the United States into World War II, and Harry Truman, who initiated the Korean War—represented the former perception.

Republican presidents—such as Herbert Hoover in the interwar years and Dwight Eisenhower after the Korean War—represented the latter.

Despite these different party factions and popular labels, members of the two parties tended to stand for the same general principles in foreign policy. As political scientist Herbert McClosky and his associates report from their 1957–1958 survey data on party leaders and followers, the differences between the parties were indeed small. In fact, the average difference between Democratic and Republican leaders was smaller in foreign policy than in any of the four domestic policy areas that McClosky and colleagues examined. Democratic and Republican followers demonstrated the same pattern generally.[11]

This **bipartisanship** was also reflected in the **policy "planks"** that each party placed in its national platforms during the Cold War years. In a systematic analysis of Democratic and Republican platforms from 1944 to 1964, political scientist Gerald Pomper reports that 47 percent of the party pledges on foreign policy were essentially the same and only 6 percent were in conflict.[12] Defense policy pledges were also quite similar: 73 percent were the same and only 2 percent were in conflict. Such bipartisanship on foreign policy was second only to that on civil rights among eight policy categories analyzed, whereas on defense policy it was tied for third position with labor and agriculture. Finally, the percentage of conflicting pledges across parties was equally low in comparison with other policy categories.

The important consequence of this bipartisanship tradition is that separate party influence, as such, seemingly did not have a strong effect on general foreign policy strategies. Instead, policy influence was mainly confined to the executive branch because the president could generally count on congressional and public support across political parties. Recall the high level of presidential success in foreign policy that we discussed in Chapter 7.

THE LIMITS OF BIPARTISANSHIP THROUGH THE VIETNAM ERA

Although *bipartisanship* was preeminent in any description of the roles of the two parties during the Cold War years and beyond, some analysts in retrospect argue (and even some at the time argued) that **partisan unity on foreign affairs was often overstated**. I. M. Destler, Anthony Lake, and Leslie Gelb best capture this alternate view in describing the first fifteen years of the Cold War:

> These were said to be the halcyon days of bipartisanship or nonpartisanship, of Democrats and Republicans putting national interests above party interests. But such a description has always been more myth than reality. Conservatives and liberals were at one another's throat constantly. There was never a time when Truman was not besieged. . . . [Adlai E.] Stevenson tried to make foreign policy a key issue in the 1956 [presidential] campaign, and Mr. Kennedy succeeded in doing so in 1960.[13]

Destler, Lake, and Gelb do acknowledge that the apparent unity in policy is partly explained by the fact that politicians primarily "rall[ied] around the President's flag in East–West confrontations," but on "second-order issues" they "squabble[d]" regularly.[14]

Two decades earlier, a prominent foreign policy analyst, Cecil Crabb, reached a similar conclusion in characterizing the bipartisanship of the late 1940s to the late 1950s.[15] After reviewing several cases of foreign policy and bipartisanship in that period, Crabb concluded that there were "relatively few genuinely bipartisan undertakings in American postwar relations." Although a bipartisan approach might provide stability and continuity in policy, he noted, it might also weaken executive leadership, reduce the vigor of debate, and even weaken the party system. Such disadvantages, of course, could ultimately be harmful to foreign policy. In short, the characterization of the period as bipartisan is not wholly accurate, nor was the attempt to achieve such a policy approach necessarily a wise one.

Partisan/Ideological Differences and Foreign Policy Issues

A closer examination of several foreign policy issues during the immediate postwar years lends credence to a more limited view of bipartisanship. **On foreign aid, military aid, defense spending, and trade issues, for example, continuous partisan divisions were evident, even at the height of presumed bipartisan cooperation**. Often, too, on these issues, the Democrats were split between their Northern wing (traditionally more liberal) and their Southern wing (traditionally more conservative). Still, even when one wing joined forces temporarily with the Republicans, there were sufficient fluctuations between issues to limit bipartisanship and produce partisan and ideological divisions.

For instance, in the 1950s, Republicans and Northern Democrats joined together ideologically to support foreign economic assistance programs, whereas Southern Democrats opposed them. In the 1960s through the early 1970s, Northern Democrats generally continued their support; Southern Democrats, their opposition. Republicans, on the other hand, fluctuated from opposition in the early 1960s to support later in the decade and into the 1970s.[16]

On the issue of military assistance, Northern Democrats in the Senate generally supported the increase or maintenance of funding levels until the early 1960s. By contrast, Southern Democrats fluctuated during the height of the Cold War but became more supportive during Vietnam. Republicans increasingly came to support such assistance over the course of the postwar period, albeit with some initial reluctance in the early 1950s. In the House, voting trends on military assistance were much more irregular across party lines, but the general direction for both parties was about the same as in the Senate.

On defense expenditures, partisan differences existed as well. More Northern Democrats in the Senate, and fewer in the House, supported increasing or at least maintaining defense spending in the 1950s, but Northern Democrats in both houses began to oppose this spending in the 1960s and 1970s. Republicans, on the other hand, opposed such expenditures in the 1950s more so than Democrats, but they tended to be much more supportive than Democrats from 1960 onward. Southern Democrats were less varied in their voting and continued to support defense expenditures during these years.

Some partisan differences on trade policy existed in the 1950s and 1960s. Democrats generally were more supportive of free trade, whereas Republicans were generally more protectionist. By the middle of the 1960s, however, these trends had reversed, with Democrats becoming more protectionist and Republicans becoming more supportive of free trade.

The upshot of these analyses is that party influence—even at the height of bipartisanship—had an impact on specific details of foreign policy. To the extent that bipartisanship existed, it necessarily had to operate within the confines of party differences. In this sense, partisan politics helped shape U.S. foreign policy behavior to a greater extent than some might wish to acknowledge. Nevertheless, as political scientist Barry Hughes and others remind us, the position and party of the president still played an important role in congressional voting results.[17]

The Effects of Vietnam

Although Destler, Gelb, and Lake acknowledge that some bipartisanship (or, more accurately, "majorityship") existed from the 1940s to the 1960s, they argue that **"Vietnam changed all this**."[18] As more young Americans were drafted and sent to Vietnam following the escalation of the war in 1965, and as the conflict became a regular feature on the evening news, President Lyndon Johnson found himself facing a domestic political problem every bit as challenging as the war itself. The effects of the war were profound on domestic harmony and on any great semblance of cooperation across party lines. As Destler, Gelb, and Lake note, "The conceptual basis of American foreign policy was now shaken, and the politics of foreign policy became more complicated."

Zbigniew Brzezinski aptly summarizes the effect of Vietnam on any domestic unity in foreign policy:

> Our foreign policy became increasingly the object of contestation, of sharp cleavage, and even of some reversal of traditional political commitments. The Democratic Party, the party of internationalism, became increasingly prone to the appeal of neo-isolationism. And the Republican Party, the party of isolationism, became increasingly prone to the appeal of militant interventionism. And both parties increasingly found their center of gravity shifting to the extreme, thereby further polarizing our public opinion.[19]

These changes in bipartisanship became evident in patterns of support for the Vietnam War within Congress. President Johnson now had to rely on the support of Republicans and conservative (largely Southern) Democrats for his Southeast Asia policy,[20] and opposition from liberals within his party and from a few Republicans began to grow. Party and ideological lines were being drawn; strong support across party lines on a major foreign policy initiative was eroding. Still, as contentious as this issue was, the Democratic-controlled Congress was never successful in defeating President Johnson or President Richard Nixon (through 1972) on a major funding bill for the war.[21] In this sense, the essence of both party loyalty and bipartisanship remained, although both forces were stretched taut.

Toward the end of the Vietnam War, bipartisanship began to wear even thinner. With a Republican president in the White House and a Congress controlled by the Democrats, the consequence was the series of foreign policy reforms discussed in Chapter 8. Although both parties supported a number of these reforms, Democrats, particularly liberal Democrats, were generally more favorable to limits on the foreign policy powers of the executive than were Republicans. Moreover, the major reforms enacted by Congress occurred when Republican presidents were in office and Democrats controlled both the Senate and the House.

Another barometer of changing foreign policy bipartisanship in the Vietnam period is the **increasing partisanship in party platforms**, especially when compared to the Cold War years. The party platforms for 1968, 1972, and 1976 indicate a marked decrease in bipartisanship,[22] with only 24 percent of foreign policy pledges and only

11 percent of defense policy pledges the same for Republicans and Democrats. (Recall that bipartisan pledges during the Cold War were about two to three times those figures.) The two parties seemed to be moving in different directions in that the preponderance of pledges on foreign and defense policy were unique to each. At the same time, the degree of conflict on pledges remained low (at about 6 percent) for each policy area. In short, bipartisanship was declining, but outright partisan conflict had yet to emerge.

By the 1980s, however, partisan divisions on foreign policy were increasing even more. Key issues such as Central America, the Middle East, and national defense elicited clashes along party and ideological lines.[23] Congressional voting on covert aid to Nicaraguan rebels, for example, often pitted Democrats against Republicans. On key defense votes, such as the MX missile, the B-1 bomber, and the Strategic Defense Initiative ("Star Wars"), the pattern was much the same.[24] In this sense, there had been clear movement away from the bipartisan tradition of the past, especially on crucial defense and foreign policy issues.

BIPARTISANSHIP AND CONGRESSIONAL FOREIGN POLICY VOTING

Academic research raises some questions about the extent to which bipartisanship *ever* actually operated, particularly with regard to policy outcome. Recall that one component of bipartisanship is a unified policy outcome across the legislative and executive branches and the two parties—that is, a majority of both parties in Congress support the president's position. Research by McCormick and Wittkopf suggests that such bipartisanship, when defined by congressional voting, was less frequent than popularly believed.[25] In several analyses of congressional foreign policy voting from the late 1940s to the late 1980s, McCormick and Wittkopf argue that partisan and ideological conflict was more often the norm than bipartisan harmony. They found, in fact, that in over 2,400 congressional foreign policy votes on which the president took a position bipartisan policy unity was as much fantasy as fact.

Figure 11.1 shows the results obtained by McCormick and Wittkopf for bipartisan voting in the House and Senate from 1947 to 1988 for eight U.S. administrations. As can be seen, with few exceptions, it was more infrequent than conventional wisdom suggests. Only during the Eisenhower administration was there bipartisan support (defined as support by the majority of both parties) across the House and Senate on more than 50 percent of foreign policy votes. The figure also shows that this support was greater in the Senate than in the House and that it was especially low in the latter chamber. Indeed, if the Eisenhower administration is excluded, no more than 50 percent of the votes in the House in any administration obtained bipartisan results. These findings hardly support the view that bipartisanship was the norm for any extended period in the post–World War II years.

In contrast, Figure 11.2 illustrates the substantial degree of partisan division in these administrations since World War II. Although greater in the House than in the Senate, partisan gaps between the parties are quite substantial. On average, the divisions in each chamber were about 20 percentage points, with only the Eisenhower administration (in both the House and the Senate) and the Johnson administration (in the Senate) obtaining noticeably smaller differences. Moreover, these partisan gaps held and were pronounced across four foreign policy issues (foreign aid, foreign

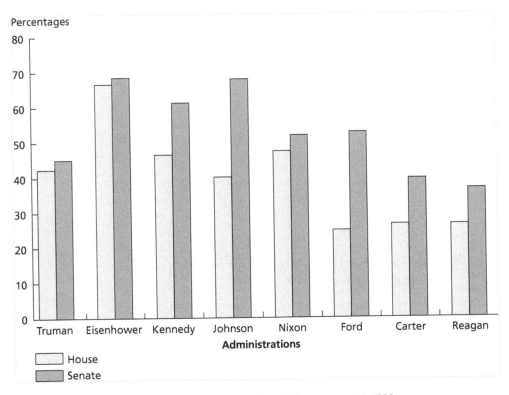

FIGURE 11.1 Bipartisan Foreign Policy Voting in Congress, 1947–1988

Note: Each bar represents the proportion of foreign policy votes on which a majority of both parties supported the president's position.

Source: James M. McCormick and Eugene R. Wittkopf, "Bipartisanship, Partisanship, and Ideology in Congressional–Executive Foreign Relations, 1947–1988," *The Journal of Politics* 52 (November 1990): 1085. Reprinted by permission of Cambridge University Press.

relations, national security, and trade). In short, the results suggest that congressional voting on foreign policy issues has always been more partisan than often portrayed.

When the Vietnam War is factored into these analyses, the overall conclusions do not change. Although partisan divisions increased somewhat in the post–Vietnam period, the impact of the war generally could not be separated from that of other factors. Only on national security voting did the pre– and post–Vietnam periods show marked differences. Overall, though, the war appeared not to be "a watershed in postwar American bipartisanship."[26] Only in combination with other changes at home and in Congress did it produce an increase in partisan and ideological divisions.

A more recent assessment by **Peter Trubowitz** and **Nicole Mellow** for a longer period of congressional voting (1889–2002) reaches the same conclusion about the decline in bipartisanship.[27] Although these analysts use a different definition of bipartisanship than that in the McCormick and Wittkopf studies (and compare both domestic and foreign policy issues), they report that bipartisanship has largely been episodic over the period of their analysis, noting that from the 1970s to the present, "the incidence of bipartisanship," whether on domestic or foreign policy issues, has

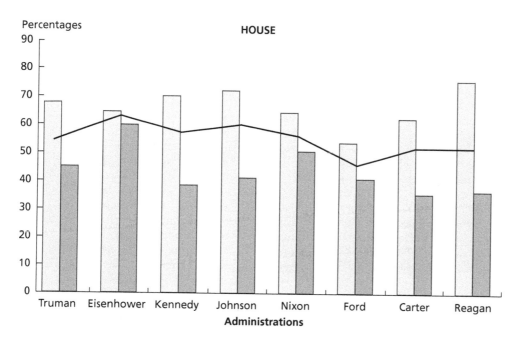

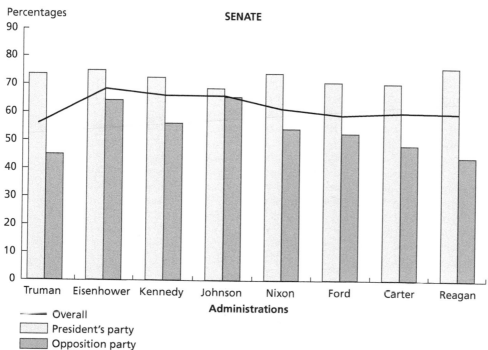

FIGURE 11.2 Partisan Differences in Congressional Voting on Foreign Policy Issues

Note: Each bar represents, for each party, the average percentage of support by members of Congress for the president's position on foreign policy votes. The overall line measures the average level of support for the president regardless of party.

Source: James M. McCormick and Eugene R. Wittkopf, "Bipartisanship, Partisanship, and Ideology in Congressional-Executive Foreign Relations, 1947–1988," "steadily eroded," and conclude that there is "strong evidence that, contrary to popular wisdom, politics do not stop at the water's edge."

These results appear to raise doubts about the degree of bipartisanship, at least as measured through formal congressional voting. However, some caution needs to be exercised in interpreting the figures and pushing them beyond what they can demonstrate about bipartisanship in U.S. foreign policy generally. For instance, the analyses do not consider the other component of bipartisanship—the process side or the degree of informal consultations between the branches—in other words, collaborative arrangements arrived at that are not (and cannot be) reflected in formal voting patterns. Further, at least for the McCormick and Wittkopf data, the analysis does not weigh the importance of particular issues to the president, even though these are the ones on which he has indicated a position. Thus, bipartisan outcomes may have been achieved for highly selective issues, especially important to the president and Congress, but bipartisan cooperation may not have been imbedded in this larger set of votes on which the president still stated a position. These necessary cautions notwithstanding, congressional voting analyses do alert us to the danger of applying too quickly and too easily the "bipartisan" label to U.S. foreign policy making during the Cold War years and after.

PARTISAN DIVISIONS: FROM THE COLD WAR TO TODAY

The debate continues over whether bipartisanship ever existed and over how much it has declined, but there is no question that partisan divisions on foreign policy issues exist today. Indeed, according to analyst Peter Beinart, "**by the time Ronald Reagan took office, foreign policy was thoroughly polarized along party lines.**"[28] Republicans had fully embraced global containment and even the rollback of communism (via the Reagan Doctrine), and Democrats had embraced détente and the promotion of global human rights as their raison d'être in foreign affairs. President Reagan recognized these partisan divisions and took at least two important steps in an effort to ameliorate them. First, he appointed bipartisan presidential commissions to garner support for both the modernization of America's strategic nuclear arsenal and his Central American policy.[29] The task of these commissions was to diffuse partisan bickering and build support across party lines. Second, he felt compelled to deliver a major foreign policy address in which he called for a return to an earlier era of executive–legislative cooperation: "We must restore America's honorable tradition of partisan politics stopping at the water's edge, Republicans and Democrats standing united in patriotism and speaking with one voice."[30] Despite this appeal, party differences in Reagan's second term actually accelerated on foreign policy, fueled largely by the controversy surrounding the Iran–Contra affair.

The George H. W. Bush Administration   When President George H. W. Bush took office, partisan accord was so low that he, like Reagan, felt it necessary to appeal for bipartisanship in foreign policy in his inaugural address:

> We need a new engagement . . . between the Executive and the Congress. . . . There's grown a certain divisiveness. . . . And our great parties have too often been far apart and untrusting of each other. . . . It's been this way since Vietnam. That war cleaves us still. . . . A new breeze is blowing—and the old bipartisanship must be made new again.[31]

Despite some initial efforts by both Republicans and Democrats and an important bipartisan Contra aid package early in 1989, Bush still faced partisan divisions over his foreign policy making. Spirited partisan and ideological debates occurred over defense expenditures, the amount of assistance to the newly independent Eastern Europe, and the response to the Chinese crackdown in Tiananmen Square. The fractious argument in January 1991 over whether to continue sanctions against Saddam Hussein's Iraq after his seizure of Kuwait or to go to war sustained these debates. In all, President Bush had bipartisan support for slightly less than one in five foreign policy votes in the House (19 percent) and less than one in three votes in the Senate (29 percent) (see Figure 11.3). These levels were lower than for Bush's three predecessors in both chambers. Partisan acrimony continued, as Figure 11.4 shows, with partisan gaps on foreign policy voting remaining as wide as during the Reagan administration—34 percent and 35 percent between Republicans and Democrats in the House and Senate, respectively, from 1989 to 1992.[32]

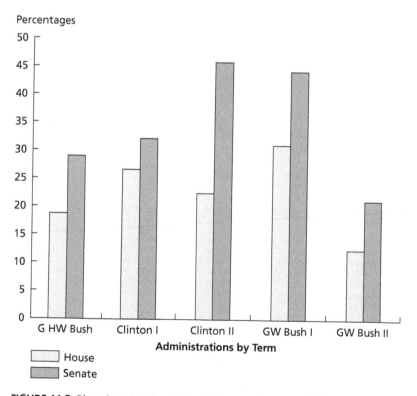

FIGURE 11.3 Bipartisan Foreign Policy Voting in Congress, 1989–2008

Note: Each bar represents the proportion of foreign policy votes on which a majority of both parties supported the president's position

Source: The table was constructed by identifying all foreign policy votes in each Congress on which the president took a position and calculating the percentage of bipartisan support across each administration's term. The data for 1989 through 1996 were taken from those reported in James M. McCormick, Eugene R. Wittkopf, and David M. Danna, "Politics and Bipartisanship at the Water's Edge: A Note on Bush and Clinton," *Polity* 30 (Fall 1997): 133–149; those for 1997 through 2008 were coded from the Congressional Almanac (various years). Thanks to Yong Ouk, Nicholas Lauen, Kirk Galster, and Robert Beyer for assistance in data collection.

Percentages

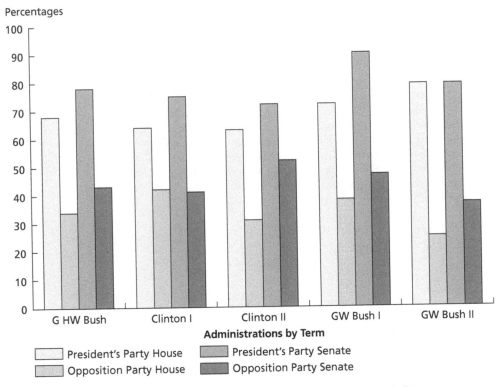

FIGURE 11.4 Partisan Differences in Congressional Voting on Foreign Policy
Issues, 1989–2008

Note: Each bar represents, for each party, the average percentage of support by members of Congress for the
president's position on foreign policy votes.

Source: The table was constructed by identifying all foreign policy votes in each Congress on which the president took
a position, calculating the support by each party for the president's position, and usually averaging them across the
Congresses for each administration's term (particularly from Clinton II through G.W. Bush II). The data for 1989 through
1996 were taken from those reported in James M. McCormick, Eugene R. Wittkopf, and David M. Danna, "Politics and
Bipartisanship at the Water's Edge: A Note on Bush and Clinton," *Polity* 30 (Fall 1997): 133–149; those for 1997 through
2008 were coded from the Congressional Almanac (various years). Thanks to Yong Ouk, Nicholas Lauen, Kirk Galster,
and Robert Beyer for assistance in data collection.

The Clinton Administration The bipartisan decline and the partisan gaps continued unabated for the Clinton administration. One analyst has suggested why:
Foreign policy divisions between Democrats and Republicans had taken on a new
form to replace the previous shapers of partisan debate: communism and the Soviet Union. On the one hand, Republicans came to define the national interest narrowly, largely to protect American actions from "a growing globalist ethic, in which
America expended blood and treasure not on its own behalf but in support of an
illusory 'international community.'"[33] On the other hand, "Democrats . . . generally
embraced stronger international institutions . . . as essential to prosperity and human
rights in a globalized age." The "Contract with America" that Republicans advanced
in the 1994 congressional elections immediately revealed this division. In it—in direct
challenges to the actions of the Clinton administration in Somalia and Bosnia—the

Republicans essentially called for limiting American commitments worldwide and for retaining American command of armed forces used in international operations.

In turn, a whole series of foreign policy issues in Congress during the Clinton administration displayed these partisan divisions, largely fought over narrowing the national interest—a position that Republicans wanted—or broadening it to include or expand support for international institutions—a position that Democrats wanted. On the use of American forces abroad, whether in Somalia, Bosnia, or Haiti, for example, Republicans were consistently less supportive than Democrats. Over the NATO air war in Kosovo in 1999, the Senate, albeit largely divided on party lines, voted to support the operation by a 58–41 margin, but the House actually rejected a resolution supporting it by a tie vote of 213–213. On the Comprehensive Nuclear Test-Ban Treaty, the Senate delivered a stinging defeat to the Clinton administration. It supported the treaty largely on a party line vote (51–48), but the vote total was 16 short of the needed 67 to win approval.[34] Trade, too, produced sharp partisan differences, with the Clinton administration ultimately relying on Republican support to gain approval of the North American Free Trade Agreement (NAFTA). Significantly, though, the Republican-controlled Congress refused fast-track trading authority for the Clinton administration, forestalling efforts to complete more trading pacts around the world.

Our summary data on the degree of bipartisan voting on foreign policy and the magnitude of the partisan gap provide a compelling picture of the sharp divide that continued between the two parties during the Clinton administration (see Figures 11.3 and 11.4). During its first term, for issues on which it took a position, the Clinton administration enjoyed bipartisan support on approximately one in four foreign policy issues in the House of Representatives, and one in three in the Senate. In its second term, the administration did slightly worse in the House (on about one in five votes) but better in the Senate (on almost one in two votes). This level of support was better than that received by the Reagan and Bush administrations in the Senate and about the same as in the House for these previous administrations. Across the two Clinton terms, the partisan gaps fluctuated considerably. In the House, the gap on foreign policy votes in the first term was 22 percent, but it increased to 32 percent in the second. In the Senate, the pattern was reversed—higher in the first term (34 percent) and lower in the second (20 percent). However we examine this partisan divide, one thing becomes clear: Democrats and Republicans were increasingly divided on foreign policy issues.

The George W. Bush Administration The George W. Bush administration came to office with a narrowly Republican-controlled Congress and initially enjoyed foreign policy support across party lines. Propelled by the events of September 11, this support accelerated, especially on security questions. Congress had moved back from its activism after the end of the Cold War and was once again more deferential to presidential wishes. Although some lawmakers may have wished to adopt a different position either for policy or party reasons, "political reality" demanded that they support the president in a time of national threat. In this sense, it had become difficult for members of Congress—of either party—to criticize a popular president confronting a foreign policy crisis,[35] and bipartisanship appeared to have been restored. Indeed, without the Iraq War, one analyst argues, "one can imagine the war on terror playing out somewhat as the early cold war did, with a broad consensus concealing differing partisan emphases."[36]

Yet the **Iraq War was initiated, and it had the effect of turning any emergent foreign policy consensus after 9/11 back into the partisan divide** among the public and in Congress that had been developing over the previous two decades. To be sure, Congress and the public were initially supportive of President Bush. After all, the Iraq Resolution was passed by wide margins in both the House and the Senate, and the public as well gave strong initial approval to the invasion.[37] However, such support can be short-lived, as Bush quickly began to learn. By the summer of 2003, as the reconstruction of Iraq began to prove more challenging, both in "blood and treasure," Bush's approval rating declined to 50 percent in one poll in September 2003; his level of support on the question of whether the Iraq War was worth fighting reached a similar level.[38] Partisan divisions among the public (and within Congress) soon emerged. Among Republican identifiers, 70 percent or more continued to assess Iraq as going well into 2004 and 2005, but among Democratic identifiers, only 30 percent (and sometimes fewer) judged the war as going well by mid-2004. That support continued to decline. Moreover, independents more closely tracked Democrats than Republicans in their assessments.[39]

Partisan divisions over foreign policy quickly resurfaced in Congress with the Iraq War, too. When we examine the degree of bipartisan voting and the partisan gap for the Bush administration in its two terms, we find much the same pattern as before. During Bush's first term, and with the events of 9/11, his bipartisan support was 31 percent in the House and 44 percent in the Senate, both figures generally higher than his father's (19 percent and 29 percent, respectively) and mainly higher than Clinton's (27 percent and 32 percent, respectively, in the first term and 22 percent and 46 percent, respectively, in the second term) but only slightly higher than Jimmy Carter's and Reagan's. Yet the partisan gap between the parties on foreign policy votes was still substantial in both chambers in the first term (34 percent in the House, 43 percent in the Senate). During Bush's second term, the bipartisan gap and partisan difference widened appreciably. On only 12 percent of the foreign policy votes in the House during 2005–2008 was there bipartisan support, and the partisan gulf in the House reached 54 percent. In the Senate, the bipartisan support was only 21 percent, and the partisan gap was somewhat smaller, although still large at 42 percent. These results generally exceed the highest percentage of partisan divisions on foreign policy of any administration since the Vietnam War.

The Obama administration has made some inroads into the lack of bipartisanship and the degree of partisanship on foreign policy in the Senate but less so in the House during its first three years in office. In the 111th Congress, for example, the Obama administration received bipartisan support on slightly more than one of four votes (27 percent) in the House, and in first year of the 112th Congress on about one in six votes (16 percent) in that chamber. By contrast, the degree of bipartisan support in the Senate was much higher for the Obama administration than other recent administrations, with 47 percent bipartisan support in the 111th Congress and 62 percent in the first year of the 112th Congress. At the same time, though, the partisan gaps for the House and Senate in the 111th Congress were still substantial, at 43 percent and 41 percent, respectively, for these two chambers, although the partisan gaps in the first year of the 112th Congress were much smaller at 7 percent and 12 percent, respectively.[40] In this sense, and although the time period is shorter than for other administrations, the Obama administration may have begun to narrow the partisan differences on foreign policy.

PARTISAN POLITICS AND THE FUTURE

Despite these recent incipient changes, bipartisanship has not been the norm over the years and remains unlikely for the foreseeable future. The more likely prospect is that partisan divisions on foreign policy will continue to be a part of the American political landscape, for several reasons. First, **divided government at the national level** over the last several decades supported a continuation and intensification of partisan conflicts, not a diminution. Republicans won nine of the fifteen presidential elections between 1952 and 2008, and Democrats won control of both chambers of Congress in twenty of the last thirty-one congressional elections between 1950 and 2010. For a majority of time, then, one party controlled the White House, and the other party controlled all or part of Congress. Even when the same party controlled both Houses of Congress and the White House (such as 2009–2010 of the Obama administration), the Senate rules, often requiring a supermajority of sixty or more votes to move legislation, hindered effective action and precipitated partisan division. In 2010, when Republicans regained control of the House (but not the Senate), a more familiar pattern of divided government between the White House and Congress was once more in place. In such a setting, partisanship, not bipartisanship, is more likely.

Second, **partisan and ideological divisions** have deepened between the major political parties over the past several decades, eroding further the prospect for bipartisan accommodation. Conservative Republicans have largely replaced conservative Democrats in the South; conservative Democrats have increasingly switched parties; and ideological preferences and party affiliations are now more closely aligned.[41] Furthermore, the parties contain fewer moderates, given the contentious issues that increasingly divide them. Put differently, Democrats are more likely to be liberal Democrats, and Republicans are more likely to be conservative Republicans across domestic and foreign policy issues. Political analysts Charles Kupchan and Peter Trubowitz have more fully outlined how these partisan differences on foreign affairs emerged in recent decades, how they have been exacerbated in the first decade of the twenty-first century, and how they should be bridged to restore a bipartisan foreign policy.[42] Such partisan cooperation will likely remain elusive, though, as long as ideology and party alignment reinforce each other within the electorate and among its leaders.

Third, the **proliferation of issues** now increasingly related to foreign policy portends more, not fewer, partisan divisions. For example, partisan debate will intensify as economic issues are increasingly viewed as having foreign and domestic policy implications, and as Americans are affected differentially by economic policy choices. Similarly, even if scientific agreement can be reached on the dimensions of such ecological challenges as acid rain, nuclear waste disposal, and global warming, common political actions to address these challenges will remain elusive and ripe for partisan discord.

Fourth, some **security issues**, and particularly the threat posed by international terrorism, may yield more temporary consensus across party lines—as the immediate aftermath of the September 11 attacks demonstrated. Yet even those issues, in the context of polarized political parties and divided government, may become divisive in a relatively short time. Indeed, partisan discord rather quickly set in over how to deal with a postwar Iraq and with the continuing war in Afghanistan. More generally, little consensus exists on how best to deal with the ongoing terrorist threats posed by numerous groups worldwide. In addition, other issues with important security components—immigration, drug trafficking, weapons of mass destruction, and territorial, ethnic, and religious conflicts—remain on the agenda and do not easily evoke a common domestic response. For instance, the major political parties are hardly in agreement on immigration and border problems and the potential security threat that they pose. Nor are Republicans and Democrats united over how to deal with the nuclear threat posed by Iran and North Korea, the rise of China, and, more generally, the future role of the United States in global affairs. These and other security concerns (as well as issues often involving more than just security) fail to evoke a common response and are becoming increasingly politicized.

Political scientist Miroslav Nincic has illustrated how imbedded these partisan foreign policy differences have become within the American electorate and the electoral system.[43] He demonstrates that Americans increasingly vote on foreign policy, in presidential and congressional elections (as the 2004 and 2008 presidential elections and the 2006 and 2010 congressional elections illustrated).[44] Second, and importantly, he shows through careful analyses of public opinion survey data that Republican and Democratic identifiers on both the means and ends of U.S. foreign policy differ significantly. Republicans embrace "goals of the self-regarding type"—"maintaining superior military power, controlling illegal immigration, and protecting American jobs." Democrats prefer "other-regarding" goals—"combating world hunger, protecting nations from aggression, and strengthening the United Nations." The adherents of the two parties also differ on how to achieve their respective goals: Democrats prefer multilateral means and more emphasis on diplomacy; Republicans prefer unilateral means and more emphasis on military measures.[45] If, indeed, these differences persist and foreign policy remains an important electoral issue, partisan politics will surely continue to influence America's actions abroad.

For several important reasons, therefore, **the influence of partisan politics on the U.S. foreign policy has become more identifiable over the past several decades**. Although the Cold War may have produced some bipartisanship, the post–Vietnam and post–Cold War years eroded any sense of unity. The 9/11 attacks may have temporarily restored some bipartisanship, but the controversies over Iraq, Afghanistan, Iran, and the rise of China have reawakened the partisan differences of a few years earlier, which are now likely to remain for the foreseeable future. This is true both because of sharp party differences and because there is now evidence that these differences are imbedded within the American electorate.

INTEREST GROUPS
AND THE FOREIGN POLICY PROCESS

The number of interest groups participating in the American political process in Washington, DC, is astounding. In 2000, by one authoritative source, there were estimated to be about 11,000 such firms or groups and 17,000 individuals with annual spending estimates of $3 billion.[46] Those numbers for groups and individuals undoubtedly are higher, although the exact totals are difficult to track precisely. Indeed, if we think more broadly about the growth of nongovernmental organizations (NGOs) worldwide (and recognize that such groups also seek to influence the political process), the number and scope of interest groups is in fact much greater than these earlier estimates, ranging from 5,600 to 25,000, and even as high as 100,000 by differing sources.[47] To be sure, the interest groups concerned either with foreign policy exclusively or with foreign and domestic policy in combination are fewer than these totals, but these numbers still convey their overall magnitude. The types of foreign policy interest groups range from the oldest—focusing on economic interests—to the newest—focusing on the interest of foreign countries. Within and between these two types, we can identify several categories, among them labor, agricultural, religious, ethnic, veteran affairs, single-issue interests, academic, and ideological.

Interest groups usually target Congress because that institution affords them more avenues of influence. There, they can seek to influence not only members but also their staffs and the staffs of various committees and subcommittees. These groups use professional lobbyists (such as lawyers or public relations firms in Washington) or their own personnel located or assigned to Washington for these efforts. In addition, a considerable portion of interest group activity may focus on influencing key foreign policy bureaucracies and, more generally, the executive branch. Important targets are the Department of Defense, the Department of State, and now the Department of Homeland Security.

Sometimes these key governmental bureaucracies (and others discussed over the last two chapters) actually lobby Congress themselves. Over a decade ago, one source listed 147 government bureaucracies, agencies, commissions, and divisions that were involved in lobbying efforts, including the Executive Office of the President, the Department of Agriculture, the Department of Commerce, the Department of State, the Department of Defense (DOD), the Agency for International Development, the CIA, and the Federal Trade Commission.[48] Indeed, each branch of the U.S. military, too, assigns staff to Capitol Hill to get its positions out. Yet, it must do so "without fingerprint," as one analyst notes, "since lobbying by government agencies is forbidden by law."[49] In all, foreign policy lobbying does not originate solely from outside the government; instead, one branch of government may seek to influence another, and the political clout of these groups should not be underestimated.

Types of Foreign Policy Interest Groups

In order to give some sense of the magnitude of nongovernmental interest groups (without attempting to provide an exhaustive list) and their foreign policy concerns, we identify several that are operating today.

Business Groups Several umbrella economic organizations lobby for business interests. The National Association of Manufacturers, the U.S. Chamber of Commerce (and its global affiliates), the Committee for Economic Development, and the Business Roundtable, among others, fit into this category.[50] Beyond these umbrella groups, particular manufacturing, industrial, and commodity interests usually engage in separate lobbying activities. The American Bankers Association, the American Petroleum Institute, the American Textile Manufacturers Institute, the American Apparel and Footwear Association, the National Cotton Council, and the American Coal Council are all examples. In addition, virtually all major corporations actively lobby for their particular foreign policy interests. These include the major defense contractors (such as General Dynamics, Lockheed Martin, Boeing, United Technologies, and General Electric), all of which target Congress and the DOD in particular. In short, virtually all major corporations on the Fortune 500 list have some kind of representation in Washington, and many of them are involved in foreign policy lobbying.

These business lobbies generally share similar foreign policy goals: they seek to increase foreign trade, to expand their own exports, and, in a number of instances, to promote a strong national defense. Moreover, most are multinational, with a presence (and headquarters) in the United States and branches in other countries. In this way, they not only impact American foreign policy at home but may also influence it with their global activities.

Labor Unions   The American labor movement actively lobbies Congress and the executive branch on foreign policy issues. Its main interests are job security and foreign imports. Specifically, the labor lobby works to protect American workers from importation of cheaper goods and the export (or outsourcing) of jobs by multinational firms seeking cheaper labor markets. As might be expected, such policy positions are often directly opposed to those of the business interest groups.

The labor unions that do the most extensive lobbying are the American Federation of Labor and Congress of Industrial Organizations (the AFL-CIO), the United Automobile Workers of America (UAW), the International Brotherhood of Teamsters, and the American Federation of State, County, and Municipal Employees (AFSCME). The AFL-CIO umbrella organization encompasses fifty-six national and international unions currently representing about 12 million workers.[51] In the early 1990s, it weighed in heavily in opposition to NAFTA, fearing the loss of jobs to cheaper labor in Mexico. Aside from NAFTA, most-favored-nation (MFN) trading status for China, and other free trade measures were important lobbying targets for the labor union movement generally. In recent years, the AFL-CIO focused its lobbying on blocking the expansion of NAFTA into Latin America and the expansion of coverage by the World Trade Organization (WTO) and opposing the passage of the Central American Free Trade Agreement and the free trade agreements with Colombia, Panama, and South Korea.

Although labor unions, like their major business interest counterparts, are primarily interested in economic issues, they also have adopted positions on other foreign policy questions. Under the longtime leadership of George Meany, the AFL-CIO was particularly known for its staunch anticommunist stance and for its effort to assist the global trade union movement in its opposition to communism during the Cold War years.[52] More recently, the AFL-CIO's concern has been to rejuvenate labor unions at home among American ethnic groups and the young, but it continues to be concerned with the Trans-Pacific Partnership agreement under development, the trade implications of Russia's membership in the WTO, and the consequences of the U.S. trade deficit with China for American workers. Finally, the AFL-CIO also has been promoting a comprehensive U.S. immigration policy.[53]

Agricultural Groups   The principal agricultural lobbying groups today are the American Farm Bureau Federation, the National Farmers Union, and the National Farmers Organization, but other such groups are also numerous in Washington.[54] By one assessment, "20–25 percent of all lobbyists in Washington, DC represent interest groups involved in the food production process."[55] Although these organizations vary in the degree to which they believe that the federal government should intervene in the market economy, they all support efforts to increase the export of farm products. They are primarily concerned with issues directly affecting agriculture, but they also take stands on other foreign policy issues that may indirectly impact farmers and producers. The American Farm Bureau Federation (AFBF), for example, routinely states its position on numerous foreign policy issues. In 2012, the AFBF outlined a number of its policy priorities, including some that supported its agricultural mission and others that seemingly went beyond it. It supported the extension of the capital gains tax reduction and the repeal of the estate tax, but it also promoted legislation to "solve the agricultural worker problem," although setting out a number of conditions for such legislation. Further, the AFBF supported permanent normal trading relations with Russia because such legislation will "improve the ability of U.S. farmers and ranchers to sell into the Russian market," and it approved of Canada as a negotiating partner in the ongoing Trans-Pacific Partnership discussion. The National Farmers Union and the National Farmers Organizations adopted a number of similar positions on foreign policy issues, especially as they relate to trade in agricultural commodities.[56]

Religious Organizations   The most prominent among these groups are the National Council of Churches (various Protestant denominations), the American Friends Service Committee (Quakers), and the United States Conference of Catholic Bishops, but other major religious groups, including the Methodists, the Unitarians, the Presbyterians, and the Baptists, have also been involved in foreign policy lobbying,[57] as have numerous of their affiliates. Several faith-based NGOs—World Vision for evangelical Protestants, World Council of Churches for mainline Protestants, and Catholic Relief Services for Roman Catholics—are important religious lobbies as well. One source listed 116 groups that were lobbying on religious questions in Washington in 2011.[58]

"Peace and justice" and "social concern" committees established by various religions inform and involve their memberships in both foreign and domestic policy matters. Indirectly, too, they assist their coreligionists in petitioning their representatives in Washington. The American Friends Service Committee (AFSC), for example, has been involved in group discussions of current international issues, has sought ways to aid the various parties in the Middle East, and has proposed ideas for canceling debt in Africa and for assisting the displaced in Burma and elsewhere. Furthermore, the AFSC has advanced proposals for resolving conflicts, whether between the Palestinians and the Israelis or within Iraq. It has also called for the withdrawal of American military forces from Iraq and Afghanistan and for the elimination of nuclear weapons.[59] In May 1983, at the time of the nuclear freeze movement worldwide, the U.S. Conference of Catholic Bishops issued its pastoral letter, *The Challenge of Peace*, on the possession and use of nuclear weapons, thus signaling foreign policy activism by the Church.[60] Largely led by members of the Catholic Church, various religious groups were also active in opposition to the Reagan administration's policy in El Salvador and Nicaragua.[61] In the 1980s, the Christian Coalition, led by Pat Robertson, became an important addition to these religious lobbying efforts through a variety of political activities. In the 1990s, religious groups lobbied on behalf of humanitarian interventions to address gross human rights violations in ethnic and religious conflicts in Bosnia, Haiti, Rwanda, and Kosovo.

In the months prior to the war with Iraq in 2003, the major religious organizations lined up to both oppose and support it. In September 2002, for instance, the president of the United States Conference of Catholic Bishops wrote to President Bush raising "serious questions about the moral legitimacy of any preemptive, unilateral use of military force to overthrow the government of Iraq."[62] Similarly, the Mennonite Central Committee, the United Church of Christ, the United Methodists, and the Quakers, among others, spoke out against going to war against Iraq. The Ethics and Religious Liberty Commission of the Southern Baptist Convention, some evangelical Christian leaders, and the Union of American Hebrew Congregations, however, supported the Bush administration's position.[63]

By late 2009, America's religious groups again weighed in over another ongoing war. Seventy-seven United Methodist bishops called on President Barack Obama for a timetable for the withdrawal of all U.S. forces from Afghanistan. The U.S. Catholic bishops wrote to General James L. Jones, the national security advisor to the president, asking the administration "to review its use of military force" to make certain that it was "proportionate and discriminate" and to "develop criteria" for ending American action there. Further, Christian magazines—*Christian Century*, *America*, and *Commonweal*—earlier had raised questions about the American approach in Afghanistan as well.[64]

In all, the nation's major religions now routinely weigh in on foreign policy issues, seeking to add their voices to the political debate.

Ethnic Groups   Ethnic groups represent another gathering of important interests active in the foreign policy arena today. Traditionally, the most active have been those of Jewish, Irish, and East European heritage, but Greeks, Hispanics, and African Americans have also sought to further their influence.[65] For example, at the end of the Cold War, Americans with Central and Eastern European roots (e.g., Armenian Americans, Czech Americans, Slovak Americans, and Hungarian Americans, among others) either revived or initiated their foreign policy activism.[66] One illustration of this activism by a relatively small ethnic group is the lobbying efforts of Armenian Americans in 2007 and 2010. It was highly instrumental in gaining passage of a resolution condemning 1917 Turkish genocide of Armenians by the House Foreign Affairs Committee, even though the Turkish lobby (and the Bush and Obama administrations) was successful in stopping the resolution from consideration on the House floor.[67]

For all of these **ethnic groups**, the dominant theme of participation in foreign affairs is usually **American policy toward the particular country or region of their ancestors' origin rather than on foreign policy in general**. On policy issues related to Israel, Ireland, Cyprus, Central America, South Africa, and Central and Eastern Europe, these groups, respectively, have been most active and have made their voices heard. Ethnic groups, as a whole, have often been identified as an especially important source of American foreign policy, and we shall have more to say about their influence later in this chapter.

Veterans Groups   Such organizations as the Veterans of Foreign Wars, the American Legion, and the American Veterans of World War II are the best known of these groups.[68] Near the end of the Vietnam War, for example, the Vietnam Veterans Against the War entered the political arena, seeking at first to end American involvement and later to petition for better treatment of Vietnam veterans. Veterans from the Persian Gulf War of 1991 raised their collective voice in calling for the government to seek the origin of the "Gulf War syndrome," which afflicted scores of military personnel who served in that conflict. Veterans from the Iraq War of 2003, including a number of activated reservists and National Guard forces, sought greater government recognition of the sacrifices that they made in that conflict and its aftermath. In 2004, the Iraq and Afghanistan Veterans of America was founded, and by 2012, it had over 200,000 members and supporters. Its goal is "to improve the lives of Iraq and Afghanistan veterans and their families" in four areas—through health, education, employment, and community.[69] One tangible, and important, indication of how effective veterans groups have been over the years is the establishment by Congress of a separate cabinet department in 1988 to serve their interests.

Ideological Groups   Although these groups are often identified with questions of domestic politics, some are also active on foreign policy issues. The most prominent of them are the Americans for Democratic Action (ADA), the principal liberal interest group in Washington politics, and the American Conservative Union (ACU), the principal conservative interest group. Both evaluate members of Congress on foreign and domestic policy from their particular perspectives and issue yearly voting "scores" for all senators and representatives. They also actively work to make known their positions on major foreign policy issues.

Many other ideological groups from both ends of the political spectrum participate in foreign affairs. Over the years, those with a conservative viewpoint have included the American Security Council, the John Birch Society, and the National Conservative Political Action Committee (NCPAC); those with a liberal viewpoint have included the Coalition for a Realistic Foreign Policy, the Women's International League for Peace and Freedom, the World Federalists, and the World Policy Institute.[70] One prominent organization usually identified with the liberal end of the political spectrum is the American Civil Liberties Union (ACLU), which has long been involved in key issues related to foreign policy and is committed to the protection of individual constitutional rights. The ACLU has been particularly involved in questioning and challenging provisions of the USA PATRIOT Act, passed by Congress in the immediate aftermath of the attacks on the World Trade Center and the Pentagon, and the use of warrantless wiretaps, which it believes to be inconsistent with the Foreign Intelligence Surveillance Act (see Chapters 7 and 10). More recently, the ACLU continues to express concerns about the "accountability for torture, detention of terrorism suspects, and the use of lethal force against civilians" during the Obama administration.[71]

Think Tanks   The numerous "think tanks" that are located primarily in Washington might not be immediately identified as interest groups.[72] These organizations are funded by individuals, corporations, and foundations that focus on analyzing a particular problem or array of problems to offer policy advice. They share their results with the congressional and executive branches through testimony on Capitol Hill, through the publication of scholarly books and articles, and through opinion pieces appearing in several elite newspapers, such as the *New York Times*, the *Wall Street Journal*, the *Washington Post*, and the *Los Angeles Times*. In these various ways, they seek to influence policy, and they have been relatively successful: "More so than in any other country," one analysis reports, American think tanks "have played an influential role in foreign policy making," largely owing to the open nature of the American political system.[73] Finally, and importantly, the scholars, analysts, and practitioners who occupy these think tanks are usually well-connected in official Washington and move in and out of government with changes in administrations. In this sense, the think tanks may seek to influence policy direction, but they may also "capture control of policy direction" when some of their (former) personnel accept a position in government.[74]

The number of think tanks is quite large and diverse, even if we consider only those devoted exclusively to foreign policy issues. They may be categorized in a variety of ways: ideologically (liberal, moderate, or conservative) or chronologically ("Old Guard," "Cold War," and now "partisan").[75] Although space precludes an exhaustive survey, a brief word or two about the major think tanks will illustrate their range and policy orientations.

The best-known conservative think tanks in Washington are the **Heritage Foundation** and the **Cato Institute**. The Heritage Foundation analyzes both domestic and foreign policy issues from a relatively hard-line conservative position. Its views are disseminated through its quarterly magazine, *Policy Review*, and through a myriad of reports on current topics. The foundation gained prominence particularly during the Reagan administration, but it remains an important and influential political force in Washington to this day. Depending on the administration in power, the Heritage Foundation is likely to be the site of an important foreign or domestic policy speech by a governmental official. In addition, though, it offers a steady series of programs and speakers on important foreign and domestic issues.[76]

The Cato Institute was established in 1977 and "owes its name to Cato's Letters, a series of essays published in 18th century England that . . . inspired the architects of the American Revolution."[77] Its libertarian orientation translates into recommendations for a more isolationist or noninterventionist U.S. approach in global affairs. On a regular basis, scholars and analysts affiliated with the Cato Institute investigate a host of foreign and domestic policy issues and disseminate their views through a number of outlets, including books, policy analysis papers, "op-ed" pieces, and testimony on Capitol Hill.

Somewhat in the middle politically is the **American Enterprise Institute for Public Policy Research (AEI)** and the **Center for Strategic and International Studies (CSIS)**. AEI defines itself as "a community of scholars and supporters committed to expanding liberty, increasing individual opportunity and strengthening free enterprise."[78] It began as a strong conservative voice on foreign policy issues (and has retained that voice on most foreign policy matters), but it has broadened its political perspective in recent years. AEI had about 185 employees, including resident and adjunct scholars/fellows, principally at major universities throughout the United States. Like the other think tanks, it produces a broad array of books and articles and an online journal, *The American*, as mechanisms to get its message out. At the same time, AEI as an institution does not take positions on national or international issues, although "AEI scholars and fellows do take positions on policy and other issues, including explicit advocacy for or against legislations currently being considered by Congress."[79]

CSIS began as an institute affiliated with Georgetown University in 1962 and became an independent institute in 1987. Although generally conservative, it has moved toward more moderation in its outlook in recent years.[80] Over the years, it has attracted many distinguished individuals to its staff, including Zbigniew Brzezinski and Henry Kissinger. Like AEI and most other think tanks, CSIS publishes a foreign policy journal, *The Washington Quarterly*, holds periodic seminars, and publishes various foreign policy materials. Unlike the other think tanks mentioned so far, it devotes its work primarily to foreign policy matters, nationally and internationally.

The best-known liberal-leaning think tank is the **Brookings Institution**, which has several divisions, including one devoted exclusively to foreign policy studies. Brookings' policy recommendations are usually moderate or liberal—indeed, it has been referred to as the "Democratic government in exile" because of the number of former officials from Democratic administrations that staff it (although in recent years this descriptor has become less appropriate). Its seminars, publications (including a wide array of foreign policy books), and conferences are highly regarded among those of all political stripes. In all, the Brookings Institution has 300 or more resident and nonresident fellows who research foreign policy, global development, economics, and domestic governance, among other issues. A former senator described it as having been "at the center of every important policy debate in this country for 90 years."[81]

Finally, two other think tanks—two of the oldest—especially deserve mention. **The Council on Foreign Relations** arose after World War I with an expressed anti-isolationist point of view. Because membership was restricted to those elected to participate, it became a rather exclusive group that reviewed and commented on foreign policy issues,[82] and it has remained so to this day. Over the years, too, the council has sponsored numerous studies and book projects on foreign policy matters, continues to publish numerous books each year, and reviews published works throughout the foreign policy and international relations field. Perhaps its most important vehicle for exercising influence is its flagship journal, *Foreign Affairs*. Without question the leading journal in the field, it has published articles that foreshadowed the change in direction of U.S. foreign policy (for example, George Kennan on containment in 1947, Richard Nixon on China in 1967), allowed policy makers to justify past actions or explain future direction (for example, Secretary of State Hillary Clinton proposing changes in State Department operations from the Quadrennial Diplomacy and Development Review), and critiqued the actions of foreign policy institutions or bureaucracies (for example, Gordon Adams and Matthew Leatherman's critique of defense policy). In this sense, although the journal is theoretically open to a wide array of contributors, it affords current and former policy makers in particular a ready venue. For an academic publication, *Foreign Affairs* has an extraordinarily large circulation, and it is widely read and quoted in official Washington.

The Carnegie Endowment for International Peace was established prior to World War I, in 1910, originally with a large gift from philanthropist Andrew Carnegie, who was interested in achieving world peace. Over the years, it has maintained that focus while evolving in various ways over the previous century. Today, its mission is "dedicated to advancing cooperation between nations and promoting active international engagement by the United States." In the past several years, the Carnegie Endowment sought to develop a global presence by opening up centers in Moscow (1993), Beijing (2004), Beirut (2006), and Brussels (2007) to complement its long-standing Washington operation. Hence, it now characterizes itself as *"the global think tank."* Books, policy analyses, and presentations are its principal ways of sharing its views.[83]

Single-Issue Groups The single-issue interest group represents somewhat of a residual category of interest groups because of its members' deeply held views on a particular policy question. Such groups range widely and include the United Nations Association of the United States, which seeks to enhance support for the UN; the Union of Concerned Scientists and the Arms Control Association, which back efforts to achieve arms limitations; and Friends of the Earth and Greenpeace, which support efforts to preserve the global environment.[84] Moreover, they probably dwarf in size any of the other categories that we might identify because they can form, lobby, and disband quickly. They can also be amalgams of interest groups that join together to lobby on a new issue on the political agenda at a particular moment in time.

Perhaps the leading exemplar of a single-issue foreign policy group in the postwar period is the anti–Vietnam War movement of the 1960s and early 1970s. This group (really a coalition of groups such as the National Mobilization to End the War, the Moratorium Movement, the War Resisters League, and even the Weathermen, the radical wing of the Students for a Democratic Society) was highly successful in rallying support among the American public and, eventually, in altering the course of American policy in Southeast Asia. In the late 1970s and early 1980s, the most prominent single-issue foreign policy groups were those either supporting or opposing the development of more nuclear weapons. The Committee on the Present Danger, composed primarily of conservative ex-government officials, was most active in opposition to the ratification of the SALT II treaty signed by President Carter. The nuclear freeze movement—a broadly based coalition of individuals from various walks of life—arose in opposition to the nuclear arms buildup by the Reagan administration and called for the enactment of a mutual and verifiable freeze on all nuclear weapons production and development.[85]

The next two decades also saw the rise of single-issue groups on foreign policy issues. By the mid-1980s, the largest set of single-issue groups united around the question of American policy in Central America. According to one study, about one hundred interest groups lobbied Congress and the president over whether to provide or withhold aid to the Nicaraguan contras.[86] In the 1990s, the question of whether Congress should give its approval to **NAFTA—establishing a free trade zone among the United States, Mexico, and Canada—sparked significant interest group activity**. Many groups from across the political spectrum participated in this debate.[87] In the early years of the twenty-first century, single-issue groups arose over the increasing globalization of the international economy and over support for and opposition to the war with Iraq. Several antiglobalization groups were internationally based (such as Third World Network, the International Forum on Globalization, and Focus on the Global South), but a prominent one, Global Exchange, maintained its headquarters in California.[88] The war against Iraq in 2003 also led a number of individuals and groups to voice their opposition in various cities around the country. Although drawn from different areas and often with an array of other interests, these various groups and individuals came together and demonstrated as a single coalition in Washington against administration policy near the outbreak of the war. By 2007, and as the Democrats gained control of the House and Senate, anti-Iraq groups coalesced under the umbrella organization, Americans Against Escalation in Iraq, whose aims were to push the Democratic Congress to pass a resolution opposing President Bush's surge strategy, cut funding for the war, and stimulate greater public opposition and protest.[89]

Foreign Lobbies   Foreign lobbies are the newest recognized lobby group on foreign policy, and their presence in Washington has grown significantly over the past three decades. In the 1970s, about 75 countries had representation in Washington. By 2011, 127 nations, both large and small and from every corner of the world, were represented by Washington lobbyists.[90] In the main, these lobbyists are often American citizens who have been hired to explain their clients' policies and to persuade Congress to give them more favorable treatment. Prominent examples are the lobbying efforts undertaken at various times by South Africa, El Salvador, Saudi Arabia, and other Third World nations. Early on, Saudi Arabia was particularly active in its lobbying efforts on the Airborne Warning and Control System (AWACS) aircraft sale in 1981, enlisting the support of several large American corporations to back its position.[91]

Perhaps the best-known (and most maligned) foreign lobby in the late 1980s and early 1990s was Japan. Over the years, Japan hired numerous former members of Congress and former administrative officials to serve as its lobbyists in influencing Congress and the executive branch on American–Japanese relations, especially regarding trade. Japan also hired some of the best-known public relations firms in Washington to get its message out. But Japan did more than lobby. It also provided research money to several Washington think tanks, such as Brookings Institution, AEI, and the CSIS, in support of various studies, conferences, and academic chairs. Although no direct Japanese benefit can be specified from such support, this approach at least raises the question of whether independent analysis can be undertaken with such arrangements.[92] All of these efforts allowed Japan access in Washington and made its lobbying effort powerful, although "the Japan lobby rarely wins battles on its own."

In the early 1990s, the republics of the former Soviet Union and the People's Republic of China were rapidly hiring Washington law and lobbying firms to promote their interests. By one assessment, Azerbaijan, Belarus, Kazakhstan, Kyrgyzstan, Latvia, Moldova, Russia, Ukraine, and Uzbekistan had hired one or more firms to represent them. In fact, within two years of the collapse of the Soviet Union, Russia and Russian firms had contracted nine different law and consulting companies.[93] China also employed a very large number of representatives to argue its case, especially on trade matters. Some high-priced and high-powered lawyers and former government officials representing U.S. businesses opened doors for Chinese officials; others represented Chinese businesses in the United States.[94] Their access to Chinese and American officials on behalf of companies in both countries was a potent political force in maintaining MFN trade status for China and eventually in achieving "permanent normal trading relations" for it in 2000. These efforts also expanded American investment in, and trade with, China.

More recently, as the genocide resolution promoted by the Armenian-American community and targeted against Turkey loomed in the Congress, former members of Congress sprang into action on Turkey's behalf, as did visits to Capitol Hill by eight Turkish parliamentarians. As one analysis put it, this debate "pitted Turkey's money and high-placed connections against a persistent and emotional campaign by Armenian-American citizens' groups." Although the lobbyists were not able to stop the passage of the resolution in the House Foreign Affairs Committee, they did keep it from a vote on the House floor.[95]

In all, the efforts by Japan, Russia, China, Turkey, and myriad other countries reflect the internationalization of lobbying that has taken place, and they illustrate how lobbying, and even foreign lobbying, has become a normal part of the U.S. foreign policy process.

THE IMPACT OF INTEREST GROUPS

How successful are these interest groups in influencing foreign policy? Unlike the president, Congress, and the foreign affairs bureaucracies that have direct control over policy, interest groups have at best only an indirect impact. By definition, they do not control policy but can only seek to influence it. In this connection, most analysts suggest that, on the whole, foreign policy groups do not do well at that task for several reasons.[96] First of all, American foreign policy tends to be made more in the executive branch than in the congressional branch, as we noted in Chapter 7, and access to the executive is more difficult than access to Congress, with its varied committee and subcommittee structures. Also, although interest groups do lobby the foreign affairs bureaucracies, their efforts may actually end up serving the bureaucracies' interests more than the lobbyists'.[97] Second, foreign policy issues and decisions are usually remote from the lives of Americans, and thus rallying public support or opposition poses a significant challenge.[98] Third, important foreign policy making is often carried out under crisis conditions—short decision time, high threat, or surprise in the executive branch—and thus it is likely to be even more elitist than normal—more confined to a few members of the executive branch and more restricted in the amount of congressional participation. In such situations, avenues of influence for interest groups are further limited. Fourth—and perhaps most pivotal—with the number of interest groups operating, it is likely that "countervailing" groups will balance each other's impact and, therefore, allow the policy makers more freedom of action.[99] Competing interest groups on NAFTA or on trade with China give members of Congress and the executive branch officials some latitude in making their own decisions on foreign policy questions. For a recent illustration of these competing interest groups over passage of the U.S.-Korea Free Trade Agreement (KORUS FTA), see Table 11.1.

Despite such difficulties, interest groups do have an impact on some key issues and under particular circumstances. The principal issues appear to be those involving long-range policy and those related to defense and foreign economic policy.[100] The former might be labeled "strategic" because they "specif[y] the goals and tactics of defense and foreign policy." Guidelines for action directed toward a particular region (such as East Asia), country (such as Russia), or issue (such as terrorism) qualify as such. The latter might be labeled "structural" because they focus on "procuring, deploying, and organizing military personnel and material . . . [and deciding] which countries will receive aid [and] what rules will govern immigration. . . ."[101] These include policy guidelines on number of military bases, the size and composition of the defense budget, and the distribution of foreign assistance.

The president often takes the lead on both strategic and structural policy questions (especially the strategic questions), but congressional approval and fine-tuning in both areas are almost always necessary. Thus, because Congress allows more avenues of access by interest groups, lobbying is likely to be more successful on these two issue types. Finally, and importantly, there is no easy or permanent demarcation between strategic and structural issues, or even crisis issues. Indeed, interest groups may even weigh in on crisis issues, especially if they are extended over time. Consider, for example, antiterrorist actions. Although the president may be given latitude to

Table 11.1 Interest Group Activity over the U.S.-Korea Free Trade Agreement (KORUS FTA)

Groups Supporting KORUS FTA	Groups Opposing KORUS FTA
U.S. Chamber of Commerce	AFL-CIO
Business Roundtable	Teamsters
National Association of Manufacturers	Friends of the Earth
Ford Motor Company	Sierra Club
American Farm Bureau Federation	National Family Farm Coalition

Sources: Office of the Press Secretary, The White House, "Statements of Support for the U.S-Korea Trade Agreement," at http://www.whitehouse.gov/the-press-office/2010/12/03/statements-support-us-korea-trade-agreement, July 3, 2012, and Citizens Trade Campaign, "Opposition to the Korea Free Trade Agreement," at http://www.citizenstrade.org/ctc/trade-policies/us-korea-free-trade-agreement/oppose-the-korea-free-trade-agreement/, July 3, 2012.

respond to terrorist attacks, over time, antiterrorism policy may become strategic or even structural. Creating new administrative structures (for example, the Department of Homeland Security) and providing new funding (for example, for port inspection technology) allows more participants to influence policy direction, including those interest groups directly affected by it. In this sense, across a broad array of foreign policy issues, active interest groups may have a role to play.

Two types of interest groups appear to be particularly influential in foreign policy, especially within Congress, and were recognized for this influence during the Cold War, as the Cold War ended, and in the post–9/11 era.[102] One type is represented by **economic groups that can be loosely identified as the "military-industrial complex"**; the other type is **ethnic groups**. The impact of the former is based on the extensive access and involvement of numerous corporations in economic and defense issues that so often arise in Congress. The impact of the latter is based on the interest that many Americans have in U.S. policy toward the country of their origin or toward a country with which they identify, such as Israel.[103] We will examine both of these types in more detail to give some sense of their relative influence.

Economic Interest Groups

Our earlier discussion highlighted the extraordinary number of economic interest groups seeking to influence foreign policy. These groups are both domestic and foreign, and in an industrial capitalist economy such as the United States their existence should not be surprising. Yet, for several decades now, the close ties between these groups and the government have raised concerns over whether this linkage so dominates the foreign policy process that American society and American democracy suffer as a result. The most often cited constellation of economic interest groups affecting, or perhaps even dominating, American foreign policy is the military-industrial complex (MIC). Today, in fact, some might prefer to call this "the military-industrial-political complex" to denote the close ties this group has with political elites. For discussion purposes, we will use the term "MIC," but this larger concept ought to be kept in mind. The origins of the MIC, and the theory underpinning it, deserve mention before we assess its degree of influence on foreign policy.

The Theory of the Military-Industrial Complex (MIC)

First introduced into the American political lexicon by President Eisenhower as he was leaving office, the term *military-industrial complex* refers to the presumed symbiotic relationship between major U.S. corporations and the American defense establishment.[104] According to this theory, these corporations are dependent on the DOD for military defense contracts and often apply pressure for a policy of strong military preparedness or even global military involvement as a means of furthering their financial well-being. More broadly, the term describes the informal ties that have developed among the top corporate sectors of society and the political-military sectors of government.[105]

The first assumption underlying the MIC theory is that there is **a unified elite within American society** that dominates all important national and foreign policy decisions. This elite is held together by interlocking structural relationships and by psychological and social constraints among occupants of key institutions.[106] In other words, the elites share similar educational and social backgrounds and frequently interact with one another.

The second assumption in this theory is that this **elite's domination of policy making produces a distinct type of foreign policy** that is consistent with its interests. Such a policy emphasizes high military spending, interventionism abroad, and the protection of private property.[107] By the pursuit of these policies, the private interests of the MIC are safeguarded, especially in a world of ideological tension such as existed during the Cold War.

Are these assumptions accurate? Does this political elite really exist? If so, is it successful in shaping policy consistent with the predictions of MIC theory? With the end of the Cold War in the early 1990s, the terrorist attacks of 2001, and the Iraq and the Afghanistan Wars in recent years, how will the MIC's influence (to the extent that it exists) change? Definitive answers to these questions are not easy to come by, even though numerous researchers have analyzed them over the years. Our review of the available evidence leads us to believe that more of a case can be made for the existence of a policy elite than for the foreign policy consequences that are presumed to follow from its influence.

Evidence for a Single, Interlocking Elite   Analyses identifying the similar backgrounds of government officials and documenting the interactions between the military and the government provide substantial support for the first assumption of the MIC theory. One of the earliest studies in this area reported that, from 1944 to 1960, 60 percent of some 234 officials, mainly in the foreign affairs bureaucracies (Department of Defense, Department of State, Central Intelligence Agency, and so on) came from important business, investment, and law firms. Moreover, a relatively small number of these individuals (84) held more than 63 percent of the positions studied.[108]

Political scientist Thomas Dye documented the background of key foreign policy officials throughout much of the post–World War II era and reached a similar conclusion about the extensive business ties of these policy makers.[109] Various secretaries of defense, for example, have had links to large American corporations. Charles E. Wilson (1953–1957) was the president and a board member of General Motors; Thomas Gates (1960–1961) was chairman of the board and chief executive officer of Morgan Guaranty Trust and served on the boards of, among others, General Electric, Bethlehem Steel, Scott Paper Company, and Insurance Company of America; Robert S. McNamara (1961–1967) was the president and a member of the board of Ford Motor Company; and Caspar Weinberger (1981–1987) was a vice president and a corporate director for Bechtel Corporation, a major global contractor, and served on the board of directors of such companies as PepsiCo and Quaker Oats.

The same pattern has held true for secretaries of state. John Foster Dulles (1953–1959) was a partner in Sullivan and Cromwell, a prominent Wall Street law firm, and was on the boards of directors for the Bank of New York, Fifth Avenue Bank, the American Cotton Oil Company, and United Railroad of St. Louis, among other firms; Dean Rusk (1961–1969 was a former president of the Rockefeller Foundation; and William P. Rogers (1969–1973) was a senior partner in Royall, Koegel, Rogers, and Wells, another prominent Wall Street law firm. Alexander Haig (1981–1982) not only served as military attaché to Henry Kissinger and as supreme allied commander of NATO but also served as an executive with United Technologies—a leading defense contractor. Before his appointment as secretary of state, George Shultz (1982–1989) was a high-ranking official with Bechtel and served on the boards of directors of Borg-Warner, General Motors, and Stein, Roe, and Farnham (a Chicago-based investment advisory firm). James Baker (1989–1992) came from a background of the law and wealth, and his father owned the Texas Commerce Bank.

The pattern continued for more recent administrations. Although, according to Dye, Clinton's top posts were largely "filled by lawyers, lobbyists, politicians, and bureaucrats,"[110] Clinton's secretaries of state, Warren Christopher and Madeleine Albright, for instance, had served in the Carter administration, and Christopher came from a prestigious law firm in California. His national security advisors—Anthony Lake and Samuel Berger—also had served in the Carter administration. Continuing the political pattern, Clinton's defense secretaries—Les Aspin, William Perry, and William Cohen—had extensive ties to Washington, Aspin and Cohen serving for many years in Congress and Perry having worked in Congress previously.

Several key appointees came with prominent business credentials as well. Clinton's first chief of staff, and later presidential counselor, Thomas McLarty, was an executive with a major natural gas company in Arkansas, and his secretary of energy, Hazel O'Leary, was an executive in a Minnesota utility company. Both of Clinton's secretaries of treasury had pronounced business ties: Lloyd Bentsen was a longtime U.S. senator from Texas, who chaired the Finance Committee, but his wealth and business holdings in Texas were extensive; and Robert Rubin was a Wall Street financier prior to his appointment as deputy secretary and then secretary of Treasury.[111]

President George W. Bush appointed similar political and business elites to key policy-making positions.[112] By one assessment, eleven of Bush's eighteen initial cabinet-level appointments gained Washington experience in earlier Republican administrations, including such key foreign policy officials as Vice President Richard Cheney, Secretary of State Colin Powell, Secretary of Defense Donald Rumsfeld, and National Security Advisor Condoleezza Rice. Individuals with extensive business ties also populated the key policy-making positions in the Bush administration. Vice President Cheney, for example, was president of Halliburton, a large oil company; Paul O'Neill, Bush's first treasury secretary, served as president of International Paper and as a key executive of Alcoa; O'Neill successor, John Snow, was chairman and chief executive of CSX Corporation, a major railroad company; and Secretary of Defense Rumsfeld was president of G.D. Searle, a leading drug company. Finally, the administration's last secretary of the treasury, Henry Paulson, former chairman of the Goldman Sachs investment firm, has been described as "probably the richest Treasury secretary in history," with a net worth totaling more than $700 million.[113]

President Obama also appointed key officials with political experience in previous administration and with business ties to key policy positions. For instance, Secretary of State Hillary Clinton served as First Lady in her husband's administration as well as in the Senate; Secretary of Defense Robert Gates not only served in the previous administration but also had served in several previous Republican administrations; Gates's successor, Leon Panetta, had a long career in Congress and an executive official in the Clinton administration. Secretary of the Treasury Timothy Geithner served as president of the Federal Reserve Bank of New York, worked at the International Monetary Fund, and held various positions in three administrations for five secretaries of the Treasury prior to his appointment. He also had worked for the consulting firm Kissinger Associates, Inc. Secretary of Commerce John Bryson was chairman and chief executive of Edison International and a former chairman of BrightSource Energy, Inc., prior to his appointment. Finally, U.S. Trade Representative Ron Kirk was a former mayor of Dallas, Texas; Texas secretary of state; and a partner in the prominent international law firm of Vinson & Elkins, LLP, before assuming this trade position.[114]

Evidence for DOD/Defense Contractor Links This first kind of study thus seems to identify some linkage between the business and political community and suggests a circulating set of policy makers. Other evidence provides support for a linkage between the military and major defense contractors—the other key component of the interlocking elite argument. An analysis from the late 1980s and early 1990s, for example, showed that the "revolving door" phenomenon between DOD personnel and defense contractors continued to operate as it had in the past.[115] In fiscal year 1987, 328 senior DOD officials and 3,199 DOD military officers who left government service went to work in the defense industry, and, in fiscal year 1993, 145 senior DOD officials and 1,164 DOD military officers who left government service did the same.[116] Although the 1987 and 1993 totals represent only 13 percent and 4 percent, respectively, of the personnel who left government service among those ranks, the top military retirees—over half of the generals and admirals in 1988 and a quarter in 1994—took defense jobs. In other words, the highest-ranking military officers continued to readily find positions with the defense industry. Importantly, as this analysis noted, "the true number of crossovers is understated because the methodology for identifying the revolving-door population only captures individuals whose employment required a security clearance.[117]

More recently, a 2008 Government Accountability Office (GAO) study found that fifty-two contractors "employed 2,435 former DOD senior and acquisition officials who had previously served as generals, admirals, senior executives, program managers, [or] contracting officers, or in other acquisition positions." Most of these (1,581) were employed by seven major defense contractors, including such prominent companies as Science Applications International, Northrop Grumman, Lockheed Martin, General Dynamics, and Raytheon. Such employment by these and other companies is not prohibited by law, but these new hires are subject to some restrictions. The GAO report also estimated that "at least 422 former DOD officials could have worked on defense contracts related to their former agencies." In fact, nine were estimated to be working on contracts for which they previously had responsibility when employed at the DOD. Such results continue to raise questions about possible conflicts of interest and provide evidence of continuing symbiotic relations between the DOD and defense contractors.[118]

In 2010 and 2011, the DOD grappled with addressing these possible conflicts of interest by issuing new rules governing military contracts, but it remains unclear how effective they will be. In December 2010, for example, DOD announced that "only contracts relating to major weapons systems and systems engineering and technical assistance" would be subject to tighter rules and thus narrowing contracts applicable to these rules. About a year later, in November 2011, the final rule issued by DOD only required "contractors bidding on solicitations to certify that former DOD officials employed or receiving compensation from the contractor" has complied with post-government employment restrictions, and this certification has only to be done once during the contract.[119]

This symbiotic relationship gains even more credence in light of the various criminal charges that have been brought against lobbyists for defense contractors and in light of the large number of revelations about cost overruns and overcharging in the defense industry. Several lobbyists have been charged and convicted of bribing DOD procurement officers to obtain lucrative contracts, for example, and major contractors (such as General Electric and the Electric Boat division of General Dynamics) have been accused of dramatic cost overruns. Still others have been accused of charging the military exorbitant prices for commonplace supplies. By one analysis, "the military paid $511 for light bulbs that cost ninety cents, $640 for toilet seats that cost $12, $7600 for coffee makers, and $900 for a plastic cap to place under the leg of a navigator's stool" in an aircraft.[120] Finally, and significantly, Representative Randy "Duke" Cunningham resigned from Congress in 2005, pleaded guilty to accepting $2.4 million in bribes "from four co-conspirators, including two defense contractors," and was subsequently sentenced to jail.[121]

On balance, these analyses provide considerable evidence for the linkage among the business, military, and political sectors in American society. What they cannot answer directly, however, is whether these common backgrounds and ties produced policy primarily meeting the interests of these elites. Presumably, shared backgrounds lead policy makers to take these elites into account in any foreign policy decisions or, at the very least, to give them access to key economic groups in order to make their case. However, more direct evidence on the second assumption of the MIC theory—the policy consequences of elite dominance—is needed to draw any firm conclusions about the role of the MIC in foreign policy.

Several studies have been undertaken to evaluate just such policy implications of the MIC theory. Unfortunately, the evidence is disparate, often focusing on various policy components and then attempting to draw larger inferences from the results obtained. Further, these policy studies have more often pointed to differing conclusions about the MIC's effect than have studies identifying close elite ties. To provide an idea of the findings on the policy effects of the MIC, we summarize some of the evidence over the past several decades.

Analyses Supporting the Influence of the MIC   Several case analyses of American foreign policy, including the Marshall Plan of 1948, the decision not to intervene in Indochina in 1954, and the decision to cut back bombing in Vietnam in 1968, provide some support for the MIC theory. According to Morton Berkowitz, P. G. Bock, and Vincent Fuccillo, "it would be difficult to point to a single decision that directly contravenes the interests of the business elite within the presidential court,"[122] although they quickly add that this elite may not have been successful on every decision. Still, "when major issues are at stake, or when its interests are clearly and incontrovertibly involved, . . . the business elite proceeds with absolute unity of purpose and action."[123] Thus, the researchers hold that the business elite view of foreign policy making provides the best explanation for America's actions abroad.

The pattern of defense contracting is often used to demonstrate the policy influence of the MIC. The prime military contractors often turn out to be among the largest industrial corporations, and they are often the same ones year in and year out. In an analysis of the largest defense contractors for fiscal year 2011, for instance, we found that eleven of the top fifty and eighteen of the top one hundred were also ranked among the one hundred largest corporations in America based on the Fortune 500 list.[124] In fact, these totals represent somewhat of an overall decline from earlier analyses: For fiscal years 1982, 1988, 1995, 2002, and 2005, this same comparison found, respectively, forty, thirty-five, twenty-three, fourteen, and eighteen of the one hundred largest corporations among the top one hundred defense contractors in those years. At the same time, it is worth keeping in mind that the spending concentration remained high, with the top ten defense contractors in fiscal year 2011 awarded 35 percent of total government contracts and the top twenty-five awarded 47 percent of total DOD contracts.

Political scientist **James Kurth** has pointed out other evidence of concentration and continuity in defense contracting. That is, **the defense contractors have largely remained the same over the last four decades**—mainly the aircraft industries and, more recently the electronics industries—and they have maintained their ties with particular military branches (such as Boeing and Rockwell International with the air force; Grumman primarily with the navy) as well as the same "product specialties"—particular types of weapons systems they manufacture.[125] The merger of Lockheed and Martin Marietta and the consolidation of control by Boeing in the aircraft industry—all major defense contractors—only reinforce the degree of concentration in these areas. Table 11.2 shows the top ten defense contractors from fiscal year 1988 to fiscal year 2011 and provides support for the argument that particular industries have continued to dominate the contracting process. Such continuity provides additional evidence on how and why certain defense systems are purchased, and on why some manufacturers are advantaged over others.

Table 11.2 Top 10 Defense Contractors for Fiscal Years 1988, 1995, 2002, 2005, and 2011 and Their Corporate Sales Rank (in parentheses) for Those Years

Rank	1988	1995	2002	2005	2011
1	McDonnell Douglas (25)	Lockheed Martin (29)	Lockheed Martin (56)	Lockheed Martin (52)	Lockheed Martin (52)
2	General Dynamics (41)	McDonnell Douglas (74)	Boeing (15)	Boeing (26)	Boeing (35)
3	General Electric (5)	Tenneco*	Northrop Grumman (99)	Northrop Grumman (67)	General Dynamics (86)
4	Tenneco (24)	General Motors (1)	Raytheon*	General Dynamics (100)	Raytheon*
5	Raytheon (53)	Northrop Grumman*	General Dynamics*	Raytheon*	Northrop Grumman (72)
6	Martin Marietta (77)	Raytheon*	United Technologies (49)	Halliburton (97)	United Technologies (44)
7	General Motors (1)	General Electric (7)	Science Applications Intl.*	BAE Systems*	Communications Holdings*
8	Lockheed Martin (33)	Loral Corporation*	TRW*	United Technologies (47)	BAE Systems*
9	United Technologies (16)	Boeing (40)	Health Net*	L-3 Comm. Holdings*	SAIC, Inc.*
10	Boeing (19)	United Technologies (30)	L-3 Comm. Holdings*	Computer Sciences Corp.*	Oshkosh Corporation*

* Companies not ranked in the top 100 U.S. companies in corporate sales in the respective years.

Sources: Defense contract rankings were taken from *100 Companies Receiving the Largest Dollar Volume of Prime Contract Awards—Fiscal Years 1982, 1988, 1995, 2002, and 2005,* at http://siadapp.dior.whs.mil/procurement/, February 27, 2007, and, for fiscal year 2011, the Federal Procurement Data System—Next Generation (under DOD), at https://www.fpds.gov/fpdsng_cms/index.php/reports, May 23, 2012. The corporate sales rankings for fiscal year 2011 were taken from "The 100 Largest US Corporations," *Fortune,* April 24, 1989; April 29, 1996; April 14, 2003; and April 17, 2006 and from CNNMoney, "Fortune 500," at http://money.cnn.com/magazines/fortune/fortune500/2011/full_list/, July 3, 2012.

Analyses Challenging the Influence of the MIC Other studies raise doubts about the success of the MIC in shaping and influencing foreign policy, especially regarding defense spending. Until its dramatic increase during the Reagan administration, defense spending, measured either as a percentage of the gross national product (GNP) or as a percentage of central government spending, had actually declined over time. For the former measure, defense spending dropped below the 6 percent level, and, for the latter, it fell to less than 25 percent. Although defense expenditures edged up during the Reagan years to about 6.6 as a percent of the GNP for 1986 and constituted 27 percent of central government expenditures, both measures dropped significantly during the administrations of Bush and Clinton. In the mid-1990s, they were just under 4 percent of GNP and around 17 to 18 percent of central government expenditures.[126] Defense spending has increased over the past decade to fight terrorism and to prosecute two wars, with expenditures increasing from 3 percent of the GDP in 2001 to 4.8 percent in 2010.[127] Yet, the aggregate clout of MIC on defense spending has been not nearly as pronounced as some think.

An analysis by political scientist Bruce Russett has cast doubt on the MIC as the sole explanation for high defense budgets. Most assuredly, the MIC contributes to continued defense spending, but other factors in combination (such as domestic bureaucratic politics, technological momentum, and international actions) are a better explanation. Russett is quick to acknowledge, however, that domestic factors tend to carry somewhat greater weight than international factors alone.[128]

Have American industries really been as dependent on defense spending for their prosperity as some think or as the analyses focusing only on defense contractors suggest? In the aggregate, as reported in a classic study by sociologist **Stanley Lieberson** near the end of the Cold War, few of the one hundred largest industrial corporations in 1968 depended on military contracts for the bulk of their sales; in fact, for seventy-eight of those, less than 10 percent of sales derived from military contracts, and for only five did military contracts account for more than 50 percent of sales.[129] In addition, Lieberson demonstrated that corporate income over time has been less dependent on military spending by the federal government than on nonmilitary spending. Finally, he shows that defense spending cutbacks seriously harm only certain sectors of the economy (aircraft, ordinance, research and development, electronics, and nonferrous metals) rather than the economy as a whole. In short, Lieberson's evidence suggests that the MIC's dominance is less than might be thought and is primarily concentrated in particular industries.

Political scientist Steve Chan has carefully surveyed and analyzed numerous studies on the relationship between the health of the economy and military spending.[130] He, too, obtained mixed and inconsistent results on the positive or negative effect of military spending overall. On the one hand, several studies that Chan researched suggest that military spending actually serves as both an "economic prop" and a "political prop." It is an economic prop because it provides jobs and cushions economic downturns, and it is a political prop because it changes according "to the rhythms of electoral cycles."[131] On the other hand, several alternative studies found no—or only limited—effects of defense spending on economic growth. More generally, as Chan notes, "there is no direct, simple link between defense spending and macroeconomic performance."[132]

In sum, these various studies over the past several decades suggest a conclusion with important ramifications for the MIC theory: **neither the dependence of the American economy on high defense spending nor such spending's**

substantial negative effects across the economy is easily demonstrable. Instead, the MIC should be seen as a convergence of defense-oriented organizations that are constantly pursuing their interests, which, moreover, has hardly been as successful as the common view holds. In short, defense spending has not been as dramatic as sometimes implied, and its negative effect on the American economy may be less than is often assumed. Further, the MIC has met public resistance and interest group opposition and continues to face such challenges to this day. Still, this amalgam of interests may continue to be viewed as a powerful foreign policy interest, especially in today's uncertain international environment.

Can these interest groups continue to affect policy and achieve their goals in this international environment, or will they meet resistance even under such circumstances? If they can succeed, perhaps the argument about the relative impact of the MIC will become clear. If they cannot, the view of those who took a more differentiated view of the power of this interest group may win out.

What should not be lost in this discussion of the MIC is the continuing size and impact of this concentration of interests. No matter what the judgment about the degree of the MIC's control, it is fair to conclude that it seems to occupy a potentially important position in the shaping of foreign policy decisions, especially when compared to other interest groups.

Ethnic Groups

The leading ethnic lobbies in recent decades are probably the Jewish and Greek communities, two relative newcomers to the American political process. The **Jewish lobby** has been able to obtain a remarkable level of economic and military assistance for Israel over the postwar years (at $2 billion to $3 billion per year) and has been able to assist in steering American policy toward support for it since 1948. Only in the past two decades or so has this strong support begun to wane. In a more limited way, the Greek lobby enjoyed policy success, especially in the middle 1970s,[133] when it was able to garner sufficient congressional support to impose an American arms embargo on Turkey despite active opposition by the executive branch.

In contrast, the influence of the older ethnic lobbies—those Americans of Irish and Eastern European descent—has generally declined over the past fifty years. The Irish enjoyed their greatest success prior to World War II, whereas the Eastern Europeans seemed most influential in the early Cold War years.[134] A new variant of the latter lobby emerged in the 1990s and once again exercised some influence.

In 1993, the Central and East European Coalition formed. Comprising sixteen American ethnic associations (among them Armenian American, Ukrainian American, Czech American, Slovak American, Polish American, Hungarian American, and Latvian American), it sought to steer American policy away from its "Russian-centered path" and toward, for example, the more rapid expansion of NATO and more aid for the former Soviet republics and the nations of Eastern Europe. Although these ethnic groups constitute only 8.5 percent of the total American population, they are concentrated in the Midwest, which gives them some influence over electoral votes in any hotly contested national election in that region. At the same time, the apparent inability of this coalition to mobilize their constituent groups may hamper the effectiveness of their lobbying.[135]

Two newer American ethnic groups—**Hispanics and African Americans**—also exercised some influence on the foreign policy process in recent decades.

TransAfrica, an organization that promotes the interests of Africans, especially in Africa and the Caribbean, was formed only in 1977, but it early on had a noticeable effect on American foreign policy.[136] The group lobbied to maintain economic sanctions on Rhodesia in the late 1970s in an effort to achieve majority rule and the creation of the nation of Zimbabwe. In conjunction with the "Free South Africa Movement," TransAfrica played an important role in prodding the Reagan administration to apply economic sanctions in 1985 and then in pushing Congress to override the Reagan veto of the Anti-Apartheid Act of 1986, a bill imposing more extensive sanctions than those called for in the 1985 measure. During the Clinton administration, TransAfrica was pivotal in keeping Haiti on the foreign policy agenda during 1993 and 1994 and in pushing the Clinton administration for stronger action against Haitian military rulers. Furthermore, it lobbied against the African Growth and Opportunity Act, although it failed to defeat its passage in Congress.[137]

More recently, TransAfrica has worked on several other issues related to America's foreign policy toward Africa. These have included calls for cancellation of debts for the poorest African countries to give them a chance at development; opposition to the establishment of the new Africa Command by the U.S. military over concerns that it will lead to greater militarization of the continent; and support for indigenous democracy in Africa, including opposition to the repressive tactics of Robert Mugabe's government in Zimbabwe.[138]

With the large percentage of Hispanics located in the South and Southwest, this ethnic group mainly focuses its attention on American policy toward Central and South America and toward such issues as immigration and refugees. So far, however, the **Cuban American National Foundation (CANF)** is the best known and most successful of the Hispanic lobbying groups. Its strong anti-Castro message has influenced both political parties over the past several decades. Although CANF has generally been more influential in Republican administrations, the Clinton administration heeded it in the 1990s—whether in halting appointments to the State Department, challenging efforts to cut funding for the anti-Castro Radio Martí, or responding to Cuba's shoot-down of two unarmed "Brothers to the Rescue" planes over international waters. In general, CANF has been instrumental in keeping sanctions on Cuba for more than four decades. It also proved instrumental in persuading Congress to pass, and President Clinton to sign, the 1996 **Helms–Burton Act**. That legislation codified the economic embargo into law (rather than an executive order) and imposed tougher economic sanctions against Cuba and against companies that deal with the Castro regime.

With the death of CANF's founder in 1997, with increased divisions between younger and older Cuban Americans, and with the rise of other lobbying groups that are more favorable to improving Cuban–American ties (such as Americans for Humanitarian Trade with Cuba, USA★Engage, and the Cuba Study Group), CANF lost some of its clout. As it shifted its position, it lost some two dozen board members, who went on to form the Cuban Liberty Council, an organization more fully committed to opposing any accommodation with the Castro regime and any negotiations with it. In other signs of divisions within the Cuban-American community in Florida, three members of Congress who traditionally supported a hard-line policy on the Castro regime were challenged in the 2008 elections, although unsuccessfully, by those favoring a different approach.[139] In short, although this lobby remains powerful, it has experienced some challenges in the past decade.

Another sizable Hispanic group, the **Mexican-American** community, has been less successful and less prominent than CANF or the Cuban-American community generally. It has had neither the same interest in nor the same effect on national policy, either toward Mexico, Central America, or elsewhere. Indeed, according to one analysis, on many issues regarding Central America, Mexican-American attitudes were not much different from those of the rest of the American public. Put differently, "Mexican-American policy preferences on major issues such as immigration and border control . . . differ from those of the Mexican government." Overall, and excluding Cuban Americans, one analysis concludes that "the Hispanic community exerts almost no systematic influence on U.S.–Latin American relations or, for that matter, on U.S. foreign policy in general."[140]

Only with their recent activism over anti-immigration legislation and over the status of NAFTA have Mexican Americans begun to make an impact. Indeed, a number of Mexican-American organizations (and allied groups) staged large demonstrations over immigration legislation that was making its way through Congress in the past decade. These groups, too, were active over an immigration law passed by the State of Arizona in 2010. As its population continues to grow across several states, with estimates of 22 million to 30 million nationwide,[141] and as immigration continues as a focal point of legislative attention, this community may play a more significant role in congressional and presidential politics.

The newest ethnic lobby is the Indian lobby, composed of Americans with ancestral ties to India. Although this lobby has existed for some time, it particularly gained prominence with the establishment of the US India Political Action Committee (USINPAC) in 2002. This committee hired staff and created a structure for effective lobbying. Furthermore, it has been able to mobilize the relative small (about 2 million) Asian Indian population, who tend to be highly educated and relatively affluent, to take effective action. It has also been able to take advantage of the changed global environment after the end of the Cold War and the event of 9/11. In such an environment, American relations with India have become more critically important in terms of stability in South Asia but in Asia generally. As a result, USINPAC was instrumental in gaining congressional passage of legislation lifting American restrictions on the selling of nuclear fuel to India, despite India's failure to sign and ratify the Nuclear Nonproliferation Treaty (NPT). Indeed, one assessment describes the Indian lobby as "the only lobby in Washington likely to acquire the strength of the Israel lobby."[142]

Why have some of these ethnic groups been so successful and others less so? How can only some 6.2 million Jewish Americans (discussed in the next section), just over 1.3 million Greek Americans, or about 1.2 million Cuban Americans exercise influence in a nation of about 300 million?[143] Although we suggested some possible reasons earlier, a brief examination of perhaps the most successful ethnic lobby, Jewish-Americans, is particularly instructive in gaining some insight in how interest group influence can occur. The ability to provide voting support in key states, make campaign contributions to candidates, and organize on key issues gives this lobby considerable political clout.[144]

The Jewish Lobby: Sources of Influence   First of all, the Jewish lobby appears to be very well organized and directs its energies primarily toward foreign policy issues related to a single state, Israel. By one estimate, there are more than seventy-five organizations that support Israel, and most are Jewish. Furthermore, these groups have two umbrella organizations to coordinate and guide their activities, the **Conference of Presidents of Major American Jewish Organizations** and the **American Israel Public Affairs Committee (AIPAC)**.[145] A more recent assessment defines this lobby as a "loose coalition of individuals and organizations that actively work to shape U.S. policy in a pro-Israel direction,"[146] and posits that it consists of several core organizations, as well as other groups seeking support for Israel, but it does not specify its exact size.

By virtually all accounts, AIPAC appears pivotal in lobbying by the Jewish community and its supporters.[147] The organization has a membership of about 100,000 with ten regional and seven satellite offices throughout the country, including Washington, D.C. Moreover, it has experienced considerable growth over the years, and its operation is well organized to facilitate maximum legislative and executive impact.[148] AIPAC maintains regular contact with its members, providing updated information and encouraging contact and involvement with local officials. It has also initiated several different types of clubs to encourage greater involvement of its membership.[149] In fact, in the estimate of one close observer from many years ago, the lobby's comprehensive organizational structure appears crucial to its overall effort: "The multitiered structural pyramid that links individual Jews in local communities across the country to centralized national foreign policy leadership groups in Washington and New York is the primary organizational factor that can explain the ability of the pro-Israel movement to mobilize rapidly and in a coordinated fashion on a national scale when important foreign policy issues arise."[150]

AIPAC's website contains summaries of key issues currently before Congress and those in development and provides policy statements on topics germane to its mission.[151] In all, then, AIPAC's activism has been pronounced, and its website touts its various legislative and policy successes.[152] Indeed, the potency of AIPAC has been recognized by the *New York Times*, which called it "the most important organization affecting America's relationship with Israel." This acclamation is prominently displayed on the organization's website.[153]

Beyond its organizational structure, AIPAC has particularly good access to Capitol Hill, although perhaps less access to the executive branch. It "is the envy of other lobbies for its easy access to the highest levels of government."[154] Through its frequent contacts with members of Congress and congressional staff, AIPAC has been able to garner remarkable levels of support for some pro-Israeli legislation and has been able to stop legislation viewed as harmful to Israel.[155] Another important indicator of its political clout is that members of Congress and the administration are highly responsive to its activities. At AIPAC's 2012 Policy Conference, for example, President Obama, Secretary of Defense Leon Panetta, and Senate minority leader, Mitch McConnell, among others, gave presentations. In addition, 2012 presidential candidates Mitt Romney, Newt Gingrich, and Rick Santorum spoke. In all, AIPAC attracts candidates across the political aisle for its major policy event and generates considerable respect from America's political elites.[156]

The Jewish lobby can also point to a number of significant legislative victories over the years. For instance, it was able to gain seventy-six co-sponsors in the Senate for the Jackson-Vanik Amendment to the Trade Act of 1974. This legislation prohibited the granting of MFN status to any state that did not have a free emigration policy and was clearly directed at the Soviet Union and its restrictions on Jewish emigration.

A few years later, an identical number of senators co-authored a letter to President Gerald Ford urging him to stand behind Israel in any search for peace in the Middle East.[157] Most significantly, of course, the lobby continues to ensure high levels of American foreign assistance for Israel year in and year out, and it has made members of Congress and the administration aware of the threats that it perceives, for example, from Iran and Syria.

AIPAC has also been able to alter or stop legislation that it does not support. Over the years, for instance, arms sales to Arab countries have been difficult to approve in Congress. When they have been, they have often required modification, consistent with AIPAC's concerns. In 1987, the Reagan administration was forced to change the composition of a proposed arms sale to Saudi Arabia to satisfy objections raised by Israel's supporters in the Senate. In 1988, Saudi Arabia completed a $30 billion arms deal with Britain rather than face potential opposition from within Congress. At about the same time, a prospective arms deal with Kuwait was altered, once again to address concerns raised by AIPAC.[158]

More significant, and less measureable, the lobby has usually been able to stop legislation that might be harmful to Israel before it advances in Congress. According to one study from the early 1970s, Senate support for Israel averaged 84 percent and existed across party lines.[159] Although this level of support probably has not been sustained over time, it is indicative of the high level of congressional support for Israel that the Jewish lobby has been able to generate.

The success of the Jewish lobby is tied to the degree of support for Israel among the American public. The American public is often sympathetic toward Israel for moral and ethical reasons. Israelis are perceived as having suffered greatly throughout history and thus as deserving of a homeland of their own. American support is also tied to political motivation. Israel represents a democratic, Western-oriented state in a region of the world that does not seem to have many of these. During the Cold War, for example, Israel was a strategic asset against the Soviet Union and communism, and it has continued to serve in that role since the Cold War ended and since the events of September 11. Further, whereas the Democratic Party has traditionally been a strong supporter of Israel, the Republican Party lately—especially among religious conservatives—has adopted pro-Israel positions.[160] In short, this latent public sympathy and support for Israel allows Jewish interest groups to obtain considerable overt support within Congress.[161]

Domestic electoral factors also contribute to politicians' support for Israel. Although the Jewish community is a small percentage of the nation's population (less than 3 percent), it is concentrated in some key states, especially along the East Coast and in California, Illinois, and Ohio.[162] As a consequence, its support can be pivotal to the success of congressional or presidential candidates in those areas. Furthermore, although AIPAC does not make direct contributions to political campaigns, it maintains "close communications with the eighty-plus PACs [political action committees] that favor the Israeli cause. Its interlocking connections and directors with these PACs provide readily available funds when necessary."[163]

AIPAC's funding and support (or opposition) were crucial in key House and Senate campaigns in the 1980s and continue to be so today.[164] For example, its lobbying was instrumental in the defeat of incumbent Senators Roger Jepsen (R–Iowa) and Charles Percy (R–Illinois), who failed to support its position on some key votes during that decade. Moreover, because the Jewish population has traditionally been politically active, there is even more incentive for potential presidents, senators, and representatives to be sympathetic to its view on Israel. Furthermore, on an electoral level, it is unlikely that any major party candidate for the presidency will not commit to support for Israel or will outline a different policy direction for the United States toward it.[165]

The relative weakness of the pro-Arab lobby, the counterpart of the pro-Israeli lobby, contributes to support for Israel. Although the **National Association of Arab Americans (NAAA)**, founded in 1972, has increased its visibility and its activism since the Arab oil embargo of 1973–1974, it remains a much less potent force than the supporters of Israel.[166] The **American–Arab Anti-Discrimination Committee (ADC)**, another lobby, has faced similar difficulties. As its former leader, former Senator James Abourezk, once indicated, it faces a formidable task of obtaining money and becoming organized: "To have influence in Congress you have to have money for candidates or control a lot of votes. We're trying to build a grass-roots network; it's difficult for us to raise money."[167] The two organizations joined together in 2002, but the Arab lobby continues to face problems in becoming politically effective and has to contend with the impression that it is more anti-Israel than pro-Arab. Although the lobby is quick to deny it, this characterization continues to plague its efforts. In addition, the Arab lobby is often divided. After all, it represents a variety of Arab nationalities with differing political traditions and with considerable rivalries.[168] A third Arab lobby, the Arab American Institute (AAI) emerged in 1985 as yet another attempt to provide a voice on Arab-American and U.S.-Arab relations.[169] Still, though, the pro-Arab lobby does not yet serve as a good counterbalance to the Jewish lobby's influence.

In a recent—and controversial—analysis of the Jewish lobby, two prominent political scientists, John Mearsheimer and Stephen Walt, concluded that its influence and effectiveness more fully explains American support for Israel than any moral or strategic arguments that might be advanced.[170] They point to its influence in Congress, but they also highlight its effectiveness with the media, think tanks, and the academic community as reasons for its considerable influence. They do not see the lobby as "a cabal or a conspiracy or anything of the sort." Instead, "it is engaged in good old-fashioned interest group politics, which is as American as apple pie." Still, they do call for more open discussion of this lobby and for more discussion of U.S. interests in the Middle East. At the same time, of course, their analysis points to the potentially powerful role that an ethnic group may have on American foreign policy.

The Jewish Lobby: Questions about Its Influence Although the Jewish lobby is usually identified as the most successful ethnic interest group, its overall influence still remains hotly debated. Especially with the changing events in the Middle East over the past three decades, new questions have been raised about its impact. To some observers, the lobby remains far from omnipotent over American policy toward Israel or the Middle East in general, as illustrated by several setbacks and conflicts with Congress and the president and within its own organization.

Prior to the late 1970s and the Camp David Accords, the Jewish lobby was generally able to forestall the provision of military supplies to the Arab states and was able to gain large military assistance for Israel from Congress. By 1978, however, success in these areas was beginning to wane as the United States sought to pursue a more even-handed policy. The Jewish lobby was unable to stop the supply of U.S. fighter aircraft to Saudi Arabia and Egypt, despite its strong efforts. More significantly, perhaps,

Congress approved the sale of AWACS and other technologically advanced aircraft equipment to the Saudis in October 1981 despite strong AIPAC lobbying. Indeed, this defeat actually motivated the organization to double its efforts for the future, but it also suggested its limitations.[171]

American presidents have challenged and criticized the Israeli government, even though they faced possible opposition from the Jewish lobby. One former Carter administration aide put it this way: "The president can take a position that Israel opposes if the American people as a whole are behind him. . . . Then the Jewish community will support him also. That happened with Ike [President Eisenhower] and the Sinai and it is still true."[172] President Reagan pursued his own extensive lobbying effort to counteract AIPAC's over the sale of arms to Saudi Arabia in 1981, and President George H.W. Bush held up $10 billion in loan guarantees to the Israeli government over the West Bank settlement issue for a time, despite considerable political pressure to do otherwise. More recently, President George W. Bush called for the creation of an independent Palestinian state in 2003—the first time that an American president did so—and opposed Israeli settlements in the West Bank. President Obama reiterated American support for a "two-state" solution in the Middle East and criticized Israel over more West Bank settlement for a time. Importantly, too, and despite Israeli opposition, Obama called for the pre-1967 borders in the Middle East as the basis for negotiations on a permanent peace in the region.

Internal discord within the American Jewish community has also weakened its lobbying effort. After the massacres at the Palestinian camps of Sabra and Shatila outside Beirut in September 1982, and the repressive response of the Israeli government to the *intifada*—the Palestinian uprisings in Israeli-occupied territories on the West Bank and the Gaza Strip beginning in 1987—fissures developed within the Jewish community, which undoubtedly weakened its overall impact in American policy making.[173]

As the peace process among Israel, its Arab neighbors, and the Palestinians evolved in the 1990s and beyond, additional divisions developed within the American Jewish community. In 1993, for example, the officers of AIPAC fired its longtime pragmatic director, Tom Dine, and moved the group toward a more hard-line stance on concessions in Middle East peace negotiations. This action divided the American Jewish community, straining AIPAC's relations with the Israeli government, and straining its ties to some members of Congress.[174] In 1995, too, Israeli Prime Minister Yitzhak Rabin publicly criticized the American Jewish community for lobbying against the policies of the Israeli government: "Never before have we witnessed an attempt by U.S. Jews to pressure Congress against the policies of a legitimate, democratically elected government."[175]

The division within the Jewish community stimulated the creation of a new lobbying group, J Street, to serve as a counterweight to AIPAC in 2008. It is an organization for "pro-Israel, pro-peace Americans fighting for the future of Israel as the democratic homeland of the Jewish people." It believes "that Israel's Jewish and democratic character depends on a two-state solution, resulting in a Palestinian state living alongside Israel in peace and security." Although it has generated a large number of supporters and has taken action to support the Obama administration's position on the Middle East, doubts remain about its long-term impact and its ability to maintain widespread support.[176] Still, the emergence of this organization suggests that American policy toward Israel and the Middle East—whether over the peace process with the Palestinians, the actions of the Israeli government, or dealing with Iran—will likely have some divisions even with the existence of a powerful lobby.

Although the evidence cited suggests that the Jewish lobby does not always succeed and may have some incipient organizational fissures, it also shows how an ethnic group may engage in the foreign policy process and, more specifically, how a well-organized and committed interest group can sometimes alter the direction of policy. Increasingly, interest groups, like political parties, are exercising an independent effect on U.S. foreign policy making.

CONCLUDING COMMENTS

Both political parties and interest groups are playing a more important role in foreign policy making today. Despite the American tradition of bipartisanship in foreign affairs, partisan differences have always been a characteristic of policy making. In recent decades, moreover, partisan (and ideological) differences on foreign policy questions have actually intensified and are likely to remain part of the American political landscape, especially as the United States confronts the dramatic changes of the twenty-first century. Interest groups, too, have become more pervasive in the foreign policy process, with both a greater number and a wider array now participating in foreign affairs. Although economic and ethnic groups remain particularly effective, foreign interests are increasingly seeking to influence policy as well.

In the next chapter, we examine the role of the media and public opinion in the making of foreign policy. These two forces usually generate different reactions among casual observers. Because the media have grown so dramatically and intrude on so many aspects of American life, their influence, even on foreign affairs, is often taken for granted. The public, on the other hand, is at such a distance from the locus of foreign policy decisions that any discussion of its role engenders considerable skepticism and many questions. We take up these concerns in Chapter 12.

Notes

1. On the various definitions of political parties and their development in America, see Marjorie Randon Hershey, *Party Politics in America*, 13th ed. (New York: Pearson Longman, 2009), pp. 5–25 or Marc J. Hetherington and William J. Keefe, *Parties, Politics, and Public Policy in America* (Washington, D.C.: CQ Press, 2007), pp. 1–7.

2. For recent discussions of the definition of interest groups and their activities, see Clive S. Thomas, "Introduction: The Study of Interest Groups," in Clive S. Thomas, ed., *Research Guide to U.S. and International Interest Groups* (Westport, CT: Praeger, 2004), pp. 3–7, and Clive S. Thomas, "Studying the Political Party-Interest Group Relationship," in Thomas, ed., *Political Parties and Interest Groups: Shaping Democratic Governance* (Boulder, CO: Lynne Rienner Publishers, 2001), pp. 6–9. For a classic treatment of the meaning of interest groups, see L. Harmon Zeigler and G. Wayne Peak, *Interest Groups in American Society*, 2nd ed. (Englewood Cliffs, NJ: Prentice Hall, 1972), p. 3.

3. Herbert McClosky, Paul J. Hoffmann, and Rosemary O'Hara, "Issue Conflict and Consensus among Party Leaders and Followers," *American Political Science Review* 14 (June 1960): 408–427.

4. The quote is taken from a speech by Senator Arthur H. Vandenberg to the Cleveland Foreign Affairs Forum. See John Felton, "The Man Who Showed Politicians the Water's Edge," *Congressional Quarterly Weekly Report*, February 18, 1989, 336.

5. For a history of bipartisanship and its various meanings, see Ellen C. Collier, ed., *Bipartisanship and the Making of Foreign Policy: A Historical Survey* (Boulder, CO: Westview Press, 1991).

6. Cecil V. Crabb, Jr., *Bipartisan Foreign Policy* (Evanston, IL: Row, Peterson and Company, 1957), p. 5.

7. Robert Dahl, *Congress and Foreign Policy* (New York: Harcourt, Brace and Company, 1950), p. 229.

8. See the Republican Party platform of 1952, which strongly attacks the Democrats, reprinted in Donald Bruce Johnson and Kirk H. Porter, *National Party Platforms, 1840–1972* (Urbana: University of Illinois Press, 1973), pp. 497–500.

9. See the 1956 party platforms in ibid., pp. 524 and 556; and the 1960 Republican platform, p. 606.

10. These trends had shifted by the 1980s (and perhaps beyond), with the Democrats more associated with peace and the Republicans with prosperity. Public opinion data on these

questions of war and peace and prosperity and recession from 1951 to 1984 are summarized in George Gallup, "GOP Edges Democrats in Poll on Prosperity Helm," *Des Moines Sunday Register*, April 29, 1984, A4.

11. See McClosky, Hoffman, and O'Hara, "Issue Conflict and Consensus Among Party Leaders and Followers," Table I, p. 410. At the same time, they argue against the view that the two parties "hold the same views" on foreign policy (p. 417). Some differences are detectable.

12. Gerald Pomper, *Elections in America: Control and Influence in Democratic Politics* (New York: Dodd, Mead & Co., 1965), p. 194.

13. I. M. Destler, Leslie H. Gelb, and Anthony Lake, *Our Own Worst Enemy: The Unmaking of American Foreign Policy* (New York: Simon & Schuster, 1984), p. 17.

14. Ibid., pp. 60–61.

15. Crabb, *Bipartisan Foreign Policy*, p. 256.

16. This discussion and the following on military assistance, defense, and trade policy are drawn from the data and discussion in Barry Hughes, *The Domestic Context of American Foreign Policy* (San Francisco: W. H. Freeman and Company, 1975), pp. 130–144. On foreign aid voting, also see Barbara Hinckley, *Stability and Change in Congress*, 3rd ed. (New York: Harper and Row, 1983), p. 272.

17. See Hughes, *The Domestic Context of American Foreign Policy*, and Hinckley, *Stability and Change in Congress*. Also see Aage R. Clausen, *How Congressmen Decide: A Policy Focus* (New York: St. Martin's Press, 1973), pp. 192–212.

18. Destler, Gelb, and Lake, *Our Own Worst Enemy*, p. 61. The quoted passage at the end of this paragraph is from the same source and at the same page (p. 61).

19. Zbigniew Brzezinski, "The Three Requirements for a Bipartisan Foreign Policy," in *The Washington Quarterly White Paper* (Washington, D.C.: Center for Strategic and International Studies, Georgetown University), pp. 14–15.

20. Leslie H. Gelb with Richard K. Betts, *The Irony of Vietnam: The System Worked* (Washington, D.C.: The Brookings Institution, 1979), p. 216.

21. "Congress Took 94 Roll-Call Votes on War 1966–1972," *Congress and the Nation, 1969–1972, Volume 3* (Washington, D.C.: Congressional Quarterly Service, 1973), p. 944.

22. The figures were computed for these years by the author from data provided in Pomper, *Elections in America*; and Gerald M. Pomper with Susan S. Lederman, *Elections in America: Control and Influence in Democratic Politics*, 2nd ed. (New York: Longman, 1980), p. 169. The former volume covered platforms from 1944 to 1964; the latter, those from 1944 to 1976.

23. One alternative explanation suggests that personal ideology more than any other factor (including party) may explain congressional voting in the post–Vietnam period. See, for example, Robert A. Bernstein and William W. Anthony, "The ABM Issue in the Senate, 1968–1970: The Importance of Ideology," *The American Political Science Review* 65 (September 1974): 1198–1206; Wayne Moyer, "House Voting on Defense: An Ideological Explanation," in Bruce M. Russett and Alfred Stepan, eds., *Military Force and American Society* (New York: Harper and Row, 1973), pp. 106–141; and James M. McCormick and Michael Black, "Ideology and Senate Voting on the Panama Canal Treaties," *Legislative Studies Quarterly* 8 (February 1983): 45–63.

24. See, for example, "House Votes to Aid El Salvador, Denies Nicaragua's Rebels," *Des Moines Register*, May 25, 1984, 1A and 20A; and "House Curbs MX, Votes $284 Billion to Military," *Des Moines Register*, June 1, 1984, 1A and 12A. For a systematic analysis of partisan differences in congressional voting on the MX missile, B-1 bomber, and Star Wars in the 1970s and 1980s, see James M. Lindsay, "Parochialism, Policy, and Constituency Constraints: Congressional Voting on Strategic Weapons, Systems," *American Journal of Political Science* 34 (November 1990): 936–960.

25. The following sections draw on these pieces of research by James M. McCormick and Eugene R. Wittkopf: "Bush and Bipartisanship: The Past as Prologue?" *Washington Quarterly* 13 (Winter 1990): 5–16; "Bipartisanship, Partisanship, and Ideology in Congressional–Executive Foreign Policy Relations, 1947–1988," *Journal of Politics* 52 (November 1990): 1077–1100; and "At the Water's Edge: The Effects of Party, Ideology and Issues on Congressional Foreign Policy Voting, 1947–1988," *American Politics Quarterly* 20 (January 1992): 26–53.

26. McCormick and Wittkopf, "Bipartisanship, Partisanship, and Ideology in Congressional–Executive Foreign Policy Relations, 1947–1988," p. 1097. For an alternate view on the impact of Vietnam, see James Meernik, "Presidential Support in Congress: Conflict and Consensus on Foreign and Defense Policy," *Journal of Politics* 55 (August 1993): 569–587.

27. Peter Trubowitz and Nicole Mellow, "'Going Bipartisan': Politics by Other Means," *Political Science Quarterly* 120 (Fall 2005): 433–453. The quoted passages are at pp. 448 and 450, respectively. This analysis importantly tests several factors that explain when bipartisanship is more likely than partisanship, both on foreign and domestic voting. These include the state of the economy, the degree of regional polarization in national politics, the existence of divided government in Washington, the impact of international crises, and the effect of congressional rules changes strengthening partisan division in Congress. For another study that questions the existence of bipartisanship in the post–World War II era as well as the wisdom of pursuing such a policy, see Leslie H. Gelb, "We Bow to the God Bipartisanship," *The National Interest* 116 (November/December 2011): 18–24.

28. Peter Beinart, "Party Politics No Longer Stops at the Water's Edge: Partisan Polarization and Foreign Policy," in Pietro S. Nivola and David W. Brady, eds., *Red and Blue Nation? Consequences and Correction of America's Polarized Politics, Volume 2* (Washington, D.C. and Stanford, CA: Brookings Institution Press and Hoover Institution Press, 2008), pp. 155–156. The quote is at p. 155.

29. See the statement by the president, "President's Commission on Strategic Forces," *Weekly Compilation of Presidential Documents* 19 (January 10, 1983): 3; and see "Summary of Kissinger Commission Report," *Congressional Quarterly Weekly Report*, January 14, 1984, 64–66, on these commissions.

30. "Excerpts from President Reagan's Speech on Foreign Policy and Congress," *New York Times*, April 7, 1984, 5.

31. These passages are taken from the inaugural address by President Bush, January 20, 1989.

32. The data and discussion on the Bush and the first term of the Clinton administrations are based on the work by the author with Eugene R. Wittkopf and David M. Danna. See our "Politics and Bipartisanship at the Water's Edge: A Note on Bush and Clinton," *Polity* 30 (Fall 1997): 133–149. Parts of the figures are taken from that work. The data and analyses for the second term of the Clinton administration and the George W. Bush administration were new calculations for this edition. See note 40 below.

33. Beinert, "Party Politics No Longer Stops at the Water's Edge: Partisan Polarization and Foreign Policy," p. 157.

34. James M. McCormick, "Clinton and Foreign Policy: Some Legacies for a New Century," in Steven E. Schier, ed., *The Postmodern Presidency* (Pittsburgh: University of Pittsburgh Press, 2000), pp. 71–73.

35. James M. Lindsay, "From Deference to Activism and Back Again: Congress and the Politics of American Foreign Policy," in Eugene R. Wittkopf and James M. McCormick, eds., *The Domestic Sources of American Foreign Policy*, 4th ed. (Lanham, MD: Rowman & Littlefield Publishers, 2004), pp. 183–195.

36. Beinert, "Party Politics No Longer Stops at the Water's Edge: Partisan Polarization and Foreign Policy," p. 158.

37. See Figure 3 in Gary C. Jacobson, "Referendum: The 2006 Midterm Congressional Elections," *Political Science Quarterly* 122 (Spring 2007): 6.

38. Richard Benedetto, "Poll: Bush Trails Clark, Kerry," *Des Moines Register*, September 23, 2003, 1A and 9A. The poll results are on p. 9A.

39. See Figure 5 in Jacobson, "Referendum: The 2006 Midterm Congressional Elections," p. 8.

40. The analyses of bipartisanship and the partisan divisions in the Obama administration for the first three years follow the calculation pattern outlined in Figures 11.3 and 11.4. That is, a bipartisan foreign policy vote was one in which the president took a position and a majority of both parties supported the president's position. The partisan gap was the average difference in support on a foreign policy vote (on which the president took a position) by members of Congress in the president's party and the opposition party. These congressional votes were drawn from the *Congressional Almanac* and *CQ Weekly* for 2009–2011. The calculations of Clinton's second term and the George W. Bush administration were compiled in a similar way and analyzed by the author, as was the Obama administration data. The comparative data for earlier administrations draw upon the author's involvement with earlier analyses cited in the figures. For the initial research report with these data from the second term of Clinton through the first two years of Obama, see James M. McCormick, "The Obama Administration, Congress, and Foreign Policy Behavior," paper presented at the annual meeting of the International Studies Association, San Diego, California, April 1-4, 2012.

41. On the degree of greater partisanship in the House in recent decades, see David W. Rohde, *Parties and Leaders in the Postreform House* (Chicago: The University of Chicago Press, 1991).

42. See Charles A. Kupchan and Peter L. Trubowitz, "Grand Strategy for a Divided America," *Foreign Affairs* 86 (July/August 2007): 71–83.

43. Miroslav Nincic, "External Affairs and the Electoral Connection," in James M. McCormick, eds., *The Domestic Sources of American Foreign Policy: Insights and Evidence*, 6th ed. (Lanham, MD: Rowman & Littlefield Publishers, 2012), pp. 139–155.

44. See ibid. for the 2004 and 2008 presidential elections and foreign policy as well as the impact of foreign policy on 2002, 2006, and 2010 congressional voting. Also see Jacobson, "Referendum: The 2006 Midterm Congressional Elections" for foreign policy and those elections.

45. Nincic, "External Affairs and the Electoral Connection," pp. 145–148.

46. J. Valerie Steel, ed., *Washington Representatives 1999*, 23rd ed. (Washington, D.C.: Columbia Books, 1999), pp. 3–4. Also see the publisher's statement for this book at amazon.com summarizing the number of organizations and individuals involved in lobbying in Washington.

47. For these estimates, see A. Leroy Bennett and James K. Oliver, *International Organizations: Principles and Issues*, 7th ed. (Upper Saddle River, NJ: Prentice Hall, 2002), p. 282; and James A. Paul, *NGOs and Global Policy-Making*, Global Policy Forum, at http://www .globalpolicy.org/ngos/analysis/ana100.htm, September 2, 2002; and Kelly-Kate S. Pease, *International Organizations: Perspectives on Governance in the Twenty-first Century*, 3rd ed. (Upper Saddle River, NJ: Prentice Hall, 2008), p. 37.

48. The count was done by the author from J. Valerie Steel, ed., *Washington Representatives 2000*, 24th ed. (Washington, D.C.: Columbia Books, 2000), pp. 703–711. (Unfortunately, the more recent edition [2007] of this source does not have a separate breakdown of executive branch and legislative offices with lobbying activities.) Of course, it should be noted that not all of these government groups are necessarily engaged in foreign policy lobbying, but several are.

49. Dana Priest, *The Mission* (New York: W.W. Norton and Company, 2003), p. 36.

50. Norman J. Ornstein and Shirley Elder, *Interest Groups, Lobbying and Policymaking* (Washington, D.C.: Congressional Quarterly Press, 1978), pp. 35–39; and Immanuel Ness, *Encyclopedia of Interest Groups and Lobbyists in the United States, Volumes 1 and 2* (Armonk, NY: Sharpe Reference, 2000). The discussion also draws on the list of organizations in Thomas L. Brewer and Lorne Teitelbaum, *American Foreign Policy: A Contemporary Introduction*, 4th ed. (Upper Saddle River, NJ: Prentice Hall, 1997), p. 141–143; it also draws on Hughes, *The Domestic Context of American Foreign Policy*, pp. 157–171, for the foreign policy goals of business, labor, and farm groups.

51. See "About the AFL-CIO," at the AFL-CIO website, http://www.afl-cio.org/About, June 26, 2012. Also see Ness, *Encyclopedia of Interest Groups and Lobbyists in the United States*, pp. 351–359 for other information in this paragraph, and Ornstein and Elder, *Interest Groups, Lobbying, and Policymaking*, p. 24.

52. For an overview of the foreign policy of the labor movement, and especially the AFL-CIO in earlier decades, see Carl Gershman, *The Foreign Policy of American Labor, The Washington Papers, Volume 3* (Beverly Hills: Sage Publications, 1975).

53. "It's Hip to Be Union," *Newsweek*, July 8, 1996, 44–45. For the current foreign policy issues of concern to the AFL-CIO, see "Issues," at http://www.aflcio.org/Issues, June 26, 2012.

54. Hughes, *The Domestic Context of American Foreign Policy*, pp. 168–171.

55. Ness, *Encyclopedia of Interest Groups and Lobbyists in the United States*, p. 209.

56. For the policy priorities of the American Farm Bureau Federation, and the sources of the quoted passages, see "Issues," at http://www.fb.org/index.php?action=issues .home, June 26, 2012. For the statement on the Trans-Pacific Partnership, see "Statement by Bob Stallman, President, American Farm Bureau Federation, Regarding Canada Joining the Trans Pacific Partnership Agreement," at http://www.fb.org/index .php?action=newsroom.news&year=2012&file=nr0621.html. For the policy position of the National Farmers Union and the National Farmers Organization, see "Legislation: International Policy" at http://nfu.org/legislation/international-policy, and the attendant links, June 26, 2012, and "About Us," at http://www.nfo.org/About_Us/Policy .aspx#international_trade, June 26, 2012.

57. *The Washington Lobby*, 4th ed. (Washington, D.C.: Congressional Quarterly, 1982), pp. 150–151, includes a list of the religious groups active over U.S. policy toward El Salvador.

58. See Valerie S. Sheridan, ed., *Washington Representatives Fall 2011* (Bethesda, MD: Columbia Books, 2011), p. 1760, for the listing of religious lobbyists. For a good source on religious organizations involved in U.S. foreign policy, see Elliott Abrams, ed., *The Influence of Faith: Religious Groups and U.S. Foreign Policy* (Lanham, MD: Rowman & Littlefield Publishers, Inc., 2001).

59. See the American Friends Service Committee website at http://ww.afsc.org for the current list of its activities and the issues that it is addressing worldwide, especially "Our Work," at http://afsc.org/our-work, July 1, 2012. For an early plan for reducing conflict in the Middle East, see the AFSC's *Search for Peace in the Middle East*, rev. ed. (Greenwich, CT: Fawcett Publications, 1970).

60. See *The Challenge of Peace: God's Promise and Our Response* (Washington, D.C.: United States Catholic Conference, May 3, 1983).

61. *The Washington Lobby*, pp. 152–153.

62. See the letter by Bishop Wilton Gregory, President of the United States Conference of Catholic Bishops to President George W. Bush, dated September 13, 2002. See http:// www.sacredheart.edu/pages/12197_u_s_bishops_write_to_president_george_w_bush_ discouraging_military_action_in_iraq.cfm, September 16, 2008.

63. For some evidence on the positions of the major religions on war with Iraq, see "Statement from Religious Leaders About Iraq," at http://www.salsa.net/peace, October 10, 2003. For those who expressed support for the war, see Laurie Goodstein, "Threats and Responses: The Religious Leaders; Evangelical Figures Oppose Religious Leaders' Broad Antiwar Sentiment," *New York Times*, October 5, 2002, A10.

64. David E. Anderson, "The Right War Gone Wrong," *Religion and Ethics Newsweekly*, November 23, 2009, at http://www.pbs.org/wnet/religionandethics/episodes/november-20-2009/the-right-war-gone-wrong/5104/. The quoted passages are from this piece or are quoted from the letters written by the religious group to General Jones.

65. For an early excellent overview of the key American ethnic groups and their role in foreign policy, see Charles McC. Mathias, Jr., "Ethnic Groups and Foreign Policy," *Foreign Affairs* 59 (Summer 1981): 975–998, but also see Abdul Aziz Said, *Ethnicity and U.S. Foreign Policy*, rev. ed. (New York: Praeger, 1981); and Tony Smith, *Foreign Attachments: The Power of Ethnic Groups in the Making of American Foreign Policy* (Cambridge, MA: Harvard University Press, 2000).

66. Dick Kirschten, "Ethnics Resurging," *National Journal*, February 25, 1995, 484–486.

67. See Jon Ward, "Genocide Resolution Advances; House Panel Defies Bush About Turkey," *The Washington Times*, October 11, 2007, p. A4, and Carl Hulse, "U.S. and Turkey Thwart Armenian Genocide Bill," *New York Times*, October 25, 2007, p. 12. On the 2010 resolution, see James M. McCormick, "Ethnic Interest Groups and American Foreign Policy: A Growing Influence?" in Allan J. Cigler and Burdett A. Loomis, eds., *Interest Group Politics*, 8th ed. (Washington, D.C.: Sage/CQ Press, 2012), pp. 317–318.

68. Hughes, *The Domestic Context of American Foreign Policy*, pp. 171–174.

69. See Iraq and Afghanistan Veterans of America, "About IAVA," at http://iava.org/about, July 1, 2012.

70. For a discussion of the development of the conservative movement and its foreign policy goals, see Richard A. Viguerie, *The New Right: We're Ready to Lead* (Falls Church, VA: The Viguerie Company, 1981); for a listing of other liberal and conservative interest groups as well as other types, see Brewer and Teitelbaum, *American Foreign Policy*, pp. 141–143; and for a listing of recent ratings of members of Congress for some of these groups, see J. Michael Sharp, ed., *Directory of Congressional Voting Scores and Interest Group Ratings, Volumes 1 and 2*, 4th ed. (Washington, D.C.: Congressional Quarterly, 2006). Also see this source for the discussion of ADA and ACU on which we draw (pp. ix–x).

71. American Civil Liberties Union, "Keep America Safe and Free," at http://www.aclu.org/keep-america-safe-free, July 1, 2012.

72. This section draws on the following sources: Arthur C. Close, Gregory C. Bologna, and Curtis W. McCormick, eds., *Washington Representatives 1990* (Washington, D.C.: Columbia Books, 1990), pp. 480, 513, 517, 518, and 520; the 1988–1989 *Annual Report of the American Enterprise Institute for Public Policy Research* (Washington, D.C.: American Enterprise Institute, 1989); Howard J. Wiarda, *Foreign Policy Without Illusion* (Glenview, IL: Scott, Foresman/Little, Brown Higher Education, 1990), pp. 162–168 for initially stimulating my interest in these groups many years ago; and many of the websites of the think tanks discussed.

73. Richard Higgott and Diane Stone, "The Limits of Influence: Foreign Policy Think Tanks in Britain and the USA," *Review of International Studies* 20 (January 1994): 32.

74. See James M. McCormick, "Decision-making Processes and Actors in American Foreign Policy Formulation: Is There a Third World Lobby?" in Jurgen Ruland, Theodor Hanf, and Eva Manske, eds., *U.S. Foreign Policy Toward the Third World* (Armonk, NY: M. E. Sharpe, 2006), p. 65. Thanks to William Quandt for bringing this point to my attention.

75. Higgott and Stone, "The Limits of Influence: Foreign Policy Think Tanks in Britain and the USA," pp. 15–34.

76. See the Heritage Foundation website, http://www.heritage.org, on its activities. For a listing of recent (and past) events, see http://www.heritage.org/events, July 1, 2012.

77. The information and quotation on the Cato Institute are taken from "About Cato," at http://www.cato.org/about.php, July 1, 2012.

78. The information on the American Enterprise Institute comes from its website at "About," at http://www.aei.org/about/aeis-organization-and-purposes, July 1, 2012.

79. Ibid.

80. See Center for Strategic & International Studies, "About Us," at http://csis.org/about-us and http://csis.org/-brief-history, July 1, 2012.

81. See the Brookings Institution's website, http://www.brookings.edu/about/reputation and http://www.brookings.edu/experts, July 2, 2012. The quoted passage is by former Senator Chuck Hagel and is from the first website.

82. Higgott and Stone, "The Limits of Influence: Foreign Policy Think Tanks in Britain and the USA," pp. 18–19.

83. See the Carnegie Endowment for International Peace, "The Global Think Tank," at http://carnegieendowment.org/about/, July 2, 2012.

84. For a compilation of categories of foreign policy interest groups (on which we partly draw), see Brewer and Teitelbaum, *American Foreign Policy: A Contemporary Introduction*, pp. 141–143.

85. Indeed, the freeze movement was very broadly based, in terms of both the kinds of groups and the individuals who participated in it. See Fox Butterfield, "Anatomy of the Nuclear Protest," *New York Times Magazine*, July 11, 1982, 14–17ff, for a discussion. For other assessments of the nuclear freeze movement, see Pam Solo, *From Protest to Policy: The Origins and Future of the Freeze Movement* (Cambridge, MA: Ballinger Publishing, 1988); and Douglas C. Waller, *Congress and the Nuclear Freeze: An Inside Look at the Politics of a Mass Movement* (Amherst: University of Massachusetts Press, 1987).

86. See Cynthia J. Arnson and Philip Brenner, "The Limits of Lobbying: Interest Groups, Congress and Aid to the Contras," paper prepared for presentation at a conference on Public Opinion and Policy Toward Central America, Princeton University, May 4–5, 1990.

87. See Box 12.2 in Stephen D. Cohen, Joel R. Paul, and Robert A. Blecker, *Fundamentals of U.S. Foreign Policy* (Boulder, CO: Westview Press, 1996), pp. 254–255, on the array of these groups.

88. A description of these antiglobalization groups is in Manfred B. Steger, *Globalism* (Lanham, MD: Rowman & Littlefield Publishers, 2002), pp. 111–112. Steger also provides a discussion of their protest activities at pp. 117–134.

89. This discussion draws from Michael Luo, "With New Clout, Antiwar Groups Push Democrats," *New York Times*, May 6, 2007, at http://www.nytimes.com/2007/05/06/washington/06left.html?scp=1&sq=With%20New%20Clout,%20Antiwar%20Groups%20Push%20Democrats&st=cse, May 6, 2007.

90. The total was compiled from the listing in Sheridan, *Washington Representatives Fall 2011*, pp. 1775–1779.

91. "How U.S. Firms Lobbied for AWACS on Saudi Orders," *Des Moines Sunday Register*, March 14, 1982, 1C.

92. The section on Japanese lobbying is based on John B. Judis, "The Japanese Megaphone," *The New Republic*, January 22, 1990, 20–25. The quoted passage is at p. 24. For a more

comprehensive and critical treatment of the lobbying efforts by Japan, see Pat Choate, *Agents of Influence* (New York: Alfred A. Knopf, 1990).

93. See the listing of countries and firms in Dick Kirschten, "Greetings, Comrades!" *National Journal*, October 2, 1993, 2191.

94. Peter H. Stone, "China Connections," *National Journal*, March 26, 1994, 708–712. For an assessment of Chinese lobby over time, see Ronald J. Hrebenar and Clive S. Thomas, "The Rise and Fall and Rise of the China Lobby in the United States," in Allan J. Cigler and Burdett A. Loomis, eds., *Interest Group Politics*, 8th ed. (Washington, D.C.: Sage/CQ Press, 2012), pp. 297–316.

95. See Marilyn W. Thompson, "An Ex-Leader in Congress Is Now Turkey's Man in the Lobbies of Capitol Hill," *New York Times*, October 17, 2007, at http://www.nytimes.com/2007/10/17/washington/17lobby.html?scp=1&sq=An+Ex-Leader+in+Congress+Is+Now&st=nyt. For the visit by Turkish parliamentarians to Capitol Hill in 2010 at the time of the second genocide resolution, see McCormick, "Ethnic Interest Groups and American Foreign Policy: A Growing Influence?" p. 317.

96. The most succinct argument for this limited influence of interest groups is in Hughes, *The Domestic Context of American Foreign Policy*, pp. 198–202, from which part of this argument is drawn. Also see, however, Bernard Cohen, *The Public's Impact on Foreign Policy* (Boston: Little, Brown and Co., 1973); and Robert H. Trice, "Domestic Interest Groups and the Arab-Israeli Conflict: A Behavioral Analysis," in Abdul Aziz Said, *Ethnicity and U.S. Foreign Policy*, pp. 128–129, on the problem of gaining access to Congress and the executive on some types of issues.

97. See Cohen, *The Public's Impact on Foreign Policy*, pp. 100–103, and his discussion of how interest groups can be used by the executive branch.

98. On this point, see Eric M. Uslaner, "All Politics Are Global: Interest Groups and the Making of Foreign Policy," in Allan J. Cigler and Burdett A. Loomis, *Interest Group Politics*, 4th ed. (Washington, D.C.: CQ Press, 1995), p. 370.

99. Brewer and Teitelbaum, *American Foreign Policy: A Contemporary Introduction*, p. 150.

100. On those points, see Hughes, *The Domestic Context of American Foreign Policy*, pp. 200–201, especially Table 7.1.

101. James M. Lindsay and Randall B. Ripley, "How Congress Influences Foreign and Defense Policy," in Randall B. Ripley and James M. Lindsay, eds., *Congress Resurgent: Foreign and Defense Policy on Capitol Hill* (Ann Arbor: The University of Michigan Press, 1993), p. 19.

102. Samuel Huntington especially notes "the displacement of national interests by commercial and ethnic interests" in recent years. See "The Erosion of American National Interests," in Wittkopf and McCormick, eds., *The Domestic Sources of American Foreign Policy*, 4th ed., pp. 55–65. The quote is at p. 64. Also see Cohen, *The Public's Impact on Foreign Policy*, p. 96, which asserts that economic and ethnic groups appear most prominently, although his analysis is based primarily on interviews with the executive branch.

103. For some reasons, for the strength of ethnic influence, see Mathias, "Ethnic Groups and Foreign Policy," pp. 980–981 and 996. Also see McCormick, "Ethnic Interest Groups and American Foreign Policy: A Growing Influence?" pp. 337–339.

104. See Dwight D. Eisenhower, "The Military Industrial Complex," in Richard Gillam, ed., *Power in Postwar America* (Boston: Little, Brown and Co., 1971), p. 158.

105. See C. Wright Mills, *The Power Elite* (New York: Oxford University Press, 1956); and Gabriel Kolko, *The Roots of American Foreign Policy* (Boston: Beacon Press, 1969).

106. For a good summary presentation of this argument, see Marc Pilisuk, with the assistance of Mehrene Larudee, *International Conflict and Social Policy* (Englewood Cliffs, NJ: Prentice Hall, 1972), pp. 108–141.

107. Ibid., pp. 113–132, especially p. 129.

108. Kolko, *The Roots of American Foreign Policy*, pp. 17–23.

109. The following data on the key foreign officials are from Thomas R. Dye, *Who's Running America? Institutional Leadership in the United States* (Englewood Cliffs, NJ: Prentice Hall, 1976), pp. 56–58; and from Dye, *Who's Running America? The Bush Era*, 5th ed. (Englewood Cliffs, NJ: Prentice Hall, 1990), pp. 89–105. The dates of service for some individuals have been corrected from what Dye reports. For a complete description of the background of Reagan administration appointees, see the national security section of Ronald Brownstein and Nina Easton, *Reagan's Ruling Class* (Washington, D.C.: The Presidential Accountability Group, 1982).

110. Thomas R. Dye, *Who's Running America? The Clinton Years*, 6th ed. (Englewood Cliffs, NJ: Prentice Hall, 1995), p. 84.

111. Ibid., pp. 84, 87, 89–91.

112. The leadership data on the George W. Bush administration is taken from Thomas R. Dye, *Who's Running America? The Bush Restoration*, 7th ed. (Upper Saddle River, NJ: Prentice Hall, 2002), pp. 77–81. In particular, see Tables 4–2 and 4–3.

113. Edmund L. Andrews, "Paulson, Taking Treasury Post, Emphasizes Global Issues," *New York Times*, July 11, 2006, C1.

114. For information on the background of Secretary Geithner, see "About: The Secretary," at http://www.treasury.gov/about/Pages/Secretary.aspx, July 2, 2012; of Secretary Bryson, see Eric Morath, "Bio: Commerce Secretary John Bryson," *Washington Wire*, June 11, 2012, at http://blogs.wsj.com/washwire/2012/06/11/bio-commerce-secretary-john-bryson/, July 2, 2012; and of USTR Kirk, see Office of the United States Trade Representative, "United States Trade Representative Ron Kirk," at http://www.ustr.gov/about-us/biographies-key-officials/united-states-trade-representative-ron-kirk, July 2, 2012.

115. See William Proxmire, "The Community of Interests in Our Defense Contract Spending," in Gilliam, ed., *Power in Postwar America*, pp. 160–166.

116. These data are taken, and in one instance recalculated, from Mark J. Eitelberg and Roger D. Little, "Influential Elites and the American Military After the Cold War," in Don M. Snider and Miranda A. Carlton-Carew, eds., *U.S. Civil-Military Relations: In Crisis or Transition?* (Washington, D.C.: The Center for Strategic and International Studies, 1995), pp. 47 and 48 (Table 3.1).

117. Ibid., p. 47.

118. Government Accountability Office, "Defense Contracting: Post-Government Employment of Former DOD Officials Needs Greater Transparency" (Washington, D.C., Government Accountability Office, May 21, 2008). The quoted passages and the principal contractors listed are from the Executive Summary; the discussion of concerns about these kinds of employments is at p. 6.

119. See Matthew Weigelt, "DOD Proposes New Conflict of Interest Rules," *Washington Technology*, April 27, 2010, at http://washingtontechnology.com/articles/2010/04/22/dod-oci-proposal.aspx, July 3, 2012; Nicole Blake Johnson, "DOD Narrows Scope of New Conflict-of-Interest Rules," *Federal Times*, December 29, 2012, at http://www.federaltimes.com/article/20101229/DEPARTMENTS01/12290302/DoD-narrows-scope-new-conflict-interest-rules, July 2, 2012, for the first quoted passage, and Federal Contractor Compliance Watch, "Department of Defense Issues Final Rule Requiring Contractors to Certify Compliance with Revolving Door Restrictions," November 21, 2011, at http://federalcontractorcompliancewatch.com/2011/11/21/department-of-defense-issues-final-rule-requiring-contractors-to-certify-compliance-with-revolving-door-restrictions/, July 3, 2012, for the second quoted passage.

120. Michael Parenti, *Democracy for the Few*, 5th ed. (New York: St. Martin's Press, 1988), p. 88.

121. Charles R. Babcock and Jonathan Weisman, "Congressman Admits Taking Bribes, Resigns," *Washingtonpost.com*, November 29, 2005, p. 1, at http://www.washingtonpost.com/wp-dyn/content/article/2005/11/28/AR2005112801827.html, June 12, 2003.

122. Morton Berkowitz, P. G. Bock, and Vincent J. Fuccillo, *The Politics of American Foreign Policy* (Englewood Cliffs, NJ: Prentice Hall, 1977), p. 289.

123. Ibid.

124. Defense contract rankings were taken from Federal Procurement Data System—Next Generation for fiscal year 2011 under Defense, at https://www.fpds.gov/fpdsng_cms/index.php/reports, May 23, 2012. The corporate sales rankings for 2011 were taken from CNNMoney, "Fortune 500," at http://money.cnn.com/magazines/fortune/fortune500/2011/full_list/, July 3, 2012. The statistics for FY1982, FY1988, FY1995, FY2002, and FY2005 are taken from earlier editions of this book.

125. For the information on the continuity and concentration in defense contracting, see James R. Kurth, "The Military-Industrial Complex Revisited," in Joseph Kruzel, ed., *1989–1990 American Defense Annual* (Lexington, MA: Lexington Books, 1989), pp. 195–215, especially pp. 196–199. The "product specialties" notion is his, at p. 198.

126. The data in this paragraph come from U.S. Bureau of the Census, *Statistical Abstract of the United States: 2008* (Washington, D.C., 2008), Table 489; U.S. Arms Control and Disarmament Agency, *World Military Expenditures and Arms Transfers 1989* (Washington, D.C.: U.S. Government Printing Office, October 1990), p. 69; and Bureau of Verification and Compliance, Department of State, *World Military Expenditures and Arms Transfers 1998* (Washington, D.C.: Government Printing Office, April 2000), p. 109.

127. For some summary aggregate data on U.S. military expenditures, see Stockholm International Peace Research Institute (SIPRI), "The SIPRI Military Expenditure Database," at http://milexdata.sipri.org/result.php4, July 3, 2012.

128. Bruce Russett, *The Prisoners of Insecurity* (San Francisco: W. H. Freeman and Company, 1983), pp. 77–96.

129. Stanley Lieberson, "An Empirical Study of Military-Industrial Linkages," *American Journal of Sociology* 76 (January 1971), especially pp. 568–572 and 575–581.

130. Steve Chan, "Grasping the Peace Dividend: Some Propositions on the Conversion of Swords into Plowshares," *Mershon International Studies Review* 39 (April 1995): 53–95. The quoted phrases are Chan's.

131. Ibid., p. 62. As Chan discusses, there are empirical studies supporting both contentions, but he specifically challenges the notion that there is evidence for "a powerful military-industrial complex" to sustain high military expenditures (p. 63).

132. Ibid., p. 68. Chan's conclusion here is drawn from a study by Stephen J. Majeski, "Defense Spending, Fiscal Policy, and Economic Performance," in Alex Mintz, ed., *The Political Economy of Military Spending in the United States* (London: Routledge, 1992), pp. 217–237. Majeski's general conclusion is at p. 231. Other studies showing different results are included in the Chan analysis, but most of the evidence seems to point in the direction of the findings reported here.

133. For a study that judges the Greek lobby second behind the Jewish lobby in influence, see Mathias, "Ethnic Groups and Foreign Policy," p. 990. Also see Morton Kondracke, "The Greek Lobby," *The New Republic*, April 29, 1978, 14–16. For two studies that raise doubts about the importance of the Greek lobby over the Turkish arms embargo issue, see Clifford Hackett, "Ethnic Politics in Congress: The Turkish Embargo Experience"; and Sallie M. Hicks and Theodore A. Couloumbis, "The 'Greek Lobby': Illusion or Reality?" in Said, ed., *Ethnicity and U.S. Foreign Policy*, pp. 33–96.

134. Mathias, "Ethnic Groups and Foreign Policy," pp. 982–987.

135. Kirschten, "Ethnics Resurging," pp. 484–486, with the quoted passage at p. 486. Also see McCormick, "Ethnic Interest Groups and American Foreign Policy: A Growing Influence?" p. 333.

136. Robert W. Walters, "African-American Influence on U.S. Foreign Policy Toward South Africa," in Mohammed E. Ahrari, ed., *Ethnic Groups and U.S. Foreign Policy* (New York: Greenwood Press, 1987), pp. 65–82.

137. See the Association of Concerned African Scholars Briefing Paper, at http://www .prairienet.org/acas/agoabm.htm, March 30, 2000, for information about these other lobbying groups on this piece of legislation.

138. These items were taken from the TransAfrica Forum's website, at http://www .transafricaforum.org, June 19, 2008. For TransAfrica Forum's current priorities, see http://transafrica.org/home/, July 4, 2012. Also see McCormick, "Ethnic Interest Groups and American Foreign Policy: A Growing Influence?" pp. 334–335.

139. Dick Kirschten, "From the K Street Corridor," *National Journal*, July 17, 1993, 1815; Philip Brenner, Patrick J. Haney, and Walter Vanderbush, "Intermestic Interests and U.S. Policy toward Cuba," in Eugene R. Wittkopf and James M. McCormick, eds., *The Domestic Sources of American Foreign Policy: Insights and Evidence*, 5th ed. (Lanham, MD: Rowman & Littlefield Publishers, 2008), pp. 70–72; Kirk Nielsen, "Cuba Libre?" *Miller-McCune* 1 (June–July 2008): 46–55, especially at pp. 50–51; Cuba Study Group, at http:// www.cubastudygroup.org/index.cgm?FuseAction=Board.Home; and Max J. Castro, "Redrawing the Lines on Cuba," *Cubanet*, December 11, 2001, at http://www.cubanet .org/CNews/y01/dec01/11e3.htm, September 16, 2008; and McCormick, "Ethnic Interest Groups and American Foreign Policy: A Growing Influence?" pp. 325–237.

140. See Damian J. Fernandez, "From Little Havana to Washington, DC: Cuban-Americans and U.S. Foreign Policy," and Rodolfo de la Garza, "U.S. Foreign Policy and the Mexican-American Political Agenda," in Mohammed E. Ahrari, ed., *Ethnic Groups and U.S. Foreign Policy* (New York: Greenwood Press, 1987), pp. 115–134 and 101–114, respectively. For the last two quotations, see Rodolfo de la Garza, "Introduction," and Peter Hakim and Carlos A. Rosales, "The Latino Foreign Policy Lobby," in Rodolfo de la Garza and Harry P. Pachon, eds., *Latinos and U.S. Foreign Policy* (Lanham, MD: Rowman & Littlefield Publishers, 2000), pp. 9 and 133, respectively.

141. For the estimates on the size of the Mexican-American community, see McCormick, "Ethnic Interest Groups and American Foreign Policy: A Growing Influence?" p. 343, note 62.

142. For a full discussion of the Indian lobby upon which we draw here, see ibid., pp. 335–337. The quoted in passage is at p. 335 and is from John Newhouse, "Diplomacy, Inc.: The Influence of Lobbies on U.S. Foreign Policy," *Foreign Affairs* 88 (May/June 2009): 81.

143. Estimates for these groups vary, of course. The data for Jewish Americans (2004) and Greek Americans (2005) were taken from U.S. Bureau of the Census, *Statistical Abstract of the United States: 2008* (Washington, D.C., 2008), Tables 76 and 51, respectively. The estimate for Cuban Americans was taken from "Cuban Americans" in *MSN Encarta*, at http://encarta.msn.com/text_761587474_0/Cuban_Americans.html, June 12, 2008.

144. See Smith, *Foreign Attachments*, pp. 85–129, for his discussion of these three means of gaining influence by ethnic groups.

145. See Trice, "Domestic Interest Groups and the Arab-Israeli Conflict," pp. 121 and 122. Also see Patrick Smyth, "The Hawkish Factions of Jewish Lobby May Be Out of Step with Members," *The Irish Times*, April 12, 2002, 11.

146. John J. Mearsheimer and Stephen M. Walt, *The Israel Lobby* (New York: Farrar, Straus, & Giroux, 2007), p. 112. For a critique of Mearsheimer and Walt's definition, see Walter Russell Mead, "Jerusalem Syndrome: Decoding The Israel Lobby," *Foreign Affairs* 86 (November/December 2007): 162. Mead's argument is that Mearsheimer and Walt

include both hawkish and dovish groups in the lobby, even though these groups "have occasionally deep divisions over exactly what policies are best for Israel."

147. See *The Middle East*, 11th ed. (Washington, D.C.: CQ Press, 2007), p. 165, for a summary discussion of AIPAC and its foreign policy role.

148. See The American Israel Public Affairs Committee, "About AIPAC" and "How We Work," at http://www.aipac.org/en/about-aipac and http://www.aipac.org/about-aipac/how-we-work, July 4, 2012. Also see Paul Findley, *Deliberate Deceptions: Facing the Facts about the U.S.-Israeli Relationship* (New York: Lawrence Hill Books, 1995), p. 95; Peter Beinart and Hanna Rosin, "AIPAC Unpacked," *The New Republic*, September 20 and 27, 1993, 22; and Hedrick Smith, *The Power Game* (New York: Ballantine Books, 1988), p. 216.

149. The American Israel Public Affairs Committee, "How We Work," at http://www.aipac.org/about-aipac/how-we-work, July 4, 2012.

150. Trice, "Domestic Interest Groups and the Arab-Israeli Conflict: A Behavioral Analysis," p. 126.

151. See The American Israel Public Affairs Committee, "Issues" and "Legislative Agenda," at http://www.aipac.org/issues and http://www.aipac.org/legislative-agenda, July 4, 2012.

152. The American Israel Public Affairs Committee, "What We've Accomplished," at http://www.aipac.org/about-aipac/what-weve-accomplished, July 4, 2012.

153. See http://www.aipac.org/en/about-aipac, where this quotation is cited from the *New York Times*.

154. Findley, *Deliberate Deception*, p. 95.

155. The American Israel Public Affairs Committee, "What We've Accomplished," at http://www.aipac.org/about-aipac/what-weve-accomplished, July 4, 2012

156. For the list of these speakers, see The American Israel Public Affairs Committee website at the following links: http://www.aipac.org/get-involved/attend-policy-conference/follow-pc/sunday-morning-plenary; http://www.aipac.org/get-involved/attend-policy-conference/follow-pc/monday-gala-plenary; and http://www.aipac.org/get-involved/attend-policy-conference/follow-pc/tuesday-morning-plenary, July 4, 2012.

157. *The Middle East: U.S. Policy, Israel, Oil and the Arabs*, 3rd ed. (Washington, D.C.: Congressional Quarterly, 1977), p. 96.

158. Harry Anderson, "Forced into British Arms," *Newsweek*, July 25, 1988, 47, and Smyth, "The Hawkish Factions of Jewish Lobby May Be Out of Step with Members," p. 11.

159. Robert H. Trice, "Congress and the Arab-Israeli Conflict: Support for Israel in the U.S. Senate, 1970–1973," *Political Science Quarterly* 92 (Fall 1977): 443–463.

160. Some of these reasons are discussed and indirectly tested in ibid. See the comments by Ron Brownstein on "CNN Live Today 10:00," April 15, 2002, at http://web.lexis-nexis.com/universe/document?_m=f30a/2da473b58abc980/cc9fcd72ace&docuum=18wchp=dGLbV/2-2SKVA&ind5=2fe2793839d2.

161. In an analysis of American support for Israel, Walter Russell Mead, a prominent foreign policy analyst, argues that such support has been historically imbedded in American society and the aggregate level of support is less the result of a Jewish lobby and more the result of a long-standing cultural and religious affinity. See his "The New Israel and the Old," *Foreign Affairs* 87 (July/August 2008): 28–46.

162. Trice, "Congress and the Arab–Israeli Conflict: Support for Israel in the U.S. Senate, 1970–1973," p. 457; and Smith, *Foreign Attachments*, at p. 99 for key states.

163. George W. Ball and Douglas B. Ball, *The Passionate Attachment* (New York: W.W. Norton and Company, 1992), p. 209.

164. Smith, *The Power Game*, pp. 228–229.

165. For a full statement of this likely commitment by presidential candidates, see Mearsheimer and Walt, *The Israel Lobby and U.S. Foreign Policy*, pp. 3–4.

166. *The Middle East: U.S. Policy, Israel, Oil and the Arabs*, pp. 102–108.

167. Christopher Madison, "Arab-American Lobby Fights Rearguard Battle to Influence U.S. Mideast Policy," *National Journal*, August 31, 1985, 1936.

168. *The Middle East*, 11th ed., p. 165.

169. On these lobbies and the AAI's aims, see McCormick, "Ethnic Interest Groups and American Foreign Policy: A Growing Influence?" pp. 323–324.

170. See Mearsheimer and Walt, *The Israel Lobby and U.S. Foreign Policy*, for a full discussion of their arguments. The quoted passage is at p. 13. An abridged version of the original article on which the book is based can be found in Wittkopf and McCormick, eds., *The Domestic Sources of American Foreign Policy*, pp. 81–95. Their article and book have raised substantial commentary and controversy. *Foreign Policy* magazine, for instance, devoted a good portion of its July/August 2006 issue to reviews of it. On the book, see reviews by Mead, "Jerusalem Syndrome: Decoding *The Israel Lobby*," pp. 160–168 and Douglas Little, "David or Goliath? The Israel Lobby and Its Critics," *Political Science Quarterly* 123 (Spring 2008): 151–156.

171. Ball and Ball, *The Passionate Attachment*, pp. 213–215; and Smith, *The Power Game*, pp. 218–221.

172. Quoted in Charlotte Saikowski, "America's Israeli Aid Budget Grows," *Christian Science Monitor*, November 30, 1983, 5. The reference is to President Eisenhower's decision to stand firm against Israel after it invaded the Sinai Peninsula and to demand its immediate withdrawal, despite a pending election.

173. For a discussion of some of the dilemmas that the Jewish community faces in its advocacy of American policy in the Middle East, see Stephen S. Rosenfeld, "Dateline Washington: Anti-Semitism and U.S. Foreign Policy," *Foreign Policy* 47 (Summer 1982): 172–183.

174. Beinart and Rosin, "AIPAC Unpacked," pp. 20–23.

175. Alison Mitchell, "Rabin Rebukes Jews in U.S. Who Lobbied Against Pact," *New York Times*, September 30, 1995, 1.

176. See McCormick, "Ethnic Interest Groups and American Foreign Policy: A Growing Influence?" pp. 324–325 for more discussion of "J Street," from which this is drawn. The quoted passages are from J Street website at "About J Street," http://jstreet.org/about, July 4, 2012. The assessment of J Street's staying power is from Newhouse, "Diplomacy, Inc.," p. 81 and cited in McCormick.

CHAPTER 12

The Media, Public Opinion, and the Foreign Policy Process

But the provision or withdrawal of legitimacy from a president
or policy, and the media's role in facilitating or undermining it, can
significantly influence foreign policy.

ROBERT M. ENTMAN, *PROJECTIONS OF POWER: FRAMING NEWS,*
PUBLIC OPINION, AND U.S. FOREIGN POLICY

2004

. . . the American public has stable, consistent,
and sensible preferences concerning a wide range of foreign policies,
and . . . those preferences are based on coherent,
logical, purposive belief systems . . .

BENJAMIN I. PAGE WITH MARSHALL M. BOUTON,
THE FOREIGN POLICY DISCONNECT

2006

The final two participants in the American foreign policy process that we will discuss are the **media** and **the public** at large. Both can and do affect the shape of U.S. foreign policy, albeit more indirectly than the other participants described so far. The foreign policy issues that the media cover, and how they cover them, can affect the policy-making process. The public's general views on foreign policy may be transmitted periodically through national polls, often conducted by the media; through contacts with their representatives at "town meetings"; through visits by executive and congressional officials as they travel across the country; and, increasingly, through new electronic media. Importantly, elections at both the congressional and presidential levels, of course, are periodic mechanisms through which the public conveys its sentiments on the direction of both foreign and domestic policy. All of these are ways in which the shaping of foreign policy can be shared by the media and the public.

In the early sections of the chapter, we consider the expansion of the media in American political life and the different roles that analysts have suggested they play in the foreign policy process. That is, do the media represent a separate actor and critic in the process (much like an interest group), or are they accomplices of the government (often championing official policy positions)? Or do the media play some combination of these roles? Further, how do the media affect the public and its views?

In the later sections, we consider the public's role in the foreign policy process and seek to answer several compelling questions about public opinion and foreign policy. Is the public largely uninformed? Are its views fickle and changeable, guided primarily by the wishes of the political leadership? Or are those views more stable and consistent on foreign policy issues than some would suggest? Does the public in fact shape the direction of foreign policy at least over the long term, if not on every decision that occurs?

THE PERVASIVENESS OF THE MEDIA

We begin our discussion of the media in the foreign policy process by considering their growth over the past few years and their place in American society. In general, media outlets of all kinds, and particularly electronic, increasingly bombard Americans. A caricature of this growth is the presumed "CNN-ization of the world," a reference to the twenty-four-hour cable news station that emerged more than three decades ago to provide instantaneous coverage of global events. Yet the electronic explosion goes beyond CNN to include the growth in radio stations, changes in programming (such as the explosion of talk radio and television news interviews and magazine programs), and the rapid expansion of cable stations and cable systems nationwide and worldwide. The development of the World Wide Web, the use of cellular phones, the growth of smartphones and applications ("apps"), the emergence of text messaging, the explosion of Facebook—all have enhanced instantaneous global communications. A few simple statistics will illustrate the kind of media transformation that has taken place over the past several decades.[1]

The Growth in Differing Media Outlets

Radio, television, and cable systems grew rapidly in recent decades. In 2009, for example, 114 million American households had access to radios, compared to 79 million in 1980. During roughly the same time span, the number of radio stations grew by about 83 percent, from 7,871 (1980) to 14,420 (2009). The number of television stations grew at almost the same pace, from 1,011 to 1,782—an increase of 76 percent. Tied to this increase is the growth of cable television systems, spreading from 4,225 in 1980 to 6,203 in 2009—an increase of 47 percent in thirty years, although declining over the past decades with increased consolidation in this industry.

By contrast, the print media has actually been contracting and consolidating. As of 2009, 1,397 daily newspapers were being published, a decline of 20 percent since 1980.[2] Fewer and fewer companies (Gannett, Tribune Company, New York Times Company, Advance Publications, News Corporation, McClatchy Company, and Media News Group, among others)[3] have gained an increasingly large national foot-hold by purchasing regional newspapers and nationalizing their circulations. The *New York Times* publishes regional daily editions in most major markets throughout the country; the *Wall Street Journal*, long available across the nation, has intensi-fied its circulation effort and its national lead; and *USA Today* has emerged as an important mass-circulation daily over the past three decades. Further, the Gannett chain (publishers of *USA Today*), News Corp, and the New York Times Company now own newspapers (and television stations) across the country. Yet these efforts at consolidation and increased national availability have not enhanced newspaper circulation, which in fact has declined from about 62.2 million readers in 1980 to 46.3 million in 2009.[4]

In addition to traditional electronic and print media, newer electronic entries have propelled the worldwide communications explosion. The facsimile, or more popularly the **fax machine**, was instrumental in fostering the democracy movement in China in the late 1980s and has revolutionized communications to virtually every corner of the globe. The impact of computer technology has been even more profound via the Internet and the World Wide Web, especially with instantaneous communications through e-mail, the impact of which in transforming global politics has indeed been revolutionary. Another entrant in this communication explosion is the **cell phone**. These are now ubiquitous—in cars, offices, and homes—with about ninety-one out of every one hundred Americans cell phone subscribers in 2009.[5] In short, then, these technologies have accelerated the pervasiveness of electronic communication world-wide as never before in human history.

Old News versus New News

The emergence of new communications and media outlets, or "new news" sources, has seemingly altered reliance on the traditional media outlets (such as network news and national newspapers), or the "old news" sources.[6] One indicator of this change is the precipitous drop in the viewership of the nightly network news broadcasts over the past three decades. In 1980, slightly more than 50 million Americans watched one of these broadcasts (ABC, CBS, or NBC). By 2011, this figure had dropped to 22.5 million, even though the U.S. population had increased over that thirty-year period. Significantly, "the average age of regular evening news consumers" in 2010 was fifty-three years of age.[7]

Other assessments support these changing trends in news viewership. In 2011, only 30 percent of Americans regularly watched the nightly network news, compared to 42 percent in 1996 and 60 percent in 1993. In the 1970s, this figure was about 80 percent.[8] Furthermore, among viewers younger than thirty, only about 14 percent watched the nightly news broadcasts on a regular basis in 2010.[9] The cable news audi-ence, however, increased, with about 39 percent of the public regularly watching one of these channels (for example, CNN and Fox), and the under-thirty audience views that source at a rate double (about 29 percent) the network nightly news. Further, in 2010, a Pew Research Center study found that "about as many young people watch the Daily Show (13%) as watch the national network evening news (14%) and the morning news shows (12%)."[10]

Another important change in news consumption—and another challenge to traditional sources—is the increasing ownership of mobile devices, which now make it easy to obtain news. According to a 2012 Pew Research Center survey, 77 percent of American adults now own a desktop or laptop computer, 44 percent own a smartphone, and 18 percent own a tablet computer. Indeed, many own two or more of these devices, with 52 percent of the desktop/laptop owners having a smartphone and 23 percent a tablet. (Only 13 percent of all Americans owned all three of these devices.) Yet, these devices are increasingly sources of news for many Americans—70 percent of desktop/laptop owners get news from their computers, 51 percent of smartphone users, and 56 percent of tablet computer users. Moreover, users of these digital devices did not restrict their news consumption to one of these devices; instead, they often use multiple devices. Nonetheless, desktop or laptop computers remain the dominant mechanism for obtaining news from these devices, with 54 percent of all Americans getting news from this source.[11]

In all, the "new news" forums and media—talk radio, comedy news shows, or use of digital devices—are challenging, and sometimes surpassing, the "old news" sources and media for viewership and listeners, but the latter continued to have a role in shaping the agenda and in stimulating discussions on the former.[12] In this sense, both traditional and new media sources play a crucial role in political and social life, but the mix is clearly changing in the early years of the twenty-first century.

The ultimate impact of this communication explosion on foreign policy is difficult to estimate. On the one hand, foreign policy coverage by the media is hardly immune to these dramatic changes in communications. Indeed, these changes are often viewed as having enhanced the American public's access to foreign affairs and, in turn, as having contributed to an enlarged role for the media in the foreign policy arena. Dramatic events worldwide bring instant and continuous coverage by the various media outlets. The use of "imbedded reporters" during the Iraq War illustrated how global events could be brought into the lives of Americans in real time—something never before seen or experienced. On the other hand, **the continuous coverage of foreign affairs by the American news media remains relatively low to modest**; 28 percent of the news analyzed by a Pew Research Center study in 2011 constituted international news. Of that 28 percent, 18 percent reported "strictly foreign events" and the other 10 percent "focused on events in which the U.S. was directly involved." Still, the 28 percent total reflected an increase from the 20 percent of international news reported in 2010.[13]

Although the implications of these changes for foreign policy should not be exaggerated, what events in the foreign policy arena are covered—and how—may have an important impact on public debate. Moreover, some recent evidence shows that "soft news" or entertainment news sources, even with its limited or indirect foreign policy coverage, can be important in informing the public at large, especially "for politically inattentive individuals, who might otherwise avoid *any* exposure to news about foreign policy."[14] In this rapidly changing environment, then, the role of the media in the foreign policy process remains a topic of continued interest and discussion.

THE ROLE OF THE MEDIA
IN THE FOREIGN POLICY PROCESS

More precise assessments of the media's role in U.S. foreign policy immediately provoke a torrent of commentary and controversy. For purposes of our discussion, we will divide these assessments into **three categories**: the **media as largely separate actors** in the foreign policy process, sometimes seeking to advance their own views among the American people; the **media as largely accomplices of the government**, more often supportive than critical of official action; and the **media and the government in a "mutually exploitative" relationship**, in which each side gains from the other.[15] These roles are often intermingled in discussions of the media and foreign policy, but the last one appears to best represent the current relationship. Before we discuss that third role, however, we first outline the two most frequently identified roles for the media in the foreign policy process and consider some criticisms that question their accuracy.

The Media as Actors

The argument here is that the media in fact shape the foreign policy agenda. Because policy makers and the public depend on them for information about global events (especially television for instantaneous communication),[16] the media are a powerful force for determining the issues considered. Put differently, what the media decide to portray (or not to portray) may have a powerful influence on the direction of American foreign policy. By extension, as a whole, they may exercise an independent effect on foreign policy making. Let us consider the evidence for and against this view.

The Vietnam War The emergence of the "media as actor" role usually dates from the Vietnam War, vivid pictures of which the media (and particularly television) provided virtually on a nightly basis for the American public and policy makers. The magnitude of the killing and the destruction on both sides became staples of the coverage, and interviews with battlefield officers and spokespersons conveyed the difficulties of the war (including a particularly memorable interview in which a military officer declared that U.S. forces had "to destroy the town to save it").[17] Protests against the war at home became standard fare as well. Such portrayals were often at odds with the upbeat assessments by American and South Vietnamese officials, who tended to laud the war's progress. In short, they often forced policy makers to explain their positions and defend their strategies, and, in this way, they ultimately had a powerful effect on the direction of policy in the Vietnam War.

The so-called **Tet offensive**—countrywide attacks across South Vietnam by Viet Cong and North Vietnamese forces beginning in late January 1968—illustrates the impact of the media on the conduct of the war and American foreign policy. Although it ultimately proved to be a military failure, Tet's physical destruction, casualties, and the widespread nature of its attacks, as portrayed by the media, conveyed another message. Indeed, the image created implied a massive defeat for South Vietnamese and American forces. Despite efforts to explain the events in other ways, the media impression produced a "profound impact on American perceptions of the war at all levels," as one analyst noted, with a sharp decline in public optimism.

In short, "the dramatic impact of the television coverage of the carnage, set against the official statements of optimism, had its effects."[18] Years later, a detailed study documented the impact of the press coverage on this crucial foreign policy episode and the misleading way in which the Tet offensive was portrayed.[19] In Tet's immediate aftermath, though, President Lyndon Johnson announced on March 31, 1968, that he would not be a candidate for president that fall. In short, the Tet offensive remains one of those events often used to convey the power of the media in affecting policy.

The Iran Hostage Crisis   In the late 1970s and early 1980s, Iranians held fifty-two Americans hostage for 444 days in the U.S. embassy in Tehran. Almost immediately, the ABC television network began broadcasting a nightly program, *America Held Hostage*, to track developments in the crisis, changing the title each night (for example, *America Held Hostage, Day 25*).[20] As the crisis wore on, seemingly without resolution, the impact of these episodes became clear: the U.S. government was powerless to intervene, and the ineptitude of the Carter administration became firmly planted in the minds of many Americans. Furthermore, the impression created was that little else mattered on the world stage. The point is not to debate whether ABC and other media outlets were seeking this outcome; what is important is that the media played a forceful role in conveying and creating a particular foreign policy image.

Ethiopia and Somalia   In the 1980s and 1990s, the media's portrayal of the death and starvation in Ethiopia and Somalia further demonstrates their power in the foreign policy arena. In the former case, journalist Peter Boyer summarized the power of a 1984 NBC report on the widening Ethiopian famine:

> It was a jarring piece, movingly narrated by BBC correspondent Michael Burk. "The faces of death in Africa," [Anchor Tom] Brokaw called it.
>
> The impact was immediate and overwhelming. The phones started ringing at NBC and at the Connecticut headquarters of Save the Children. . . . The next night, NBC aired another BBC report and, again, the response was staggering. CBS and ABC a week later aired more reports on the famine—with even more response, more reports. The story had exploded.[21]

In 1991 and 1992, the media prodded the Bush administration to take more vigorous actions about the starvation and suffering in Somalia. Former Secretary of State Lawrence Eagleburger described the impact of television over Somalia in this way:

> I will tell you quite frankly television had a great deal to do with President Bush's decision to go in the first place, and, I will tell you equally frankly, I was one of those two or three that was strongly recommending he do it, and it was very much because of the television pictures of these starving kids, substantial pressures from the Congress that comes from the same source, and my honest belief that we could do this. . . .[22]

The media's riveting portrayal of the suffering in that country ultimately led to the dispatch of American military forces to help with the distribution of food and needed supplies. Indeed, "among the most vivid scenes from that operation was the look of startled Navy seals in war paint hitting the beaches which had already been secured by television news crews to record the landing."[23] Such a scene was a dramatic and stark illustration of the power of the media in setting the foreign policy agenda and even in the stage management of a foreign policy action.

The Iraq War In the fall of 2003, the Bush administration and its supporters laid a severe charge against the national news media for their portrayal of the attacks on Americans in Iraq, the instability within the country, and the difficulty faced in the reconstruction efforts. The claim was that the media was highlighting the attacks and the problems of reconstruction and not telling the full story and that, in doing so, they were contributing to a decline in support for the administration's policy at home and abroad. Put differently, the media were conveying neither the political and social achievements in much of the country nor the overall stability of Iraqi life.

In an effort to combat this imagery, President George W. Bush met with reporters from regional media around the country to convey his views on the situation in Iraq, and several administration officials were dispatched on speaking engagements to get the message out about the "real" conditions in Iraq. Some of these same administration officials also went to Iraq in an effort to portray the story more favorably from that venue. These actions were taken to combat what was seen as the media serving as an actor by seemingly setting the agenda on Iraq.

On occasion, too, *individual members of the media* can play an even more direct role in the foreign policy process—a role that media analyst Doris Graber has called "media diplomacy."[24] Four examples in recent decades illustrate this aspect of media as actors.

The Cuban Missile Crisis ABC television reporter **John Scali** is often given considerable credit for aiding in the peaceful resolution of the nuclear standoff between the United States and the Soviet Union during the Cuban Missile Crisis of October 1962. He had been asked by a Soviet official to transmit a proposal for ending the crisis to Washington—one that ultimately bore a resemblance to the final outcome.[25]

Sadat and Begin[26] During a CBS evening news broadcast anchored by **Walter Cronkite** a month or so before Anwar Sadat's visit to Israel in November 1977, Sadat and Prime Minister Menachem Begin were simultaneously interviewed by Cronkite from their home countries, Egypt and Israel, respectively. During the interview, Cronkite encouraged Begin to issue an invitation to Sadat. Begin did so, and Sadat's path-breaking trip to Jerusalem was initiated—on U.S. television.

The Persian Gulf War A reporter for CNN, Peter Arnett, was in Baghdad prior to the outbreak of the Gulf War and stayed on during the conflict.[27] He gained both notoriety and political attacks in the United States for his continuous reporting. As virtually the only Western source in Baghdad once the war broke out, Arnett became a lightning rod for critics of the media and foreign policy for seemingly taking at face value the Iraqi explanations of events. He was also criticized by many "when he engaged Iraqi president Saddam Hussein in a long television interview" because it appeared to offer Hussein a ready "propaganda forum."[28]

The Iraq War During March and April 2003, the media were deeply involved in portraying the Iraq War because they had been "imbedded" in numerous military units. (Indeed, many had undergone some combat training before taking part in the advance on Baghdad from Kuwait.) In this sense, the media were real-time participants and actors who, although under particular restrictions (for example, they were prohibited from identifying their exact locations during combat), were in a position to convey a wartime situation to the American public and policy makers as never before. In addition, a few reporters stayed in Baghdad or went into Iraq during the fighting outside of the officially sanctioned units to provide important images and commentaries on the action. Finally, of course, during the reconstruction of Iraq, the degree of independent reporting on the situation there led the Bush administration to go on its "media offensive," as we noted.

Other Interpretations of the Role of the Media Despite the examples just given, several analysts doubt the accuracy of describing the media as separate foreign policy actors. Instead, they point to other explanations for the changing media coverage of foreign policy events. Daniel C. Hallin, a leading media analyst, disputes the idea that an "oppositional media" developed over Vietnam and the Tet offensive in particular.[29] Although acknowledging that coverage was more critical of policy after Tet than before, he sees the reason as not that the media had changed its role but that domestic consensus had evaporated, bringing more and more criticism of government policy.[30] As a result, the members of the media, relying on their norm of objective journalism, gave more and more coverage to the emerging controversy. Furthermore, as Hallin endeavors to show, the media continued to convey official government statements about the Vietnam War, made about the same ratio of comments about antiwar and war supporters after Tet, and offered little explicit independent commentary on the war.[31] He notes:

> The case of Vietnam suggests that whether the media tend to be supporting or critical of government policies depends on the degree of consensus those policies enjoy, particularly within the political establishment. . . . News content may not mirror the facts, but the media, as institutions, do reflect the prevailing pattern of political debate: when consensus is strong, they tend to stay within the limits of the political discussion it defines; when it begins to break down, coverage becomes increasingly critical and diverse in the viewpoints it represents, and increasingly difficult for officials to control.[32]

Some analysts question that the media shaped the coverage of the Iran hostage crisis. Instead, they point to the Carter administration for producing the significant media emphasis on this event.[33] Because President Carter treated the hostage taking as the most important problem facing the country and refused to leave Washington to campaign until it was resolved (the so-called Rose Garden strategy), the media necessarily gave the crisis more and more attention. This argument surely has some attraction as an alternate explanation; however, it fails to explain the sustained coverage in Tehran by American media outlets.

Furthermore, significant media coverage does *not* always produce a foreign policy response by the United States. Consider the cases of Cambodia (Kampuchea), Bosnia, and Rwanda over recent decades and the case of Syria in the current one.

Despite the Cambodian "killing fields" in the late 1970s, and the media coverage of the two million people massacred by the Pol Pot regime, American foreign policy toward that country changed very little with increased media coverage. Instead, because of the aftermath of the Vietnam War, the United States took a less assertive stance. Similarly, despite dramatic television pictures from Bosnia revealing the killings in the markets of Sarajevo, the haunting figures of starving men held in prisoner of war camps, and wholesale killings and rapes in the name of ethnic cleansing in the early 1990s, American policy makers were slow to change direction. It was not until mid-1995 that the Clinton administration took a more determined stance. The ethnic slaughter of Tutsis in Rwanda in 1994 and its vivid portrayal by the media brought only a limited policy response, too. Finally, despite media portrayals (primarily clandestinely by journalists) of the killings in Syria by the Bashar al-Assad government, the Obama administration has been reluctant to take actions beyond diplomatic condemnations due to international and domestic constraints.

In contrast, though, consider instances when the United States acted without being prodded by television coverage or remained steadfast in its position, despite media coverage. In humanitarian disasters, whether in Africa (such as Sierra Leone or Liberia) or Southeast Asia (such as East Timor), American assistance often arrived before, or with, the reporters and the cameras. Despite the criticism of Peter Arnett's reporting in Iraq during the Persian Gulf War, no evidence exists that he changed U.S. policy in any significant way. Similarly, the George W. Bush administration remained steadfast to its policy course in Iraq in the face of sustained media criticism and criticism from the American public and the international community.

The Liberal Media? Another aspect of this media as actor view focuses on the ideological characteristics of the journalists themselves and the possible bias that they bring to their reporting. The American public often views the media as being elitist, as possessing a liberal political bias, and as trying to foist such views on policy.

The media as a group are largely elitist demographically and do not reflect the American public as a whole. One major study reported that the media elite (both print and electronic) largely came from the northeast and north-central part of the country, had urban and ethnic roots, were highly educated, were "mostly well off, highly educated members of the upper middle class," and had primarily "secular roots" (only half were religious believers and less than 10 percent attended church).[34] Also, they were largely liberal in orientation (54 percent describing themselves as left of center; 17 percent, as right of center). A study of the Washington press corps at about the same time found that 42 percent were liberal and 19 percent were conservative,[35] and that their partisan orientation tended to be skewed in one direction, with more than four-fifths of those surveyed supporting Democratic presidential candidates Johnson, Hubert Humphrey, George McGovern, and Jimmy Carter in the elections immediately prior to the survey.[36]

Two decades later, a 2004 survey of 547 national and local reporters also revealed a tilt toward the liberal side of the political spectrum.[37] Thirty-four percent of national journalists described themselves as liberals compared to 23 percent of local journalists. In contrast, only 7 percent of national journalists and 12 percent of local journalists described themselves as conservatives. To be sure, the majority of both groups, 54 percent national and 61 percent local, described themselves as moderates. Nonetheless, the small percentage of conservatives as compared to liberals and to conservatives in the general public (33 percent at the time) remains striking.

In another recent study of the media, political scientist Tim Groseclose and economist Jeffrey Milyo estimated an ideological score for major media outlets and found that all reflected a "strong liberal bias." *The CBS Evening News* and the *New York Times* had the highest left-of-center scores; only *Fox News Special Report* and the *Washington Times* were the exceptions to this liberal direction. The television programs that scored more toward the center were *PBS NewsHour*, *CNN's Newsnight* (CNN's evening news program at the time), and *ABC's Good Morning America*; *USA Today* was more toward the center among print media.[38]

Finally, in a 2011 Gallup survey, 60 percent of the American public continued to perceive bias in the media, with 47 percent saying the media are too liberal and 13 percent saying they are too conservative. Only a third of the public (36 percent) viewed the media as "just about right." By party, Republicans and independents particularly view the media as too liberal, 75 percent and 50 percent, respectively; by ideology, 75 percent of conservatives view the media as too liberal, whereas the modal response by moderates and liberal is that the media is just about right.[39] Moreover, the modal perception of the media as too liberal goes back at least to 2002, based on earlier Gallup results.[40]

The important question is whether these personal characteristics mattered in what was reported or how it was reported. Many members of the media would argue that their journalistic training directs them to be fair and to prevent their personal beliefs and background from affecting their work. Thus, their sociopolitical background or political leanings would not significantly alter their reporting on domestic or foreign policy matters. Moreover, some of these liberal members of the media work for conservative organizations whose principal goals are increasing their share of the market among American viewers and listeners and enhancing corporate profits. In such an environment, reporters must follow a "good story" despite their political leanings.

Others disagree strongly over claims that members of the media do not allow their personal views to intrude on their reporting. Indeed, one prominent political scientist and media analyst calls this argument "absurd." Instead, he argues, this liberal bias comes into play "more in the setting of the agenda than in the reporting of particular facts. What they choose to cover, what they think is important is the liberal agenda."[41] Bernard Goldberg, former CBS reporter and author of a major book on the media, also disagrees. As he puts it, "Liberal bias is the result of how they [the media] see the world," which, in turn, affects the way that they report the news.[42] Liberals, however, would point to the impact that Fox News has had on the media environment in offering a conservative viewpoint and possessing a conservative bias.[43] In his 2011 book examining the media (and built on his analysis cited above), Tim Groseclose concludes that "the reporting by journalist is *very* susceptible to their political opinions. Namely, such opinion can easily influence . . . the topics they cover, the experts they choose to quote, the language they use, and the facts they include or omit from their reports."[44]

In this sense, we are back to where we started this discussion. That is, the media are important in setting the foreign policy agenda, as a recent study by Stuart N. Soroka has demonstrated empirically for recent decades.[45] How much the media set the agenda and how much they influence policy remain hotly debated questions. Longtime media analyst Bernard Cohen, writing more than four decades ago about the press and foreign policy, still offers an apt summary of this role of the media as actors:

> [T]he press is significantly more than a purveyor of information and opinion. It may not be successful much of the time in telling people what to think, but it is stunningly successful in telling its readers what to think *about*.[46]

The Media as Accomplices

A second role for the media might be stated most strongly as one wholly at variance with the first: **The media**, knowingly or not, act as **accomplices of the government**. That is, they become the "handmaidens" of the government in the portrayal of news and information.[47] At least three kinds of evidence support this view. First, the media are ultimately dependent on the government for information and for providing sources of information on many foreign policy questions. Second, the media elite often share similar values and beliefs about foreign policy with the political elite. As such, they will give credence to policy makers' positions. Third, government officials often try to use the media for promotion of particular policies, and they are increasingly trained to do so.[48]

Media Dependency   The American interventions in Grenada (1983) and Panama (1989) as well as the Persian Gulf War (1990–1991) and the Iraq War (2003) illustrate the problems that the media have in playing an independent role and reveal how dependent they may become on the government for information. During the American intervention in Grenada in October 1983, and with the memory of the media's role in Vietnam in mind, the Reagan administration decided to exclude journalists from the invasion and sent home those who had reached the island nation on their own.[49] In this instance, information was tightly channeled so as to control it, leaving the media largely to report what officials wanted.

After this episode, a commission was established to arrange a new relationship between the media and the government (in this case, the Pentagon) over future foreign engagements. The result was a "pool" of reporters that would accompany future military actions,[50] and the intervention in Panama in December 1989 was its first test. On the one hand, the pool system largely failed in the view of the media because they were kept under close scrutiny and control by Pentagon officials and were not allowed in combat areas for long periods. On the other hand, it succeeded in the view of the military and the government because the picture of the intervention conveyed was the one that they wanted.

The Persian Gulf War of 1990–1991 produced even greater government efforts to control and shape information. Indeed, here the Pentagon actually outlined detailed "ground rules" for journalists.[51] For example, sizes of American and coalition units and their military components could not be disclosed, future operational plans were forbidden, and exact locations of forces could not be revealed. News "pool" operations were once again established, and "they became the essential mode of operation."[52] The daily military briefings on the Persian Gulf operations, generally carried live on CNN, were the primary sources of information for the many news organizations in Saudi Arabia. The efforts to shape the story in a way that the government wanted proved largely successful.

The Iraq War that began in 2003 extended this governmental involvement in media reporting. Once again, the Pentagon provided media summaries of battlefield actions on a daily basis from the Department of Defense's Central Command headquarters located in Qatar or from the Pentagon. In addition, and as we discussed earlier, the military took its relationship with the media a step further by "imbedding" reporters in fighting units. With video phones and satellite capabilities, these reporters could send back real-time battlefield images to the American public. Reporters were under severe strictures, however; they could not identify their precise location, and they were limited in the kind of images that they could show. Presumably, they were conveying the story that the military wanted told. (Note that this discussion, too, illustrates the difficulties of separating out the role of media as actors from that of media as government accomplices.)

The Afghanistan War continued this pattern, especially given the dangerous environment there. The degree of restrictions on reporting may have been somewhat less than in earlier wars, but the media remained largely dependent for both access to particular areas and information on the government. In this sense, the media would have a challenge, albeit not insurmountable, in reporting on this war.

Close Personal and Working Relationships Although these illustrations are recent instances of the ability of the government to use the media in a way favorable to it, other mechanisms are available and have operated for some time. Often, members of the media and public officials form close personal and working relationships and can thus use each other to get a particular message to the public and other policy makers. The leaking of information to particular reporters is the obvious and most direct way to achieve this end. Just as "sources" for the media develop in the government, foreign policy officials may use their media "contacts" to make their case to the American people. Some of these contacts become "Washington insiders" with easy contact and access to policy makers (although they do not always comply with the officials' wishes).

A pure example of the Washington insider is difficult to identify (because few media people would accept this characterization), but the late James Reston, longtime columnist for the *New York Times*, fits the portrait, in part. A first-rate reporter and columnist on foreign and domestic issues, Reston was also closely tied with and highly trusted by Washington officials—he was "the quintessential Washington insider," in one commentator's judgment. In fact, in that analyst's view, he was too close to key officials: "Officials used him to test out new ideas on the public or to drop leaks for which they did not want to be held accountable. Because of his high position at the *Times* and his personal integrity, he was trusted both by those who provided the news and by those who read it."[53] On at least one important occasion, Reston was willing, after a presidential phone call, to withhold a story—in this case, involving the emplacement of Soviet missiles in Cuba in 1962, at a time when the crisis had yet to become public.

Another reporter with apparent good governmental access is *Washington Post* reporter Bob Woodward. Although he gained fame (with Carl Bernstein) with the disclosures of White House wrongdoing during the Watergate episode in the early 1970s, more recently he has written "insider" accounts of White House decision making after the attacks of September 11 during the George W. Bush administration (*Bush at War*) and over the Afghanistan War during the Barack Obama administration (*Obama's Wars*). For these accounts, he needed (and apparently received) access to top Washington officials. Whether he was acting in any way as an accomplice to the White House would be denied by him, but his access was surely important in developing these accounts.

At a more general level, media representatives and public officials have often worked closely together to gain information and have relied on and trusted one another. The extent of this cooperation abroad is considerable because an American embassy or consulate is the primary source of information for many reporters. This collaboration may include a reporter reading American embassy cable traffic on a regular basis in an African country, another reporter withholding information about secret negotiations over Afghanistan at the request of an ambassador, or a Washington columnist using information from a White House source to influence the foreign policy debate on Iraq.[54] At the very least, though, the collaboration often involves a regular and sustained exchange of information.

Government Use of the Media The government has increasingly sought to establish ground rules for dealing with the media, not just interventions or wars as the Grenada, Persian Gulf, or Iraq cases suggest, but on a more ongoing basis. A former assistant secretary of state for inter-American affairs made the point bluntly about the need by government officials to shape the message emanating from the media: "We are not taught about the press as an instrument of foreign policy execution, and that is crucial. . . . You have to use the press, and when I say 'use,' I don't mean cynically, in the sense of hoodwinking. I mean use it in the sense that it's an instrument that is there for you."[55] As a result, in recent years, the Department of State has developed an extensive series of guidelines for dealing with the media and has offered stern warnings about what and what not to say.[56] In fact, government officials now receive both formal and informal training in media relations.

Critics raised this charge of government use of the media in mid-2012 when disclosures about a highly classified secret "kill list" against al-Qaeda suspects by the Obama administration and about American involvement in cyber attacks against Iran's computer system appeared in *New York Times* articles. The reporters acknowledged that they had talked to current advisors and "participants in the many Situation Room meetings" in developing their reporting.[57] Such details about these governmental actions raised questions about whether this information was purposefully leaked by the administration to bolster the president's standing on foreign policy, even at the expense of national security. Although the administration denied such action, investigations were subsequently initiated over such leaks.

Much as with the role of media as actors, though, some analysts warn about relying too fully on the role of media as accomplices to explain the media–policy maker relationship. First, however much journalists are dependent on the "golden triangle" (White House, Pentagon, and State Department) for gathering news (which is why the official government position often receives considerable attention), a "professional norm" exists that "discourages taking sides by looking to report different sides of a debate."[58] As the policy debate among officials emerges—whether between the Pentagon and State or between the White House and Congress—the media are able to do more than just report the officially stated government position. "When official conflict is sustained, the news gates tend to open to grass-roots groups, interest groups, opinion polls, and broader social participation."[59] In this way, the media are increasingly successful as more than just accomplices of the government. Second, journalists are fully aware of official *spinning*—the strategy of conveying a particular image or interpretation of foreign policy events and having the media report it[60]—and they take precautions to guard against it. Furthermore, as foreign policy issues become increasingly contentious and partisan, journalists seek out alternate interpretations from various sources.

The Media and the Government: Mutually Exploitative?

As criticism of the media as accomplice role illustrates, an increasing tension has developed in the relationship between the media and the foreign policy community, suggesting a third possible relationship between the two that strikes a middle ground. That is, **the media and the government both seek to take advantage of their relationship**. One analyst has aptly described this as "mutually exploitative":

> Both organizations [the U.S. foreign policy community and the media] promote their own version of reality around the world; the foreign policy apparatus does so to serve its own policy interests; the media do so because that is what they do. Both are adept at supporting, manipulating, or attacking the other. The relationship is sometimes competitive and sometimes cooperative, but that is only incidental to its central driving force: self-interest.[61]

In particular, recent foreign policy and media activities, most notably in connection with the Iraq War, give credence to this characterization. Although the media were eager to take advantage of "imbedded" reporters to cover the war, the military and policy makers saw this arrangement as a way to maintain some stake in the reporting. After the ground war was over in Iraq, coverage of the reconstruction efforts—and the differences over it between policy makers and the media—again illustrated the efforts by both participants to shape the coverage. In 2007 and 2008, the seemingly limited media coverage of the success of the "surge strategy" in Iraq in dampening down violence provides yet another example of the continuing sparring between government and the media to shape the portrait conveyed to the American public.

The success of the media versus the policy makers, however, varies by issue.[62] On the environment, human rights, and human interest stories generally, sometimes called "low politics" issues, the media are more effective in influencing the policy process. Human rights violations of ethnic minorities and the struggle for freedom and independence by indigenous groups are often easily portrayed through the medium of television with compelling visual images. On arms control or the accuracy of weapons systems, sometimes called "high politics" issues, policy makers may have an advantage. Consider the media's difficulty in reporting the debate for and against arms control agreements without official arguments, or strategies against international terrorism without military input. As a long-time foreign policy journalist noted: "Media technology is rarely as powerful in the hands of journalists as it is in the hands of political figures who can summon the talent to exploit the new invention."[63]

In sum, then, the media and the foreign policy community may well feed off each other's skills as both seek to promote their interests. In many ways, "mutually exploitative" may be a more accurate way to think about the relationship between these two organizations, rather than simply trying to characterize the media as always independent actors or always government accomplices.

THE MEDIA'S IMPACT ON THE PUBLIC

The final topic to consider is the media's effects on the views and opinions of the public. Suffice it to say here the media obviously have some impact on the public's perceptions as it forms those opinions. In a real sense, of course, the public depends heavily on the kind and extent of information that the media provide it. As political scientists Benjamin Page and Robert Shapiro note, "Many events—especially distant happenings in foreign affairs—do not directly and immediately affect ordinary citizens, and therefore, do not speak for themselves." Instead, they must be reported and "*interpreted*."[64] In this sense, the media matter, but how much and to what degree?

In a study covering a fifteen-year period (1969–1983), Page and Shapiro have begun to sort out the media's role by assessing the impact of several providers of news on television, such as "the president, members of his administration and fellow partisans, members of the opposing party, interest groups, . . . experts, network commentators or reporters . . . foreign nations or individuals, unfriendly states," and others on the changes in the public's view of foreign and domestic policies.[65] From their analyses, two important findings emerge. First, the public's views were relatively stable over time (only changing about 50 percent of the time over the years), even given a variety of interpreters of television news. Second, when opinion change did occur in the short term, news commentators—more than any of the other providers of news—produced most of it. In this sense, the media, and especially news commentators, mattered in affecting the public's views more than presidents, policy experts, and foreign nations.

In another study, Stuart Soroka looked at the effect of media content on foreign policy opinion. After systematically examining the foreign and domestic policy contents in the *New York Times* and the *Times* of London between 1981 and 2002 on the British and American public, Soroka concluded that there is a **remarkably powerful effect of media content on the salience of foreign affairs for the public.**[66] That is, foreign affairs coverage raises the importance of these issues for the public, which is hardly unexpected or exceptional in light of what we have been discussing. What Soroka also demonstrates, however, is important: there is a media effect in addition to the impact of the events themselves. In turn, such issue salience affects how the public evaluates governments and political leaders. In this sense, media reporting of foreign affairs—beyond the events themselves—can be crucial to the nature of public opinion within a country. Finally, Shapiro and Page add some important cautions about the relationship between the media and foreign policy opinion. They note, for example, that "gradual social and economic trends, and world and national events—which have some unmediated impact" combine with those reported through the mass media to affect opinion change.[67] In addition, although the public's foreign policy views are often interpreted through the media by elites, "people seem to have reacted directly to events themselves, sometimes going against elite interpretations."[68] The evidence is quite strong that **the public is not made up of mindless robots** wholly swayed by the latest media pictures and portrayals; opinion change among the public comes from many sources and not exclusively from the media.[69]

PUBLIC OPINION AND FOREIGN POLICY: ALTERNATE VIEWS

With an understanding of the role of the media, we now examine more directly the public's role in the foreign policy process. We divide our discussion and analysis between two perspectives about public opinion and foreign policy and evaluate the evidence for each of them. We conclude by judging which perspective seems more appropriate.

According to the **first perspective, the public is uninterested, ill informed, and subject to being led from the top**. In the strongest form of this position, public opinion is less a shaper of foreign policy and more likely to be shaped by it. As a consequence, it plays little or no role in its formulation. According to the **second perspective, the public plays a somewhat larger, albeit still limited, role**. Although it may not be fully informed on foreign policy and may lack sustained interest in it, the public's views are more structured and consistent over time than many have previously contended. As such, the public can affect foreign policy making, especially over the long haul.

In the course of this discussion, we evaluate how much impact public opinion has on policy making—indirectly through presidential and congressional elections and directly through current policy actions—as a way to gain some insight into the utility of these two alternate perspectives.

FOREIGN POLICY OPINION: UNINFORMED AND MOODISH

In this first view, except for very rare occurrences, public opinion has limited impact on the foreign policy process. Only during wars or international crises is the public sufficiently concerned about foreign policy to affect it directly. **The principal reason for this limited impact is the public's lack of interest in, and knowledge about, foreign affairs.** Even when specific foreign policy views of the public are expressed, they often prove susceptible to short-term shifts—produced, for example, by presidential leadership, the wording of questions in public opinion polls, or rapidly changing international events. In this context, public opinion serves as a relatively weak restraint on policy makers.

Public Interest and Knowledge of Foreign Affairs

Low levels of public understanding of and concern about foreign policy issues have existed since America's sustained global involvement began after World War II. A 1947 study of Cincinnati, Ohio, for instance, showed that only 30 percent of the public were able to explain in a simple way what the United Nations did. An analysis two years later revealed that the public was equally uninformed. By this assessment, only 25 percent were judged to possess reasonably developed opinions, 45 percent had only limited knowledge of world affairs, and 30 percent were classified as uninformed.[70]

Throughout the three decades prior to the events of September 11, 2001, the level of interest in foreign affairs did not change appreciably—even in the context of a more educated electorate. Based on the seven quadrennial surveys of the American public on foreign policy issues conducted by The Chicago Council on Foreign Relations from 1974 to 1998, local community news received the highest level of interest (between 55 and 65 percent over the years), whereas news about other countries was much lower (about 31 percent on average).[71] News about America's relations with other countries ranked a bit higher, ranging from 44 to 53 percent across the surveys. It is interesting that news about U.S. relations with other countries stimulated more interest than simply news about other countries, but it still trailed interest in local community affairs. Figure 12.1 is a comparison of interest in different types of news across these surveys.

After September 11, however, the public's interest in news about U.S. relations with other countries jumped to 61 percent, about the same level of interest in local community news and national news, whereas interest in news about other countries rose to 42 percent. (See Figure 12.1 for complete 2002 data.) In this sense, September 11 had a profound effect on the public's level of interest in foreign affairs. Indeed, the 2002 Chicago Council survey points to this change as one of its key findings: "Public interest in world news is the strongest it has been in the last three decades of Council surveys."[72] Unfortunately, subsequent biennial Chicago Council surveys did not include the same battery of questions that tapped interest in these various types of news.[73] Instead, respondents were asked only one—on the degree of public interest in news about U.S. relations with other countries. In 2004, 53 percent were "very interested," but in 2006 that figure was only 38 percent. That figure dropped to 31 percent in 2008 and rose to only 32 percent in 2010.[74] At least by this indicator, the American public's interest in foreign affairs by end of the decade had reverted to past patterns.

Percentages

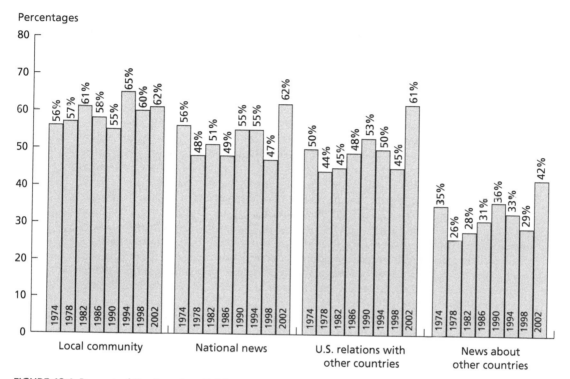

FIGURE 12.1 Percent of the American Public Very Interested in Various Types of News, 1974–2002

Source: Marshall M. Routon and Benjamin I. Page, eds., *Worldviews 2002: American Public Opinion & Foreign Policy* (Chicago: The Chicago Council on Foreign Relations, 2002), Figure 1–6, p. 13. Adapted with permission.

Overall, interest in foreign affairs may have increased temporarily in the immediate post–9/11 years, but the **level of knowledge about foreign affairs has not**. In fact, the Chicago Council surveys over the years generally conclude that only about 20 to 25 percent of Americans are fully informed on foreign policy matters; they constitute what has been called the "attentive public." The results for 1990 were a little higher, with 29 percent characterized as "high attentives," although the criteria for attentiveness were less demanding in this survey than in earlier ones.[75] Furthermore, as the 1998 survey noted, the "'don't know' responses among the public are not uncommon, especially on specific foreign policy issues requiring more detailed information," and the level of this kind of response has remained about the same over the years.

In the Pew Center's 2011 News IQ survey, the public's knowledge of national and international affairs remains modest, whether they were asked verbal or visual questions. The average score on the nineteen-item survey (with about half on foreign affairs) was 11.5 correct or 60 percent, with a greater number correct for visual than verbal questions. The results differed modestly by partisanship (Republicans doing better than Democrats), by age (older people doing better than younger people), and education (college-educated doing better than those with some college or high school or less). The 2011 results for the public had not changed markedly from the results reported by the Pew Research Center in 2007, and the 2007 respondents, in fact, did slightly less well than the results reported in a 1989 survey.[76] In all, the expansion of information outlets discussed earlier, and the increase in educational attainment has not led to a more informed public.

We can demonstrate the public's paucity of foreign affairs knowledge more concretely by considering the accuracy of the public's information about different kinds of foreign policy activities and about the high level of "don't know" or "no opinion" answers to foreign policy questions. An often-used example deals with the amount of foreign aid that the United States provides. Although such aid is hardly a new item on the foreign policy agenda (it has been a staple of U.S. foreign policy since the end of World War II), the public has a low level of knowledge about how much the United States actually dispenses. In a 2002 survey by The Chicago Council on Foreign Relations, the public's median estimate of the percent of the federal budget spent on foreign aid was 25 percent. In reality, it is about 1 percent and has been at that level for a long time. Only 2 percent of the public knew this.[77] In fairness (and perhaps the reason for the confusion in responding to this question), the United States has always been the leading or second leading donor (after Japan) in terms of total dollar amount of foreign assistance. Yet the public's inability to differentiate between total versus relative amounts of aid clearly shows a lack of knowledge about this foreign policy item.

Other examples illustrate the same degree of limited knowledge among the public, even about international events in the news.[78] In February 1999, when Kosovo and its ethnic conflicts had been in the news for some time and only one month prior to U.S. military action there, a Gallup poll asked a sample of Americans "to choose which of four geographic locations best described Kosovo." Forty-two percent correctly chose the Balkans, 26 percent placed the province in the former Soviet Union, 8 percent placed it in Africa or Southeast Asia, and 24 percent responded "don't know." For another ongoing dispute, the public was even less informed. When asked by Gallup in late 1999 what country East Timor was having a dispute with, two-thirds of the American public did not have an answer, and only 20 percent (that is, the "attentive public") answered correctly (Indonesia).

These disputes might be regarded as off the radar for most Americans, but the public also displays limited knowledge of the European Union and key foreign policy makers at home and abroad. In a May 2004 survey about the European Union (EU), 77 percent acknowledged that they knew little or nothing about it, although over 20 percent correctly noted that the population of the EU was larger than that of the United States.[79] About a year earlier (February 2003), 37 percent of the public had "no opinion" when asked the name of the current secretary of state. Only 6 percent could identify the prime minister of Canada, and 92 percent had "no opinion." Similarly, 57 percent had "no opinion" when asked to name the president of Russia and 46 percent responded similarly when asked the name of the prime minister of England—at a time when the United States and Great Britain were on the verge of going to war against Iraq.[80] In another Gallup survey in February 2006, only 37 percent could name the president of Russia (at the time), Vladimir Putin; only 29 percent, the president of Mexico (at the time), Vicente Fox; and only 4 percent, the chancellor of Germany, Angela Merkel.[81] In Pew's 2011 News IQ quiz, though, 61 percent of the respondents correctly identified Greece as an indebted country, but only 38 percent correctly identified David Cameron as Britain's prime minister.[82]

Foreign Policy as an Important Issue

Despite the low level of knowledge and interest in international affairs over past decades, the public still views foreign policy as an important issue facing the country at various times. During portions of the last six decades, for example, foreign policy has been identified as the most important issue facing the nation, but during the past forty years or so, economic or domestic concerns (such as crime, unemployment, inflation) were generally regarded as the principal issue. After 9/11, unsurprisingly, terrorism quickly became the key issue, with 36 percent of the public listing it as one of the two or three biggest problems. By 2003, the economy once again matched that issue as most important,[83] but the Iraq War soon became the most important problem and narrowly continued to lead the economy through at least the fall of 2007.[84] By early 2008, the "economy in general" (35 percent) outdistanced the "situation in Iraq/War" (21 percent) when the American public was asked the "most important problem facing the country."[85] By 2012, the economy and unemployment/jobs were mentioned by 57 percent of the public as the most important problem, with only one issue related to foreign policy (immigration) reaching mention by 3 percent of the public. Instead, the Great Recession of 2008 and 2009 continued to dominate the agenda.[86]

Figure 12.2 graphically portrays the extent to which the public identified foreign policy–related problems as the most important problem or problems facing the country over the most recent thirty-year period. Between 1978 and 1998, foreign policy problems as a percentage of the total ranged from a low of 7 percent in 1998 to a high of 26 percent in 1986, but the average foreign policy mentions over those years were only 13 percent. In the wake of September 11, foreign policy problems constituted 41 percent of the mentions in 2002—a very dramatic increase from the 7 percent of 1998 or even the 26 percent of 1986.[87]

Unfortunately, the Chicago Council did not use this same question and analysis in their 2004, 2006, 2008, or 2010 surveys.[88] However, in an effort to gauge the relative importance of foreign policy problems, we used three surveys by the Gallup organization on the most important problems for the country (one in December 2005; a second in March 2008, and a third in June 2012) and report the percentages for foreign policy issues mentioned by the public's responses.[89] The results are reported in the last three columns of Figure 12.2. What these results suggest is that foreign policy issues continued to be quite important after 9/11, declined somewhat by 2008, and were negligible by mid-2012. Perhaps as America's economic woes recede or international events change, foreign policy will return as the most important problem, but it is likely to lag domestic economic concerns, much as in the past.

Finally, and importantly, if foreign policy has occasionally captured a portion of the public's attention, why has the public not been more informed and more influential in shaping policy? Part of the explanation rests in the two earlier items we discussed: the low level of *sustained* interest in foreign policy over the years and the low level of foreign policy knowledge generally. Because the public's concern has largely been episodic and tied to particular international events, and because the public's knowledge of foreign policy has remained relatively low, its ability to influence policy arguably has remained relatively weak.

Presidential Leadership

Another important factor in the public's lack of influence is its susceptibility to presidential leadership. According to evidence provided by political scientist John Mueller, the president has often been the most admired person in the country.[90] As

Percentages

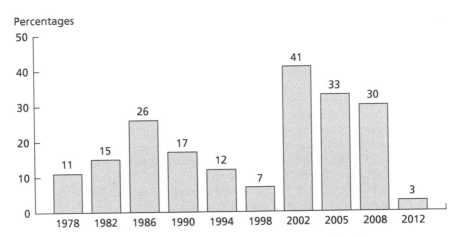

FIGURE 12.2 Relative Percentage of Foreign Policy Problems as Most Important Problem(s) Facing the Country Identified by the American Public, 1978–2012

Sources: Marshall M. Bouton and Benjamin L Page, eds., *Worldviews 2002: American Public Opinion & Foreign Policy* (Chicago: The Chicago Council on Foreign Relations, 2002), Figure 1-3, p. 11, for the years 1978 through 2002. Adapted with permission. The data for those years asked the public for the two or three biggest problems facing the country. The data for 2005 were from Joseph Carroll, "Most Important Problem," January 10, 2006, at **http:// www.gallup.comlpoi/l74338/Most-Important-Prob/em.aspx**, July 18, 2012, and was the sum of mentions of the Iraq War, terrorism, and immigration as foreign policy issues. Mention of all issues totaled 80 percent in this report. The data for 2008 were from Dennis Jacobe, "Economy Widely Viewed as Most Important Problem," March 13, 2008, at **http:// www.gallup.com/poi/1704959/Economy-Widely-Viewed-Most-Important-Prob/em.aspx**, July 18, 2012, and was the sum of mentions of the Iraq War, national security, terrorism, foreign aid/focus overseas, and international issues/problems. Mentions of all issues totaled 128 percent in this report. The data for 2012 were from Lydia Saad, "In U.S., Jobs a More Glaring Issue for Some Groups Than Others," June 27, 2012, at **http://www.gallup.com/poll/155375/Jobs**-Glaring-Issue-Groups-Others.aspx, July 13, 2012. Immigration (at 3 percent) is the only foreign policy–related issue among the top ten responses reported. Mentions for these responses totaled 103 percent. For 2005, 2008, and 2012, the respondents were asked to identify "the most important problem facing this country today."

a consequence, because the public is not well informed on foreign policy issues, a tendency has developed for it to defer to the president's judgment on such matters. Several examples illustrate this phenomenon.

When President Johnson changed his Vietnam strategy, the public generally was willing to shift to support it—even if the policy was a reversal of his earlier expressed position. Prior to the bombing of oil depots around Hanoi and Haiphong, a majority of the public opposed such bombing. After the bombing began, however, 85 percent supported it. A similar shift, dictated by a presidential initiative, occurred later in the war. Before Johnson halted the bombing in 1968, 51 percent of the public supported it. After Johnson announced a partial bombing halt, a majority (64 percent) favored this decision.[91] In both instances, then, the American public was very susceptible to presidential leadership.

A similar phenomenon occurred during President Richard Nixon's handling of the war. Just prior to the American invasion of Cambodia in 1970, a Harris Poll asked whether the public supported the commitment of U.S. forces there. Only 7 percent did. Yet after Nixon went on national television to explain his decision to send troops into Cambodia, another Harris Poll indicated that 50 percent of the American public supported him.[92] In other words, in a matter of three weeks, public opinion turned around dramatically, with only the president's speech as the important intervening event.

In the post-Vietnam and post–Cold War periods, such ready acceptance of presidential leadership might have seemed more difficult to obtain, but, in fact, it continued. Prior to the seizure of American hostages in Iran in November 1979, President Carter's approval rating was only 32 percent. By the end of December, his approval had jumped to 61 percent. Furthermore, Carter initially got high marks from the public over his handling of the Iranian situation, with 82 percent applauding his actions.[93] Although this "rallying around the president" could be short-lived, as Carter was to find out, it nevertheless allowed the executive considerable latitude in initiating foreign policy without suffering any immediate domestic repercussions.

President Ronald Reagan also influenced public opinion on foreign policy issues by exercising presidential leadership. Although he met resistance on several issues—sending American forces into Lebanon in 1982, backing the Contras in Central America, and opposing a nuclear freeze—Reagan was still able to increase support for his policy positions. After the terrorist bombing of the marine headquarters in Beirut, Lebanon, in October 1983, with the loss of 241 Americans, the public's approval of U.S. troops stationed in that country increased from 36 percent in late September to 48 percent by late October of 1983. Similarly, Reagan's decision to send U.S. troops to Grenada won quick approval from the American public, with 55 percent supporting this action and 31 percent opposing it. Both shows of support for the president were accompanied by an increase in overall approval of his handling of the presidency.[94]

President George H. W. Bush was also able to use his foreign policy actions to gain public support. In the first two years of his term, he generally enjoyed strong foreign policy support, yet his decisions to intervene in Panama in December 1989 to topple and seize Manuel Noriega and to respond with military force to Saddam Hussein's invasion of Kuwait in August 1990 won him even greater approval. After the U.S. assault on Panama, Bush's approval rating went up to 80 percent in January 1990, and after his decision on August 8, 1990, to send American forces to support Saudi Arabia against Saddam Hussein, it shot up again, reaching 77 percent in mid-August 1990.[95] After Congress approved the use of force in the Gulf against the Iraqis in January 1991, and as first the air war and then the ground war began, it shot up once again. Indeed, his popularity had reached about 90 percent by the time of the cease-fire in March 1991.[96] Dramatic and decisive foreign policy actions often rally support for the president, and in this, Bush, was no exception.

President Bill Clinton experienced the same "rallying around the flag" over his Haitian actions during the fall of 1994. As the military government in Haiti remained steadfast in its resistance to restoring the democratically elected government, the Clinton administration increasingly hinted that military action would be required and gained prior UN authorization for it. However, the American public was skeptical, with only a little more than one-third supporting this option.[97] Overall approval "of the way Bill Clinton is handling the situation in Haiti" was equally low (27 percent) in early September 1994, and was only slightly higher (35 percent) on September 14, 1994, the day before the president's nationwide address pledging to use force to remove the Haitian military regime. After that speech, however, the poll results demonstrated the potency of presidential leadership, with Clinton's approval shooting up to 53 percent; it was still at 48 percent at the end of September.[98]

After September 11, 2001, President George W. Bush experienced the **greatest "rally effect"** of any president in polling history, when his approval rating soared from 51 percent just before 9/11 to 86 percent approval after. The rally effect of thirty-five points was the largest ever found by the Gallup polling organization, and within a matter of days, Bush's rating had reached 90 percent, surpassing that of his father during the Gulf War.[99] Furthermore, in the four months after 9/11, his average approval rating was 84 percent and, on September 11, 2002, was still at 70 percent. By one analysis, this average level of public support during Bush's first eighteen months was 72 percent—the highest average of a U.S. president since Vietnam and the third highest among post–World War II presidents. Such a long rally effect was unusual, and Bush's support did eventually decline in 2003 prior to the Iraq War, then increased when the war broke out, and declined again in the summer and fall of 2003 as the reconstruction effort proved daunting. By the end of 2003, Bush's level of support was at about 50 percent or slightly higher—virtually the same as it was pre–9/11.[100]

The killing of Osama bin Laden by the United States in May 2011 increased the American public's approval rating of President Obama, too. His approval rating went from an average approval rate of 44 percent in the week before bin Laden's death to 51 percent in the week after. Much of this increase in approval came from Republicans and independents, revealing the tendency to rally around the president across party lines over international events.[101]

In sum, the potency of the presidency as a shaper of foreign policy opinion has been important in particular circumstances, and it can serve as an important restraint on the effectiveness of overall public sentiment in directing foreign policy making. However, such presidential power is also contingent on the public's general approval of the policy direction being pursued. In this sense, the presidency is not all encompassing, as we will show later in this chapter.

Gauging Public Opinion

Other difficulties seemingly diminish the effectiveness of public opinion. Because the public's views are not always well developed or firmly held, **question wording and even the terms used in public opinion polls can alter them from survey to survey**. As Milton Rosenberg, Sidney Verba, and Philip Converse hypothesized, the concepts used to describe American involvement in Vietnam could influence the level of its public support or opposition. If negative terms were used (such as "defeat" or "Communist takeover"), the public would likely be more defensive and hawkish in its response. If other negative terms were used ("the increase in killings" or "the continued costs of the war"), the public might respond in a more dovish or conciliatory manner.[102]

A study of the various public opinion polls regarding aid to the Nicaraguan Contras in the 1980s confirmed the effects of question wording. When the public was asked about funding the Contras and specific references were made to "President Reagan," "the Contras," or the "Marxist government" in Nicaragua, support for aid was generally higher than when such references were left out. By contrast, when references were made to the amount of money involved in supporting the Contras, or when the question format was more "balanced" in treating the competing parties, support was lower. Although the overall effect of question wording on support or opposition to Contra aid was relatively modest, it did have a discernible effect.[103]

The **number of options**, as well as question wording, that are presented to a respondent can be important in affecting polling results. In 2002 survey results asking the public whether they favored or opposed U.S. military action against Iraq, different options and different wording cues produced differing results. When the general question was asked (favor or oppose such action), 57 percent favored military action against Iraq and 38 percent opposed it. When the question wording was changed to "if the United Nations supports invading Iraq," the results were 79 percent favorable and 19 percent unfavorable. When the same question was asked with a different conditionality ("if the United States has to invade alone"), 59 percent opposed and 38 percent favored—a virtual reversal of the answer given when the question was asked without any qualifiers.[104]

A somewhat similar result occurred in 2007 surveys on the withdrawal of American troops from Iraq. When the public was asked whether to keep troops in Iraq or to set a timetable for removing them, in three surveys from early September 2007 through December 2007, a majority supported the timetable by a rough 60 percent to 38 percent margin. When the respondents who supported a withdrawal were probed, the results were instructive. Between 17 and 21 percent wanted a withdrawal "as soon as possible," but 39 to 42 percent called for a "gradual withdrawal."[105]

The results were comparable when the American public was asked about President Obama's withdrawal plan for U.S. forces from Afghanistan. When the public was asked whether they "favor" or "oppose" the president's plan to pull out 10,000 troops in 2011, 20,000 by the end of the summer of 2012, and the rest by the end of 2014, the public favored the plan by a margin of 72–23 percent. When the public was probed on the president's timetable and given three options ("agree with the timetable," "should withdraw sooner," or "should not set timetable for withdrawal"), the public divided remarkably evenly among these options (30 percent, 33 percent, and 31 percent, respectively).[106] Although the results obtained with more options (and similar to the case of the question on Iraq withdrawal) may not change the overall policy preferences of the public, they do suggest a different policy emphasis than that revealed when only two dichotomous options were considered.

In sum, we might view these differing responses as reflecting a sophisticated and informed public (as we will discuss in the next section), but the alternate results achieved with differing question wording or number of options allow policy makers to select the poll results most favorable to their intended policy actions, and thus they are less constrained by the public's views. Hence, in an environment of limited foreign policy knowledge and a variety of options, different responses to survey questions are possible. This once again raises doubts about how much credence officials give to competing survey results. In this sense, surveys and polls may erode the impact of public opinion on foreign policy.

Public Opinion and Fluctuating Moods

Gabriel Almond, an early pioneer in the analysis of public attitudes toward foreign policy, has aptly summarized the portrait of American public opinion that we have sketched so far. The American public view is essentially **a "mood" toward foreign affairs that lacks "intellectual structure and factual content."** This mood is largely "superficial and fluctuating," "permissive," and subject to elite leadership influence "if they [the policy makers] demonstrate unity and resolution."[107]

With these fluctuating and permissive moods, the role of public opinion as a shaper of foreign policy is surely diminished. Although the public can exercise some impact during periods of crises or wars, in general, it is more apt to follow its leaders. Similarly, although the fluctuation in moods may not be as great as it once was, as Almond later acknowledged, public opinion is still largely unstable and unstructured. Consequently, as Almond put it, public opinion "cannot be viewed as standing in the way of foreign policy decisions by American governmental leaders."

The influential American journalist and student of public opinion Walter Lippmann took an equally dim view of the role of public opinion in foreign policy, but he saw it as far more dangerous than Almond did. As one analyst put it, Lippmann saw "the mass public as not merely uninterested and uninformed, but as a powerful force that was so out of synch with reality as to constitute a massive and potentially fatal threat to effective government and policies."[108] As Lippmann himself wrote, "The people have impressed a critical veto on the judgments of informed and responsible officials. They have compelled the government, which usually knew what would have been wiser, or was necessary, or what was more expedient, to be late with too little, or too long with too much, too pacifist in peace and too bellicose in war. . . ."[109]

Some scholarly evidence seems to counter Lippmann's fears.[110] One scholar, for example, found that the public's views were not consistent or "constrained." That is, an individual's views in one area did not correlate well with views in another. In other words, the American public seemed to lack any underlying structures, at least according to the 1950s and 1960s data. As a result, mass opinion, with such disparate and changeable views across individuals, could hardly serve as a restraining force on policy makers. Many scholars have also questioned whether public opinion really affects foreign policy. Whether these analysts studied Congress or the executive, only the most tenuous link (or none at all) existed between opinion and policy. In short, little compelling evidence could be summoned to suggest that public opinion mattered much in foreign policy making.

FOREIGN POLICY OPINION: STRUCTURED AND STABLE

Recent research is less pessimistic about public opinion and its role in the foreign policy process. Even in the context of a relatively uninformed public that is susceptible to elite or presidential leadership, foreign policy attitudes of the American public are not always irrelevant to policy making. At least two interrelated factors support this view: (1) the public's attitudes are more structured and stable than has often been assumed; and (2) the public mood is more identifiable and less shiftable and potentially more constraining on policy makers' actions than is sometimes suggested.

The Structure of Foreign Policy Opinions

How is it possible that opinions can be structured and stable if, as we demonstrated earlier, knowledge and interest in foreign affairs are so relatively low among the American public? Political scientists Jon Hurwitz and Mark Peffley have begun to untangle this apparent anomaly, arguing that individuals use **information short-cuts to make political judgments** and **extrapolate preferences from general attitudes**. Paradoxically, ordinary citizens can maintain coherent attitude structures, even though they lack detailed knowledge about foreign policy. As Hurwitz and Peffley write:

> Individuals organize information because such organization helps to simplify the world. Thus, a paucity of information does not *impede* structure and consistency; on the contrary, it *motivates* the development and employment of structure. Thus, we see individuals as attempting to cope with an extraordinarily confusing world (with limited resources to pay information costs) by structuring views about specific foreign policies according to their more *general and abstract beliefs*.[111]

Political scientists Benjamin Page, Robert Shapiro, and Eugene Wittkopf have demonstrated more fully the accuracy of this position. In extensive analyses of public opinion surveys from the 1930s to the 1980s, Shapiro and Page showed that public opinion has changed relatively slowly over time. "When it has changed, it has done so by responding in rational ways to international and domestic events. . . ." In their view, public opinion is not "volatile," nor does it "fluctuate wildly." Instead, "collective opinion tends to be rather stable; it sometimes changes abruptly, but usually by only small amounts; and it rarely fluctuates."[112] In short, the public is markedly "rational" and stable in its foreign policy beliefs.

Through comprehensive analyses of the Chicago Council on Foreign Relations surveys, Wittkopf determined the structure of American foreign policy opinion and demonstrated its stability over a three-decade period.[113] These analyses reveal that the American people have been divided not only over *whether* the United States should be involved in foreign affairs (the traditional isolationism/internationalist dimension) but also over *how* it should be involved (the cooperative/militant dimension). These divisions, moreover, have remained remarkably consistent over the years.

More specifically, **the American public is divided along two continua: *cooperative internationalism* and *militant internationalism*.** Where the public falls on these continua depends on its attitudes and opinions "about how broad or narrow the range of U.S. foreign policy goals should be; about the particular countries in which the United States has vital interests; and about the use of force to protect others."[114] The intersection of those two continua produces four distinct belief systems and best describes the structure of American foreign policy opinion today.

Wittkopf labeled the four segments of the public holding these belief systems as *internationalists, isolationists, accommodationists,* and *hardliners*.[115] Figure 12.3 displays the belief systems in each quadrant based on the intersection of these two continua.[116]

Internationalists support both cooperative and militant approaches to global affairs and are largely reflective of American attitudes prior to the Vietnam War. Both unilateral use of U.S. force and cooperative efforts through the United Nations find support among this segment of the public. In the Persian Gulf War of 1991, for example, internationalists likely supported both UN efforts to resolve the conflict over Kuwait and the use of U.S. and coalition forces to expel Iraq from Kuwait. With the Afghanistan War of 2001 or the Iraq War of 2003, internationalists probably supported initial involvement, but they would have supported withdrawal from Iraq and would also support a gradual withdrawal from Afghanistan.

Isolationists reject both cooperative internationalism and militant internationalism and favor a reduced role for the United States in global affairs. They would not have supported the use of force against Iraq in the Persian Gulf War, nor would they have believed that a vital interest was at stake over the seizure of Kuwait. Isolationists undoubtedly opposed the Bush administration's attack on Iraq in 2003, and they would have counseled for immediate withdrawal of U.S. troops. The same arguments would likely apply to addressing the war in Afghanistan. In their view, Iraq and Afghanistan posed no direct threat to America's interests.

Accommodationists favor cooperative internationalism and oppose militant internationalism. They would have supported the use of economic sanctions against Iraq over Kuwait in 1990 but would not have supported the use of force in early 1991. On Iraq, accommodationists would have preferred tightening sanctions against Saddam Hussein and more international inspections to uncover weapons of mass destruction in 2002–2003. They undoubtedly supported an immediate withdrawal of forces and

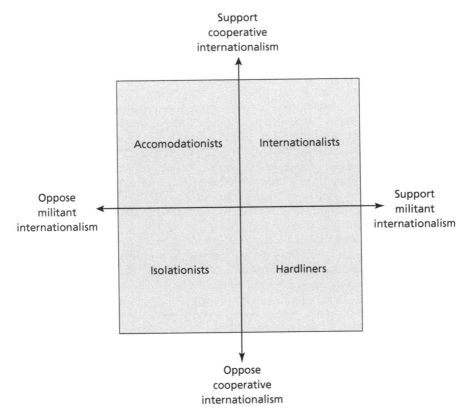

FIGURE 12.3 Distribution of the Public among Four Types of Foreign Policy
Belief Systems by Cooperative and Militant Internationalism

Source: Adapted from the diagram in Eugene R. Wittkopf, *Faces of Internationalism: Public Opinion and American Foreign Policy,* p. 26. Copyright @ 1990, Duke University Press. Reprinted by permission of the publisher.

greater reliance on the international community in Iraq reconstruction efforts. In Afghanistan, accommodationists would have preferred an international solution to the issue of international terrorism emanating from that country.

Hardliners favor militant internationalism and oppose cooperative internationalism. In the case of the Persian Gulf War, they undoubtedly supported the early use of force and preferred that option over diplomacy. They would have favored the initiation of the Iraq War. Hardliners also would have favored keeping American troops in Iraq until the situation improved. For Afghanistan, hardliners would have favored the "surge strategy" and would oppose any early withdrawal of American forces from that country.

Because these four underlying belief systems have been rather evenly distributed among the public,[117] they are important for understanding the nature of public attitudes toward foreign policy and for understanding how they might constrain policy makers for several different reasons. First, these belief systems are highly predictive of what *specific* policies these segments of the public will support. For example, over 80 percent of internationalists and over 60 percent of accommodationists were supporters of U.S.

participation in peacekeeping operations; isolationists and hardliners were not. Internationalists and accommodationists strongly supported continuing or increasing aid to Russia at the end of the Cold War; once again, hardliners and isolationists did not. In contemplating another kind of action in Europe—the use of American troops—internationalists and hardliners were the strongest proponents; accommodationists and isolationists were the weakest. Similarly, an overwhelming majority of both internationalists and hardliners strongly supported coming to the aid of Japan if it were invaded, but only a minority of accommodationists and isolationists did.[118] In this sense, these groups or coalition of groups may support or oppose particular policies of administration and hence serve as a constraint on foreign policy options.

Second, the four belief systems are closely tied and held together by a number of other sociopolitical characteristics of the American public. As such, they are deeply ingrained within the American political landscape and may persist for some time. In particular, the political ideology of an individual and his or her level of education are good predictors of where that individual falls along the two continua.[119] Political liberals, for instance, tend to be accommodationists, political conservatives tend to be hardliners, and political moderates tend to be internationalists. College-educated individuals tend to be both internationalists and accommodationists, those with a high school education tend to be both internationalists and hardliners, and those with less than a high school education tend to be hardliners. As one of Wittkopf's analyses reveals, respondents who "describe themselves as either very conservative or very liberal both reveal strong isolationist tendencies—the only political groups that do."[120]

The patterns are less clear-cut by region and party. The East is, by and large, composed of accommodationists; the Midwest and West fluctuate among accommodationists, internationalists, and hardliners; the South varies between hardliners and internationalists. Most interestingly, though, these belief systems are not closely tied to partisanship. Although there was some tendency for hardliners and internationalists to be Republicans and accommodationists and internationalists to be Democrats, the differences were sufficiently blurred across the parties to make accurate predictions difficult.

A more recent survey of studies analyzing the source and structure of foreign policy attitudes both specifies and partially supports Wittkopf's principal findings about the factors shaping these belief systems. After reviewing several studies of age, gender, race, education, party, and ideology as determinants of foreign policy attitudes, political scientist Ole Holsti concluded that "[T]he closely linked attributes of ideology and party identification consistently have been the most powerful correlates of attitudes on a wide range of foreign policy issues . . . ."[121] Thus, these two political variables are consistently important predictors for identifying and structuring the foreign policy beliefs of the American public.

Third, and in sum, because these divisions among belief systems exist and have been consistent over time, political leaders perhaps are now more constrained than some might argue. Foreign policy decision makers must now gauge which groups will support or oppose particular foreign policy actions and must calculate the acceptable limits of those actions. In any earlier era, if research findings are accurate portrayals of the public, the president, for example, did not have to make such calculations; instead, he could routinely count on public support. With these persistent divisions, though, that support is less assured.

Although recent Chicago Council surveys have not been analyzed in the same way that the earlier ones were,[122] there is reason to believe that the same underlying processes are still at work—at least as the events of September 11 recede somewhat—for at least two reasons. Public support for a vigorous U.S. response to the terrorist attacks cut across all four belief systems—except perhaps isolationists—but the situation appears to have changed for the Iraq and Afghanistan wars and their aftermath. For instance, public divisions between the so-called unilateralists and multilateralists over the proper direction for U.S. foreign policy incorporate the competing public belief systems just outlined. Support for the unilateralist position appears to be drawn from hardliners and internationalists, whereas support for multilateralists appears to be drawn from accommodationists and to a lesser extent from internationalists. Furthermore, with the overall decline in support, first for the Iraq War and now the Afghanistan Wars, the hardliners appear to be the only segment of the public that remains steadfast in support of the military option. In this sense, the public divisions over the direction of U.S. foreign policy seem to be continuing in the post–9/11 and the post-Iraq world.

Finally, another study informed by Wittkopf's work and other research on public opinion also found structure and stability in public beliefs regarding foreign policy. Through a careful analysis of the 2002 Chicago Council survey, Benjamin Page and Marshall Bouton demonstrate that Americans "hold coherent, *purposive belief systems* concerning foreign policy, which (when individuals' opinions are aggregated) contribute to the existence of a coherent and consistent set of policy preferences at the aggregate level."[123] Moreover, these belief systems are based on "sets of attitudes, beliefs, and orientations concerning world affairs," which in turn "are linked both logically and empirically with support for particular policy alternatives."[124] In short, structure and stability continue to characterize public opinion on foreign policy questions.

AN ALTERNATIVE VIEW OF THE PUBLIC MOOD

If we take this initial conclusion about public's restraints on policy makers one step further, we can begin to suggest a somewhat larger role for the "public mood" in the policy process. Bernard Cohen and V. O. Key, writing separately shortly after Almond's initial work on the public "mood" and foreign policy, suggest as much with their concepts of "climate of opinion" and the "context of public opinion."

Bernard Cohen introduced the concept of "**climate of opinion**" to summarize the public's view on foreign policy actions. This notion refers to the decision-making environment that, "by creating in the policymaker an impression of a public attitude or attitudes, or by becoming part of the environment and cultural milieu that help to shape his own thinking, may consciously affect his official behavior."[125] A few years later, V. O. Key expanded this notion by introducing what he called the "**context of public opinion**," which suggests how the public's overall views can affect government action, including foreign policy. Key's description of this concept and how it operates are worth quoting at some length:

> That context is not a rigid matrix that fixes a precise form for government action. Nor is it unchangeable. It consists of opinion irregularly distributed among the people and of varying intensity, of attitudes of differing convertibility into votes, and of sentiments not always readily capable of appraisal. Yet that context, as it is perceived by those responsible for action, conditions many of the acts of those who must make what we may call "opinion-related decisions." The opinion context may affect the substance of action, the form of action, or the manner of action.[126]

These alternate views of the "public mood" suggest that the foreign policy opinions of the American people form a part of the political milieu. In this way, they might be thought of as setting the broad outlines of "acceptable" policy without necessarily dictating the day-to-day policy choices of decision makers. Thus, gauging the public mood, and acting within its constraints, becomes an important task for successful policy makers. A brief survey of recent public moods or climates of opinion, gleaned from several sources, will illustrate their relationship to, and impact on, American foreign policy. It must be kept in mind, however, that policy makers will try to alter or adjust that public mood to their liking, much as Almond and others have suggested.

The Cold War Mood During the height of the Cold War, **the public expressed strong support for an active American role in global affairs.** This support was also quite predictive of public commitment to the Marshall Plan, NATO, and the use of military action to stop communism. In fact, after examining a number of public opinion polls for the late 1940s through the early 1960s, political scientist William Caspary concluded that the American public demonstrated a "*strong* and *stable* 'permissive mood' toward international involvements."[127] Another analyst saw the Cold War period as one in which "policymakers became imprisoned by popular anticommunism even though, in most cases, [they] were too sophisticated really to share the popular perspective."[128] Thus, the values of the postwar consensus (see Chapter 2) were firmly embedded in the minds of the public and policy makers alike and largely shaped the policy choices.

The "Vietnam Syndrome" The "searing effects" of the Vietnam War on the beliefs of the American public toward international affairs have also been widely analyzed.[129] **In the immediate post-Vietnam period, for instance, there was a decided turn inward on several important dimensions of foreign and military involvement.** In late 1974, roughly one-third of the American public favored a cutback in the defense budget, and over 50 percent believed that "we should build up our own defenses and let the world take care of itself."[130] In addition, there was considerable public aversion to sending U.S. troops to support friendly nations that had been attacked or even to providing them military and economic aid. Only in the case of an attack on Canada did a majority of the public (77 percent) support American military involvement. Support for military and economic aid to help friendly countries that had been attacked was equally low—only 37 percent. Finally, the American public favored a cutback in military aid and opposed CIA political operations, presumably because these options further involved the United States abroad.

Although the public mood tended to reject an active military and political involvement in international affairs in the immediate post-Vietnam period, this should not imply an abandonment of an "active role" for the United States in world affairs. In fact, 66 percent of the public still supported a continued global role for the United States but in a different form than that prescribed by the Cold War consensus. When asked to rank the importance of a variety of goals for the United States, the public placed greatest importance on keeping the peace and promoting and defending America's security. Next, however, the public indicated that the United States should concentrate on a large number of domestic and global economic problems, such as securing adequate energy supplies, protecting American jobs, and solving global food, inflation, and energy problems. Most important, perhaps, the traditional goals of the Cold War period, such as containing communism, defending allies, and helping to spread democracy and capitalism abroad, were ranked relatively low. This mood seemed to have a dampening effect on the actions of both the Ford and Carter administrations, sharply reducing their ability to use force and to intervene globally. The Ford administration, for example, was unable to win any public (or congressional) support for last-minute aid to South Vietnam and Cambodia prior to their collapse in 1975 or for vigorous action on behalf of the National Front for the Liberation of Angola in its struggle with the Soviet-backed Popular Movement for the Liberation of Angola. Given this foreign policy mood, the appeal of Carter's presidential candidacy is quite understandable. With his call for an emphasis on global issues that downplayed the East–West dispute, and for universal human rights, Carter fit the public mood in the mid-1970s.

The "Self-Interest" Mood[131] The public mood changed somewhat by the late 1970s, especially as the relationship between the United States and the Soviet Union began to deteriorate during the second and third years of the Carter administration. Indeed, there was an increased perception of a Soviet threat. By one analysis, concern over the power of the Soviet Union had replaced Vietnam as the "central preoccupation of American foreign policy."[132] As a result, the public mood began to move away, albeit slowly, from the limits of the Vietnam syndrome.

The public was now more willing to increase defense expenditures, support American military actions abroad, and tolerate CIA activities in other nations.[133] At the same time, there was a **certain amount of ambivalence about any rekindling of past crusading efforts on the part of the United States**. Although some Cold War goals (such as protecting allies and containing communism) had increased in importance from their 1974 levels, the domestic and foreign economic concerns remained most important for the American public (such as "keeping up the value of the dollar," "securing adequate supplies of energy," and "protecting the jobs of American workers").[134]

This ambivalence was especially visible in the mixed reaction to the Soviet Union. Although 56 percent of the public believed that the United States was "falling behind the Soviet Union in power and influence," as a whole, it remained committed to greater cooperation through joint energy efforts, joint scholarly exchanges, and arms limitations.[135] In short, sentiment for détente was in place, especially among the attentive public.[136]

In sum, by the late 1970s, the public mood was for a more "self-interested" and nationalistic foreign policy than in 1974. Furthermore, the public continued to be "wary of direct involvement that characterized United States policy in the 1960s," but it remained determined to defend important commitments in the world.[137]

The Public Mood in the 1980s The public mood of the 1980s changed little from that of the late 1970s. The Reagan administration, however, adopted some policies that were at variance with it.

Foreign policy goals, as expressed in two national polls conducted in late 1982 and late 1986, remained essentially the same as in 1978.[138] Global and domestic economic concerns continued to have the highest priority, whereas containing communism and defending allies still ranked somewhat lower. At the same time, the public expressed a slight increase in support for interventionism. On the question of the Soviet Union in 1982 and 1986, the public remained ambivalent, much as it had earlier. Although the Soviet Union came in last or second to last of any nation (after Iran) when states were ranked on a "thermometer scale," the public remained committed to seeking better ties with it.[139]

This public mood generally clashed with the priorities of the Reagan administration, especially during its first term.[140] President Reagan brought back some of the rhetoric and policies of the Cold War consensus, but the public opposed several of them. For example, the administration wanted to increase defense spending and engage in a defense buildup; the public was content to keep the budget as it was and seek arms control agreements instead. The administration also wanted a more confrontational policy toward the Soviet Union; the public wanted more cooperative exchanges with it. The administration wanted to increase military assistance; the public, by a wide margin, continued to oppose such aid. Such disagreements between the public mood and public policy undoubtedly put some restraints on Reagan's plans for foreign policy. In this sense, they contributed to a political climate that ultimately facilitated accommodation with the Soviet Union on the one hand and constrained the policy course pursued toward Nicaragua on the other.

The Public Mood in the 1990s The repercussions from the dramatic events of 1989–1991 (the fall of the Berlin Wall, the emergence of democracy in Eastern Europe, the unification of Germany, the Iraqi invasion of Kuwait, and the collapse of the Soviet Union) caused the public mood to evolve into what has been described as **"pragmatic internationalism"** and later as **"guarded engagement."**[141] About two-thirds of the public remained committed to an active role for the United States in global affairs, but Americans continued to be more concerned about domestic economic and social problems than foreign policy and appeared less willing to intervene in the affairs of other states. The public did not reject global leadership, but it sought a greater sharing of it through multilateral organizations, and it wanted the United States to be more selective in the actions it took abroad.

Perhaps a better indicator of the public's mood toward international affairs during this period was where individuals believed that American interests lay. Interestingly, Russia held an important place after the Cold War, although the public still viewed that country with both friendliness and wariness. Russia was viewed in a more favorable light than in the past, but even as the public expressed these views, a substantial majority (81 percent in 1994) believed "that the military power of Russia represents either a critical or an important possible threat to the vital interests of the United States in the next 10 years."[142]

In other ways, though, the post–Cold War era evoked different priorities. In 1994, the public ranked Japan, Saudi Arabia, Kuwait, and Mexico as vital interests. Japan remained an important ally in a region of increasing problems, but its economic competitiveness continued to be a concern.[143] Saudi Arabia and Kuwait also ranked as vital interests owing to their vast supply of oil, their proximity to troublesome states in the Middle East—Iran and Iraq—and questions about their domestic political stability. Mexico, too, emerged as a vital interest, not only because it borders the United States but also because, with the North American Free Trade Agreement in effect, its fortunes were linked with those of America as never before. By mid-decade, China emerged as a vital interest—almost three-fifths of the public viewed its emergence as a world power as a "critical" threat and two-thirds believed that its significance in global affairs was growing.[144] By the end of the decade, Great Britain, Germany, Russia, Japan, Israel, and China, among a few others, were viewed as being in the vital interest of the United States, with Europe generally more crucial than Asia.

Several traditional security concerns continued, and the public remained cautious about American interventions abroad. Indeed, on defense spending, the public's views stabilized, with general support for increasing or maintaining it and for maintaining America's NATO commitment.[145] The public also reiterated its commitment to multilateralism in efforts abroad and looked warily on the use of force. At the same time, though, a majority expressed support for a range of options to address international terrorism, from diplomacy to closing terrorist camps to using military air strikes against such facilities. Moreover, a majority supported "assassination of individual terrorist leaders." In short, the public remained cautious and selective about where it would support the use of American military force abroad, but, and perhaps foreshadowing the post–9/11 period, supported vigorous actions against international terrorism.

The Post–September 11/Iraq War Mood[146] Immediately after September 11, the public seemed to shift in several significant ways to a mood that has been described as "**refocused internationalism**"—that is, an internationalism "refocused on containing and defeating the international threat."[147] Significantly, of course, the focus was on international terrorism, but it was also concerned with the threats posed by other nations obtaining nuclear weapons and the dangers posed by the spread of chemical and biological weapons. This sense of threat among the public diminished in the 2004 and 2006 Chicago Council surveys, but the public continued to view terrorism, the potential acquisition of nuclear weapons by other states, and weapons of mass destruction as "critical threats" to U.S. vital interests.[148]

Despite this sense of threat, the public's commitment to internationalism after 9/11 and with the onset of the Iraq War and beyond continued at remarkably high levels. Seventy-one percent in 2002, 67 percent in 2004, and 69 percent in 2006 were committed to an "active role in world affairs."[149] Although international terrorism largely ranked as the dominant threat and issue during this period, the public continued to identify several other foreign policy goals as "very important"—and these were goals that had generally been on its agenda for several decades: "Protecting the jobs of American workers," "preventing the spread of nuclear weapons," "securing adequate supplies of energy," and "promoting economic growth."[150]

One change in public attitudes after 9/11, however, was the increased level of public support for American military power, although the intensity of that support seemingly weakened by 2006 in light of the Iraq War.[151] Even as the American public indicated a willingness to support a more activist and militant approach to the international system, it also remained strongly committed to multilateralism in the years immediately after 9/11 and during the Iraq War. A very large percentage of the American people (about 75 percent) opposed a U.S. role of "world policeman."[152] Instead, most (about 78 and 75 percent in 2004 and 2006, respectively) supported a multilateral approach.[153] Furthermore, they remained supportive of international institutions (such as the United Nations, the World Trade Organization), international agreements, and the use of diplomatic measures, and they believed that the United States should abide by the decisions of the international organizations, even if they were not the ones most favored by the American government.[154]

Attitudes toward the global economy changed only slightly after September 11, and they remained largely the same during the Iraq War. The American people still viewed globalization as "mostly good," but international trade as an admixture of good and bad.[155] A majority of Americans in 2006 believed that international trade raises the American standard of living and helps the economy and U.S. companies. They also believed that it was bad for the environment, for American jobs, and for

American security. However, the public did not opt for protectionism, but, rather, largely supported more assistance to those displaced by the impact of globalization.[156] Immigration also became an issue of concern for the American public, but it was largely tied to attitudes about job security and possible terrorism.[157]

A Mood of "Constrained Internationalism" By the end of the first decade of the twenty-first century, the public mood on foreign policy evolved from what is was only a decade earlier, despite the lingering impact of the events of 9/11. With the continuing recession that had begun in 2008, the explosion of government debt in subsequent years, the continuing war in Afghanistan, and the rise of other states in the international system, the American public by 2010 began to "scale back their ambitions and become more selective in what they will support in terms of blood and treasure." In this sense, as the 2010 Chicago Council on Global Affairs labels it, the mood of American public is toward a "constrained internationalism."[158]

To be sure, the American public (with a 67 percent majority) continues to believe that the United States should "take an active part in world affairs," a level of support consistent with the public's view over the past several decades. At the same time, the public now perceives that the U.S. influence has eroded (especially in comparison with China), that American power has been constrained by unresolved international problems (and the U.S. inability to make headway on them) and by the severe economic problems at home. In fact, only 24 percent of the public "think the United States plays a more important and powerful role as a world leader [in 2010] compared to ten years ago."[159] As a result, the American public are "fairly accepting of the prospect of the United States playing a less dominant role" and more supportive of "more selective engagement" abroad. In this sense, the public provides the most support to threats perceived as vital to America's national interest (such as international terrorism, nuclear proliferation) and that involve "low-risk, low-cost humanitarian actions" (such as stopping a government from committing genocide).[160]

The public, however, also appears to want "to selectively scale back ambitions internationally." This change is most evident in the degree of support for long-term military basing commitments around the world, but it is also evident in the desire for the United States not to become involved in a conflict that does not directly threaten the country (such as possible conflict between Iran and Israel, confrontations between North and South Korea, and the promotion of democracy in a Muslim country).[161] This more constrained mood among the public has also led to a somewhat reduced support for "upgrading international institutions." That is, a rather sharp drop in support has occurred for strengthening the United Nations and the World Health Organization (WHO), even as majority support continued for such actions for both. On the other hand, pluralities of the public now oppose the strengthening of the World Trade Organization, the World Bank, and the International Monetary Fund. Even as the public takes a more skeptical view of strengthening these organizations, majorities still support taking actions through the United Nations to address a variety of problems (investigating human rights violations, creating an international marshals service to apprehend those responsible for genocide, or using the United Nations to "control nuclear fuel" or "to regulate the international sale of arms," for example).[162]

In short, the current mood is not abandoning an international role for the United States. Instead, it calls for lessening U.S. involvement on some issues, being more "selective" on others, and utilizing multilateral actions on still others.

Evidence of Stability and Consistency in Public Opinion

As these summaries suggest, the public mood does change over time, but it seems to do so in reasonable and predictable ways. Yet, several researchers have found that the public remains equally "coherent," "consistent," and "stable" when considering several salient issues. Shapiro and Page are leading proponents of this view, and their work is worth citing in some detail.

In an important analysis, for example, these scholars report that, "the proportions of Americans thinking the United States should sell arms varied markedly from one country to another" from 1975 to 1985, yet they also contend that this variation always occurred in a coherent way.[163] Whereas sales to some countries (such as England and West Germany) received more support than sales to others (such as Greece, Turkey, and Iran), the patterns were markedly the same or consistent across the years. A similar consistency occurred regarding aid to El Salvador during the early to middle 1980s. Support for and opposition to foreign aid generally, the building of the MX missile in the 1980s, free trade, and other foreign policy issues exhibit the same stability over different time periods. Thus, Shapiro and Page conclude that "Stability is the rule for foreign as well as domestic issues. When opinion changes do occur, many do so quite gradually. . . ."[164] They add that Americans—even in the face of new information and new global conditions—"are regular, predictable, and generally sensible" in their opinions.[165]

In another context, several political scientists and analysts illustrate the consistency and stability of public opinion on a highly salient issue—the use of American military force abroad. In a detailed analysis of public opinion polls on nine different uses of American force in the 1980s and early 1990s (including the Persian Gulf War in 1990–1991), for example, Bruce Jentleson finds that public support or opposition is closely tied to the *"principal policy objective."* In instances of *"foreign policy restraint"*—the use of force to stop "aggressive actions against the United States or its interests"—public support is generally always higher than for instances of *"internal political change"*—the use of force to support a friendly government in power or to overthrow an unfriendly regime. Although those findings in themselves are of interest, the important implication for public opinion and foreign policy is that the public is not always swayed by presidential leadership and is not "as boorish, overreactive, and generally the bane of those who would pursue an effective foreign policy." Instead, Jentleson says, the public is "pretty prudent" and, we might add, pretty consistent in its foreign policy beliefs.[166]

Another study by Andrew Kohut and Robert Toth focused exclusively on the early to middle 1990s, including the Gulf War, Somalia, and Bosnia, and also generally found that public opinion on the use of force was consistent. In particular, Kohut and Toth report that the American public was willing to use force in only two situations: "[I]f it feels America's vital interests are at stake, and if American military force can provide humanitarian assistance without becoming engaged in a protracted conflict."[167] Once again, their analysis suggests that the policy objective is crucial (albeit a bit broader than what Jentleson found) to the level of support and that the public does not blindly follow its leaders (as it did not in the expansion of American involvement in Somalia in 1993). At the same time, they point out that the ability of leaders (such as President George H. W. Bush over the Persian Gulf) to explain their objectives to the American people is important in gaining support.[168]

Other studies also reveal the stability and consistency of the public regarding military action abroad. Political scientist John Mueller documented consistent support for what has come to be called the "casualty tolerance" hypothesis among the American public. He found that public support for the Korean and the Vietnam wars was closely linked to the number of American casualties. As casualties increased in those wars (albeit with a logarithmic function of the number of casualties related to the degree of support), public support declined. He demonstrated the same phenomenon for the Iraq War, although he points out that the casualty tolerance was even lower among the public for Iraq than Korea and Vietnam.[169] Other scholars have sought to specify this hypothesis by, for example, evaluating whether domestic elite support for a military mission weakens the relationship or whether the expectation of success has an impact on the relationship as well.[170] Still another recent study questions these event-based theories of public opinion on military action abroad. Instead, support or opposition in this view derives from domestic politics—and particularly the positions articulated by partisan elites on the current conflict. That is, the public tends to adopt the positions of their preferred Republican or Democratic partisans, and they thus in turn convey a sense of stability and consistency in their views as a result.[171]

Other research points to public opinion stability beyond political–military issues. Research on support for or opposition to trade and globalization points to consistency in public opinion on these topics as well. One study, for example, found that skilled workers are more likely to support trade liberalization and unskilled workers are more likely to oppose it. Apparently, skilled workers believe that they can compete successfully in such an environment, whereas unskilled workers are concerned about job security. A similar level of stability in opinion occurred when trade attitudes were analyzed for workers as a different kind of consumers. Those workers who are "consumers of exportable goods are more protectionists than those who tend to consume imports." In all, as one important analysis concluded, the "American voters have well-informed attitudes about international trade and . . . they ground these attitudes prudently in terms of the material consequences of trade for themselves and their families."[172]

A final example of the public's stability and consistency is its continuous **support for multilateralism** in addressing global problems. Indeed, the public has a long history of support for the United Nations since the inception of the quadrennial surveys conducted by The Chicago Council on Foreign Relations in 1974 and right through 1998—and that support has been much higher than that expressed by U.S. policy makers. What is interesting, however, is the continued support for multilateralism after September 11.[173] By 2010, there was some erosion in support for strengthening the United Nations, as we noted earlier, but the support for using a multilateral approach to solve global issues remained robust: 71 percent of Americans in a 2010 survey again supported the view that the United States "share in efforts to solve international problems together with other countries."[174]

THE IMPACT OF PUBLIC OPINION ON FOREIGN POLICY

One of the most difficult analytic tasks is to assess the overall effect of public opinion on foreign policy. Even if public opinion can be characterized as structured and stable, as we have suggested, some fundamental questions remain: How much difference does public opinion make in the foreign policy process? Are congressional and presidential elections mechanisms of popular control over foreign policy issues? Are the policy choices of Congress or the president really constrained by what the public thinks? In spite of recent analyses that provide partial answers, these questions remain important subjects of debate.

Foreign Policy Opinion and Presidential Elections

One way for public opinion to register an impact on foreign policy is through the electoral process, and especially through presidential elections. In this way, the electorate can use their votes to punish political candidates with unpopular foreign policy views and reward those with whom they agree. **Yet numerous analyses have raised doubts about whether presidential elections are true referenda on foreign policy.**

First, for example, presidential elections are rarely fought on foreign policy issues. Instead, domestic issues, and especially domestic economic issues, have dominated American presidential campaigns in the post–World War II years. By most assessments, only in 1952 and 1972 was foreign policy a central campaign issue between the candidates. Both of these elections, however, occurred during U.S. involvement in two highly unpopular wars, Korea and Vietnam. The 2004 presidential election probably should be added to this list because the Iraq War and global terrorism "formed an important backdrop" for that contest and "proved crucial for some voters." By one assessment, in fact, three in ten voters saw these kinds of foreign policy issues as the most important in the election.[175] In all, and noting these exceptions, the consensus has often been that foreign policy is not crucial for presidential elections.

Second, even when foreign policy might be an issue in a presidential election, the stances of the candidates are not sufficiently different for the public to distinguish between them. In the 1968 presidential campaign, for example, the Vietnam War was an issue, but candidates Nixon and Humphrey were not perceived to be markedly different in their positions on it.[176] As a result, foreign policy did not turn out to be decisive in how the public voted in that campaign.

Even if the public views foreign policy as salient, its overall effect on the election outcome is quite small. In a classic analysis on this point, Warren Miller reported that the decline in support for Republican candidates from 1956 to 1960 based on their respective foreign policy stances was minuscule—one-half of 1 percent. Thus, instead of Republicans having a 2.5 percent vote advantage because of their foreign policy position in 1956, they had only a 2 percent advantage in 1960.[177] Two decades later, in the 1980 contest between Carter and Reagan, a similar small effect was reported. Despite the popular impression that the Iran hostage situation would severely hurt Carter's reelection prospects, a careful analysis of voting behavior in that election found otherwise. Reagan's issue position on foreign and domestic matters produced a difference in the vote outcome of only about 1 percent. Instead, the voters' decisions were more fully related to overall dissatisfaction with President Carter's performance in office and to their doubts "about his competence as a political leader."[178]

Left unanswered by these and similar analyses, however, is whether even these small differences between the candidates in the aggregate affected the outcome in *particular states*, and hence the *electoral votes* of one presidential candidate over the other. Especially in a close national election, such as the one between Kennedy and Nixon in 1960, in which less than one percentage point separated the candidates, foreign policy opinion may have mattered. More recently, of course, it may have mattered in the 2000 presidential election, especially in key states such as Florida. Put more precisely, in close state votes, a swing of even a few percentage points can dramatically affect the national electoral vote count. To date, however, detailed state studies of presidential elections, including the role of foreign policy issues, are not available to answer such questions.

Also left unanswered by these analyses is whether the foreign policy of incumbents contributes to an image of competence or incompetence that can affect the outcome of elections. Although specific foreign policy opinion may not be a central factor in voting decisions, presidential actions in the global arena can convey a general impression of effectiveness. This seems to fit what happened in 1980, when President Carter's inability to manage foreign affairs probably hurt him at the polls. In this (albeit indirect) way, foreign policy mattered. Conversely, President Clinton seemingly sought to be "Peacemaker in Chief" with his actions in Haiti, Bosnia, and Northern Ireland. By taking these actions, according to one analysis, the "president hope[d] to do well with voters by doing good on the international stage."[179] The presidential election of 2004 surely revolved in part around the ability of the candidates to deal with global security in the face of international terrorism;[180] the principal party candidates in 2008 vied to convey competence on national security as well; and President Obama in the 2012 election campaign sought to utilize the killing of Osama bin Laden, the use of drone attacks against terrorists, and perhaps the leaking of information about the cyber attacks on Iran (albeit denied by the administration) to portray a sense of foreign policy effectiveness to the public. (By contrast, too much emphasis by an incumbent president or a challenger on foreign affairs may also have an effect electorally. In 1992, President Bush's perceived excessive attention on foreign affairs, and his perceived inattention to domestic policy, proved costly among voters.)

Over the past decade or two, and especially since 9/11 and the onset of the Iraq War, however, **research studies have begun to reconsider the relationship between foreign policy opinion and presidential elections**. One analysis suggests that when candidate differences are large and foreign policy issues are salient, the public's views do affect election outcomes. These conditions not only existed in 1952 and 1972, as has been noted, but also were prevalent in 1964, 1980, and 1984,[181] when public opinion probably did make a difference. Voters could see differences between the candidates, and these differences influenced voting decisions.

More recent analyses by political scientist Miroslav Nincic argue that foreign policy matters both directly and indirectly in presidential elections. In a direct way, foreign policy mattered because about 10 percent of the public identified "foreign affairs" as the most important issue in their voting decisions in the 1988 and 2000 elections.[182] In the 2004 election, Nincic reports that "*fully half of the electorate* considered foreign policy the most important influence on their presidential voting decision."[183] By the 2008 election, the percentage of the public who viewed foreign policy issues as most crucial to their voting decision had returned to "10-15 percent of U.S. voters." Nincic thus argues that foreign policy can be important in all types of presidential elections. He makes this point in this way: "During halcyon times, foreign policy can affect the electoral balance in a tight election; in troubled time, it may play a decisive role."[184] In an indirect way, as suggested by our earlier discussion, Nincic argued that a candidate's stance on foreign affairs "can create an impression of leadership, decisiveness, and forcefulness" to the American people.[185] If a candidate can convey a familiarity with the issues and a degree of confidence in dealing with them, he or she can gain public acceptance and support. In this way, too, the public's view of a candidate or his/her party may affect electoral outcomes.

Two recent studies of the impact of the Iraq War on presidential voting in 2004 reinforce Nincic's results. A study by Christopher Gelpi, Peter Feaver, and Jason Reifler reveals "that about one-third of the voters stated that foreign policy issues were the most important factor in determining their vote choice." A related study by the same authors also found that "attitudes toward the Iraq war had a substantial impact on vote choice—more substantial than their attitudes regarding which candidate would be more effective in handling the economy or social issues."[186]

Foreign Policy Opinion and Congressional Elections

Congressional elections are rarely considered referenda on foreign policy questions. This is particularly true for the House of Representatives, and only occasionally are foreign policy questions salient in U.S. Senate races. In both instances, the foreign policy positions of candidates are likely to be marginal to their campaigns.

Still, foreign policy may play a role in these elections in some negative and positive ways. On the one hand, if an incumbent is perceived as too involved in foreign affairs or spends too much time on them, he or she could be subject to electoral punishment for neglecting the "folks back home." When Congressman Frank McCloskey (D-Indiana) appeared to focus more on global human rights than on his district, his Republican opponent seized on this perception and defeated him in 1994. The *Indianapolis Star* summed up McCloskey's defeat in this way: "Hoosiers were much more interested in local events than the problems of a region half a world away."[187]

On the other hand, congressional candidates in their state or district often make sure to be on the "right" side of particular foreign affairs issues in order to avoid electoral punishment. Those from districts or states with substantial military installations are unlikely to oppose military spending; candidates with large Jewish constituencies are likely to be very supportive of Israel; and candidates from south Florida districts, for example, are likely to be strongly opposed to any compromise policy with Fidel Castro. It was perhaps no accident that in the 1990s, a Democratic congressman and later senator from New Jersey, which has a large Hispanic population, was a leading proponent of a tougher policy toward Cuba.

On occasion, too, foreign policy issues may take on an important *symbolic* importance in congressional races, even if their substantive importance is less clear. A special congressional election in Oklahoma in May 1994 makes this point.[188] In this race, the Democratic candidate stated that he did not object to UN command of American troops in a peacekeeping operation. How important or salient this issue was to Oklahoma congressional voters is unclear (although large percentages, when asked, said they opposed this position), but the Republican candidate seized on his opponent's statement to portray him as out of touch with voters of his home state. Through a mailing that targeted a particularly sensitive group (in this case, young Republicans), he was able to spark interest and concern over this foreign policy issue among voters who responded. In this way, the issue of foreign command of U.S. troops assumed a much greater importance than its substance warranted, and the Republican candidate was able to paint his opponent as too closely tied to Washington and the Clinton administration and not sufficiently tied to Oklahomans.

At least two recent congressional elections point to the significant effect of foreign policy on voting outcomes. In the 2002 congressional elections, for example, security matters were at least partially on the minds of the American voters.[189] One national poll in that year found that "fully 46 percent [of the public] would be guided by foreign policy and national security issues, such as terrorism and the war in Afghanistan."[190] President Bush took advantage of these foreign policy concerns by campaigning in key congressional districts and key states to maintain his party's control of the House of Representatives and to regain control of the Senate. Some analysts saw his campaigning on national security issues in closely contested states and districts as partly responsible for his party's success.

In the 2006 congressional elections, foreign policy made an even greater difference in voting outcomes. As political scientist Gary Jacobson argues, "the primary source of the pro-Democratic tide in 2006 was public unhappiness with the Iraq War and its originator, George W. Bush."[191] Importantly, Jacobson's analyses demonstrate empirically that trends in support for the war and in presidential popularity closely tracked each other: as support for the war declined, so did presidential popularity. Furthermore, Jacobson shows that these two factors—support or opposition to the war and approval or disapproval of President Bush—were closely related to how Republicans, Democrats, and independents voted in the 2006 congressional elections in both the House and the Senate. Although other factors affected voters' choices, approval or disapproval of the Iraq War was highly significant.[192]

In sum, although analysts generally do not characterize congressional elections as foreign policy referenda, the particular context of such elections can *occasionally* render foreign policy issues central to their outcome.

Foreign Policy Opinion and Policy Choices

If it is difficult to argue that elections are *routinely* referenda on foreign policy opinion, it is perhaps even more difficult to sustain the view that foreign policy opinion shapes particular policy choices. Only in rare instances, for example, when the public has been mobilized by the president via a nationwide television address or by particular interest groups over an upcoming vote in Congress, does public opinion seem to matter in an immediate foreign policy decision facing the country. Rather, the **effect of public opinion on individual policy decisions appears to be sporadic and exceptional**.

The last four decades witnessed examples of such sporadic events, although the public's success in controlling their outcomes was mixed. In the late 1970s, public opinion, as expressed in various polls, was strongly opposed to the return of the Panama Canal to Panama by the year 2000. As a result, President Carter had a difficult time gaining Senate approval for the treaties that would accomplish this. Despite his initial opposition to any changes in the treaties, he was forced to accept several understandings and amendments to make them more acceptable at home. He was also forced to lobby hard for their passage in the Senate, and even then, he barely squeaked out the required two-thirds majority, 68–32. Although public opinion did not ultimately stop these treaties, it affected the nature of the debate and their final provisions.

President Reagan had a similar experience over the issue of aid to the Nicaraguan Contras. He appealed several times on nationwide television for public support for increased Contra funding, but he was not always successful in obtaining it. Indeed, in the aggregate, public opinion remained opposed, and Congress generally gave him much less than he asked for. In this particular case, more than in the Panama Canal debate, public opinion ultimately contributed to a change in policy course by the Reagan administration and later by the Bush administration.

Two recent studies examining a series of cases over several decades came to different conclusions about the overall effect of public opinion on foreign policy. In an examination of Vietnam in the 1960s and 1970s, Nicaragua in the 1980s, and the Gulf War and Bosnia in the 1990s, Richard Sobel concluded, "public opinion . . . constrained the decision-making process."[193] That effect was often manifested more in policy restraint (that is, eliminating options for decision makers) than in policy setting (that is, prescribing precise options). Furthermore, Sobel argues, public opinion is now playing an "increasing role . . . in foreign policymaking."

By contrast, Douglas Foyle, examining a longer time frame and more cases extending from Harry Truman through Clinton,[194] came to a more cautious conclusion than Sobel's. He concluded that "the public's influence can be *generally* described as no-impact or constraint during crises and elite efforts to lead public opinion on longer-term decisions." Ultimately, though, the impact of public opinion is a function of the policy makers' belief systems and particular policy context—that is, how receptive policy makers are to public opinion and how the decision setting allows the public to influence policy. Among recent presidents, for example, President Clinton was receptive to public opinion and that opinion in turn affected his policy response to Somalia and Bosnia; President Reagan tended to reject the importance of public opinion in policy making or of responding to it, as his actions demonstrated in the withdrawal of marines from Lebanon in 1983 and in the announcement of the Strategic Defense Initiative that same year.

Political scientists Page and Shapiro, to whom we referred earlier, also provide important insights on the long-term trends in the relationship between the public and their leaders. In their massive analysis of the directional changes in public opinion and public policy over five decades (1935 to 1979), they sought to answer a central question: When public opinion moved in one direction on an issue, did public policy follow? What they found was that **policy changes generally *did* follow the direction of opinion in both domestic and foreign affairs** in the period of their analysis. In particular, policy and opinion were congruent in 62 percent of the cases examined. Further, policy really did seem to follow opinion rather than the other way around. As they conclude, "it is reasonable in most of these cases to infer that opinion change was a *cause* of policy change, or at least a proximate or intervening factor leading to government action, if not the ultimate cause."[195] Nonetheless, they acknowledge that their analysis could not and did not answer how much opinion was affected by the efforts of politicians and interest groups. Although normatively optimistic about the effect of public opinion on policy formation, they caution that not all intervening linkages between opinion and policy have been fully explored.

In his examination of the impact of public opinion on arms control, however, political scientist Thomas Graham has begun to specify these linkages. He identifies four factors necessary for public opinion to affect foreign policy making at the executive and congressional level.[196] First, the magnitude of public opinion on a foreign policy issue must be substantial. He estimates that "public opinion must reach at least consensus levels (60 percent and higher) before it begins to have a discernible effect on decision making."[197] Second, public opinion can be most effective when it succeeds in placing an issue on the decision-making agenda (such as public support for arms control talks) and during the ratification process (such as support or opposition to arms control treaties). Third, the effectiveness of public opinion is contingent on political elites evaluating and understanding the public's view. In Graham's view, it is the level of understanding by the executive, not the public, that poses a formidable barrier to policy impact. Fourth, the president or the political elites must be effective in translating the public's views into "articulate themes" that reinforce or elicit public support. Graham concludes that although these factors pose problems for the impact of public opinion, "public opinion has had a significant impact on decision making for several decades, and it can be documented as far back as Franklin D. Roosevelt."[198]

After a comprehensive review of public opinion and foreign policy studies over the past several decades, political scientist Ole Holsti concluded that more work is needed to assess the causal linkage between public opinion and policy outcome. He also noted that "case studies employing archival research, interviews with policymakers, or both, are virtually indispensable for assessing the impact of public opinion."[199] As Holsti also reminds us, we need further research on whether policy makers perceive public opinion on particular issues, whether they are affected by such views, and how such views impact the policy decisions they make.

Analyses by political scientist Philip Powlick also provide some sense of the work that remains to be done—and the challenge that public opinion still faces in the policy arena. Powlick assessed the attention that foreign policy makers in Washington were paying to public opinion and found that National Security Council staffers and State Department officials generally held a skeptical view of the public's knowledge and sophistication but were receptive to incorporating public opinion into the foreign policy process.[200] As he reported: "Among the foreign policy officials interviewed for this study, the notion that public support of policy is a sine qua non—and that it must therefore be a major factor in policy decisions—is so widespread as to suggest the existence of a 'norm' within the bureaucratic subculture."[201] These officials, however, often rely on Congress, the news media, interest groups, and other elites to gauge "public opinion," rather than "unmediated opinion" (for example, public opinion polls) alone. Thus, although the amount of unmediated opinion transmitted to the policy makers appears to be greater than in earlier decades, and public opinion appears to be more important as well, the level of "filtered" opinion remains an obstacle for sustained public impact. As a result, foreign policy makers can "justify their policy decisions as having been made after taking public opinion into account, whether or not such decisions necessarily reflect the opinions of the mass public."[202]

CONCLUDING COMMENTS

Both the media and the foreign policy opinions of the American people play a part in the making of U.S. foreign policy. Some characterize the media as both separate actors and critics, others see them as accomplices of government, and still others view them as vying with governmental officials to serve their own purposes. This last view appears to best describe the media's true role. Furthermore, although the media have an important impact on how the public views global affairs, the public makes its own independent assessment of foreign policy actions.

Public opinion matters in shaping foreign policy, but the magnitude of its impact remains a source of debate. One view sees it as "moodish," relatively shiftable, and subject to leadership from the top; another sees it as structured and relatively stable and capable of setting limits on executive (or even congressional) action. Differing views also exist on the overall influence of public opinion on specific foreign policy decisions and on general policies adopted by the government. Although its continuous impact on presidential and congressional elections remains unclear, it may be crucial to electoral outcomes in particular contexts. In short, then, the precise impact of public opinion on foreign policy may still be debated, but the fact remains that political leaders, or those who hope to become leaders, cannot (and do not) wholly ignore the public's views—even on seemingly distant foreign policy issues.

Notes

1. The earlier comparison data are from previous editions of this book. The recent data on the media reported here are taken from the U.S. Bureau of the Census, 2012 *Statistical Abstract of the United States* (Washington, D.C., 2012), Table 1132, at http://www.census .gov/compendia/statab/2012/tables/12s1132.pdf, July 8, 2012. The change percentages were calculated by the author.

2. Ibid., Table 1135, for the decline in newspaper circulation in recent years as well as the comparison with 1980. The percentage change was calculated by the author. Also see David D. Newsom, *The Public Dimension of Foreign Policy* (Bloomington and Indianapolis: Indiana University Press, 1996), pp. 45 and 240, note 3, for information on media size and coverage.

3. For a list of the top ten newspaper companies in 2009 and 2010, see Bradley Johnson, "100 Leading Media Companies," *Advertising Age* 82 (October 3, 2011), pp. 44–54.

4. The 2012 *Statistical Abstract of the United States*, Table 1135.

5. See Table 1392 in The 2012 Statistical Abstract—U.S. Census Bureau, "Telecommunications, Computers," at http://www.census.gov/compendia/statab/2012/tables/12s1392 .pdf, July 18, 2012.

6. The title of the section and the initial information draws from "Old News Ain't Beat Yet," *The Economist*, May 18, 1996, 32.

7. Emily Guskin and Tom Rosenstiel, "Network: By the Numbers," The Pew Research Center's Project for Excellence in Journalism, The State of the News Media 2012, at http://stateofthemedia.org/2012/network-news-the-pace-of-change-accelerates/ network-by-the-numbers/http, July 10, 2012.

8. See ibid., for the latest data. See "Old News Ain't Beat Yet," and *Americans Lack Background to Follow International News: Public's News Habits Little Changed by Sept. 11* (Washington, D.C.: The Pew Research Center for the People and the Press, 2002), pp. 1–4, for the earlier data.

9. Pew Research Center for the People and the Press, "Americans Spending More Time Following the News," September 12, 2010, at http://www.people-press.org/ 2010/09/12/americans-spending-more-time-following-the-news/, July 10, 2012.

10. Ibid.

11. The data in this paragraph are taken from the discussion and analysis in Amy Mitchell, Tom Rosenstiel, and Leah Christian, "Mobile Devices and News Consumption: Some Good Signs for Journalism," *The State of the News Media 2012,* at http://stateofthemedia.org/2012/mobile-devices-and-news-consumption-some-good-signs-for-journalism/, July 9, 2012.

12. See "Old News Ain't Beat Yet" and *Americans Lack Background to Follow International News,* but also see Mitchell, Rosenstiel, and Christian, "Mobile Devices and News Consumption: Some Good Signs for Journalism," which notes that even those who use digital devices for news usually rely on the sites of established news organizations.

13. Pew Research Center's Project for Excellence in Journalism, "The Year in News 2011: Coverage of Economy and International News Jump in a Year of Major Breaking Stories," at http://journalism.org/print/27799, July 12, 2012.

14. Matthew A. Baum, *Soft News Goes to War: Public Opinion and American Foreign Policy in the New Media Age* (Princeton: Princeton University Press, 2003), p 13. Emphasis in original. This volume outlines how soft news sources provide foreign policy information to the public, particularly the so-called inattentive public.

15. For an early analysis of different roles of the press in the foreign policy process, see Bernard Cohen, *The Press and Foreign Policy* (Princeton, NJ: Princeton University Press, 1963), pp. 4–5; for a more recent analysis, see John T. Rourke, Ralph G. Carter, and Mark A. Boyer, *Making American Foreign Policy* (Guilford, CT: The Dushkin Publishing Group, 1994), pp. 338–354. Another study that identifies the first two roles and analyzes them for the *New York Times* can be found in Nicholas O. Berry, *Foreign Policy and the Press* (Westport, CT: Greenwood Press, 1990). Also see Bill Kovach, "Do the News Media Make Foreign Policy?" *Foreign Policy* 102 (Spring 1996): 169–179. All of these studies aided our thinking about these roles.

16. It is not an accident that the Communications Center at the Department of State in Washington always has a television set available (and usually on), even as cables from American posts around the world are being sorted and distributed to the appropriate bureau, office, or desk.

17. Quoted in Leslie H. Gelb with Richard K. Betts, *The Irony of Vietnam: The System Worked* (Washington, D.C.: The Brookings Institution, 1979), p. 171.

18. Both quotes are from Timothy J. Lomperis, *The War Everyone Lost—and Won* (Washington, D.C.: CQ Press, 1993), p. 78.

19. See Peter Braestrup, *Big Story: How the American Press and Television Reported and Interpreted the Crisis of Tet 1968, Volumes 1 and 2* (Boulder, CO: Westview Press, 1977), as cited in ibid.

20. Interestingly, this program evolved into the late-night ABC program *Nightline,* which continues to this day as a news and analysis forum.

21. Quoted in Newsom, *The Public Dimension of Foreign Policy,* pp. 47–48.

22. Quoted in Stephen Hess, *International News & Foreign Correspondents* (Washington, D.C.: The Brookings Institution, 1996), pp. 1–2. The passage originally came from the CNN program *Reliable Sources,* October 6, 1994.

23. W. Lance Bennett, "The News about Foreign Policy," in W. Lance Bennett and David L. Paletz, eds., *Taken by Storm: The Media, Public Opinion, and U.S. Foreign Policy in the Gulf War* (Chicago and London: The University of Chicago Press, 1994), p. 12.

24. Doris A. Graber, *Mass Media and American Politics,* 5th ed. (Washington, D.C.: CQ Press, 1997), p. 349.

25. Robert F. Kennedy, *Thirteen Days* (New York: W.W. Norton and Company, 1969), pp. 90–91. Although Soviet withdrawal of missiles for an American pledge not to invade Cuba was the proposal, the ultimate settlement also involved the American withdrawal of missiles from Turkey.

26. See Graber, *Mass Media and American Politics*, pp. 349–350, for a discussion of this episode.

27. See Peter Arnett's detailed description of his time in Baghdad in his *Live From the Battle-field* (New York: Simon & Schuster, 1994). Arnett's flight jacket from the war was put on display at CNN headquarters in Atlanta after his return to the United States.

28. Graber, *Mass Media and American Politics*, 5th ed., p. 351.

29. Daniel C. Hallin, *We Keep America on Top of the World: Television and the Public Sphere* (London and New York: Routledge, 1994), pp. 40–57.

30. Ibid., at pp. 44–48 and 52–53.

31. Ibid., at pp. 48–50, 51, and 50, respectively.

32. Ibid., p. 55. For a similar conclusion on how the media "index" news coverage "to the intensity and duration of official conflicts," see W. Lance Bennett, "The Media and the Foreign Policy Process," in David A. Deese, ed., *The New Politics of American Foreign Policy* (New York: St. Martin's Press, 1994), pp. 168–188, especially pp. 179–181.

33. I am grateful to James M. Lindsay for bringing this argument to my attention.

34. S. Robert Lichter, Stanley Rothman, and Linda S. Lichter, *The Media Elite* (Bethesda, MD: Adler & Adler, 1986), pp. 21–23. The quoted passages are at p. 23.

35. The first study reported is from ibid., p. 28; the second is from a study by Stephen Hess of the Brookings Institution and is quoted in ibid., p. 40.

36. Ibid., p. 30.

37. See "Bottom-Line Pressures Now Hurting Coverage, Say Journalists," May 23, 2004, at http://people-press.org/report/214/bottom-line-pressures-now-hurting-coverage-say-journalists, June 25, 2008.

38. Tim Groseclose and Jeffrey Milyo, "A Measure of Media Bias," *The Quarterly Journal of Economics* 120 (November 2005): 1191–1237. The summary of the study draws from that abstract at p. 1191 and the discussion in the article. The measure used to assess the symmetry is the degree of congruence between the ideological orientations of members of Congress in citing particular think tanks and how much media outlet cite those "various think tanks and policy groups" (p. 1191).

39. Lymari Morales, "Majority in U.S. Continues to Distrust the Media, Perceive Bias," Gallup, September 22, 2011, at http://www.gallup.com/poll/149624/Majority-Continue-Distrust-Media-Perceive-Bias.aspx, July 9, 2012.

40. See the chart back to 2002 on media bias in Lymari Morales, "Distrust in U.S. Media Edges Up to Record High," Gallup, September 29, 2010, at http://www.gallup.com/poll/143267/Distrust-Media-Edges-Record-High.aspx, July 9, 2012.

41. The media argument is taken from James Glassman, "The Press: Obvious Bias . . . ," *Washington Post*, May 7, 1996, A19, as is the quotation, which is from Larry Sabato.

42. Bernard Goldberg, *Bias: A CBS Insider Exposes How the Media Distort the News* (Washington, D.C.: Regnery Publishing, 2002), p. 221.

43. Jeremy D. Mayer, *American Media Politics in Transition* (Boston: McGraw Hill, 2008), p. 34.

44. Tim Groseclose, *Left Turn: How the Liberal Media Bias Distorts the American Mind* (New York: St. Martin's Press, 2011), p. 254. Emphasis in original.

45. Stuart N. Soroka, "Media, Public Opinion, and Foreign Policy," *Harvard International Journal of Press/Politics* 9 (Winter 2003): 27–48.

46. Cohen, *The Press and Foreign Policy*, p. 13. Emphasis in original.

47. The term is from Patrick O'Heffernan, "A Mutual Exploitation Model of Media Influence in U.S. Foreign Policy," in Bennett and Paletz, eds., *Taken by Storm*, p. 231, in which he summarizes Bernard Cohen's conclusion of his 1963 book.

48. See, for example, David D. Pearce, *Wary Partners: Diplomats and the Media* (Washington, D.C.: Congressional Quarterly, 1995).

49. Newsom, *The Public Dimension of Foreign Policy*, p. 86. For a scathing account of press deference during the Reagan administration, see Mark Hertsgaard, *On Bended Knee: The Press and the Reagan Presidency* (New York: Farrar, Straus & Giroux, 1988).

50. Johanna Neuman, *Lights, Camera, War* (New York: St. Martin's Press, 1996), pp. 207–208. The "pool" term is quoted from Neuman at p. 207.

51. These are outlined in Pete Williams, "Ground Rules and Guidelines for Desert Shield," in Hedrick Smith, ed., *The Media and the Gulf War* (Washington, D.C.: Seven Locks Press, 1992), pp. 4–12.

52. Hedrick Smith, Preface, in Smith, ed., *The Media and the Gulf War*, p. xviii.

53. R. W. Apple, Jr., "James Reston, a Journalist Nonpareil, Dies at 86," *New York Times*, December 7, 1995, B19. The commentator quoted was Ronald Steel.

54. The first two examples are from Pearce, *Wary Partners*, pp. 1–3.

55. Ambassador Alexander Watson is quoted in ibid., p. 10.

56. See the various appendices in ibid., pp. 169–186.

57. See Jo Becker and Scott Shane, "Secret "Kill List' Proves a Test of Obama's Principles and Will," *New York Times*, May 29, 2012, at http://www.nytimes.com/2012/05/29/world/obamas-leadership-in-war-on-al-qaeda.html?pagewanted=all, May 29, 2012, and David E. Sanger, "Obama Order Sped Up Wave of Cyberattacks Against Iran," *New York Times*, June 1, 2012, at http://www.nytimes.com/2012/06/01/world/middleeast/obama-ordered-wave-of-cyberattacks-against-iran.html?pagewanted=all, June 10, 2012, on these stories.

58. Bennett, "The Media and the Foreign Policy Process," p. 179.

59. Ibid.

60. On the problems for the media in this connection, see ibid., pp. 180–181.

61. O'Heffernan, "A Mutual Exploitation Model of Media Influence in U.S. Foreign Policy," pp. 232–233.

62. The discussion of issues draws on ibid., p. 240.

63. Journalist Johanna Neuman is quoted in Kovach, "Do the News Media Make Foreign Policy?" p. 171. The comment is originally from Neuman, *Lights, Camera, War*, p. 8.

64. Benjamin I. Page and Robert Y. Shapiro, *The Rational Public: Fifty Trends in Americans' Policy Preferences* (Chicago and London: The University of Chicago Press, 1992), p. 321. Emphasis in original.

65. Ibid., p. 342. The discussion of the findings is drawn from pp. 341–347.

66. Soroka, "Media, Public Opinion, and Foreign Policy," p. 43.

67. Page and Shapiro, *The Rational Public*, p. 353.

68. Ibid., p. 354.

69. Ibid.

70. These data are from Gabriel A. Almond, *The American People and Foreign Policy* (New York: Praeger, 1960), p. 82.

71. See the following publications, edited by John E. Rielly and published by The Chicago Council on Foreign Relations: *American Public Opinion and U.S. Foreign Policy 1987*, p. 8; *American Public Opinion and U.S. Foreign Policy 1991*, p. 9; *American Public Opinion and U.S. Foreign Policy 1995*, p. 9; and *American Public Opinion and U.S. Foreign Policy 1999*, p. 6. The data for the period from 1974 through 2002 are

summarized in Marshall M. Bouton and Benjamin I. Page, eds., *Worldviews 2002: American Public Opinion & Foreign Policy* (Chicago: The Chicago Council on Foreign Relations, 2002), p. 13.

72. Ibid., p. 5.

73. We verified with the Chicago Council (now The Chicago Council on Global Affairs), on June 25, 2008, that these questions were not asked via a phone interview.

74. See The Chicago Council on Foreign Relations' *Global Views 2004* report *U.S. Public Topline Report*, September 2004, p.1, at http://www.thechicagocouncil.org/past_pos.php, September 22, 2008; *Global Views 2006* report and Public Opinion Survey 2006 Topline Report, at http://www.thechicagocouncil.org/dynamic_page.php?id=56, September 22, 2008; *Global Views 2008, U.S. Topline Report*, July, 2008, at http://www.thechicagocouncil. org/UserFiles/File/POS_Topline%20Reports/POS%202008/2008%20Public%20Opin-ion_US%20Topline.pdf, July 13, 2012; and *Global Views 2010, U.S. Topline Report*, September 22, 2010, at http://www.thechicagocouncil.org/UserFiles/File/POS_Topline%20 Reports/POS%202010/Global%20Views%202010_USTopline.pdf, July 13, 2012.

75. Rielly, ed., *American Public Opinion and U.S. Foreign Policy 1987*, p. 9, and *American Public Opinion and U.S. Foreign Policy 1983* (Chicago: The Chicago Council on Foreign Relations, 1983), p. 9. The results for 1990 can be found in Rielly, ed., *American Public Opinion and U.S. Foreign Policy 1991*, p. 9. The 1995 survey did not indicate the size of the attentive public for the 1994 data. Given the modest changes overall in the latest survey, the percentage estimate from the early surveys appears to hold. The quotation from the 1998 survey can be found in Rielly, *American Public Opinion and U.S. Foreign Policy, 1999*, p. 9.

76. The results of the 2011 survey are reported in the Pew Research Center for the People and the Press, "What the Public Knows—In Words and Pictures," November 7, 2011, at http://pewresearch.org/pubs/2125/news-iq-quiz-current-events, July 13, 2012, and the results for 2007 and the comparison with 1989 are reported in The Pew Research Center for the People and the Press, *What Americans Know: 1989–2007: Public Knowledge of Current Affairs Little Changed by News and Information Revolution*, at http://people-press.org/files/legacy-pdf/319.pdf, July 13, 2012.

77. Bouton and Page, *Worldviews 2002*, pp. 43–44.

78. On the events and the public's knowledge about them, see Mark Gillespie, "New Poll Shows Support for Peacekeeping in Kosovo," February 22, 1999, at http://www.gallup .com/poll/4060/New-Poll-Shows-Support-Peacekeeping-Role-Kosovo.aspx, September 25, 2008, and Frank Newport, "East Timor Has Yet to Register Strongly on Americans' Consciousness," October 4, 1999, http://www.gallup.com/poll/3559/ East-Timor-Has-Yet-Register-Strongly-Americans-Consciousness.aspx, September 25, 2008.

79. Alec Gallup and Lydia Saad, "Americans Know Little about European Union," June 14, 2004, at http://www.gallup.com/poll/12043/Americans-Know-Little-About-European-Union.aspx, June 26, 2008.

80. See Darren K. Carlson, "Can Americans Name Key Foreign Leaders?" Gallup Poll Tuesday Briefing, March 4, 2003, online. Available at http://www.gallup.com/poll/tb/ goverpubli/20030304b.asp.

81. Jeffrey M. Jones, "Gallup Quizzes Americans on Knowledge of World Leaders," February 20, 2006, at http://www.gallup.com/poll/21541/Gallup-Quizzes-Americans-Knowledge-World-Leaders.aspx, June 26, 2008.

82. The Pew Research Center for the People and the Press, "What the Public Knows—In Words and Pictures."

83. See Bouton and Page, *Worldviews 2002*, pp. 10–11, for the top problem about one year after September 11. For the return of the economy as a top issue, see Frank Newport,

"Americans Clear That Economy Is Most Important Problem Facing Country," May 12, 2003, at http://www.gallup.com/poll/8368/Americans-Clear-Economy-Most-Important-Problem-Facing-Country.aspx, September 17, 2008.

84. Joseph Carroll, "Iraq Remains Top Problem Facing the Nation," September 21, 2007, at http://www.gallup.com/poll/28759/Gallup-Update-Iraq-Remains-Top-Problem-Facing-Nation.aspx, June 26, 2008.

85. Dennis Jacobe, "Economy Widely Viewed as Most Important Problem," March 13, 2008, at http://www.gallup.com/poll/104959/Economy-Widely-Viewed-Most-Important-Problem.aspx, June 24, 2008.

86. See Lydia Saad, "In U.S., Jobs a More Glaring Issue for Some Groups Than Others," June 27, 2012, at http://www.gallup.com/poll/155375/Jobs-Glaring-Issue-Groups-Others.aspx, July 13, 2012.

87. See Bouton and Page, *Worldviews 2002*, p. 11. The data for those years asked the public for the two or three biggest problems facing the country.

88. Via a phone interview on June 25, 2008, with an official at the Chicago Council, we verified that these questions and analyses were not done for 2004 and 2006. No questions on this topic were shown in the *Global Views 2008, U.S. Topline Report*, July, 2008, or the *Global Views 2010, U.S. Topline Report*, September 22, 2010.

89. The data for 2005 were from Joseph Carroll, "Most Important Problem," January 10, 2006, at http://www.gallup.com/poi/!74338/Most-Important-Problem.aspx, July 18, 2012, and was the sum of mentions of the Iraq War, terrorism, and immigration as foreign policy issues. Mention of all issues totaled 80 percent in this report. The data for 2008 were from Dennis Jacobe, "Economy Widely Viewed as Most Important Problem," March 13, 2008, http://www.gallup.com/poi/1704959/Economy-Widely-Viewed-Most-Important-Problem.aspx, July 18, 2012, and was the sum of mentions of the Iraq War, national security, terrorism, foreign aid/focus overseas, and international issues/problems. Mentions of all issues totaled 128 percent in this report. The data for 2012 were from Lydia Saad, "In U.S., Jobs a More Glaring Issue for Some Groups Than Others," June 27, 2012, at http://www.gallup.com/poll/155375/Jobs-Glaring-Issue-Groups-Others.aspx, July 13, 2012. Immigration (at 3 percent) is the only foreign policy–related issue among the top ten responses reported. Mentions for these responses totaled 103 percent. For 2005, 2008, and 2012, the respondents were asked to identify "the most important problem facing this country today."

90. John E. Mueller, *War, Presidents and Public Opinion* (New York: John Wiley and Sons, 1973), chap. 8.

91. Ibid., pp. 70–74.

92. Milton J. Rosenberg, Sidney Verba, and Philip E. Converse, *Vietnam and the Silent Majority* (New York: Harper and Row, 1970), pp. 26–28.

93. See "Opinion Roundup," *Public Opinion* 3 (February/March 1980), pp. 27 and 29.

94. These *New York Times*/CBS News Poll results are reported in David Shribman, "Poll Shows Support for Presence of U.S. Troops in Lebanon and Grenada," *New York Times*, October 29, 1983, 9.

95. These data are taken from Michael Oreskes, "Support for Bush Declines in Poll," *New York Times*, July 11, 1990, A8; and Andrew H. Malcolm, "Opponents to U.S. Move Have Poverty in Common," *New York Times*, September 8, 1990, 6.

96. On the patterns in President Bush's popularity, see Robin Toner, "Did Someone Say 'Domestic Policy'?" *New York Times*, March 3, 1991, 1E and 2E. A CNN (Cable News Network) poll and a *Newsweek* poll placed President Bush's popularity at about 90 percent at the immediate end of the Persian Gulf War. See Ann McDaniel and Evan Thomas with Howard Fineman, "The Rewards of Leadership," *Newsweek*, March 11, 1991, 30.

97. Andrew Kohut and Robert C. Toth, "Arms and the People," *Foreign Affairs* 73 (November/December 1994): 60.

98. Gallup, *The Gallup Poll: Public Opinion 1994*, pp. 141, 145, and 148.

99. On these data and trends, see Shoon Kathleen Murray and Christopher Spinosa, "The Post-9/11 Shift in Public Opinion: How Long Will It Last?" in Eugene R. Wittkopf and James M. McCormick, eds., *The Domestic Sources of American Foreign Policy: Insights and Evidence*, 4th ed. (Lanham, MD: Rowman & Littlefield Publishers, 2004), pp. 97–115; Frank Newport, "Terrorism Fades as Nation's Most Important Problem," January 14, 2002, at http://www.gallup.com/poll/5170/Terrorism-Fades-Nations-Most-Important-Problem.aspx, September 17, 2008; and "Rallying behind the Country's Leaders and Institutions," September 25, 2001, *TuesdayBriefing@Gallup.com*.

100. For the changing trends, see Lydia Saad, "Iraq War Triggers Major Rally Effect," March 25, 2003, at http://www.gallup.com/poll/releases/pr0300325.asp; and Lydia Saad, "Bush's Job Rating Still Above 60%," July 2, 2003, at http://www.gallup.com/poll/releases/pr030702.asp. For a poll near the end of 2003, see "State of the Nation," November 25, 2003, at http://www.gallup.com/poll/stateNation.

101. Lydia Saad, "Obama's Approval Bump Hasn't Transferred to 2012 Prospects," Gallup, May 11, 2011, at http://www.gallup.com/poll/147500/Obama-Approval-Bump-Hasnt-Transferred-2012-Prospects.aspx, July 13, 2012.

102. Rosenberg, Verba, and Converse, *Vietnam and the Silent Majority*, pp. 24–25. The authors do not actually use poll data to make this point about question wording; instead, they rely on these hypothetical examples to demonstrate the underlying argument.

103. Brad Lockerbie and Stephen A. Borrelli, "Question Wording and Public Support for Contra Aid, 1983–1986," *Public Opinion Quarterly* 54 (Summer 1990): 195–208.

104. For the alternate responses and level of public support for each, see Frank Newport and Lydia Saad, "Americans' View: U.S. Should Not Go It Alone in Iraq," September 24, 2002, at http://www.gallup.com/poll/6874/Americans-View-US-Should-Alone-Iraq.aspx, September 17, 2008.

105. These question options and results are reported in Joseph Carroll, "Public Continues to Favor Timetable for Iraq Withdrawal," Gallup Poll, December 11, 2007, at http://www.gallup.com/poll/103159/Public-Continues-Favor-Timetable-Iraq-Withdrawal.aspx, June 27, 2008.

106. Lydia Saad, "Americans Broadly Favor Obama's Afghanistan Pullout Plan," Gallup, June 29, 2011, at http://www.gallup.com/poll/148313/Americans-Broadly-Favor-Obama-Afghanistan-Pullout-Plan.aspx, July 15, 2012.

107. Gabriel A. Almond, *The American People and Foreign Policy* (New York: Frederick A. Praeger, 1960), pp. 53, 69, and 88. Harcourt, Brace, and Company published the original edition of this book in 1950.

108. Ole R. Holsti, "Public Opinion and Foreign Policy: Challenges to the Almond-Lippmann Consensus," *International Studies Quarterly* 36 (December 1992): 442.

109. Quoted in ibid.

110. Ibid., pp. 443–444. The studies referred to in this paragraph from Holsti are Philip E. Converse, "The Nature of Belief Systems in Mass Publics," in David E. Apter, ed., *Ideology and Discontent* (New York: Free Press, 1964), pp. 206–261; Bernard C. Cohen, *The Public's Impact on Foreign Policy* (Boston: Little, Brown and Co., 1973); and Warren E. Miller and Donald E. Stokes, "Constituency Influence in Congress," *American Political Science Review* 57 (March 1963): 45–56.

111. Jon Hurwitz and Mark Peffley, "How Are Foreign Policy Attitudes Structured? A Hierarchical Model," *American Political Science Review* 81 (December 1987): 1114. First two emphases in original; last one has been added here.

112. Robert Y. Shapiro and Benjamin I. Page, "Foreign Policy and the Rational Public," *Journal of Conflict Resolution* 32 (June 1988): 211 and 243. A more complete statement of their views can be found in their *The Rational Public*.

113. Eugene R. Wittkopf, *Faces of Internationalism: Public Opinion and American Foreign Policy* (Durham, NC: Duke University Press, 1990), pp. 25–33. Analyses of the more recent Chicago Council surveys by Wittkopf may be found in Eugene R. Wittkopf, "Faces of Internationalism in a Transitional Environment," *Journal of Conflict Resolution* 38 (September 1994): 376–401, for the 1990 survey; and Eugene R. Wittkopf, "What Americans Really Think About Foreign Policy," *The Washington Quarterly* 19 (Summer 1996): 91–106.

114. These are the items used for the analysis of the 1994 survey in ibid., p. 94. Slightly different ones were used for analyzing the 1990 survey; see Wittkopf, "Faces of Internationalism in a Transitional Environment," p. 381. For the 1974 through 1986 surveys, these underlying attitudes were largely tapped by questions about the use of American force abroad, communism, and American–Soviet relations. See Wittkopf, *Faces of Internationalism: Public Opinion and American Foreign Policy*, p. 25. The end of the Cold War necessitated the use of different items because the attitudes toward communism and American–Soviet relations were no longer appropriate.

115. Wittkopf, *Faces of Internationalism*, pp. 25–30. Our application of Wittkopf's typology to the Persian Gulf War was aided by a personal communication with him.

116. Wittkopf published the results for 1974–1986 in ibid., p. 26. See Wittkopf, "Faces of Internationalism in a Transitional Environment," pp. 376–401, for the 1990 results. He had also done the same kind of analysis for the 1998 Chicago Council data with generally the same kind of results as reported for these earlier surveys, but those results were not published to the best of my knowledge. Personal communication with Eugene R. Wittkopf, September 19, 2003.

117. On the evenness and stability of the distribution of the public among these four groups, see Wittkopf, *Faces of Internationalism*, p. 26; Wittkopf, "Faces of Internationalism in a Transitional Environment," pp. 376–401, for the 1990 results; and personal communication with Eugene R. Wittkopf for the 1994 data. The numbers are rough averages within each quadrant across the surveys. The technique of factor analysis contributes to the more even distribution among the four quadrants, although differences exist among the groupings.

118. These examples are drawn from Wittkopf, "What Americans Really Think about Foreign Policy," pp. 95–99; and Wittkopf, *Faces of Internationalism*, pp. 27–32, especially the table at p. 28 and the discussion at p. 30.

119. Ibid., pp. 44–49.

120. Wittkopf, "What Americans Really Think About Foreign Policy," p. 103. His 1994 analysis of the other sociodemographic characteristics of the public for these belief systems (reported at pp. 103–104) generally supports the results from his earlier work.

121. Ole R. Holsti, *Public Opinion and American Foreign Policy*, rev. ed. (Ann Arbor: The University of Michigan Press, 2004), pp. 231–232.

122. Unfortunately, the 2002 Chicago Council survey results, for example, were not susceptible to the same analysis because the appropriate questions were not included in the survey instrument. Personal Communication with Eugene R. Wittkopf on September 19, 2003. Thanks to him for the insight into the current distribution of opinion summarized in this paragraph.

123. Benjamin I. Page with Marshall M. Bouton, *The Foreign Policy Disconnect* (Chicago and London: The University of Chicago Press, 2006), p. 28. Emphasis in original.

124. Ibid., p. 236.

125. Bernard Cohen, *The Political Process and Foreign Policy: The Making of the Japanese Peace Settlement* (Princeton, NJ: Princeton University Press, 1957), p. 29. We should note, however, that Cohen is relatively skeptical about the impact of public opinion overall. See note 36.

126. V. O. Key, Jr., *Public Opinion and American Democracy* (New York: Alfred A. Knopf, 1961), p. 423.

127. William R. Caspary, "The 'Mood Theory': A Study of Public Opinion and Foreign Policy," *The American Political Science Review* 54 (June 1970): 546. Emphasis in original.

128. Bruce Russett, "The Americans' Retreat from World Power," *Political Science Quarterly* 90 (Spring 1975): 9.

129. The phrase is from ibid., p. 8. For other judgments of the Vietnam War and its impact on the foreign policy beliefs of the American public and its leaders, see, for instance, Eugene R. Wittkopf and Michael A. Maggiotto, "Elites and Masses: A Comparative Analysis of Attitudes Toward America's World Role," *The Journal of Politics* 45 (May 1983): 303–334; and Ole R. Holsti and James N. Rosenau, "Vietnam, Consensus, and the Belief Systems of American Leaders," *World Politics* 32 (October 1979): 1–56.

130. Rielly, ed., *American Public Opinion and U.S. Foreign Policy 1975*, p. 12. All other data in this section are from this report. The national sample survey was conducted in December 1974 by Harris and Associates for The Chicago Council on Foreign Relations.

131. The title is from John E. Rielly, "The American Mood: A Policy of Self-Interest," *Foreign Policy* 34 (Spring 1979): 74–86.

132. Rielly, ed., *American Public Opinion and U.S. Foreign Policy 1979*, p. 4.

133. The data on the public's support for these actions are outlined in the report in ibid. Also, see a Harris survey in early 1980 that showed majority public support for use of U.S. troops if the Soviets attacked the Persian Gulf area, Iran, or Pakistan. See "Use of U.S. Troops to Defend Invaded Countries Endorsed," *Houston Post*, February 26, 1980, 3C.

134. Rielly, ed., *American Public Opinion and U.S. Foreign Policy 1979*, p. 12.

135. Ibid., p. 15.

136. Ibid., p. 12.

137. Ibid., p. 7. Also Rielly, "The American Mood: A Foreign Policy of Self-Interest," pp. 74–75.

138. Rielly, ed., *American Public Opinion and U.S. Foreign Policy 1983*, and Rielly, ed., *American Public Opinion and U.S. Foreign Policy 1987,* for the discussion of this mood.

139. See Rielly, ed., *American Public Opinion and U.S. Foreign Policy 1983*, p. 32; and *American Public Opinion and U.S. Foreign Policy 1987*, p. 31.

140. See the tables in Rielly, ed., *American Public Opinion and U.S. Foreign Policy 1983*, p. 35; and *American Public Opinion and U.S. Foreign Policy 1987*, p. 35, which compare the public's views with those of the Reagan administration. Also, see p. 29 of the latter source for a discussion of public attitudes on military expenditures.

141. The summary of this mood is based on John E. Rielly, "The Public Mood at Mid-Decade," *Foreign Policy* 98 (Spring 1995): 76–93; Rielly, ed., *American Public Opinion and U.S. Foreign Policy 1995*, and *American Public Opinion and U.S. Foreign Policy 1999.* The title of the moods comes from these sources.

142. See Figure III-3 in Rielly, ed., *American Public Opinion and U.S. Foreign Policy 1995*, p. 22, and the discussion on p. 21. For the 1998 data, see Rielly, ed., *American Public Opinion and U.S. Foreign Policy, 1999*, p. 28 and Figure 5–1. The quoted passage is from Rielly, ed., *American Public Opinion and U.S. Foreign Policy, 1995*, p. 21. Also see the tables on the public's views toward Russia on pp. 24–25.

143. Ibid., p. 23.

144. Ibid., pp. 23 and 25; and Rielly, ed., *American Public Opinion and U.S. Foreign Policy, 1999*, pp. 12–14 for the 1998 ("end of the decade") data.

145. John E. Rielly, "Public Opinion: The Pulse of the '90s," *Foreign Policy* 82 (Spring 1991): 83, 86, and 89; Rielly, ed., *American Public Opinion and U.S. Foreign Policy 1995*, p. 34; and Rielly, ed., *American Public Opinion and U.S. Foreign Policy 1999*, pp. 24–27.

146. The discussion of the public mood after September 11 and with the Iraq War is drawn from the data and analysis in Bouton and Page, *Worldviews 2002*; Marshall M. Bouton and Benjamin I. Page, eds., *Global Views 2004: American Public Opinion and Foreign Policy* (Chicago: The Chicago Council on Foreign Relations, 2004); and Bouton and Page, eds., *Global Views 2006: The United States and the Rise of China and India; Results of a 2006 Multination Survey of Public Opinion* (Chicago: The Chicago Council on Global Affairs, 2006). The quoted passages throughout this discussion are from these sources as indicated.

147. *Worldviews 2002*, p. 11.

148. Ibid., p. 16; *Global Views 2004*, p. 12; and *Global Views 2006*, p. 16.

149. Ibid., p. 14; *Global Views 2004*, p. 17; and *Worldviews 2002*, p. 13.

150. See *Global Views 2006*, p. 17.

151. For the specific changes in attitude on the use of American military power over this period, see *Worldviews 2002*, pp. 23-24, *Global Views 2004*, p. 29, and *Global Views 2006*, pp. 21-22.

152. Ibid., p. 14.

153. Ibid.

154. Ibid., pp. 18–19. Also see, *Global Views 2004*, pp. 20 and 36; and *Worldviews 2002*, p. 33 for the specific international initiatives supported by the public at that time.

155. *Global Views 2006: The United States and the Rise of China and India; Results of a 2006 Multination Survey of Public Opinion*, p. 23.

156. Ibid., pp. 23–24.

157. Ibid., p. 25.

158. Marshall M. Bouton, ed., *Global Views 2010: Constrained Internationalism: Adapting to New Realities* (Chicago: The Chicago Council on Global Affairs, 2010), p. 11. The last quoted phrase and the section title are from the title of this report.

159. Ibid. The quoted passages are at p. 15 and p. 12, respectively.

160. Ibid. The quoted passages are at pp. 17 and 19.

161. Ibid., pp. 20–21. The quoted passage is at p. 20.

162. Ibid., pp. 20–23. The quoted passages are at p. 20 and p. 23, respectively.

163. Robert Y. Shapiro and Benjamin I. Page, "Foreign Policy and Public Opinion," in David A. Deese, ed., *The New Politics of American Foreign Policy* (New York: St. Martin's Press, 1994), pp. 216–235. The quote is from p. 218.

164. Ibid., p. 223.

165. Ibid., p. 226.

166. Bruce W. Jentleson, "The Pretty Prudent Public: Post Post-Vietnam American Opinion on the Use of Military Force," *International Studies Quarterly* 36 (March 1992): 49–74. The quoted passages are from pp. 50 and 71, respectively. Emphasis in the original.

167. Kohut and Toth, "Arms and the People," p. 47.

168. Ibid., p. 50.

169. The results for the Korean and Vietnam Wars are reported in Mueller, *War, Presidents, and Public Opinion*, pp. 23–65, in particular, but the entire volume is instructive; the results

for the Iraq War (as well as the comparison with those earlier wars) can be found in John Mueller, "The Iraq Syndrome," in Eugene R. Wittkopf and James M. McCormick, eds., *The Domestic Sources of American Foreign Policy*, 5th ed. (Lanham, MD: Rowman & Littlefield Publishers, Inc., 2008), pp. 115–124. The more rapid erosion in the level of support for Iraq and the reasons for it is at pp. 116–117.

170. See the discussion of these studies in John H. Aldrich, Christopher Gelpi, Peter Feaver, Jason Reifler, and Kristin Thompson Sharp, "Foreign Policy and the Electoral Connection," *Annual Review of Political Science* 9 (2006): 477–502. The specific discussion is at pp. 482–483.

171. On the "elite cue" theory, see Adam J. Berinsky, "Events, Elites, and American Public Support for Military Conflict," in James M. McCormick, ed., *The Domestic Sources of American Foreign Policy: Insights and Evidence*, 6th ed. (Lanham, MD: Rowman & Littlefield Publishers, Inc., 2012), pp. 123–138. Also see "Part I: Introduction" in James M. McCormick, ed., *The Domestic Sources of American Foreign Policy: Insights and Evidence*, 6th ed. (Lanham, MD: Rowman & Littlefield Publishers, Inc., 2012), pp. 29–30 for a further description of this theory.

172. The studies are discussed and cited in Aldrich, Gelpi, Feaver, Reifler, and Sharp, "Foreign Policy and the Electoral Connection," pp. 483–484. The quoted passages are at p. 484.

173. See Benjamin I. Page and Jason Barabas, "Foreign Policy Gaps Between Citizens and Leaders," *International Studies Quarterly* 44 (September 2000): 339–364, especially p. 358; Rielly, ed., *American Public Opinion and U.S. Foreign Policy 1995*, and his *American Public Opinion and U.S. Foreign Policy 1999* for discussion of multilateral support more recently. For post–September 11 support for multilateralism, see Bouton and Page, *Worldviews 2002*, p. 27, for the quotation and data, their *Global Views 2004*, p. 24, for data, and their *Global Views 2006*, pp. 18–21, for the commitment to multilateralism by the public.

174. See Bouton, *Global Views 2010: Constrained Internationalism: Adapting to New Realities* and the chart on p. 15 with this quotation and these results.

175. See the discussion in James M. McCormick, "Domestic Politics and US Leadership after September 11," in David B. MacDonald, Dirk Nabers, and Robert G. Patman, eds., *The Bush Leadership, the Power of Ideas, and the War on Terror* (Farnham, UK: Ashgate Publishing Limited, 2012), pp. 163–164. The assessment of the importance of foreign policy for three in ten votes is from Paul R. Abramson, John H. Aldrich, and David W. Rohde, "The 2004 Presidential Election: The Emergence of a Permanent Majority?" *Political Science Quarterly* 120, no. 1, pp. 53–54.

176. See John H. Aldrich, John L. Sullivan, and Eugene Borgida, "Foreign Affairs and Issue Voting: Do Presidential Candidates 'Waltz Before a Blind Audience'?" *American Political Science Review* 83 (March 1989): 136.

177. Warren E. Miller, "Voting and Foreign Policy," in James N. Rosenau, ed., *Domestic Sources of Foreign Policy* (New York: The Free Press, 1967), p. 226. Also see John Spanier and Eric M. Uslaner, *American Foreign Policy Making and the Democratic Dilemmas* (Pacific Grove, CA: Brooks/Cole Publishing Company, 1989), p. 216.

178. Gregory B. Markus, "Political Attitudes During an Election Year: A Report on the 1980 NES Panel Study," *American Political Science Review* 76 (September 1982): 558. This point is also discussed in Spanier and Uslaner, *American Foreign Policy Making and the Democratic Dilemmas*, p. 216, from which we draw.

179. R. W. Apple, Jr., "Clinton's Peace Strategy," *New York Times*, December 2, 1995, 1.

180. The Democratic candidates for the 2004 nominations started early in the campaign cycle focusing on foreign policy issues, especially the situation in Iraq. In turn, the Republican National Committee began airing campaign advertisements defending the Bush administration's antiterrorism policy. Such an early focus on foreign policy ensured its centrality in the 2004 election.

181. See the chart in Aldrich, Sullivan, and Borgida, "Foreign Affairs and Issue Voting," p. 136.

182. Miroslav Nincic, "Elections and Foreign Policy," in Eugene R. Wittkopf and James M. McCormick, eds., *The Domestic Sources of American Foreign Policy: Insights and Evidence*, 4th ed. (Lanham, MD: Rowman & Littlefield Publishers, 2004), pp. 118–119.

183. Miroslav Nincic, "External Affairs and the Electoral Connection," in Eugene R. Wittkopf and James M. McCormick, eds., *The Domestic Sources of American Foreign Policy: Insights and Evidence*, 5th ed. (Lanham, MD: Rowman & Littlefield Publishers, 2008), p. 129. Emphasis added.

184. Miroslav Nincic, "External Affairs and the Electoral Connection," in James M. McCormick, eds., *The Domestic Sources of American Foreign Policy: Insights and Evidence*, 6th ed. (Lanham, MD: Rowman & Littlefield Publishers, 2008), pp. 143–144.

185. Nincic, "Elections and Foreign Policy," p. 119.

186. Both studies, and the quotations, are cited in Aldrich, Gelpi, Feaver, Reifler, and Sharp, p. 490. One of the studies has been published in the journal *International Security*; the other is unpublished.

187. See James M. McCormick and Neil J. Mitchell, "Commitments, Transnational Interests, and Congress," *Political Research Quarterly* 60 (December 2007): 580, for this example. The episode was originally recounted in Samantha Power, *A Problem from Hell: American and the Age of Genocide* (New York: Basic Books, 2002), pp. 324–325.

188. The discussion in this paragraph draws on the description and analysis of the Oklahoma case provided in Jeremy Rosner, "The Know-Nothings Know Something," *Foreign Policy* 101 (Winter 1995–1996): 116–127.

189. Although many issues were in the public mind at the midterm congressional elections, concerns about terrorism, war, and international issues were mentioned slightly more frequently than economic issues. See Lydia Saad, "Americans Troubled by Issues, Upbeat About Leaders This Election Day," November 5, 2002, at http://www.gallup.com/poll/7159/Americans-Troubled-Issues-Upbeat-About-Leaders-Election-Day.aspx, September 17, 2008.

190. Cited in Nincic, "External Affairs and the Electoral Connection," *The Domestic Sources of American Foreign Policy: Insights and Evidence*, 5th edition, p. 129.

191. Gary C. Jacobson, "Referendum: The 2006 Midterm Congressional Elections," *Political Science Quarterly* 122 (Spring 2007): 5.

192. The voting analyses are reported in Gary C. Jacobson, "The War, the President, and the 2006 Midterm Congressional Elections," paper presented at the annual meeting of the Midwest Political Science Association, Chicago, Illinois, April 12–15, 2007.

193. Richard Sobel, *The Impact of Public Opinion on U.S. Foreign Policy: Constraining the Colossus* (New York: Oxford University Press, 2001). The quoted passages are at p. 240 and p. 234, respectively.

194. Douglas C. Foyle, *Counting the Public In: Presidents, Public Opinion, and Foreign Policy* (New York: Oxford University Press, 1999). See especially pp. 257–289. The quoted passage is at p. 259 with the emphasis in the original.

195. Benjamin I. Page and Robert Y. Shapiro, "Effects of Public Opinion on Policy," *American Political Science Review* 77 (March 1983): 186. Emphasis in the original. The discussion here is drawn from this article. For a more recent summary of their work on foreign policy, see Page and Shapiro, *The Rational Public*, pp. 172–320.

196. Thomas Graham, "Public Opinion and U.S. Foreign Policy Decision Making," in David A. Deese, ed., *The New Politics of American Foreign Policy* (New York: St. Martin's Press, 1994), pp. 190–215.

197. Ibid., p. 196. These four factors are discussed at pp. 195–199, from which we draw.

198. Ibid., p. 195.

199. See Holsti, *Public Opinion and American Foreign Policy*, rev. ed. The quoted passage is at p. 299. The last sentence in the paragraph draws on Holsti's discussion at p. 65 of his book.

200. Philip J. Powlick, "The Attitudinal Bases for Responsiveness to Public Opinion among American Foreign Policy Officials," *Journal of Conflict Resolution* 35 (December 1991): 611–641; and Philip J. Powlick, "The Sources of Public Opinion for American Foreign Policy Officials," *International Studies Quarterly* 39 (December 1995): 427–451.

201. Powlick, "The Attitudinal Bases for Responsiveness to Public Opinion among American Foreign Policy Officials," p. 634. This finding stands in sharp contrast to analyses of four decades earlier, when public opinion seemed to matter little. On this point, see all of Bernard C. Cohen, *The Public's Impact on Foreign Policy*, but especially some of his analyses and conclusions at pp. 184–200.

202. Powlick, "The Sources of Public Opinion for American Foreign Policy Officials," p. 447.

PART III

Conclusion

In Part I, we demonstrated that the formulation of American foreign policy had been marked by a considerable degree of value consensus prior to the Vietnam War and has been subject to a substantial amount of value shifts from one administration to the next ever since. In Part II, an important message was that the various political institutions—the executive, Congress, and the bureaucracies, for example—have become increasingly competitive in seeking to promote their values and beliefs in foreign policy making. As a result of these two patterns, the direction of American foreign policy and the values that the United States seeks to promote remain a source of debate. In Part III, the concluding chapter, we examine the nature of the debate among elites and between the elites and American mass public and outline some possible alternative directions for American foreign policy in the future. These alternatives will not necessarily resolve this debate over what values should be promoted in American foreign policy, but they should bring the value and policy differences into sharper focus as the public and their leaders consider policy choices in the years ahead.

CHAPTER 13

American Foreign Policy Values and the Future

The problem of American power in the twenty-first century . . . is
not of decline but what to do in light of the realization that even
the largest country cannot achieve the outcomes it wants
without the help of others.

JOSEPH NYE
"THE FUTURE OF AMERICAN POWER," 2010

. . . America will never again experience
the global dominance it enjoyed in the seventeen years
between the Soviet Union's collapse in 1991
and the financial crisis of 2008.
Those days are over.

GIDEON RACHMAN
"THINK AGAIN: AMERICAN DECLINE," 2011

As we move through the second decade of the twenty-first century, a consensus among the American people on the role of the United States in world affairs remains elusive. Although the events of September 11, 2001, seemingly produced a temporary unity among the American people and its leaders, the legacies of two wars in Iraq and Afghanistan, the continuing economic problems of recession and debt at home, and the emergence of new states abroad has produced a cacophony of voices arguing over decline of the United States in global affairs and the need for a new direction in American foreign policy. In such an environment is a new approach possible and desirable? And what should the new approach be?

In this last chapter, we discuss the challenges that exist in gaining a consensus, or even adequate support, for the United States to pursue a new foreign policy direction. The differences among elites and between elites and the American public about the appropriate role for the United States are two crucial and important hurdles. Further, both major political parties hold increasingly differing views, both on the principal goals and principal means for conducting American foreign policy. As a result of these divisions, the alternative approaches that the United States should adopt vary considerably. We begin by identifying more fully the extent of underlying value conflicts among the American leaders and the public in recent years. Then we turn to evaluating the problems of, and prospects for, developing a new foreign policy direction at this juncture of the twenty-first century and sketch out some alternative future courses that students and analysts of U.S. foreign policy might consider.

A NATION DIVIDED

An abundance of evidence exists at both the mass and elite levels on the degree of value conflict over the direction of foreign policy. The United States has witnessed discernible shifts in its foreign policy approach with the coming of each new administration over the past four decades that we have discussed. Recall the rejection of the Cold War consensus, the power politics of Richard Nixon and Henry Kissinger, the idealism of Jimmy Carter, the revival of containment during the Ronald Reagan years, the modified realism of George H. W. Bush, the liberal internationalism of Bill Clinton, the neoconservatism of George W. Bush, and revival of liberal internationalism by Barack Obama. Although some would argue that significant underlying stability in goals and objectives largely characterized policy over much of the past half century or more, that view fails to account for the changes in emphasis from one administration to the next.[1] Further, it fails to help us understand the pervasive divisions in value orientation among the leadership (the foreign policy elites) and the American people, beginning in the post-Vietnam era and continuing, and arguably expanding, today.

Several longitudinal surveys of American leaders and the public are available to help us gauge the degree of consensus or division among the leadership and the public since the end of the Vietnam War to the 1990s.[2] Using the results of these surveys, and supplementing them with the surveys by the Chicago Council on Foreign Relations (now the Chicago Council on Global Affairs) and Pew Research Center data from the present era, we can evaluate the degree of consensus or dissensus both among America's foreign policy leaders and between these leaders and the public. Such information is crucial for understanding the challenges for developing a new direction in an American foreign policy that has the prospect of gaining public and elite support in the future.

VALUE DIFFERENCES WITHIN ELITES

The results of periodic leadership surveys by political scientists Ole Holsti and James Rosenau provide compelling evidence of divisions among foreign policy leaders, or elites. These divisions emerged after the Vietnam War, and, as we shall show, continue to the present. Employing the fourfold analytic categories of isolationists, hardliners, accommodationists, and internationalists developed to assess public opinion (see Chapter 12), Holsti and Rosenau's evaluation of four foreign policy leadership opinion surveys from 1984 through 1996 found significant elite divisions across those four categories. Moreover, the divisions were reasonably constant from one survey to the next, with the elites perhaps more divided recently.[3] Accommodationists and internationalists turn out to be the two largest components of those leaders surveyed, with the former constituting 48 percent and the latter 29 percent in 1996. Hardliners and isolationists, by contrast, form much smaller components, with 13 percent and 10 percent, respectively.[4]

Largely consistent with the earlier analyses of the public with these four categories, these analysts report that "partisan, ideological and, to a less degree, occupational differences" account for these differing belief systems.[5] On a partisan level, for instance, they found that hardliners were Republicans and accommodationists were Democrats among the 1996 respondents. "To a less dramatic extent," they report, "internationalists and isolationists preferred the GOP to the Democratic Party." On an ideological level, the hardliners tended to be conservatives and the accommodationists tended to be liberals; the internationalists and isolationists "tended to tilt toward the conservative end of the ideological self-identification scale."[6]

Furthermore, in a related set of analyses, Holsti demonstrated that **partisan differences among elites have existed across a series of specific foreign policy issues**, beginning with a 1976 survey and continuing through five other quadrennial surveys from 1980 through 1996. Indeed, his data "offer only modest evidence that the end of the Cold War has resurrected a foreign policy consensus among opinion leaders." Instead, and especially important to note, "partisan cleavages are evident on a great many issues," although "trade stands out as an exception."[7] On that issue, liberal Democrats and conservative Republicans came together to oppose trade liberalization, albeit for different reasons.

In short, partisan differences divide elites on foreign policy—and have for a considerable time. In Holsti's summary of a large array of sources of foreign policy attitudes, including age, gender, education, region, and race, for both the public and its leaders, he concludes that *ideology* and *party identification* remain the principal correlate in accounting for foreign policy attitudes.[8]

More recent surveys support these earlier findings about elite divisions on foreign policy. The 2002 Chicago Council leadership survey, for example, a survey composed of knowledgeable Americans from government, business, labor, communications, education, religious groups, and foreign policy interest groups, points to clear divisions among specific leadership groups within and outside of government on a variety of specific foreign policy issues.[9]

On the question of whether the United States should act alone in international affairs, for example, elite groups from outside the government believed that the United States generally needed the support of its allies, but majorities from three government institutions (House, Senate, and the administration) supported the right of Americans to act alone. On the Kyoto treaty and the International Criminal Court (ICC), the elites were also split. Regarding Kyoto, majorities from American business, the Senate, and the Bush administration were opposed; other elites were in favor. For the ICC, the split was largely the same, with the Bush administration and House and Senate elites opposed and other elites in favor. Finally, most American elites favored the United States' siding with neither Israel nor the Palestinians in the Middle East conflict. Yet elites from the Senate were divided on the issue, and most U.S. religious leaders tilted toward Israel.[10]

A 2005 survey conducted by the Pew Research Center also uncovered some differences among opinion leaders on important foreign policy questions.[11] Pew's survey consisted of "520 men and women chosen from recognized lists of top individuals within their fields and/or those who hold key leadership positions." The fields covered included members of the news media, foreign affairs specialists, security specialists, state and local officials, academic and think tank leaders, religious leaders, scientists and engineers, and retired military officers. Although these opinion leaders did not differ on all issues (for instance, 60 to 80 percent identified China as "a serious problem but not an adversary"), they disagreed on several. For example, state and local officials and members of the military were the most optimistic about "efforts to establish a stable democracy" in Iraq (51 percent and 64 percent, respectively), but scientists/engineers, security officials, and foreign policy specialists, by large margins, thought such efforts would fail (84, 71, and 71 percent, respectively).

On whether the United States should remain the "only military superpower," divisions were also evident. A majority of state and local officials, military officers, and foreign affairs specialists were in favor, whereas a majority of academic and think tank officials, religious leaders, and scientists/engineers believed that it would be satisfactory if "another country became as powerful." Similarly, these groups differed over the utility of public diplomacy to change the image of the United States in the Middle East. Fifty percent or more of religious leaders and state and local officials believed that public diplomacy could be beneficial; the other opinion leaders did not, ranging from 51 percent of military officers to 79 percent of security officials. Finally, although a plurality or majority of the opinion leaders believed that the impact of NAFTA was "good," the levels of support ranged broadly from 44 percent of religious leaders and 59 percent of foreign affairs specialists to 87 percent of military officers and 93 percent of security officials.

In all, these examples highlight the diversity and division of opinions among leaders on select issues. They also show that leadership differences continue in the present era and complicate the shaping of American foreign policy.

VALUE DIFFERENCES BETWEEN ELITES AND MASSES

The lack of consensus among the elites is complicated in two other aspects: (1) the failure of leaders and masses to share the four belief systems in roughly the same proportion and (2) the sustained differences between leaders and the public on key foreign policy questions.

On the first aspect, empirical research found that, despite the fact that the attitudes of elites and masses are similarly structured into comparable belief systems, not all of these belief systems are held in the same proportion by each group. For instance, **the American leadership tends to be much more internationalist than the public** (in both the militant and cooperative varieties). In contrast, **the public tends**

to favor more hardline and isolationist policies (i.e., a more militant internationalism).[12] Such disparities seemingly reduce the prospect of making foreign policy with widespread support.

On the second aspect, the Chicago Council surveys for 1974 through 2002 systematically reported the **"policy gap" (policy differences) between the leadership and public opinion at large** in their surveys. These differences, moreover, **were consistent and quite large across several policy areas**. Table 13.1 provides an illustration of these differences by comparing the responses to several foreign policy questions in a general public survey to those in a leadership survey.[13] As the table shows, the public's attitudes toward the world and toward specific policy questions differed significantly from those of their leaders. The public, for instance, was less committed to an active world role than were leaders, but it was more committed than the foreign policy elites to strengthening the United Nations. The differences between the public and leaders on these two questions were wide, at 23 and

**Table 13.1 Policy Differences between
the Leaders and the Public in 2002 (Percentages)**

	Public	Leaders	Gap (leaders minus public)
Diplomatic Involvement Abroad			
Take an active part in world affairs	74	97	+23
Strengthening the United Nations a very important goal	58	28	−30
Foreign Aid			
Favor increasing aid to other countries	14	59	+45
Increase aid to Palestinians	13	43	+30
Increase aid to Afghanistan	23	67	+44
Increase aid to Africa	37	75	+38
Use of Force/Protecting the Homeland			
Favor use of U.S. troops if North Korea invades South Korea	39	83	+44
Favor use of U.S. troops if Arab Forces invade Israel	52	79	+27
Favor use of U.S. troops if China invades Taiwan	35	54	+19
Favor sharing intelligence information against terrorism	60	94	+34
Trade/Immigration			
View protecting jobs as a very important goal	85	35	−50
View immigration and refugees as critical threat to United States	60	14	−40

Note: percentages are of those holding an opinion.

Source: Constructed from discussion, tables, and questions in Marshall M. Bouton and Benjamin I. Page, eds., *Worldviews 2002: American Public Opinion & Foreign Policy* (Chicago: The Chicago Council on Foreign Relations, 2002), pp. 69–72.

30 percentage points, respectively. Leaders (or elites) were more willing than the public to increase aid to other countries generally and to several countries specifically.[14]
On these particular questions, the gaps between leaders and the public were even
wider, ranging from 30 to 45 percent.

Leaders were also much more willing than the public to use force and to share
intelligence information on terrorism. For example, a majority of Americans favored
sending troops if Arab forces attacked Israel, whereas the majority of leaders supported
using troops in several different scenarios. Sixty percent of the public supported sharing intelligence information on matters dealing with terrorism; an overwhelming
94 percent of leaders did so. As with the other issues, the gap between the groups
surveyed was markedly wide.

On two other important issues, trade and immigration/refugees, the public and
the leadership were likewise divided—and by a considerable margin. Eighty-five percent of the public as opposed to 35 percent of leaders viewed protecting U.S. jobs as
a very important goal of U.S. foreign policy. In contrast, 60 percent saw immigration
and refugees as a critical threat to the United States whereas only 14 percent of leaders were concerned about either issue.

Two public opinion analysts, Benjamin Page and Marshall Bouton, **provide
an even broader picture of elite/mass public differences in _The Foreign Policy
Disconnect_.**[15] Through careful and detailed analysis of all the quadrennial Chicago
Council leadership and public opinion surveys from 1974 through 2002, they illustrate just how dramatic—and persistent—these elite/mass differences were over a
thirty-year period. Utilizing all identically worded questions in the two surveys for
each year and defining a disagreement between leaders and the public as 10 percentage points or more, they discovered that, from 1974 through 2002, the leaders and the
public disagreed on 73 percent of those questions. The lowest level of disagreement
was 68 percent in 1986; the highest was 78 percent in 1990. When Page and Bouton
employed a stricter criterion for disagreement—a majority of the public and a majority of the leaders in disagreement—they still found that the two groups disagreed
26 percent of the time. These differences occurred across three policy areas, economic,
defense, and diplomatic, with the largest gulf on economic policy and the smallest on
diplomatic policy. Clearly, the leadership and public gap continues.

The 2005 Pew Research Center survey, referred to earlier, also revealed this continuing leader–public gap. Although its results showed some congruence between
leaders and the public on "protecting against terrorism and preventing the spread of
weapons of mass destruction," divisions existed over trade policy and protection of
U.S. jobs. On NAFTA, for example, only 44 percent of the public saw it as "good" for
the country; all of the leaders except one group viewed it much more positively. Furthermore, the public was more favorable than leaders toward the use of military force
and more tolerant of the use of torture.

In sum, major analyses of elite, or leadership, opinion offer the same picture of
America's foreign policy leaders: an elite often divided over how the United States
ought to act in the world. These studies also highlight the continuing divisions between leaders and the public on a number of important foreign policy questions.
Furthermore, there appears little reason to believe that these policy gaps have lessened
as the Afghanistan War lingers on and as the economic problems at home and abroad
deepen. In addition, partisan divisions on foreign policy, to which we now turn, have
reinforced and perhaps surpassed the elite–mass divisions that we have been witnessing over the past several decades.

PARTISAN DIVISIONS
ON FOREIGN POLICY

As several scholars have noted (and as we discussed in Chapter 11), **partisan divisions on foreign policy have more often been the norm rather than the exception**, despite the reluctance of some to acknowledge them on foreign policy. Indeed, as Miroslav Nincic has aptly noted, foreign policy issues "have been a big part of national election campaigns since the country's rise to superpower status." These issues are likely to continue to be a source of contention in elections and beyond— and thus also complicate foreign policy making for a fundamental reason. That is, the two political parties are now increasingly divided over both the ends and means of American foreign policy. Regarding the ends of foreign policy, those who identify themselves as Republicans tend to prefer foreign policy goals of a "self-regarding" type, such as "maintaining superior military power, controlling illegal immigration, and protecting American jobs." Those who identify themselves as Democrats tend to prefer foreign policy goals of an "other regarding" type, such as "combating world hunger, protecting weak nations from aggression, and strengthening the United Nations." Regarding the means of foreign policy, the differences are equally stark between party identifiers: Democrats prefer multilateral means and diplomacy as their preferred methods, and Republicans prefer unilateral means and military measures as their preferred methods.[16] In such an environment, cooperation across foreign policy issues remains a serious challenge for policy makers.

In a 2010 survey conducted by the Chicago Council on Global Affairs, these partisan differences were brought into sharp relief on several key foreign policy issues. Table 13.2 reproduces some of the "partisan gaps" between Republicans and

Table 13.2 Partisan Differences on Selected Foreign Policy Issues

Selected Issues	Rep. (%)	Dem. (%)	Diff. (%)
Immigration			
Percentage who see large numbers of immigrants and refugees coming into the United States as a "critical" threat to the vital interest in the next ten years.	63	40	23
Percentage who see the goal of controlling and reducing illegal immigration as a "very important" foreign policy goal for the United States.	74	47	27
Percentage who say illegal immigrants mostly take away jobs from Americans who need them.	63	37	26
Globalization			
Percentage who say that globalization, especially the increasing connections of our economy with others around the world, is "mostly good" for the United States.	49	67	−18

(Continued)

Selected Issues	Rep. (%)	Dem. (%)	Diff. (%)
Percentage who say that overall globalization is "good" for creating jobs in the United States.	27	46	−19
Percentage who say that overall globalization is "good" for the next generation of Americans.	36	57	−21
Climate Change			
Percentage who see climate change as a "critical" threat to the vital interest of the United States in the next ten years.	16	48	−32
Percentage who see the goal of limiting climate change as a "very important" foreign policy goal for the United States.	17	50	−33
Percentage who say protection of the environment should be given priority even at the risk of curbing economic growth.	40	69	−29
Percentage who say the United States should participate in a new international treaty to address climate change by reducing greenhouse gas emissions.	50	85	−35
International Institutions			
Percentage who agree that when dealing with international problems, the United States should be more willing to make decisions within the United Nations even if this means that the United States will sometimes have to go along with a policy that is not its first choice.	35	62	−27
Percentage who see the goal of strengthening the UN as a "very important" foreign policy goal for the United States.	24	50	−26
Torture			
Percentage who favor using torture to extract information from suspected terrorists in order to combat international terrorism	53	29	24
Percentage who agree that rules against torture should be maintained because torture is morally wrong and weakening these rules may lead to the torture of U.S. soldiers who are held prisoner abroad.	41	74	−33

Source: Taken from Marshall M. Bouton, ed., *Global Views 2010: Constrained Internationalism: Adapting to New Realities* (Chicago: The Chicago Council on Global Affairs, 2010), pp. 80-81.

Democrats on the issues of immigration, globalization, climate change, and the use of torture from the survey.[17] **What is most compelling about these results is the magnitude of the differences between the political parties,** as indicated by the size of the difference score in the last column of this table. The smallest difference between the parties across these issues was 18 percent and the largest was 35 percent, and the average differences on these policy questions was in the middle 20 percent range. The largest differences deal with questions about climate change and how that issue should be viewed and addressed, followed by the differences over immigration and the use of international institutions. The use of torture, too, deeply divides the parties, whether asked about using it as a method to extract information or over maintaining rules against its use because it is morally wrong. Among these items, the least divisive set of questions occurs for those about the benefits of globalization, where slightly less than 20 percentage points separated party adherents from one another. Nonetheless, this partisan gap is still considerable, and it is not something that can easily be bridged.

To be sure, and despite these increasing differences in orientation by the two major political parties, some "cross-party" consensus does exist. Both Democrats and Republicans support the view that the United States should take an "active part" in global affairs; both party adherents view terrorism and nuclear proliferation as "critical" threats; and both see protecting the job of American workers as a "very important" goal. Both sets of partisans continue to show agreement on the use of American forces and on maintaining U.S. bases overseas. Similarly, both groups view Iran and China as crucial foreign policy concerns.[18] Indeed, in a 2012 Gallup survey, Republicans, Independents, and Democrats viewed Iran and China as the top enemies of the United States, although Republicans were slightly more likely to identify these two countries as the principal adversaries.[19] In all, then, there exist some commonalities, despite the gulf outlined earlier, and hence some opportunities to forge a new direction.

A NEW FOREIGN POLICY CONSENSUS?

The shifts in policy from one president to another and the divisions that developed among American leaders and between those leaders and the public point to the need for a new foreign policy consensus. In the international system that exists today, this need is greater than ever. A new consensus could engender widespread support among the American people and lend coherence and direction to U.S. policy. This is not the first time there have been calls for a new consensus—they were heard after the Vietnam War, after September 11, and as the Iraq War dragged on. Indeed, the number of proposals for altering the direction of American foreign policy over recent decades has escalated from one time period to the next.

Calls for a New Consensus

Prior to becoming national security advisor in the Carter administration, Zbigniew Brzezinski, for example, argued that the Vietnam experience had shattered the WASP foreign policy elite and that Henry Kissinger's global design had failed to replace it. Thus, he contended, there was a "need for national leadership that was capable of defining politically and morally compelling directions to which the public might then positively respond."[20] A bit later, another foreign policy analyst lamented that a consensus had not emerged and that the United States was experiencing a foreign policy "crack-up."[21] With the demise of communism in Eastern Europe and the collapse of the Soviet Union, calls for a new consensus, or at least new approaches, were once again widespread.[22] In the immediate aftermath of the events of September 11, too, the prospects for a new consensus were quickly discussed and debated. In a provocative essay, James Steinberg, then director of the foreign policy program at the Brookings Institution, asked whether counterterrorism was "a new organizing principle for American national security."[23]

As the Iraq War dragged on and U.S. foreign policy became increasingly divisive at home and abroad, more proposals were advanced to unite foreign policy around a set of ideas, values, or norms that Americans could embrace. Two analysts called for the reemergence of the "rational center" to bring stability to policy;[24] another proposed a reformulated containment policy as the best way to replace the Bush Doctrine;[25] a third called for learning from the Cold War, both how to defend the country from terrorism and how to defeat an adversary;[26] a fourth proposed the adoption of "security first" as a policy guide.[27] After reviewing several such proposals, eminent international relations scholar Joseph S. Nye concluded that "there is clearly no consensus in academe about the future of American foreign policy."[28]

More recently, several prominent analysts have yet again outlined new grand strategies for the United States: Fareed Zakaria has proposed how the United States should respond to the "rise of the rest." G. John Ikenberry has offered a series of prescriptions for how the United States can engage in "liberal order building" to sustain the present global order and improve on it. And Charles Kupchan argues that a "global turn" is taking place with the emergence of an international system with multiple centers of power. If the United States is going to play a role in this new order, it must "retrench" at home by restoring "economic and political solvency" and creating a "domestic consensus."[29]

A new consensus remains a formidable challenge for American foreign policy for several reasons. First, some have long doubted that a new consensus can be created and believe that any short-term consensus may be detrimental to sound foreign policy. Second, the foreign policy interests of the United States today are too diverse to be summarized under a single rubric, like anticommunism during the height of the Cold War, antiterrorism under the Bush administration, or even under "partnership" during the Obama years. Third, domestic interests are now often perceived as closely linked to foreign policy (such as trade and domestic employment), so foreign policy actions under such a rubric might only reinforce existing domestic divisions rather than promote a wider "national interest."[30] And finally, "while a consensus may make a country easier to govern, it does not necessarily make for good policy,"[31] especially in a changing global environment.

Less demanding than seeking an overarching consensus—but more than a case-by-case approach—would be to identify and obtain agreement on dealing with key issues or key nations.[32] For instance, a consensus might be built on agreeing to common policies for addressing terrorism, drug trafficking, or nuclear proliferation, regardless of differences on other issues. Similarly, it might be possible to gain consensus only on relations with specific countries or regions (such as Iran, North Korea, or China). In short, an intermediate approach to consensus building would be less demanding and perhaps more achievable.

If a consensus were to emerge, however, dangers might accompany it. A premature consensus—one that is not firmly embedded in both the leadership and the public—might be just a set of simple moral slogans that do not reflect the complexity of policy needed for today's world.[33] A premature consensus could easily turn out to be a target for those opposed to a particular approach. A related and more critical danger for any consensus has been aptly summarized by analysts Leslie Gelb and Richard Betts in the wake of the Vietnam War, but it remains applicable today: "Doctrine and consensus are the midwives to necessity and the enemy of dissent and choice."[34] That is, once beliefs become so dominant in the policy process, movement away from them becomes extraordinarily difficult. In large measure, this is what occurred with Iraq for the Bush administration, and the same concern might be raised about Afghanistan during the Obama administration as well.

Developing a New Consensus

Can a workable foreign policy consensus emerge that takes into account these possible dangers? The answer, of course, is still very much up in the air. Yet as one proponent argued many years ago, "there is no sensible alternative but to try."[35] **At a minimum, though, certain requirements must be met to achieve a new consensus.**

First, political leadership will be a fundamental necessity. This leadership, however, must not be one that yearns for past glory; instead, it must accept the changed global reality—a world increasingly divided—and be willing to evoke change by pursuing a more differentiated foreign policy. Second, the leadership must be willing to educate the public continuously on foreign policy. That is, leaders must be willing to explain their policy and the rationale for their actions on a regular basis. Third, and crucially important, the public must evaluate its beliefs and values regarding what the United States should stand for in the world, the extent to which domestic values should shape American policy, and the degree to which various political, economic, and military instruments are acceptable for implementing it.

None of these requisites will be easy to achieve. Political leaders often opt for domestically attractive foreign policy stances because they find educating the public on the issues difficult. Similarly, the public has too often shown little interest in or knowledge of foreign affairs. A coherent foreign policy, however, requires that the leadership and the public make such an effort. The leadership task is especially difficult today because the elite–public value divisions are ideologically and partisan-based and exist within rather than across generations. Thus, simple appeals to only one segment of the American public will not suffice; the leadership must instead be much more creative in identifying values and policies that will appeal across generations and groups.

In addition, creating a domestic consensus is made perhaps even more difficult today due to the challenges posed by the current international system—with the rise of new states, the impact of the global economic crisis of recent years, and the perceived decline in American influence abroad. For instance, the emergence of China and India in Asia, the rise of Brazil in Latin America, and the increase in influence of Turkey in the Middle East, among others, may portend the rise of a new international order without Western (or American) leadership. Indeed, the future has been dubbed as "no-one's world" by one analyst—a world order with perhaps multiple orders led by various states.[36] Further, the rise of these new states has occurred largely in conjunction with an economic crisis, particularly within Western states from 2007 onward, that has paralyzed the West's responses to these global changes. In turn, this environment has led to the resurrection of debate over the decline of the United States, and the perception by some that America's role in global politics will never be the same as it was after the collapse of the Soviet Union in 1991. (See the competing views on decline in the opening quotations of this chapter to gain some sense of this division.) In short, both domestic *and* international factors make developing a foreign policy consensus difficult.

Alternate Visions of a New Foreign Policy Consensus

What, then, are some alternative approaches that have been advanced for creating a new consensus, and what are their prospects for gaining support across groups and generations? Numerous proposals have been offered over recent decades, but in a short space we cannot do justice to them. Instead, what we can do is outline three kinds of alternatives that encapsulate the gist of the competing visions that have been advanced (a foreign policy of American realism and primacy, a foreign policy of American multilateralism and cooperation, and a foreign policy of American retrenchment and limits). These alternatives should hopefully stimulate debate among students and analysts about the future direction of American foreign policy.

A Foreign Policy of American Realism and Primacy

Several analysts call for greater realism—an approach in which the United States would remain engaged in the world, albeit more selectively and with greater self-interest than in the past. Variants of this approach called for more unilateralism, including recognition of America's hegemonic role in global politics, whereas others advocate a more focused and selective involvement with other states and organizations (while largely preserving America's autonomy of action).

The most forceful statement of a more focused realism was the neo-conservative approach first advanced by William Kristol and Robert Kagan in the years immediately after the Cold War in which they called for a "benevolent global hegemony" by the United States.[37] In this approach, U.S. power and influence would be largely generous and unselfish in leading and promoting global order. A principal aim would be to preserve American predominance around the world through "strengthening [its] security, supporting its friends, advancing its interests, and standing up for its principles."[38] To sustain and promote this global role, the United States would also need to pursue a policy of "military supremacy and moral confidence" by enhancing defense spending, increasing citizen awareness of America's international role, and pursuing actions abroad "based on the understanding that its moral goals and its fundamental national interests are almost always in harmony."[39] In large measure, of course, this approach was embraced by members of the George W. Bush administration, and the Bush Doctrine was one manifestation of it (see Chapter 5).

Other recent analysts also point to American primacy as central to global order and stability. Political scientist Robert Lieber, for example, has argued for American primacy and questions the declinist argument about the loss of American power. American primacy will likely continue, he contends, because the United States had no real challengers and because American leadership has been the "necessary catalyst" for effective global action, including "international collaboration."[40] The "declinists"—those who see American hegemony waning as other countries rise in power and as America's domestic problems increase—are wrong as well. They fail to understand the problems still faced by the likely challengers and the resiliency of the United States in several areas. Russia, China, and India among others have domestic and international problems that prevent them from being "major power challengers" in the near term. In contrast, America's "structural advantages," its size, its wealth and resources, and its "remarkable flexibility, dynamism, and capacity for reinvention" sustain its central role in global affairs.[41]

Political scientist Michael Mandelbaum makes the case for a sustained hegemonic role for the United States in another way: **America has largely operated as the "world's government" by providing political and economic security over** the decades.[42] In this sense, "Goliath" matters in global affairs. Although other states will continue to criticize American preeminence, Mandelbaum argues, they would soon miss its stabilizing influence if it were to lose its dominant role. In this sense, U.S. primacy or hegemony in foreign affairs remains an attractive, even an indispensable, option for shaping future policy.

Still another analyst, writing from the realist perspective, **proposed the continuation of American leadership but in a much less hegemonic and unilateral way than called for by others**.[43] Under his design, "the priority for American foreign policy should be to integrate other states into American-sponsored or American-supported efforts to deal with the challenges of globalization."[44] This cooperation cannot be achieved by coercion but only through the consent of other states. The fundamental focus would be on building "cooperative relations" among major powers, which would commit "to promoting certain principles and outcomes." In turn, these commitments would expand "into effective arrangements and actions" that would incorporate "other countries, organizations, and peoples." The ultimate goal would be a more integrated and cooperative international community.[45] Such an approach would involve a "little less sovereignty" for the United States and for other nations, but it would have the advantage of enhancing the legitimacy of American actions as well as those of others.[46]

Although this first approach appeals to American exceptionalism and America's traditional role over the past several decades, it also bumps up against a public that has largely rejected such an approach shortly after the initiation of the Iraq War. In this sense, whatever the benefits of sustained American hegemony, and there are many as the various proponents contend, it must confront an American public consistently committed to multilateral effort to address global problems and unwilling to be the "world police officer." Finally, too stark an emphasis on realist principles—acting only on narrow national interests to create global stability and order—without reliance on guiding moral principles runs the risk of increasing public cynicism about the short-term motivations of politicians and of affronting the ethical impulses toward foreign affairs still prevalent among Americans.

A Foreign Policy of American Multilateralism and Cooperation

A second approach for building a new consensus focuses more on the use of multilateralism and global cooperation in carrying out American foreign policy and represents a sharp departure from the realism and primacy of the first approach. Indeed, it connotes a sense of idealism in the conduct of policy through the attempt to spread American values in the international system. It also comports with some of the components of the Obama administration's initial liberal internationalist approach (see Chapter 6).

About a decade ago, political analysts Ivo H. Daalder and James M. Lindsay in particular emphasized **the need for American foreign policy to move beyond unilateralism to a greater multilateralism during the present era of globalization**.[47] They acknowledged that the unilateralists are correct in recognizing that "power remains the coin of the realm in international politics," that "the wise application of American primacy can further U.S. values and interests," and that the United States differs from past hegemons "in not seeking to expand its power through territorial gains." However, they maintained that American primacy and power are not sufficient and have clear limits. "Some crucial problems do defy unilateral solution," whether they are global warming, international terrorism, or a whole range of other issues tied to globalization. As such, international "cooperation can extend the life of American primacy" and manage some of globalization's positive and negative effects. "By creating international regimes and organizations," these analysts argue, "Washington can imbed its interests and values in institutions that will shape and constrain countries for decades, regardless of the vicissitudes of American power." In this sense, it is in the U.S. national interest to create a global order "based on democracy, human rights, and free enterprise. By doing so, the United States enhances its own liberty, security, and prosperity."[48]

Writing at about the same time, Joseph S. Nye, Jr., largely proposed the same prescription, albeit with a more expansive design.[49] The essential challenge for the United States, Nye argued, was to "define our national interest to include global interests."[50] To do so, **the United States will need to pursue interests and values that will have broad appeal, and it will need to build a global community that is compatible and supportive of such values.** A unilateral or hegemonic approach is not sufficient to achieve those ends; instead, one that weds unilateralism and multilateralism, albeit with an emphasis on the latter, is his essential prescription for the future.

Nye's "grand strategy" has several important components for future policy.[51] Although he acknowledges that protecting vital interests is at the core of his approach (and these interests can and should be defended unilaterally), the national interest also includes the values that the people believe "are so important to our identity or sense of who we are that people are willing to pay a price to promote them."[52] Thus, the United States must work to create three important "global public goods." In particular, it must maintain "regional balances of power" as a way to reduce the incentive for states or groups to try to change international borders, to promote "an open international economic system" as it serves both the interests of the United States and the rest of the world, and to keep open the global commons (such as freedom of the seas, "global climate change, preservation of endangered species, and the uses of outer space, as well as the virtual commons of cyberspace").[53] Third, the United States should promote human rights and democracy. These values should be a part of America's foreign policy, but their promotion must also be integrated into larger foreign policy considerations in dealing with a country or region. Furthermore, Nye set out "rules of prudence" for when humanitarian interventions should come to the defense of human rights. Standing for, and promoting, these values globally would enhance America's soft power, as would the promotion of democracy, but "the role of force is usually less central" to this goal, "and the process [of democratization] is of a longer-term nature."[54]

A more recent, and perhaps the strongest, statement of this multilateral approach has been advanced by G. John Ikenberry in his *Liberal Leviathan*. In that volume, he urges the United States to engage in a grand strategy of "**liberal order building**."[55] Such a strategy would involve the United States taking the lead in building "institutional cooperation to strengthen the capacity of governments and the international community" to address a series of transnational problems (such as food shortages, epidemics, mass migrations); the rebuilding of American security alliances worldwide and "making new compromises over the distribution of formal rights and responsibilities" within such alliances; reforming and creating "global institutions that foster and legitimate collective action"; and "[accommodating] and institutionally [engaging] China." Finally, and crucially, Ikenberry argues that America's elites "should reclaim a liberal internationalist public philosophy."[56] What that philosophy means in practice is "a vision of multilateral partnership, cooperative security, and collective action" in the conduct of American foreign policy—and, in essence, a rejection of the unilateralism of the recent past.[57]

On one level, of course, these calls for multilateralism may be met with considerable receptivity by both the public and its leaders. After all, the public has consistently supported an active role for the United States in global affairs and for multilateral approaches to address global issues—and that support continues today. On another level, though, there are questions to be answered about the patience and long-term support required for this approach to be fully implemented—as well as the resources to do so today. Further, this general approach carries with it some loss of national sovereignty and a movement in the direction of the United States as an ordinary, not extraordinary, nation in global politics. As such, this approach may generate some backlash among the public. Finally, one recent study suggests that the depth of public support for multilateralism and for some international institutions is soft and sometimes exists more in the abstract than in practice.[58] This might be an obstacle as well. In all, sustained leadership would be required to turn this approach for American foreign policy into a reality.

A Foreign Policy of Retrenchment and Limits

Charles Kupchan and Peter Trubowitz proposed yet a **third kind of approach** for the future, one that they describe as **a more "politically solvent strategy" for American foreign policy, which would allow a "judicious retrenchment" without a return to isolationism**.[59] This is an approach somewhere between the realism and primacy of the first approach and the multilateralism and global cooperation of the second approach. The rationale for this more restrained foreign policy approach rests on the polarized nature of domestic politics and the need to advance a foreign policy that would foster more bipartisanship at home.

With Republicans showing "little patience for cooperative multilateralism" and Democrats "readying ambitious plans to breathe new life into international institutions," these analysts call for "a new grand strategy that is politically solvent"[60]—that is, a strategy that would meet the power demands of Republicans and the partnership demands of Democrats.[61] To achieve this kind of foreign policy compromise, they argue that U.S. commitments must be brought into line with American political means. The United States thus ought to pursue "a strategy that is as judicious and selective as it is purposeful."[62]

In particular, they suggest several principles to meet those requirements and manage the constraints imposed by domestic politics. They include the encouragement of greater burden sharing and self-reliance by other states, abandoning efforts at regime change, the rebuilding of America's military readiness, seeking to dampen major power competition through "shrewd diplomacy," reducing reliance on foreign oil, and "favor[ing] pragmatic partnerships over the formalized international institutions of the Cold War era."[63]

In a more recent volume, Kupchan reinforced this need for a more modest U.S. foreign policy for the future.[64] Moreover, he points out that the recent "fiscal and political constraints on U.S. strategy may be a blessing in disguise." As a result, the focus of American foreign policy should now return to great power rivalries, with an abandonment of the nation building activities of the past decade and the use of force "in a surgical fashion to combat terrorists." Further, under a policy of retrenchment, the United States "would also devolve rights and responsibilities to emerging powers looking to wield influence commensurate with their growing capabilities."[65]

Finally, Michael Mandelbaum in *The Frugal Superpower* echoes this call for foreign policy retrenchment.[66] As we noted earlier, Mandelbaum has long espoused the importance of the United States (as "Goliath") in global governance, and, indeed, he contended that the United States functioned "as the world's de facto government" through global public goods that it provided. Yet with America's fiscal crisis, beginning in September 2008 and continuing to the present, his position now more closely mirrors that of Kupchan and Trubowitz on several issues. Mandelbaum now judges that **it will be necessary for the United States to eschew humanitarian interventions, nation building, and effort to impose democracy in light of America's fiscal constraint**. Depending on how much the U.S. military is maintained or rebuilt in this current era, the focus will more likely be on "ensuring security in Europe and East Asia, opposing the spread of nuclear weapons, and guaranteeing a secure geopolitical background for international commerce." Finally, and importantly, he advocates a "new containment" policy to reduce American (and Western countries) dependence on imported petroleum as perhaps the most important step to managing American foreign policy for the future.

As we noted earlier, the retrenchment approach falls somewhere between the emphasis on realism and primacy and multilateralism and cooperation approaches, even as it seeks to utilize elements from both approaches in its implementation. In this sense, the approach may draw elites from both of these earlier approaches to its side. Furthermore, the approach comports with the current public mood in its call for a more selective and limited involvement on the part of the United States (see Chapter 12).[67] As a result, the public may be drawn to it. Yet, the approach may have some downsides. A policy of retrenchment appears to satisfy neither those who seek to maintain American exceptionalism nor those who seek to promote greater American multilateralism in foreign policy. With the public (and leaders) divided by ideology and partisanship, as we noted earlier, the challenge for this approach is whether the "middle" of American politics is still sufficiently large and supple to enable this approach to gain the necessary political traction to be implemented.

The 2012 Elections and Future American Foreign Policy

The 2012 presidential and congressional elections did not resolve the ongoing debate among these alternative visions over the direction of American foreign policy. Instead, the results were largely a reaffirmation of the status quo. On November 6, President Barack Obama was reelected by a narrow margin in the popular vote (51%-48%) and a larger victory in the Electoral College (332-206) over former Massachusetts Governor Mitt Romney. In the congressional elections, the Republicans maintained control of the U.S. House of Representatives and the Democrats, the U.S. Senate. Thus, neither party could claim a clear mandate for the future policy, and especially foreign policy. Indeed, exit poll results revealed that foreign policy was the most important issue for only about four or five percent of the American public in the presidential election. Instead, these elections were largely fought over issues of the economy, the levels of trust of the candidates, and the power of incumbency.

As a result, American foreign policy will likely follow the same general direction that President Obama set out in 2009 and 2010 (see Chapter 6), albeit now within limits. The administration will continue to foster American "partnerships" around the world in an effort to address problems of common global interests with other, and, in that sense, it will adhere to the second alternative vision outlined above—an emphasis on multilateralism and cooperation with others. Now, however, important domestic constraints will limit the extent of American-led actions abroad. In foreign policy surveys in 2010 and 2012, the American public made it clear that it is increasing wary (and weary) over commitments abroad and supports more "selective engagement."

Further, even if Americans were willing to engage extensively abroad, the "wallet" to do so is now lacking. With a national debt of $16 trillion, and yearly budget deficits of $1 trillion, the administration will necessarily need to pursue elements of the third alternative vision discussed earlier—retrenchment and limits.

The only area of the world where the Obama administration is likely to expand American involvement in the near term is in the Asia-Pacific region. With the increasing strategic and economic importance of the nations in that part of the world (e.g., the rise of China, India, Indonesia) and the potential for conflict and instability there (e.g., island disputes in the South and East China Sea), the Obama administration announced in late 2011 and early 2012 a foreign policy "pivot" toward that area. A series of military, economic, and diplomatic actions were accelerated toward that region by the United States, and such actions are only likely to intensify in a second term. Many of these initiatives have been to enhance partnerships with friends and allies there. In this sense, this approach will likely be more consistent with limiting direct American involvements in regional issues and fostering greater burden-sharing by other states—a strategy that will likely be well received by the American public.

CONCLUDING COMMENTS

Which approach or combination of approaches (if any) will emerge as the basis of a new foreign policy consensus? We obviously cannot say with any certainty because the public and elite debate continues. Nevertheless, these contrasting approaches continue to highlight one important component of the historical American debate that has largely been resolved, and another that goes on: it is generally agreed that continued American engagement in world affairs is necessary, albeit in sharply different degrees. The question is still open on the extent to which domestic moral values should act as an overarching guide to policy actions and on what those values should be.

Such debates over fundamental values need not be debilitating for American foreign policy. Instead, they can strengthen Americans' unity and resolve in addressing their common foreign policy concerns, even as American society seeks to determine the values it wants to promote in the global arena. The role of values in foreign policy deliberations has perhaps never been more pronounced. As noted a few years ago, "the rise of ethics in foreign policy" has become increasingly crucial, and, by this assessment, we are in a new era:

> We have passed from an era in which ideals were flatly opposed to self-interests into an era in which tension remains between the two, but the stark juxtaposition of the past has largely subsided. Now ideals and self-interests are generally considered necessary ingredients of the national interest.[68]

Notes

1. See Eugene R. Wittkopf, Charles W. Kegley, and James M. Scott, *American Foreign Policy: Pattern and Process*, 6th ed. (Belmont, CA: Wadsworth, 2003), pp. 14–15, for an argument along these lines.

2. Political scientists Ole Holsti and James Rosenau conducted six Foreign Policy Leadership Project (FPLP) surveys every four years from 1976 through 1996; the Chicago Council on Foreign Relations (now the Chicago Council on Global Affairs) conducted eight quadrennial leadership surveys in parallel with their public opinion surveys from 1974 through 1992. For a discussion of first set of surveys, see Ole R. Holsti, *Public Opinion and American Foreign Policy*, rev. ed. (Ann Arbor: The University of Michigan Press, 2004), pp. 99–106 and Table 4.1 at pp. 104–105, for a description of the samples used. For access to the Chicago Council surveys, see its website under "Studies and Publications" for the "Chicago Council surveys" link at http://www.thechicagocouncil.org/files/Surveys/ Chicago_Council_Survey_Home/files/Studies_Publications/POS/Public_Opinion.aspx.

3. Ole R. Holsti and James N. Rosenau, "The Political Foundations of Elites' Domestic and Foreign-Policy Beliefs," in Eugene R. Wittkopf and James M. McCormick, eds., *The Domestic Sources of American Foreign Policy: Insights and Evidence*, 3rd ed. (Lanham, MD: Rowman & Littlefield Publishers, 1999), pp. 33–50.

4. Ibid., p. 37. When all of the surveys are analyzed, including 1976 and 1980, the results do not change much. For example, hard liners made up 20 percent of the leaders in 1976 and 1980; isolationists, 8 percent and 7 percent; internationalists, 30 percent and 33 percent; and accommodationists, 42 percent and 41 percent. the results for the other years (1984, 1988, and 1992) are largely comparable. See Holsti, *Public Opinion and American Foreign Policy*, Table 4.5 at p. 134 for the complete data for all these years.

5. Holsti and Rosenau, "The Political Foundations of Elites' Domestic and Foreign-Policy Beliefs," p. 42.

6. Ibid., p. 46.

7. Ole R. Holsti, "Public Opinion and Foreign Policy," in Robert J. Lieber, ed., *Eagle Rules? Foreign Policy and American Primacy in the Twenty-first Century* (Upper Saddle River, NJ: Prentice Hall, 2002), pp. 16–46. The quoted passages are at p. 39. Other post-Vietnam analyses of elite beliefs by Wittkopf have largely confirmed and more fully specified the foreign policy divisions that Holsti and Rosenau initially suggested. (See Eugene

R. Wittkopf, *Faces of Internationalism: Public Opinion and American Foreign Policy* [Durham, NC: Duke University Press, 1990], pp. 107–133.)

8. See Holsti, *Public Opinion and Foreign Policy*, pp. 231–232, for this summary statement. Emphasis added.

9. Marshall M. Bouton and Benjamin I. Page, eds., *Worldviews 2002: American Public Opinion & Foreign Policy* (Chicago: The Chicago Council on Foreign Relations, 2002), pp. 63–72. Here is how Bouton and Page describe the components of the leadership survey: "Administration officials in the State, Treasury, Commerce, and other departments, and agencies dealing with foreign policy; members of the House and Senate or their senior staff with committee responsibilities in foreign affairs, senior business executives from Fortune 1000 firms who deal with international matters; university administrators and academics who teach in the area of international relations; presidents of major organizations or large interest groups active in foreign affairs; presidents of the largest labor unions; religious leaders; and journalists and editorial staff who handle international news" (p. 63).

10. Ibid., pp. 66–68.

11. The results reported here are taken from "Opinion Leaders Turn Cautious, Public Looks Homeward," The Pew Research Center for the People and the Press, at http://people -press.org/report/263/opinion-leaders-turn-cautious-public-looks-homeward, July 7, 2008.

12. See Eugene R. Wittkopf and Michael A. Maggiotto, "Elites and Masses: A Comparative Analysis of Attitudes Toward America's World Role," *The Journal of Politics* 45 (May 1983): pp. 312–323; Eugene R. Wittkopf, "Elites and Masses: Constancy and Change in Public Attitudes Toward America's World Role," a paper delivered at the annual meeting of the Southern Political Science Association, Birmingham, Alabama, November 1983; and Wittkopf, *Faces of Internationalism*, pp. 134–165.

13. See Bouton and Page, *Worldviews 2002: American Public Opinion & Foreign Policy*, pp. 66–73.

14. See ibid. at pp. 69–72. The data discussed here are summarized in Table 13.2.

15. Benjamin I. Page with Marshall M. Bouton, *The Foreign Policy Disconnect* (Chicago and London: The University of Chicago Press, 2006). The discussion and data are taken from pp. 207–215. This chapter of the book was written with Lawrence R. Jacobs.

16. Miroslav Nincic, "External Affairs and the Electoral Connection," in James M. McCormick, ed., *The Domestic Sources of American Foreign Policy: Insights and Evidence* (Lanham, MD: Rowman and Littlefield Publishers, Inc., 2012), pp. 139, 145–148.

17. See Marshall M. Bouton, ed., *Global Views 2010: Constrained Internationalism: Adapting to New Realities* (Chicago: The Chicago Council on Global Affairs, 2010), pp. 80–81 for the complete list of policy issues and party differences.

18. Ibid., p. 79.

19. Frank Newport, "American Still Rate Iran Top U.S. Enemy," Gallup, February 20, 2012, at http://www.gallup.com/poll/152786/Americans-Rate-Iran-Top-Enemy.aspx, July 24, 2012.

20. Zbigniew Brzezinski, "America in a Hostile World," *Foreign Policy* 23 (Summer 1976): 89. For a sample of the Vietnam-era calls for a new consensus, see, for example, Lincoln P. Bloomfield, "Foreign Policy for Disillusioned Liberals," *Foreign Policy* 9 (Winter 1972–73): 55–68; Thomas L. Hughes, "The Flight from Foreign Policy," *Foreign Policy* 10 (Spring 1973): 141–156; and Philip Windsor, "America's Moral Confusion: Separating the Should from the Good," *Foreign Policy* 13 (Winter 1973–74): 139–153.

21. Thomas L. Hughes, "The Crack-Up: The Price of Collective Irresponsibility," *Foreign Policy* 40 (Fall 1980): 33–60.

22. See, for example, Graham Allison and Gregory F. Treverton, eds., *Rethinking America's Security: Beyond Cold War to New World Order* (New York: W.W. Norton and Company, 1992); Terry L. Deibel, "Strategies Before Containment: Patterns for the Future," *International Security* 16 (Spring 1992): 79–108; John Lewis Gaddis, *The United States and the End of the Cold War: Implications, Reconsiderations, and Provocations* (New York: Oxford University Press, 1992); Zalmay Khalilzad, "Losing the Moment? The United States and the World After the Cold War," *The Washington Quarterly* 18 (Spring 1995): 87–107; Richard A. Melanson, *American Foreign Policy Since the Vietnam War: The Search for Consensus from Nixon to Clinton*, 2nd ed. (Armonk, NY: M. E. Sharpe, 1996); and Andrew Rosenthal, "Farewell, Red Menace," *New York Times*, September 1, 1991, 1 and 14. There are many others.

23. James Steinberg, "Counterterrorism," *Brookings Review* 20 (Summer 2002): 4–7.

24. Stefan Halper and Jonathan Clarke, *The Silence of the Rational Center* (New York: Basic Books, 2007). See pp. 1–20 for the essential argument, but the entire book addresses this issue.

25. Ian Shapiro, *Containment: Rebuilding a Strategy against Global Terror* (Princeton and Oxford: Princeton University Press, 2007).

26. Philip Gordon, *Winning the Right War* (New York: Times Books, 2007).

27. Amitai Etzioni, *Security First* (New Haven and London: Yale University Press, 2007).

28. Joseph S. Nye, "American Foreign Policy after Iraq," *The Chronicle Review*, July 27, 2007, B6–B8. The quote is at p. B8. Nye reviews the Halper and Clarke, Shapiro, and Etzioni books as well as a volume by Chalmers Johnson in this essay. We used this essay as well.

29. Fareed Zakaria, The Post-American World (New York: Norton, 2008); G. John Ikenberry, *Liberal Leviathan: The Origins, Crisis, and Transformation of the American World Order* (Princeton and Oxford: Princeton University Press, 2011); and Charles A. Kupchan, *No One's World: The West, The Rising Rest, and the Coming Global Turn* (New York: Oxford University Press, 2012). The quoted passages from Kupchan are at p. 203.

30. On how American foreign policy has become captive to domestic interests at the expense of the "national interest," see Samuel P. Huntington, "The Erosion of American National Interests," in Eugene R. Wittkopf and James M. McCormick, eds., *The Domestic Sources of American Foreign Policy: Insights and Evidence*, 4th ed. (Lanham, MD: Rowman & Littlefield Publishers, 2004), pp. 55–65.

31. See James Chace, "Is a Foreign Policy Consensus Possible?" *Foreign Affairs* 57 (Fall 1978): 16, for the view advanced at the beginning of this paragraph. For Chace's later view, including this quotation, see James Chace, "The Dangers of a Foreign Policy Consensus," *World Policy Journal* 13 (Winter 1996–1997): 97.

32. I am indebted to Professor Ole Holsti of Duke University for suggesting this point about consensus on issues.

33. Chace, "Is a Foreign Policy Consensus Possible?" p. 15. Actually, Chace quotes from Stanley Hoffmann's *Primacy or World Order* (New York: McGraw-Hill, 1978) to make this point.

34. Leslie H. Gelb with Richard K. Betts, *The Irony of Vietnam: The System Worked* (Washington, D.C.: The Brookings Institution, 1979), pp. 365–369.

35. Hughes, "The Crack-Up: The Price of Collective Irresponsibility," p. 59.

36. See Kupchan, *No One's World: The West, The Rising Rest, and the Coming Global Turn*.

37. William Kristol and Robert Kagan, "Toward a Neo-Reaganite Foreign Policy," *Foreign Affairs* 75 (July/August 1996): 18–32. The quoted passage is at p. 20.

38. Ibid., p. 23.

39. Ibid., pp. 23, 27.

40. Robert J. Lieber, "Foreign Policy and American Primacy," in Lieber, ed., *Eagle Rules? Foreign Policy and American Primacy in the Twenty-first Century*, pp. 1–15. The quoted passages are at p. 5. For an extended statement of his views on American primary, see Robert J. Lieber, *The American Era: Power and Strategy for the 21st Century* (New York: Cambridge University Press, 2005).

41. Robert J. Lieber, "Falling Upwards: Declinism, The Box Set," *World Affairs*, Summer 2008, at http://www.worldaffairsjournal.org/2008%20-%20Summer/full-Lieber.html, July 2, 2008. More recently, Lieber argues that "to the extent that limits to American primacy do exist, they are just as likely to be ideational as they are material." See Robert J. Lieber, "Staying Power and the American Future: Problems of Primacy, Policy and Grand Strategy," *Journal of Strategic Studies* 34, no. 4 (2011): 510.

42. See Michael Mandelbaum, "The Benefits of Goliath," in Eugene R. Wittkopf and James M. McCormick, eds., *The Domestic Sources of American Foreign Policy: Insights and Evidence*, 5th ed. (Lanham, MD: Rowman & Littlefield Publishers, 2008), pp. 55–64. His larger work on this topic is *The Case for Goliath: How America Acts as the World's Government in the Twenty-first Century* (New York: Public Affairs, 2005). Recently, Mandelbaum has modified his position somewhat, especially in light of the American economic difficulties, and called for some foreign policy retrenchment as a result (which we will take up below). See Michael Mandelbaum, *The Frugal Superpower* (New York: Public Affairs, 2010).

43. Richard N. Haass, "Defining U.S. Foreign Policy in a Post-Post–Cold War World," The 2002 Arthur Ross Lecture, Remarks to the Foreign Policy Association, New York, April 22, 2002, at http://2001-2009.state.gov/s/p/rem/9632.htm, August 4, 2012.

44. Richard N. Haass, *The Opportunity* (New York: Public Affairs, 2005), p. 23.

45. Ibid., p. 24.

46. See the chapter entitled "A Little Less Sovereignty" in ibid, pp. 33–50 and the discussion of "legitimacy" at p. 23 and Iraq at pp. 168–194.

47. Ivo H. Daalder and James M. Lindsay, "The Globalization of Politics: American Foreign Policy for a New Century," *Brookings Review* 21 (Winter 2003): 12–17.

48. Ibid., pp. 16 and 17 for the quotations in this paragraph.

49. Joseph S. Nye, Jr., *The Paradox of American Power: Why the World's Superpower Can't Go It Alone* (New York: Oxford University Press, 2002). The entire volume sets out his design, but Chapter 5 ("Redefining the National Interest"), pp. 137–171, especially sets out some specific policy recommendations.

50. Ibid., p. xiv.

51. Ibid., pp. 141–153.

52. The quotation is from ibid., at p. 139.

53. The quotations are from ibid., pp. 144–145.

54. The previous quotations in this paragraph are from ibid., pp. 152–153.

55. G. John Ikenberry, *Liberal Leviathan* (Princeton and Oxford: Princeton University Press, 2011, p. 353.

56. Ibid., pp. 354, 355, and 356.

57. Ibid., p. 355 on unilateralism, and p. 356 for the quoted passage.

58. See Daniel W. Drezner, "The Realist Tradition in American Public Opinion," *Perspectives on Politics* 6 (March 2008): 51–70, especially p. 57.

59. Charles A. Kupchan and Peter L. Trubowitz, "Grand Strategy for a Divided America," *Foreign Affairs* 86 (July/August 2007): 71–83. The quotations are at pp. 72 and 82, respectively.

60. Ibid. The quoted passages are at pp. 79 and 80, respectively.

61. Ibid., p. 77.

62. Ibid., p. 80.

63. These principles are from ibid., pp. 80–82 with all quoted passages at pp. 81 and 82.

64. See Kupchan, *No One's World: The West, The Rising Rest, and the Coming Global Turn.*

65. Ibid. The quoted passages in the paragraph are at pp. 204 and 203, respectively.

66. Mandelbaum, *The Frugal Superpower.* The quoted passages are at pp. 5–6. For the other arguments here, see pp. 182–194 and pp. 165–180.

67. See Bouton, *Global Views 2010: Constrained Internationalism: Adapting to New Realities* for a summary of the current public mood.

68. Leslie H. Gelb and Justine A. Rosenthal, "The Rise of Ethics in Foreign Policy: Reaching a Values Consensus," *Foreign Affairs* 82 (May/June 2003): 2–7. The first quote is from the title of the article at p. 2; the second is from p. 7.

A Selected Bibliography

Abrams, Elliott, ed. *The Influence of Faith: Religious Groups and U.S. Foreign Policy.* Lanham, MD: Rowman & Littlefield Publishers, Inc., 2001.

Acheson, Dean. *Present at the Creation.* New York: W. W. Norton and Company, 1969.

Adams, Gordon, and Matthew Leatherman. "A Leaner and Meaner Defense." In *The Domestic Sources of American Foreign Policy: Insights and Evidence.* 6th ed. James M. McCormick, ed. Lanham, MD: Rowman & Littlefield Publishers, Inc., 2012.

Adler, David Gray. "The Constitution and Presidential Warmaking: The Enduring Debate." *Political Science Quarterly* 103 (Spring 1988): 1–36.

Aldrich, John H., Christopher Gelpi, Peter Feaver, Jason Reifler, and Kristin Thompson Sharp. "Foreign Policy and the Electoral Connection." *Annual Review of Political Science* 9 (2006): 477–502.

———, John L. Sullivan, and Eugene Borgida. "Foreign Affairs and Issue Voting: Do Presidential Candidates 'Waltz Before a Blind Audience'?" *American Political Science Review* 83 (March 1989). 123–141.

———, and Philip Zelikow. *Essence of Decision: Explaining the Cuban Missile Crisis.* 2nd ed. New York: Longman, 1999.

Almond, Gabriel A. *The American People and Foreign Policy.* New York: Praeger, 1960.

Ambrose, Stephen E. *Rise to Globalism: American Foreign Policy 1938–1976.* New York: Penguin Books, 1976.

Anderson, David E. "The Right War Gone Wrong." *Religion and Ethics Newsweekly,* November 23, 2009, at http://www.pbs.org/wnet/religionandethics/episodes/november-20-2009/the-right-war-gone-wrong/5104/.

Arnett, Peter. *Live from the Battlefield.* New York: Simon & Schuster, 1994.

Baker, James A., III, and Lee H. Hamilton. *The Iraq Study Group Report.* New York: Vintage Books, 2006.

———, with Thomas M. DeFrank. *The Politics of Diplomacy: Revolution, War and Peace, 1989–1992.* New York: G. P. Putnam's Sons, 1995.

Ball, George W., and Douglas B. Ball. *The Passionate Attachment.* New York: W. W. Norton and Company, 1992.

Barry, John, Richard Wolffe, and Evan Thomas (with Dan Ephron and Michael Hirsch). "Stealth Warrior." *Newsweek* (March 19, 2007): 28–35.

Baum, Matthew A. *Soft News Goes to War: Public Opinion and American Foreign Policy in the New Media Age.* Princeton, NJ: Princeton University Press, 2003.

Bazan, Elizabeth B., and Jennifer K. Elsea. "P.L. 110-55, the Protect America Act of 2007: Modifications to the Foreign

Intelligence Surveillance Act." CRS Report to Congress, Washington, DC, Congressional Research Service, The Library of Congress, February 14, 2008.

———. "Presidential Authority to Conduct Warrantless Electronic Surveillance to Gather Foreign Intelligence Information." CRS Report to Congress. Washington, DC, Congressional Research Service, The Library of Congress, January 5, 2006.

———. "The U.S. Foreign Intelligence Surveillance Court and the U.S. Foreign Intelligence Surveillance Court of Review: An Overview." CRS Report to Congress. Washington, DC, Congressional Research Service, The Library of Congress, January 24, 2007.

Becker, Jo, and Scott Shane, "Secret 'Kill List' Proves a Test of Obama's Principles and Will," *New York Times*, May 29, 2012, at http://www.nytimes.com/2012/05/29/world/obamas-leadership-in-war-on-al-qaeda.html?pagewanted=all.

Beinert, Peter. "Party Politics No Longer Stops at the Water's Edge: Partisan Polarization and Foreign Policy," In *Red and Blue Nation? Consequences and Correction of America's Polarized Politics, Volume Two.* Pietro S. Nivola and David W. Brady, eds. Washington, DC and Stanford, CA: Brookings Institution Press and Hoover Institution Press, 2008.

Bennett, A. Leroy, and James K. Oliver. *International Organizations: Principles and Issues.* 7th ed. Upper Saddle River, NJ: Prentice Hall, 2002.

Bennett, W. Lance. "The Media and the Foreign Policy Process." In *The New Politics of American Foreign Policy.* David A. Deese, ed. New York: St. Martin's Press, 1994.

———, and David L. Paletz, eds. *Taken by Storm: The Media Public, Opinion, and U.S. Foreign Policy in the Gulf War.* Chicago and London: The University of Chicago Press, 1994.

Berger, Samuel R. "A Foreign Policy for a Global Age." *Foreign Affairs* 79 (November/December 2000): 22–39.

Berinsky, Adam J. "Events, Elites, and American Public Support for Military Conflict." In *The Domestic Sources of American Foreign Policy: Insights and Evidence.* 6th ed. James M. McCormick, ed. Lanham, MD: Rowman & Littlefield Publishers, Inc., 2012.

Berkowitz, Bruce. "Information Age Intelligence." *Foreign Policy* 103 (Summer 1996): 35–50.

Bernstein, Robert A., and William W. Anthony. "The ABM Issue in the Senate, 1968–1970: The Importance of Ideology." *American Political Science Review* 68 (September 1974): 1198–1206.

———. *Foreign Policy and the Press.* Westport, CT: Greenwood Press, 1990.

Best, Jr., Richard A. "Covert Action: Legislative Background and Possible Policy Questions." CRS Report to Congress. Washington, DC, Congressional Research Service, The Library of Congress, December 27, 2011.

Blechman, Barry M., and Stephen S. Kaplan. *Force Without War.* Washington, DC: The Brookings Institution, 1978.

Blight, James G., and David A. Welch. *On the Brink: Americans and Soviets Reexamine the Cuban Missile Crisis.* 2nd ed. New York: The Noonday Press, 1990.

Bliss, Howard, and M. Glen Johnson. *Beyond the Water's Edge: America's Foreign Policies.* Philadelphia, PA: J. B. Lippincott Co., 1975.

———. *In Search of American Foreign Policy.* New York: Oxford University Press, 1974.

Bond, Jon R., and Richard Fleisher. *The President in the Legislative Arena.* Chicago: The University of Chicago Press, 1990.

Bouton, Marshall M. *Global Views 2010: Constrained Internationalism: Adapting to New Realities.* Chicago: The Chicago Council on Global Affairs, 2010.

———, and Benjamin I. Page. *Worldviews 2002: American Public Opinion & Foreign Policy.* Chicago: The Chicago Council on Foreign Relations, 2002.

Braestrup, Peter. *Big Story: How the American Press and Television Reported and Interpreted the Crisis of Tet 1968, Volumes 1 and 2.* Boulder, CO: Westview Press, 1977.

Brenner, Philip, Patrick J. Haney, and Walter Vanderbush. "Intermestic Interests and U.S. Policy toward Cuba." In *The Domestic Sources of American Foreign Policy: Insights and Evidence*. 5th ed. Eugene R. Wittkopf and James M. McCormick, eds. Lanham, MD: Rowman & Littlefield Publishers, Inc., 2008.

Brewer, Thomas L and Lorne Teitelbaum. *American Foreign Policy: A Contemporary Introduction*. 4th ed. Upper Saddle River, NJ: Prentice Hall, 1997.

Brown, Seyom. *The Faces of Power: Constancy and Change in United States Foreign Policy from Truman to Reagan*. New York: Columbia University Press, 1983.

Browne, Marjorie Ann. "Executive Agreements and the Congress." *Issues Brief*, IB75035. Washington, DC: The Library of Congress, 1981.

Brzezinski, Zbigniew. "America in a Hostile World." *Foreign Policy* 23 (Summer 1976): 65–96.

———. "How the Cold War Was Played." *Foreign Affairs* 51 (October 1972): 181–204.

———. *Power and Principle: Memoirs of the National Security Advisor, 1977–1981*. New York: Farrar, Straus & Giroux, 1983.

Buckley, William F., Jr. "Human Rights and Foreign Policy." *Foreign Affairs* 58 (Spring 1980): 775–796.

Bureau of the Census. *Statistical Abstract of the United States: 2002*. Washington, DC: Bureau of the Census, 2002.

———. *Statistical Abstract of the United States: 2008*. Washington, DC: Bureau of the Census, 2008.

———. *Statistical Abstract of the United States: 2008*. Washington, DC: Bureau of the Census, 2012.

Burgin, Eileen. "Congress and Foreign Policy: The Misperceptions." In *Congress Reconsidered*. Lawrence C. Dodd and Bruce I. Oppenheimer, eds. Washington, DC: CQ Press, 1993.

Bush, George W. "A Distinctly American Internationalism." Speech delivered at the Ronald Reagan Presidential Library, November 19, 1999, at http://www.georgewbush.com/speeches/foreign-policy/foreignpolicy.asp.

———. "Address to a Joint Session of Congress and the American People." Delivered on September 20, 2001, at http://www.whitehouse.gov/news/releases/2001/09/20010920–8.html.

———. "President's Remarks at the United Nations General Assembly." Delivered September 12, 2002, at http://www.whitehouse.gov/news/releases/2002/09/2002/09.

———. "President Says Saddam Hussein Must Leave Iraq Within 48 Hours." March 17, 2003, at http://www.whitehouse.gov/news/releases/2003/03/20030317–7.html.

Cameron, Maxwell A., and Brian W. Tomlin. *The Making of NAFTA: How the Deal Was Done*. Ithaca, NY, and London: Cornell University Press, 2000.

Campbell, John Franklin. "The Disorganization of State." In *Problems of American Foreign Policy*. 2nd ed. Martin B. Hickman, ed. Beverly Hills, CA: Glencoe Press, 1975.

Carroll, Holbert N. *The House of Representatives and Foreign Affairs*. Pittsburgh, CA: University of Pittsburgh Press, 1958.

Carter, Jimmy. *Keeping Faith*. New York: Bantam Books, 1982.

Carter, Ralph G., and James M. Scott. "Funding the IMF: Congress versus the White House." In *Contemporary Cases in U.S. Foreign Policy: From Terrorism to Trade*. Ralph G. Carter, ed. Washington, DC: CQ Press, 2002.

Caspary, William R. "The 'Mood Theory': A Study of Public Opinion and Foreign Policy." *American Political Science Review* 54 (June 1970): 536–547.

Center for Strategic and International Studies. *CSIS Commission on Smart Power: A Smarter, More Secure America*. Co-chairs Richard L. Armitage and Joseph S. Nye, Jr. Washington, DC: Center for Strategic and International Studies, 2007.

Chace, James. "The Dangers of a Foreign Policy Consensus." *World Policy Journal* 13 (Winter 1996–1997): 97–99.

_____. "Is a Foreign Policy Consensus Possible?" *Foreign Affairs* 57 (Fall 1978): 1–16.

Chan, Steve. "Grasping the Peace Dividend: Some Propositions on the Conversion of Swords into Plowshares." *Mershon International Studies Review* 39 (April 1995): 53–95.

Christopher, Warren. "Ceasefire Between the Branches: A Compact in Foreign Affairs." *Foreign Affairs* 60 (Summer 1982): 989–1005.

_____, and Bruce Stokes. *Democratizing U.S. Trade Policy.* New York: Council on Foreign Relations, 2001.

Clark, Duncan L. "Why State Can't Lead." *Foreign Policy* 66 (Spring 1987): 128–142.

Clinton, Hillary R. "Leading Through Civilian Power." *Foreign Affairs* (November–December 2010): 13–14. Print.

Cohen, Bernard. *The Political Process and Foreign Policy: The Making of the Japanese Settlement.* Princeton, NJ: Princeton University Press, 1957.

_____. *The Press and Foreign Policy.* Princeton, NJ: Princeton University Press, 1963.

_____. *The Public's Impact on Foreign Policy.* Boston, MA: Little, Brown and Co., 1973.

Cohen, Stephen D. *The Making of United States International Economic Policy.* 3rd ed. New York: Praeger, 1988.

_____. *The Making of United States International Economic Policy.* 4th ed. Westport, CT: Praeger, 1994.

_____. *The Making of United States International Economic Policy.* 5th ed. Westport, CT: Praeger, 2000.

_____, Joel R. Paul, and Robert A. Blecker. *Fundamentals of U.S. Foreign Trade Policy.* Boulder, CO: Westview Press, 1996.

_____, Robert A. Blecker, and Peter D. Whitney. *Fundamentals of U.S. Foreign Trade Policy.* 2nd ed. Boulder, CO: Westview, 2003.

Collier, Ellen C. "Foreign Policy by Reporting Requirement." *The Washington Quarterly* 11 (Winter 1988): 75–84.

Commission on CIA Activities. *Report to the President by the Commission on CIA Activities Within the United States.* Washington, DC: Government Printing Office, June 1975.

Committee on Foreign Relations, United States Senate. *Treaties and Other International Agreements: The Role of the United States Senate.* A Study Prepared for the Committee on Foreign Relations, United States Senate, by the Congressional Research Service, The Library of Congress, Washington, DC: Government Printing Office, January 2001.

Cooper, Chester L. "The CIA and Decisionmaking." *Foreign Affairs* 50 (January 1972): 221–236.

Cooper, Joseph, and Patricia A. Hurley. "The Legislative Veto: A Policy Analysis." *Congress & the Presidency* 10 (Spring 1983): 1–24.

Cooper, Philip J. "George W. Bush, Edgar Allan Poe, and the Use and Abuse of Presidential Signing Statements." *Presidential Studies Quarterly* 35 (September 2005): 515–532.

Corwin, Edward S. *The President: Office and Powers 1787–1957.* New York: New York University Press, 1957.

CQ Press Staff. *The Middle East.* 11th ed. Washington, DC: CQ Press, 2007.

Crabb, Cecil V., Jr. *Policymakers and Critics: Conflicting Theories of American Foreign Policy.* New York: Frederick A. Praeger, 1976.

_____, and Pat M. Holt. *Invitation to Struggle: Congress, the President, and Foreign Policy.* Washington, DC: Congressional Quarterly Press, 1980.

Craig, Gordon A., and Alexander L. George. *Force and Statecraft.* 3rd ed. New York and Oxford: Oxford University Press, 1995.

Cumings, Bruce. *The Origins of the Korean War. Volume II: The Roaring of the Cataract, 1947–1950.* Princeton, NJ: Princeton University Press, 1990.

Cummings, Alfred. "Covert Action: Legislative Background and Possible Policy Questions." CRS Report for Congress. Washington, DC: Congressional

Research Service, The Library of Congress, January 28, 2008.

Daalder, Ivo H., and I. M. Destler "Advisors, Czars, and Councils," *The National Interest* 68 (Summer 2002): 66–78.

_____. "How National Security Advisers See Their Role." In *The Domestic Sources of American Foreign Policy: Insights and Evidence.* 5th ed. Eugene R. Wittkopf and James M. McCormick, eds. Lanham, MD: Rowman & Littlefield Publishers, Inc., 2008.

_____. "A New NSC for a New Administration," *Brookings Policy Brief #68*, at http://www.brook.edu.dybdocroot/comm/policybriefs/pb068/pb68.htm.

Daalder, Ivo H., and James M. Lindsay. *America Unbound: The Bush Revolution in Foreign Policy.* Washington, DC: Brookings Institution, 2003.

_____. "Bush's Foreign Policy Revolution." In *The George W. Bush Presidency: An Early Assessment.* Fred I. Greenstein, ed. Baltimore and London: The Johns Hopkins University Press, 2003.

_____. "The Globalization of Politics: American Foreign Policy for a New Century." *Brookings Review* 21 (Winter 2003): 12–17.

_____, and James B. Steinberg "Hard Choices: National Security and the War on Terrorism." *Current History* 101 (December 2002): 409–413.

Dahl, Robert A. *Congress and Foreign Policy.* New York: Harcourt, Brace and Company, 1950.

Dallek, Robert. *The American Style of Foreign Policy.* New York: Alfred A. Knopf, 1983.

Deibel, Terry L. "Strategies Before Containment: Patterns for the Future." *International Security* 16 (Spring 1992): 79–108.

De la Garza, and Rodolfo O. "U.S. Foreign Policy and the Mexican-American Political Agenda." In *Ethnic Groups and U.S. Foreign Policy.* Mohammed E. Ahrari, ed. New York: Greenwood Press, 1987.

_____, and Harry P. Pachon. *Latinos and U.S. Foreign Policy.* Lanham, MD: Rowman & Littlefield Publishers, Inc., 2000.

De Long, Bradford, Christopher De Long, and Sherman Robinson. "The Case for Mexico's Rescue." *Foreign Affairs* 75 (May/June 1996): 8–14.

Department of State. *State 2000: A New Model for Managing Foreign Affairs.* Washington, DC: Department of State. State 2000: A New Model for Managing Foreign Affairs, January 1993.

_____, and Office of the Historian. "The United States and the Global Coalition Against Terrorism, September–December 2001: A Chronology." December 31, 2001, at http://www.state.gov/r/pa/ho/pubs/fs/5889.htm.

Desch, Michael C. "Bush and the Generals." *Foreign Affairs* 86 (May/June 2007): 97–108.

Destler, I. M. *American Trade Politics.* Washington, DC: Institute of International Economics, and New York: The Twentieth Century Fund, 1992.

_____. "How National Security Advisers See Their Role." In *The Domestic Sources of American Foreign Policy: Insights and Evidence.* 6th ed. James M. McCormick, ed. Lanham, MD: Rowman & Littlefield Publishers, Inc., 2012.

_____, Leslie H. Gelb, and Anthony Lake. *Our Own Worst Enemy: The Unmaking of American Foreign Policy.* New York: Simon & Schuster, 1984.

De Tocqueville, Alexis. *Democracy in America.* Richard D. Heffner, ed. New York: New American Library, 1956.

Deutsch, Karl W. "External Influence on the Internal Behavior of States." In *Approaches to Comparative and International Politics.* R. Barry Farrell, ed. Evanston, IL: Northwestern University Press, 1966.

De Young, Karen. "After Attempted Airline Bombing, Effectiveness of Intelligence Reforms Questioned." *Washington Post.* January 7, 2010. Web, at http://www.washingtonpost.com/wp-dyn/content/article/2010/01/06/AR2010010605158.html, June 13, 2012.

_____, and Steven Mufson. "A Leaner and Less Visible NSC Reorganization Will Emphasize Defense, Global Economics." *Washington Post* (February 10, 2001): A1 and A6.

Dorrien, Gary, "Axis of One." *Christian Century* 120 (March 8, 2003): 30–35.

_____. *On the Edge: The Clinton Presidency.* New York: Simon & Schuster, 1994.

Drezner, Daniel W. "The Realist Tradition in American Public Opinion." *Perspectives on Politics* 6 (March 2008): 51–70.

Dye, Thomas R. *Who's Running America? The Bush Era.* Englewood Cliffs, NJ: Prentice Hall, 1990.

_____. *Who's Running America? The Clinton Years.* 6th ed. Englewood Cliffs, NJ: Prentice Hall, 1995.

_____. *Who's Running America? The Bush Restoration.* 7th ed. Upper Saddle River, NJ: Prentice Hall, 2002.

Easton, David. *The Political System.* New York: Alfred A. Knopf, 1953.

Eisenhower, Dwight D. "The Military–Industrial Complex." In *Power in Postwar America.* Richard Gillam, ed. Boston, MA: Little, Brown and Co., 1971.

Elsea, Jennifer K., Michael John Garcia, and Thomas J. Nicola. "Congressional Authority to Limit U.S. Military Operations in Iraq." CRS Report to Congress. Washington, DC: Congressional Research Service, The Library of Congress, July 11, 2007.

Entman, Robert. *Projections of Power: Framing News, Public Opinion, and U.S. Foreign Policy.* Chicago and London: The University of Chicago Press, 2004.

Esterline, John H., and Robert B. Black. *Inside Foreign Policy: The Department of State Political System and Its Subsystems.* Palo Alto, CA: Mayfield Publishing Company, 1975.

Executive Legislative Consultation on Foreign Policy. *Strengthening Foreign Policy Information Sources for Congress.* Washington, DC: Government Printing Office, February 1982.

Executive Order 12333 (2003), 13355 (2004), and 13470 (2008), at https://www.cia.gov/about-cia/eo12333.html.

Executive Orders 13491, 13492, and 13493. January 22, 2009. *Federal Register* 74, no. 16 (January 27): 4893–4902, at http://www.archives.gov/federal-register/executive-orders/2009-obama.html.

Falk, Richard A. "What's Wrong with Henry Kissinger's Foreign Policy." *Alternatives* 1 (March 1975): 79–100.

Fenno, Richard F., Jr. *Congressmen in Committees.* Boston, MA: Little, Brown and Co., 1973.

Ferrell, Robert H. *American Diplomacy: A History.* 3rd ed. New York: W. W. Norton and Company, 1975.

_____. *American Diplomacy: The Twentieth Century.* New York: W. W. Norton and Company, 1988.

Findley, Paul. *Deliberate Deceptions: Facing the Facts about the U.S.–Israeli Relationship.* New York: Lawrence Hill Books, 1995.

Fisher, Louis. *Presidential War Power.* Lawrence: University Press of Kansas, 1995.

Fleisher, Richard, and Jon R. Bond. "Are There Two Presidencies? Yes, But Only for Republicans." *The Journal of Politics* 50 (August 1988): 747–767.

_____, Jon R. Bond, Glen S. Krutz, and Stephen Hanna. "The Demise of the Two Presidencies." *American Politics Quarterly* 28 (January 2000): 14–23.

Foyle, Douglas C. *Counting the Public In: Presidents, Public Opinion, and Foreign Policy.* New York: Oxford University Press, 1999.

Franck, Thomas M., and Edward Weisband. *Foreign Policy by Congress.* New York: Oxford University Press, 1979.

Frye, Alton. *Humanitarian Intervention: Crafting a Workable Doctrine.* New York: Council on Foreign Relations, 2000.

Fukuyama, Francis. *America at the Crossroads: Democracy, Power and the Neoconservative Legacy.* New Haven and London: Yale University Press, 2006.

Fulbright, J. William. *The Arrogance of Power.* New York: Vintage Books, 1966.

Gaddis, John Lewis, *The Cold War: A New History,* New York: The Penguin Press, 2005.

_____. "A Grand Strategy." *Foreign Policy* (November/December 2002): 50–57.

_____. *Strategies of Containment.* New York: Oxford University Press, 1982.

_____. *The United States and the End of the Cold War: Implications, Reconsiderations, and Provocations.* New York: Oxford University Press, 1992.

_____. *The United States and the Origins of the Cold War 1941–1947.* New York and London: Columbia University Press, 1972.

Gelb, Leslie H. "We Bow to the God Bipartisanship." *The National Interest* 116 (November/December 2011): 18–24.

_____, with Richard K. Betts. *The Irony of Vietnam: The System Worked.* Washington, DC: The Brookings Institution, 1979.

_____, and Justine A. Rosenthal, "The Rise of Ethics in Foreign Policy: Reaching a Values Consensus." *Foreign Affairs* 82 (May/June 2003): 2–7.

Gibson, Martha Liebler. "Managing Conflict: The Role of the Legislative Veto in American Foreign Policy." *Polity* 26 (Spring 1994): 441–472.

_____. *Weapons of Influence: The Legislative Veto, American Foreign Policy, and the Irony of Reform.* Boulder, CO: Westview Press, 1992.

Glennon, Michael. *Constitutional Diplomacy.* Princeton, NJ: Princeton University Press, 1990.

Global Views 2004: American Public Opinion and Foreign Policy. Chicago: The Chicago Council on Foreign Relations, 2004.

Global Views 2006: The United States and the Rise of China and India; Results of a 2006 Multination Survey of Public Opinion. Chicago: Chicago Council on Global Affairs, 2006.

Global Views 2008: Anxious Americans Seek a New Direction in U.S. Foreign Policy. Chicago: Chicago Council on Global Affairs, 2008.

Goldberg, Bernard. *Bias: A CBS Insider Exposes How the Media Distort the News.* Washington, DC: Regnery Publishing, 2002.

Goldstein, Judith, and Robert O. Keohane, eds. *Ideas and Foreign Policy: Beliefs, Institutions, and Political Change.* Ithaca, NY, and London: Cornell University Press, 1993.

Goncharov, Sergei N., John W. Lewis, and Xue Litai. *Uncertain Partners: Stalin, Mao, and the Korean War.* Stanford, CA: Stanford University Press, 1993.

Gordon, Philip. "Can the War on Terror Be Won?" *Foreign Affairs* 86 (November/December 2007): 53–66.

_____. "The End of the Bush Revolution." *Foreign Affairs* 85 (July/August 2006): 75–86.

_____. *Winning the Right War.* New York: Times Books, 2007.

Government Accountability Office. "Securing, Stabilizing, and Rebuilding Iraq," GAO-07-1195. Washington, DC: Government Accountability Office, September, 2007.

Graber, Doris A. *Mass Media and American Politics.* 5th ed. Washington, DC: CQ Press, 1997.

_____. *Mass Media and American Politics.* 7th ed. Washington, DC: CQ Press, 2006.

Graham, Thomas. "Public Opinion and U.S. Foreign Policy Decision Making." In *The New Politics of American Foreign Policy.* David A. Deese, ed. New York: St. Martin's Press, 1994.

Grier, Peter, and Amelia Newcomb. "US, China Find a New Middle Way." *Christian Science Monitor* (December 11, 2003): 1.

Grimmett, Richard F. *War Powers Resolution: After Twenty Eight Years.* Washington, DC: Congressional Research Service, The Library of Congress, November 30, 2001.

_____. *War Powers Resolution: Presidential Compliance.* Washington, DC: Congressional Research Service, February 1, 2012 and September 25, 2012.

Groseclose, Tim. *Left Turn: How the Liberal Media Bias Distorts the American Mind.* New York: St. Martin's Press, 2011.

_____, and Jeffrey Milyo. "A Measure of Media Bias." *The Quarterly Journal of Economics* 120 (November 2005): 1191–1237.

Haass, Richard N. "The Age of Nonpolarity: What Will Follow U.S. Dominance." *Foreign Affairs* 87 (May/June 2008): 44–56.

_____. "Defining U.S. Foreign Policy in a Post-Post–Cold War World." The 2002 Arthur Ross Lecture to the Foreign Policy Association, New York, April 22, 2002, at http://www.state.gov/s/p/rem/9632.htm.

_____. *The Opportunity.* New York: Public Affairs, 2005.

Haig, Alexander. *A Strategic Approach to American Foreign Policy.* Washington, DC: Bureau of Public Affairs, Department of State, August 11, 1981.

Hakim, Peter, and Carlos A. Rosales. "The Latino Foreign Policy Lobby." In *Latinos and U.S. Foreign Policy.* Rodolfo de la Garza and Harry P. Pachon, eds. Lanham, MD: Rowman & Littlefield Publishers, Inc., 2000.

Hallin, Daniel C. *We Keep America on Top of the World: Television Journalism and the Public Sphere.* New York: Routledge, 1994.

Halper, Stephen, and Jonathan Clarke. *The Silence of the Rational Center.* New York: Basic Books, 2007.

Hamilton, Lee. "The Role of the U.S. Congress in American Foreign Policy." *Elliott School Special Lectures Series,* The George Washington University, 1999–2000.

Hanrahan, Charles E. "Agricultural Export and Food Aid Programs." CRS Report to Congress. Washington, DC: Congressional Research Service, The Library of Congress, April 15, 2008.

Hanson, Elizabeth C. *The Information Revolution and World Politics.* Lanham, MD: Rowman & Littlefield Publishers, Inc., 2008.

Hartley, Thomas, and Bruce Russett. "Public Opinion and the Common Defense: Who Governs Military Spending in the United States?" *American Political Science Review* 86 (December 1992): 905–915.

Hendrickson, David C. *Union, Nation, or Empire: The American Debate over International Relations, 1789–1941.* Lawrence: University Press of Kansas, 2009.

Hendrickson, Ryan. *The Clinton Wars: The Constitution, Congress and War Powers.* Nashville: Vanderbilt University Press, 2002.

Henkin, Louis. "Foreign Affairs and the Constitution." *Foreign Affairs* 66 (Winter 1987–1988): 284–310.

_____. *Foreign Affairs and the Constitution.* Mineola, NY: The Foundation Press, 1972.

Herring, George C. *America's Longest War: The United States and Vietnam 1950–1975.* Philadelphia, PA: Temple University Press, 1986.

_____. *LBJ and Vietnam: A Different Kind of War.* Austin, TX: University of Texas Press, 1994.

Hersh, Seymour M. "Last Stand." In *The Domestic Sources of American Foreign Policy: Insights and Evidence.* 6th ed. James M. McCormick, ed. Lanham, MD: Rowman & Littlefield Publishers, Inc., 2012.

Hersman, Rebecca K. C. *Friends and Foes.* Washington, DC: The Brookings Institution, 2000.

Hess, Stephen. *International News & Foreign Correspondents.* Washington, DC: The Brookings Institution, 1996.

Hetherington, Marc J., and William J. Keefe. *Parties, Politics, and Public Policy in America.* Washington, DC: CQ Press, 2007.

Higgott, Richard, and Diane Stone. "Does the CIA Still Have a Role?" *Foreign Affairs* 74 (September/October 1995): 104–116.

_____. "The Limits of Influence: Foreign Policy Think Tanks in Britain and the USA." *Review of International Studies* 20 (January 1994): 15–34.

Hinckley, Barbara. *Less Than Meets the Eye.* Chicago and London: The University of Chicago Press, 1994.

Hoffmann, Stanley. *Gulliver's Troubles, or the Setting of American Foreign Policy.* New York: McGraw-Hill, 1968.

_____. *Primacy or World Order.* New York: McGraw-Hill, 1978.

_____. "Requiem." *Foreign Policy* 42 (Spring 1981): 3–26.

Holloway, David. "Gorbachev's New Thinking." In *America and the World 1988/89.* William P. Bundy, ed. New York: Council on Foreign Relations, 1989.

Holmes, Jennifer S. "Colombia and U.S. Foreign Policy: Coca, Security, and Human Rights." In *Contemporary Cases in U.S. Foreign Policy: From Terrorism to Trade.* Ralph G. Carter, ed. Washington, DC: CQ Press, 2011.

Holsti, Ole R. *Public Opinion and American Foreign Policy.* Rev. ed. Ann Arbor, MI: The University of Michigan Press, 2004.

_____. "Public Opinion and Foreign Policy." In *Eagle Rules? Foreign Policy and American Primacy in the Twenty-first Century.* Robert J. Lieber, ed. Upper Saddle River, NJ: Prentice Hall, 2002.

_____. "Public Opinion and Foreign Policy: Challenges to the Almond-Lippmann Consensus." *International Studies Quarterly* 36 (December 1992): 439–466.

_____, and James N. Rosenau. *American Leadership in World Affairs.* Boston, MA: Allen & Unwin, 1984.

_____. "The Structure of Foreign Policy Attitudes Among Leaders." *Journal of Politics* 52 (February 1990): 94–125.

_____. "The Structure of Foreign Policy Beliefs Among American Opinion Leaders After the Cold War." *Millennium* 22 (Summer 1993): 235–278.

Holt, Pat. *Secret Intelligence and Public Policy.* Washington, DC: CQ Press, 1995.

Hoopes, Townsend. *The Limits of Intervention.* New York: David McKay, 1968.

House and Senate Select Committees on Intelligence. "Report of the Joint Inquiry into the Terrorist Attacks of September 11, 2001." July 24, 2003, at http://new.findlaw.com/cnn/docs/911rpt/index.html.

Howell, William G., and Jon C. Pevehouse. "When Congress Stops Wars: Partisan Politics and Presidential Power." *Foreign Affairs* 86 (September/October 2007): 95–107.

Hrebenar, Ronald J., and Clive S. Thomas, "The Rise and Fall and Rise of the China Lobby in the United States."

In *Interest Group Politics.* 8th ed. Allan J. Cigler and Burdett A. Loomis, eds. Washington, DC: Sage/CQ Press, 2012.

Hughes, Barry B. *The Domestic Context of American Foreign Policy.* San Francisco, CA: Freeman, 1978.

Hult, Karen M. "The Bush White House in Comparative Perspective." In *The George W. Bush Presidency: An Early Assessment.* Fred I. Greenstein, ed. Baltimore and London: The Johns Hopkins University Press, 2003.

Hunt, Michael H. *Ideology and U.S. Foreign Policy.* New Haven, CT: Yale University Press, 1987.

Huntington, Samuel P. "The Erosion of American National Interests." In *The Domestic Sources of American Foreign Policy: Insights and Evidence.* 4th ed. Eugene R. Wittkopf and James M. McCormick, eds. Lanham, MD: Rowman & Littlefield Publishers, Inc., 2004.

Hurwitz, Jon, and Mark Peffley. "How Are Foreign Policy Attitudes Structured? A Hierarchical Model." *American Political Science Review* 81 (December 1987): 1099–1120.

Ikenberry, G. John. *Liberal Leviathan: The Origins, Crisis, and Transformation of the American World Order.* Princeton and Oxford: Princeton University Press, 2011.

Isaacson, Walter. *Kissinger: A Biography.* New York: Simon & Schuster, 1992.

Jacobson, Gary C. "Referendum: The 2006 Midterm Congressional Elections," *Political Science Quarterly* 122 (Spring 2007): 1–24.

Jensen, Kenneth M., ed. *Origins of the Cold War: The Novikov, Kennan, and Roberts' "Long Telegrams" of 1946.* Washington, DC: United States Institute of Peace, 1991.

_____. *Origins of the Cold War: The Novikov, Kennan, and Roberts' "Long Telegrams" of 1946.* Rev. ed. Washington, DC: United States Institute of Peace, 1993.

Jentleson, Bruce W. "The Pretty Prudent Public: Post Post-Vietnam American Opinion on the Use of Military Force." *International Studies Quarterly* 36 (March 1992): 49–74.

_____. *With Friends Like These.* New York and London: W. W. Norton and Company, 1994.

Jervis, Robert. "The Impact of the Korean War on the Cold War." *The Journal of Conflict Resolution* 24 (December 1980): 563–592.

_____. "Why Intelligence and Policymakers Clash." In *The Domestic Sources of American Foreign Policy: Insights and Evidence.* 6th ed. James M. McCormick, ed. Lanham, MD: Rowman & Littlefield, Inc., 2012.

Johnson, Loch, and James M. McCormick. "Foreign Policy by Executive Fiat." *Foreign Policy* 28 (Fall 1977): 117–138.

_____. "The Making of International Agreements: A Reappraisal of Congressional Involvement." *The Journal of Politics* 40 (May 1978): 468–478.

Jones, Christopher M. "Roles, Politics, and the Survival of the V-22 Osprey." In *The Domestic Sources of American Foreign Policy: Insights and Evidence.* 6th ed. James M. McCormick, ed. Lanham, MD: Rowman & Littlefield Publishers, Inc., 2012.

Jones, General James L. USMC (Ret.), Chairman. "The Report of the Independent Commission on the Security Forces of Iraq." September 6, 2007, at http://www.csis.org/component/option,com_csis_progj/task,view/id,1028/, September 22, 2008.

Jones, Joseph M. *The Fifteen Weeks.* Chicago: Harcourt, Brace and World, 1955.

_____, and Lawrence J. Korb. *American National Security: Policy and Process.* 4th ed. Baltimore, MD: The Johns Hopkins University Press, 1993.

Kaiser, Fred. "Congressional Control of Executive Actions in the Aftermath of the Chadha Decision." *Administrative Law Review* 36 (Summer 1984): 239–274.

Karnow, Stanley. *Vietnam: A History.* New York: The Viking Press, 1983.

Katzman, Kenneth. "Iran Sanctions." CRS Report for Congress. Washington, DC: Congressional Research Service, April 26, 2012.

Katzmann, Robert A. "War Powers: Toward a New Accommodation," In *A Question of Balance.* Thomas E. Mann, ed. Washington, DC: The Brookings Institution, 1990.

Kaufman, Natalie Hevener. *Human Rights Treaties and the Senate.* Chapel Hill and London: The University of North Carolina Press, 1990.

Kegley, Charles W., and Eugene R. Wittkopf. *American Foreign Policy: Pattern and Process.* 5th ed. New York: St. Martin's Press, 1991.

Kellerman, Barbara, and Ryan J. Barilleaux. *The President as World Leader.* New York: St. Martin's Press, 1991.

Kennan, George. *American Diplomacy 1900–1950.* New York: Mentor Books, 1951.

_____. "Containment Then and Now." *Foreign Affairs* 65 (Spring 1987): 885–890.

_____. "Is Detente Worth Saving?" *Saturday Review* (March 6, 1976): 12–17.

_____. *Memoirs 1925–1950.* Boston, MA: Little, Brown and Co., 1967.

_____. "The Sources of Soviet Conduct." *Foreign Affairs* 25 (July 1947): 566–582.

Kennedy, Robert F. *Thirteen Days.* New York: Signet Books, 1969.

Kihl, Young Whan. "Nuclear Issues in U.S.–Korea Relations: An Uncertain Security Future." *International Journal of Korean Studies* 7 (Spring/Summer 2003): 79–97.

Kirkpatrick, Jeanne J. "Dictatorships and Double Standards." *Commentary* 68 (November 1979): 34–45.

Kissinger, Henry A. *American Foreign Policy.* 3rd ed. New York: W. W. Norton and Company, 1977.

_____. *Diplomacy.* New York: Simon & Schuster, 1994.

Koh, Harold Hongju. *The National Security Constitution.* New Haven, CT: Yale University Press, 1992.

Kohut, Andrew, and Robert C. Toth. "Arms and the People." *Foreign Affairs* 73 (November/December 1994): 47–61.

Kolko, Gabriel. *The Roots of American Foreign Policy.* Boston, MA: Beacon Press, 1969.

Korb, Lawrence. "The Joint Chiefs of Staff: Access and Impact in Foreign Policy." *Policy Studies Journal* 3 (Winter 1974): 170–173.

_____. "Political Generals," *Foreign Affairs* 86 (September/October 2007). 152–153.

Korb, Lawrence, and Caroline Wadhams. "A Critique of the Bush Administration's National Security Strategy." *Policy Analysis Brief.* Muscatine, IA: The Stanley Foundation, June, 2006.

Korn, Jessica. *The Power of Separation.* Princeton, NJ: Princeton University Press, 1996.

Kovach, Bill. "Do the New Media Make Foreign Policy?" *Foreign Policy* 102 (Spring 1996): 169–179.

Krass, Caroline D. "Authority to Use Military Force in Libya." United States Attorney General, Apri. July 5, 2012, at http://www.justice.gov/olc/2011/authority-military-use-in-libya.pdf.

Kristol, William, and Robert Kagan. "Toward a Neo-Reaganite Foreign Policy." *Foreign Affairs* 75 (July/August 1996): 18–32.

Kull, Steven. "What the Public Knows That Washington Doesn't," *Foreign Policy* 101 (Winter 1995–1996): 102–115.

Kupchan, Charles A. *No One's World: The West, The Rising Rest, and the Coming Global Turn.* New York: Oxford University Press, 2012.

_____, and Peter L. Trubowitz. "Grand Strategy for a Divided America," *Foreign Affairs* 86 (July/August 2007): 71–83.

Ladd, Everett., Jr. *The American Age: United States Foreign Policy at Home and Abroad since 1750.* New York: W. W. Norton and Company, 1989.

_____, "Traditional Values Regnant." *Public Opinion* 1 (March/April 1978): 45–49.

Lake, David A. "Powerful Pacifists: Democratic States and War." *American Political Science Review* 86 (March 1992): 24–37.

Landler, Mark. "Obama Signs Pact in Kabul, Turning Page in Long War." *New York Times,* May 2, 2012, at http://www.nytimes.com/2012/05/02/world/asia/obama-lands-in-kabul-on-unannounced-visit.html?_r=1.

Leffler, Melvyn P., and David S. Painter, eds. *Origins of the Cold War: An International History.* London and New York: Routledge, 1994.

LeLoup, Lance T., and Steven A. Shull. "Congress Versus the Executive: The 'Two Presidencies' Reconsidered." *Social Science Quarterly* 59 (March 1979): 704–719.

Levgold, Robert. "The Revolution in Soviet Foreign Policy." In *America and the World 1988/89.* William P. Bundy, ed. New York: Council on Foreign Relations, 1989.

Lichter, S. Robert, Stanley Rothman, and Linda S. Lichter, *The Media Elite.* Bethesda, MD: Adler & Adler, 1986.

Lieber, Robert J. *The American Era: Power and Strategy for the 21st Century.* New York: Cambridge University Press, 2005.

_____. "Falling Upwards: Declinism, The Box Set." *World Affairs* (Summer 2008), at http://www.worldaffairsjournal.org/2008%20-%20Summer/full-Lieber.html.

_____. "Foreign Policy and American Primacy." In *Eagle Rules? Foreign Policy and American Primacy in the Twenty-first Century.* Robert J. Lieber, ed. Upper Saddle River, NJ: Prentice Hall, 2002.

_____. "Staying Power and the American Future: Problems of Primacy, Policy and Grand Strategy." *Journal of Strategic Studies* 34, no.4 (2011).

Lieberson, Stanley. "An Empirical Study of Military-Industrial Linkages." *American Journal of Sociology* 76 (January 1971): 562–584.

Lieberthal, Kenneth. "A New China Strategy." *Foreign Affairs* 74 (November/December 1995): 35–49.

Lindsay, James M. "Congress and Defense Policy: 1961 to 1986." *Armed Forces and Society* 13 (Spring 1987): 371–401.

_____. *Congress and the Politics of U.S. Foreign Policy.* Baltimore and London: The Johns Hopkins University Press, 1994.

————. "The Shifting Pendulum of Power: Executive-Legislative Relations on American Foreign Policy." In *The Domestic Sources of American Foreign Policy: Insights and Evidence.* 6th ed. James M. McCormick, ed. Lanham, MD: Rowman & Littlefield, Inc., 2012.

Lipset, Seymour Martin. *The First New Nation.* Garden City, NY: Anchor Books, 1967.

Little, Douglas. "David or Goliath? The Israel Lobby and Its Critics." *Political Science Quarterly* 123 (Spring 2008): 151–156.

Locke, John. *The Second Treatise of Government.* Oxford: Basil Blackwell, 1966.

Lomperis, Timothy J. *The War Everyone Lost—and Won.* Washington, DC: CQ Press, 1984.

Lowenthal, Mark M. *Intelligence: From Secrets to Policy.* 3rd ed. Washington DC: CQ Press, 2006.

Majeski, Stephen J. "Defense Spending, Fiscal Policy, and Economic Performance." In *The Political Economy of Military Spending in the United States.* Alex Mintz, ed. London: Routledge, 1992.

Madelbaum, Michael. "The Benefits of Goliath." In *The Domestic Sources of American Foreign Policy: Insights and Evidence.* 5th ed. Eugene R. Wittkopf and James M. McCormick, eds. Lanham, MD: Rowman & Littlefield Publishers, Inc., 2008.

————. *The Case for Goliath: How America Acts as the World's Government in the Twenty-first Century.* New York: Public Affairs, 2005.

————. "Foreign Policy as Social Work." *Foreign Affairs* 75 (January/February 1996): 16–32.

————. *The Frugal Superpower.* New York: Public Affairs, 2010.

Mansfield, Edward, and Jack Snyder. "Democratization and War." *Foreign Affairs* 74 (May/June 1995): 79–97.

Maoz, Zeev, and Bruce Russett. "Normative and Structural Causes of Democratic Peace, 1946–1986." *American Political Science Review* 87 (September 1993): 624–638.

Marchetti, Victor, and John D. Marks. *The CIA and the Cult of Intelligence.* New York: Dell, 1974.

Mathias, Charles M., Jr. "Ethnic Groups and Foreign Policy." *Foreign Affairs* 59 (Summer 1981): 975–998.

May, Ernest R. *"Lessons" of the Past: The Use and Misuse of History in American Foreign Policy.* New York: Oxford University Press, 1973.

Mayer, Jeremy D. *American Media Politics in Transition.* Boston, MA: McGraw Hill, 2008.

Mayer, Kenneth R., and Kevin Price. "Unilateral Presidential Powers: Significant Executive Orders, 1949–99," *Presidential Studies Quarterly* 32 (June 2002): 367–386.

Mayne, Richard. *The Recovery of Europe 1945–1973.* Garden City, NY: Anchor Books, 1973.

Maynes, Charles W. "America Without the Cold War," *Foreign Policy* 78 (Spring 1990): 3–25.

McClosky, Herbert, Paul J. Hoffmann, and Rosemary O'Hara. "Issue Conflict and Consensus Among Party Leaders and Followers." *American Political Science Review* 14 (June 1960): 408–427.

McCormick, James M. "Assessing Clinton's Foreign Policy at Midterm." *Current History* 94 (November 1995): 370–374.

————. "Clinton and Foreign Policy: Some Legacies for a New Century." In *The Postmodern Presidency.* Steven E. Schier, ed. Pittsburgh, CA: University of Pittsburgh Press, 2000.

————. "Congressional Voting on the Nuclear Freeze Resolutions." *American Politics Quarterly* 13 (January 1985): 122–136.

————. "Decision Making in the Foreign Affairs and Foreign Relations Committees." In *Congress Resurgent: Foreign and Defense Policy on Capitol Hill.* Randall B. Ripley and James M. Lindsay, eds. Ann Arbor, MI: The University of Michigan Press, 1993.

————. "Decision-Making Processes and Actors in American Foreign Policy Formulation: Is There a Third World

Lobby." In *U.S. Foreign Policy Toward the Third World*. Jurgen Ruland, Theodor Hanf, and Eva Manske, eds. Armonk, NY: M. E. Sharpe, 2006.

———. "Diplomatic History." In *Routledge Handbook of American Foreign Policy*. Steven W. Hook and Christopher M. Jones, eds. New York and London: Routledge, 2012.

———. "Domestic Politics and US Leadership after September 11." In *The Bush Leadership, the Power of Ideas, and the War on Terror.* David B. MacDonald, Dirk Nabers, and Robert G. Patman, eds. Farham, UK: Ashgate Publishing Limited, 2012.

———. ed. *The Domestic Sources of American Foreign Policy: Insights and Evidence.* Lanham, MD: Rowman & Littlefield, Inc., 2012.

———. "Ethnic Interest Groups and American Foreign Policy: A Growing Influence?" In *Interest Groups Politics.* 8th ed. Allan J. Cigler and Burdett A. Loomis, eds. Washington, DC: Sage/CQ Press, 2012.

———. "Human Rights and the Clinton Administration: American Policy at the Dawn of a New Century." In *Universal Human Rights?* Robert G. Patman, ed. New York: St. Martin's Press, 2000.

———. "The War on Terror and Contemporary U.S.–European Relations." *Politics and Policy* 34 (June 2006): 426–450.

———, and Eugene R. Wittkopf. "At the Water's Edge: The Effects of Party, Ideology, and Issues on Congressional Foreign Policy Voting, 1947–1988." *American Politics Quarterly* 20 (January 1992): 26–53.

———, and Michael Black. "Ideology and Voting on the Panama Canal Treaties." *Legislative Studies Quarterly* 8 (February 1983): 45–63.

———, and Neil J. Mitchell. "Commitments, Transnational Interests, and Congress." *Political Science Quarterly* 60 (December 2007): 579–592.

———. "Human Rights and Foreign Assistance: An Update." *Social Science Quarterly* 70 (December 1989): 969–979.

———, and Steven S. Smith. "The Iran Arms Sale and the Intelligence Oversight Act of 1980." *PS* 20 (Winter 1987): 29–37.

———. "Bipartisanship, Partisanship, and Ideology in Congressional–Executive Foreign Policy Relations, 1947–1988." *The Journal of Politics* 52 (November 1990): 1077–1100.

———, Eugene R. Wittkopf, and David M. Danna. "Politics and Bipartisanship at the Water's Edge: A Note on Bush and Clinton." *Polity* 30 (Fall 1997): 133–149.

McElroy, Robert W. *Morality and American Foreign Policy: The Role of Ethics in International Affairs.* Princeton, NJ: Princeton University Press, 1992.

McMahon, Robert. "Book Review of *Union, Nation, or Empire: The American Debate over International Relations, 1789–1941.*" *Political Science Quarterly* 125 (Spring 2010): 168–169.

Meacham, Jon. *American Gospel.* New York: Random House, 2006.

Mead, Walter Russell. "Jerusalem Syndrome: Decoding 'The Israel Lobby.'" *Foreign Affairs* 86 (November/December 2007): 160–168.

———. "The New Israel and the Old." *Foreign Affairs* 87 (July/August 2008): 28–46.

———. *Power, Terror, Peace, and War: America's Grand Strategy in a World at Risk.* New York: Vintage Books, 2005.

———. *Special Providence.* New York: Alfred A. Knopf, 2001.

Mearsheimer, John J., and Stephen M. Walt. *The Israel Lobby.* New York: Farrar, Straus & Giroux, 2007.

———. "The Israel Lobby." In *The Domestic Sources of American Foreign Policy: Insights and Evidence.* 6th ed. James M. McCormick, ed. Lanham, MD: Rowman & Littlefield Publishers, Inc., 2012.

Meernik, James. "Presidential Support in Congress: Conflict and Consensus on Foreign and Defense Policy." *Journal of Politics* 55 (August 1993): 569–587.

Melanson, Richard A. *American Foreign Policy Since the Vietnam War: The Search for Consensus from Nixon to Clinton.* 2nd ed. Armonk, NY: M. E. Sharpe, 1996.

Merrill, John. *Korea: The Peninsular Origins of the War.* Newark: University of Delaware Press, 1989.

Miller, Robert Hopkins. *Inside an Embassy: The Political Role of Diplomats Abroad.* Washington, DC: Congressional Quarterly, 1992.

Miller, Warren E., and Donald E. Stokes. "Constituency Influence in Congress." *American Political Science Review* 57 (March 1963): 45–56.

Mills, C. Wright. *The Power Elite.* New York: Oxford University Press, 1956.

———. "The Structure of Power in American Society." In *Power in Postwar America.* Richard Gillam, ed. Boston, MA: Little, Brown and Co., 1971.

Mitchell, Amy, Tom Rosenstiel, and Leah Christian. "Mobile Devices and News Consumption: Some Good Signs for Journalism," *The State of the News Media 2012,* at http://stateofthemedia.org/2012/mobile-devices-and-news-consumption-some-good-signs-for-journalism/.

Mitnick, Joshua. "After GOP Victory, Emboldened Israel Declares New Building in East Jerusalem." *Christian Science Monitor,* November 8, 2010, at http://www.csmonitor.com/World/Middle-East/2010/1108/After-GOP-victory-emboldened-Israel-declares-new-building-in-East-Jerusalem.

Mohamed et al. v. Jeppesen Dataplan, Inc. American Civil Liberties Union, at http://www.aclu.org/national-security/mohamed-et-al-v-jeppesen-dataplan-inc.

Morales, Lymari. "Distrust in U.S. Media Edges Up to Record High." Gallup, September 29, 2010, at http://www.gallup.com/poll/143267/Distrust-Media-Edges-Record-High.aspx.

———. "Majority in U.S. Continues to Distrust the Media, Perceive Bias." Gallup, September 22, 2011, at http://www.gallup.com/poll/149624/Majority-Continue-Distrust-Media-Perceive-Bias.aspx.

Morgenthau, Hans J. "The Mainsprings of American Foreign Policy." In *A Reader in American Foreign Policy.* James M. McCormick, ed. Itasca, IL: F. E. Peacock, 1986.

———. *Politics Among Nations: The Struggle for Power and Peace.* New York: Alfred A. Knopf, 1973.

Moyer, Wayne, and Timothy E. Josling. *Agricultural Policy Reform: Politics and Process in the EC and the USA.* New York: Harvester/Wheatsheaf, 1990.

Mueller, John. "The Iraq Syndrome." In *The Domestic Sources of American Foreign Policy: Insights and Evidence.* 5th ed. Eugene R. Wittkopf and James M. McCormick, eds. Lanham, MD: Rowman & Littlefield Publishers, Inc., 2008.

———. *War, Presidents and Public Opinion.* New York: John Wiley and Sons, 1973.

Myers, Richard B., and Richard H. Kohn. "The Military's Place." *Foreign Affairs* 86 (September/October 2007): 147–149.

Nash, Henry T. *American Foreign Policy: Changing Perspectives on National Security.* Homewood, IL: The Dorsey Press, 1978.

National Commission on Terrorist Attacks. *The 9/11 Commission Report: Final Report of the National Commission on Terrorist Attacks upon the United States.* New York: W. W. Norton & Company, 2004.

National Security Preparedness Group. "Tenth Anniversary Report Card: The Status of the 9/11 Commission Recommendations." August 31, 2011, at http://bipartisanpolicy.org/sites/default/files/CommissionRecommendations.pdf.

Nelson, Michael, ed. *Congressional Quarterly's Guide to the Presidency.* Washington, DC: Congressional Quarterly, 1989.

Ness, Immanuel. *Encyclopedia of Interest Groups and Lobbyists in the United States, Volumes 1 and 2.* Armonk, NY: Sharpe Reference, 2000.

Neuman, Johanna. *Lights, Camera, War.* New York: St. Martin's Press, 1996.

Newsom, David C. *The Public Dimension of Foreign Policy.* Bloomington and Indianapolis: Indiana University Press, 1996.

Nincic, Miroslav. "External Affairs and the Electoral Connection." In *The Domestic Sources of American Foreign Policy: Insights and Evidence.* 6th ed. James M. McCormick, ed. Lanham, MD: Rowman & Littlefield Publishers, Inc., 2012.

Nivola, Pietro S. "Trade Policy: Refereeing the Playing Field." In *A Question of Balance*. Thomas E. Mann, ed. Washington, DC: The Brookings Institution, 1990.

Nixon, Richard M. "Asia After Viet Nam." *Foreign Affairs* 46 (October 1967): 111–125.

Nye, Joseph S. "American Foreign Policy After Iraq," *The Chronicle Review* (July 27, 2007): B6–B8.

Nye, Joseph S. Jr. "The Case for Deep Engagement." *Foreign Affairs* 74 (July/August 1995): 90–102.

_____. *The Paradox of American Power: Why the World's Only Superpower Can't Go It Alone.* New York: Oxford University Press, 2002.

_____. "Peering into the Future." *Foreign Affairs* 73 (July/August 1994): 82–93.

Office of the President. *The National Security Strategy of the United States of America.* September 17, 2002, at http://www.whitehouse.gov/usc/nss.html.

_____. "The National Security Strategy." May 27, 2010, at http://www.whitehouse.gov/sites/default/files/rss_viewer/national_security_strategy.pdf.

O'Halloran, Sharyn. "Congress and Foreign Trade Policy." In *Congress Resurgent: Foreign and Defense Policy on Capitol Hill.* Randall B. Ripley and James M. Lindsay, eds. Ann Arbor, MI: The University of Michigan Press, 1993.

O'Heffernan, Patrick. "A Mutual Exploitation Model of Media Influence in U.S. Foreign Policy." In *Taken by Storm: The Media, Public Opinion, and U.S. Foreign Policy in the Gulf War.* W. Lance Bennett and David L. Paletz, eds. Chicago and London: The University of Chicago Press, 1994.

Oldfield, Duane M., and Aaron Wildavsky. "Reconsidering the Two Presidencies." *Society* 26 (July/August 1989): 54–59.

Oneal, James R., Brad Lian, and James H. Joyner. "Are the American People 'Pretty Prudent'? Public Responses to U.S. Uses of Force, 1950–1988." *International Studies Quarterly* 40 (June 1996): 261–280.

Ornstein, Norman J., and Thomas E. Mann. "When Congress Checks Out." *Foreign Affairs* 85 (November/December 2006): 67–82.

Osgood, Robert E. *Ideals and Self-Interest in America's Foreign Relations.* Chicago: The University of Chicago Press, 1953.

Page, Benjamin I., with Marshall M. Bouton. *The Foreign Policy Disconnect.* Chicago and London: The University of Chicago Press, 2006.

_____, and Robert Y. Shapiro. "Effects of Public Opinion on Policy." *American Political Science Review* 77 (March 1983): 175–190.

_____. *The Rational Public: Fifty Years of Trends in Americans' Policy Preferences.* Chicago: The University of Chicago Press, 1992.

_____, and Jason Barabas. "Foreign Policy Gaps Between Citizens and Leaders." *International Studies Quarterly* 44 (September 2000): 339–364.

Pastor, Robert. *Congress and the Politics of U.S. Foreign Economic Policy 1929–1976.* Berkeley, CA: University of California Press, 1980.

Payne, James L. *The American Threat.* College Station, TX: Lytton Publishing Company, 1981.

Pearce, David C. *Wary Partners: Diplomats and the Media.* Washington, DC: Congressional Quarterly, 1995.

Pease, Kelly-Kate S. *International Organizations: Perspectives on Governance in the Twenty-first Century.* 3rd ed. Upper Saddle River, NJ: Prentice Hall, 2008.

Percy, Charles H. "The Partisan Gap." *Foreign Policy* 45 (Winter 1981–1982): 3–15.

Perkins, Dexter. *The American Approach to Foreign Policy.* Cambridge, MA: Harvard University Press, 1962.

Pew Global Attitudes Project. *America's Image Slips, But Allies Share U.S. Concerns over Iran.* Washington, DC: The Pew Research Center for the People & the Press, 2006.

_____. "Arab Spring Fails to Improve U.S. Image," May 17, 2011, at http://www.pewglobal.org/2011/05/17/arab-spring-fails-to-improve-us-image/.

_____. "Obama More Popular Abroad than At Home, Global Image of U.S. Continues to Benefit." June 17, 2010, at http://pewglobal.org/2010/06/17/obama-more-popular-abroad-than-at-home/

_____. *Views of a Changing World June 2003*. Washington, DC: The Pew Research Center for the People & the Press, 2003.

Pew Research Center for the People and the Press. *Americans Lack Background to Follow International News: Public's News Habits Little Changed by Sept. 11*. Washington, DC: The Pew Research Center for the People and the Press, 2002.

_____. "Americans Spending More Time Following the News." September 12, 2010, at http://www.people-press.org/2010/09/12/americans-spending-more-time-following-the-news/.

_____. *What Americans Know: 1989–2007: Public Knowledge of Current Affairs Little Changed by News and Information Revolutions*. Washington, DC: The Pew Research Center for the People & the Press, April 15, 2007.

Pillar, Paul R. "Intelligent Design? The Unending Saga of Intelligence Reform." *Foreign Affairs* 87 (March/April 2008): 138–144.

Powlick, Philip J. "The Attitudinal Bases for Responsiveness to Public Opinion Among American Foreign Policy Officials." *Journal of Conflict Resolution* 35 (December 1991): 611–641.

_____. "The Sources of Public Opinion for American Foreign Policy Officials." *International Studies Quarterly* 39 (December 1995): 427–451.

"Presidential Policy Directive-1." The White House, Washington, DC, February 13, 2009, at http://www.fas.org/irp/off-docs/ppd/ppd-1.pdf.

President's Special Review Board (Tower Commission). *Report of the President's Special Review Board (Tower Commission Report)*. Washington, DC: Government Printing Office, February 26, 1987.

Priest, Dana. *The Mission*. New York: W. W. Norton and Company, 2003.

Pringle, Robert. "Creeping Irrelevance at Foggy Bottom." *Foreign Policy* 29 (Winter 1977–1978): 128–139.

Renshon, Stanley A. *National Security in the Obama Administration: Reassessing the Bush Doctrine*. New York and London: Routledge, 2010.

Report of the Congressional Committees Investigating the Iran-Contra Affair. Washington, DC: Government Printing Office, November 1987.

Rice, Condoleezza. "Promoting the National Interest." *Foreign Affairs* 79 (January/February 2000): 45–62.

_____. "Rethinking the National Interest: American Realism for a New World." *Foreign Affairs* 87 (July/August 2008): 2–26.

Richelson, Jeffrey T. *The U.S. Intelligence Community*. 3rd ed. Boulder, CO: Westview Press, 1995.

_____. *The U.S. Intelligence Community*. 4th ed. Boulder CO: Westview Press, 1999.

_____. *The U.S. Intelligence Community*. 5th ed. Boulder, CO: Westview Press, 2008.

_____. *The U.S. Intelligence Community*. 6th ed. Boulder, CO: Westview Press, 2012.

Rielly, John E. "The American Mood: A Foreign Policy of Self Interest." *Foreign Policy* 34 (Spring 1979): 74–86.

_____. "American Opinion: Continuity, Not Reaganism." *Foreign Policy* 50 (Spring 1983): 86–104.

_____. "America's State of Mind." *Foreign Policy* 66 (Spring 1987): 39–56.

_____. "The Public Mood at Mid-Decade." *Foreign Policy* 96 (Spring 1995): 76–93.

_____. "Public Opinion: The Pulse of the '90s." *Foreign Policy* 82 (Spring 1991): 79–96.

_____, ed. *American Public Opinion and U.S. Foreign Policy 1975*. Chicago: The Chicago Council on Foreign Relations, 1975.

_____, ed. *American Public Opinion and U.S. Foreign Policy 1979*. Chicago: The Chicago Council on Foreign Relations, 1979.

_____, ed. *American Public Opinion and U.S. Foreign Policy 1983*. Chicago: The Chicago Council on Foreign Relations, 1983.

_____, ed. *American Public Opinion and U.S. Foreign Policy 1987*. Chicago: The Chicago Council on Foreign Relations, 1987.

_____, ed. *American Public Opinion and U.S. Foreign Policy 1991*. Chicago: The Chicago Council on Foreign Relations, 1991.

_____, ed. *American Public Opinion and U.S. Foreign Policy 1995*. Chicago: The Chicago Council on Foreign Relations, 1995.

_____, ed. *American Public Opinion and U.S. Foreign Policy 1999*. Chicago: The Chicago Council on Foreign Relations, 1999.

Ripley, Randall B., and James M. Lindsay, eds. *Congress Resurgent: Foreign and Defense Policy on Capitol Hill*. Ann Arbor, MI: The University of Michigan Press, 1993.

Robinson, James A. *Congress and Foreign Policy-Making*. Rev. ed. Homewood, IL: The Dorsey Press, 1967.

Rockman, Bert A. "America's Departments of State: Irregular and Regular Syndromes of Policymaking." *American Political Science Review* 75 (December 1981): 911–927.

Rohde, David. "The Obama Doctrine." *Foreign Policy* (March/April 2012), at http://www.foreignpolicy.com/articles/2012/02/27/the_obama_doctrine.

Rohde, David W. *Parties and Leaders in the Postreform House*. Chicago: The University of Chicago Press, 1991.

Rosenberg, Milton J., Sidney Verba, and Philip E. Converse. *Vietnam and the Silent Majority*. New York: Harper and Row, 1970.

Rosner, Jeremy D. "The Know-Nothings Know Something." *Foreign Policy* 101 (Winter 1995–1996): 116–129.

_____. *The New Tug-of-War: Congress, the Executive Branch, and National Security*. Washington, DC: Carnegie Endowment for International Peace, 1995.

Russet, Bruce. *Grasping the Democratic Peace: Principles for a Post-Cold War World*. Princeton, NJ: Princeton University Press, 1993.

_____, and Donald R. Deluca. "'Don't Tread on Me': Public Opinion and Foreign Policy in the Eighties." *Political Science Quarterly* 96 (Fall 1981): 381–399.

_____, and Elizabeth C. Hanson. *Interest and Ideology: The Foreign Policy Beliefs of American Businessmen*. San Francisco, CA: W. H. Freeman, 1975.

_____, Harvey Starr, and David Kinsella. *World Politics: The Menu for Choice*. 9th ed. Boston, MA: Cengage/Wadsworth, 2009.

Saad, Lydia. "Americans Broadly Favor Obama's Afghanistan Pullout Plan." Gallup. June 29, 2011, at http://www.gallup.com/poll/148313/Americans-Broadly-Favor-Obama-Afghanistan-Pullout-Plan.aspx

_____. "Obama's Approval Bump Hasn't Transferred to 2012 Prospects." Gallup. May 11, 2011, at http://www.gallup.com/poll/147500/Obama-Approval-Bump-Hasnt-Transferred-2012-Prospects.aspx.

Sagan, Scott. *The Limits of Safety: Organizations, Accidents, and Nuclear Weapons*. Princeton, NJ: Princeton University Press, 1993.

Saideman, Stephen M., "More than Advice? The Role of the Joint Staff in the American Foreign Policy Process." Paper presented at the annual meeting of the American Political Science Association, Chicago, August 30, 2007.

Sanger, David E. "Obama Order Sped Up Wave of Cyberattacks Against Iran." *New York Times*, June 1, 2012, at http://www.nytimes.com/2012/06/01/world/middleeast/obama-ordered-wave-of-cyberattacks-against-iran.html?pagewanted=all.

Schier, Steven E. *Transforming America*. Lanham, MD: Rowman & Littlefield Publishers, Inc., 2011.

Schlesinger, Arthur, M., Jr. "Congress and the Making of American Foreign Policy." *Foreign Affairs* 51 (October 1972): 78–113.

_____. "Foreign Policy and the American Character." *Foreign Affairs* 62 (Fall 1983): 1–16.

_____. "Human Rights and the American Tradition." *Foreign Affairs* 57 (Winter 1978–1979): 503–526.

_____. *The Imperial Presidency.* Boston, MA: Houghton Mifflin Company, 1973.

Schlesinger, James. "The Role of the Secretary of Defense." In *Reorganizing America's Defense: Leadership in War and Peace.* Robert J. Art, Vincent Davis, and Samuel P. Huntington, eds. Washington, DC: Pergamon-Brassey's, 1985.

Schraufnagel, Scot, and Stephen M. Shellman. "The Two Presidencies, 1984–1998: A Replication and Extension." *Presidential Studies Quarterly* 31 (December 2001): 699–707.

Scott, Andrew M. "The Department of State: Formal Organization and Informal Culture." *International Studies Quarterly* 13 (March 1969): 1–18.

_____. "The Problem of the State Department." In *Problems of American Foreign Policy.* 2nd ed. Martin B. Hickman, ed. Beverly Hills: Glencoe Press, 1975.

Scott, James M. "Trade and Trade-Offs: The Clinton Administration and the 'Big Emerging Markets' Strategy." *Futures Research Quarterly* 13 (Summer 1997): 37–66.

Scott, Len, and Steve Smith. "Political Scientists, Policy-Makers, and the Cuban Missile Crisis." *International Affairs* 70 (October 1994): 659–684.

Shapiro, Ian. *Containment: Rebuilding a Strategy Against Global Terror.* Princeton and Oxford: Princeton University Press, 2007.

Shapiro, Robert Y., and Benjamin I. Page. "Foreign Policy and Public Opinion." In *The New Politics of American Foreign Policy.* David A. Deese, ed. New York: St. Martin's Press, 1994.

_____. "Foreign Policy and the Rational Public." *Journal of Conflict Resolution* 32 (June 1988): 211–247.

Sharp, J. Michael, ed. *Directory of Congressional Voting Scores and Interest Group Ratings, Volumes 1 and 2.* 4th ed. Washington, DC: Congressional Quarterly, 2006.

Sheehan, Neil, Hedrick Smith, E. W. Kenworthy, and Fox Butterfield. *The Pentagon Papers as Published by the New York Times.* New York: Bantam Books, 1971.

Sheridan, Valerie S., ed. *Washington Representatives Spring 2007.* 31st ed. Bethesda, MD: Columbia Books, 2007.

_____, *Washington Representatives Fall 2011.* Bethesda, MD: Columbia Books, 2011.

Shull, Steven A. *Presidential-Congressional Relations: Policy and Time Approaches.* Ann Arbor, MI: The University of Michigan Press, 1997.

_____, ed. *The Two Presidencies: A Quarter Century Assessment.* Chicago: Nelson/Hall Publishers, 1991.

Sigelman, Lee. "A Reassessment of the Two Presidencies Thesis." *The Journal of Politics* 41 (November 1979): 1195–1205.

Silverstein, Gordon. *Imbalance of Powers: Constitutional Interpretation and the Making of American Foreign Policy.* New York: Oxford University Press, 1997.

_____. "Judicial Enhancement of Executive Power." In *The President, The Congress, and the Making of Foreign Policy.* Paul E. Peterson, ed. Norman and London: University of Oklahoma Press, 1994.

Smith, Hedrick. *The Media and the Gulf War.* Washington, DC: Seven Locks, 1992.

Smith, Jean Edward. *The Constitution and American Foreign Policy.* St. Paul, MN: West Publishing Company, 1989.

Smith, Tony. *Foreign Attachments: The Power of Ethnic Groups in the Making of American Foreign Policy.* Cambridge, MA: Harvard University Press, 2000.

Snider, Don M., and Miranda A. Carlton-Carew, eds. *U.S. Civil–Military Relations: In Crisis or Transitions?* Washington, DC: The Center for Strategic & International Studies, 1995.

Snyder, Jack. "One World, Rival Theories." *Foreign Policy* 145 (November/December 2004): 53–62.

Sobel, Richard. "Public Opinion about United States Intervention in El Salvador and Nicaragua." *Public Opinion Quarterly* 53 (Spring 1989): 114–128.

_____, ed. *The Impact of Public Opinion on U.S. Foreign Policy: Constraining the Colossus.* New York: Oxford University Press, 1999.

_____ *Public Opinion in U.S. Foreign Policy: The Controversy over Contra Aid.* Lanham, MD: Rowman & Littlefield Publishers, Inc., 1993.

Solo, Pam. *From Protest to Policy: The Origins and Future of the Freeze Movement.* Cambridge, MA: Ballinger Publishing, 1988.

Soroka, Stuart N. "Media, Public Opinion, and Foreign Policy." *Harvard International Journal of Press/Politics* 9 (Winter 2003): 27–48.

Spanier, John. *American Foreign Policy since World War II.* 9th ed. New York: Holt, Rinehart and Winston, 1982.

Steel, J. Valerie, ed. *Washington Representatives 1999.* 23rd ed. Washington, DC: Columbia Books, 1999.

_____. *Washington Representatives 2000.* 24th ed. Washington, DC: Columbia Books, 2000.

Steger, Manfred B. *Globalism.* Lanham, MD: Rowman & Littlefield Publishers, Inc., 2002.

Stiglitz, Joseph E. *Globalization and Its Discontents.* New York: W. W. Norton and Company, 2002.

Stockton, Paul. "Beyond Micromanagement: Congressional Budgeting for a Post–Cold War Military." *Political Science Quarterly* 110 (Summer 1995): 233–259.

_____. "Congress and U.S. Military Policy Beyond the Cold War." In *Congress Resurgent: Foreign and Defense Policy on Capitol Hill.* Randall B. Ripley and James M. Lindsay, eds. Ann Arbor, MI: The University of Michigan Press, 1993.

Stokes, Bruce, and Pat Choate. *Democratizing U.S. Trade Policy.* New York: Council on Foreign Relations, 2001.

Strobel, Warren P. *Late-Breaking Foreign Policy.* Washington, DC: United States Institute of Peace, 1997.

Sundquist, James L. *The Decline and Resurgence of Congress.* Washington, DC: The Brookings Institution, 1981.

Talbott, Strobe. *Deadly Gambits: The Reagan Administration and the Stalemate in Nuclear Arms Control.* New York: Vintage Books, 1985.

_____. "Globalization and Diplomacy: The View from Foggy Bottom," In *The*

Domestic Sources of American Foreign Policy: Insights and Evidence. 4th ed. Eugene R. Wittkopf and James M. McCormick, eds. Lanham, MD: Rowman & Littlefield Publishers, Inc., 2004.

Tananbaum, Duane. *The Bricker Amendment Controversy: A Test of Eisenhower's Political Leadership.* Ithaca, NY, and London: Cornell University Press, 1988.

Terhune, Kenneth W. "From National Character to National Behavior: A Reformulation." *Journal of Conflict Resolution* 14 (June 1970): 203–264.

Tower, John G. "Congress Versus the President: The Formulation and Implementation of American Foreign Policy." *Foreign Affairs* 60 (Winter 1981–1982): 229–246.

Trice, Robert H. "Congress and the Arab–Israeli Conflict: Support for Israel in the U.S. Senate, 1970–1973." *Political Science Quarterly* 92 (Fall 1977): 443–463.

_____. "Domestic Interest Groups and the Arab–Israeli Conflict: A Behavioral Analysis." In *Ethnicity and U.S. Foreign Policy.* Rev. ed. Abdul Aziz Said, ed. New York: Praeger, 1981.

Trubowitz, Peter, and Nicole Mellow. "'Going Bipartisan': Politics by Other Means." *Political Science Quarterly* 120 (Fall 2005): 433–453.

Truman, Harry S. *Year of Decision.* New York: Doubleday & Co., 1955.

_____, and David C. Hendrickson. "Thomas Jefferson and American Foreign Policy." *Foreign Affairs* 69 (Spring 1990): 135–156.

Veillette, Connie, and Susan B. Epstein. "State, Foreign Operations, and Related Programs: FY2008 Appropriations." CRS Report to Congress. Washington, DC: Congressional Research Service, The Library of Congress, December 14, 2007.

Walt, Stephen M. "Two Cheers for Clinton's Foreign Policy." *Foreign Affairs* 79 (March/April 2000): 63–79.

Walters, Robert W. "African-American Influence on U.S. Foreign Policy Toward South Africa." In *Ethnic Groups and U.S. Foreign Policy.* Mohammed E. Ahrari, ed. New York: Greenwood Press, 1987.

Weiner, Tim, David Johnston, and Neil A. Lewis. *Betrayal: The Story of Aldrich Ames, An American Spy.* New York: Random House, 1995.

Whittaker, Alan G., Shannon A. Brown, Frederick C. Smith, and Ambassador Elizabeth McKune. "The National Security Policy Process: The National Security Council and Interagency System," Research Report, August 15, 2011, Annual Update. Washington, DC: Industrial College of the Armed Forces, National Defense University, U.S. Department of Defense, 2011.

Wiarda, Howard J. *Foreign Policy Without Illusion.* Glenview, IL: Scott Foresman/ Little, Brown Higher Education, 1990.

Wildavsky, Aaron. "The Two Presidencies." *Transaction* 3 (December 1966): 7–14.

Willetts, Peter. *The Non-Aligned Movement: The Origins of a Third World Alliance.* London: Frances Pinter, Ltd., 1979.

Wise, David. *Nightmover: How Aldrich Ames Sold the CIA to the KGB for $4.6 Million.* New York: HarperCollins, 1995.

Wittkopf, Eugene R. *Faces of Internationalism: Public Opinion and American Foreign Policy.* Durham, NC: Duke University Press, 1990.

_____. "Faces of Internationalism in a Transitional Environment." *Journal of Conflict Resolution* 38 (September 1994): 376–401.

_____. "What Americans Really Think about Foreign Policy." *The Washington Quarterly* 19 (Summer 1996): 91–106.

_____, Charles W. Kegley, Jr., and James M. Scott. *American Foreign Policy: Pattern and Process.* 6th ed. Belmont, CA: Wadsworth, 2003.

_____, and James M. McCormick. "The Cold War Consensus: Did It Exist?" *Polity* 22 (Summer 1990): 627–653.

_____. "The Domestic Politics of Contra Aid: Public Opinion, Congress, and the President." In *Public Opinion in U.S. Foreign Policy: The Controversy over Contra Aid.* Richard Sobel, ed. Lanham, MD: Rowman & Littlefield Publishers, Inc., 1993.

_____, eds. *The Domestic Sources of American Foreign Policy: Insights and Evidence.* 5th ed. Lanham, MD: Rowman & Littlefield Publishers, Inc., 2008.

Woodward, Bob. *Bush at War.* New York: Simon & Schuster, 2002.

_____. *Obama's Wars.* New York: Simon & Schuster, 2010.

_____. *Veil: The Secret Wars of the CIA, 1981– 1987.* New York: Pocket Books, 1987.

Wooldridge, Adrian. "After Bush: A Special Report on America and the World." *The Economist* (March 29): 3–16.

Woolley, John, and Gerhard Peters. "Presidential Signing Statements." The American Presidency Project, at http://www.presidency.ucsb.edu/signingstatements.php?year=2009.

Yarmolinsky, Adam. *The Military Establishment: Its Impact on American Society.* New York: Harper and Row, 1971.

Yergin, Daniel. *Shattered Peace. The Origins of the Cold War and the National Security State.* Boston, MA: Houghton Mifflin Company, 1977.

Zakaria, Fareed. *From Wealth to Power: The Unusual Origins of America's World Role.* Princeton, NJ: Princeton University Press, 1998.

_____. *The Post-American World.* New York: Norton, 2008.

Zelikow, Philip D. "The United States and the Use of Force: A Historical Summary." In *Democracy, Strategy, and Vietnam.* George K. Osborn, Asa A. Clark IV, Daniel J. Kaufman, and Douglas E. Lute, eds. Lexington, MA: D. C. Heath and Company, 1987.

☆
Name Index

Subject Index

CPSIA information can be obtained
at www.ICGtesting.com
Printed in the USA
FFHW011008291219
57321827-62817FF

9 781435 462724